P9-CQE-378

THESE UNITED STATES

James P. Shenton   Judith R. Benson   Robert E. Jakoubek

THESE UNITED STATES

HOUGHTON MIFFLIN COMPANY · BOSTON

Atlanta   Dallas   Geneva, Illinois   Hopewell, New Jersey   Palo Alto   Toronto

AUTHORS

James P. Shenton is Professor of History at Columbia University. He has lectured on American history for educational television and been a member of the Passaic, New Jersey, School Board. Professor Shenton has also conducted summer institutes for secondary school teachers in New York State and Puerto Rico. He is the author of *Robert John Walker: A Politician from Jackson to Lincoln, Reconstruction: The South After the War, An Historian's History of the United States,* and *The Melting Pot.*

Judith R. Benson teaches social studies at Cedar Falls High School, Cedar Falls, Iowa. She has also taught in California, where she earned her M.A. at Stanford. As a SEATO intern, Mrs. Benson has worked in Thailand and traveled in the Far East.

Robert E. Jakoubek has degrees from Indiana University and from Columbia where he is specializing in twentieth century United States history. Mr. Jakoubek has published articles on John W. Davis and the New Deal.

EDITORIAL ADVISER

Howard D. Mehlinger is Professor of History and Education at Indiana University and serves as Editorial Adviser for Houghton Mifflin Social Studies programs.

CONSULTANTS

Roger E. Johnson, Professor of Education, University of South Florida, and a consultant on reading and readability
Hollis R. Lynch, Professor of History and a member and former Director of the Institute of African Studies, Columbia University
Anne Firor Scott, Professor of History, Duke University, editor of *Women in American Life* and *The American Woman, Who Was She?*

TEACHER-ADVISERS

María Velia Cárdenas, Sam Houston High School, San Antonio, Texas
Carol Dodge, Native American Teacher Corps, Keshena, Wisconsin
Virginia Edwards, Windsor Forest High School, Savannah, Georgia
Gary Yamashiro, Hillcrest High School, Midvale, Utah

Verses by Claude McKay on page 491 are from the poem "If We Must Die," published in *Selected Poems of Claude McKay.* Copyright 1953 by Twayne Publishers, Inc., and reprinted with permission of Twayne Publishers, A division of G. K. Hall & Co., Boston.

Copyright © 1978 by Houghton Mifflin Company

All rights reserved. No part of this work may be reproduced or transmitted in any form or by any means, electronic or mechanical, including photocopying and recording, or by any information storage or retrieval system, without permission in writing from the publisher.

Printed in the U.S.A.
Library of Congress Catalog Card Number: 76-58080
ISBN: 0-395-24224-X

j 973
J S5462t
c.2

CONTENTS

A NEW WORLD

I

II A NEW NATION

III

A TIME OF TRIAL

Collection of the Henry Ford Museum.

A TIME OF CHANGE

IV

V

A WORLD POWER

NRA
MEMBER

U.S.

WE DO OUR PART

VI

A
WORLD
LEADER

WENDELL WILLKIE

AMERICA
NEEDS HIM
in the

WE THE PEOPLE
WANT WILLKIE

A NEW DIRECTION

VII

APPENDIX

MAPS

CHARTS AND GRAPHS

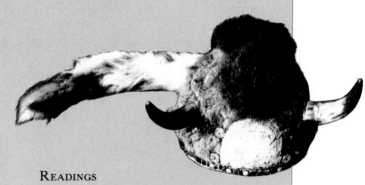

FEATURES

PROLOGUE

In the beginning the land was clean. Clear water washed the shores of Lake Michigan and Lake Erie and plunged thundering over Niagara Falls. Clean air blew across the sagebrush deserts of Southern California and rose in morning mists off the Hudson River.

The North American forest began almost at water's edge and rolled in endless acres to mid-continent. There it gave way to a silent sea of grass. Buffalo by the millions wandered over the plains, and passenger pigeons by the billions darkened the skies.

The land was both new and very old. Within living memory, volcanoes had poured out lava, and forest fires had left still-smoldering scars. Yet the Colorado River, cutting deep into the Grand Canyon, showed rocks a billion years old.

The land was harsh as well as mild. Blizzards whipped through the Dakotas at seventy below zero, while parts of Arizona simmered at 130 degrees. But on a March morning in the Carolinas or an October afternoon on Cape Cod anyone would forget all other seasons.

The land was both poor and very rich. It included endless miles of Nevada desert and the fertile black topsoil of Illinois. The first inhabitants told of a mysterious liquid that would float on water and burn when set ablaze. Others would call it petroleum. The Mesabi Range of Minnesota hid mountains of iron ore, and in the pebbly creeks of the Rockies there was the gleam of gold.

The land seemed nearly empty. Here and there an observer might have noticed a totem, a passing canoe, or the flicker of a campfire. Among the rock formations of the Mesa Verde were certain regular shapes that could only have been made by human beings. And on the high plateau of Mexico was the outline of a sizable city. But no structure as large—or as dramatic—as the Great Wall of China broke the North American landscape.

This New World seemed incomplete, infinite, and mysterious. And it more than matched the first explorers' capacity for wonder.

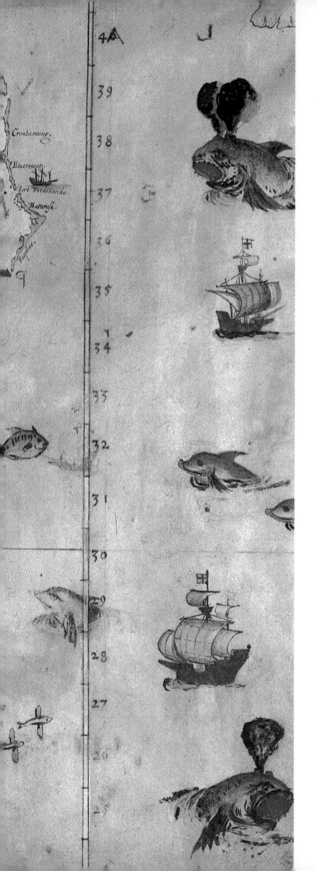

I

A NEW WORLD

After many years have passed, a time will come when the ocean will loosen the chains in which it holds us, and a great land will be revealed. Then will we learn of new worlds and find that our farthest boundary is no longer the end of the earth.

Seneca, *Medea*   17

The Old World
Finds the New

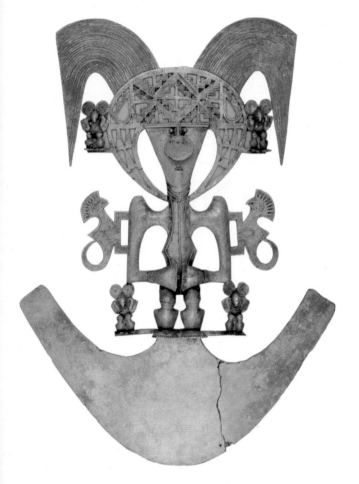

Made in America—perhaps a thousand years ago—this golden knife is now in a European museum. What marvelously clever people could have done work like this? Where did they get such quantities of gold? How did the knife find its way to far-off Europe? Chapter 1 starts the story.

1. THE EARLIEST AMERICANS

Europe, Asia, Africa. In Columbus's day, as in ancient times, these were the continents known to the Old World. Europeans knew of Africa and the slave trade. They had heard of Asia Minor. Its capital, Constantinople, had fallen to the Turks in 1453. Europeans traded with India, and from travelers like Marco Polo they even heard accounts of China and Japan.

But America was a surprise. Explorers stumbled on it while searching for a new route to India and China. To the settlers who followed the explorers, the people already living in the new land were a mystery. At first the Europeans called them "noble savages" and thought they needed only the benefit of Christian teaching. Soon, however, they were looked upon as murderous devils, treacherous and best shot or driven away. The descendants of the Europeans are only now beginning to understand these American Indians.

A people from Asia. The American Indian, like the European settler, migrated from the Old World. No fossil remains have yet been found to show that human life began independently in the Americas. Scientists who study such questions believe instead that the first Americans crossed from eastern Siberia to Alaska. The latest methods of scientific dating keep pushing back the time of this migration. But it was at least 25,000 years ago and may have been over 50,000.

For several thousand years Asian peoples crossed Alaska and wandered slowly southward along the west coast of North America. Some traveled eastward toward the Atlantic, settling beside rivers and lakes. Others migrated into Central and South America. In fact, some did not end their journey down the South American continent until they stood at Cape Horn, its southern tip.

Different life-styles. North American Indians lived in varied ways. These ranged from great stone cities, built by the Aztecs of Mexico, to tepees, the mobile homes of the Plains Indians. Indian tribes were usually organized around a chief or king, and many had tribal councils in which each clan, or family group, was represented.

North of what is now Mexico, the Indians had little metal and made their tools and weapons out of stone. When they wanted to clear part of a forest, they killed the trees by simply peeling away a ring of bark. But even in this northern area there were many differences in Indian culture. For example, 56 families of North American languages and hundreds of dialects have been identified.

———•◆•———

Read here of how

The first Americans came from Asia.
They took up different ways of living.
But all stayed close to nature.
Europeans and Indians influenced one another.

———•◆•———

TIME CHART

1488	Portuguese round the tip of Africa.
1492	Columbus makes his first voyage.
1513	Ponce de León discovers Florida.
1519	Cortés finds Mexico City.
1565	St. Augustine, Florida, founded.
1585	The first English colony is started.
1588	The Spanish Armada is defeated.
1603	Champlain explores the northeast.
1608	The French found Quebec.
1624	Dutch establish New Amsterdam.

———◆———

Of about twenty million Indians who lived in the New World just before the Europeans arrived, there were perhaps 300,000 east of the Mississippi. Most of these had built permanent settlements and lived by farming. The women among them tended the fields, while the men added to the food supply by hunting and fishing. Some Indian settlements included regular streets, well-managed gardens, and large social and religious centers.

Beyond the Mississippi, on the Great Plains, tribes of wandering Indians followed the buffalo herds year after year. From the herds they got not only their food but their clothing, fuel, and shelter.

In the Southwest there was a more settled agricultural life, although the Navaho and Apache of that region were good hunters. The Pueblo Indians of the Southwest built community houses on plateaus that were easy to defend. There they wove cloth and grew a variety of crops.

European influence. It is hard to imagine some of these Indian cultures as they must have been before the coming of the whites. In some cases the cultures no longer

19

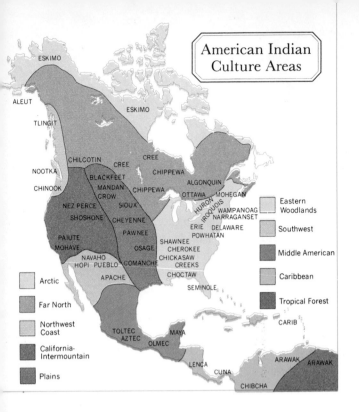

American Indian Culture Areas

ESKIMO
ALEUT
TLINGIT
ESKIMO
CHILCOTIN
NOOTKA
CREE
CREE
CHIPPEWA
CHINOOK
BLACKFEET
ALGONQUIN
MANDAN
CHIPPEWA
OTTAWA
MOHEGAN
CROW
HURON
NEZ PERCE
SIOUX
IROQUOIS
WAMPANOAG
SHOSHONE
CHEYENNE
NARRAGANSET
PAWNEE
ERIE
DELAWARE
PAIUTE
POWHATAN
MOHAVE
SHAWNEE
OSAGE
CHEROKEE
NAVAHO
CHICKASAW
HOPI PUEBLO
COMANCHE
CREEKS
APACHE
CHOCTAW
SEMINOLE
CARIB
TOLTEC
MAYA
AZTEC
OLMEC
LENCA
ARAWAK
ARAWAK
CUNA
CHIBCHA

Eastern Woodlands

Southwest

Middle American

Caribbean

Tropical Forest

Arctic

Far North

Northwest Coast

California-Intermountain

Plains

exist. In others the Europeans changed the Indians' way of living even before coming in contact with them. For instance, when we think of the Plains people, we picture a culture that made use of horses for migration, for war, and for hunting buffalo. Yet horses had died out in North America during the Ice Age. American Indians knew nothing of them until they were brought here by the Spaniards.

The Indians had used dogs to haul their goods until they caught wild horses that were born of European runaways. Suddenly the people of the Plains had the speed and ease of movement that later explorers saw in the 1800s. They assumed it must be something timeless and entirely American. Actually, it was a recent and highly creative change in the Indian methods of hunting and traveling—a sort of technological revolution.

20   Another example of the way Indian

civilization could adapt was in its methods of government. Five Indian tribes or nations—the Mohawk, Cayuga, Oneida, Onandaga, and Seneca—formed the Iroquois confederacy. This very complicated system of government had existed before the French and English came. But the fur trade with these Europeans made the confederacy far more powerful. Very quickly it came to dominate all the tribes of the Northeast. So the popular idea of Indians living in a changeless, unprogressive, Stone Age culture simply does not fit the facts.

THE INDIAN AND THE EUROPEAN

Just as Indians adapted to the coming of the Europeans, Europeans learned from the Indians. Indians taught the newcomers how to live in the forest: how to clear it; how to hunt and trap game; how to fashion moccasins, snowshoes, and canoes. They introduced the whites to corn, sweet potatoes, tobacco, cotton, lima beans, peanuts, and maple sugar. It was only by eating Indian corn that the earliest settlers managed to survive their first terrible winters in North America.

The Indian and nature. Toward the wilderness of the eastern woodlands, the animals and forests within it, the plains stretching westward, and the sky that covered all, Indians held feelings unlike those of Europeans. The land was an important part of the Indians' religion, and religion made the Indians one with the forces of nature. It bound them to the moon, stars, wind, and rain. It bound them to the deer to which they addressed a prayer of apology as they drew back their arrows to shoot it. It bound them to the sun that they called "my relative."

The Art of the First Americans

The figures above are clay whistles, the toys of some child who lived in Mexico long before the time of Columbus. The kneeling figure and the bowl (below) are the work of the Mound Builders, an advanced people about whom we know little. They lived in the central and southeastern United States before the Europeans came.

The vividly painted buckskin used for ceremonial dances shows signs and symbols of nature.

Whites, on the other hand, claimed that their religion encouraged them to conquer the earth and expand their settlements. The Bible said that God had commanded: "Be fruitful and increase and fill the earth and subdue it. Rule over . . . every living thing." (Genesis 1:28.)

The Indians felt that they were temporary residents on the land, that they were its caretakers. The Omaha warrior sang, "I shall vanish and be no more, but the land over which I now roam shall remain and change not." Most tribes held goods in common, and some lacked the idea of private property altogether. Tribal ownership of land merely meant the right to use it. Indians were willing to share that use with others. But they simply could not accept the European idea of real estate as something fenced off for one's exclusive use.

English settlers thought themselves wonderfully generous if they were willing to buy land. But their offers always astonished the Indians. "Sell the country?" exclaimed the warrior chief Tecumseh. "Why not sell the air, the clouds, the Great Sea?" For their part, whites never understood that the chief of a tribe could not sell them land owned by the tribe as a whole. Yet by hook or by crook these settlers managed to "buy" or take away most of it.

The clash of two cultures. The saddest thing about the struggle between Indian and European settler was that it seemed impossible to avoid. Here, on an untouched continent, two peoples met and clashed. The Europeans came first to look for gold and later to build towns, plantations, shipyards, and in time factories. Everywhere that the settler advanced, the Indian was forced to withdraw. And so in the course of the hundreds of years it took the frontier to move from the Atlantic Ocean to the Pacific, the Indians were finally conquered and driven from their homelands.

 TRY THIS!

List these numbers on a sheet of paper; then beside each write an *I* if the sentence would be more true of American Indians, an *E* if it would be more true of European settlers, or a *B* if it would be true of both. **1.** They spoke hundreds of different languages. **2.** They saw themselves as caretakers of the land. **3.** They felt it was their right and duty to control nature. **4.** They adopted new ways of living from the other group. **5.** They are only now beginning to understand the others' history and culture.

2. A NEW EUROPE TAKES SHAPE

When Columbus and his tiny crew sighted land on October 12, 1492, they set off a chain of events that changed the rest of human history. Columbus's discovery started a westward movement of people that still continues. It freed millions of Europeans, enslaved millions of Africans, and killed millions of Indians. It also began a power struggle among western European nations, that finally spread throughout the world.

Exploration, trade, and conquests. By 1492 Europe itself was rapidly becoming a new world. It had entered a time of expansion and change. This drive found a natural outlet in the opening of America for exploration, trade, and conquest.

European merchants were eagerly taking advantage of trade possibilities in distant Russia, the Middle East, India, China, and the coastland of Africa. The European population that had been mostly rural now felt the influence of booming cities like Paris, London, Amsterdam, and Cologne. Landholding lords came under attack from both townspeople and kings.

Martin Luther's challenge. In the same year that Columbus discovered America, Pope Alexander VI was crowned in Rome. Under his rule and that of several popes who followed him, the Roman Catholic Church reached a peak of lavish wealth and display. The very splendor of the papacy laid it open to attacks for "worldliness."

In 1517, the German monk Martin Luther was insisting that the Church badly needed reform. In particular he denounced a practice by which the Church appeared to be selling forgiveness for sin. Furthermore, he said that the Bible was the only reliable source of religious truth. Luther made the Bible available to the people by translating it into ordinary German. It was no longer necessary to understand Latin to read and interpret it.

Some twenty years later, John Calvin was preaching that those who lived thrifty, industrious, sober, and responsible lives were likely to be chosen for salvation. His views were especially attractive to the new middle class of merchants and businessmen who were proud of their thrift and hard work.

After the Reformation. Those who followed Luther and Calvin called themselves *Protestants.* The Catholic Church responded to Protestantism with its own reformation. Old abuses were corrected. A new religious society, the Jesuits, worked to uphold the power of the Pope.

Within Protestantism radical groups were soon questioning all religious authority, and this led to bloody persecutions. Small, persecuted groups were the ones that most often moved to America. They had a great effect on religion in the United States. For instance, they insisted on freedom of conscience and developed ideas on the separation of church and state. They were also the first to spread the idea that America was a haven for those who could find no place in the Old World.

Read here of how

Europe, in 1492, was ready for change.
Europeans were eagerly looking for new routes to the East.
Columbus had a daring plan for getting there.
And the rulers of Spain gambled on his idea.

The spread of information and knowledge. Columbus's discovery of America was triggered by the competition of European countries for the rich trade of the Far East. Marco Polo had journeyed by land to China toward the end of the 1200s, when he was only twelve years old. He was in the East for twenty years, and his accounts inspired other European adventurers.

Marco Polo wrote that in Japan, "the quantity of gold they have is endless." As for Java: "The treasure of this island is so great as to be past telling." His descriptions of Oriental merchants making large profits from the sale of gold, pearls, and spices stirred the envy of European businessmen. For some time they had been importing luxurious fabrics, rare gems, exotic perfumes, and a wide variety of spices from the Middle East. Now they longed to make direct contact with the distant Eastern markets that Marco Polo described.

During the 1300s and 1400s the Italian city-states of Genoa and Venice dominated Eastern trade. They had close ties with the Arabs and with Constantinople, but their overland route to the Orient was long and difficult. By the time goods reached western Europe, only the wealthiest people could afford them.

The first Europeans to look for a better route to the East were the Portuguese. Portugal's rulers dreamed not only of trade and profits but of spreading the Christian gospel to distant lands. Fifty years before Columbus, Portuguese sea captains were

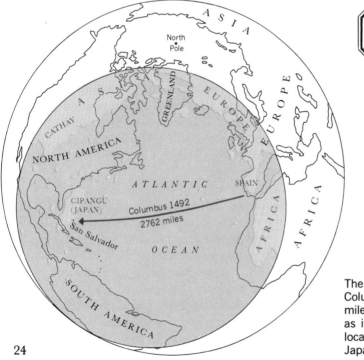

Columbus Misjudges the Distance to Asia

The inner circle of the map shows the world as Columbus believed it to be, with Japan only 2,762 miles west of Spain. The outer circle is the world as it really is. The islands of the Caribbean are located where Columbus expected to find Japan. Japan is really over 14,000 miles west of Spain!

discovering islands in the Atlantic and sailing down the coast of Africa. In 1488 Bartholomeu Dias rounded the tip of that continent. Ten years later Vasco da Gama reached India.

But long before that, the Portuguese set up trading posts along the African coast. Gold and slaves soon poured into Portugal. A system had begun that was to have terrible effects on Africa and the New World.

As western Europeans began their search for a water route to the Orient, new technical developments appeared. Inventions like the magnetic compass, which had been known since the 1100s but little used, were finally put to work. Small, seaworthy sailing vessels called *caravels* allowed longer and swifter ocean voyages. By 1450 accurate maps of the European coastlines existed. Finally the German Johann Gutenberg invented a way of printing with movable type. This was a discovery of supreme importance in human history. It made possible the spread of information and knowledge. And it enabled explorers everywhere to benefit from one another's experience.

West to the Orient. Christopher Columbus was a sea captain from Genoa, Italy. He had wandered through the courts of Europe for almost ten years, trying to raise money for a plan to reach the Orient by sailing westward from Europe. He knew a great deal about sailing, and his idea rested on firm scientific knowledge.

Columbus's knowledge was wrong in only one important detail. Sailors and learned men had never lost sight of the fact that the world was round. The earth that the Italian poet Dante described in his *Divine Comedy* (written about 1300) was a globe, and anyone who lived on a seacoast could watch ships going down over the ho-

rizon. But the size of the earth was still in doubt. A Greek geographer had accurately worked out its circumference almost two thousand years before. But Columbus either did not know about that measurement or didn't believe it. Instead, he accepted a calculation by later geographers that made the earth very much smaller than it actually is. A globe manufactured by a German in 1492 showed the earth as one-third its actual size. Armed with this kind of misinformation, Columbus assumed that India was comparatively near Europe.

The Spanish venture. In 1492 King Ferdinand and Queen Isabella of Spain agreed to back Columbus. They would pay for an expedition that would carry him westward to India and China. Their sup-

---

 THE FAILURE OF A DREAM

Columbus founded two colonies on the island he called Hispaniola (Santo Domingo). The first was destroyed by the Indians, and he lost command of the second. At one point he was even shipped back to Spain in chains by an official sent to investigate complaints against him.

When he died, Columbus was so completely forgotten that it is not even known for sure where his bones are buried. For a long time they were thought to be beneath a religious shrine in Spain. But the government of the Dominican Republic claimed that it had found them in a plain casket within a walled-off section of an old mission.

This might have been the final revenge of Christopher Columbus's angry followers.

port enabled him to set out with three ships, the *Niña*, the *Pinta*, and the *Santa Maria*, manned by a crew of ninety. It was a voyage that would transform the world.

Columbus first sighted land on San Salvador—probably Watling's Island in the Bahamas—on October 12, 1492. His journal records that the people there "traded and gave everything they had, with good will. But it appeared to me that these people were poor in everything."

After a brief stay Columbus sailed on to discover Cuba and Hispaniola (the island of Santo Domingo). These islands became a jumping-off point later for Spanish conquests. They lay about where Columbus had expected to find the coast of Asia. This convinced him that he was only a short distance from the riches of China and Japan. He returned to Europe with a few natives he had kidnapped and whose strange appearance caused a sensation in Spain.

Between 1493 and 1504, Columbus returned three more times to the New World. In the fall of 1502 he sailed along the Central American coast and informed King Ferdinand he was exploring the Malay Peninsula. He never lost his belief that the islands he had discovered were on the outskirts of China and Japan.

 TRY THIS!

1. Explain how Europeans might have discovered the New World even if the compass, the caravel, or the art of printing had never been invented. 2. Suppose you had been the ruler of Spain in 1492. List the reasons you might have had for going along with Columbus's plan. What were some arguments against it? 3. Using an outline map of the world, show just how Columbus made his great mistake about America.

3. THE SPANIARDS IN THE NEW WORLD

Within a year of Columbus's voyage, his letters to King Ferdinand and Queen Isabella had been translated into twelve languages. It was not long before Europeans began to realize that he had stumbled on a new world. Amerigo Vespucci (ves-POO-chee), an Italian explorer, went along on one of the Spanish voyages to the New World. Vespucci's accounts were widely read, and this probably caused his name to be given to the continents of the Western Hemisphere. Otherwise they might have been called North and South Columbia.

Between 1519 and 1522, a ship of Ferdinand Magellan, also sailing for Spain, voyaged around the world. (Magellan himself was killed in the Philippines.) His crew

established that the ancient Greek geographer (page 25) had been right after all about the size of the earth. It was considerably larger than Columbus had thought, and the westward route was no short cut to the Indies.

———— ◆●◆ ————

Read here of how

Spanish conquerors built a mighty empire.
Many Indians were enslaved and died.
An Indian civilization was destroyed.
Spanish power spread but then was checked.

———— ◆●◆ ————

EARLY EXPLORERS OF NORTH AMERICA

	Year	Country	Part of Present United States Explored
Juan Ponce de Léon	1513	Spain	Florida
Giovanni da Verrazano	1524	France	Atlantic coast from Virginia to Canada
Hernando de Soto	1539–1542	Spain	Southeastern United States to Mississippi R.
Francisco Coronado	1540–1542	Spain	Texas, Oklahoma, Kansas
Francis Drake	1577–1579	England	California coast
Samuel de Champlain	1603–1607, 1615–1616	France	New England coast, Lake Champlain, Great Lakes
Henry Hudson	1609	Dutch	Hudson River
Louis Joliet	1669, 1672–1674	France	Great Lakes Mississippi R. and valley to Arkansas R.
Jacques Marquette	1672–1674	France	(with Joliet) Mississippi R. and valley
Robert La Salle	1682	France	Mississippi R. to mouth

Nonetheless, within ten years of being discovered, the New World had become the goal of colonists and treasure-seekers alike. Less than fifty years after Columbus's voyages, Spain had established an empire stretching from Florida and California to Cape Horn. Spanish historians have called the 1500s *el siglo de oro,* "the century of gold."

"They live in a golden age." The wealth that poured into Spain from the New World stirred the imagination of its ambitious young men. They turned their eyes westward and became *conquistadors* (kon-KWISS-tuh-dorz)—adventurers licensed by the king but paying their own way. In time they carried the Spanish flag, the sword, and the cross into the farthest parts of the Americas. They agreed to set aside for the king of Spain a share of any wealth they might discover or that their colonies might produce. The conquistadors were certain that they would still become rich through what they were allowed to keep.

To the Spanish, as to so many tourists in our own day, the islands of the Caribbean seemed like a Garden of Eden. Their reports spread the belief that the Indian was a "noble savage." "The islanders of Hispaniola," wrote one Spaniard, "go naked. They know neither weights nor measures nor the source of all misfortunes, money. They live in a golden age, without

27

In the drawing above are Spaniards and an Aztec before a temple in Tenochtitlán. Right is a breast ornament in the form of a fire serpent.

duced by whites thinned the Indian population. Between 1492 and 1509 the numbers in Hispaniola alone fell from a million to barely 14,000.

Even the passionate pleas of a missionary priest, Bartolomé de Las Casas, a few years later, could not put an end to the brutal treatment of the Indians. "The Spaniards' conduct towards these people," he declared to the king, "their robberies, murders . . . has brought great infamy on the name of Jesus and the Christian religion. . . . I believe that because of these [terrible] acts, God will visit His wrath upon Spain."

"We must depart forever." Two thousand miles beyond the home of the simple people of the Caribbean, in what is now Mexico City, lay the capital of the highly developed Aztec civilization. The Aztecs arrived in Mexico sometime in the early 1300s. They had been hunters, but they borrowed from and built upon the culture of the Mayas and others who flourished in

laws, without lying judges, without books, satisfied with their life, and in no way concerned for the future."

A great infamy. Yet the Spaniards had not come as tourists; they came to conquer. They enslaved the natives and forced them to mine the gold, which was plentiful on the mainland but in short supply on the islands. And the conquistadors punished their new subjects cruelly when the right amount of gold was not delivered. Their savage treatment drove many Indians to suicide. At the same time, diseases intro-

Central America. Then they turned to founding a mighty empire.

Among the achievements of the Aztecs were beautiful metalwork, unusual sculpture, a remarkable way of weaving, and engineering skills by which they built a city on a marshy lake. This was Mexico City, or Tenochtitlán (tay-nohch-tee-TLAHN). The Aztecs also appear to have had a system by which everyone could obtain an education.

The Aztecs' worship of the war god Huitzilopochtli (weet-see-loh-POCH-tlee) was extremely cruel. On his altars they offered up still-beating hearts torn from the bodies of their prisoners of war.

In the 1500s the Aztecs' neighbors joined with Hernán Cortés, greatest of the conquistadors, against the Aztec ruler, Moctezuma (mokt-uh-ZOO-muh). In the decisive battle Cortés had only a thousand Spaniards and twelve horses. Yet his leadership was so effective that with the aid of his Indian allies he was able to topple the

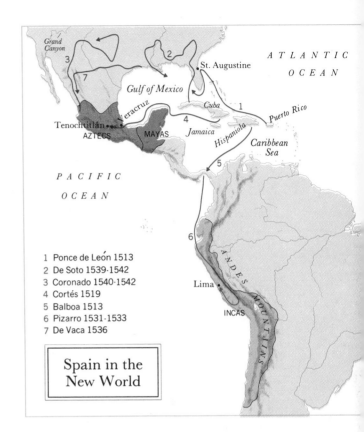

1 Ponce de León 1513
2 De Soto 1539-1542
3 Coronado 1540-1542
4 Cortés 1519
5 Balboa 1513
6 Pizarro 1531-1533
7 De Vaca 1536

Spain in the New World

vast Aztec empire. He destroyed it, together with its capital city, Tenochtitlán.

"I lift my voice in wailing, I am afflicted," lamented the Aztec, "as I remember that we must leave the beautiful flowers, the noble songs. Let us enjoy ourselves for a while, let us sing, for we must depart forever, we are to be destroyed in our dwelling place."

The pursuit of gold and glory. Early in 1521, just as the Aztecs were surrendering to the Spaniards, the conquistador Juan Ponce de León died trying to invade Florida. Ponce de León had come to America on Columbus's second voyage and afterwards seized Puerto Rico. But tribal groups in Florida proved more difficult than those in the Caribbean and Mexico, and it was

29

A SPANISH SOLDIER ENTERS MEXICO CITY

We went along the causeway, which is eight paces wide at that point and runs straight into the City of Mexico (Tenochtitlán). Wide as it is, it was so crowded with people that there was hardly room for all of them. Besides those who came out to see us, some were leaving the city and others returning to it, so that we were hardly able to pass. The towers and pyramidlike temples were full of people too, and so were the canoes that came from all parts of the lake. It was not surprising, for none had ever before seen horses, or men like us.

Gazing at such wonderful sights, we did not know what to say, or whether what we saw was real. On the land were great buildings and on the lake ever so many more. The lake itself was crowded with canoes. And in front of us stood the great City of Mexico. We, on the other hand, did not number 400 soldiers! Then we remembered the warnings that had been given us not to enter Mexico City because the people would kill us as soon as they had us inside.

Think, readers, what I am saying. What other men have shown such daring?

After Bernal Diaz del Castillo,
The Conquest of New Spain.

This mirror frame of cast and hammered gold was made for the Incas by Chimu artisans.

another forty years before the Spanish were able to establish a permanent colony. They called it St. Augustine, and its date—1565—makes it the oldest European settlement in the United States.

In the 1530s the conquistadors subdued the Inca empire in the part of South America where Peru and Ecuador are now. The Incas had developed an empire of many tribes, numerous languages, and a system of splendid roads. Along these roads, many of which still exist, relays of runners carried messages to and from government officials.

In metalwork the Incas moved ahead of the Aztecs and earlier Mayas. But they had a fatal weakness. They were blindly obedient to the authority of their god-em-

When we drew near the city, the great Moctezuma appeared and got down from his litter, helped by his chiefs. They stood by him beneath a rich canopy of green-colored feathers, with gold and silver embroidery, and with pearls hanging from the border. Moctezuma was richly dressed and wearing sandals with soles of gold, decorated with precious stones.

When Cortés learned that Moctezuma was approaching, he got down from his horse and they greeted each other. It seemed to me that our Cortés offered him his right hand and Moctezuma did not want to take it. But then he did give his hand to Cortés. Then Cortés brought out a necklace made of colored glass stones strung on a perfumed cord of gold. But when he went to embrace Moctezuma, the chiefs held Cortés back, considering it beneath the emperor's dignity to be so treated.

Later, after having thought about all that we had seen, some of our soldiers who had been in many parts of the world, to Constantinople and all over Italy and in Rome, said that they had never before seen so large a place, one so full of people and yet so well run.

peror. This allowed immediate transfer of control to the Spanish conquerors, once Pizarro had seized the Incas' supreme ruler.

Meanwhile, other conquistadors were pursuing gold and glory elsewhere, in North America. These adventurers were often lured by tales of fabulous cities of gold. Such stories were given out by Indians, who would tell the Spaniards anything that might make them go somewhere else. Conquistadors ranged from the Blue Ridge Mountains of the eastern United States to Drake's Bay, California. In 1539 Francisco Vásquez de Coronado set out to conquer the mythical Seven Cities of Cíbola. They turned out to be Zuni Indian villages, but on that trip one of Coronado's men discovered the Grand Canyon.

English sea dogs. Through the 1500s Spain seemed all-powerful, but appearances were deceiving. Spanish wealth had attracted the interest of English adventurers. The Spaniards called them pirates, and their attacks on the treasure fleets from the West Indies were increasingly costly. An angry King Philip II of Spain further complained that Queen Elizabeth I of England had secretly helped the Dutch in a successful revolt against his rule.

The English monarch had also done something even more objectionable. She had financed many of the attacks on the Spanish treasure fleet in exchange for a share of the loot. Moreover, Elizabeth's steady refusal to return to the Catholic faith had infuriated Philip II.

In 1588, to destroy the English menace forever, Philip ordered a fleet into English waters. This vast Armada, made up of 132 ships carrying over 3,000 cannon, was the largest that had ever been assembled. But swift-moving English warships commanded

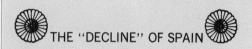

THE "DECLINE" OF SPAIN

Though Spain's power shrank after 1600, the Spanish empire in America continued to grow. A Spanish colony in New Mexico lasted from 1598 to 1680. Missionaries like the Franciscan priest Junipero Serra helped to spread Spain's influence. He founded a chain of missions that stretched northward through what is now California, from San Diego to San Francisco. In 1776, just as the American Revolution was beginning, Spain's expansion in the New World reached its peak. In that year Juan Bautista de Anza led a hardy group of permanent settlers to the San Francisco Bay area.

by men like Francis Drake and Gilbert Hawkins totally destroyed it. The English "sea dogs" who had robbed King Philip's treasure had now stolen his power. Never again did Spain regain its old supremacy, but its mark upon the New World was permanent.

TRY THIS!

1. Look up the meaning of the Spanish word *conquistador*. Why was it applied to men like Cortés, Pizarro, Ponce de León, and Coronado? **2.** Describe the city of the Aztecs as it must have looked to Cortés and his followers. **3.** Explain how a handful of Spanish soldiers were able to overthrow the Aztec empire, while Spain's mighty Armada was defeated by a small island kingdom.

4.   OTHER EUROPEANS IN AMERICA

Hope of profit brought Europeans to America. This was true of the great nations and of the lesser ones as well.

A sharp-tongued governor. In 1624 the Dutch West India Company founded their colony of New Amsterdam on the present site of New York City. To encourage settlement they offered large estates along the Hudson River to anyone who brought fifty families to America.

The most memorable leader of New Amsterdam was its one-legged, sharp-tongued governor Peter Stuyvesant (STY-vuh-s'nt). To those who criticized him Stuyvesant said, "We derive our authority from God and the Company, not from a few ignorant subjects." But when he tried to impose the Dutch Reformed faith on the German, English, Jewish, and Dutch popu-

lation of the colony, the Company quickly overruled him. It had no interest in letting religious squabbles interfere with the flow of profits from the fur trade.

Stuyvesant was more successful when he seized the colony of New Sweden. This settlement was located in the lower Delaware valley. It had barely survived until

Read here of how

The Dutch came to the New World.
The French claimed part of North America.
The English failed to find a northwest passage.
And lost a colony as well.

Stuyvesant snuffed out its existence in 1655. However, the Swedes had already made an important gift to America: the log cabin.

Stuyvesant finally had to surrender his colony to the English in 1664.

France in Canada. The French first began to explore America in the early 1600s. It was then that the brilliant Samuel de Champlain (sham-PLAYN) gave them their claim to Canada. Champlain explored the New York lake named for him and then went on to the Great Lakes. At the same time, he created a chain of bases that secured French supremacy in the St. Lawrence and upper Mississippi valleys.

But Champlain's most important act was founding the fortress of Quebec. Begun in 1608, it remained a French stronghold for 150 years. Champlain's most serious mistake was allying himself with the weaker Huron Indians against the powerful Iroquois. Later on, the alliance of the Iroquois with the English helped to give Britain military victory over France in the New World.

"History written on a beaver skin." The explorations of Champlain and of La Salle, who followed him, were extended by Jesuit priest-explorers. One of these, named Louis Hennepin, gave Europeans their first account of Niagara Falls; another, Jacques Marquette, explored the

Fish and furs were the mainstay of New France.

33

upper reaches of the Mississippi. There were many more. Such men were searching not for gold, but for souls. "You must have sincere affection for the savages," wrote Father Jean de Brébeuf (bray-BERF) in his instructions to newly arrived Jesuit missionaries, "looking upon them as our brothers with whom we are to pass the rest of our lives."

The missionaries' affectionate concern for the Indians was not always returned. Father Brébeuf was slowly tortured to death when he fell into the hands of the Iroquois in 1649. In upstate New York today the National Shrine of the North American Martyrs marks the spot where Isaac Jogues (ZHOHG) and two other French missionaries met a similar fate. Jogues and Brébeuf were later declared saints by their Church.

But other French-Indian relations were friendly. Fair dealing with the Algonquin and Huron Indians gave the French a secure place in North America's interior (map on page 74). The fur trade also happened to be good business. In return for tools, guns, brandy, and cloth, the Indians supplied the newcomers with valuable furs. It has even been said that "the history of North America can be written on a beaver skin."

From the beginning the French settlement suffered from underpopulation. The king would not allow French Protestants to settle there, and few others were willing to. The colony reflected the needs of the handful of businessmen who ran the fur trade. Furs provided a lot of money for the mother country, but sending out the profits did not make for a prosperous colony. By 1700 only 7,000 French lived in the New World—a handful in possession of the heartland of North America.

Fool's gold. Seventy-five years after Columbus, an English navigator named Sir Humphrey Gilbert described America as an island. He argued that it would be possible to sail around it to the Orient. In other words, he claimed that there must be a northwest passage.

The possibility fascinated Martin Frobisher. Frobisher was one of the English sea dogs who later helped to defeat the Spanish Armada. He made three voyages (1576–1578) looking for the northwest passage, but he never found it. What he did find, in northern Canada, was the shiny worthless substance called iron pyrites, or fool's gold. It put the whole idea of northern exploration under a cloud for a few years.

However, in 1608, 1609, and 1610 another Englishman, Henry Hudson, tried to find a northern route. On his second voyage he explored the Hudson River for the Dutch East India Company. His third voyage brought him into Hudson Bay, also named for him. It was his last trip. On the way home in 1611, Hudson's crew mutinied and set him adrift in a small boat. No trace of him was ever found.

A doomed colony. Earlier, Sir Walter Raleigh—soldier, writer, adventurer, and half brother of Sir Humphrey Gilbert—became interested in colonizing America. In 1584, two ships sailing under his orders had returned with news of a vast and grand region, a land "most plentiful, sweet, fruitful, and wholesome of all the world." They reported that the people there lived "void of all guile and treason . . . after the manner of the golden age."

The artist John White (page 36) painted this village scene showing houses, plantings, and ceremonies of tribal groups on the Virginia coast.

Their greene corne

Corne newly sprong.

Their sittinge at meate

The place of solemne prayer

horse wherin the Tombe of their Herounds standeth.

SECOTON.

A Ceremony in their prayers wt strange testurs and songs dansing abowt posts carued on the topps lyke mens faces.

Raleigh promptly named the new country Virginia in honor of the Virgin Queen Elizabeth I. He also saw the chance of wealth. Even though the Queen refused to invest in his expedition, Raleigh raised enough to send out a fleet of seven ships. The year was 1585, and he was about to found the first English colony in the New World, at Roanoke.

Nearly 200 men made the voyage, including Thomas Hariot, a writer, and John White, an artist. Their writings and drawings provided the first accurate and detailed picture of this part of North America. But the colonists' experience was so terrible that when their leader returned to England for reinforcements, they sailed home on the remaining ships. The colony was renewed with an even larger group, including the parents of Virginia Dare, the first English child born in America. But in 1590, when the next English ships put in at Roanoke, the entire colony had vanished—its fate a mystery that has not been solved to this day. Another seventeen years passed before the English planted a successful colony in North America.

 TRY THIS!

1. Make a chart showing the explorations and colonies of the Dutch, the Swedes, and the French. Show what happened to their colonies.   **2.** Compare the early French and Spanish treatment of the Indians.   **3.** Draw a map of North America as Sir Humphrey Gilbert might have imagined it. Show why this view was so appealing to the English.

5.   AFRICA AND THE SLAVE TRADE

Europe had always known that south of the Mediterranean and the great sea of sand called the Sahara was the world of black Africa. There in vast grasslands had flourished the empires of Ghana, Mali, and Songhai (SON-guy).

Lands beyond the Sahara. Arabs and other followers of Mohammed reached the interior of Africa in the 700s. There they found rich farmlands producing grain, cotton, and other crops. Cattle-raising was the specialty of one people living there; the nomadic Fulani. Their vast herds provided meat and dairy products, as well as hides to be worked into leather goods. In many towns cloth-weaving and work in metals, including iron, employed thousands. Caravans moved across the Sahara carrying gold, ivory, hides, and slaves. These were traded for salt, swords, silks, woolen blankets, beads, and other ornaments.

The legend of African cities in which gold was so plentiful it was used to pave streets excited awe and greed. Throughout Europe the prosperous city of Timbuktu (tim-buk-TOO) on the Niger River helped to inspire these legends. There was a flourishing trade in its great markets. Its schools

---

Read here of how

Civilizations flourished in ancient Africa.
Gold and slaves attracted Europeans.
The New World's need for workers expanded
   the African slave trade.

---

were centers of learning and scholarship. Visitors occasionally reported the existence of splendid palaces and mosques. These were the places of worship for the Muslims—the followers of Mohammed. Visitors to Timbuktu were especially impressed by the complicated system of irrigation. It allowed farming to flourish even on the edge of the Sahara.

Black gold. As traders from Portugal made their way along the coast of west Africa, they came upon a number of seaports. None was more surprising than the city of Benin in the Niger valley. Its walls stretched for 25 miles, and within them was a city of palaces, wide avenues, and comfortable homes. Benin's prosperity was based on manufacturing and farming.

The Portuguese were astonished when they noted the absence of beggars. Benin had a system of social security that guaranteed everyone the essentials of life. Everywhere Europeans went in West Africa, they found plenty of evidence that here were prosperous societies and civilizations.

One thing was missing. Unlike the Europeans, the Africans had not developed a technology of guns. In the conflict between African and European, the gun was the key to victory. The goods of Africa attracted white attention. But as Europeans expanded their empires in the New World, they more and more needed Africa's man and woman power. This was the "black gold" that drew first the Portuguese and then the Spanish, French, Dutch, and English into the slave trade. Between 1450 and 1850, the trade in human beings condemned at least ten million to slavery.

Benin was noted for its bronze work, as can be seen from the figure of a musician above and the head of a young queen below.

37

This watercolor was done by a British navy officer—the only picture of a slave ship made from life.

NEW-WORLD SLAVERY

Slavery did not begin in the Americas. The Bible speaks of it. The Greeks and Romans practiced it. Throughout the Middle Ages it existed in southern Europe as a holdover from ancient times. In the 1300s and 1400s Italian merchants, who dominated Mediterranean shipping, also carried on a busy trade in white slaves from southeastern Europe. A mild form of slavery existed in Africa long before the coming of the Europeans. African slaves were generally criminals, debtors, or prisoners of war. But in many cases they had the right to own property, marry free persons, or buy their way out of slavery. They were often considered part of the family that owned them. Some slaves even rose to positions of leadership in African communities. This slavery had nothing to do with race.

In the New World the Europeans at first enslaved the Indians. Those living in the Caribbean were special targets. As slaves, the Indians were generally put to work on their own islands. They were expected to produce gold and other valuables. But the land contained little of either, and so they grew desperate. Many committed suicide; others fled into the interior of their islands only to be pursued by hunters and large dogs. As we have seen, the death rate among the Indians was fearful (page 28). By 1540 the Spaniards were looking for replacements from Africa. Increasingly, blacks began appearing in the Caribbean to mine precious metals and produce sugar on the plantations.

The slave/gun cycle. The European powers established forts and trading posts on the West African coast, but they rarely ventured inland. It was the African rulers of coastal regions who sent raiding parties into the interior to capture slaves, and marched them back to the coast chained to each other in long lines or *coffles.* The rulers then sold them to Europeans for guns. In this way they saved their own people from slavery.

The slaves were loaded onto slave ships and sent to America. This terrible voyage was called the Middle Passage. A quarter of the human cargo regularly died in the overcrowded, disease-ridden ships. The shipowners found it more profitable to let some slaves die than to load fewer of them onto the vessels.

On the islands or coast of the New World, the slaves were "seasoned." This process was supposed to break their will to resist. When the earliest slaves reached areas like Brazil, their life span was usually no more than seven years.

The slave trade was disastrous for African society. Firearms introduced by the Europeans set off the grim "slave/gun cycle." African rulers who received guns were able to attack their neighbors and capture more slaves. West Africans quickly understood the importance of the gun: it spelled the difference between freedom and slavery. To protect themselves they entered the trade. The result was that in a steadily widening area of West Africa, raids and wars to obtain slaves became a normal part of life. No one knows for sure how many people died in these struggles, but the numbers probably ran into millions. Vast areas were emptied, and where once there had been flourishing societies, there was a wasteland. Men had made a new kind of Sahara.

Riches for some. African slaves were valuable workers because they knew how to farm and had other skills. By the end of the 1600s slavery had reached every colony of North and South America. Beginning in the mid-1600s, and increasing in the 1700s, over 400,000 slaves were brought to those English colonies that would become part of the United States. A good deal of the trade between English North America and Europe involved the transportation and sale of slaves. Great fortunes were earned from the trade, and cities like Liverpool, England, became the centers from which it was run. It was quickly realized by those who bought slaves that the African slave trade could make them rich. Profits encouraged its steady growth.

Once black men, women, and children were enslaved, it was only a matter of time before whites began to think slavery was the natural condition of blacks. Within the New World, a monster was being born: racism. And it remained to plague the nation long after the trade that caused it had ended.

 TRY THIS!

1. Compare the culture that grew up in Africa, south of the Sahara, with that of the Aztecs. Does either one seem superior? Did one develop anything that the other lacked?
2. Describe the slave trade as it might have appeared to a European sea captain, a West African chieftain, a landowner in the West Indies, and an American Indian of Central America.

39

ROUNDUP

Who?

Martin Luther
Marco Polo
Amerigo Vespucci
Bartolomé de Las Casas
Samuel de Champlain

What?

Iroquois confederacy
Algonquin
Sioux
Navaho
Reformation
northwest passage
Middle Passage

Where?

the Bahamas
Tenochtitlán
St. Augustine
Roanoke
Timbuktu

KNOW THIS

The Earliest Americans

1. What do today's scientists think about the origins of the earliest Americans?
2. List three differences in culture among Indian tribes of North America.
3. Explain how the American Indians and the European settlers were both borrowers and lenders of culture.
4. What evidence is there that the Indians did not live in a "changeless, unproductive, Stone Age culture"?

A New Europe Takes Shape

1. What was the Reformation? Why did it occur when the Catholic Church seemed at the height of its power?
2. How did Europeans learn about the rich trade opportunities in the Orient?
3. Identify three inventions that helped promote European exploration.
4. Describe Columbus's plan for reaching the East.

The Spaniards in the New World

1. Describe the attitudes and behavior of the conquistadors towards the Indians of the Caribbean.
2. Why do we consider Aztec civilization advanced?
3. Explain how the Aztec empire was overthrown.
4. What event reduced Spain's hold on the New World?

Other Europeans in North America

1. Who was Peter Stuyvesant? What sort of person was he?
2. What territories did Champlain claim for France?
3. What important mistake did Champlain make?
4. In what sense was the history of French North America "written on a beaver skin"?
5. Identify two "firsts" of Raleigh's colony at Roanoke.

Africa and the Slave Trade

1. What were some of the goods produced by the African states south of the Sahara?
2. How did the slave trade become part of life in West Africa?
3. What made the slave trade so profitable for Europeans?
4. Why had the Spaniards enslaved the Indians of the Caribbean?
5. How did the slave trade destroy African culture?

DIG HERE

The following guide will help you to examine in depth the career of one of the New World explorers.

A. List five characteristics related to the explorer's achievements. Cite specific examples.
B. Include facts about a) the physical environments in which the explorer lived and later worked, b) his family background, c) his occupation, d) his social class.
C. Can you show any connections between the explorer's life and his achievements?
D. Describe historical conditions at the time the explorer lived. Which events are related to his achievements? What values or beliefs did people hold at the time?
E. On the explorer's most important expedition, a) What problems did he face? How did he meet them? b) What people or events helped him? c) What important discoveries resulted from the explorer's efforts?
F. Final Evaluation
   Does history make special people, or do special people make history? Were this explorer's accomplishments a result of character, behavior, and background, or of the general conditions of the time in which he lived? If the explorer had been born three hundred years earlier, would he have done something similar?

Useful sources are Brebner, *Explorers of North America,* Doubleday; *Discoverers of the New World,* Am. Her.; Hale, *Age of Exploration,* Time Inc.

THINK ABOUT IT

1. Just how did the magnetic compass, the caravel, and the printing press contribute to the European discovery and exploration of America? Could they have taken place without any one of the inventions? Explain.
2. How good were the European claims to various parts of America? Should the Europeans have respected the rights of the Indians? Since they didn't, should something be done now? What?
3. Should something be done now to make up for the injustices of the slave trade? If so, what? Who should benefit? Who should pay? Give reasons for your answers.

DO IT!

1. With a classmate, look up one of these: Marco Polo, European trade with the East, Moctezuma, the defeat of the Armada. Report to the class in the form of a TV interview, with one of you as a reporter and the other as Marco Polo, a Portuguese sea captain, Moctezuma, or an English sailor.
2. Invite an archaeologist or archaeology student to tell the class about the methods, tools, and procedures used on a dig.

THEN AND NOW

What are some of the problems arising from our use of the environment? Do we have anything to learn about ecology from the American Indians? If the problem is not new, why is it getting so much attention now? Explain.

A Colonial People Sink Their Roots

2

Had it not been for the tobacco plant, Jamestown might have failed as had earlier settlements. For the English colony, tobacco was like the Spaniards' gold and the furs of the French—something Europe wanted. If England's colonies had sent it gold or furs, would the mother country have been so careless about them?

The English who came to America brought with them a long tradition of individual rights. They firmly believed that the power of government should be strictly limited and that people were capable of running their own affairs. On such traditions and beliefs, colonial society was built.

The earliest English settlements were made, only a few years apart, in Virginia and in New England. Yet each developed differently, and each set the pattern for future colonies in its own region. In a sense Virginia was the mother of what we today call the South, and New England the father of today's North. Both began very small.

1.   A BEGINNING IN VIRGINIA

Near the end of 1606, 144 men set sail from England in three small ships. The Virginia Company of London was sending them to start an English colony in the New World—the first one that succeeded. By the time the men sailed up the James River, May 24, 1607, only 104 were still living. They landed sick and worn from their five-month journey.

Survival. The colonists selected a spot thirty miles from the sea so that they would be safe from the Spaniards and from pirates. They also chose a place easy to defend against Indians. But they paid a price. Jamestown, as they called their settlement, was surrounded by mosquito-filled forests and swamps. Almost at once the settlers began dying of malaria and yellow fever. No one knew that the mosquitoes carried the diseases.

There were other problems as well. Too many of the colonists were gentlemen and adventurers, mostly interested in hunting for gold and silver. The merchants and other wealthy men of the Virginia Company who had put up the money for the colony encouraged the search for riches. All hoped their colony would produce the same kind of wealth that had made Spain so rich. But the new settlers soon learned that if they were to survive, they must grow food. And too few of them were experienced farmers.

A lesson for America. Jamestown would probably have died out altogether if John Smith had not set about correcting its problems. He was a short, muscular man who had had a colorful career as a soldier fighting the Turks. Smith was tough and disciplined, and he laid down a blunt rule: those who would not work would not eat.

Smith added to the food supply by trading with the Indians. Once he was captured by the local chief, Powhatan; the

---

Read here of how

The English planted a colony at Jamestown.
They learned to produce tobacco.
They were prosperous and self-governing.
But their wealth was based on slavery.

TIME CHART

1607   Jamestown is founded.
1619   The House of Burgesses meets.
1619   The first blacks arrive at
       Jamestown.
1620   Plymouth is founded.
1630   Puritans settle Boston.
1664   The English take New Netherland.
1692   Witchcraft trials are held in
       Massachusetts.
1704   The Boston *News-Letter* appears.
1735   John Peter Zenger is tried for libel.

---

chief's daughter Pocahontas saved his life. After being released, he again barely escaped death. Some of the Jamestown colonists wanted him executed for having lost two men on that trading trip.

When not saving the colony, Smith was busy exploring and mapping the interior of Virginia. By the time he left for England in 1609, it seemed likely that Jamestown would survive. Smith's toughness had shown that in a new settlement hard work and self-denial were what counted. It was a lesson that frontier America never forgot.

Harsh discipline. The colonists went through another terrible winter, another "starving time." There was sickness and there were Indian attacks, but mostly the settlers died of hunger. However, five hundred more settlers, this time including some women and children, arrived in 1610.

With the new arrivals and some better management, Jamestown slowly began to grow. A pattern of life took shape. Instead of working only for the common store, each man received three acres for his own use. In return he gave three months' service to

43

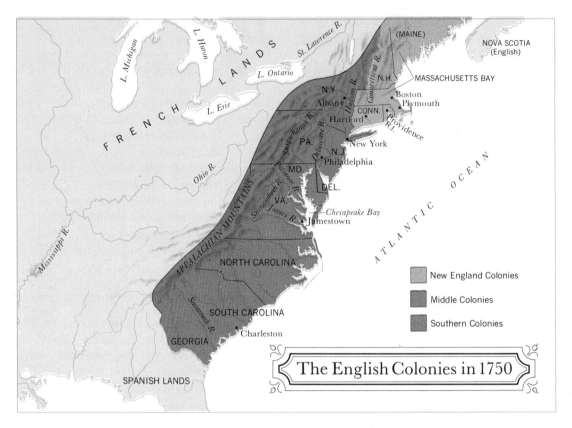

The English Colonies in 1750

the colony. Settlers rose early each day to work their fields, then met for morning prayers. After prayers the colonists went back to their fields or worked on fortifications or on their homes.

This strict routine had been laid out to end quarreling and disorder, which had threatened to destroy the settlement. Those who failed to go along drew swift punishment. The discipline was painful, but it guaranteed the future of the colony.

Success at last. Almost from the beginning the prosperity of the Virginia colony depended on tobacco. This plant had long been used by the Indians. Spaniards learned to grow it in the West Indies, and by the late 1500s it had become popular throughout Europe.

The kind of tobacco that grew in Virginia was coarse and bitter. No one in England would have liked it. Then, in 1612, the colonist John Rolfe succeeded in growing the finer West Indian tobacco near Jamestown. The first shipment to England a few years later was an instant success. Soon the Virginia settlers were so taken up with growing and drying the profitable leaf that they had to be ordered to plant food as well. Otherwise, they would have starved.

"Two shiploads every year." Growing tobacco brought a pressing need for more workers. In 1618, to attract settlers, Virginia adopted a revolutionary new plan. By the *headright system* anyone who migrated to the colony or paid the passage for someone else was given fifty acres of land.

Those whose passage was paid by someone else became *indentured servants.* That is, they worked for a period of years (usually seven) to repay their debt. At the end of their *indenture,* the servants too became eligible for fifty acres of land.

Virginia planters were soon importing as many indentured servants as they could. One large landowner wrote home, "I am pretty confident I could dispose of two shiploads every year." The Virginia Company itself sent over many servants to work its own lands. So that settlers already in America would not feel cheated, the Company also gave each of them a hundred acres or more. In this way, from the very beginning, it was assured that ownership of land would be spread among large numbers of people—an entirely different situation from that in Europe.

Without legal standing. Virginia's demand for workers could not be satisfied by indentured servants from England. In 1619 John Rolfe recorded the arrival of a Dutch ship whose cargo included twenty blacks. This was the beginning of the use of blacks from Africa as workers. Throughout the 1600s the number of black workers slowly grew until at the end of the century more than one out of every three Virginians was a black.

At first blacks seem to have been treated as indentured servants. As late as 1651 some blacks were being given land as free men when they finished their indentures. But there is also evidence that as early as 1640 some blacks were being held as slaves for life. Slavery was not recognized in the laws of Virginia until 1661. Those laws did not affect blacks who were already free.

A group apart. Certainly, from the beginning, white Virginians regarded blacks as outsiders and as inferior. Even when there were only 200 blacks in the colony, they were treated as a group apart. In 1639 blacks were barred from entering the militia or from owning arms. In the 1640s black indentured servants who tried to run away were made to serve for life. This was not true of white indentured servants.

Rights and freedom. In 1619, the year after they began giving land to settlers, the owners of the Virginia Company established the House of Burgesses (citizens). It was the first system of representative government in English America. Under it landowners in each settlement of the colony chose two people who met with the other "burgesses" at Jamestown. The House of Burgesses was intended to give the colonists a chance to express their opinions. In no time at all it had taken over the power to make the colony's laws.

The old regulations were now relaxed. The king's charter promised all Virginians the same rights and freedoms, as though they were living "within this our Realm of England." Education was encouraged, and there was an attempt to introduce other means of making a living besides tobacco growing. Iron works, brick manufacturing, and fur trading were promoted. But as demand for tobacco spread in England and throughout Europe, the colony's dependence on it increased.

An Indian hostage. The first Virginians settled in an area controlled by the mighty chief Powhatan. This powerful leader ruled a confederacy of some thirty tribes. Powhatan's people lived by fishing, hunting, and growing corn. At first their relations with the whites were fairly friendly. The Indians helped the whites to survive during the first terrible years. And they liked getting European goods and weapons.

45

But as whites prospered and tried to crowd the Indians off their lands, tensions grew. These seemed to quiet down when the tobacco planter John Rolfe married Powhatan's daughter Pocahontas in 1614. The famous romance was a great advantage to the colonists, for it gave them a hostage who assured that Powhatan would not attack them. But Pocahontas died in 1617, followed a year later by her father.

"Bloody and barbarous hands." Powhatan's brother took command of the confederacy in 1618. He watched angrily as more and more Indian lands were planted with tobacco. Virginia enjoyed the

This deerskin cloak with shell decorations may have belonged to Powhatan.

new prosperity and neglected its defenses. Then, on a Friday morning in March of 1622, some Indians came to Jamestown as though to trade. Instead, they attacked. The official account read: "There fell under the bloody and barbarous hands of that perfidious and inhumane people . . . 347 men, women, and children, mostly by their own weapons." In all nearly a quarter of the colonists were killed.

The Indian attack is called the Massacre of 1622. (Indian victories are always referred to as "massacres.") The settlers struck back ruthlessly, driving the Indians out of the whole region near the shore.

Once again, in 1644, the Indians tried to seize Jamestown. This time their leader was captured and killed. By 1665 the governor of Virginia was appointing the chiefs of Powhatan's confederacy. In time, the tribes retreated westward.

A model colony. In England, the Virginia Company was bankrupted by the Indian attack of 1622. King James I, who was unhappy with the independent attitude of the House of Burgesses, took away the Company's charter. Virginia then became the first royal colony; that is, the first one directly controlled by the English government.

Only 1,200 settlers remained of the thousands who came to Virginia between 1607 and 1623. However, the colony was making money and it had the beginnings of self-government. As a royal colony it continued to thrive. But its success had been marred by its violent treatment of the local Indians and by the introduction of African slaves.

By 1660 Virginia was well established. It served as a model for later colonies in the southern part of British America. Maryland, North and South Carolina, and

Georgia followed Virginia's lead in most matters.

All of the southern colonies prospered by growing crops for sale and export, and all depended more and more on slavery. In none of them was there much town life. The class of people who owned large plantations were the ones who controlled public affairs. The South was on its way to becoming a distinct and different section.

TRY THIS!

1. Compare the experiences of the earliest English settlers with those of the Spaniards (page 26). How were they alike? How different? 2. Write your opinion of John Smith as a colonial leader. Imagine that you served under him at Jamestown and have been asked for your views by the directors of the Virginia Company. 3. Explain the difference between an indentured servant and a slave.

2. TWO NEW ENGLAND SETTLEMENTS

On the rocky coast of New England there was a society quite unlike the one growing up in Virginia. It was started by a group of people we have come to call the *Pilgrims.* They were religious reformers who believed a true church was not one officially recognized by the government. It was a body of faithful souls that elected its own pastor and made its own rules.

"A special instrument of God." Twelve years earlier the Pilgrims had left England, where their religious practices were illegal. They settled for a while in the Netherlands but were not happy there. So 35 of them risked the voyage to the New World.

Late in the fall of 1620 their ship, the *Mayflower,* landed on Cape Cod and settled at a place called Plymouth. During the

---

Read here of how

The Pilgrims settled in New England.
The Puritans followed them to Massachusetts Bay.
They were hard with any who opposed them.
And that included the Indians.

---

first winter, the Plymouth colony, like the one at Jamestown, suffered starvation, disease, and death. It survived only because of what its leader, William Bradford, called "a special instrument of God." An Indian named Squanto taught them how to hunt in the forest and how to grow corn.

Dishonesty and bad luck. From the beginning the Pilgrims quarreled with the Plymouth Company in England which had paid for their voyage. In 1625, the settlers agreed to buy up the company's shares and pay back its debt. But they were dogged by poor management, dishonest merchants, and plain bad luck. (One year a ship loaded with beaver skins was lost at sea.)

By 1648, when the debt was finally paid, the settlers were self-sufficient. They had given up common ownership of the land for individual holdings. That system worked much better, just as it had in Jamestown. Within a short time twenty other towns had grown up around Plymouth.

Plymouth was taken over by a larger neighbor, the Massachusetts Bay Colony, in 1691. But to this day the southeastern part of Massachusetts is sometimes called the Old Colony.

The Pilgrims proved that a colony could survive in rocky, rugged New England. They pioneered in self-government also. Their governor and his seven councilors were chosen every year by a vote of all free men. Although they did not believe in complete religious liberty, the Pilgrims were more tolerant than the settlers in Boston. For instance, Quakers were allowed to live in peace at Plymouth during the same time that three of them were hanged on Boston Common.

THE MASSACHUSETTS BAY COLONY

The people who followed the Pilgrims to New England were *Puritans*. Their religious ideas were slightly different from those of the Pilgrims. The Puritans believed that instead of separating from the Church of England, they should work to *purify* it of its errors.

"A city upon a hill." The Puritans were a tough lot, absolutely convinced that they were a chosen people. In England they fought and won a civil war against King Charles I, then chopped off his head. Some of them decided even before the English civil war to move to the New World. There, after risking the ocean storms, they hoped to build a government based on the teachings of the Bible. It would be, they said, like "a city upon a hill," for the rest of the world to gaze upon.

This group of Puritans formed a company of the kind that had founded Jamestown and Plymouth, but with an important difference. The charter of the Massachusetts Bay Company did not say that its directors had to meet in England to elect officers and conduct the company's business. The members seized on this point and decided to take the charter with them to Massachusetts and hold their meetings there. In this way they could govern their colony alone, without interference from the king or anyone else.

Early in the spring of 1630 over a thousand Puritans set sail in eleven ships under their able leader, John Winthrop. In a few months they had established Boston and other communities around Massachusetts Bay. The first settlers suffered some hunger and disease, but it was nothing like that at Jamestown and Plymouth. In ten years 20,000 other English, not all of them Puritans, followed. By then there were offshoots of the colony, in Rhode Island and Connecticut and northward into New Hampshire and Maine.

Common sense. The founders of the Massachusetts Bay Colony never thought that all people were equal. As their governor, John Winthrop, warned them, "In all times some must be rich, some poor, some high . . . others mean and in subjection." Governor Winthrop also believed that officials had to be chosen by the people. However, he said, once they had been chosen, officials drew their authority from God. For this reason they had to be obeyed unquestioningly.

But common sense soon undercut Winthrop's high and mighty views. Most of the settlers were too busy building new lives in the wilderness to pay much attention to government affairs. As one of them is said to have reminded John Winthrop, "Sir, we came hither not to praise God but to catch fish."

By 1664 the eighteen-man General Court had become a two-house legislature. And because of its unusual charter, Massachusetts was more like a self-sufficient small nation than a colony.

Dividing the land. New Englanders were generally more interested in town or village government than in the affairs of the colony. And it was for good reason. The town played a leading part in giving out land.

Usually the General Court granted land to a group of fifty or so families who were organized as a church congregation. The families then "gathered" with their minister on their new tract and divided it, leaving the poorest land as a "common" for pasture. Then they built a meetinghouse and their own homes, close to it, around a village green.

At town meetings all important issues (and a lot of unimportant ones) were thoroughly discussed. The meetings also elected delegates to represent the town in the General Court. At first only men who were church members could vote, but soon all adult males could do so. However, many never bothered to attend the meetings unless something of vital interest (like the distribution of land) was under discussion.

Then the whole male population turned out.

A model of honesty and fairness. Though no one ever planned it so, the town meeting system encouraged equality and a fierce defense of individual rights. *Dissent,* the statement of contrary or unpopular opinions, was part of the colony's life from its first days.

Probably the ablest and most brilliant dissenter was Roger Williams. Not only did he insist on complete separation from the Church of England, he spoke out against any official church, including the one in Massachusetts. As though that were not enough, he denounced the colony's charter, saying that only the Indians, not the king, had the right to give away Indian lands.

Williams was put on trial and banished in 1635. In the dead of winter, with a handful of followers, he traveled south to Rhode Island. There he established the colony of Providence, with a government that reflected his beliefs. Members of any religious group were accepted, including

This first map of the New England settlements shows how rapidly the region filled with people.

Jews and Catholics. Williams's dealings with the Indians were a model of Christian honesty and fairness.

"Ready wit and bold spirit." The next challenger was Anne Hutchinson. Even Governor Winthrop called her "a woman of ready wit and bold spirit." She was accused of believing that it was not necessary to attend a church, or belong to one, in order to win a place in heaven. She even questioned the need to obey the law.

Mrs. Hutchinson's following was much larger than Roger Williams's had been. So the dispute over her teachings split the Massachusetts Colony into warring camps. In a sense Anne Hutchinson was also an early victim of discrimination. Much of the hostility to her was due not only to the fact that she was teaching false doctrines, but that she was teaching them to men. "We do not mean to [argue] with those of your sex," Governor Winthrop huffed at her trial.

Although she answered the charges against her with brilliance, Anne Hutchinson was banished by the court. She wandered with her followers first to Rhode Island, then to New York. There she and her children died in an Indian attack.

Masters of guerrilla warfare. In their own eyes New Englanders always dealt fairly with the Indians. They tried to convert them to Christianity, and they usually paid something for the Indian lands they took. But as in Virginia, they disrupted the Indians' lives. From time to time there were outbreaks of fighting, and these always ended in the same way: the Indians were totally defeated and immediately lost their lands to the whites.

The last great Indian war in New England took place in the 1670s. A local chief, King Philip, was a gifted leader. He believed the Indians had to make a stand against the white advance before it was too late. Then, in 1675, the colonists executed three of Philip's tribesmen for killing an Indian who had been helpful to them. The war that followed almost wiped out the colony. The Indians were masters of guerrilla warfare. They burned towns and killed whites, but they would not be drawn into a pitched battle.

Slowly, however, the settlers gained the upper hand. Philip was hunted down and killed. The remainder of his tribe, even his wife and son, were sold into slavery in the West Indies. By 1678, the Indian defeat was total.

Like the Virginians to their south, the New Englanders were now in complete control of the country around their settlements. But they, too, paid a price. One sixteenth of the white population perished, and the military costs equalled millions of dollars in modern money.

 TRY THIS!

List the numbers of these sentences on a piece of paper. Beside each write a *P* if the sentence is true of the people of Plymouth, an *M* if it is true of those at Massachusetts Bay, a *J* if it is true of those at Jamestown, and an *O* if it is true of none of them. **1.** They wished to separate from the Church of England. **2.** They dealt harshly with those whose religious views were unlike their own. **3.** They came to depend heavily on slaves from Africa. **4.** They lived in peace with their Indian neighbors. **5.** They came to the New World in a large, well-financed movement. **6.** They tried to buy out the company that sent them. **7.** They had the first representative government in British America. **8.** They were strictly controlled by the king. **9.** They moved westward as groups of church members. **10.** Their charter made them almost self-governing.

3. PEOPLE OF THE ENGLISH COLONIES

In 1664 the English took New Netherlands from the Dutch, immediately renaming it New York and New Jersey (page 33). England then controlled most of the eastern shore of North America. Its colonies stretched from the French lands on the St. Lawrence River in the north to Spanish Florida in the south (map on page 44).

Eighteen years later, William Penn began settling Pennsylvania. Penn was as firm a believer in religious liberty as Roger Williams (page 49). His tolerant attitude drew people who were suffering religious persecution; they came from all parts of northwestern Europe. Non-English additions were making the middle colonies what all America would one day become: a land of many peoples, races, and religions.

Steadiness and hard work. The population of the English colonies grew fantastically (graph on page 52). Part of the growth came about because the birth rate was much higher than the death rate, but there was another reason.

Around 1700 England developed a greater need for skilled workers and laborers. So it stopped encouraging migration to America. But as the colonies still needed people, existing laws against non-English people in the New World were eased. After 1700 a rising tide of immigrants from other parts of Europe outstripped those from England.

In the 1600s Germany had been the scene of ferocious religious wars. A few Germans came to English America at that time to escape persecution. William Penn was especially impressed by their steadiness and hard work, and he tried to attract more of them with pamphlets in the German and Dutch languages. Between 1710 and 1770 almost a quarter of a million more Germans, called Pennsylvania Dutch, came to America. (The name was misleading; they left from the Netherlands, but not all had lived there.) The Pennsylvania Dutch came for religious freedom

The Pennsylvania Dutch brought their music and dancing to the New World.

Read here of how

The English controlled the Atlantic seaboard.
Their colonies attracted other Europeans.
Women had advantages in colonial times.
American society differed from European.

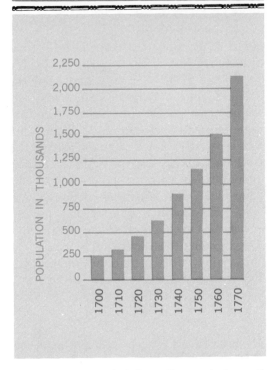

POPULATION GROWTH IN THE ENGLISH COLONIES 1700-1770

Which ten-year period shows the greatest growth in numbers? In percentage?

and to share in the fertile lands of the Susquehanna Valley. By the 1740s increasing numbers of them also made their way along the Shenandoah River into the backcountry of the South (map on page 44).

All of Ireland. The Scots-Irish too came in great numbers. They were *Presbyterians* (strict Protestants like the Puritans). The English government had moved them from Scotland to Northern Ireland to help control the Irish Catholics. The Scots-Irish were willing to leave their second home and seek a third one for a number of reasons. They had not been welcomed by their Irish neighbors (naturally). They hated the Church of England and their English landlords (who kept raising their rents). And the English, being worried about their own

weavers, killed off a flourishing textile trade of Northern Ireland.

So the Scots-Irish poured into the New World, especially to the middle and southern colonies. One Pennsylvanian exclaimed, "It looks as if Ireland is ready to send all its inhabitants hither." These new Americans were self-reliant, but they disliked authority of any kind. Settling on the frontier, they began at once to stir up trouble with the Indians.

Badly needed skills. Sizable numbers of French *Huguenots* (HYOO-guh-nots), Welsh miners, and others also found their way to America. And hundreds of Scots captured in rebellion against the English were sent as indentured servants.

The Huguenots were French Protestants. After 1685 they were no longer tolerated in their mostly Catholic homeland, and thousands of them came to the English colonies. They were townspeople, well trained in trade, crafts, and business—just what the new land needed most. Some settled in New York; an even larger group of Huguenots went to Charleston, South Carolina.

Small numbers of Spanish and Portuguese Jews also arrived. Most of them settled in New York and in Newport, Rhode Island.

All of the newcomers brought badly needed skills and labor. Their presence added color and variety to the colonial population. And they further weakened the ties between England and the colonies.

Scattered families. Once in America the English and other Europeans changed many of their attitudes and ways of living. Even their views of the family were likely to be different. As they moved farther west into the interior of the country, still deeper changes took place.

For instance, in Europe not only sons

and daughters but other relatives as well might live together in a single household. In America this arrangement occurred less often. The difference came about because land was so plentiful. Sons did not have to stay home waiting to inherit the family farm before marrying. They could strike out for themselves. And families did not live for generations in the same area; they scattered across the country.

The families were larger than in Europe. Early marriages may have accounted for that. But undoubtedly the plentiful supply of food helped as well. And because there was so much work to be done in the new country, children were valued, especially on family farms. At the same time, the high death rate among infants meant that a family had to have many children, as few lived to adulthood. Paul Revere, the Boston silversmith and Revolutionary hero, married twice. In all he had sixteen children, but only four of them lived to grow up.

Almost every occupation. In colonial times men and woman worked together to produce needed goods and services. Certain things were considered "women's work." Spinning, sewing, raising poultry, making cheese and beer were among them. But there was almost no work men did that some women (especially widows) did not do too. They ran farms and plantations, kept shops, supervised blacksmithing, shoemaking, and other crafts.

Women filled almost every occupation at one time or another. Most medical care was in their hands. They appeared in court on their own account or to represent their husbands. In New York there were famous women merchants and shipowners. In some religious groups women were preachers and missionaries.

In short, it's likely that women ac-counted for more than half the goods and services produced. In textiles alone their output would equal that of a very large factory in later times.

"The best poor man's country." From the beginning, colonial society had no fixed class structure. A few upper-class people led the migrations to America, but most of those who came had been farmers or craftsmen.

Once ashore or free of their indenture, they took up land. This was true even of those who continued to work at their trade. Landholding had always meant a great deal in Europe. In the New World it also gave a man the vote and opened the way to public office.

There were even greater opportunities in business. Robert Buchanan, a Scotsman, came to America in 1760 as an apprentice. Six years later he was a partner in a large business. Bernard Corey, an Irish cloth

In the colonies, as in England, businesses were run in small shops by masters and apprentices. Some "masters" were women.

53

COLONIAL SETTLEMENT

Colony	*Founder*	*Date*	*Reasons*	*Early History*
Virginia	London (Virginia) Company	1607	Trade, furs, gold and silver	Tobacco, 1612; slavery, 1619; colonial assembly, 1619
Massachusetts	Plymouth Company	1620	Religion, trade	Mayflower Compact, refuge for Pilgrims
	Massachusetts Bay Company	1630	Religion	Self-government; Congregational churches; first school, college; refuge for Puritans
New Hampshire	Mass. Bay settlers	1623	Land	
New York	Dutch West India Company	1624	Furs	Dutch influence in American life
New Jersey	Dutch West India Company	1624	Trade	Owned by Duke of York, various noblemen, a group of Quakers
Maryland	Lord Baltimore	1634	Religion, tobacco	Act of Toleration, 1649; refuge for Catholics
Connecticut	Thomas Hooker, Mass. Bay settlers	1634	Religion, land	Fundamental Orders, 1639 (written constitution)
Rhode Island	Roger Williams	1636	Religion	Religious tolerance; separation of church and state
Delaware	Swedish trading company	1638	Trade	The log cabin
Pennsylvania	William Penn	1682	Religion	Refuge for Quakers
North Carolina	Virginia settlers	1653	Land	Military buffer against Spain
South Carolina	English noblemen	1670	Land	Rice cultivation
Georgia	James Oglethorpe	1732	Land, charity	Military buffer against Spain; refuge for poor and debtors

dealer, arrived in 1766 with a little money. In ten years he owned 6,000 acres of land and a large herd of livestock. "America," as one Englishman said, "is one of the best poor man's countries in the world."

There was still plenty of poverty. In the backcountry tens of thousands had barely enough to keep them alive. By 1730 there was also a class of poor people in the towns. But most colonists were farmers living above the poverty level. As one South Carolinian explained, "My farm gave me a good living. Nothing to wear, eat, or drink was purchased as my farm provided all."

American society was made up of middle-sized property owners and self-employed farmers. Most of them enjoyed a higher standard of living than ordinary people anywhere else in the world.

 TRY THIS!

1. Explain how the population of the American colonies became more varied in the 1700s. 2. Show why the easy availability of land changed the settlers' patterns of living. 3. Name and describe some of the groups in colonial society.

4. LIFE IN COLONIAL TIMES

In spite of some broad resemblances, the three parts of English America—New England, the middle colonies, and the South—differed from each other as much as they did from England. Many of the Pilgrims and Puritans who first settled New England had worked at manufacturing, shipbuilding, and other trades before leaving their homeland. Arriving in the New World, they first took up farming but soon saw that the soil was thin and rocky. So they turned to the sea. Fishing and trade gave them the living that they could not gain from the land.

———————◆■◆———————

Read here of how

New Englanders took to the sea.
The middle colonies produced food.
Frontier settlers were angry and distrustful.
The South had a rich and varied society.
But depended heavily on slavery.

———————◆■◆———————

A tightly knit upper class. Trade and commerce were their lifeblood. Well before the end of the 1600s, New Englanders had gained a reputation for shrewd, sharp business deals. By the 1700s they had produced a prosperous class of *merchants.* (We would call them shippers, importers, and wholesalers.) Merchants put their profits into large estates, fine town houses, and great commercial undertakings.

There were a number of good seaports in New England, but Boston outclassed them all. There the wealthy merchants gained the same kind of political influence that the prominent ministers and royal officials enjoyed. Together these three groups formed a tightly knit upper class. Their homes were so splendid and their manners so elegant that one English visitor commented, "A gentleman from London would almost think himself at home in Boston." The official tax returns for 1687 show that even then the wealthiest 5 per cent of Bostonians owned more than 25 per cent of the town's property.

By the mid-1700s business was prosperous and life was pleasant.

At the other end of the social scale were laborers, indentured servants, and a few slaves. The same 1687 tax returns show that the bottom 20 per cent of the population owned only 2 per cent of the town.

Between the two groups were the great majority who earned their living as seamen, in the shipbuilding or export trades, or by providing some service. Life in Boston was typical of that in most New England ports.

The breadbasket of English America. The middle colonies had fertile soil and a longer growing season, so they could grow wheat and other grains. The average farmer might produce fruit, vegetables, or livestock, but he depended on wheat to bring in money. The middle colonies were the breadbasket of English America, and they made New York and Philadelphia booming centers of trade. The region supplied meat products, corn, oats, peas, beans, and even horses, for the West Indies.

But the wheat alone was worth four or five times as much as all the rest together.

A tolerant religious group. Philadelphia was the queen of colonial cities. With 23,000 inhabitants, it was the largest urban center in English America and second only to London in the whole Empire. The *Quakers* who founded Philadelphia made it a distinctly different place. Quakers were a very tolerant religious group who did not believe in churches or ceremonies and would not fight for any reason. They dressed very plainly and called one another "thee" and "thou." Quakers were in control of the colonial assembly and ran the government of Philadelphia.

Many early settlers of Philadelphia rose to the rank of master craftsmen, giving the city a large middle class. But as in other towns, a small group of wealthy merchants controlled economic and social life.

Fair treatment or bullets? Life in the backcountry of Pennsylvania was very different from that in Philadelphia. The country people were largely Scots-Irish (page 52), and they resented the city's control of colonial affairs. They were particularly angry at the assembly's failure to defend the frontier against Indian raids. William Penn had made a treaty with the Delaware Indians, and for fifty years Pennsylvania lived in peace with them. But now the Scots-Irish were displacing the Indians, who began to fight back.

The Quaker-controlled assembly would not put up money to fortify the frontier because many Quakers refused on principle to finance a war. Many also suspected that problems were being caused more by the Scots-Irish than by the Indians. The Quakers believed that fair treatment would do more good than bullets.

The cry of the slave auctioneer. Some slavery existed in every English colony. Prejudice against people with black skins allowed most Americans to accept slavery as part of the natural order of things. And for the owners of slaves, there were profits. John Adams, the second President, hated slavery and refused to have anything to do with it. Yet he believed that he could have saved thousands of dollars by owning slaves instead of hiring free men as farm workers and servants.

The northern and middle colonies never had as many slaves as the South. And their slavery was a much milder kind. New York, where 15 per cent of the population was black, had the largest number of slaves outside the South. In New York slaves often worked as craftsmen, had the right of trial by jury, and could sometimes choose their own masters.

However, in 1712, when nine whites were killed during a slave uprising in New York City, the punishment was savage.

Twenty-one slaves were burned alive, hanged, or broken on the wheel. (The last was an especially brutal punishment for treason.) Six others killed themselves.

Pennsylvania had hardly any slaves, and neither did New England. A few families there owned one or two. They might work as house servants, farm laborers, or skilled craftsmen. In New England slaves had a number of important legal rights. They could sue people in the courts, testify in cases involving whites, and enter legal marriages. Nevertheless, New England was deeply involved in the profitable slave trade. Even in Newport, Rhode Island, which had been founded in the cause of freedom, the cry of the slave auctioneer could be heard.

LIFE IN THE SOUTH

There were three strikingly different types of society in the South. Each had its own geography: the tidewater region, the backcountry, and the Piedmont.

Three regions. The term *tidewater* refers to the area near the sea. This coastal land is so flat that ocean tides can carry ships far up its rivers. Tidewater soil is especially rich, and the tobacco and rice grown there could be loaded aboard ocean-going vessels at the planter's own docks. Tidewater planters were the wealthiest and best educated people in the southern colonies. Needless to say, the political and social leaders of the South came from the tidewater region.

The *backcountry* was the frontier region, stretching westward through the valleys of the Appalachian Mountains and beyond. Its rough-and-tumble ways differed sharply from the polite society of the tidewater.

57

The *Piedmont* was the foothill region on the eastern slopes of the Appalachians. Life in the Piedmont combined the qualities of the tidewater and the backcountry. There were good-sized plantations, but there were also small farms producing only enough for the owners and their families.

Getting elected. It would have been possible for a tidewater planter to live very much apart from his neighbors. The plantation supplied all his daily needs. The ships that carried away his tobacco or rice also brought imported goods to his wharves. But planters led very active social lives. "They live," an English visitor said, "more like country gentlemen than any other settlers . . . their labor being done mostly by slaves."

Tidewater planters also gave their time to colonial government. They ran the House of Burgesses—the colonial assembly (page 45)—and decided who should hold local offices. However, to get into the Burgesses, a planter still had to be elected. There was a property qualification for voting, but it was low. About 65 per cent of all white males were allowed to vote. As a result, a planter sometimes had to campaign hard in order to gain office.

Candidates were likely to spend a lot of money on barbecues and liquor. In 1758 young George Washington, in his first successful campaign for the House of Burgesses, passed out 28 gallons of rum, 50 gallons of rum punch, 34 gallons of wine, 46 gallons of beer, and two gallons of cider. This amounted to a quart and a half for each voter. On seeing the bill, Washington said only that he hoped everyone had had enough and that his supporters hadn't "spent with too sparing a hand."

A candidate could be sure that his generosity paid off because there were no pa-per ballots. Each voter stepped forward and announced his choice for all to hear. Few who owed a planter anything would risk voting against him.

A web of intermarriages. One reason for seeking office was that it often led to wealth. A member of the governor's council or of the Burgesses could easily acquire land. Such men thought of public office as their natural right. Yet they did take their duties seriously.

A planter might also "marry money." From time to time colonial letters and diaries mention the marriage of a planter's young son to some elderly, wealthy widow. By the time of the Revolution, the planter class was tied together by a web of intermarriages. At many weddings the bride and groom were cousins.

Cheaper than free labor. Between 1660 and 1700, slaves became the chief workers on the tobacco plantations. By 1700 Virginia alone had 6,000 of them. The number grew rapidly.

It cost more to buy a slave than an indentured servant, but slaves remained for life. And they were cheaper to keep, since they could be given coarser food and poorer clothes and housing. They could also be disciplined more harshly, and they would increase their own numbers. Most owners believed, even if they did not approve of slavery itself, that slaves were cheaper than free labor.

Moreover, slaves often had skills or could quickly learn them. Plantations prided themselves on having a good blacksmith, mason, and shoemaker.

A "kindly" master. By 1705 Virginia had a system of laws that strictly regulated slave life. It laid down severe punishments for running away, keeping arms, or striking a white person. Masters were given complete ownership of their slaves and of all the slaves' descendants. Fifty years later, throughout the South, the law generally defined slaves as *chattels* (pieces of property). Since they were property, slaves themselves had no protection from the law. A master could mistreat them or punish them as he saw fit.

The cruelest means were used to maintain discipline among the slaves. William Byrd of Virginia considered himself a kindly master. Yet about once a month he found it necessary to have some slave whipped, beaten, or branded with a hot iron.

We can only guess how slaves learned to hide their feelings at the treatment they received. The number of slave rebellions and uprisings shows that sometimes they were unable to do so.

 TRY THIS!

Write the diary of an imaginary journey through the American colonies in the 1700s (map on page 44). How would you travel? What route would you follow? What places might you visit? What would you want to see? What kind of people would you meet?

A fine tidewater plantation with its own warehouse and wharf.

Town and Country

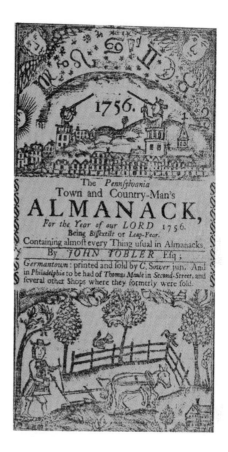

The painting below was made for the owners of the farm. They are shown standing in front of it. The events they are watching may be those they described to the painter, the recollections of a year—or longer.

Town life was more exciting—and dangerous. When the Hand-to-Hand Fire Company of New York City was called out, most members passed buckets to fill the pumper, which four others worked while a fifth aimed the hose. Still others prepared to mount ladders and pull down blazing walls. The captain directed all with his speaking trumpet.

Next to the Bible, almanacs were the favorite reading matter in town and country. Published annually, they contained a jumble of astronomical facts, weather misinformation, health hints, bad jokes, and wise sayings.

5. THE MIND OF COLONIAL AMERICA

The religious life of the American colonists was not like that of their European cousins. And by the 1700s, even in New England, it was not what it had been in earlier days. Disputes like those involving Roger Williams and Anne Hutchinson no longer rocked the colonies.

The first witch hunt. In part at least, the change was due to a series of events that took place in 1692, in a small town just north of Boston. Two young girls of Salem, in the Bay Colony, had happened to read a book about witchcraft written by a Puritan minister. The book had a powerful effect. The girls began to act out what they had read and to accuse people of having bewitched them. A female slave may also have told the girls about practices in her homeland. They were soon accusing old women and other innocent people of being witches. The whole community was swept up in the hysteria; one woman even described how she had sold her soul to the devil.

The governor of Massachusetts sent a group of officials to Salem to investigate the charges. But they too caught the general infection. The officials imprisoned hundreds of suspects and hanged fourteen women and six men for practicing witchcraft.

Read here of how

The colonists changed religious ideas.
And started a system of public education.
The first newspapers appeared.
Benjamin Franklin put science to work.

Finally, respectable merchants, even ministers and the governor's wife, were accused. Something had to be done. Wealthy and important people began to speak out against the trials and hangings, and the accusations stopped as suddenly as they had begun.

A few years later Samuel Sewall, the leading judge at the trials, stood in church while his apology for what he had done was read aloud. Twenty years after that the General Court also admitted the mistake and voted to set aside the convictions. To this day the term *witch hunt* stands for the irresponsible harassment of innocent people.

Some who had suffered and survived began to question the judgment and intelligence of their ministers. These men, who had been unquestioned leaders of the colony, lost some of the awe and respect with which they had once been regarded.

A fiery preacher. One result of the witchcraft trials was an increase in religious toleration. But toleration is likely in any society where there is no one religion to which most people belong. America was rapidly becoming that kind of society.

Throughout the middle colonies and the backcountry, Baptists, Presbyterians, Lutherans, and Mennonites were thrown together. In the south the Church of England was *established* (it was supported out of tax funds) as were the Congregationalists in New England. But even here greater tolerance was shown to other religious groups. No longer were Quakers hanged in Boston; some Baptists still met only in private homes though.

Part of the new tolerance came about simply because people no longer cared to

A minister's gravestone. The stones often show the deceased's work or profession.

quarrel over religion. However, in the 1740s and 1750s a great religious revival swept the colonies. It began in England as Methodism and in America as the Great Awakening. In New England it was inspired by the fiery preaching of Jonathan Edwards.

The message was clear. Edwards was descended from a long line of Puritan clergymen. He was serving in Northampton, Massachusetts, when he began to question whether anyone could know for certain if he or she was saved. Such ideas filled his listeners with fear. They were in the hands of God, Edwards told them, and could only cling to their faith and pray that He would hear them. "Oh sinner! Consider the fearful danger you are in. It is a great furnace of wrath, a wide and bottomless pit, full of the fire of wrath, that you are held over in the hand of God."

Jonathan Edwards and others like him were imitating a famous English preacher, George Whitefield, who visited the colonies in 1738. But his message was a kindlier and more reassuring one. Crowds listened entranced as Whitefield asked, "Father Abraham, whom have you in heaven? Any Episcopalians? 'No.' Any Presbyterians? 'No.' Have you any Independents or Seceders? 'No.' Have you any Methodists? 'No, no, no!' Whom have you there? 'We don't know those names here. . . .'" The message was clear: religious denominations were not important; everyone could be saved.

As long-established religious beliefs were questioned, so were political and social ideas. When people began to doubt the ministers of religion, it was not long before they challenged those who governed them.

A schoolteacher in every town. Americans in the colonial period still looked to Europe for guidance in art, science, and education. Upper-class southerners sent their sons to England for their education, or had them tutored at home. The middle colonies had a system of education that was

63

available to almost everyone. However, the upper classes there followed the South's example.

Only in New England was there a solid system of common education. In the Bible commonwealth of Massachusetts, every town was required to provide a schoolmaster for its children. The purpose of this first American school law was to make sure that all children could read the scriptures.

In New England there were also a few

A teacher brings the fruit of knowledge within the reach of an eager student.

"grammar" or "Latin" schools to prepare boys for college. By the 1700s these had been joined by private "academies." The academies gave advanced work to those not wishing to attend college and lifted the level of general education in all the colonies.

The chief purpose of the early colleges was to train ministers for the colonial churches. So all of them were founded by, or had some close connection with, a religious group. The Congregationalists set up Harvard (1636), Yale (1701), and Dartmouth (1769). The Presbyterians founded Princeton (1746); the Episcopalians, William and Mary (1693) and Columbia (1754); and the Baptists, Brown (1764).

Local gossip and a lot of advertising. Better-educated Americans were familiar with a large number of books. But most others got along with just the Bible. *Pilgrim's Progress*—a religious work by John Bunyan, or the English *Book of Common Prayer* might also be found in colonial homes, as well as some sort of text from which children could be taught the "three R's." Benjamin Franklin's *Poor Richard's Almanac* was also widely circulated.

The Boston *News-Letter* appeared in 1704. It was the first successful American newspaper. By 1765 there were 25 like it in the colonies. The papers came out each week and were usually four pages long. They included local gossip, foreign news, essays on a variety of subjects, shipping news, and a lot of advertising.

A case of libel. The papers were careful not to offend any political leaders. Government printing work was an important part of their income, and they did not want to risk losing it.

When John Peter Zenger, publisher of the *New York Weekly Journal*, attacked government officials in 1735, he was tried for *libel* (printing statements that unjustly damage someone's reputation). The jury acquitted Zenger on grounds that what he had written was true, but that did not make it safe for a newspaper to criticize political leaders. In 1769 the New York legislature jailed an editor for questioning its decision to quarter troops in the colony. Nevertheless, in spite of their limitations, colonial newspapers kept Americans informed about daily affairs.

An inventive printer. Americans have always been a practical people. Since the colonists lived a stone's throw from the wilderness, they prized practical inventions that would make their lives richer and more comfortable. They respected those scientists who could convert theory into something useful.

The best-known American scientist of his day was Benjamin Franklin. He was mostly self-educated, and as a boy, had been apprenticed to a printer. At seventeen he moved from Boston to Philadelphia to take up his trade and was highly successful there. Franklin was a born organizer. He gave Philadelphia its first police force and fire company, as well as a circulating library and city hospital. He formed a debating society to discuss scientific subjects, when he was 21.

The Franklin stove (much more efficient for home heating than a fireplace) and bifocal eyeglasses were only two of the famous Philadelphian's inventions. His proof that lightning was a form of electricity had an important practical result: lightning rods that would protect homes and buildings. Immediate usefulness was what counted. If life could be made easier, safer, or more comfortable, then scientific knowledge was worthwhile.

A century later, Philadelphia firefighters still honored their founder.

Franklin believed in the future. And he found nothing wrong with changing his mind if what he had thought was true proved to be false. His attitude was shared by many Americans, and so were his views of kings and governments. In the later 1700s it was much easier for Americans to think about revolution and act as revolutionaries.

 TRY THIS!

1. Suggest how each of these may have made it natural for Americans to become revolutionaries: (a) their religious backgrounds, (b) their newspapers, (c) their attitude towards science. **2.** Tell how one of Benjamin Franklin's inventions helped to make life easier, safer, or more comfortable for his fellow Americans.

ROUNDUP

Who?
John Smith
Powhatan
Pocahontas
John Rolfe
Anne Hutchinson
Roger Williams
King Philip
William Penn
Jonathan Edwards
Benjamin Franklin

What?
headright
indentured servant
House of Burgesses
Puritan
Quaker
Piedmont
established church

Where?
Jamestown
Plymouth
Boston
New York
Philadelphia

KNOW THIS

A Beginning in Virginia

1. How did the pattern of life at Jamestown help the colony to survive?
2. What was the headright system? How did it affect the future of the Virginia colony?
3. How do we know that slavery existed in Virginia before it became legal in 1660?
4. Name two Virginia "firsts" in American history.

Two New England Settlements

1. How were Plymouth and Massachusetts Bay alike? How did their governments and religion differ?
2. What was the New England system of land distribution?
3. Describe the views of Roger Williams and Anne Hutchinson.
4. Compare the experiences of the New England settlers and the Virginians in dealing with the Indians.

People of the English Colonies

1. Explain the population growth of the English colonies.
2. Why did each of these groups come to America in the 1600s: the Germans, Scots-Irish, French Huguenots, Jews from Spain and Portugal?
3. Where did each of the groups in Question 2 settle? What effect did each have on the English colonies?
4. How did women fare in colonial America?
5. Why was America a good "poor man's country"?

Life in Colonial Times

1. What were some ways of making a living in New England, the middle colonies, and the South?
2. Describe the social classes found in all the colonies.
3. What are some Quaker beliefs?
4. How were the tidewater, the Piedmont, and the back-country of the South unlike one another?
5. Describe the slave system in the South.

The Mind of Colonial America

1. How did the witchcraft trials affect the colonies?
2. What was the Great Awakening?
3. Compare the educational systems in New England, the middle colonies, and the South.
4. How did newspapers help to educate the colonists?
5. What did the colonists think about science? How did Benjamin Franklin's career illustrate their attitude?

DIG HERE!

Choose some aspect of everyday life in colonial America and prepare a detailed report about it. Consider expanding your written description with models, diagrams, sketches, or demonstrations. For example, if your topic is food, you might prepare a recipe for your classmates to sample. Or you might make models of different kinds of boats the colonists used. Here are some possible topics:

Types of houses, home furnishings, food and recipes, meals (when, what, how much), textiles (wool and flax), fashions (for men, women, children), home crafts (quilting, broommaking, candlemaking, soap-making, needlework), transportation, taverns and inns, sports and recreation (hunting and fishing, storytelling, dancing, horse racing, cock fighting, ice skating), trades and occupations. When you have told about the topic or topics chosen, list as many contrasts as you can between the everyday life of colonial America and that of today. You might write about attitudes toward work, amount and use of leisure time, self-sufficiency of individuals, families, and communities, necessities versus luxuries, or the family as a social unit.

For sources of the information you need, use the books listed at the end of this unit (page 117). The books by Blow, Earle, Hawkes, Tunis, and Wright should be especially useful.

THINK ABOUT IT

1. Why was the life of Virginia so widely copied throughout the South? Why was it *not* copied in the North? Consider the type of colonists in each section, their reasons for coming to America, and their life styles.
2. Family life and the roles of women were quite different in America and Europe. Is there a connection between these two facts? Explain.

DO IT!

1. Re-enact the trial of Peter Zenger. Students can take the parts of judge, defendant, defense attorney, prosecutor and witnesses. Have the class act as jury.
2. Report to the class on why you would or would not have liked being a teenager in colonial America.

THEN AND NOW

Compare the roles of women in America during colonial times and today. Did women have any advantages in colonial times that they lack now? What were they? Can you explain the difference? How?

Revolution Makes a New Nation

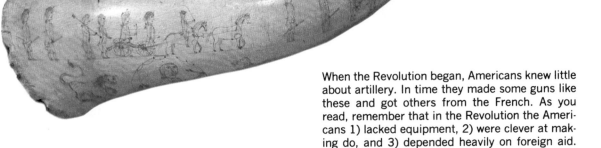

3

When the Revolution began, Americans knew little about artillery. In time they made some guns like these and got others from the French. As you read, remember that in the Revolution the Americans 1) lacked equipment, 2) were clever at making do, and 3) depended heavily on foreign aid.

1. FROM COLONY TO PROVINCE

England's New World empire grew in a haphazard fashion. During the 1600s the colonies were not run; they were allowed to run themselves. Except for the tobacco and rice lands of the South, the mainland colonies were considered less valuable than the sugar islands of the West Indies. (The tiny island of Barbados—166 square miles—was worth more to England than all of New England, New York, and Pennsylvania together.)

By the 1700s bigger and better ships made the voyage to America safer, but it could still take several weeks. The British government had to leave many decisions to those on the spot. During the early days the colonies saw to their own defense and looked for trade wherever they could. They were free because they were too far away to be controlled.

Later an English prime minister called this policy *salutary neglect* (neglect that is helpful or healthy). The policy allowed the colonies to flourish and grow strong. But it also made them all the more resentful when controls had to be applied.

The most valuable product. In the direct trade between England and her American mainland colonies, England supplied manufactured goods to the colonies.

They, in turn, sent tobacco, rice, furs, and timber to the mother country. However, after 1740 all of the colonies' products were less than enough to pay for their imports. In the later 1700s the trade became more and more out of balance (graph on page 73).

The most valuable product of the New World was West Indies sugar. Sugar plantations, like those that grew tobacco and rice, were carefully organized businesses. The hard and monotonous work on the plantations was done by large gangs of slaves. The work was so hard, in fact, and so unhealthy, that the slaves lived only about seven years. Vast numbers of them had to be imported from Africa.

In addition, sugar land was too valuable to be wasted on growing food. So food had to be brought in too. As sugar and molasses were shipped to Europe in barrels, there was also a great demand in the islands for wood products.

Big business in New England. The mainland colonies, especially New England, played an important part in supplying the West Indies' needs. Slaves from Africa, dried fish from New England, grain, other food, and wood from the middle colonies found ready markets in the sugar islands. All were likely to be carried there by New England ships.

Read here of how

The colonists sold goods to Europe and the West Indies.
But England tried to control their trade.
The colonies ran their own governments.
And fought four wars with the French.

TIME CHART

1759	Wolfe captures Quebec.
1763	Britain controls North America.
1765	The Stamp Act Congress meets.
1773	The Boston Tea Party is held.
1775	Fighting breaks out between colonists and British.
1775	Washington commands the Continental Army.
1776	Independence is declared.
1777	The Battle of Saratoga is won.
1778	The French Alliance is signed.
1781	Cornwallis surrenders at Yorktown.
1783	The Treaty of Paris is signed.

Payment for goods sent to the West Indies was often in sugar and molasses. A New England sea captain might then carry the sugar to Europe or return to New England with it. In New England, sugar products were turned into rum, which could be shipped to Africa and exchanged for slaves. Slaving was a big business in New England, even though there were hardly any slaves there.

As can be seen from the maps on pages 70 and 71, there were many different patterns in the triangular trades. Much of the trade was illegal (such as selling rice to the Mediterranean countries in return for wines and other luxury goods). And more of it became illegal as England tried to tighten control of its empire.

No competition. During the colonial period several Navigation Acts restricted colonial trade to English or American ships. The acts also listed "enumerated

69

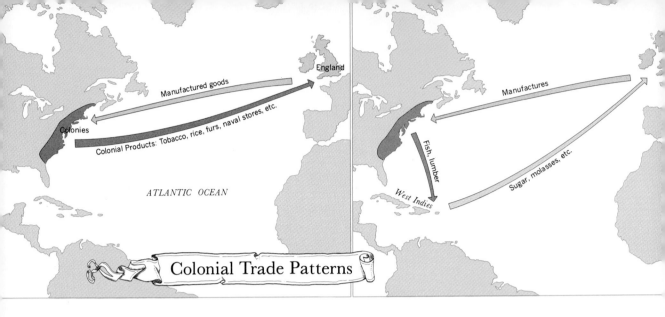

Manufactured goods

England

Colonies

Colonial Products: Tobacco, rice, furs, naval stores, etc.

ATLANTIC OCEAN

Manufactures

Fish, lumber

West Indies

Sugar, molasses, etc.

Colonial Trade Patterns

International trade is seldom one-to-one. A third party is often involved. How many "triangles" can you identify? Note the importance of Britain and the West Indies for colonial trade.

articles." These products could be sold only to England for use or resale to other countries. Among them were tobacco, sugar, wool, and cotton. Rice, copper, furs, and *naval stores* were added later. (Naval stores were goods used on sailing ships: pitch, tar, and masts. Most of these products came from pine trees.)

By the time of the Revolution, just about everything the colonies produced was an "enumerated article." Not being able to sell their most valuable goods to other countries was a real hardship for the colonists. And English prices were so low that many planters went bankrupt.

Other acts tried to keep the colonies from producing goods that England specialized in. Wool in any form was one of these; hats and finished iron goods were others.

Parliament had two reasons for wanting to control trade in this way: to step up production of goods England needed or could sell in Europe and to discourage products that would compete with English manufactures.

Buckskins and wampum. But the most unfair of all restrictions were those on paper or metal money. In every colony there was a shortage of ready cash. Yet the colonists were forbidden to mint coins or print paper money. Without either one, it was extremely hard to carry on any kind of business.

For day-to-day purposes all kinds of substitute money were tried. In backwoods Pennsylvania buckskins were used. In New York it was beaver pelts. In South Carolina rice was bartered for every other kind of goods. Indian wampum (shell beads strung together) served as money in New England. And some colonies got around the law by issuing various kinds of paper credit.

Merchants doing business with the Spanish colonies were paid in silver coins. But the Navigation Acts made that trade illegal. So it was safer to melt the coins down and make teapots than to spend the silver.

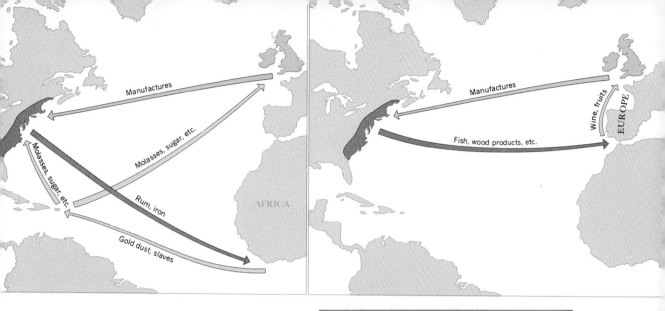

As the balance of trade with England became more unfavorable (graph on page 73), some way had to be found to pay for goods the colonists were importing from the mother country.

A nation of smugglers. It is hard to weigh the advantages and disadvantages of England's trade regulations. Some laws discriminated against all parts of the empire for the benefit of England. The restrictions on manufacturing and coinage were among these.

Other laws favored one colony against others. An act of 1733 put a heavy tax on any molasses produced outside the British West Indies. New Englanders who made rum had to either buy high-priced molasses from those British islands or smuggle in the cheaper French, Dutch, or Spanish molasses.

Some laws helped and hurt at the same time. The Iron Act of 1750 stopped Americans from making finished iron products, but it gave them a protected market in England for smelted iron. By the time of the Revolution, the colonies were producing one seventh of the world's unfinished iron.

 HOW SWEET IT WAS

In 1742 sugar was selling in the London market for several dollars a pound. That was down considerably from its price a few years earlier. When the future Austrian Empress Maria Theresa married in 1736, sugar was listed as one of her wedding gifts—among the precious stones!

Moorish conquerors carried "the honey-bearing reeds" into Spain in the 800s. Until the discovery of the New World the only sugar Europeans ever saw was produced in and near Spain or imported at great cost from the Orient.

Columbus brought sugarcane plants to Hispaniola on his second voyage. From there sugar growing spread to the other islands of the Caribbean. By the late 1700s, thanks to these islands, sugar was in use all over Europe.

Some medical historians say that in the 1700s, with all that sugar, Europeans got something else they never had before—bad teeth.

Certainly, the Navigation Acts helped New England shipbuilders. At the end of the colonial period almost a third of all the empire's shipping was American.

But New Englanders especially resented the business regulations because their region depended so much on trade. As a result, they became heavily involved in smuggling. One governor of Virginia complained, "We are most obedient to all laws while the New England men break them and trade to any place their interest leads them."

Miniature Parliaments. The thirteen colonies began in different ways, at different times, and for different reasons. But gradually their governments became more and more alike. By the mid-1700s nine were royal. That is, their governors were appointed by the king. Of the other four, Pennsylvania and Maryland were still controlled by the heirs of the Penn and Calvert families that had founded them. In Connecticut and Rhode Island the governors were elected. And all colonies had an elected assembly and an appointed council.

The governor could summon and dismiss the assembly. He could also veto its acts if he thought they were illegal under the colony's charter, or if they were against his instructions from the king.

Colonial governors often became very rich. All land grants had to have their signatures. In a single year the fees for signing land grants could add up to a fortune.

Some governors got along well with the assemblies and were liked by the colonists. But this was not usually the case. The colonists felt that most of these men were strangers sent to govern them. Benjamin Franklin claimed that many governors were "men of vicious characters and broken fortunes, sent [to America] to get them out of the way."

Merchants and wealthy landowners made up the governors' councils. They generally cooperated with the governors in order to get land grants or other benefits.

In spite of all this, throughout the 1700s the assemblies became more powerful while the governors and councils grew

ENGLAND OR BRITAIN?

In early times English rulers were sneered at as "kings of half an island," since Scotland was an independent country. Later, for over a hundred years the kings or queens of England ruled both lands separately.

However, in 1707 an Act of Union joined the two kingdoms under the name of Great Britain. So after 1707 *Britain* is the more correct term, while before that date *England* is.

To mark the joining of the two countries the "Union Jack" was adopted as the national flag. It unites the cross of St. George (England) with the cross of St. Andrew (Scotland).

As American population grew, so did the demand for English goods. English demand for American goods remained steady. What years was trade most out of balance? Can you give a reason for this?

weaker. This was chiefly because the assemblies controlled the raising and spending of tax money, including the governors' salaries. Control of the "purse strings" was the chief source of the assemblies' power. Most governors sooner or later gave in to them in order to get the money they needed to run the colony, and to have necessary laws passed.

Colonial assemblies liked to think of themselves as miniature Parliaments. In England Parliament was increasing its power over the king, and the assemblies tried to do something similar with the royal governors. They also saw themselves as standing in the same relation to the king as Parliament did. That was one reason why they resisted so fiercely whenever Parliament tried to exercise power over them.

There was a long standing English tradition that owning land carried with it the right to vote. Since landowning was open to so many in America, there was a large number of voters. On the other hand, the requirements for holding office were stiff. Government positions were generally limited to wealthy merchants and planters. Nevertheless, the colonies had a form of self-government with ever-growing responsibilities. That was a development the authorities in London never seemed to understand.

Sideshows. Throughout the 1700s there was a continuing struggle for control of North America. The French went on exploring and laying claim to the interior of the continent (pages 33 and 34). As they moved into the Mississippi Valley and the

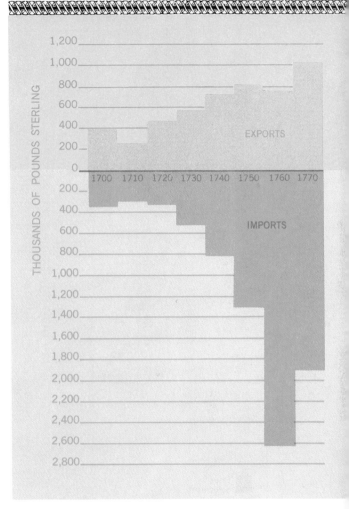

COLONIAL BALANCE OF TRADE 1700-1770

Hudson Bay area, there were frequent clashes with the English.

But these were just sideshows to much larger European conflicts. Whenever France and Britain went to war, the fighting spilled over into the New World. In America the English usually called the wars by the name of the ruling monarch: King William's War (1689-1697), Queen Anne's War (1702-1713), and King George's War (1740-1748).

73

The Old World in the New

ALASKA

Claimed by Russia, Spain, and Britain

UNEXPLORED

PACIFIC OCEAN

Hudson Bay

Newfoundland

Ft. Louisburg

Wolfe 1759

Montreal • Quebec

NEW FRANCE

St. Laurence R.

Acadia (Nova Scotia)

L. Superior

L. Huron

L. Michigan

L. Ontario

L. Erie

LOUISIANA

Detroit

Ft. Duquesne

Braddock 1755

† San Francisco 1776

Colorado R.

Ohio R.

Mississippi R.

ATLANTIC OCEAN

San Diego 1769 †

† Sante Fe 1607

NEW

† El Paso 1659

Natchez

SPANISH FLORIDA

St. Augustine 1565

San Antonio 1718

Rio Grande

Mobile

New Orleans

SPAIN

Monterrey

Gulf of Mexico

Bahama Islands

Cuba

Hispaniola

Puerto Rico

Mexico City • • Veracruz

West Indies

Jamaica

Guadeloupe

Martinique

Caribbean Sea

Barbados

Trinidad

Legend:
- British settlement
- British territory
- × British fort
- French settlement
- French territory
- × French fort
- Spanish territory
- † Spanish mission

74   Which nation held the smallest area? Which area, do you think, had the largest number of people?

Settlement of these conflicts took place in Europe. And more than once a treaty forced the colonials to give up forts or territory they had fought hard to win. It did not help their relations with the mother country. They were convinced that Britain cared little about the colonies.

A turn in the tide. The last struggle with France was the French and Indian War (1754–1763). Unlike the earlier struggles, this one began in North America. The French had built Fort Duquesne (doo-KAYN) at the key location (Pittsburgh) where two rivers meet to form the Ohio; the British sent General Edward Braddock to America with an army of regulars to drive them out. But Braddock was ambushed and killed by French and Indians. A young Virginian, George Washington, distinguished himself by leading the survivors to safety.

Throughout 1757 the British and the colonists suffered defeats. Then, in 1758, a new British government with William Pitt as prime minister took control. Young, energetic officers were sent to America and the tide began to turn. The climax came on September 12, 1759. All through that long night a steady stream of small boats carried an army of British soldiers past the massive cliffs along the St. Lawrence River. Above them loomed the great French fortress of Quebec (page 33). Before dawn the British force scaled the cliff and stood on the Plains of Abraham outside the city. The youthful British general, James Wolfe, had finally cornered the French army commanded by Montcalm.

Foundation for rebellion. The outnumbered French were no match for their attackers. In the short, fierce battle that followed, both Montcalm and Wolfe were killed. But the British won. Five days later

The success of the British was their undoing. The problems of ruling such a large empire, with so many people, were too great.

Quebec surrendered. In a year all of Canada was in British hands.

A century-long struggle had ended. The British flag flew from the Gulf of Mexico to the Arctic (map on this page). But barely fifteen years later the American colonies were in rebellion.

 TRY THIS!

1. Write a letter about English trade regulations that might have come from (a) a West Indies sugar planter, (b) a Pennsylvania iron maker, or (c) a New England customs collector. 2. Give some of the reasons why one sugar island was worth more than all of New England, New York, and Pennsylvania. 3. Using a map, explain the importance of Fort Duquesne (Pittsburgh).

75

2. GROWING POLITICAL UNREST

Britain's successful wars with France lasted from 1689 to 1763—almost a hundred years. Once the glow of victory died away, Britain faced some grim problems. The government had borrowed heavily to pay for the war and had a huge national debt. The taxes were staggering. Many in Britain felt that the colonists too should help to pay the costs of running the empire. Furthermore, the colonists were pressing for western lands. This, the British feared, would only lead to more and bigger Indian wars.

The government in London barely understood even the size of its vast new empire. But it did realize that the time had come for something more than "salutary neglect" (page 68).

Anyone who had dealt with colonial assemblies (pages 72-73) knew they would not willingly allow themselves to be taxed. And some British leaders were wise enough to see that any policy threatening colonial rights would cause the colonies to unite against the mother country. In the long run only cautious methods were likely to succeed.

Different reactions. The British government had no wish to add to the tax burdens of its people, and renewed warfare with the Indians of the Ohio Valley would have meant just that. The best western policy seemed to be one that would halt or slow the rush for land and the disruption of Indian life.

Then suddenly, in May of 1763, the Ottawa Indians of the Northwest rose up under their leader, Pontiac. The tribes and their allies captured every English post in the region and laid siege to Detroit. It took several thousand British troops until September 1764 to restore peace.

The reaction to the uprising was different in the colonies and in London. Frontiersmen denounced the colonial authorities for not giving them protection. In Pennsylvania a western vigilante group called the Paxton Boys massacred a group of Indians, then marched on Philadelphia. They went home only after the colonial government had given in to some of their demands.

In London the British authorities had responded to the uprising by issuing the Proclamation of 1763. It ordered the royal governors to keep settlers and land companies out of the region west of a line along the peaks of the Appalachian Mountains. King George's proclamation ended: "It is just and reasonable and essential to our interest and that [the Indians] who live under our protection should not be molested or disturbed in . . . their hunting grounds."

The colonials felt they had helped Britain to win the land they were now forbidden to occupy (map on page 75). So there were protests throughout the colonies. Virginia, in particular, denounced the Proclamation as a violation of its charter rights (map on page 75). Some saw it as an attempt to shut them off from the profitable fur trade.

But others realized that the rule could not be enforced for very long. And London soon found out that it was easier to issue

---

Read here of how

Britain tried to run its new empire.
Americans objected to trade regulations.
And found a way to fight back.

---

such rulings than it was to make them stick.

"Neglect, connivance and fraud." Besides dealing with the land problem, the new British prime minister, Lord Grenville, felt that he must enforce the trade regulations. He had found out that the customs service in America was costing more to run than it was taking in. This was due, a report told him, to "neglect, connivance, and fraud." Grenville ordered the Royal Navy to enforce the customs acts and to help in arresting smugglers.

He also put through the Sugar Act of 1764. It was supposed to raise money to pay for soldiers on the western frontier. To do so, the act cut the duties on foreign molasses in half (page 71) and increased those on fine cloth, coffee, and dyes. It also increased the list of enumerated articles that could be shipped only to England (pages 69-70) and forbade most trade with the French, Dutch, or Spanish West Indies.

Each of these regulations would interfere with one or more of the colonial trade patterns (page 69). Worse still, colonists accused of breaking any of them would not be tried in their own courts before their own judges and juries. They would be tried in admiralty courts with British judges and no juries.

"No taxation without representation." Nothing angered the Americans more than the infamous Stamp Act of 1765. The provisions of the Sugar Act had called for indirect, or hidden, taxes, passed on to the consumer of sugar, cloth, and other goods. They could be explained as necessary for regulating trade within the British Empire. But Americans would be reminded of the stamp tax every time they had to pay it.

And they would be paying it often. The Stamp Act laid a small but unavoidable tax on legal papers such as wills, mort-gages, and property deeds, and on newspapers, pamphlets, and even playing cards. The same kind of tax was being collected in the mother country without difficulty, so no one in the British government expected any trouble. Even Benjamin Franklin encouraged his friends and relatives to get themselves appointed stamp distributors.

But the Stamp Act directly hit all the most influential people in the colonies: businessmen, lawyers, newspaper publishers, even ministers. The cry went up, "No taxation without representation." Violence shook the colonial communities, especially Boston. There the Sons of Liberty, a sort of underground organization, forced the stamp distributor to resign. Stamp agents everywhere did the same, making it impossible to enforce the act. In Boston, too, a mob wrecked the home of Thomas Hutchinson, the royal governor of Massachusetts. All efforts to catch or punish the rioters failed. Britain was stunned.

 THOSE ADMIRALTY COURTS

Admiralty courts try cases under the laws of the sea. Sea law is extremely complicated and well outside the experience of most citizens. For that reason admiralty cases are usually decided by judges alone. Juries are not used.

In colonial New England almost everyone was involved, directly or indirectly, in breaking the trade laws. So admiralty courts were good places in which to try those who got caught. After all, how could the authorities ever win a guilty verdict for smuggling from a jury made up of twelve smugglers?

A powerful weapon. In October 1765 a Stamp Act Congress met at New York. Nine of the thirteen colonies were represented. After eleven days of debate, the Congress passed a fairly mild resolution. It promised allegiance to the king but demanded from him all "the rights and privileges of natural-born subjects." The resolutions particularly mentioned trial by jury (page 77) and the right of the colonists to be taxed only by their own legislatures.

The protest was not all talk and resolutions. Colonial merchants made *nonimportation* agreements to boycott British goods. At once imports dropped by half a million pounds (the equal of several million dollars in present-day money). Even wealthy Americans wore homemade clothing to show that they supported the boycott.

English merchants were badly hurt, and they let their anger be known. In March of 1766 a bill to repeal the Stamp Act swept through Parliament. But at the same time, Parliament reaffirmed the right to tax the colonies "in all cases." The great statesman William Pitt told Parliament that he doubted the wisdom of its claim. He said: "The forefathers of the Americans did not leave their native country and subject themselves to every danger and distress to be reduced to slavery."

The colonists were triumphant. Whatever Parliament might declare, they knew that they had a powerful weapon. By cutting off trade, they had made the British government back down.

A drop in trade. However, the following year, 1767, Britain found itself in a business depression. The government was unable to meet its bills. So the treasury chief, Charles Townshend, had to cut expenses somehow. To pay the salaries of colonial officials and the cost of defending the American frontier he pushed through new taxes on glass, tea, lead, and paper.

The London authorities also established new agencies to enforce the Townshend duties and the earlier Sugar and Navigation Acts. New admiralty courts were set up. And the governor of New York had to shut down the colonial assembly because it refused to pay for the support of British troops.

Once more there was bitter resentment; once more the cry "No taxation without representation." Worst of all, the new measures really worked. Ships and cargoes were seized and sold. And income from customs rose from nothing to thousands of dollars in present-day money.

Boycotting English goods again was the least anyone thought of doing. Agitators like Sam Adams of Boston were calling for more violent steps. British trade with the colonies now fell off by almost 40 per cent. When customs officers seized a ship belonging to the popular Boston merchant John Hancock, a mob chased them out of town to an island in the harbor.

A fateful night. The British sent four more regiments of troops to Boston to join the two already there, and order was restored. But there were several clashes between the Bostonians and the red-coats. On March 5, 1770, the violence climaxed in the Boston Massacre.

That night some boys and men were throwing snowballs (some with rocks in them) at a British sentry. When a squad of troops under Captain Thomas Preston arrived, the crowd attacked them. In the resulting riot, shots were fired, and five members of the crowd fell. The first to die was a black man, Crispus Attucks.

Sam Adams quickly accused the soldiers of murder. But at their trial John Adams and Josiah Quincy, both patriots, won acquittal for all but two of the defendants. The soldiers were withdrawn to an island in the harbor.

In the meantime, the boycott was once more hurting the British merchants, and again the government gave in to their demands. All the Townshend duties were repealed except the one on tea (which no one was paying anyway). Peace seemed to have been restored.

 **TRY THIS!**

1. Show how each of these added to the ill feeling between Britain and the American colonies: a) the Proclamation of 1763, b) the Sugar Act of 1764, c) the Stamp Act, d) the Townshend duties, e) the Boston Massacre. **2.** Find out why two patriots like John Adams and Josiah Quincy defended the British soldiers accused in the Boston Massacre.

3. FIRST BATTLES OF THE REVOLUTION

The final stage of the revolutionary crisis between Britain and its colonies began with an effort to save the East India Company. Through corruption and bad management the Company was facing bankruptcy. But it held 17 million pounds of tea in its warehouses.

A family quarrel. In May 1773 the government agreed to let the Company sell its tea tax-free to American storekeepers. Parliament thought the colonists would be overjoyed at getting cheaper tea. It had guessed wrong again. American merchants (that is, wholesalers) would be undercut by competition from the cheaper tea. Other colonials thought it must be a trick to make them pay the tea tax.

Read here of how

A quarrel began over the tax on tea.
Push came to shove in Massachusetts.
The king offered the colonists a hard choice.
They decided to fight.

In every American port except Charleston, efforts to unload the tea failed. (In Charleston it was locked in a warehouse and finally sold to help pay for the American Revolution.) Everywhere, people sang:

"There was an old lady lived over the sea,
And she was an island queen;
Her daughter lived off in a new countree
With an ocean of water between."

The song ended with the daughter's refusing to pay a tax on her mother's tea, even though the mother threatened, "I'll half-whip your life away."

In Boston, Sam Adams, the fiery rebel, took the lead. On the night of December 16, 1773, the tea ships waited to unload. Adams led the Sons of Liberty, disguised as Indians, aboard one of the ships. As a crowd watched, they dumped the chests of tea overboard.

Was any colony safe? News of the Boston Tea Party spread, and it was soon imitated in New York City and Annapolis, Maryland. In London an angry govern-

The colonists took action because in a few days the tea would have been unloaded. This picture of the event was published in England.

ment passed a series of acts intended to punish Boston.

Americans called these the Intolerable Acts. The first, the Boston Port Act, closed the town's harbor until the tea was paid for. The second, the Massachusetts Act, suspended self-government in the colony. It limited town meetings and jury selection. The third Intolerable Act allowed the king to move the trial of an accused official to another colony. And the Quartering Act allowed the placing of troops in private homes. There was also a Quebec Act which the colonists were sure would give away their western lands.

Nothing did more to unite American feelings against Britain than these five acts. If Parliament could change the constitution of one colony, Americans asked, was any colony safe? From far down the Atlantic seaboard, food and other supplies poured into Boston. A British officer re-

ported that the Bostonians were soon as "sleek and round as robins."

Meanwhile, the British made a military man, General Thomas Gage, governor of Massachusetts. "The colonies," said King George III, "must either triumph or submit." No one argued with that. But Lord North, the king's chief minister, was getting "expert" advice from General Gage. He urged a test of strength at once. Bostonians, Gage said, would prove "very meek" when they were punished.

No retreat. Rebel leaders everywhere took heart. Each colony had its Sons of Liberty and its Committee of Correspondence. The committees formed an information network guaranteed to give the widest publicity to every new British outrage.

In the spring of 1774 Massachusetts asked for a general meeting of all the colonies. Every one but Georgia accepted, and the First Continental Congress met at Philadelphia in September 1774. John Adams called the 55 delegates "a collection of the greatest men on this continent."

After much discussion the Congress issued a declaration denouncing all the acts of Parliament for the preceding eleven years. Six days later it organized an *embargo* (boycott) to "wring immediate concessions" from the British government. In London George III said, "We must not retreat." But the statesman Edmund Burke, an old friend of America, grumbled, "A great empire and little minds go ill together." In Massachusetts, General Gage was ordered to restore British authority by force if necessary. The time for talk had passed.

"In the king's name." Gage was in a bad position. In Boston there was a hostile crowd of tradesmen and sailors. They had been thrown out of work by the closing of the port. Outside the town, patriot "minutemen" patrolled the roads, ready for anything. Arms and ammunition were hidden everywhere.

Finally, Gage sent 800 troops to seize military supplies at Concord, eighteen miles from Boston. The British tried to keep the expedition secret, but two horsemen, Paul Revere and Thomas Dawes, slipped out of town and spread the alarm.

The British route took them through the village of Lexington. There, on the morning of April 19, 1775, some fifty minutemen had hastily gathered. At dawn the British advance column came into view. The colonials were ordered to lay down their arms "in the king's name." They refused to do so, and there was a brief exchange of shots. Eight Americans were killed; ten others and one redcoat were wounded.

"Americans to arms!" The British pushed on to Concord. There they destroyed some military supplies and prepared to return to Boston. Meanwhile, word of the Lexington affair spread throughout the countryside. At a bridge just outside Concord, a platoon of British were attacked. Then, all the way back to Boston, the outnumbered British were picked off by snipers from all sides.

Once the British reached the safety of the town, they were sealed inside by the angry minutemen. Later that spring as the spirit of rebellion spread, thousands of other colonial troops joined them. In New York patriot forces seized British supplies. And a Philadelphia woman wrote, "The universal cry is, 'Americans, to arms!'"

In May of 1775 the Second Continental Congress met at Philadelphia. Most of the delegates still hoped for some kind of agreement with Britain. But the same day the Congress met, 300 Green Mountain

PARTICULAR CARE

No one would believe that Abigail Adams could not read Latin—or do anything else she wanted to. She had taught herself French, and she ran the farm and business and raised the children, while husband John served the country in Philadelphia, Paris, and London. She did it so well that he never became poor, as other Revolutionary leaders did.

What letters they wrote! She warned him that Congress should give more power to women. "If particular care . . . is not paid to the ladies," she wrote, "we are determined to [start] a rebellion, and we will not hold ourselves bound by any law in which we have no voice or representation."

She toned down John's rough edges. (He had plenty.) And she built his self-confidence. (Few people were aware he needed any.)

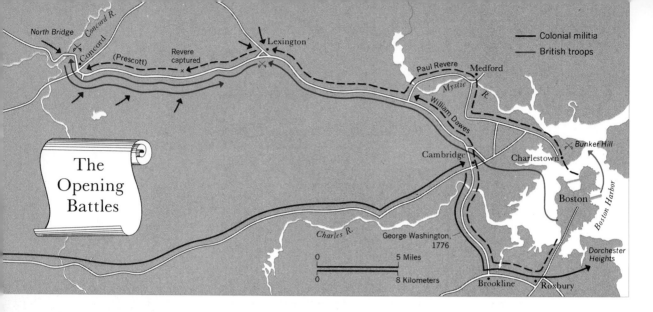

The Opening Battles

North Bridge · Concord R. · Concord · (Prescott) · Revere captured · Lexington · Paul Revere · Medford · Mystic R. · William Dawes · Cambridge · Charlestown · Bunker Hill · Boston · Boston Harbor · Charles R. · George Washington, 1776 · Dorchester Heights · Brookline · Roxbury

Colonial militia
British troops

0   5 Miles
0   8 Kilometers

As it was almost an island, Boston would be hard to take by assault. How could it be supplied? How would cannon on Bunker Hill or Dorchester heights make the town hard to hold?

Boys from Vermont captured the fort at Ticonderoga (tigh-con-duh-ROH-guh), New York. Their leaders, Ethan Allen and Benedict Arnold, had cut the invasion route from Canada (map on page 90).

The Congress selected George Washington, a wealthy Virginia planter, to lead the American forces. It was a wise choice. Having Washington as commander helped to gain the support of Virginia, the largest and richest of the colonies. Furthermore, though he sometimes failed in battle, Washington's leadership improved as the struggle grew worse. And he understood the strategy needed for victory.

A costly victory. Before Washington could take over his command, the American cause was greatly aided by a British "victory." One night in June of 1775, 1,500 Americans fortified a hill overlooking Boston Harbor. The next morning 2,500 redcoats marched up the hill in the face of a withering fire. The British finally took the

hill on the third attempt, but only after the Americans ran out of ammunition and slipped away.

The Battle of Bunker Hill cost the British 1,400 dead and wounded—over half their force. The Americans escaped with only 400 casualties. For the first time, colonists had stood up against British regulars in a pitched battle. And they gave a good account of themselves.

The following March (1776), in a better planned operation, Washington forced the British to leave Boston. Over a thousand loyalists went with them to Canada.

The hope of independence. In the summer of 1776 Congress sent King George an "Olive Branch Petition." They assured him of their loyalty and promised to restore good relations if his unjust laws were repealed. At the same time Congress drew up a more radical document. It explained why Americans had been forced to take up arms. The spirit of independence was rising.

George III and Lord North met the petitions of Congress by hiring Hessian soldiers from Germany. News soon reached London that royal governors were being

82

overthrown in one colony after another.

Some petitions denounced Britain for encouraging slave revolts. Lord Dunmore, the last royal governor of Virginia, had in fact invited slaves to act against their rebel masters. In return they were to receive their freedom. But for white Americans the hope of independence did not mean freedom for blacks.

 TRY THIS!

1. Trace the chain of events leading from the problems of the East India Company to the Battle of Bunker Hill. Show how each led to the next. **2.** Arrange a panel discussion that could have taken place between members of the Second Continental Congress and the British Parliament.

The Americans were in a bad place. Warships could have cut off their retreat (map on page 82).

BOSTON

CHARLES TOWN

4. THE DEBATE OVER INDEPENDENCE

Most Americans took their ideas about government from John Locke and the other writers who had lived through the English revolution of 1688. In that Glorious Rebellion, as it was sometimes called, Parliament got rid of one king (James II) and put another (William III) in his place. In doing so Parliament, for all time, made itself superior to the king—as every English ruler since has realized.

Necessary and reasonable laws. Locke explained the English revolution in terms of basic human rights that no government could ever take away. By Locke's theory James II had interfered with the basic rights of his subjects, and they had overthrown him. Even a king, Locke said, must have the "consent" of his people.

Well before the American Revolution, Locke's ideas were accepted on both sides of the Atlantic. But they meant different things in England and in America. For instance, King George III believed that he governed with the consent of his people, as Locke said he should. He fully accepted Parliament's power and respected the rights of his subjects.

Americans, on the other hand, took the words of Locke to mean that governments should serve rather than rule their people. There would always be a struggle, they felt, between the citizen and the state.

The king and his ministers were puzzled at the way Americans reacted to necessary and reasonable laws. If Parliament could not rule the colonies, they wondered, who could? And what exactly did tie together the mother country and its far-flung possessions?

A new kind of empire. Benjamin Franklin had one answer. He felt that Parliament should have no power within the colonies. Instead, they should be "so many separate states, only subject to the same king." (It was on this basis that the British Commonwealth of Nations was to be built many years later.) Americans were still loyal to their king. But when he refused to accept their view of the empire, that link too gave way.

Meanwhile the country was divided on the issue of independence. Among the members of the Second Continental Congress were fiery radicals who wanted a break with England, and moderates who still looked for compromise. But all opposed the authority of Parliament. And none believed that the empire could go on any longer in the old way.

A powerful change. As Americans in and out of Congress continued to debate, a fresh new voice was heard across the land. In January 1776, a pamphlet titled *Common Sense* appeared. Its author was Thomas Paine, an Englishman who had just arrived in the New World. Of America's connection with the mother country, Paine said, "'Tis time to part." He went on:

A government of our own is our natural right. And when a man seriously reflects on . . . human af-

---◆---

Read here of how

British and Americans agreed about rights and revolution.
But disagreed about their application.
Tom Paine wrote *Common Sense.*
And Jefferson wrote a Declaration.

---◆---

fairs, he will become convinced that it is infinitely wiser and safer to form a constitution of our own in a cool and deliberate manner . . . than to trust such an interesting event to time and chance. . . .

Instead of pretending that George III was a good king misled by wicked advisers, Paine called him "the royal brute of Great Britain." Paine argued that the republican form of government was far better than monarchy. It was readily suited, he said, to American conditions.

Paine's writing style was simple and easy to understand. And he was telling Americans many things they already believed. Within a brief time over 100,000 copies of *Common Sense* were sold. General Washington said that it worked "a powerful change in the minds of many."

Free and independent states. In colony after colony, as the royal governors were driven out (page 83), new Republican constitutions were approved. South Carolina accused the king of attacking his own people. North Carolina and Rhode Island told their delegates to work for independence. In Massachusetts one town meeting after another called for cutting all ties with Britain. Finally, in mid-May, Virginia too demanded a declaration of independence.

Richard Henry Lee of Virginia, rose in the Congress on June 7, 1776. Following his state's orders, he introduced a resolution declaring that the colonies "are and of right ought to be free and independent states."

The opinions of mankind. Congress appointed a committee of five members to draw up a declaration formally breaking its ties with Britain. Two of the committee members, John Adams and Benjamin Franklin, had minor suggestions about the document. Otherwise, it was entirely the work of Thomas Jefferson.

The tall, soft-spoken Virginian made the declaration a classic statement of human freedom. In setting out the reasons for the split with Britain, Jefferson drew heavily on the ideas of John Locke (page 84). The English philosopher had said that life, liberty, and property were natural rights. Jefferson used the words *life, liberty,* and *pursuit of happiness.* Americans, he insisted, were not asking for anything new or revolutionary. They were claiming rights that belonged to all human beings and could not be taken away by any government.

The Declaration listed a long series of charges and abuses to prove that the British government intended to stamp out American liberties. But it blamed everything on "the present king of Great Britain." This restated the American view that he was their only link with England. It was a powerful case Jefferson put before "the opinions of mankind."

The possibility of change. Jefferson knew that many Americans opposed rebellion against the king. So he took care to use only the most familiar terms. As he explained many years later, "The object of the Declaration of Independence [was] not to find out new principles or new arguments never before thought of . . . but to place before mankind the common sense of the subject, in terms so plain and firm as to command their assent." It was to be, he concluded, "an expression of the American mind."

Many Americans no doubt considered Jefferson's opinions too radical. Few were ready to accept the statement that "all men are created equal." For example, Jefferson originally charged George III with encouraging slavery and the slave trade.

In putting their names to the Declaration, the signers committed "high treason."

holder, saw that slavery denied the most sacred rights of life and liberty. Perhaps change was possible even here.

Two peoples. When Congress voted to adopt Jefferson's Declaration, on July 4, 1776, the break with Britain was complete. Americans had embraced a new idea, that "supreme power . . . resides always in the body of the people; and it never was or can be delegated to one man or a few."

As John Adams noted "The revolution was complete in the minds of the people and the union of the colonies before the war commenced in the skirmishes of Concord and Lexington." There were now two peoples, one British and one American.

TRY THIS!

Explain how Americans came to adopt a different view of human rights from that held by their English cousins. What circumstances and experiences could have caused the change?

But this had been taken out to avoid offending South Carolina and Georgia.

There were few who would admit that slavery presented a serious problem for a democratic society. But Jefferson, a slave-

5. A FIGHT TO THE FINISH

The colonists who took part in the American Revolution understood that they had begun a dangerous journey. They knew that Britain apparently had every advantage. The British army was well-trained, and it was backed by a navy of more than 800 ships. British forces could land anywhere along the coast, choosing the time and place of attack. Furthermore, Britain could count on 30,000 hired Germans and thousands of Indian allies. It could also raise far more money than the Continental Congress.

The American cause looked grim by contrast. Congress had no power to tax or

Read here of how

The British had many advantages in the Revolution.
But the Americans had a few more.
The French were persuaded to help them.
And the world turned upside down.

to draft troops. General Washington was forced to plead repeatedly for men and supplies. And he had to depend on poorly trained militia who often refused to fight outside their own states.

The American army was in constant danger of falling to pieces. Desertions were so common that Washington rarely commanded more than 8,000 men. But those he had remained loyal even under the worst circumstances.

Too many troops. The British had their problems too. They had to fight in a hostile and unfamiliar country 3,000 miles from home. Their supply problems were staggering. Though they won almost every major battle, they could never capture or destroy Washington's army. Final victory kept escaping them. The Americans could always retreat deeper into the country, wearing the British down. It slowly dawned on them that they would have to occupy the entire country in order to win. That would take too many troops, more than they could afford.

The American cause was also helped by divided opinion among the British public. The English Whig Party opposed the war and would not support it. The Whig leader Lord Chatham refused to "contribute . . . a single shilling" to win the war. Distinguished generals from the French and Indian War refused to accept commands in America. Businessmen, university people, and ordinary citizens had doubts about what their country was doing.

A hundred thousand exiles. In America too there was lack of support for the war. About a third of the colonists stayed loyal to the king. Some of these were judges or royal officials and their families. Merchants and landholders often joined with them.

Sizable numbers of workmen and farmers could also be found among the loyalists. This was especially true on the frontier and in the seaports of the middle colonies. But only in the middle colonies were the loyalists, or Tories equal in numbers to the patriots. They were a quarter of the popula-

Americans like the rifleman (far left) and the black infantryman (left center) were sometimes roughly dressed. British troops (right center) and Hessians (far right) were well trained and smartly uniformed.

87

A VETERAN OF THE REVOLUTION

Wives of Revolutionary soldiers often marched with them on campaigns. Sometimes they did work for which they got rations and pay.

Not unheard-of were women who served in the ranks as soldiers. One of them was Deborah Sampson of Plymouth, Massachusetts. In 1782, using a man's name, Deborah enlisted. She stood five feet seven inches, which was tall for a woman of those times.

The young soldier served with distinction in several battles, before being badly wounded. At a Philadelphia hospital Deborah Sampson's secret was discovered. She was honorably discharged and returned to Massachusetts. In 1792 she asked for a soldier's pension and got one.

tion in the South but only a tenth of it in New England.

American loyalists, or Tories, were often persecuted. Some were forced to take oaths supporting the Revolution. Many were jailed, driven from their homes, tarred and feathered. But loss of property was their greatest hardship. A number of them joined the British forces. When the war ended, over 100,000 Tories went into exile, giving up all they owned.

A rifleman behind every tree. Washington had many faults as a commander, but they often worked out to his advantage. His ignorance of conventional military tactics led him to fight in ways the British could never understand. Very early he got the idea that the war in America would have to be fought differently from one in Europe. By using swift-moving light infantry and by sharing his men's discomforts, Washington built the first revolutionary colonial army.

The British might hold the seaports, but they were soon convinced that going out into the countryside was dangerous for them. They came to believe that every tree, bush, or stone wall hid an American rifleman.

A bad mistake. Their navy gave the British the power to strike wherever they wanted. Washington could only guess where the next blow might fall. In 1776, with Boston abandoned (page 82), New York City seemed a likely target. Washington worked hard to fortify it. As summer opened, a fleet of more than 100 ships landed over 30,000 troops under Sir William Howe, Sir Henry Clinton, and Lord Cornwallis on Staten Island in New York Harbor.

In trying to defend the city, Washington made the bad mistake of splitting his

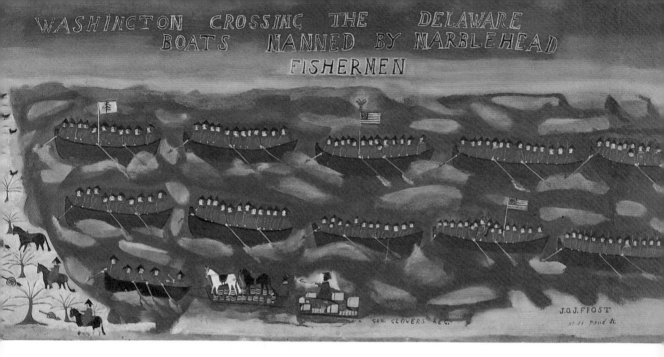

The "artist" was justly proud of what his townsmen had done.

army. He placed one force at Brooklyn Heights and the other in lower Manhattan (map on page 90). Howe easily defeated Washington at Brooklyn. But he allowed the American force to escape across the East River to Manhattan. Washington first retreated up to Harlem and White Plains, then crossed into New Jersey. The British had taken New York without difficulty, and they continued to hold it throughout the war.

A daring move. American morale was at its lowest point. Desertions soared, and Washington was close to despair. He was nearly captured retreating across New Jersey and Pennsylvania. But as winter closed in, he made a daring decision. He would attack.

Washington chose Christmas night, 1776, for his surprise move. He crossed the ice-filled Delaware River and fell upon a force of Hessians at Trenton. With a loss of only five men, he captured 1,900 Germans. The British reacted at once, but not

quickly enough. Washington was able to smash a British force at Princeton, then dig in for the winter at Morristown, New Jersey.

When spring came, the American army was still intact. It had not melted away as Howe had hoped. Clearly the British needed a larger plan.

Guerrilla action. The plan that emerged was a disaster for Britain. In the summer of 1777 three British armies were to meet at Albany on the Hudson River (map on page 90). One of these would march south from Canada under General John Burgoyne. A second force, under Colonel Barry St. Leger, was to move along the Mohawk Valley. Howe was to send a third body of troops up the Hudson River from New York.

If the three armies had met, they would have cut the colonies in half. However, they never did. St. Leger was stopped at Oriskany by New York militia. His Indian allies deserted and his army fled. Burgoyne had even greater trouble. At first he moved south without difficulty. He captured Ticonderoga, New York (page 82), in July but soon found himself running out of supplies. At the same time American sharpshooters and guerrilla-type forces dogged his army.

The turning point. Howe was completely involved in capturing Philadelphia and never did send any troops northward to join Burgoyne. (In taking the colonial capital, Howe defeated Washington again at Brandywine and Germantown.) Meanwhile, Burgoyne woke up to the fact that he was outnumbered and entirely cut off. Finally, in October 1777, he lost the Battle of Bemis Heights. On October 16 he surrendered at Saratoga, New York, to General Horatio Gates. It was the turning point of the war.

Britain's enemies in Europe now believed that the Americans could win. France had been secretly supplying arms and other material. After the Saratoga victory a formal alliance was drawn up and signed in February 1778. Within a year Spain and the Netherlands joined France on the American side.

The European powers entered the war for their own good. An American victory would strengthen them by weakening Britain. And French and Dutch loans gave the Americans badly needed funds. News of the French alliance helped American morale during the terrible winter at Valley Forge. And the British retreated from Philadelphia so that they could concentrate their forces in New York against an expected French attack.

Washington could have lost his army and the war in 1776. The following year brought victory, renewed hope, and the French alliance. The Hudson River/Lake Champlain route was the Great Warpath.

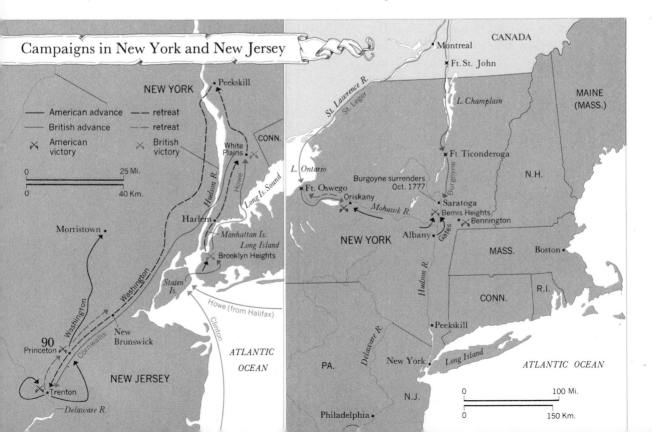

Campaigns in New York and New Jersey

A hard winter march. On the ocean the Americans scored few victories. Britain still ruled the waves and successfully supplied its forces in New York. John Paul Jones managed to carry the war into British waters, but this did not affect the final outcome.

The rest of 1778, while the Americans waited for the buildup of French aid, was a period of stalemate. Both sides tried to break it. Beyond the Allegheny Mountains, frontiersmen joined the Virginia militia under George Rogers Clark. By mid-1778 Clark had seized the whole Illinois country. In early 1779 he made a hard winter march of almost 200 miles and captured Vincennes. For the rest of the war bitter and bloody fighting raged along the frontier.

A British Saratoga. By 1778 the British had turned their efforts to the South. They had been unable to conquer the North, and they believed that there was a lot of loyalist support in the southern colonies (pages 87–88).

Sir Henry Clinton sent a force from New York to capture Savannah in December 1778. Early in 1780 he overwhelmed the local militia and captured Charleston. It was as great a victory for the British as Saratoga had been for the Americans. The British took 5,000 prisoners and 300 cannon that the Americans could never replace.

Loyalist cavalry under Colonel Banastre Tarleton terrorized the countryside. Carolina loyalists and patriots looted each other's houses and slaughtered one another in a brief but savage civil war. A number of old quarrels having nothing to do with the war were settled in the fighting.

At Camden, South Carolina, another group of militia panicked and ran away.

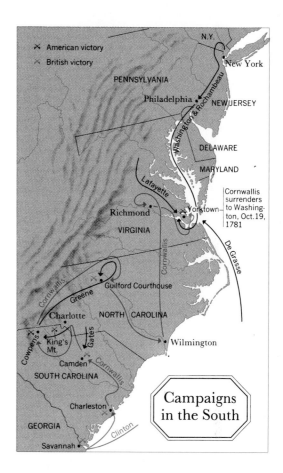

Nathanael Greene was one of the best American generals. Cornwallis, heading for the sea at Yorktown, Virginia, found a French fleet, not the British, waiting for him.

The British under Cornwallis then pursued the clever American general Nathanael Greene across North Carolina. As he advanced (map on this page), Cornwallis was stretching his supply lines and being constantly harassed by guerrilla-like cavalry under Francis Marion and Thomas Sumter.

"The World Turned Upside Down." In Virginia the American traitor Benedict Arnold captured Richmond for the British.

Like Abigail Adams (page 81) these southern women ran farms and businesses.

(He had fled to their lines after trying to sell them the fortress at West Point, New York.) Cornwallis and his army settled into Yorktown (map on page 91).

Cornwallis had no idea that Washington, with a French army of 5,000, was moving south to trap him. Furthermore, a French fleet had temporarily cut the British navy's supply lines to Yorktown. Cornwallis was soon facing a French and American force of nearly double his strength.

On October 10, 1781, after some unsuccessful attempts to break away, Cornwallis surrendered his army to George Washington. As the British troops marched out to lay down their arms, the band played "The World Turned Upside Down," a popular tune of the day. In London, Lord North moaned, "It is all over."

Independence the issue. But the war was not really over. The fighting had almost stopped, but it took another two years to make peace.

The American peace team, John Adams, John Jay, Benjamin Franklin, and Henry Laurens, got little help from the wartime allies. Neither one wanted a powerful new republic in America. Spain was hoping to get back Florida and parts of the Mississippi Valley. By the Treaty of Alliance the United States and France were supposed to agree on peace terms. But France would not even insist that the British recognize American independence before beginning discussions with them.

Adams and Jay stubbornly insisted that independence was the chief issue. When the British agreed to a separate peace with the United States, they accepted. The Treaty of Paris that was finally signed September 3, 1783, fully recognized the independence of the United States. It made Canada in the north, Florida in the south, and the Mississippi River in the west the boundaries of the new country (map on page 101). Congress agreed to urge payment of the debts that Americans owed to British merchants and to ask the states to pay the loyalists whose property had been taken. And Americans could fish off Newfoundland.

In a separate treaty with Britain, Spain got Florida. The long struggle was finally finished.

 TRY THIS!

1. Show that Washington was (a) often a poor tactician, (b) always an indispensable leader. **2.** Using the maps on pages 82, 90, and 91, explain the strategy that made it possible for America to win the Revolution. **3.** Tell why the United States got little help from its allies in the peace of 1783.

92

The siege of Yorktown.

ROUNDUP

Who?

John Adams
Sam Adams
Crispus Attucks
Paul Revere
Thomas Paine
Thomas Jefferson
Sir Henry Clinton
George Rogers Clark

What?

salutary neglect
triangular trades
enumerated articles
Navigation Acts
Proclamation of 1763
Stamp Act
Sons of Liberty
Intolerable Acts
Continental Congress
Declaration of
    Independence
Tories

Where?

Fort Duquesne
Quebec
Fort Ticonderoga
Saratoga
Savannah
Charleston
Yorktown

KNOW THIS

From Colony to Province

1. What was New England's part in the triangular trades?
2. What three restrictions did Britain place on colonial trade? What was the effect of each?
3. In what ways did colonial assemblies act like "miniature Parliaments"? Why did they?
4. How did the British victories in 1759 change the map of North America?

Growing Political Unrest

1. What was the purpose of the Proclamation Line? How did the American colonists regard it?
2. Was the Sugar Act good for the colonies? Explain.
3. Why was there strong reaction to the Stamp Act?
4. How was it that the Boston Massacre was followed by a period of peace and quiet?
5. How did victory in 1763 hasten the Revolution?

First Battles of the Revolution

1. What brought about the Boston Tea Party? How did the British government react to it?
2. How did each Intolerable Act punish Massachusetts?
3. Describe the events at Lexington and Concord.
4. Why was Washington a good choice for commander of the American forces?

The Debate over Independence

1. What was Locke's view of government and revolution?
2. How did British and Americans view his ideas?
3. How did Thomas Paine help the United States to gain its independence?
4. Describe the manner in which the Declaration of Independence came to be written.
5. Why was the writing style so important in *Common Sense* and the *Declaration of Independence?*

A Fight to the Finish

1. Why did the British expect to win a quick victory in the Revolution?
2. To what extent did Americans support the war?
3. Why is the Battle of Saratoga considered the turning point of the Revolution?
4. How important was foreign aid to the United States in the Revolution? What did France provide?
5. On what terms did the British and Americans make peace in 1783?

DIG HERE!

By yourself or with one or two classmates, look into the details of one engagement or campaign of the Revolution: Lexington/Concord, Kings Mountain, Cowpens, *Bonhomme Richard–Serapis,* Yorktown, or some other.

A. Prepare a map showing the location of the battle and also the countryside. Did geography affect the outcome? Explain.
B. Who were the commanders? Describe their earlier careers. How effective were they in this battle?
C. What tactics were used by each side? If possible, show them on your map.
D. Can you explain the victory? How?
E. How important was this battle to the whole war effort? Was it decisive? Explain.

After you and the other students have reported on your research, discuss the reasons for the final American victory. In particular, consider these words of the historian Edmund Morgan: "The American Revolution was a people's war, and it is doubtful that the British could ever have won more than a stalemate."

What is a "people's war"? Has Morgan explained the outcome of this conflict? See pages 87–88.

These books will be especially helpful: four books by Donald Barr Chidsey, *The Siege of Boston; July 4, 1776; The War in the North; Victory at Yorktown;* also, Life Reprint #72, *Great Battles of the American Revolution* (Life Educational Materials Center).

THINK ABOUT IT

1. Why is "the power of the purse" (control of spending) so important for a legislative body? How did it help colonial assemblies?
2. It appears that before the Revolution, British officials failed to understand the American colonies. How did the policies of Lord Grenville, Charles Townshend, Thomas Gage, and George III bear this out? Give examples.

DO IT!

1. With three or four classmates, research, write, and tape-record a series of interviews for a radio program titled "Revolutionary Profiles." You might include Baron Von Steuben, Ethan Allen, Deborah Sampson, John Paul Jones, Benedict Arnold, Lafayette, or Benjamin Franklin.
2. The Declaration states that "all men are created equal." Some important groups have not felt included: women, blacks, Indians, and others. Report to the class on the role played in the Revolution by members of one or more of these groups. Or create a wall mural designed to tell their story.

THEN AND NOW

Were John Adams and his partner right in defending the British soldiers in the Boston Massacre? Is every accused person entitled to the best possible defense? Why? If you were a lawyer, would you take the cases of those accused of especially evil crimes? Why, or why not?

95

The Government of a Free People

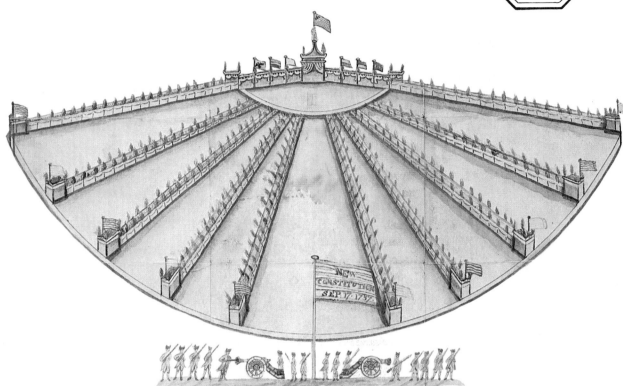

4

Acceptance of the United States Constitution by New York State assured it of a start. New York City strongly favored adoption and showed it by celebrating three days early with parades and fireworks and by feasting and speechmaking for 6,000 in this banquet pavilion.

1. A SOCIAL REVOLUTION

Today the American Revolution would be called a "war of national liberation." Its chief purpose was to win independence. Nevertheless, the Revolution accomplished far more. It affected people's everyday lives, and it changed relationships among the social classes. The Revolution also opened greater business opportunities to some citizens and established new methods of landholding. Finally, the Revolution made politics noticeably freer and more democratic.

New voters. When the royal governments were overthrown, new constitutions had to be drawn up in every colony except Connecticut and Rhode Island. (These colonies had been self-governing even before the Revolution—page 72.) Most of the new constitutions lowered property qualifications for voting, and this increased the number of people taking part in elections.

Many jobs that had been filled by appointment were voted on by the people under the new state constitutions. Terms of office were short; usually a year. And governors had at most only a limited power to veto acts of the assemblies. Several states, beginning with Massachusetts in 1780, adopted a Bill of Rights as part of their constitutions.

A new business class. During the Revolution great tracts of land were taken away from the loyalists. The Penn family alone lost 21 million acres in Pennsylvania. Much of the loyalists' land found its way into the hands of important patriots. But some of it was also sold to poorer farmers.

Numbers of Tory merchants lost their fortunes or fled the country. A new merchant class rose to take their places. They were people who had grown rich through filling government contracts, buying up loyalist property, and *privateering*.

Privateers were merchant ships armed and sent out to attack the merchant ships of enemy nations. The vessels they captured were sold and the profits divided among the crew of the privateer, its owners, and the government. Many New England

---

Read here of how

Revolution changed American society.
Slavery disappeared in the North.
But was more widespread in the South.

TIME CHART

1777	Congress proposes the Articles of Confederation.
1781	Virginia leads in giving up western lands.
1785	A land ordinance is adopted for the Northwest.
1786	The Annapolis Convention meets.
1786	Shays' Rebellion takes place in Massachusetts.
1787	The Constitutional Convention meets.
1788	The Constitution is ratified.
1793	Eli Whitney invents the cotton gin.

---

families built their fortunes on privateering during the Revolution.

The ending of the Navigation Acts (pages 69-70) and the closing of British ports to American shipping affected American trade and industry. New England began to develop its own textile manufacturing, and New England merchants looked for new markets in the Far East and Europe.

Black troops. By the time of the Revolution there were about 500,000 slaves in the thirteen colonies, mainly on the plantations of the South. At that time no one but a few Quakers took stands publicly against slavery. But in the crisis of the 1770s numbers of Americans began to see the contradiction between slaveholding and human or natural rights. It was no accident that the first antislavery society was begun in Philadelphia five days before the Battle of Lexington.

Because of pressure from the South, George Washington at first refused to have

97

The China Trade

With independence, the United States lost its West Indies trade. Merchants turned to China. Furs found a ready market there. They were bought from the Indians of the Pacific Northwest and exchanged for tea, silks, and fine porcelain. The Chinese sold tea (above) and made articles just for the U. S. market. The vase (right) shows the signing of the Declaration. Dislike of westerners is seen in the Chinese picture (far right) of a sailor, hairy and spewing tobacco smoke.

black soldiers in the Continental Army. He changed his mind when the British commander in Virginia offered freedom to any slaves who escaped to his lines. Washington then allowed the enlistment of blacks. But only Maryland, among the southern states, used many black troops.

Whenever the American forces in the South lost a battle, thousands of slaves went over to the British to gain their freedom. On withdrawing from Savannah and Charleston the British took these former slaves with them.

A different situation. The spread of revolutionary ideas, and the service of about 5,000 blacks in the army, led many northern states to do away with slavery. There were so few slaves in the North that this could take place without any disruption.

The situation in the South was radically different. There slaves were the very basis of the region's economic life. The closest any southern state came to doing away with slavery was in a Virginia law of 1781. It merely encouraged owners to free their slaves voluntarily. Nevertheless,

10,000 Virginia slaves were set free by their masters in the 1780s. So were a number of blacks in Maryland and Delaware. Elsewhere, things continued unchanged.

A new source of wealth. In 1793 the cotton gin appeared. It was the invention of a northerner, Eli Whitney. At about the same time, improvements were made in the machinery for spinning cotton thread. Together, these two developments opened the way for a new kind of cotton production.

For years a limited amount of fine, long-fibered cotton had been grown along the coast of Georgia and South Carolina. It was called sea island cotton. Now it was possible to make money growing coarser, short-fibered, upland cotton that could be produced wherever rainfall was moderate and there were 200 days free of frost. In other words, this cotton could be grown throughout much of the lower South.

A new kind of plantation began to appear, one that grew cotton for an expanding world market. In a few years the white fiber became the most important source of wealth in the South. And as cotton growing spread, so did the idea that slavery must be kept and protected.

But the Revolution had given birth to a belief in human equality. That belief would be a mighty weapon in the future struggle against human bondage.

 TRY THIS!

1. Compare the everyday life of Americans before and after the Revolution. Show how each of the following had changed: a) politics, b) landholding, c) trade, d) slaveholding. **2.** Explain the effect of the cotton gin on slavery.

2. THE ARTICLES OF CONFEDERATION

While the Revolution was still going on, Americans recognized the need for a stronger government. At the same time, they were suspicious of central power. In fact, it was British efforts to increase control of the colonies that had caused them to revolt in the first place. The Continental Congress was a good example of this confusion of ideas. It had the task of supplying the army. But at the same time, it was forbidden to tax.

Congress met the need for money by using the printing presses. Paper money poured out at a rate that soon reduced its value and brought on soaring inflation. Price controls might have helped, but the states rejected them. And to make matters worse the states were printing their own paper money. If it had not been for loans of French gold and silver, the country's finances would have been a complete mess.

The first government. The first central government of any kind the United States had was under a written constitution called the Articles of Confederation. The Continental Congress drew up the Articles shortly after declaring independence, and in November 1777, it sent them to the states to be *ratified* (accepted or agreed to).

The Articles gave the Congress control of foreign affairs and the power to make

———————————◆———◆———————————

Read here of how

Articles of Confederation were drawn up.
The Ordinance of 1785 set land policy.
The Northwest was organized.
The period after the Revolution came to be called "critical."

war and to settle disputes among the states. The Congress could also coin money and borrow to pay its bills.

Each state was to have one vote in the Congress. Ordinary questions could be decided by a simple majority. Important ones required nine votes. To *amend* (change) the Articles, all thirteen states had to agree. Any powers not given to the Congress remained with the states.

The Articles seemed to make Congress quite strong. But, as noted, it lacked the power to tax. It could only ask the states for the money it needed, and it had no way of enforcing its decisions.

"For the good of the Union." Final ratification of the Articles proposed in 1777 was delayed until 1781, due to disputes over western lands (map on page 101). Maryland and Delaware insisted that Congress be given control of the territory beyond the Appalachian Mountains. The colonial charters of Maryland and Delaware gave them no rights in the region, and they feared that the states having claims (Massachusetts, Connecticut, Virginia, the Carolinas, and Georgia) would become too powerful. Maryland argued that the lands had been won from Britain in a common effort and should belong to all.

Finally, in January of 1781, Virginia agreed to give up its claim "for the good of the Union." The other states with western territory followed Virginia's lead, and on March 11 the Articles were ratified. The Continental Congress could now call itself "The United States of America in Congress Assembled."

A dollar an acre. The western lands that the Congress received from the states gave it control of a vast region. At once

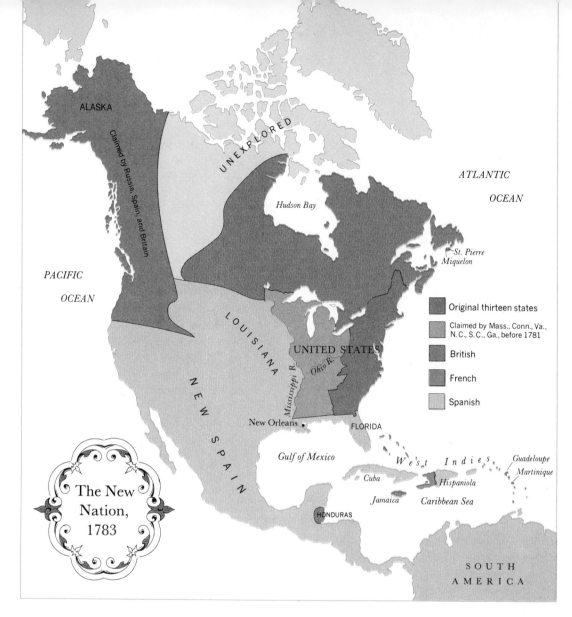

The New
Nation,
1783

ALASKA

Claimed by Russia, Spain, and Britain

UNEXPLORED

Hudson Bay

ATLANTIC

OCEAN

St. Pierre
Miquelon

PACIFIC

OCEAN

LOUISIANA

UNITED STATES

Ohio R.

Mississippi R.

NEW

SPAIN

New Orleans •

FLORIDA

Gulf of Mexico

West Indies

Guadeloupe
Martinique

Cuba

Hispaniola

Jamaica

Caribbean Sea

HONDURAS

SOUTH

AMERICA

	Original thirteen states
	Claimed by Mass., Conn., Va., N.C., S.C., Ga., before 1781
	British
	French
	Spanish

The first boundaries of the United States were set by the Treaty of 1783 with Britain. It was a magnificent territory. Compare this map with the one on page 75.

there was a dispute over how the new territory was to be settled. Two methods were possible. On the one hand there was the New England system, whereby a large group of people moved into new country and set up a town (page 49). On the other was the southern way, by which individuals or small groups bought or claimed land.

As a result of the debate over the two plans, the Ordinance of 1785 was adopted. It called for surveying the land *before* it was occupied. The survey divided the new territory into townships, each one being six miles long by six miles wide (36 square

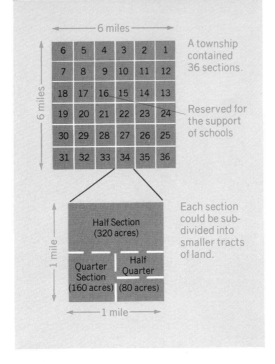

<table>
<tr><td colspan="6">← 6 miles →</td></tr>
<tr><td>6</td><td>5</td><td>4</td><td>3</td><td>2</td><td>1</td></tr>
<tr><td>7</td><td>8</td><td>9</td><td>10</td><td>11</td><td>12</td></tr>
<tr><td>18</td><td>17</td><td>16</td><td>15</td><td>14</td><td>13</td></tr>
<tr><td>19</td><td>20</td><td>21</td><td>22</td><td>23</td><td>24</td></tr>
<tr><td>30</td><td>29</td><td>28</td><td>27</td><td>26</td><td>25</td></tr>
<tr><td>31</td><td>32</td><td>33</td><td>34</td><td>35</td><td>36</td></tr>
</table>

A township contained 36 sections.

Reserved for the support of schools

Half Section (320 acres)

Quarter Section (160 acres)

Half Quarter (80 acres)

Each section could be subdivided into smaller tracts of land.

Sections of a township were numbered this way. The one for schools was always 16 whether its soil was good or poor. The 640 acres in a square mile might be divided as shown.

miles). Each square mile (640 acres) was called a *section* (see chart above). One section in each township (number 16) was set aside to support education. That is, money received from selling that section would help pay for public schools.

The land was auctioned off by sections and by townships. The smallest price allowed was a dollar an acre. Good land cost much more. Thus the smallest price for a section would be 640 dollars—a lot of money for ordinary people. Those who benefited first from the land sales were *speculators*. (A speculator buys something, not for use but in the hope of selling it at a higher price.) Many of them paid for their pur-

chases with the valueless paper money Congress had issued.

Orderly growth. Congress provided a government for its new lands by passing the Northwest Ordinance in 1787. It allowed for no fewer than three states or no more than five in the territory north of the Ohio River (map on page 101). It also provided for gradual self-government in the region.

First, Congress was to appoint a governor, a secretary, and three judges for a territory. When it contained 5,000 adult males, they could elect a legislature and send one nonvoting delegate to Congress. When the territory had a population of 60,000 people, it entered a third stage. It could then apply for statehood on the same basis as the original thirteen states.

The Northwest Ordinance also supported fair treatment for the Indians, religious freedom, and public education. And it prohibited slavery in the Northwest.

In some ways the Northwest Ordinance was one of the most far-reaching pieces of legislation ever passed in the United States. As the country grew, the Ordinance's main provisions were copied all the way across the continent. This made it certain that new territories would come into the Union as full-fledged states. The nation had provided for its own orderly growth.

A CRITICAL PERIOD?

Until recently the period after the Revolution has been called the "Critical Period." It used to be taken for granted that in the 1780s the government under the Articles of Confederation was falling apart. Supposedly, it was working so badly that a new constitution was needed to save the country from collapse.

Lately this grim view has been challenged. Historians have pointed to the successes of the Confederation. Under it Congress developed a land policy for the young nation (the Ordinance of 1785). And the business depression that began when the fighting ended in 1781 was overcome. Manufacturing was encouraged, and Americans consumed more products made in their own country. Flourishing growth existed on all sides, but it is true that there were signs of discontent. Some of it was felt by people of power and influence.

An empty show of sovereignty. Alexander Hamilton was a bright young New York lawyer who had served as an aide to Washington during the Revolution. Both Hamilton and his former chief felt that the Confederation would never become a true central government. It was too weak, they said, and Congress was fast losing what little respect it had.

The powerlessness of Congress was most clearly seen in Europe. Thomas Jefferson, representing the United States in France, was all but ignored. John Adams, in London, could not get a trade agreement or persuade the British to give up their posts in the Northwest Territory. Spain denied the new country full use of the Mississippi by closing off the port of New Orleans (map on page 101). Hamilton summed up the situation when he wrote, "Our ambassadors abroad are mere pageants of mimic sovereignty." (In other words, they were just going through an empty show or make-believe.)

High taxes and low prices. Well-to-do citizens were disturbed because some state governments seemed to be growing indifferent to property rights. Rhode Island, for instance, allowed its people to pay their debts in nearly worthless paper money. This drove some of their creditors into bankruptcy.

In western Massachusetts Daniel Shays, a former Revolutionary officer, roused the local farmers. They were discontented at the high taxes they had to pay and the low prices brought by their goods. (The low prices were partly due to the loss of British and West Indian trade.) Shays and his followers attacked the courthouses to stop foreclosures on farm property. Only the state militia kept them from seizing the arsenal at Springfield, Massachusetts.

State officials quickly recognized that there was some justice in Shays' Rebellion. They cut court costs, held off on raising taxes, and eased the debt laws. They also pardoned Daniel Shays.

"A little rebellion." But throughout the country Shays' Rebellion was seen as an attack on private property. Abigail Adams, the outspoken wife of John Adams, said the whole thing was the work of "ignorant, restless desperadoes without conscience or principles." Some Americans thought they must be living on the edge of a general uprising.

From abroad, Jefferson tried to reassure them by saying, "I hold that a little rebellion now and then is a good thing, as necessary in the political world as storms in the physical." But few were convinced. Those who worried about the nation's survival were ready to support a new government.

 TRY THIS!

1. Explain why the lack of power to tax was Congress's greatest weakness. **2.** Show how the Northwest Ordinance grew out of the American colonies' experience with British rule.

3. TOWARD A MORE PERFECT UNION

Two documents shaped the beginning stages of United States history. The Declaration of Independence was the first. It set out the reasons for the American rebellion. It also defined the beliefs on which the new republic was based. But the Declaration did not create a government.

In 1787 a group of Americans gathered once more in the place where they had declared their independence, to draw up a new system of laws for the government of their republic. Two years later the new Constitution was accepted, and the federal Union took its place among the free nations of the world. Though no one realized it at the time, that Union would shape the destiny of half the world.

Sweeping proposals. During the Confederation period the problem of strengthening the government was made worse by sharp disagreements among the states. Some of these were about trade. For example, Maryland and Virginia were taxing each other's shipping. George Washington and a young Virginian, James Madison, wanted to settle the quarrel. In 1784 they invited representatives of the two states to meet at Washington's home. There the representatives agreed to have a committee regulate commerce and defense.

Read here of how

Trade problems troubled the states.
A Convention was held at Philadelphia.
The large and small states were at odds.
Connecticut found a way to satisfy both.

Both state legislatures went along with the agreement. But they soon saw that if it was going to work, their neighbors Pennsylvania and Delaware would have to be brought in too. Virginia proposed a meeting of all thirteen states to discuss trade and other problems.

That meeting was called at Annapolis, Maryland, in May 1786. Only New York, New Jersey, Pennsylvania, Delaware, and Virginia showed up. Even Maryland, the host state, failed to send anyone. New Jersey proposed that instead of talking about trade, the states should discuss ways to strengthen the Articles of Confederation. James Madison agreed with this plan and spoke up for a more powerful central government. Alexander Hamilton of New York wanted the Articles completely overhauled. A Delaware member even proposed doing away with the state governments altogether.

The forces favoring change. None of these actions could be taken by the few states present at Annapolis. So Hamilton proposed a meeting of all the states to discuss the serious issues facing the country. After much debate, the Annapolis Convention asked Congress to call a meeting at Philadelphia. It would be authorized to change the government to meet the needs of the times.

Late in February 1787 the Congress reluctantly agreed to the meeting. Virginia, Pennsylvania, New Jersey, Delaware, and North Carolina swiftly appointed delegates to meet at Philadelphia that spring. In the end every state but Rhode Island sent someone. Many of the representatives were opposed to changing the Articles, but more favored doing so. Those wanting change were led by Washington, the head of the Virginia delegation. He was determined to have a complete change in the Articles. His choice as President of the Convention guaranteed that the forces favoring change would be in control.

Only by give and take. On May 25, 1787, the delegates got down to business in Philadelphia's Independence Hall. The 55 delegates who took part at one time or another were a talented group. The youngest was Jonathan Dayton of New Jersey, who was 26; the oldest was Benjamin Franklin, aged 81. Such important Revolutionary leaders as John Hancock and Samuel Adams of Massachusetts, and Patrick Henry of Virginia, were absent. Patrick Henry said he "smelled a rat" in the call for a

convention and refused to attend. Thomas Jefferson and John Adams were representing the country in Europe and could not be there. But both men were kept fully informed of the Convention's work.

Most of the 55 delegates had been in government, and more than half had gone to college. Most were lawyers, planters, or merchants. Many had loaned money to the government during the Revolution. A number were speculators in western lands.

Naturally, those who had loaned money wanted to be repaid. The government under the Articles could not raise the money to meet its debts. So one thing the founders wanted was a stronger central government with the power to tax and to repay its debts.

George Washington inspired such awe among the delegates that some were afraid to address him.

Throughout the country the most active supporters of a stronger national administration were merchants, businessmen, and skilled workers. They hoped the new government would aid commercial growth and trade. They realized that to do so the government would need the power to tax, to regulate trade, to build roads and other internal improvements, and to issue sound money. In time all these provisions were included in the new Constitution of the United States.

Almost from the beginning, it was clear that most of those at the Convention were interested in setting up an entirely new government. It was also clear that a lot of compromises would have to be made. Only by give-and-take would the various states be persuaded to ratify the new Constitution. To make compromises easier to find, the delegates voted to keep their sessions secret.

A central government in control. As soon as the delegates settled down to business, Edmund Randolph proposed the Virginia Plan. Its real author was James Madison. The plan called for the creation of a new government with a two-house legislature. Representation in both houses was to be according to population. Thus the large states would have more members than the small ones. Virginia, for instance, might have twice as many as New York and ten times as many as Rhode Island or Delaware.

Under the Virginia Plan, the lower house would be elected by popular vote; the upper house was to be chosen by the lower house from a list of candidates selected by state legislatures. No member was to serve two terms in a row, and each was to have one vote. The legislature was to elect a President or Chief Executive who was to have a single term. The proposal also called for a system of federal courts.

If the Virginia Plan had been carried out, it would have given the central government complete control of the states. Among other things, the national legislature would have had the right to override the acts of state legislatures. The new central government would also have been able to use military force to make a state obey its orders. But the delegates from the smaller states realized that if they accepted the Virginia Plan, Massachusetts, Pennsylvania, and Virginia would be running the Union. John Dickinson of Delaware protested, "We would sooner submit to a foreign power than . . . be thrown under the domination of the large states."

Protection for the small states. On June 15 William Paterson of New Jersey moved to offer another plan. He told Madison that unless concessions were made to the smaller states, the Convention would end in disaster. Instead of replacing the Confederation, the New Jersey Plan proposed changing it in some important ways. Congress would be given the power to tax and to regulate both interstate and foreign commerce. Instead of a single President or Chief Executive, there would be a Board of Directors that would serve for only one term. The Board was to fill all civil, military, and judicial positions by appointment. And there would be a Supreme Court. Of great importance was the Plan's provision that all laws and treaties made by Congress would be "the supreme law of the land."

Paterson bluntly warned that the Virginia Plan would never receive popular approval. Unless they were given an equal vote, it was unlikely that the smaller states would ever accept the Constitution.

Satisfaction for large and small. Although the Virginia Plan had wider backing, everyone realized that a compromise between the interests of the large and small states was necessary. James Madison defined the problem when he said, "The great difficulty lies in the affair of representation; and if this could be adjusted, all others would be surmountable."

Roger Sherman of Connecticut set forth the outlines of a solution. He proposed "that the proportion of the [vote] in the first branch should be according to the respective number of free inhabitants; and that in the second branch . . . each state should have one vote and no more."

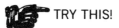 TRY THIS!

1. Trace the role of George Washington in setting up a new government for the United States. 2. Outline some of the arguments that might have been given in the Constitutional Convention by a) a delegate from the large state of Pennsylvania and b) one from the small state of Georgia.

4. THE FRAMEWORK OF GOVERNMENT

Once the delegates had accepted Roger Sherman's compromise plan, they quickly agreed on two important points. There would be a House of Representatives with members elected by population. And there would be a Senate made up of two members from each state. Representatives were to be chosen by the people of the states for two-year terms. State legislatures would elect the senators, who would serve for six years.

The Connecticut Compromise, or Great Compromise, as the agreement was called, satisfied the larger states because it allowed representation by size in the

---•◆•---

Read here of how

The Constitution provided a legislature.
As well as a President and court system.
It had a trade and commerce section.
But it dodged the slavery issue.

---•◆•---

House. The smaller states were happy with their equal representation in the Senate.

Representatives of the people. Article One of the Constitution gives Congress the power to make laws. The House alone can introduce bills to tax the citizens. When Jefferson was told of this provision, he immediately approved. It was his belief that only those directly representing the people should tax them.

By Article One, Congress is authorized to control commerce both at home and abroad. It can coin and print money, and it can borrow on the credit of the United States. The army and navy are supported by Congress, and it alone can declare war. The Senate has the right to approve treaties by a two-thirds vote.

A very important authority was given to Congress in Article One, Section 8, paragraph r. It is allowed "To make all laws which shall be necessary and proper for carrying into execution the foregoing powers." On this part of the Constitution rest the Congress's *implied powers.* Congress can do whatever is necessary to carry out any of its powers, as long as what it does is not forbidden by another part of the Constitution. For example, Congress has established the Federal Reserve System in order to carry out its power to regulate the value of money.

Chosen by the states and the people. The creation of the office of President shows how compromise entered into the writing of the Constitution. Originally Madison had proposed that the Chief Executive be elected by the Congress for a single term of seven years. But some delegates argued that the states should have a role in the choice. Another group proposed that the people should help choose the President. Finally a committee was formed which came up with a compromise—an Electoral College. It allows the people to vote for the electors, who then choose the President.

Representation in the Electoral College is based on the number of each state's representatives and senators. In this way the larger states play an important role in the selection process. And the smallest state has at least three electoral votes. To win, a candidate must get more than half the votes of the Electoral College.

The Commander-in-Chief. Article Two of the Constitution says that a President must be at least 35 years old and a native-born citizen of the United States. Should the presidential office fall vacant, the Vice President becomes President.

Originally no limits were placed on the number of four-year terms a President could have. When Jefferson decided to serve only two terms and cited Washington's example, this established a two-term tradition. That ended in 1940, when Franklin D. Roosevelt won a third term.

Since 1951, the Twenty-second Amendment to the Constitution has limited a President to two elected terms.

The chief task of the President is to carry out the laws passed by Congress. However, he can veto legislation he thinks undesirable. To check excessive use of this power, Congress may then override the veto if two thirds of both houses agree.

The President is the Commander-in-Chief of the armed forces. He has the power to make treaties, with the agreement of two thirds of the Senate. And with the agreement of the Senate, he appoints federal judges, ambassadors, and other key officials.

Responsibility to the law. A final provision in Article Two describes how a President or other high official can be removed from office by the process called *impeachment*. Under it any President, federal judge, or other official accused of breaking the law is first impeached by the House of Representatives. In other words, the House first establishes whether the official might have broken the law. If the House thinks that this happened, the Senate conducts a trial.

Should two-thirds of the senators find the official guilty, he is removed from office. It was the founders' way of saying that no matter how powerful an office may be, its holder is still responsible to the law.

A court system that grew in power. Article Three established the Supreme Court and other federal courts. Unable to decide exactly how to organize the federal court system, the Convention left that up to Congress. But it said that federal judges were to hold their office for life, as long as they did not break the law. They too could be impeached and removed if convicted.

The Convention was careful to guarantee that the federal laws would be enforced equally in all the states. That and all questions about the Constitution or treaties and legal disputes involving the states were placed under the control of the federal *judiciary* (court system). Some opponents feared that the courts might become too powerful. In fact, Chief Justice John Marshall did rule in 1803 that the Supreme Court had the power to declare acts of Congress and the President unconstitutional (page 175). From that time on, the power of the Supreme Court has grown year by year.

Trade and manufacturing. Nothing in the Constitution has had more far-reaching results than the clause giving the federal government the power to regulate trade. It assured that from the beginning there would be a "common market" throughout the United States. There can be no tax on goods moving from one state to another (Article One, Section 10, paragraph b). Raw materials and finished products flow easily. A paper manufacturer in Massachusetts knows that he can sell his goods in Georgia or Ohio. And an Iowa farmer knows that his hogs will have a market in New York or Rhode Island.

This great economic strength of the new republic was not achieved without a fight. A number of disputes arose when the suggestion was made that Congress should have the right to regulate commerce. The southern states feared that Congress would use the power to end the slave trade. Southerners were also fearful that taxes might be used to favor northern industry at the expense of southern exports.

These difficulties were resolved, as one delegate explained, in "a bargain among

The women and men of Philadelphia did much of their buying and selling on the streets of the town.

the northern and southern states." Southern delegates agreed to have trade regulations settled by a majority of Congress rather than by a two-thirds vote. In return the northerners agreed not to interfere with the slave trade until 1808 (Article One, Section 9, paragraph a).

"Persons held to service or labor." One of the disturbing things in the Constitution was its handling of slavery. The word *slave* was carefully left out of the document. This was done to make it easier for northerners to support the Constitution. Some founders admitted being ashamed of not having taken firm action against slavery. Nonetheless, the basis of representation and taxation was settled by another compromise between the sections. It provided that all "free persons" and three fifths of "other persons" be counted. By "other persons" the founders meant slaves.

Article Four, Section 2 came to be known as the Fugitive Slave clause. It stated that any "person held to service or labor" who fled from one state to another was to be returned to his or her owner.

Why were the founders so cautious in dealing with the slavery question? Some felt that an attack on slavery would make it difficult to get the Constitution ratified. Others feared that to attack one form of property would lead to attacks on other forms. Few believed that if the slaves were freed, blacks and whites could live together in a just and peaceful society.

But whatever their beliefs, many of the delegates had the uneasy feeling that slavery threatened the freedom of all. Jefferson knew that the day of reckoning on this most dangerous of issues had only been postponed. "I tremble for my country," he wrote, "when I reflect that God is just, and that his justice cannot sleep forever."

 TRY THIS!

List these numbers on a sheet of paper. Beside each one write a *C* if the statement refers to the Congress, a *P* if it refers to the President, and an *S* if it refers to the Supreme Court. **1.** Commands the armed forces. **2.** Declares war. **3.** Votes on taxes. **4.** Settles disputes between states. **5.** Appoints judges. **6.** Coins money. **7.** Impeaches the President. **8.** Declares laws unconstitutional. **9.** Controls commerce. **10.** Settles disputes under the Constitution.

5. A FEDERAL REPUBLIC ESTABLISHED

The men who drew up the Constitution did not know they were establishing a government that would still exist two centuries later. What explains their success?

First of all, the Constitution was written in general terms. It did not try to spell out every last detail of government. And the founders knew how much they could not foresee. The implied-powers clause (pages

Read here of how

The Constitution created a federal system.
And made good use of checks and balances.
A Bill of Rights was added to it.
Federalists got the Constitution ratified.

107–108) was helpful in meeting such unexpected developments as railroads, electricity, television, and nuclear energy.

A government for all time. A second strength of the Constitution was in its system of checks and balances. For instance, the *federal* idea created a dual citizenship. Americans are citizens both of the United States and of the states in which they live. Another example of federalism is seen in the Tenth Amendment, which states that "powers not delegated to the United States by the Constitution, nor prohibited by it to the states, are reserved to the states respectively, or to the people." Out of this developed the concept of states' rights. It allows the citizens of a state to meet their special problems.

A good example of the way the federalist system works is the organization of public education. Each state decides how to maintain and regulate its educational system. It says which requirements must be met to graduate from high school. And it determines what must be done for admission to a state university.

A many-layered system. There are also limits on the powers of the states. The Constitution forbids them to place tariffs on goods brought in from another state, to engage in war, or to make treaties with foreign countries (Article One, Section 10).

In addition, the states are allowed to exercise certain regulatory powers not forbidden by Congress. So for many years it was possible for state banks to issue paper money. But in 1865 Congress acted against such currency. Today our money is issued only by the national government.

In other areas both the federal and state governments have responsibility. The best example is the police power. Unlike most other countries, the United States does not have a national police force. Local police are controlled by the city or town. Most states have state troopers. Some counties have their own police forces or sheriffs' deputies. At the same time, the federal government has the Federal Bureau of Investigation, Treasury agents, and the Secret Service. This many-layered system means that no single authority controls all the police. If such control existed, it would give whoever had it very great power over the everyday lives of citizens.

A bill becomes a law. In addition to the checks and balances that the state and federal governments exercise on one another, the Constitution has a carefully worked out system of checks and balances within the federal government. The best way to understand the process is to explore how a bill becomes a law.

The process begins when one house of Congress passes a bill. It then goes to the other house, which must vote it out in exactly the same form. Then the President can sign it, or if he thinks it unnecessary or wrong for the people, he can veto it.

Congress can override the President's veto if two thirds of the members in each house vote for the bill a second time. If they do not, the bill dies. Once a bill has been approved by Congress and the President has signed it into law, a citizen who questions whether or not it is constitutional can appeal to the Supreme Court. If the Supreme Court upholds the law, then it remains in force.

The system of checks and balances was designed to assure that government powers would be kept separate. No one branch of government and no one person can dominate the whole system. The founders feared power. They saw it as the greatest threat to liberty. To keep power under control, they

111

The Bald Eagle Our National Bird

Benjamin Franklin was distressed at the choice of the bald eagle as our national bird. "He is," Franklin said, "a bird of bad moral character; he does not get his living honestly." He charged the eagle with being a thief and a coward easily frightened by smaller fowl.

Franklin favored the turkey, an American species, as the national bird. He claimed that the turkey was "a little vain and silly" but "a bird of courage," one that "would not hesitate to attack a grenadier of British Guards who would presume to invade his farmyard with a *red* coat on."

divided it. Under their system Congress and the President keep an eye on each other. And the Supreme Court watches and is watched by both of them.

"If men were angels." The final check on government is with the people. The Constitution states that its power comes from them. When the Constitution went to the states for ratification, special conventions had to be called in all the states to vote on it (Article Seven). As one of the conditions for the states' agreeing to its ratification, the people demanded that the Bill of Rights be included.

This was done by amendment. The Constitution is amended when two thirds of both House and Senate propose a change, and three fourths of the states agree to it. (Article Five).

The Bill of Rights can be found in the first ten amendments to the Constitution. It guarantees the freedoms of religion, speech, and the press; the right to a fair trial; protection from the government itself; and other rights that United States citizens take for granted.

Few of the founders thought that people could become perfect. Madison observed that the system of checks and balances might be seen as a criticism of human nature. But he added, "If men were angels, no government would be necessary." The Constitution tried to create a political system that would give Americans both freedom *and* security.

"They will swallow us up!" Once it had been approved in Philadelphia, the Constitution passed to the states for ratification. Unlike the changes in the Articles of Confederation, the Constitution would not require the agreement of every state (Article Seven). As soon as nine states ratified, it would become the supreme law of the land.

In the nine months that followed, the American public was treated to a brilliant defense of the new document against the attacks of a large group of *Antifederalists.* These opponents of the Constitution feared that those who drew it up intended, as one of them from Massachusetts argued, to "get all the power and all the money into their own hands, and then . . . swallow up us little folks like . . . the whale swallowed up Jonah!" It was these Antifederalist fears that led to the Bill of Rights.

Other reasons for Antifederalist opposition were more selfish. Much of it came from state officeholders who saw no reason to reduce the power of their own governments. Some were fearful that land claims they held from state grants would be lost. And other were just old-fashioned. They feared change. For them, the old, tried, and familiar were what counted.

Nine agree. Despite the opposition, the *Federalists,* who favored the Constitution,

THE NEW CONSTITUTION

You say that I have been dished up to you as an Antifederalist and ask me if it be just. . . . If I could not go to heaven but with a party, I would not go there at all. Therefore, I am not of the party of the Federalists.

But I am much farther from that of the Antifederalists. I approved from the first moment the great mass of what is in the new Constitution: the consolidation of the government; the organization into executive, legislative, and [courts]; the subdivision of the legislative [into House and Senate]; the voting by persons instead of by states; the [limited veto] on laws given to the executive. . . .

What I disapproved from the first moment . . . was the want of a Bill of Rights to guard liberty. . . . I disapproved also [the lack of a limit on the President's terms]. . . .

These, my opinions, I wrote within a few hours after I had read the Constitution. . . . I had not then read a single word printed on the subject.

Letter from Thomas Jefferson to Francis Hopkinson, March 13, 1789.

carried the day. In the month of December 1787, Delaware, Pennsylvania, and New Jersey ratified the document. In Philadelphia, a ruthless Federalist party rammed ratification through before their opponents had a chance to organize. The smaller states of Delaware and New Jersey saw the Constitution as protection from their larger neighbors. And New Jersey, which had suffered heavy destruction during the Revolutionary War, hoped the new government would help it rebuild.

In January 1788 the Georgians ratified unanimously. They were exposed to the attacks of Indians and Spaniards, and they hoped the new Union would give them greater security. Two days later Connecticut, one of the smaller states, ratified overwhelmingly. Massachusetts, in February 1788, narrowly ratified after skillful maneuvering by the Federalists. Among other things, they dangled the plum of the Presidency before John Hancock. In late April, Maryland approved by a vote of more than six to one. South Carolina gave a thumping two-to-one endorsement. In June, New Hampshire made it nine. Like Georgia, it too had a powerful neighbor. British Canada was to its north.

Self-interest of the largest number. In theory the Constitution had been ratified. But everyone knew the key states were Virginia and New York. Virginia was the largest and richest state, and if New York did not join, the nation would be divided (map on page 101).

Through June a brilliant debate raged in Virginia. Patrick Henry used every argument he could think of to denounce the new government. And promptly James Madison and John Marshall, then a young lawyer, answered him. In late June, by a narrow vote, Virginia ratified. As the largest state, its decision had an effect in New York. In addition, New York City was threatening to secede from the rest of the state and join the new Union.

New York voters were kept fully informed of the arguments in the 85 *Federalist Papers*. Although no one knew it at the time, these excellent essays were written by James Madison, Alexander Hamilton, and the New Yorker John Jay. They explained the Constitution and gave every reason for accepting it.

Alexander Hamilton, who had originally thought the Constitution was not good enough, changed his mind. He now argued that it was the best possible result, given the way most Americans felt about their government. For him half a loaf was better than none.

James Madison, in Federalist Paper Number Ten, argued forcefully in favor of the Constitution. The key to its success, he said, would be its appeal to the self-interest of the largest number of Americans. On July 25, 1788, by a three-vote margin, New York voted ratification.

A rising sun. Another year elapsed before North Carolina joined. Little Rhode Island held out until May 1790. In the end the pressure of its neighbors was too strong; it entered the Union. The experiment in a federal republic was launched. Thoughtful citizens realized that its success would show whether the American Revolution had been worth fighting.

All through the original debates over the Constitution in Independence Hall, the aged, arthritic Franklin had been wondering whether the half sun emblazoned on Washington's chair was rising or setting. As he put his trembling signature to the paper, he finally decided it was a rising sun. Two hundred years later, no one could doubt that he was right.

 TRY THIS!

1. Compare the Constitution of the United States and the Articles of Confederation. What are the strongest features of each? The weakest? **2.** Write a report of the secret sessions of the Constitutional Convention that might have been "leaked" to an "investigative journalist."

ROUNDUP

Who?

Eli Whitney
Alexander Hamilton
Daniel Shays
James Madison
Edmund Randolph
William Paterson
Roger Sherman
John Jay

What?

Articles of
    Confederation
Ordinance of 1785
Northwest Ordinance
    of 1787
"Critical Period"
Shays' Rebellion
Constitutional
    Convention
Virginia Plan
New Jersey Plan
Great Compromise
Electoral College
Bill of Rights
Federalists
Antifederalists
Federalist Papers

Where?

Northwest Territory
Annapolis
Philadelphia

KNOW THIS

A Social Revolution

1. How did democracy increase after the Revolution?
2. Explain the shift in property-holding following the war.
3. Where did some American merchants go to make up for their lost trade with the West Indies?
4. How did the Revolution affect the position of slaves in the northern states?
5. Why did slavery expand in the South after that war?

The Articles of Confederation

1. Which five powers was Congress given under the Articles of Confederation?
2. What important power was Congress not given?
3. What were the provisions of the Ordinance of 1785?
4. How did the Northwest Ordinance of 1787 provide for governing the Northwest Territory?
5. Explain why the term *Critical Period* was used to describe the years between 1781 and 1789. Which events support this description? Which do not?

Toward a More Perfect Union

1. Trace the developments leading to the Constitutional Convention of 1787.
2. Why was the selection of George Washington as president of the Convention important?
3. What three groups supported a stronger government?
4. List the main provisions of the Virginia Plan.
5. Which states opposed the Virginia Plan? What did they propose in its place?

The Framework of Government

1. How was the question of representation settled?
2. What method of selecting a President was chosen?
3. What compromises were made about trade and manufacturing?
4. Why is Article One, Section 8, of the Constitution so important?
5. How does Congress check the power of the President?

A Federal Republic Established

1. What is a "federal system of government"? Give two examples of federalism under the Constitution.
2. Why does the Constitution have a system of checks and balances?
3. How was the Constitution ratified?
4. Why were New York and Virginia essential to the success of the new government?

DIG HERE!

This activity will allow you to explore present-day applications of constitutional principles. Choose *one* of the topics listed in italics. Read as many newspaper or newsmagazine articles as you can—on *one* of the current issues listed with it. Draw up a report along the lines suggested at the end of this activity.

Bill of Rights: freedom of the press, court gag orders, rights of the accused, capital punishment, gun control, demonstrations and protests.
Implied powers: energy crises, environmental controls, welfare system.
Federal system: civil rights, busing, federal aid to schools.
Checks and balances: presidential vetoes, court rulings on constitutionality of laws, executive privilege.

A. Briefly summarize the events and describe the people involved in your issue.
B. How does your issue relate to the United States Constitution? Depending on the constitutional principle involved: Which provision of the Bill of Rights is at stake? How do Congress's implied powers apply to the issue? How does the issue show the working of the federal system? Which branch of government is being checked? Which is doing the checking?
C. From the facts you have gathered about the issue, and from your understanding of the Constitution, are the Constitution's principles being applied as those who wrote the Constitution intended? If not, what would you do about it?

THINK ABOUT IT

1. Some historians have claimed that the Articles of Confederation would have gradually developed into a stronger government, even if there had been no Constitutional Convention. Do you agree?
2. A federal system is much more complicated than one with a single authority and a single set of laws. What are some advantages of federalism? Are they worth the trouble? Explain.
3. It has been said that if the Bill of Rights was put to a vote today, it would not pass. Do you think this is true? How would you vote on the First and Fifth Amendments?

DO IT!

1. Look up the life of Daniel Boone. Create a comic-strip biography telling the story of his career.
2. Design a display on the Northwest Territory. Include a map, and a model of an early settlement.
3. Write a newspaper feature story on Shays' Rebellion. Include an interview with Daniel Shays.

THEN AND NOW

Has the Constitution, written almost two hundred years ago, failed to keep up with the times? Should the states call a convention, as allowed in Article Five, to overhaul the document? Are there ways, do you feel, the government doesn't work as well or as quickly or as fairly as it should? Would a new Constitution be the best way to solve such problems? Explain.

TEST YOUR HISTORY

1. What cultural differences led to conflict between American Indians and European settlers?
2. Why did Europeans, in the 1500s, come to America?
3. What four nations sent explorers to America? Name one for each nation.
4. How and why did the African slave trade begin?
5. What was the position of blacks in the colonies by 1700?
6. Compare the three English colonial regions of America.
7. What nationalities other than English were colonists?
8. How did Williams, Hutchinson, Quakers, and the "Salem witches" aid religious toleration?
9. Why was colonial America a good "poor man's country"?
10. What were the colonists' complaints about trade?
11. How was independence promoted by a) British leaders, b) different views on government, and c) propaganda?
12. How did British and American military strategies differ?
13. What role did France play during a) the 1700s and b) the war?
14. Why did slavery expand in the South after the Revolution?
15. How did the Northwest Ordinance aid the nation's growth?
16. What groups wanted a new constitution? Did not want one?
17. What constitutional compromise settled representation?
18. What checks and balances were provided by the Constitution?
19. How was ratification of the Constitution accomplished?

I

REVIEW

FURTHER READING

Andrist, R., *American Heritage History of the Making of a Nation.* Am. Heritage, 1968.

Athearn, R.G., *American Heritage New Illustrated History of the United States,* Vol. 1. Dell, 1963.

Blow, M., ed., *American Heritage History of the Thirteen Colonies.* Am. Heritage, 1967.

Earle, A.M., *Home Life in Colonial Days.* Berkshire, 1974.

Evans, E., *Weathering the Storm: Women of the American Revolution.* Scribner, 1975.

Hale, J.R., *Age of Exploration.* Time, 1966. (Great Ages of Man)

Hawkes, D. *The Colonial Experience.* Bobbs, 1966.

Ketchum, R.M., ed., *American Heritage Book of the Revolution.* Am. Heritage, 1958.

Leonard, E., *Dear-Bought Heritage.* U. Penna., 1965.

Tunis, E., *Colonial Craftsmen.* World, 1967.

A
NEW
NATION

I have often inquired of myself what great principle or idea it was that kept this confederacy so long together. It was not the mere matter of separation of the colonies from the motherland, but something in the Declaration of Independence which gave liberty, not alone to the people of this country, but hope to the world for all future time.

Abraham Lincoln, Address, February 22, 1861   119

A Federal Republic
Is Established

5

In 1793 balloon ascents were new and startling. So were governments with written constitutions and elected heads. George Washington watched as this balloon took off. Could its flight have reminded him of the new government he was trying to launch?

1.   LAUNCHING THE NEW GOVERNMENT

Even before the Confederation disappeared as a government in 1789, it had about stopped working. Its only representatives in foreign countries were John Adams in London and Thomas Jefferson in Paris. Its dealings with other nations were handled by one man with the aid of a few clerks. The Treasury Board had no problems, because it had no money. The Confederation's reputation was not good, for as one congressional committee found, it had "many strong marks of a want of responsibility."

The new nation was almost without defense, as there were just 840 men in its army. The twelve clerks who were its only employees grumbled because their salaries had not been paid. Meanwhile, the Continental Congress simply fell apart. Only seven states were represented at the last meeting, on Friday, October 10, 1788. All government then stopped until the new federal Congress met on March 4, 1789.

Most people realized that the new government would have its work cut out. It would have to find out just how much the

Confederation owed, come up with sources of money, and restore government credit.

The first President. Once Congress came together, it had to inaugurate the new President. George Washington, the unanimous choice of the electors, finally took the oath of office in New York City on April 30, 1789. Alone among Americans, the great Revolutionary leader had universal respect. "No man has ever appeared upon the theater of public action," an early biographer said, "whose . . . principles were more perfectly free from selfish and unworthy passions."

In his first inaugural address, Washington clearly stated the challenge facing the new government: "The preservation of the sacred fire of liberty and the destiny of the republican model of government are . . . entrusted to . . . the American people."

Time and time again Washington said that he wanted to give an example of the proper use of presidential authority. He never let himself forget that everything he did was an example or rule for the future. When later Presidents were faced with problems like his, they would look at what he had done and be guided by it. He was sure that authority used cautiously but firmly would create respect for the office and lighten the burden of future Presidents.

Washington also knew that the sections of the country were deeply divided. By re-

---

Read here of how

Washington became the first President.
The new government was organized.
Hamilton was its most important Secretary.
Hamilton and Jefferson disagreed.

TIME CHART

1789	Washington is inaugurated. The new government begins.
1790	The public debt is reorganized.
1793	Neutrality is proclaimed.
1794	Western Pennsylvania farmers rebel.
1795	Jay's, Pinckney's, and the Greenville Treaties are ratified.
1796	Adams is elected the second President.
1798	The Alien and Sedition Acts are passed; the Kentucky and Virginia Resolutions are adopted.
1800	The undeclared war with France is ended.
1801	Jefferson is elected the third President.

---

maining above their quarrels he hoped to build public confidence and respect for the new government. "With me," he was to say in his Farewell Address, "a predominant motive has been . . . to gain time for our country to settle and mature . . . and to progress without interruption to . . . the command of its own fortunes."

The most important department. To assist the President, Congress in 1789 set up three departments of government: State, Treasury, and War. A little later, the office of Attorney General was created to give him legal advice. To head these new departments Washington appointed Thomas Jefferson (State), Alexander Hamilton (Treasury), Henry Knox (War), and Edmund Randolph (Attorney General).

121

The first presidential inauguration, Federal Hall, New York City, April 30, 1789.

Like everyone else in the government, Alexander Hamilton realized that the Treasury was the most important department. Size alone would have caused it to overshadow all others. Under its head there were an assistant secretary, a controller, a treasurer, an auditor, a registrar, thirty clerks, and about a thousand customs officials and revenue collectors. (By comparison, the State Department had six employees, and the War Department got along with three clerks.) The size of the Treasury was enough to worry people who believed that government should be small. So was its influence on business. In addi-

tion, the Treasury's control of the Post Office meant that it could give out jobs and so create a group of loyal followers.

The powers of the federal courts. Of all the branches of the new government, none was more loosely defined than the federal courts. The Constitution simply stated that there would be a Supreme Court, but left its organization and the establishment of lower courts to Congress. The Judiciary Act of 1789 set up a six-judge Supreme Court as well as sixteen lower federal courts. As soon as it was passed, Washington named John Jay the first Chief Justice of the United States.

I think I knew General Washington intimately and thoroughly; and were I called on to [describe] his character, it would be in terms like these.

His mind was great and powerful without being of the very first order . . . and as far as he saw, no judgment was ever sounder. . . . Hence the common remark of his officers of the advantages he derived from councils of war, where hearing all suggestions, he selected whatever was best. And certainly no general ever planned his battles more judiciously, but if . . . any [part] of his plan was dislocated by sudden circumstances, he was slow in a readjustment. . . .

He was incapable of fear, meeting personal dangers with the calmest unconcern. Perhaps the strongest feature of his character was prudence, never acting until every circumstance, every consideration, was maturely weighed, refraining if he saw a doubt, but when once decided, going through with his purpose, whatever obstacles opposed. His integrity was most pure, his justice the most inflexible I have ever known. . . . He was indeed in every sense of the words a wise, a good, and a great man.

His temper was naturally irritable . . . but reflection and resolution had obtained a firm [control] over it. If, however, it broke its bonds, he was tremendous in his wrath. . . . His heart was not warm in its affections, but he exactly calculated every man's value and gave him a solid esteem proportioned to it. . . .

His person, you know, was fine, his stature exactly what one would wish, his deportment easy, erect, and noble. [He was] the best horseman of his age, and the most graceful figure that could be seen on horseback. . . . In public, when called on for a sudden opinion, he was unready, short, and embarrassed. Yet he wrote readily . . . in an easy and correct style. This he had acquired [through practice], for his education was merely reading, writing, and common arithmetic, to which he added surveying at a later day.

On the whole his character was . . . perfect, in nothing bad, in few points indifferent. And it may be said that never did nature and fortune combine more perfectly to make a man great. . . . For his was the singular destiny and merit of leading the armies of his country through an arduous war . . . of conducting its councils through the birth of a government . . . and of [carefully] obeying the laws . . . through the whole of his career. [Of this] the history of the world furnishes no other example.

JEFFERSON REMEMBERS GEORGE WASHINGTON

Letter to Walter Jones,
January 2, 1814.

123

For the first ten years of its existence the Supreme Court was caught in a disagreement over the powers of the federal courts. Those who feared the authority of the new government insisted that the state courts had a position equal or superior to that of the federal courts. Not until the appointment of Chief Justice John Marshall in 1801 did the Supreme Court begin to assert its supremacy.

Two clever competitors. Throughout American history not many rivals have been as different as Alexander Hamilton and Thomas Jefferson. Both were brilliant, but there the similarity ended. Hamilton was twelve years younger than Jefferson. Short and handsome, he was also a self-made man. He had been born in the West Indies of uncertain parentage and had come to New York as a young boy. He had agreed to go to Columbia College only if he would be allowed to finish in half the usual time. During the Revolution he had acted as Washington's trusted aide. Then, after the war, he married into the prominent and wealthy Schuyler (SKY-lur) family.

In public life Hamilton's razor-sharp mind made it hard for him to get along with those less clever than he. Above all, he believed in a government by the privileged and well-born. For him *democracy* was a frightening word.

Jefferson, in contrast, was a member of the Virginia gentry. From birth he had been connected with people of wealth and power. But as with most landowners, he was uneasy with businessmen like those from the seaport towns. He was most at home among farmers. It was his firm political faith that a government rooted in the people was best. Democracy might present problems, he believed, but it made government responsible to the governed.

Jefferson and Hamilton had another quality in common. They both were immensely ambitious.

A center of disagreement. From the moment Hamilton took over the Treasury, Jefferson knew that his rival was working to expand its power. Hamilton had always claimed that the national government needed to be strengthened. His one fear was that its power might be used too cautiously. He was determined, through the Treasury Department, to stretch the authority of the federal government. This, of course, made him a center of disagreement in Washington's Administration.

Jefferson suspected Hamilton of gathering power into his own hands for dishonest purposes. He had great influence with Congress, and this bothered Jefferson because it threatened to upset the proper balance between the executive and legislative branches. As Jefferson later explained it, his opposition to Hamilton arose from the determination "to preserve the legislature pure and independent of the executive, to keep the Administration to republican forms and principles, and not permit the Constitution to be changed into a monarchy." The differences between the two men became sharper as the Treasury chief set out new financial policies.

 TRY THIS!

List the numbers of these sentences on a piece of paper. Beside each write a *W* if the sentence is most true of Washington, a *J* if it is most true of Jefferson, an *H* if it is most true of Hamilton, and an *N* if it is true of none of them. **1.** He wanted to expand federal power. **2.** He believed in using presidential authority cautiously. **3.** He deeply distrusted the new government. **4.** He believed government should be rooted in the people. **5.** He controlled the largest department of the federal government.

2. HAMILTON'S FINANCIAL SYSTEM

Nothing the founders of the Republic did was more important than setting up a dependable system of federal financing. This helped the new government to gain the confidence of its own citizens and also of investors overseas. It made the United States look like a sound proposition and the federal government like a going concern.

The federal war debts. Alexander Hamilton recognized that the United States was an underdeveloped country. He knew it must have good credit if it was to attract money from other nations. Most of what the government owed had been borrowed during the Revolution. It had come partly from the American people and partly from other governments. The total

---

Read here of how

Hamilton planned to pay the public debt.
He set up a United States Bank.
His actions were opposed by many.
But they were favored by people of wealth.

---

amount of this debt was over 55 million dollars, including unpaid interest. Hamilton insisted that all of it must be paid back for the sake of the government's credit at home and abroad.

A special problem was the 42 million dollars originally owed to the American people: Revolutionary veterans, farmers, and others who had furnished money or supplies to the Continental Congress. After the war, many of these people sold the notes and bills for a small part of their real value. Some were unable to wait for payment. Others may have doubted that the government would ever make good on what it owed.

But people who had more faith in the new government, or who were better off, bought up these notes and bills at reduced prices. They were willing to take a chance on getting more money back at some future time.

Many senators and representatives

A merchant's office, or "counting house." Merchants were the nation's first business leaders. Many of them were holders of government notes.

opposed paying this part of the debt at full value. If the government did that, they argued, the speculators would get rich, while those who had helped the cause of liberty would get nothing.

Hamilton's ideas about federal finances were explained in his *Report on Public Credit*. He saw that his first job was to draw the loyalties of Americans away from their home states and to the federal government. The best way to achieve this, he said, was to tie the public interest to the new country's finances. By paying the outstanding public debt in full the government would please people with property. It would give them a stake in the nation's future and be sure to win their support.

The war debts of the states. The most surprising part of Hamilton's plan was his proposal to take over the debts contracted by the states during the Revolution. They amounted to over 25 million dollars. Added to what the Confederation owed, they would bring the total debt of the new government to about 80 million dollars.

Opposition to this part of Hamilton's plan was particularly strong in states that had few debts or none at all, since they would be taxed to pay off what the other states owed. Hamilton argued that the burdens of the Revolution should be shared by all as part of a common effort.

The public argument that followed was bitter. North Carolina, Maryland, and Georgia, all nearly debt-free, opposed federal takeover. Pennsylvania, owing two million dollars, was divided. South Carolina, the New England states, New Jersey, and New York, all with heavy debts, strongly supported this part of Hamilton's plan.

Virginia's original war debt had been over six million dollars. But that had been almost halved by selling land in Kentucky.

A good part of the southern state debts had found their way into the hands of northern speculators, and this added bitter sharpness to the debate. There was even talk of breaking up the Union.

A political bargain. Hamilton understood that his financial program had reached a dead end. Only a political deal would settle the argument. In April the House of Representatives had narrowly voted against taking on state debts. In the summer of 1790 Hamilton went to Jefferson and Madison and suggested a bargain. He offered to swing northern votes behind a move to locate the national capital on the Potomac River. In return Jefferson agreed to persuade several southern congressmen to vote for the takeover of state debts.

Finally, the seat of federal government was moved from New York to Philadelphia for ten years. During that time a location on the Potomac River would be made ready. A debt program passed in which the states owing small amounts got additional federal grants to make up for what they would lose through taxes.

Jefferson had been responsible for Hamilton's triumph. He had some second thoughts about it. But he saw that a capital on the Potomac would form a tie between the South and the growing West.

Interest-bearing bonds, fully guaranteed by the government, were issued to cover the total debt of over 80 million dollars. In a single stroke, thanks to Hamilton, lending to the federal government became one of the safest investments possible.

Hamilton's Bank. Settling the federal debt in this way caused Hamilton to think increasingly of the need for a central bank. He drew largely upon the Bank of England for ideas as to how it would be run, but there would be differences. In the Bank of the United States, unlike the Bank of England, the public would be heavily represented. The Bank was to be a mixed corporation. It would take deposits of government funds, manage domestic and foreign operations for the Treasury, and regulate state banking. The Bank was further allowed to issue paper currency that could be redeemed in gold or silver and was acceptable as payment of federal debts. This would expand the amount of money circulating in the new republic. And it would further strengthen the tie between leading property owners and the government.

Hamilton's Bank plan stirred up great opposition, especially among congressmen from farm districts. One Georgian bluntly argued: "The bank is calculated to benefit a small part of the United States—the mercantile interest only. The farmers . . . will derive no advantage from it." James Madison, who was increasingly uneasy about a strong central government, doubted that the Bank was constitutional. But the opposition proved fruitless. The Senate voted for the Bank in January 1791, and shortly afterwards the House added its approval. The vote had been by sections of the country, with most of the Bank's support coming from the North and opposition from the South.

President Washington was in great doubt. He was flatly advised by both Jefferson and Attorney General Edmund Randolph that the Bank went far beyond the intent of the Constitution. Hamilton replied with the argument that the government had the power to do whatever was necessary to carry out the powers it had been given (pages 107-108). Washington was convinced and signed the bill.

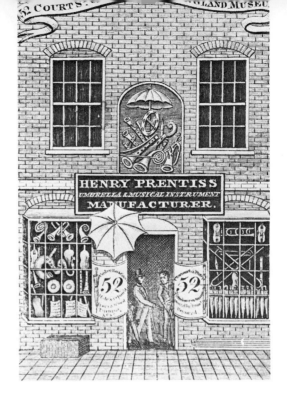

Promoting manufactures. Throughout the war years Hamilton had often noted the weakness of American industry. Lack of manufactured goods had left soldiers and country at the mercy of foreign powers. In December 1791 he presented to Congress a *Report on Manufactures.* It stated that the government ought to encourage industry in the United States, and it could do so partly by means of a *protective tariff.* This would make foreign goods more expensive by taxing them as they entered the country.

Hamilton argued that doing its own manufacturing would cut down American dependence on Europe and would reduce ill feeling between the sections of the country as well. Northern factories would provide a ready market for the South's farm products, and the South would buy northern goods. All this would help Hamilton in his unending struggle to strengthen "the engine of government," as he called the federal Union.

127

Most manufactured goods were imported. Some were made in the colonies.

BOUGHT OF

Jonathan Harris,

WHO HAS FOR SALE

At his SHOP No. 24, Cornhill, BOSTON,

AND STORE ADJOINING,

ENGLISH GOODS

OF EVERY KIND. Alfo,

INDIA, FRENCH, DUTCH and SPANISH GOODS;
with Braziery, Cutlery, and other Hard Wares by
Wholefale and Retail.   ** *Cheap as ufual.*

Madison condemned the tariff proposals, but his arguments fell on deaf ears. In his State of the Union address, Washington had already called on the nation to promote manufacturing. It was hardly surprising that in general, Congress accepted Hamilton's proposal.

Tariffs were to be a central issue of United States politics well into the 1900s. In this and in other ways Mr. Hamilton left his mark forever on the Republic.

TRY THIS!

Show how each of the three people listed here might have felt about a) payment of war debts owed to people in the United States, b) takeover of state debts by the federal government, c) setting up a United States Bank, d) encouraging manufactures through a protective tariff: **1.** A Virginia planter. **2.** A New York merchant. **3.** A Pennsylvania farmer.

3.   THE EARLIEST POLITICAL PARTIES

Nowhere does the Constitution say anything about political parties. The founders had expected that people would divide into

interest groups on various issues. But they thought that these groups would come together only for short periods of time. In fact, the founders viewed permanent parties as very bad for a republic. Political parties, they believed, meant only division and strife. None of them could foresee that Hamilton's program would lead to an opposition movement, and that by the end of the 1790s there would be two political parties: Hamilton's Federalists and Jefferson's Republicans.

Two warring Cabinet members. The rivalry of Jefferson and Hamilton pointed up the many differences between them. For instance, they held opposite views on the revolution that began in France in 1789. When that revolution led to war between France and Britain in 1793, the strain increased. Hamilton's sympathies were with the British; Jefferson's, with the French. Although Jefferson was Secretary of State, Hamilton had frequent meetings with the British minister. In addition, Washington accepted Hamilton's view on how to enforce United States neutrality. Jefferson was greatly upset when the President arranged for customs agents from Hamilton's Treasury Department to take on the job. He seriously wondered whether Hamilton might be trying to absorb the State Department into the Treasury.

Further quarrels broke out over the distribution of jobs. When Hamilton gained control of the Post Office, Jefferson complained to Washington: "The Department of Treasury possesses already such an influence as to swallow up the whole executive powers." He was so annoyed as to hint that Hamilton and a "corrupt squadron" in Congress might be making personal profits from the new financial policies. He even charged that Hamilton intended to set up a monarchy. Washington dismissed this notion along with the idea of corruption in Congress.

Because they could not persuade Washington to lessen Hamilton's influence, Jefferson's followers started their own newspaper, the *National Gazette*. Madison got the poet Philip Freneau to edit it. Jefferson then put Freneau on the State Department payroll to assure him of an income. Hamilton answered Jefferson's paper with the *Gazette of the United States*, a newspaper edited by his friend John Fenno and supported by Treasury Department printing contracts. The country was treated to the spectacle of two Cabinet members denouncing each other in print. The seeds of two political parties were being sown.

Party strife. As Hamilton's financial policies took shape, an opposition grew in Congress. It surprised Hamilton that the spokesman for this opposition was James Madison. Madison was a small man and he was not a very good speaker. But he combined a shrewd mind with great energy. Time and time again Madison took to the floor of the House of Representatives to denounce Hamilton's proposals. Specifically, he called for a hands-off policy toward business.

Into the growing opposition came Aaron Burr of New York, a man of unlimited ambition. So did James Monroe of Virginia. He was a strong rival of Madison, but for the time he put aside his feelings. The Republican Party was an alliance between middle-state and southern politicians. By 1793 it was so strong that the

---

Read here of how

The first political parties were formed.
A near revolution broke out.
New voters joined Jefferson's party.

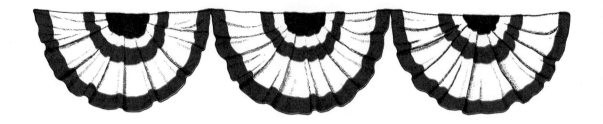

THE FIRST POLITICAL PARTIES

Politics has been defined as a way of deciding who gets what and how they get it. If we ask three questions about the political parties that were started by the followers of Alexander Hamilton and Thomas Jefferson, the answers are these:

	The Federalists	*The Republicans*
WHO WERE THEY?	Merchants of the seaport towns, businessmen, holders of federal and state government bonds, owners of large plantations, ex-officers of the Continental Army, Episcopal and Congregational ministers, important lawyers, workers in the shipping industry, farmers growing crops for export.	Small farmers, North and South, who grew crops for their own use; carpenters, shoemakers, and other tradesmen of the towns; the less important lawyers; Baptist and Methodist ministers; most westerners (i.e., anyone living very far from the eastern seaboard).
WHAT DID THEY WANT?	A central government strong enough to keep order, collect taxes, pay its debts, and provide a sound, stable money supply; friendly relations with Britain, America's biggest trading partner; support and encouragement for commerce and manufacturing.	Individual liberty; protection from the rich and powerful, especially those of the towns and great plantations along the seaboard; freedom from all but the most necessary taxes; an end to the public debt; and opposition to British power.
HOW DID THEY HOPE TO GET IT?	By accepting the leadership of those Hamilton called the rich, the well-born, and the able; by maintaining a United States Bank; by allowing the federal courts to interpret the Constitution broadly, or loosely, so that the federal government could take any necessary action not clearly forbidden; by making sure that the federal government was stronger than the states; and by keeping out "dangerous" democratic ideas, especially those from revolutionary France.	By having strong state governments, firmly in the hands of the common people; by careful control of the federal courts; by a strict, or narrow, interpretation of the Constitution, so the federal government could only do what was carefully spelled out for it, thus limiting its powers; by following the leadership of Jefferson and Madison.

Federalist Fisher Ames charged, "Madison is become a desperate party leader."

As word got around that Jefferson was leading the opposition to Hamilton within the Cabinet, Jefferson and Madison were increasingly linked. Finally, unable to tolerate Hamilton's high position, Jefferson resigned from the Cabinet.

The first Democratic-Republican Societies were established in 1793. They endorsed candidates, attacked Federalists, and in hotly fought races they made sure the voting was fair. Although not officially a party, the Societies spread Republican views. They were effective enough by 1794 for President Washington to denounce them. Federalists charged that they were out to overthrow the nation.

The whiskey tax. The worst Federalist fears seemed to come true when the Whiskey Rebellion broke out. Washington called it "the first formidable fruit of the Democratic Societies." In fact, the true cause of the Rebellion had been a 25 cent tax that Hamilton proposed placing on each gallon of whiskey. The tax put a special burden on those farmers who made their surplus grain into whiskey, so that it

could more easily be moved to market. The farmers' discontent burst into violence during the summer of 1794. In western Pennsylvania tax collectors were terrorized, and federal judges there decided to drop court proceedings. The rebels even halted mail delivery.

When Pittsburgh joined the uprising, President Washington acted. Convinced that federal authority was at stake, he called upon the states for militia. The response was overwhelming. With Washington and Hamilton in command the militia crushed the rebellion. Federal authority had been upheld, and Hamilton viewed it as a major triumph. But it had a price. As one Federalist noted, "Elective rulers can scarcely ever employ the physical force of a democracy without turning . . . the power of public opinion against the government." A strong opposition to Hamilton took shape within the Federalist Party.

New voters. Another long-range threat to the Federalists came from the new states that soon joined the original thirteen. Vermont was admitted in 1791, Kentucky in 1792, and Tennessee in 1796. Unlike the older states, Vermont and Kentucky had

Washington reviews the troops being sent to put down the Whiskey Rebellion.

constitutions that allowed all adult males to vote, whether or not they owned property. Tennessee's did much the same.

Most of the voters in the new states felt more at home with the views of Thomas Jefferson than with those of Alexander Hamilton. Their electors added to the strength of the Democratic-Republicans.

 TRY THIS!

Show how each of the following helped the early growth of political parties: **1.** The rivalry of Hamilton and Jefferson. **2.** Reaction in Congress to Hamilton's policies. **3.** The Democratic-Republican Societies. **4.** The Whiskey Rebellion.

4.   WAR IN EUROPE—TROUBLE AT HOME

Beginning in 1789, a revolution swept France, and its effects were felt throughout the world. As we have seen, it deeply divided Jefferson and Hamilton. Most Americans, however, probably felt sympathy for the French. They remembered the aid from France that had helped them win their own Revolution. And they felt proud when France in 1793 chose to imitate them and become a republic.

Gratitude to France. When France declared war on Britain in 1793, both Jefferson and Hamilton agreed that the United States should remain neutral. However, they disagreed sharply on how this should be done. Jefferson, as Secretary of State, felt bound by the Treaty of Alliance with France made during the American Revolution. It pledged the United States to help France defend its West Indian islands and to allow French warships the use of American ports.

President Washington, trying to maintain a balance between Jefferson and Hamilton, hoped to satisfy both. He gave recognition to the representative of the revolutionary government, Edmond Genêt (jzhuh-NAY), and kept the French treaty in force. At the same time, he insisted that the United States remain neutral. Some pro-French Americans denounced the United States for deserting France in its hour of need, but Hamilton pointed out that France had helped America for its own reasons. He reminded Americans that gratitude had very little to do with foreign policy.

French interference. Citizen Genêt, as the French minister was called, soon gave the people of the United States a lesson in foreign affairs. He announced that the government's neutrality was a fraud. And Genêt made it clear that whether President Washington approved or not, he intended to make the United States a base of operations against the British.

Americans greeted French victories

Read here of how

France and Britain went to war.
The United States was almost drawn into it.
John Jay made an unsatisfactory treaty.
Thomas Pinckney made a much better one.
The Indians lost out again.

132

over the British with enthusiasm, and they gave Genêt the warmest receptions wherever he traveled. This led the Frenchman to make a bad mistake. He assumed that he could force President Washington to do what he wanted. He also misunderstood Jefferson, who had been friendly and had even revealed to him what had been discussed in Cabinet meetings.

Thus encouraged, Genêt decided to send out twelve American privateers to attack British shipping and bring captured British vessels into American ports for sale. This clearly would have been an act of war. At once Jefferson ended his ties with the peppery Frenchman. Genêt then demanded that Congress be called together to choose between neutrality and aid to France. He even threatened to carry his case to the American public.

The government was suddenly rid of Genêt when a new and more radical group took power in France and ordered the minister home. Genêt had no wish to go, because he knew he faced trial and probable execution. Being a man without a country, he asked for and was given the right to stay in the United States. A danger had passed, but larger problems loomed.

A chance for peace with Britain. As the war between France and Great Britain spread, United States difficulties also grew. In November 1793 the British directed their navy to seize all shipping entering or leaving the French West Indies. Since United States merchant vessels carried the largest share of this trade, they were the chief target of the English order. Some 250 ships were seized, and relations between the two countries almost reached the breaking point.

More trouble arose because the British failed to turn over the Northwest military outposts, as they had promised in the treaty ending the Revolution. Americans soon learned that the British were giving guns and ammunition to the Indians along the Canadian border. As frequent Indian attacks began to result in heavy losses, Americans demanded action. Congress authorized the building of a navy and expansion of the militia, but Washington wanted to avoid an open conflict. When the British withdrew their naval order in January 1794, Hamilton saw a chance to keep the peace.

A storm of protest. Hamilton had always understood that if his financial plans were to succeed, there would have to be peace. Only a steady income from tariff collections would allow the government to pay the interest on its bonds. So Hamilton favored sending Chief Justice John Jay as a special representative to London. There Jay was to draw up a peaceful settlement of all the disputes between the United States and Britain.

Jay arrived in England in June of 1795. By the end of the year he had what he thought was a satisfactory agreement. Britain was to grant the United States very limited trading rights in the West Indies, to pay for the American ships destroyed in the Revolution, and to get out of the Northwest posts by June 1796. Jay had also been told to arrange payment for the slaves the British army had taken at the close of the Revolution. But the stiff and proper New Yorker was so deeply opposed to slavery that he couldn't bring himself to raise the question. Jay's Treaty wasn't a very good one. Certainly it was no triumph for the United States. But it probably gave the new republic as much as it could expect in the circumstances.

However, as soon as the public understood the terms of Jay's Treaty, a storm of protest rose against it. Jay had done nothing about the seizure of American vessels in the French West Indies (page 133). And the treaty limited trade with the British West Indies to one very small ship a year. (The provision was so stingy that the Senate considered it an insult and struck it out before ratifying the treaty.) Furthermore, in the South there was much resentment that the question of the captured slaves had been ignored.

But President Washington used his powerful influence, and after some wrangling the Senate accepted Jay's Treaty. The Republicans in the House then tried to hold back the money needed to carry out the treaty. After a bitter debate, this was finally approved by an almost straight party vote. Jay's Treaty secured an uneasy peace with Britain. But it also drew the lines separating Republican and Federalist more sharply than ever.

A treaty with Spain. Americans were also looking with increased concern at their southwestern frontier. Settlers in the West objected to Spain's control of New Orleans, and United States merchants had many claims against the Spaniards. To Spain Jay's Treaty looked like the beginning of an alliance between the United States and Britain. The chief minister of the Spanish king was already talking about a settlement with the special United States envoy, Thomas Pinckney. They set to work on an agreement.

The treaty with Spain that was signed

Besides the Treaty of Greenville, four others "extinguished" Indian claims in the Northwest. Not all tribes accepted these settlements. Some resisted fiercely.

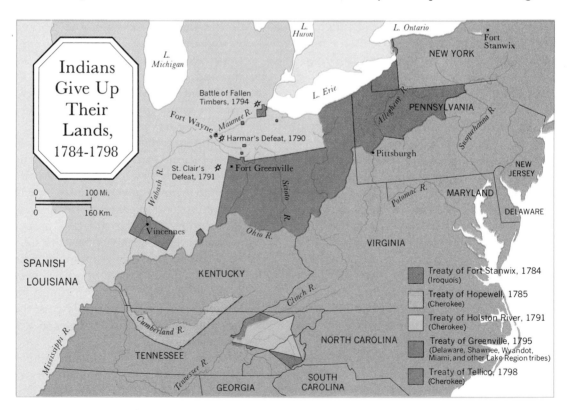

Indians Give Up Their Lands, 1784-1798

100 Mi.
160 Km.

Treaty of Fort Stanwix, 1784 (Iroquois)
Treaty of Hopewell, 1785 (Cherokee)
Treaty of Holston River, 1791 (Cherokee)
Treaty of Greenville, 1795 (Delaware, Shawnee, Wyandot, Miami, and other Lake Region tribes)
Treaty of Tellico, 1798 (Cherokee)

in October 1795 met practically every American wish. It opened the Mississippi to western shipping for three years, after which there could be a renewal. Under the agreement the United States got the *right of deposit* at New Orleans. This meant that goods being shipped to or from the United States could be landed at New Orleans and shipped out again without payment of any Spanish taxes. Furthermore, the southern boundary with Florida was drawn at 31° north latitude, and the Spaniards agreed to keep the Indians of their territory from raiding the United States. The treaty was soothing to American pride, and the Senate approved it unanimously. It was so popular that Thomas Pinckney suddenly emerged as a possible candidate for President in 1796.

An Indian defeat. The Pinckney Treaty was pleasing to westerners since it opened the Mississippi to their trade. Even Jay's Treaty helped them by cutting down British influence in the Northwest. But another treaty accepted by Congress in the same year of 1795 did even more to open land west of the Appalachians to settlers.

By the Treaty of Greenville the Indian tribes living in the Northwest Territory gave up the southern half of what is now Ohio (map on page 134). The treaty followed the Battle of Fallen Timbers, fought in 1794. The United States had been at war with these Indians since 1790. In 1791 some militia had been ambushed and badly beaten by them. Then Washington made General Wayne, a hero of the Revolution, governor of the territory.

General "Mad Anthony" Wayne had gotten his nickname because of his rashness and hasty action against the British. But this time he insisted on having regular enlisted troops instead of militia, and he trained for two years before marching north to meet the Indians. The battle Wayne fought at the rapids of the Maumee River ended Indian influence in the region for another twenty years.

TRY THIS!

1. Explain how Citizen Genêt's activities were dangerous to the United States.   **2.** Tell why Hamilton was eager to keep peace with Britain, and why other Americans wanted to help France.   **3.** Show what Jay's Treaty, the Pinckney Treaty, and the Treaty of Greenville did to help the West.

5.   THE DECLINE OF THE FEDERALISTS

Read here of how

John Adams had a difficult administration.
He managed to prevent a war with France.
Federalists tried to crush Republicans.
But their plans backfired.
Then the election of 1800 caused a crisis.

In 1792 George Washington accepted a second term as President. He did so only because he was convinced that this would strengthen the government. At the end of those four years he decided that the most dangerous problems had been solved. So he set about composing a last speech to the nation. His Farewell Address contained ideas from both Madison and Hamilton. By drawing on the ideas of both these men,

135

Washington plainly showed that he wished to reduce ill feelings between the parties.

The second President. The retirement of Washington meant that the Federalists had to find a replacement. With some doubts they settled on John Adams. His fiery temper and stubborn self-assurance did not make him well liked by other Federalists. Hamilton, who had left the Cabinet, tried to push the candidacy of Thomas Pinckney. His treaty with Spain had made him very popular (pages 134–135).

Once Adams's nomination had been settled upon, the campaign went smoothly. But Hamilton was still a power among the Federalists. It was a poor beginning for the new Administration. Both parties were at a critical point. The Republicans controlled the House of Representatives; the Federalists retained a slim hold on the Senate. But the Federalists were divided.

Adams made the mistake of keeping all of Washington's Cabinet. Its leading members, Secretary of State Timothy Pickering and Secretary of Treasury Oliver Wolcott, looked to Hamilton for guidance. For his part Hamilton had no intention of allowing Adams too much executive power. For Adams, the pro-British feelings of Hamilton were just as dangerous to the country as Jefferson's sympathy for France. He feared that both threatened United States neutrality.

"Not one cent for tribute." Relations with France were very bad, due to the continued seizure of American ships. They had become worse after August 1796, when Washington withdrew James Monroe as minister to Paris. The French refused to accept his replacement, Charles C. Pinckney. Adams sent to France a special mission made up of Pinckney, John Marshall, and Elbridge Gerry.

The representatives soon learned that the French were not ready to compromise. They did not believe that the United States had the power to protect its own interests. The commissioners were shocked when three French agents informed them that paying 250,000 dollars might smooth the way to a settlement. Even more insulting was the fact that part of the sum would be a bribe to the French foreign minister. The response of Pinckney was firm. "It is no, no," he said, "not a sixpence." When this became known in the United States, it gave rise to the popular slogan "Millions for defense, but not one cent for tribute."

When Adams told Congress about the commissioners' experience in Paris, he referred to the French agents only as X, Y, and Z. The XYZ Affair rocked the nation. The President considered war but then held back. The state of American defenses, he knew, was very poor. Adams, however, did order that commercial vessels be armed, and he called for the construction of warships and coastal defenses. Congress approved Adams's request for 27 ships, and the public quickly bought up war bonds to build them. After news of the American commissioners' experience had been fully reported, even Republicans rallied to the cause.

An undeclared war. "It is too late to preach peace and to say we do not think of war. A defensive war must be waged, whether it is formally proclaimed or not," declared the Federalist Fisher Ames in April 1798. The only other choice was to give in, and no American was prepared to argue for that. An army of ten thousand was authorized, and Washington was called out of retirement to serve as commander-in-chief. Adams, however, objected to Hamilton's being his second-in-command. When Washington urged that Hamilton be appointed, Adams unwillingly agreed, but he condemned Hamilton privately for "selfish vanity and aspiring ambition."

The Administration pushed mostly for action at sea, and soon a fleet of privateers was operating against the French. In a few months the powerful warships *Constellation* and *United States,* later joined by the *Constitution,* gave muscle to the new navy.

If nothing else, the French government learned a hard lesson: the United States refused to be bullied. As 1798 closed, the French concluded that peace could be restored only if they were prepared to treat the young republic as an equal. Feelers were sent out, and Adams replied favorably by sending another mission to Paris. He did so without consulting his Cabinet, since he was sure that they would oppose his action. The Republicans, on the other hand, were overjoyed.

In the long, difficult negotiations that ended in September 1800, both sides gave up something. The Americans surrendered their claims for damage to their ships, and the French admitted that the Alliance of 1778 was no longer binding on the United States.

DEFEAT FOR THE FEDERALISTS

Adams and the Federalists were anxious to strengthen their party, so they used the war emergency as an excuse for attacking the Republicans. The Federalists organized committees to keep a check on all prominent Republicans, including Jefferson. Anyone who questioned government policy was suspected of being disloyal, if not an outright traitor. To keep their opponents down, the Federalists drew up a number of new laws.

The Naturalization, Alien, and Sedition Acts. Nothing bothered the Federalists more than the way in which immigrants to the United States rushed to join the Republican Party. To slow them down, Congress approved a naturalization act that increased the years of residence required to become a citizen from five to fourteen. At the same time six states called for a Constitutional amendment that would bar any naturalized citizen from holding office.

Just as bad in Federalist eyes was the number of foreigners who worked for the Republican cause. (Even the French minister had campaigned for Jefferson in the 1796 election!) So the Federalists also passed the Alien and Alien Enemies Acts. These gave the President the authority to expel any alien he judged "dangerous to the peace and safety of the United States."

But the greatest uproar was caused by the Sedition Act. Although Adams had not asked for this law, he never questioned its

137

RE-ELECTED—FROM PRISON

Matthew Lyon was an Irishman, and a rebel by choice. His father had been executed for plotting against the British government.

Matthew came to America as an indentured servant, married a relative of Ethan Allen, fought in the Revolution, was elected to Congress from Vermont, and got entangled with the Sedition Act. He accused President John Adams of having "an unbounded thirst for ridiculous pomp, foolish adulation, and selfish avarice."

For this a jury well-packed with Federalists found Lyon guilty of sedition, and a staunch Federalist judge gave him four months in jail and fined him one thousand dollars. However, the Vermont voters overwhelmingly re-elected their jailed congressman. And George Mason collected money for Lyon's fine from the people of Virginia.

being constitutional. The Act seriously restricted both freedom of speech and freedom of the press. It said that anyone making a "false, scandalous, and malicious" statement or publishing anything "against the government of the United States" was subject to a fine of up to 2,000 dollars and a prison term of as much as two years. The Act did, however, provide for jury trials.

In time 25 people were arrested under the Sedition Act, of whom ten were convicted. Among those seized were four Republican editors and congressmen. But Americans in general believed that they had the right to express freewheeling opinions of the government, and by the time the Act ran out in 1801, the Federalists realized they had made a major and lasting mistake. It was one from which they never fully recovered.

Unconstitutional laws. Jefferson and Madison saw in the Alien and Sedition Acts a chance to end once and for all the danger that the federal government might "swallow up the state sovereignties." They laid out their ideas in the Kentucky and Virginia Resolutions. The first of these were written by Jefferson and passed by the Kentucky legislature in November 1798. They stated that federal power was limited and that each state had the right to decide for itself whether the central government was acting against the Constitution.

Kentucky asked that the states combine to force the repeal of the Alien and Sedition Acts. Less than a month later the Virginia Resolutions appeared. They were the work of James Madison, and they argued that states could block the enforcement of unconstitutional federal laws within their own boundaries.

Seven state legislatures refused to accept the theory of the Resolutions. They claimed that the Supreme Court alone had the power to declare a law unconstitutional. Jefferson, knowing that most members of the Court were Federalists, took a more radical stand. In a second set of Kentucky Resolutions, he stated that a single state could *nullify* (set aside or make as nothing) unconstitutional actions of the federal government.

In this way the idea of *nullification* was first introduced. In time it was to do great harm, even helping to bring about the Civil War.

The election of 1800. When the election year opened, the Federalists were in confusion. Adams's and Hamilton's followers were hopelessly split. The Republicans could see an opportunity in these divisions, and chose as their candidates Thomas Jefferson and Aaron Burr of New York.

The Federalists nominated John Adams and South Carolina's Charles C. Pinckney, but Hamilton had other ideas. Although he knew that many in the party supported Adams, Hamilton publicly denounced the President as arrogant, narrow, stubborn, and vain. Adams replied with savage directness, dismissing Hamilton as the illegitimate son of a "Scots peddler." Many longtime Federalists were shocked at this behavior and withdrew from politics.

When the Electoral College finally met, Jefferson and his running mate, Aaron Burr, both had 73 electoral votes; John Adams had 65, and his running mate, Pinckney, had 64. Before the Twelfth Amendment was adopted, electors voted for two candidates. The candidate receiving the largest number of votes became President, and whoever got the second largest number became Vice President. If two candidates were tied, like Jefferson and Burr, or if no one had a majority, the final decision went to the House of Representatives. There each state had one vote, and a majority of a state's delegation decided who got it. Nine states were needed for election, and as the Federalists were firmly in control of the House, they could block Jefferson's election.

Hamilton's solution. To Hamilton's dismay the Federalists considered supporting Burr, who in his eyes was a raving radical. On the other hand, though the former Treasury chief had little love for Jefferson, he believed that once in power Jefferson would not change the system. But the Federalists stuck to their course, driving Hamilton to describe himself as in "the awkward situation of a man who continues sober after the company are drunk."

Burr remained aloof, doing nothing to aid the Federalists. The standoff ended in February 1801, after the Federalists learned that Jefferson had privately promised he would not try to change the existing government. His pledge reassured the Federalists, and Jefferson was finally elected.

Never again would the Federalists gain national dominance, but the system they had built would endure.

 TRY THIS!

1. Tell what qualities especially fitted John Adams to be President. Which qualities worked against him? 2. Make a list of the things that prevented the Federalists from electing a President after John Adams. 3. Describe the way in which an act of Congress would have been declared unconstitutional under the Kentucky and Virginia Resolutions. 4. Explain the mix-up that took place in the election of 1800. You may want to look up Article Two, Section 1, of the Constitution, and the Twelfth Amendment.

ROUNDUP

Who?
>   Alexander Hamilton
>   Citizen Genêt
>   John Jay
>   Thomas Pinckney
>   John Adams
>   Aaron Burr

What?
>   First Bank of the
>   United States
>   *Report on Manufactures*
>   Whiskey Rebellion
>   Democratic-Republican
>   Societies
>   XYZ Affair
>   Alien and Sedition Acts
>   Virginia and Kentucky
>   Resolutions
>   nullification

Where?
>   Potomac River
>   Fallen Timbers

KNOW THIS

Launching the New Government

1. What was the condition of the United States government just before March 4, 1789?
2. Which of the executive departments set up in 1789 had the most power? Why?
3. Compare Hamilton's and Jefferson's family backgrounds, political beliefs, and theories of government.
4. How were the federal courts organized?

Hamilton's Financial System

1. What did Hamilton hope to accomplish by his financial measures?
2. How big was the government debt left over from the Confederation? What part of it presented the greatest problem? Why?
3. Why was the debate over state war debts so angry?
4. What did the First Bank of the United States do?
5. Why did Hamilton want to encourage manufactures?

The Earliest Political Parties

1. How did the nation's founders view political parties?
2. How did Hamilton and Jefferson make their disagreements known to the public?
3. Why was the whiskey tax especially hard on the farmers of western Pennsylvania?
4. What effect did the Whiskey Rebellion have on the Federalist Party?

War in Europe—Trouble at Home

1. What was the official United States position on the undeclared war between France and Britain?
2. Outline the provisions of Jay's Treaty. Why was it so unpopular?
3. How did Jay's Treaty make Pinckney's task easier?
4. Why was the right of deposit needed at New Orleans?
5. What resulted from the Battle of Fallen Timbers?

The Decline of the Federalists

1. Why was it a "fatal mistake" for Adams to keep Washington's Cabinet?
2. What was the XYZ Affair? Who were involved?
3. What were the provisions of the Naturalization, Alien and Alien Enemies, and Sedition Acts?
4. At whom were the Alien and Sedition Acts aimed? How did they backfire on the Federalists?
5. What part did Hamilton play in the election of 1800?

DIG HERE!

You could call this report "A Tale of Two Cities." It will be about Philadelphia and Washington, the second and third capitals of the United States, as they were in 1800. Be sure to point out common features as well as obvious differences. For instance, both were early examples of city planning.

Here are some of the topics you can investigate:

A. The plans of the two cities.
B. Distinctive landmarks, streets, and buildings. (Washington's were still on the drawing board in 1800.)
C. Those responsible for the plans.
D. Leading citizens in 1800. (Philadelphia only.)
E. Populations. How many and what kinds of people lived in each?
F. What was the standard of living in each city?
G. Were there marked social classes? If so, what were they?

There are four excellent articles for this project in *American Heritage* magazine: Mary Cable, "Main Street of America," February 1969; John Dos Passos, "Builders for a Golden Age," August 1959; Marshall B. Davidson, "Penn's City: American Athens," February 1961; and Paul F. Norton and E. M. Cassidy, "Latrobe's America," August 1962. (The last article has information and pictures on both cities.) The subject catalog of your school or local library will lead you to further information.

THINK ABOUT IT

1. Some historians say that though Washington was not brilliant, he was "the right man, in the right place, at the right time." What do they mean? What did Washington bring to the Presidency? Suppose he had been the twenty-first President (or the forty-first) instead of the first. Would he have been as successful? Explain.
2. What was the political idea behind the Kentucky and Virginia Resolutions? You might look up *nullification* in an unabridged dictionary. How, do you think, could nullification have helped to bring on the Civil War?

DO IT!

1. Write an eyewitness account of the Battle of Fallen Timbers for a news syndicate. Be sure to include an interview with "Mad Anthony" Wayne in your report.
2. Look up the achievements of the two great industrialists of the 1790s, Eli Whitney and Samuel Slater. Report to the class on the way they changed American life. Diagrams or models of their work would add a lot to your report.

THEN AND NOW

Are political parties good or bad? Or are they a necessary evil? What useful tasks do they perform? Could this work be done in any other way? Some observers say that the party system is dying. They point to the ever-rising number of independent voters, those who belong to no party. Is this trend good or bad? Explain.

The Jeffersonians
Champion Democracy

How did the nation accept its first change of government? What new ideas did Jefferson bring?

When Thomas Jefferson was sworn in as President, he clearly showed that political power could be transferred from one party to another without violence. The defeated Federalists expected wholesale removals from office, or worse. To their amazement Jefferson stated in his inaugural address that "the minority possess their equal rights, which equal laws must protect, and to violate which would be oppression." Although Jefferson's followers had overwhelming majorities in Congress, they made no effort to overturn the republic that Washington, Hamilton, and Adams had built. Jefferson did, however, give the government a new tone. He believed that the people were the source of all power. This belief was his constant guide.

1. THE REVOLUTION OF 1800

Historians have often described Thomas Jefferson's coming to power as "the revolution of 1800." It was a revolution in which no shots were fired, but in which the new republic was set on the path to democracy. It brought to head the nation one who believed in government of, by, and for the people. Of course Jefferson's idea of democracy did not include blacks or Indians.

A man of contradictions. Thomas Jefferson was a very complicated human being. Tall, redheaded, bony, he reminded many who met him of a scarecrow. He didn't care much for appearances. In the White House he was often seen wearing "a blue coat, a thick gray-colored hairy waistcoat with a red underwaistcoat lapped over it, green velveteen breeches with pearl buttons, yarn stockings, and slippers [worn] down at the heels."

Jefferson never hid the fact that for him comfort came first. And public speaking was something he did not find comfortable. His low voice made it almost impossible for anyone beyond the first rows to hear him. Since he liked conversation much better than public speaking, he made very few speeches. Instead, he gave dinner parties at which he charmed his guests with lively talk, good food, and fine wines.

When he was not busy with politics, Jefferson followed a variety of interests that amazed the people of his day. Agriculture, languages, literature, music, history, architecture, science, political philosophy, geography, clothing design, and inventions were all among the things that fascinated

---

Read here of how

Jefferson was a new kind of President.
He lost some followers but gained others.
And he kept many Federalist ideas.
But he tried to change their courts.

TIME CHART

1803	Louisiana is purchased from France.
1804–1806	Lewis and Clark explore the West.
1805	Britain begins seizing U.S. ships.
1807	Aaron Burr is tried for treason.
1807	France declares Britain blockaded.
1807	The *Leopard* attacks the *Chesapeake.*
1807	An embargo stops trade with Europe.
1808	Madison is elected fourth President.
1811	Tecumseh is defeated at Tippecanoe.
1812	A second war with England begins.
1814	The capital is attacked and burned.
1815	The Treaty of Ghent ends the war.

---

him. He carried on a vast correspondence with people from all parts of the world.

Many noted that Jefferson's words and deeds were often contradictory, but he never allowed what he had said to keep him from doing anything that needed to be done. Although he preached equality, Jefferson never thought of blacks as the equals of whites. He disliked slavery, but he could not imagine a different system so long as there were blacks in America. He believed in states' rights, but as President he insisted on a large measure of executive power. He opposed federal laws to control the press, but supported state laws to regulate it. All this makes more sense if you remember that he believed firmly in change. For him change was the necessary law of society.

143

A party split. The new President's democratic attitude attracted most Americans. It stressed the value of rural, agricultural life. In fact, throughout his lifetime Jefferson viewed a self-sufficient farm population as the chief guardian of liberty. "Those who labor in the earth," he believed, "are the chosen people of God." At the same time he was fearful of cities and urban dwellers.

An interesting crew rallied to Jefferson's support. Its most prominent member was James Madison, who had played such an important part in drawing up the Constitution. He became Secretary of State. Less known was Albert Gallatin, a shrewd, Swiss-born banker whom Jefferson made his Secretary of the Treasury. Then there was John Randolph, the outspoken leader of Jefferson's party in the House of Representatives, and the pamphlet writer John Taylor of Caroline, whose ideas on the superiority of country life were much like those of Jefferson. James Monroe, later the fifth President, was another follower. He represented the United States in a number of European capitals.

But Jefferson's followers were split between those who insisted on keeping rural America intact and those who believed a powerful nation would need factories, cities, and a strong federal government. Typical of the first group was John Randolph. (Above all, Randolph was colorful. At more than one meeting of the House of Representatives, he arrived in full hunting dress, carrying a dog whip, and followed by his favorite hounds.)

Randolph held to the old Jeffersonian principles: peace, states' rights, a weak Presidency, a balanced budget, no standing army, and no interference with personal liberty. In time Randolph and others like him drifted away from Jefferson as the President expanded the power of the executive office.

The party split began over Jefferson's first inaugural address. Alexander Hamilton happily described it as "a pledge . . . that the new President will not lend himself to dangerous innovations, but in essential points tread in the steps of his predecessors." Because Jefferson kept to the principles on which the Federalists had started the government, there was a steady movement of Federalists into Republican ranks. But there was also a departure of the "Old Republicans" from the party. For them Jefferson's policies were "very like a compromise with Mr. Hamilton's" (pages 125-128). However, the loss was more than balanced by gains from the Federalists.

A new capital, a new Administration. The Washington to which Jefferson brought his government was a rough-hewn settlement. One visitor complained, "The federal city is in reality neither town nor village. It has two or three vast [buildings] upon distant hills but nothing . . . between them." The White House was only half built, and the roof leaked, causing damage to ceilings and furniture. Congress rarely voted more than a thousand dollars a year to keep up the building, and this added to the feeling that nothing in the new capital was complete.

Jefferson and his Secretary of the Treasury, Albert Gallatin, immediately set to work to pay off the national debt. Both men preached government economy, balanced budgets, and lower taxes. They also reduced spending on the army and navy, leading John Adams to fear that Jefferson might abolish the navy. But the new President did not go that far.

To the delight of Federalist officehold-

The capitol in 1800. George Washington chose the stone from a Virginia quarry.

ers, only those who were incompetent or openly opposed to the Administration were removed. This did not please Jeffersonians who had expected jobs in return for their support. The demand of his followers for government jobs was so heavy that Jefferson sadly complained, "If a due participation of office is a matter of right, how are vacancies to be obtained? Those by death are few; by resignation none."

Keeping party discipline was also difficult. The congressmen of each party met in what was called a *caucus* (KAW-kuss), but this rarely did anything except choose the party's presidential nominees. Congressmen gave their loyalties first to their states and then to their sections. It was clear that these local feelings might harm the nation, and that they could one day lead to a civil war.

Acceptance of the Bank. Jefferson had never accepted the First Bank of the United States (page 127). It seemed to him to threaten the very safety of the government. The Bank's system of branches doing business in the states made him suspicious. So did the fact that much of its stock was owned by foreigners.

But Gallatin opposed doing away with the Bank. He felt that it was needed to regulate the nation's money system. In time Jefferson accepted Gallatin's view. He was pleased to know that the national debt would be reduced by one half by the end of his Presidency. To the "Old Republicans" Jefferson's acceptance of the Bank was one more proof of how far he had strayed from his beliefs.

A powerful court system. The Federalists passed the Judiciary Act of 1801 before

145

they turned over control of Congress to the followers of Jefferson. The Act changed the organization of the federal courts and added 23 new federal jobs. Jefferson was able to force a repeal of these Federalist changes through Congress, but one appointment escaped him. John Marshall was still Chief Justice.

Marshall was a craggy, self-assured Virginian. On the surface he looked easygoing, but the appearance hid a sharp, shrewd mind. He knew how to expand the power of the court, and he disliked Jefferson, who he feared meant to undermine "the foundation principles of the government." For Jefferson, Marshall's great sin had been promoting the Federalist Party in Virginia. Perhaps the real trouble between them was that they were very much alike. (The Chief Justice too sometimes appeared in public with patches on his pants.)

Jefferson first attacked the Supreme Court indirectly. One justice, Samuel Chase, was such a devoted Federalist that he always seemed to rule against Republican defendants. When Jefferson proposed

that he ought to be impeached and removed, the Republicans in the House of Representatives readily agreed.

It was the Senate, however, that had to try Chase (page 108). John Marshall was such a strong witness for the impeached justice that to President Jefferson's dismay the Senate acquitted Chase. Everyone had realized that if Chase were removed, the stage would be set for the impeachment of Marshall. But Marshall took care not to give Jefferson any opportunities. Instead, he stuck to the letter of the law as he laid the foundations for a powerful and independent court system.

 TRY THIS!

Make a list of the personal characteristics that describe Thomas Jefferson. Put a + beside each characteristic that you think was an advantage to him as President. Put a − beside each characteristic that you think was a disadvantage to him.

2. LOUISIANA AND THE WEST

Just as Jefferson reluctantly accepted Hamilton's financial system, he also spectacularly increased the size of the country. When Spain gave Louisiana to France in 1800, it was disturbing news. Then France announced that it would close the port of New Orleans to the United States. "The day that France takes possession of New Orleans," Jefferson warned, "from that moment, we must marry ourselves to the British fleet and nation." To prevent France from carrying out its intention, Jefferson and Madison decided to see if they could buy the port of New Orleans.

The United States effort was helped by events in the French colony on the island of Santo Domingo. A slave uprising there led by a brilliant black man, Toussaint L'Ouverture, had overturned French control. In

———————●———————

Read here of how

The United States bought Louisiana.
Lewis and Clark explored the new territory.
Pike found the "Great American Desert."
Aaron Burr was tried for treason.

———————●———————

146

1801 the French ruler, Napoleon, sent a large force to win back the island. L'Ouverture was treacherously seized—even though he had been promised fair treatment—and sent to France, where he died in prison. However, the fierce resistance of the former slaves and an epidemic of yellow fever all but destroyed the French force. Discouraged, Napoleon directed his foreign minister Talleyrand to offer the United States all of Louisiana.

A wonderful bargain. The United States minister Robert Livingston and James Monroe, who had been sent to France by Jefferson to arrange the purchase, quickly accepted Talleyrand's offer. In 1803, without approval of Congress, they agreed to pay France fifteen million dollars. Jefferson, when he received the news, readily accepted this wonderful bargain. In a single stroke the country had been more than doubled in size. Federalists denounced the purchase, but the decision won popular approval.

By the Louisiana Purchase Jefferson had extended presidential power beyond the wildest dreams of the Federalists. He admitted that he had stretched the Constitution to the breaking point, but he defended this as necessary for the good of the country.

Two unusual men. Jefferson knew that the government had only a general idea of what was in the Louisiana Territory it had bought. He and Congress immediately set up an expedition to explore the vast new lands. He chose two young army officers, Meriwether Lewis and William Clark, to lead it.

Lewis and Clark were unusual men. The intense, thoughtful Lewis had been Jefferson's private secretary. In the course of the explorations he kept a careful diary in which he described the animal and plant life found along the way. Redheaded William Clark was the younger brother of George Rogers Clark, who had conquered the Northwest Territory (page 91). The rough-hewn Clark knew the frontier like the back of his hand. He was in sharp contrast to the more polished Lewis.

From the outset of the exploration Jefferson and a number of leading American scientists planned its purposes down to the smallest detail. Lewis and Clark were to explore the Missouri and Columbia river basins to find the quickest overland water route to the Pacific. They were also to map the regions they passed through, and to record information on various Indian tribes. Similarly, the explorers were to note every detail of the plant, forest, animal, and mineral resources they found. Even temperature records were to be kept.

The immediate interest of the government was to develop the fur trade. A long-term and much more important concern was to find out how the new lands could most quickly be opened for settlement. Lewis and Clark were to map an empire

A horned toad (left) was sent back by Lewis and Clark. The pheasant (right) was sketched by them.

147

148

Life on the Frontier

The first 300 miles of westward movement took 150 years; a thousand more took another century. Thirty years later it was all over. The frontier was closed. The cabin (above left) might have belonged to Daniel Boone (1734–1820). He felt crowded when he could see the smoke from a neighbor's chimney. Later, fierce frontier independence gave way to cooperation and socializing at barn raisings, quilting parties (above right), and during logging (left).

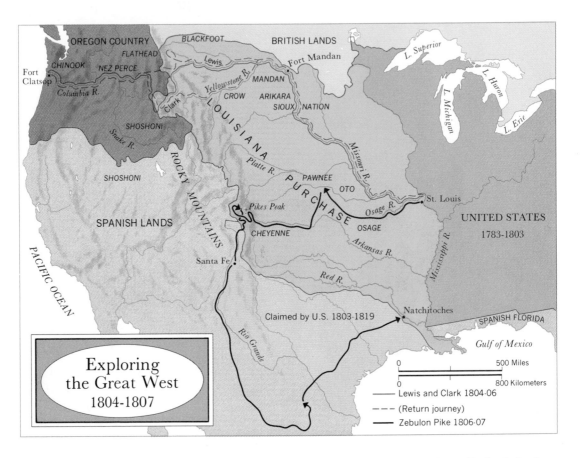

OREGON COUNTRY
FLATHEAD
BLACKFOOT
BRITISH LANDS
L. Superior
CHINOOK
NEZ PERCE
Lewis
Fort Mandan
L. Huron
Fort Clatsop
Columbia R.
Yellowstone R.
MANDAN
CROW
ARIKARA
SIOUX
NATION
L. Michigan
L. Erie
Clark
Snake R.
SHOSHONI
LOUISIANA
Missouri R.
SHOSHONI
ROCKY MOUNTAINS
Platte R.
PURCHASE
PAWNEE
OTO
St. Louis
UNITED STATES
1783-1803
Pikes Peak
Osage R.
SPANISH LANDS
CHEYENNE
OSAGE
PACIFIC OCEAN
Santa Fe
Arkansas R.
Mississippi R.
Red R.
Claimed by U.S. 1803-1819
Natchitoches
SPANISH FLORIDA
Rio Grande
Gulf of Mexico
0   500 Miles
0   800 Kilometers
—— Lewis and Clark 1804-06
- - - (Return journey)
—— Zebulon Pike 1806-07

Exploring the Great West 1804-1807

Like earlier explorers, Lewis and Clark hoped to find a water route to the Pacific. Both they and Pike pushed beyond United States lands.

and provide information for the conquest of the West.

"By land from the U. States." The expedition that set out in 1804 numbered 23 soldiers, three interpreters, and one slave. Probably the most useful member of the party was the Indian guide and interpreter Sacajawea (SAH-kuh-juh-WEE-uh). Without her help in dealing with the Shoshone and other Indians, Lewis and Clark might never have gotten as far as they did. For two and a half years they sailed the Missouri, Snake, and Columbia rivers;

crossed the endless plains; climbed the jagged, towering peaks of the West. They were threatened with attack by the Sioux and other tribes that they encountered along the way.

In the letters Lewis and Clark sent back, Jefferson read with excitement Lewis's description of what they had found. When one of their boats returned, the President had a chance to view animal skins, horns, and skeletons, mineral and plant specimens, and even some living animals they had collected. Clark prepared remarkable maps of the new country. The exploration reached its climax one day in a slashing rainstorm. That day Clark carved on a tall yellow pine overlooking the Pacific: "William Clark December 3rd 1805. By land from the U. States in 1804 and 1805." The nation had extended its claims to the edge of the continent.

A "Great American Desert." In 1806 Zebulon Pike, an adventurous army officer, extended the explorations of the Louisiana Territory. He entered New Mexico and Colorado and discovered the peak that bears his name. His reports first mentioned the possibility of a southern route to California and the Spanish trading posts of the Southwest. However, in one respect Pike was an obstacle to further exploration of the region. He described much of the Southwest as a desert, and for several decades United States maps labeled the region that way—as the Great American Desert. The myth of such a desert lasted until the later 1840s.

But the Lewis and Clark expedition and the Pike expedition provided the federal government with vital details on geography, natural resources, and the Indian population. They reinforced United States claims to the Oregon Country and the Southwest and gathered knowledge necessary for the great push westward. For most of the 1800s the West was the place of national expansion, and Jefferson was truly the father of that interest.

The troublesome Aaron Burr. Even as the West was being explored, it became the scene of a supposed conspiracy. Aaron Burr lost the Vice Presidency in 1804. Jefferson always suspected Burr of secretly plotting with the Federalists to get the Presidency for himself in the election tie of 1800 (page 139). Then Burr had become even more notorious in 1804, when he killed Alexander Hamilton in a duel. Their quarrel had to do with New York State politics and Burr's effort to make a political comeback by being elected governor of New York.

Having lost that election, Burr felt he no longer had a political future in the East. He turned then to Louisiana. In one of the new states to be carved out of the vast territory, he might be elected to Congress or make a fortune dealing in land. But Jefferson and his friends came to believe that Burr had another purpose. They felt he meant to detach part of the region from the United States and make it a separate nation. This supposed plan led to Burr's trial for treason.

The first hint of Burr's secret purpose came from James Wilkinson. He was the governor of the Louisiana Territory. In 1806, newspapers began carrying stories mentioning an old plan of General Wilkinson's to form a separate government west of the Appalachian Mountains. Burr's name kept coming up in these stories. One had him scheming to seize power in New Orleans. Another said that he would overthrow Spanish authority in Florida. Most surprisingly, one reported his planning an invasion of Mexico. Rumors increased until it looked as though Burr had a force of thousands awaiting his command. In late December of 1806 Jefferson issued a proclamation warning citizens to stay clear of any Burr scheme involving Spanish territory.

A trial for treason. Burr was arrested, but a jury in the Mississippi Territory refused to indict him. He later made an unsuccessful effort to escape into West Florida. All this time Burr insisted that he had never had more than a hundred men at his command. They were to be used, he said, to explore the new western territories and seek out valuable tracts for settlement. Some evidence indicated that Wilkinson had planned secession and had decided to

151

protect himself by shifting blame to Burr.

Whatever the truth, Jefferson saw a chance to get rid of Burr once and for all, so he ordered him moved to Richmond, Virginia, to stand trial for treason. Chief Justice John Marshall presided at the trial. (In those days the Supreme Court had little to do, so its justices sometimes served as trial judges.)

After sifting through a mass of hearsay and contradictory evidence, Marshall made a decision in Burr's favor. He noted that the rules of evidence for treason were very strict (see the Constitution, Article Three, Section 3) and that the case against the former Vice President was not very good. Marshall's decision caused Jefferson to dislike the Chief Justice even more.

For the remainder of his life a dark shadow hung over Aaron Burr. His name was enough to strike fear wherever he went. Even now no one knows for certain the true story of his strange career.

 TRY THIS!

1. List the five purposes of the Lewis and Clark expedition in what you see as their order of importance for the country's future.
2. Show the relationship of each of the following to the treason trial of Aaron Burr: the Louisiana Territory, James Wilkinson, Thomas Jefferson, newspapers, John Marshall.

3.   TROUBLE WITH FOREIGN COUNTRIES

Although Thomas Jefferson had been sympathetic to revolutionary France in the 1790s, he was totally committed to keeping the United States out of European wars. Once he was in office, his policy toward the great powers was one of caution and restraint. Even when both the British and French provoked him severely, he looked for solutions short of war. Toward lesser powers, such as those on the northern coast of Africa, he turned a hard face. There he was ready to fight for American interests and honor.

A 60,000-dollar ransom. In the early 1800s the Mediterranean shore of North Africa was called the Barbary Coast. Rulers of the Barbary states demanded payment from any countries trading in their waters. The United States and various European countries gave money to these Barbary pirates, as they were called, so that their ships would not be attacked.

In 1801 the ruler of Tripoli, one of the Barbary states, demanded a larger tribute payment. Jefferson answered by sending four frigates to the Mediterranean to protect American shipping.

When Tripoli seized the warship *Philadelphia,* a force of U. S. Marines invaded the country. Peace was restored when Tripoli agreed to return to the old scale of tribute. But the United States had to pay a 60,000-dollar ransom for the release of its captured sailors.

———————— ◆ ————————

Read here of how

Barbary pirates challenged the U.S.
War in Europe again caused trouble.
Jefferson tried to stop all trade with Europe.
Madison ended it with Britain and France.
Neither plan worked.

———————— ◆ ————————

Sea fights often ended in hand-to-hand combat with cutlasses, pistols, and knives.

It was a small war, but an important new principle had been established. In spite of what the Constitution said (Article One, Section 8, paragraph k), a war could be fought under the direction of the President without a vote by Congress.

A question of citizenship. French and British interference with United States shipping was a more dangerous threat to peace than the Barbary pirates. Britain and France were almost continually at war during the administrations of Jefferson and Madison. The English attacks on American ships were especially annoying, since they reminded Americans of Britain's tyranny before the Revolution. The country did not seem completely independent as long as England could seize American ships and American sailors and get away with it.

Captains of British warships were desperate for manpower in their struggle with France. Often they stopped United States merchant vessels to search for deserters from the British navy. They sometimes also took men they judged to be British subjects. This process was called *impressment*. It was an especially sore point because it meant that British officers refused to admit that the men were United States citizens.

When France and England began fighting in 1803 after a brief peace, the English decided to halt the trade of all countries with the French and Spanish colonies in the New World. The action struck at the profits of American shippers. It also raised a serious question as to whether the United States could stay clear of war.

Heavier losses. First Jefferson, then Madison, struggled unsuccessfully to make Britain recognize United States rights. Finally the Americans resorted to a method that had been used with good results before the Revolution. The government placed a ban on all trade with Britain. In 1806 the Non-Importation Act was passed. It forbade entry of a wide range of British manufactures but left the President to determine how and when the ban would go into effect. It also gave him the power to end the ban if the English agreed to recognize United States rights at sea.

When the English asked for a postponement of the Non-Importation Act, it seemed as if the plan might work. But Britain was convinced that the United States would not be able to enforce its wishes. Efforts by an American delegation to end the impressment of American sailors failed.

Through 1807, as the war between England and France heated up, the problems of the United States grew. An English blockade of the coast of Europe was met by a French decree commanding the French navy to seize any ships bound for the British Isles.

Between 1803 and 1806 the United

States lost 528 ships to the English and 206 to the French. In the next six years another 389 ships were lost to the English, while 469 were seized by the French and their allies. As the attacks of the European enemies grew sharper, the United States staggered under heavier losses. Jefferson's policy ran into a stubborn fact: the English and French were locked in a death struggle and were unwilling to give up any advantage, no matter who got hurt.

National outrage. To make matters worse, Jefferson had ruthlessly cut naval spending in order to pay off the national debt. He had not foreseen that an English fleet might anchor outside the ports of the United States and inspect every ship sailing outward. When one did, Americans were outraged, but the government lacked the strength to make the English withdraw.

To sit by and allow merchant ships to be inspected seemed bad enough. To allow warships to be searched would seem like the end of independence. In 1807 the English frigate *Leopard* attacked the *U.S.S. Chesapeake* after its commander refused to allow inspection of the ship for deserters. The country was outraged. Even diehard Federalists demanded revenge, but Jefferson still tried to avoid war. He closed American waters to English warships and instructed the United States Minister to London, James Monroe, to demand payment for the losses on the *Chesapeake* and an end to impressment. The English government refused.

Jefferson's failure. Left with few choices other than war, Jefferson decided to stop all United States trade with Britain. The *Embargo,* as it was called, was aimed at reaching the London government through the English merchants. They were already cut off from much of Europe, so Jefferson believed they would not risk their American market. The stopping of United States grain exports might also increase the problem of feeding the English population. Jefferson guessed wrong. England was fighting a war for survival and was prepared to tighten its belt a little more. There was another difficulty as well: Americans also would have to make heavy sacrifices.

In much of New England and the Middle Atlantic states merchants and tradesmen set about breaking the Embargo. New Englanders had goods shipped to Canada and then smuggled across the unguarded border. Secretary of the Treasury Gallatin admitted that the Embargo was impossible to enforce. Jefferson reacted with a call for stricter controls and got Congress to allow the government to seize any ships violating the Embargo.

The reaction in the Northeast was violent. Massachusetts refused to allow the measure to be enforced within its boundaries. As support for the Federalist Party grew, Republicans swung behind James Monroe, who openly criticized the Embargo. It looked as though Jefferson's supposed successor, James Madison, might not get the presidential nomination. Great numbers of Republicans joined with the Federalists in Congress to repeal the measure, and Jefferson had to admit failure.

A course that could lead only to war. James Madison was elected in 1808, and he wished to open his administration on a soothing note. He therefore proposed to repeal the Embargo and pass instead the Non-Intercourse Act. This would authorize trade with every nation but England and France. It offered to trade with these two countries as well, once they agreed to respect the rights of the United States as a neutral nation.

154

BRIEF HOUR OF TRIUMPH

United States frigates of the *Constitution* ("Old Iron-sides") class were the most advanced naval vessels of their day. First there were the armaments. They carried more guns (44 in the case of the *Constitution*) than anything else afloat except a full man-of-war (which usually had 73). Then there was the design. The hulls and rigging of these frigates were such that they could outsail any ships except those much smaller than themselves.

Because of these clever innovations, a United States frigate of this class could outgun anything it could not outrun and outrun anything it could not outgun. No wonder the ships were a sore trial to the British navy during the one glorious year that they roamed the oceans of the world!

But the frigates' hour of triumph was brief. Because the frigates were outnumbered, the British were able to run them, one by one, into various ports and pin them there until the war was over.

For a time it looked as though the British might give in, and Madison promptly lifted the trade restrictions. But England had no intention of ending its harassments of American trade. The two countries were on a course that could lead only to war.

"A prisoner released from his chains." Jefferson was determined to retire at the end of his second term. He called attention to the fact that Washington had served only two terms. With his old friend Madison in the White House, Jefferson felt that the republic was in safe hands. The wreck of his Embargo policy made his departure a happy escape. "Never did a prisoner released from his chains," he admitted, "feel such relief as I . . . on shaking off the shackles of power."

Nevertheless, power had taught the author of the Declaration many lessons. He gave up his opposition to manufactures, as he saw how the nation's dependence on foreign goods had put it at the mercy of the British. "Experience has taught me," he admitted, "that manufactures are now as necessary to our independence as to our comfort." This shift was typical of Jefferson. He never let a previous theory trap him when experience showed it to be faulty. Unwilling to be confined by unthinking prejudice, he threw open the windows of today to the winds of tomorrow.

TRY THIS!

1. Look again at your assessment of Jefferson (page 146). Now that you have learned more about him, would you want to change your opinion of any of his characteristics? Why? **2.** List the points you would have made in a letter of protest to the British government in 1808. **3.** Defend the Embargo as a loyal follower of Thomas Jefferson might have.

155

4. THE WAR OF 1812

James Madison came to the Presidency after a long training. He was physically small and a poor speaker, but his work at the Constitutional Convention and on the *Federalist Papers* (page 114) would have made him famous. Furthermore, in the 1790s he had played a key role in shaping the political party system.

"The war spirit is increasing." Once in the Presidency, Madison continued his search for a way to avoid war. He tried to play off England and France by offering to trade with whichever first respected American rights, but this was a total failure. Madison found himself increasingly denounced by a group of congressmen because United States rights were so easily violated. The sharp-tongued John Randolph (page 144) called this group the War Hawks.

In the congressional elections of 1810 many voters agreed with the Pennsylvania congressman who complained: "The people are sick of embargoes and non-intercourse laws—the war spirit is increasing." When the votes were counted, the group in the Twelfth Congress favoring war was a minority, but it had one advantage: among its members was that group of outspoken, energetic young leaders called War Hawks. They included Henry Clay of Kentucky and John Calhoun of South Carolina. These two men would be prominent political leaders for the next forty years.

The War Hawks understood the desire of Americans for some action that would make up for the shame of the past decade. Once people were convinced that there was no other choice but war, the War Hawks were ready to step forward and speak up for it. The same group was also eager to increase westward migration. The biggest obstacle to that was the Indians, and a major confrontation with them was shaping up.

Indian conflict. The history of the United States' treatment of the Indians does not make very pleasant reading. Again and again, despite treaty guarantees, the Indians were driven from their lands. In 1809 Governor William Henry Harrison of the Indiana Territory got the Indians living there to hand over almost three million acres. But white settlement was blocked when the Shawnee leader Tecumseh and his brother, called the Prophet, organized the local tribes.

Whites quickly guessed from the activities of the Indians that they were getting help and encouragement from the English in Canada. When Tecumseh went south to get other tribes to join his movement, Harrison decided to strike. The Battle of Tippecanoe (1811) was a bloody victory for Harrison and the United States. It took the lives of 200 soldiers. Andrew Jackson of Tennessee bluntly said, "Our murdered countrymen must be revenged." With war

---

Read here of how

Harrison crushed Indian resistance.
The nation was ill prepared to fight Britain.
It suffered defeats on land.
But won great victories at sea.
And emerged stronger and more united.

Major Battles 1811–1815

Map legend:
- ⚔ American land victory
- ⚔ British land victory
- ☆ Indian battle
- ⚓ American naval victory
- ⚓ British naval victory
- ⚓ British blockade

Map labels:
- CANADA (Great Britain)
- L. Superior
- L. Huron
- L. Michigan
- MICHIGAN TERRITORY
- York (Toronto) 1813
- Thames River 1813
- Detroit 1812
- L. Erie
- Lake Erie 1813
- Lake Champlain 1814
- Montreal
- St. Lawrence R.
- MAINE
- N.H.
- VT.
- NEW YORK
- MASS.
- CONN.
- R.I.
- Boston
- New York
- Philadelphia
- PENNSYLVANIA
- N.J.
- DEL.
- MD.
- Baltimore
- Fort McHenry 1814
- Washington, D.C. 1814
- VIRGINIA
- ILLINOIS TERRITORY
- OHIO
- INDIANA TERR.
- Tippecanoe 1811
- KENTUCKY
- MISSOURI TERRITORY
- Mississippi R.
- TENNESSEE
- NORTH CAROLINA
- SOUTH CAROLINA
- Charleston
- GEORGIA
- Savannah
- MISSISSIPPI TERRITORY
- Horseshoe Bend 1814
- LOUISIANA
- Mobile
- New Orleans 1815
- Gulf of Mexico
- FLORIDA (Spain)
- ATLANTIC OCEAN
- Constitution – Guerrière 1812
- Enterprise – Boxer 1813
- Shannon – Chesapeake 1813
- President – Belvidera 1812
- President – Endymion 1815
- Wasp – Frolic 1812
- Peacock – Epervier 1814

Scale: 500 Mi. / 800 Km.

Why were Lakes Erie, Ontario, and Champlain the key to invasion of the United States from Canada? When the British lost control of the lakes, the Duke of Wellington said, "Make peace."

against Britain likely, it looked as though a widespread Indian conflict could not be avoided either. Defeat of the Indians would also open the Mississippi Valley to settlement.

One War Hawk, Peter Porter of New York, declared in Congress that the time was coming when America must seize Canada. Such an action, he said, would "put it out of the power of Great Britain or of any British agent, trader, or . . . company . . . to supply Indian tribes with arms or ammunition, to instigate and incite Indians to disturb and harass our frontiers. . . ." The War Hawks made the annexation of Canada seem like the simplest of tasks. According to them, merely by walking through the Canadian countryside, the American army could take over that land.

Meanwhile, Tecumseh saw that no matter where the United States moved, Indians would be forced off their lands. He chose to ally himself with Britain.

157

MILITARY OPERATIONS

Even as the United States declared war on Britain, June 18, 1812, England revoked its *Orders in Council,* the acts by which it had been stopping all ships bound for ports under French control. (They were England's worst interference with United States trade.) The war also got under way just as Napoleon launched an invasion of Russia. So any hope that France might shield the United States from the full weight of British power was lost. Finally, much to the surprise of the United States, the British decided to defend Canada against invasion. The War of 1812, as it came to be called, turned into a continual series of disasters for the United States.

United States defenses. Americans might dream of gaining endless new lands from the war, but they were badly equipped to fight it. The United States was still suffering from Jefferson's belief that a standing army and navy were "dangerous to the liberty of a free people." The Secretary of War had only twelve clerks to assist him, and even the Inspector General was not sure of the army's size. He guessed that there were about 6,700 troops scattered among 23 forts and army posts. Fewer than 900 of these were assigned to the defense of New York City.

To fight the war, Congress authorized the enlistment of 50,000 men, but only 10,000 volunteered. Even the danger of a British invasion failed to bring in more recruits. The Administration considered a draft, but Congress refused to approve one. Finally the government proposed increasing the amount of free land being given to those who volunteered. The result of this move was truly discouraging. Thousands of those already in the armed forces deserted so that they could re-enlist and get bigger rewards.

The navy, with only sixteen major ships against an English fleet of 600, was hardly better off than the army. It had in addition some 200 gunboats, but these were unseaworthy.

Bankruptcy. Money was also a problem. In 1811 Congress had refused to recharter the First Bank of the United States, making it much harder to sell government bonds. Of 61 million dollars in bonds authorized by Congress, only two thirds were bought, often at heavy discounts. Northerners, especially, saw the conflict as one more interference with trade. And New England, then the nation's financial center, refused to lend money to the government. One Maryland congressman sadly informed his constituents, "The Department of State is so bare of money as to be unable even to pay its stationery bill." In the final year of the war the banks stopped paying out gold and silver, leaving the country with hardly any circulating currency.

The war finally made it necessary for Jeffersonians to restore what their old enemy Hamilton had created. In 1816 they chartered the Second Bank of the United States.

"On to Canada!" The war opened with an invasion of Canada that was quickly thrown back. A force of 7,000 British regulars backed by Canadian militia proved more than a match for the United States. William Hull, governor of the Michigan Territory, had badly overestimated British strength, but he did think that he could force the British to abandon Upper Canada. Unfortunately his plans for invasion fell into the hands of the British commander, Isaac Brock. Brock cleverly exploited Hull's fear of his superior numbers and maneuvered him into surrendering Detroit and his entire force.

The performance of the Americans improved on September 10, 1813, when a small United States naval force under Captain Oliver Hazard Perry won a smashing victory on Lake Erie. The nation's pride swelled as it read Perry's dispatch to General William Henry Harrison: "We have met the enemy and they are ours."

The British forces withdrew to the Thames River in Upper Canada, allowing a large force of militia under Harrison to reoccupy Detroit. Harrison then pushed on

On Lake Erie, Perry had to change flagships when his first one sank. But he fought on to victory.

to the Thames where on October 5, 1813, the Americans won a thumping victory.

The successful war at sea. At the outbreak of the war, the small fleet of United States vessels put to sea. Knowing that they were somewhere on the ocean forced the English to keep large forces busy searching for them. In a number of encounters, the frigates *Constitution* and *Essex,* as well as the sloop *Hornet,* won spectacular victories. Even the loss of the frigate *Chesapeake* stirred Americans' pride as they repeated Captain James Lawrence's famous dying words, "Don't give up the ship. Fight her till she sinks."

As 1814 opened, the British government decided that only a full military effort would bring the United States to

British officers ate President Madison's dinner before they set fire to his house.

terms. An English fleet was ordered to blockade the Atlantic and Gulf coasts. Gangs of English sailors landed anywhere they liked, to seize food and supplies. Worse threatened. The veterans of England's recent victory over the French in Spain were shipped across the sea to begin a major invasion of the United States.

The English decided to strike at Washington, D. C. The city fell on August 24, 1814, and English troops set fire to the White House, the Capitol, and other government buildings. Madison and Congress fled the ruined city. The federal government was homeless, and antiwar sentiment grew rapidly.

The Federalists destroyed. In the congressional elections of 1814 the Federalists made large plans. Discontent took threat-

ening shape in New England, where the Federalist Party was strongest. Massachusetts and Connecticut refused to allow their militia to serve under federal direction. It seemed that the Union was about to come apart. The Massachusetts legislature sent out a call to the rest of New England to take steps to end the war, and delegates from Connecticut and Rhode Island, plus a scattering from Vermont and New Hampshire, attended a convention at Hartford. The meeting agreed that Congress's war-making power needed radical reform. If the changes the Federalists wanted were not made, they wished to end the Union.

Only news that the war had ended spared the nation a major crisis. But the events at Hartford also destroyed the Federalist Party. It was now permanently identified in the American mind with treason.

A Christmas peace. War had scarcely begun before the Madison Administration began searching for a way to make peace. But only in 1814 were both sides convinced that neither could win a complete victory. During the summer of 1814 the United States was doing badly; so Madison decided not to force the issue of impressment—one of the chief causes of the war. At Ghent, Belgium, a delegation led by John Quincy Adams and Albert Gallatin began serious negotiations with representatives of Britain. The ever-present chance that Napoleon might return caused the English to soften their terms as well. Their great military hero, the Duke of Wellington, convinced them that a peace with the United States was urgent. Finally, on Christmas Eve of 1814, a treaty was signed restoring everything to just what it had been at the outbreak of fighting. (The treaty reached the United States in February, 1815.) Since Britain was no longer in a life-or-death struggle with France, impressments of American sailors and seizures of United States ships simply stopped. The War of 1812 ended in a draw.

A new folk hero. Fifteen days after the treaty of peace had been signed, a British force, unaware that the war was over, launched an attack on New Orleans. It had been planned as the final stage of British strategy. The British knew that port was the key to America's heartland. By occupying it a British army would strike a powerful blow against the United States.

However, the English had not calculated on Andrew Jackson, a general of the Tennessee militia. To meet the British at New Orleans, he threw together a colorful force of New Orleans residents, pirates, slaves, and about a thousand Kentuckians. With them he repulsed the invasion force. News of Jackson's victory stirred national pride. The Battle of New Orleans lifted Americans from a feeling of humiliation and made Jackson a hero. Thirteen years later it helped him win the Presidency.

Stronger national ties. For the first quarter-century of its existence the United States had lived in a time of international upheaval. Still a weak, neutral country, it had suffered humiliating attacks on its pride. Reluctantly, it had fought a war. Now, though the war had ended in a draw, England was finally convinced that it could never get back its former colonies. The warring countries decided that peaceful negotiations were the most sensible way to settle future quarrels.

United States control of the Mississippi and Missouri valleys was settled, and never again would an invading force set foot on its soil. The war had also strengthened national ties and freed American energies to subdue a continent. The Atlantic Ocean was a barrier behind which the United States could march to the Pacific without fear. For Americans the future lay under the western star. A continent beckoned them, and they meant to master it.

 TRY THIS!

1. Show the connection between the fight with Tecumseh and the war with England. If there had been no trouble with the Indians, would the United States have gone to war with England? Explain. **2.** List all the examples you can of the United States' lack of preparation for war with England. **3.** Using a map, indicate why control of the Great Lakes played such an important part in the War of 1812.

ROUNDUP

Who?
> Albert Gallatin
> John Randolph
> John Marshall
> Meriwether Lewis
> William Clark
> Sacajawea
> Tecumseh
> the Prophet
> Andrew Jackson
> William Henry
>   Harrison

What?
> Revolution of 1800
> Non-Importation Act
> Embargo
> Non-Intercourse Act
> War Hawks
> Orders in Council
> Treaty of Ghent

Where?
> New Orleans
> Great American Desert
> Pike's Peak
> Barbary Coast
> Tippecanoe

KNOW THIS

The Revolution of 1800

1. What do historians mean by "the Revolution of 1800"?
2. What economic group did Jefferson believe to be the foundation of a strong democracy?
3. How did Jefferson's leadership divide the Republican Party?
4. Briefly explain the policies of the Jefferson Administration on the national debt, government jobs, and the Bank.

Louisiana and the West

1. Why did Jefferson want to buy French lands in America?
2. How did the purchase of Louisiana affect the American Presidency?
3. What error did Zebulon Pike make in his reports?
4. How did the explorations of Lewis and Clark and those of Pike affect the history of the United States?

Trouble with Foreign Countries

1. Compare Jefferson's policy toward large, powerful nations with his policy toward smaller, weaker ones.
2. How did the *Chesapeake-Leopard* affair challenge United States sovereignty?
3. Give two reasons why the Embargo failed to protect United States rights.
4. How did developments during Jefferson's second term change his ideas about manufactures?

The War of 1812

1. How was President James Madison's foreign policy a failure?
2. Why were the War Hawks so important, even though they were only a minority in Congress?
3. Who did the United States think was aiding Tecumseh and his Indian allies?
4. Discuss the United States' lack of preparation for the War of 1812.
5. Briefly summarize the results of the War of 1812.

DIG HERE!

In American architecture and decoration, the time from 1785 to 1820 is called the Federal period. Among architects using the style were Thomas Jefferson (Monticello, University of Virginia), Benjamin Latrobe (United States Capitol), Charles Bulfinch (Massachusetts State House), Joseph Mangin (New York City Hall). Builders of fine houses also used the style for southern mansions and for the homes of rich merchants in such New England seaports as Boston, Salem, and Newburyport. Using the books below, write a report answering these questions:

A. What earlier styles of buildings or furniture is the Federal style based on? What periods of the past seem to have most attracted architects and designers in the Federal period? Can you find a reason for this?

B. What descriptive words come to your mind as you look at Federal buildings? What kinds of lines, forms, and materials did these architects favor? Are the same lines and forms carried out in the furniture and interiors of these buildings?

C. Are there present-day buildings in your own or nearby communities that show traces of the Federal style? (Sometimes it is mistakenly called "Colonial.") Why is the style still copied today?

These American Heritage books will help you: *Book of Historic Places, Guide to Historic Houses, Guide to Antiques, Notable American Houses.*

THINK ABOUT IT

1. Compare Chief Justice John Marshall and Thomas Jefferson as men and as political leaders. Consider such things as physical appearance, family background, ability to use political power, and political beliefs. Do you agree with the text that "perhaps the real trouble between them was that they were very much alike"? Explain.

2. The Northeast suffered most from English actions before the War of 1812, yet this section was most opposed to the war. Why? How do you explain the fact that the West and South wanted war?

DO IT!

1. Construct a "museum display" on the Lewis and Clark expedition or that of Zebulon Pike, or even of both. Include maps and pictures of their routes and the territory they explored, reproductions of their charts and sketches, and reports on the Indians they encountered.

2. Write a magazine article, "Inside the White House with Dolley Madison" (James Madison's wife). How does she view her role as First Lady?

THEN AND NOW

Why were people surprised at the peaceful transfer of power from Adams to Jefferson? Why do people today accept the election of candidates whom they may have worked against and voted against?

The Nation Begins to Grow

7

Why did national growth depend on transportation? Why did better transportation depend on technology? Without good transportation, could the country have remained united?

In 1815 peace returned to the United States, as it did to the rest of the world. It was a time of growing nationalism. Americans developed confidence in themselves and showed it in their dealings with other nations. New and better means of transportation drew the sections of the country together. Under John Marshall the Supreme Court reduced the power of the states to control business and so gave industry a freer hand to grow and prosper.

In some ways the sections of the country were also drawing apart. They had different interests in party politics and in the disputes over slavery and the tariff. Good transportation helped the West to grow, but this caused some jealousy in older sections. And it raised the problem of how public land was to be made available to settlers.

It was a confusing, but fascinating, period of history.

1. STRENGTHENING THE BOUNDARIES

Both before and after the War of 1812, a number of events increased the size of the United States and helped to improve its defenses.

Andrew Jackson and the Creeks.
When the War of 1812 began, the Creeks and other Indians of the Old Southwest seemed to threaten New Orleans. The Old Southwest was the region east of the Mississippi River. Creeks and other tribal groups living there blocked white occupation of the rich lands of Alabama.

The Creeks were settled, civilized people whose society was based on farming. Many of them had been Christians for many years. In 1811 the leader Tecumseh (page 156) had visited the Creeks and deeply stirred many of their younger warriors. A remarkable young chief, William Weatherford, had been especially impressed. Weatherford, who was a mixture of Creek, French, Spanish, and Scottish, was also called Red Eagle because of his red hair.

In 1813 a band of Creeks was attacked by white settlers. In revenge a force of Indians commanded by Weatherford killed about five hundred militia and refugees at Fort Mims, Alabama. News of these deaths reached Andrew Jackson as he was recovering from wounds received in a duel, but he took immediate action. He was merciless to the Creeks. At Horseshoe Bend in Alabama, and in a number of other battles, his forces defeated them completely. In August 1814 the Creeks surrendered.

Jackson forced the Creeks to give up territory that made up one fifth of Georgia

----

Read here of how

Andrew Jackson fought the Creeks.
The United States got Florida.
And drew the boundaries of Louisiana.
President Monroe issued a famous doctrine.

TIME CHART

1803	*Marbury v. Madison* is decided.
1816	A Second U.S. Bank is chartered.
1816	James Monroe is elected fifth President.
1818	Jackson invades East Florida.
1819	The Adams-Onís Treaty is signed.
1820	A Missouri Compromise is agreed upon.
1823	The Monroe Doctrine is announced.
1824	John Quincy Adams is elected the sixth President.
1825	The Erie Canal is completed.
1828	The Tariff of Abominations is passed.
1828	Andrew Jackson is elected the seventh President.

----

and three fifths of Alabama. Those who had not fought against the United States protested the loss of their lands. They were bluntly told that they could migrate to Florida. In a country starved for news of military victory Jackson's conquest sent the spirits of white settlers soaring.

An annoyance to the United States.
Once the War of 1812 was over, Jackson and many other people in the United States demanded the annexation of East Florida (the Florida peninsula). Hostile Indians living there often raided across the border. Furthermore, the planters of South Carolina and Georgia saw the Florida swamps and forests as a haven for runaway slaves. President-elect James Monroe believed that Spain would soon have to give up control of the territory.

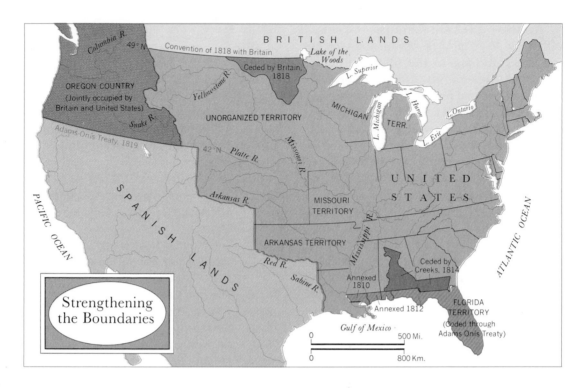

Note that the "steps-and-stairs" Adams-Onís line does away with both the United States claim to Texas and the Spanish claim to Oregon.

As the border raids continued, President Monroe's Secretary of War, John C. Calhoun, ordered Jackson to put an end to the Indian threat but not to interfere with Spanish sovereignty. Jackson asked the President to give him greater authority. He wrote, "Let it be signified to me through any channel . . . that the possession of Florida would be desirable to the United States, and in sixty days it will be accomplished."

Monroe's answer was not very clear, but Jackson swept through East Florida with 3,000 men. When his troops captured two British adventurers, Jackson tried and executed both. The British government was well aware that the two men had been

encouraging Indian raids and made no protest.

The reaction in Washington was different. Secretary of War Calhoun wanted to have Jackson court-martialed. Other Cabinet members agreed. Only Secretary of State John Quincy Adams defended Jackson. To Spanish demands that the United States punish him, Adams responded:

Spain must [decide] either to place a force in Florida adequate . . . to the protection of her territory . . . or cede to the United States a province . . . which is in fact a derelict, open to the occupancy of every enemy . . . of the United States and serving no other earthly purpose than as a post of annoyance to them.

Spain understood that it could either surrender Florida for a price or lose it by military action and gain nothing in return. In

February 1819 the territory was transferred to the United States. The United States then promised to pay five million dollars to American citizens for claims against Spain.

A new future. The annexation of Florida was part of a wider agreement between the United States and Spain. The settlement drew a clear boundary line between the Louisiana Purchase and the Spanish lands to the west. In addition the United States agreed that Texas had not been included in the Louisiana Purchase, and Spain gave up any claim to the Oregon Country. All of these matters were worked out by Secretary of State Adams and the Spanish minister, Luis de Onís. The Adams-Onís Treaty was ratified by the Senate in February 1819. At long last the South was safe from attack (map on page 166).

Even before the United States finally settled its problems with Spain, it had reached two agreements with Britain. The first of these was the Rush-Bagot Agreement of 1817. Under it the United States and Britain limited their naval strength on Lake Champlain and on the Great Lakes. Neither country would have more than one small warship on Lake Champlain and three others on the Great Lakes. This was one of the first and most successful of all disarmament treaties. Of course it was easy to enforce. It's hard to hide a warship.

The next year the United States came to an understanding with Britain over part of the Canadian boundary. The line would follow the line of 49° north latitude from the Lake of the Woods to the peaks of the Rocky Mountains (map on page 166). West of the Rockies, the Oregon Country was to be occupied, for the time being, by people of both the United States and Britain. This Convention of 1818 settled the northern boundary of the Louisiana Purchase.

Americans could now look westward to the vast country that Lewis and Clark had explored. There a new future beckoned.

No new colonial establishments. As the United States stretched its boundaries, it also began taking a bigger part in international affairs. The wars in Europe had produced an unexpected result: a revolution against Spanish control of Latin America. As John Quincy Adams noted, "Our national sympathy with the patriots of South America is natural and inevitable." Most Americans also asked the same question that he did: "How shall we be affected?"

President Monroe was worried about the Latin American upheaval, but he followed Secretary of State Adams's advice to remain neutral. By 1821 most of South America, as well as Central America and Mexico, had won independence. Adams now insisted that the American continents should no longer be open to conquest or colonization by any European country. It was a big claim.

The United States looked forward to a Western Hemisphere free of foreign interference. At the same time Britain was concerned that European nations might interfere in Latin America. As American and British interests were the same, the British suggested that both countries together speak out in favor of Latin American independence. They further urged that any interference there be regarded as a hostile act.

Former President Madison favored the British proposal, but Monroe and Adams seized the chance for the United States to act independently. Instead of making an agreement with the British, they committed the United States alone to enforcing a hands-off policy in the Western Hemisphere. The result was the statement to Congress known as the Monroe Doctrine.

"Honest friendship with all nations, entangling alliances with none." In his State of the Union message, delivered in December 1823, President Monroe stated that the United States no longer considered the American continents "subjects for colonization by any European power." To be sure that there was no doubt about the American position, Monroe said that any attempt to spread foreign control into the Western Hemisphere would be viewed as "dangerous to our peace and safety." This, of course, included any effort to restore Spain's control over its former colonies. It also took in any possible move by Russia down the Pacific Coast from Alaska. At the same time, the United States pledged noninterference in the affairs of Europe.

Monroe's policy had clear advantages.

Without entering a formal alliance with Britain, the United States had committed itself to a stand that it knew the British navy would defend. It was claiming to be first in the Western Hemisphere.

The Monroe Doctrine was firmly anchored to a principle of Thomas Jefferson: "Peace, commerce, and honest friendship with all nations, entangling alliances with none."

 TRY THIS!

1. Describe the life-style of the Creek Indians. Mention such things as the way they earned their living.   **2.** Explain how both Andrew Jackson and Secretary of State John Quincy Adams helped persuade Spain to transfer Florida to the United States. **3.** Identify the major points of the Monroe Doctrine.

2.   TRANSPORTATION OPENS THE WEST

When the country began, the founders doubted that it could hold its distant territories together. Westward migration raised the question of how new states could be brought into the Union. However, the drafters of the Articles of Confederation had allowed for their admission as fully equal partners with the older ones. By accepting this principle, the Constitution guaranteed the western settler an equal citizenship (page 102).

Rival sections. To strengthen the bonds of union, President Madison in 1815 asked support for a federal road-building program. He urged "the great importance of establishing throughout our country the roads and canals that can best be built un-

der national authority." In particular, Madison wanted to continue construction of the National Road. Begun in 1811, it was to run from Cumberland, Maryland, to Wheeling, in the western part of Virginia (map on page 172). By 1822 a well-paved highway was carrying heavy Cones-

---

Read here of how

The sections grew jealous of one another.
But roads and canals drew them together.
Steamboats revolutionized river travel.
The West's population grew.

Highways and bridges meant that coaches could travel at night. Boston to New York in 39 hours!

toga wagons through the Cumberland Gap of the Appalachians and tying together the Potomac and Ohio rivers.

But Madison's proposal aroused deep-seated fears. The South was suspicious of any measure that might increase the power of the federal government. New England was ready to invest in its own improvements but was unwilling to develop the frontier regions. New Englanders feared that such aid would drain away population. Also, they did not want Boston's trade to be endangered and that of Philadelphia, Baltimore, or New York to be helped. All three of these ports had shorter routes to the interior of the United States than Boston (map on page 172).

In a curious way two different and contradictory attitudes were growing in the country. One favored uniting the nation more fully; the other sought to prevent the power of the federal government from growing. This was particularly noticeable where actions of the federal government might help one section to get ahead of another. As we have just seen, it caused some sections to work against federal road-building at the very time state governments and private business were struggling to improve transportation so that people could make better use of the nation's resources.

On the corduroy roads. From the earliest settlements, Americans had moved into the interior along lines of least resistance. Wherever a river cut across the Appalachian Mountains, settlers poured through the gap into the western valleys. Indian

169

trails running through the Great Valley of the Appalachians provided the route for the Great Wagon Road connecting Philadelphia and the foothills of South Carolina. Running off this highway was a network of country roads linking farms to the outside world.

Usually the country roads looked like obstacle courses. They were often cluttered with tree stumps and deeply rutted from wagon traffic. Where swamps blocked the way, logs were put down to form "corduroy roads." These gave floating support to foot travelers. Most Americans took it for granted that the weather would interrupt travel. But they also longed for better roads and good bridges, and they pressured their states to get them.

These aids to transportation were called *internal improvements*. In the West especially they became a political issue, as western farmers expected the federal government to pay for them.

The rage for turnpikes. In the last years of the 1700s New England state governments began constructing *turnpikes*. These were toll roads paid for partly by the state and partly by bonds sold to private investors. Users paid tolls, so in time the investors got their money back.

At the end of the War of 1812 New York had a turnpike system that extended from Massachusetts to Lake Erie. New Jersey added a stretch of turnpike that would allow quick movement from New York to Philadelphia. Farther south, turnpikes did not receive much support, and except in Maryland southern roads remained in poor condition. But the National Road through the Cumberland Gap into Kentucky made the way west easier for southerners.

As the 1830s opened, the rage for roads and turnpikes faded, and public attention turned first to canals and then to railroads.

A frenzy of canal-building. In 1817 New York State started building a canal to connect Buffalo on Lake Erie with Albany on the Hudson River. The lake reached most of the way across Ohio, and the Hudson emptied into New York Harbor, so a

A typical busy scene on the Erie Canal. Note the variety of goods and activities at this port.

Canal boats were towed by horses and raised or lowered by systems of locks (right center).

canal joining them would mean an all-water route from the Old Northwest to the Atlantic Coast (map on page 172).

The 364-mile Erie Canal was an enormous success. Before it was built, shipping goods from Buffalo to New York City had cost 100 dollars and taken twenty days. Immediately, the canal cut the cost to ten dollars a ton and the time to eight days. Rates continued to drop, and ten years after it was finished, the canal had to be enlarged. The tonnage passing through it kept right on growing until 1880.

The great success of the Erie Canal set off a nationwide frenzy of canal-building. The people of the United States built 3,326 miles of them at a cost of 125 million dollars, mostly to expand the use of rivers and streams. Canals connecting eastern rivers with the Mississippi and Ohio valleys were common. They were followed by an extensive system to unite the rivers with the Great Lakes.

Some of the canals, especially the ones serving the coal fields of eastern Pennsylvania, returned excellent profits. Elsewhere the results were not as good. Many canals were built where there was little real need for them, and few could compete with the railroads when they came along. Yet canals drastically cut transportation costs and opened vast areas of the West to settlement and farming for profit.

Floating on a heavy dew. From the earliest times people had clustered along the rivers, depending on them for a link to the outside world. On crudely built flatboats and rafts they moved vast quantities of western farm produce down the Ohio and Mississippi rivers. The method worked, but it was time-consuming. A journey from Pittsburgh to New Orleans took no less than four months. So it's hardly surprising that many Americans looked for ways to speed up river travel.

In 1807 Robert Fulton introduced a steamboat that could move at a speed of five miles an hour against the current of the Hudson River. Two years later a man named John Stevens had a similar success on the Delaware. Steamboats able to carry large cargoes and many passengers were soon moving along the majestic rivers of both East and West.

Americans boasted that they had "leveled the Appalachian Mountains." Had they? Using this map, show why they thought so.

The steamboat revolutionized travel on western streams. As early as 1811 one was running between New Orleans and Pittsburgh. The number increased, until on the eve of the Civil War 727 of the vessels worked the Ohio, Mississippi, and Missouri rivers. Here, too, the drop in fares and freight rates was dramatic.

Steamboat travel was hazardous. There was danger from ice in winter, from sandbars in summer when the water was low, and from hidden snags at all times. Furthermore, riverboat captains had the dangerous habit of racing one another and trying to set speed records. No less than 30 per cent of western steamboats were lost in accidents before 1848.

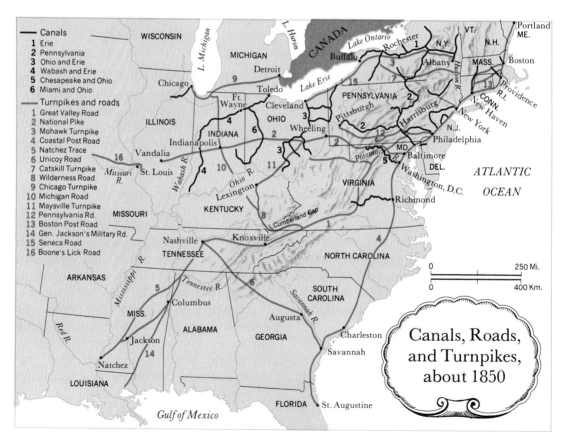

Canals, Roads, and Turnpikes, about 1850

Canals
1 Erie
2 Pennsylvania
3 Ohio and Erie
4 Wabash and Erie
5 Chesapeake and Ohio
6 Miami and Ohio

Turnpikes and roads
1 Great Valley Road
2 National Pike
3 Mohawk Turnpike
4 Coastal Post Road
5 Natchez Trace
6 Unicoy Road
7 Catskill Turnpike
8 Wilderness Road
9 Chicago Turnpike
10 Michigan Road
11 Maysville Turnpike
12 Pennsylvania Rd.
13 Boston Post Road
14 Gen. Jackson's Military Rd.
15 Seneca Road
16 Boone's Lick Road

Fulton's *Clermont* made rivers an important link in the nation's transportation network.

But the risks encouraged development of craft suited to western needs. Masters of steamboat construction produced vessels they claimed could "float on a heavy dew." They were wooden and needed as little as thirty inches of water to move successfully. Carrying much of the heavy cargo of both the West and the South, steamboats held their own against the railroads until the 1860s. When they disappeared after the Civil War, they left romantic legends that still linger.

A land policy for westerners. Part of the drive to improve transportation came from the need to open the West for settlement. Closely tied in was the question of how western land should be sold. Speculators who hoped to get rich by buying and selling lands constantly pressured the government to make purchase and payment terms easier.

As with so many other questions, the country divided, on its land policy, along sectional lines. Easterners wanted land to make money for the federal government,

and they wished the settlement of the West to be slow and orderly. Meanwhile, westerners were demanding that land be cheap and easy to obtain. In a series of land acts the westerners slowly won out.

The Land Act of 1796 copied the Ordinance of 1785 (pages 101-102). It made townships of six square miles each, half of which were divided into 640-acre sections. But nothing smaller than a section could be sold, and the sale price was two dollars an acre, to be paid at once. This discouraged buyers. In 1800, payment over a four-year period was allowed. Then the price was cut to a $1.64 an acre, and sale of quarter sections (160 acres) was permitted.

The government had trouble collecting on its credit sales, so in 1820 Congress did away with them. However, it also cut the price of public land to $1.25 an acre. At the same time, Congress made sales of as few as eighty acres legal. Finally, beginning

173

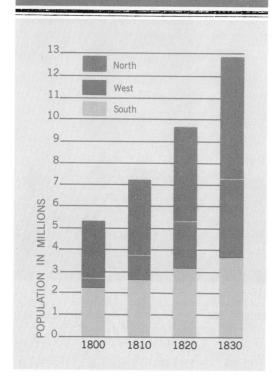

POPULATION IN MILLIONS

13
12 ■ North
11 ■ West
10 ■ South
9
8
7
6
5
4
3
2
1
0

1800   1810   1820   1830

As United States population boomed, which section was growing fastest? Which grew least? Can you think why this was so?

in 1841, "squatters" (those who settled on public lands without permission) were given the right to purchase the land ahead of anyone else.

Mind-boggling growth. Federal land policies encouraged an enormous migration westward. So great was it that one traveler exclaimed, "Old America seems to be breaking up and moving westward." Often the migrants were parents leading swarms of children, guaranteeing that the population would expand rapidly.

The growth of western population was mind-boggling. Ohio's alone went up by over 450 per cent between 1800 and 1810; Indiana's grew by over 500 per cent from 1820 to 1830; and Arkansas had a startling 1,250 per cent rise in population between 1810 and 1820.

Westerners were independent-minded and insisted on their natural rights. None of these was dearer to them than their right to land, and the vast federal domain gave the government the means to satisfy their longing. The rising states of the West added a vigorous new element to the early republic. But because they were eager to re-create the same kind of society left behind in the East, westerners helped to assure the unity of the nation.

 TRY THIS!

1. Explain what President Madison meant when he spoke of "the great importance of establishing throughout our country the roads and canals that can best be built under national authority." **2.** Compare turnpikes and canals as early means of transportation. Which were easier to build? Which could carry more goods and people? Which had a greater effect on the country? **3.** Trace the changes in land policy from 1796 to 1841.

3.   JOHN MARSHALL AND FEDERAL POWER

As the United States expanded, the federal government kept growing in power. The Supreme Court had a lot to do with this development. Under its greatest Chief Justice, John Marshall (page 146), it cut back the influence of the states, especially over business. In fact, the decisions that it made in those early days affect business and commerce right down to our own times. The case of *Marbury v. Madison,* in 1803, made it certain that the Court's later decisions would have lasting effect.

A defeat for President Jefferson. The *Marbury v. Madison* case began during the final days of John Adams's administration. As one of his last acts, President Adams had signed the appointments of 42 District of Columbia justices of the peace. All of them were loyal Federalists, but the outgoing Secretary of State failed to hand over the appointments. When Jefferson took office, he refused to release them.

William Marbury and three other people who had been appointed sued for the release of the appointments, naming the new Secretary of State, James Madison, as the person responsible. Jefferson expected the Supreme Court to order their delivery, and he did not intend to obey. Since Marshall did not have the power to enforce a decision, Jefferson looked forward to giving the Court a real setback.

Marshall, however, had no intention of getting into a hopeless battle with the new President. When the Court decided the case in February 1803, it did so in an unexpected way. The Chief Justice declared that the Judiciary Act of 1789, which gave the Court the power to act in cases like Marbury's, was unconstitutional. The Constitution carefully listed the kinds of cases

---

Read here of how

Jefferson hoped to reduce the power of the Supreme Court.
Marshall made the courts a strong branch of government.
The states lost some control of business.

---

the Supreme Court could hear, and this was not one of them. Marshall added that although the Court could not order the appointment of Marbury, it thought that he was legally entitled to the job.

In a single opinion the clever Chief Justice had managed to lecture the President on his duties, assert the power of the Court to review existing laws, and at the same time avoid a direct conflict with Jefferson. The Court did not again declare an act of Congress unconstitutional until the Dred Scott case in 1857, but a powerful precedent had been established.

No changes in contracts. In a number of major cases beginning in 1819 the Marshall Court laid the foundations for the federal government's right to make laws for business. The Constitution specifically gives Congress the right "to regulate commerce with foreign nations and among the several states . . ." (Article One, Section 8, paragraph c). The Constitution also does not allow the states to pass laws that change what a person must do after he has made a contract (Article One, Section 10, paragraph a). These two provisions, as the Supreme Court has interpreted them, are the basis of the federal government's power to regulate commerce and protect property.

As early as the *Fletcher v. Peck* case of 1810, the Court had upheld certain land grants made by the Georgia legislature. Persons voting for the grants had been bribed by the land companies receiving them. When a new legislature voted to take back the grants, these companies sued. The Court concluded that the original grants had been contracts, and so Georgia was bound to make good on them.

A more important decision on contracts came in *Dartmouth College v. Woodward* (1819). The New Hampshire legislature had tried to change the charter of the col-

175

lege. Marshall's Court ruled that charters were contracts, which states could not change.

Three weeks after the Dartmouth College decision the Court decided in *Sturges v. Crowninshield* that a state legislature could not act to free a debtor of what he owed. Both of these decisions were reassuring to anyone who wanted to invest money in business. The Supreme Court had made it clear that contracts, once made, could not be changed by state legislatures.

Federal supremacy in matters of business. At least as significant as cases dealing with the regulation of commerce are those dealing with the United States Bank and with contracts. A business panic in 1819 led several states to pass laws directing the Second Bank of the United States to pay heavy taxes on Bank branches. These states wanted to make it impossible for the Bank to do business within their borders.

Bank officials refused to pay the taxes. Among them was James W. McCulloch, cashier of the Maryland branch, and so Maryland sued to force him to pay. Marshall found in the *McCulloch v. Maryland* case that a state lacked the power to block the operation of a federally authorized agency. "The power to tax," as Marshall remarked, "is the power to destroy."

By ruling in this way Marshall was also declaring the Bank constitutional. In doing so he laid down the doctrine of implied powers (page 107). "Let the end be legitimate," he wrote, "let it be within the scope of the Constitution, and all means which are appropriate, which are plainly adapted to that end, which are not prohibited, but agree with the letter and spirit of the Constitution, are constitutional." *McCulloch v. Maryland* greatly expanded federal power. States'-rights southerners were deeply dis-

turbed. As a Virginia judge warned, "It is high time for the states to tremble . . . all their great rights may be swept away one by one."

Five years later the Court again expanded federal power. In 1808 New York State had given Robert Fulton, inventor of the steamboat, and his partner, Robert Livingston, a monopoly for operating steam vessels (see page 172). Then Robert Livingston granted former Governor Aaron Ogden of New Jersey the exclusive right to run steamboats between New Jersey and New York. In 1818 Thomas Gibbons started a competing line, and Ogden sued to shut it down. In 1824 John Marshall delivered the *Gibbons v. Ogden* decision. The Court declared that Fulton's and Livingston's original monopoly was illegal, since only the federal government had the power to regulate commerce between states. Federal supremacy in interstate commerce had been established.

In the years to come, both supporters of free enterprise and supporters of government control of business would draw their arguments from the decisions of John Marshall's Court.

TRY THIS!

Name the Supreme Court case to which each statement refers: **1.** A state legislature tried to take away a charter. **2.** The Second Bank of the United States was declared constitutional. **3.** For the first time the Court declared an act of Congress unconstitutional. **4.** Even if you have friends in the state legislature, you still have to pay what you owe. **5.** But if your friends in the legislature sell you land, you can keep it. **6.** On the other hand, if your friends in the legislature try to sell you a steamboat monopoly, watch out!

4. POLITICS IN A TIME OF CHANGE

As the nation's boundaries filled out, political hatreds appeared to fade away. A country that had seemed to be falling apart in the last months of the War of 1812 emerged from the war more united than ever.

An "Era of Good Feelings." The newly elected President, James Monroe, worked hard to strengthen the Union. It looked as though the Federalists, who had been accused of disloyalty for opposing the War of 1812, were going to disappear as a party. At the same time the Republicans adopted such Federalist ideas as the United States Bank and the protective tariff. In Congress the Federalists gave up all organized opposition. They even cast their ballots for Monroe in the 1816 election, giving him a near-unanimous vote. Once in office, the new President worked to do away with all parties.

President Monroe's objective seemed to be reached in 1820 when he won re-election with only one electoral vote cast against him. In Congress the Republican caucus (page 145) controlled lawmaking. The same was true in most state legislatures, so the triumph of Jefferson's party appeared to be complete. But lack of opposition led to indifference among voters. Of a total population of 12,067 in Richmond,

---

Read here of how

Politics became quite peaceful after 1815. But there was a disputed election in 1824. John Quincy Adams failed as President. The Democratic Party was born.

---

only seventeen persons went to the polls in 1820. In Providence, Rhode Island, 11,000 inhabitants produced only 81 votes. State performance was just as bad. Out of Virginia's 600,000 voters, a mere 4,321 chose to cast ballots.

Meanwhile, the party caucuses in Congress were attacked more and more for the lack of democracy. One Marylander complained that although democracy "did once mean . . . a government originating with and controlled and protected by the people," it had degenerated into "a government originating with the few, in which the people have no share, in which they have no voice, no power, no rights."

But the calm of this Era of Good Feelings, as it has been called, was all on the surface. The Republicans soon broke apart into squabbling factions. The time was ripe for a major reorganization of political parties.

An exciting sense of democracy. On all sides there were signs of change in voting procedures and voting restrictions. In 1800 only two states chose their presidential electors by popular vote, but by 1824 all but six had switched to that method. Eight years later only South Carolina was still leaving the choice to its legislature. For most people, voice voting had given way to a printed ballot, which ensured privacy, and the increase in polling places made voting easier. The rapid growth of newspapers and magazines gave candidates easy means of communication. Steamboats, canals, and finally railroads also widened political contacts. Public interest in politics was greatly stirred by rallies, barbecues, and conventions.

More important were the changes made in state constitutions. Most of these were intended to increase the people's control of government. Between 1816 and 1820, as the states of Illinois, Alabama, Indiana, Mississippi, Maine, and Missouri entered the Union, each gave the vote to all white adult males. Of the older states only Maryland had such liberal rules. Pressure grew to bring the older states' constitutions into line with the newer ones'. The principle behind these changes had been laid down by Jefferson when he said that "governments are republican only . . . as they embody the will of their people and execute it."

With office-seekers appealing directly to the voters, an exciting sense of democracy spread throughout the country. It made itself felt for the first time in the election of 1824.

"If my country wants my services, she must ask for them." As the administration of James Monroe ended, Republican Party divisions grew wider. Secretary of the Treasury William Crawford, although he was half paralyzed and nearly blind, managed to win the presidential nomination of the party leaders. But their backing no longer meant much. The South's John C. Calhoun, the West's Henry Clay, the Northeast's John Quincy Adams, and Andrew Jackson of Tennessee quickly challenged Crawford. Each had strong support in his own section, but only Jackson had anything like nationwide backing.

The voters had their doubts about the headstrong Hero of New Orleans (page 161), but they liked his independence. Well before the voting, Calhoun withdrew in favor of Jackson, leaving Clay and Adams as his strongest opponents. Clay was a firm supporter of internal improvements,

the roads and bridges that meant so much to westerners. On the other hand, Adams's long career and achievements made him the best-qualified candidate for the Presidency. But Adams had one drawback: he would not play up to the voters. "If my country wants my services," he wrote, "she must ask for them." Before the campaign was over, Adams bent this principle to win, and the results were disastrous for his administration.

A very close vote. The campaign was peaceful. Slightly more than 356,000 voters cast presidential ballots. Jackson led with 43 per cent of the total vote, followed by Adams with 30 per cent, Crawford with 14 per cent, and Clay with 13 per cent. The electoral votes were similarly divided as Jackson received 99, Adams 84, Crawford

This thread box with its picture of John Quincy Adams was a souvenir given out in the presidential campaign of 1824.

41, and Clay 37. Since no candidate had the 131 votes then needed for an electoral majority, the House of Representatives had to choose a President from among the top three candidates (Twelfth Amendment).

All the candidates—even the stiff, unbending John Quincy Adams—worked to win over the various state delegations. Early in January, Clay agreed to support Adams. He seemed to have been promised in return the post of Secretary of State. In no time Washington buzzed with talk of a "corrupt bargain." Adams was also made to look bad when he promised Daniel Webster that former Federalists would receive some government jobs.

For weeks the politicking went on. Finally, on a snowy February day in 1825, the House of Representatives met and by a very close vote chose John Quincy Adams as the sixth President of the United States.

The vision of a better America. John Quincy Adams was a model of proper behavior, but he entered the White House under a cloud. Although his talents were impressive, the new President soon found that he did not have popular support. Once he had actually made Henry Clay Secretary of State, it was generally felt that there had indeed been a "corrupt bargain." The defeated Andrew Jackson seemed to accept Adams's election, but privately he referred to Clay as "the Judas of the West."

The new President held definite ideas about government. He argued that it was the government's job to protect both the people and their property, but he had doubts about the effectiveness of democracy. His views on slavery were not well known, but they would have frightened white southerners out of their wits. Adams was convinced that in the end slavery would tear the Union apart and lead to war between the sections. He expected that war to be long and bloody, but he also believed that it would destroy slavery. "As God shall judge me," he had written in 1820, "I dare not say that [such a war] is not to be desired."

In the first months of his administration Adams painted a vision of a better America. He called for a vast program of internal improvements as well as for the establishment of a national university and an observatory, a standardized system of weights and measures, and patent-law reforms.

Unfortunately, Adams's program inspired deep fears of federal power. The aged Jefferson warned that it would be the beginning of an aristocracy of bankers and merchants. Adams had given the opposition a rallying cry. From every side came the charge that he intended to make the federal government the center of all power. A suspicious public thought they smelled tyranny.

A new political organization. From the moment he lost the election of 1824, Jackson and his friends set about to win in 1828. By the time the voters were ready to go to the polls, Adams had no hope of re-election. Nevertheless, the campaign was bitter, with slanderous charges hurled by both sides. As the returns poured in, Jackson won an overwhelming victory.

In the four years between elections presidential voting had completely changed. The popular vote increased by almost 300 per cent, and on the surface it seemed that the country had now become more democratic. Yet this was not really fair. Competition between the parties was what had encouraged many more people to vote. In 1828 voters were convinced that they had a real choice for the Presidency.

Jackson's election promised further changes. The lean old general set to work to revive "a plain system, void of pomp, protecting all, and granting favor to none." To achieve this result his followers formed a new political organization. They called it the Democratic Party, and it would control national political life for most of the next thirty years.

 TRY THIS!

1. Explain why the years of President Monroe's administration were called an Era of Good Feelings. 2. List the important changes in voting procedures in the early 1800s. Tell why you have listed each. 3. Explain why John Quincy Adams was an unpopular President and why he was unable to achieve his goals.

5.   INCREASING SECTIONAL STRIFE

The United States seemed peaceful and calm in the years following the War of 1812. But deep and barely hidden disagreement threatened the Union. From time to time rivalries between the sections broke into bitter quarrels over the tariff. Even more threatening were the disputes concerning slavery. Shortly after the Revolution the country had divided into slave and free states (page 99). This brought on a series of crises that finally led to civil war.

The great danger. For a while, each time a crisis threatened, Congress managed to work out some sort of a political compromise. The earliest, in 1820, provided a model for later settlements. It seemed that as long as some agreement was possible, the nation would remain at peace. But the compromises only postponed resolving a basic contradiction: the existence of slavery within a nation claiming that all men were created equal.

The authors of the federal Constitution had been careful to protect the institution of slavery. For instance, Article One, Section 2, gave southern whites three-fifths representation for their slaves; Article One, Section 9, provided for the return of runaway slaves.

The slavery provisions were part of a compromise between northern and southern states worked out during the Constitutional Convention at Philadelphia (page 110). At that time James Madison had explained, "The great danger to our general government is the great southern and northern interests of the continent being opposed to each other." But a Maryland delegate, Luther Martin, had angrily asserted that the Constitution was an "insult to that God . . . who views with equal eye the poor African slave and his American master."

In spite of the Constitution many remained uneasy. Slavery roused the consciences of thoughtful people and the fears of others. In the early years southerners generally were still sensitive about slavery, which they sometimes called their "peculiar institution." As late as 1828 a South

Read here of how

Slavery became a national issue.
The Missouri Compromise was adopted.
The tariff of 1828 angered the South.
The Compromise of 1833 avoided a crisis.

180

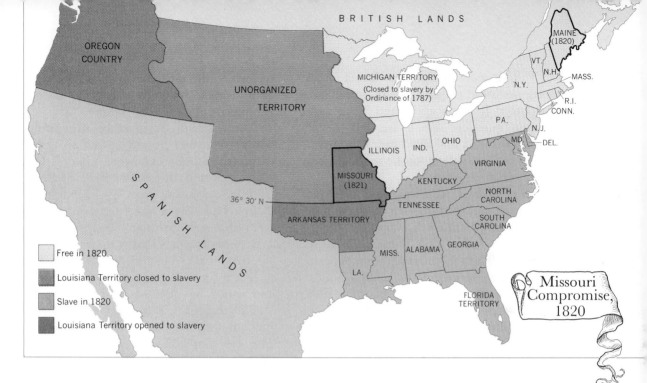

BRITISH LANDS

OREGON COUNTRY

UNORGANIZED TERRITORY

MICHIGAN TERRITORY
(Closed to slavery by Ordinance of 1787)

MAINE (1820)

VT.
N.H.
MASS.
N.Y.
R.I.
CONN.
PA.
N.J.
DEL.
MD.

S P A N I S H   L A N D S

36° 30′ N

ILLINOIS   IND.   OHIO

MISSOURI (1821)

KENTUCKY

VIRGINIA

NORTH CAROLINA

ARKANSAS TERRITORY

TENNESSEE

SOUTH CAROLINA

MISS.   ALABAMA   GEORGIA

LA.

FLORIDA TERRITORY

Free in 1820

Louisiana Territory closed to slavery

Slave in 1820

Louisiana Territory opened to slavery

Missouri Compromise, 1820

What seeds of future conflict between North and South can you see in this compromise? Which side seems to have gotten a better bargain? Why?

Carolinian told Congress that he "condemned and abhorred" slavery. But a different attitude was growing. Lush profits from raising cotton were strengthening the slave system.

"A fire bell in the night." The first conflict over slavery came unexpectedly in 1819. In that year James Tallmadge, a New York congressman, brought in a bill to admit Missouri to the Union. The measure also provided that "further introduction of slavery or involuntary servitude" be forbidden in the new state. At the same time Maine applied for admission. To accept either Missouri or Maine as a free state would upset the balance of eleven free and eleven slave states in the Senate. The House, because of the swiftly growing northern population, already had 105 free-state to 81 slave-state representatives. An angry sectional dispute took place. It

clearly showed the depths of passion behind the slavery issue.

In defending slavery southerners used a variety of arguments. They said that it was recognized in the Bible, and they claimed, "There is no place for free blacks in the United States." On the other hand John Quincy Adams concluded that "The bargain between freedom and slavery contained in the Constitution of the United States is morally and politically vicious. ..." The disagreement over slavery showed how Thomas Jefferson's Republican Party was falling apart.

But the issue of statehood for Missouri and Maine was peacefully settled under the guidance of Speaker of the House Henry Clay. In the late winter of 1820 Congress agreed to admit Maine as a free state and Missouri as a slave state. It also laid down the rule that in the future slavery would be prohibited north of 36° 30′ north latitude. The 36° 30′ line was also the southern boundary of Missouri (map on this page).

181

The Missouri Compromise lasted for 34 years, but it did not solve the real problem. A troubled Jefferson exclaimed, "This momentous question, like a fire bell in the night, awakened and filled me with terror. . . . It is hushed indeed for the moment, but this is only a reprieve."

The Tariff of Abominations. No issue was more continually before the nation in the nineteenth century than that of the protective tariff (page 127). Time and again, from the 1790s to the early 1900s, it blew up to divide the people of the United States. Debate over the Tariff of 1828 became part of the presidential campaign and added to the sectional rivalry.

As the election year of 1828 opened, the supporters of Andrew Jackson were well organized in almost every state. One opponent grudgingly admitted, "Say what you will, these Jacksonians are excellent politicians." The accuracy of his remark was fully revealed in the maneuvering over the Tariff of 1828. As proposed, the measure put heavy duties on all imported woolen and iron products. Merchants in the Northeast felt threatened, and southern planters would be denied cheaper manufactured goods from abroad. Because of such provisions the measure was called the Tariff of Abominations, and many expected it to be voted down. But they were wrong. The protective features of the bill appealed to a good number of people, and it finally got through Congress. President Adams, a longtime supporter of protection, signed it into law.

The Tariff of 1828 certainly destroyed whatever chance Adams had to gain southern support for re-election. It also added to the avalanche of votes that soon put Jackson in the White House. But the split between the South and the rest of the country, which the tariff brought into the open, grew deeper. It finally shook the Jackson Administration and the nation.

"Our Union: It must be preserved." Southerners had no choice but to accept the Tariff of Abominations. John C. Calhoun reflected the deep anger of South Carolina when he wrote his *Exposition and Protest*. This was a closely reasoned argument that a state might "nullify," or set aside, a federal act that it found to be unconstitutional (page 138).

For a time Calhoun set aside his doubts and joined the Jackson Administration as Vice President. But relations between Jackson and Calhoun were always distant. The Hero of New Orleans had learned how Calhoun failed to support him when he seized Florida (page 166), and this he could never forgive. Their feud finally broke into public view in 1830.

Jackson was bothered more and more by the nullification statements of Calhoun and his South Carolina followers. So at the 1830 Jefferson Day dinner, when he was called on for a toast, the stern President boomed forth, "Our Union: It must be preserved." The crowd fell silent. Calhoun, white-faced and trembling, replied, "The Union, next to our liberty, most dear." The nullifiers and Andrew Jackson were on a collision course.

"Disunion by armed forces is treason." Confrontation did not come about at once. In 1832 Congress passed a lower tariff, which Jackson considered a great improvement over the Tariff of 1828. Calhoun and his supporters thought otherwise. The South Carolinian continued to claim that nullification was the proper step for a state or section to take whenever it was threatened or injured by the federal government. He made it clear that he considered any

WE GO FOR THE UNION

The painting shows Jackson's opposition to nullification and his wide support among the people.

protective tariff reason enough for nullification.

In that same year South Carolina called a statewide convention that declared the tariffs of 1828 and 1832 "null, void, and no law" in the state after February 1, 1833. If the federal government tried to enforce the tariff, South Carolina said that it would declare its independence.

At first Jackson did not react as he might have been expected to. He remained calm in his annual message to Congress, but privately he fumed and prepared for drastic action. If the nullifiers persisted in their madness, he warned, "I will . . . have the leaders arrested and arraigned for treason." To back up this threat he pledged to send 100,000 men to put down resistance in South Carolina.

To the people of the rebellious state, he said: "The laws of the United States must be executed. . . . Those who told you that you might peaceably prevent their execution deceived you. . . . Their object is disunion. But do not be deceived by names. Disunion by armed forces is treason. Are you really ready to incur this guilt?"

Another compromise. To support his position Jackson got Congress to pass a "Force Bill." It authorized the federal government to defend its constitutional rights, but Jackson was reluctant to risk all-out war. When Henry Clay proposed a gradual lowering of tariffs, Jackson agreed and signed the bill into law. South Carolina replied by approving this compromise tariff of 1833, and voting to nullify the Force Bill.

An open break had been avoided by the Compromise of 1833. But again, as in the Missouri Compromise, the issues raised by the crisis remained to trouble the country. South Carolina had challenged the federal government and won concessions. The question of states' rights was still unsettled. An even more threatening issue remained: Could freedom and slavery coexist?

 TRY THIS!

1. Make a list of the events, decisions, and government actions that widened the gap between North and South from 1815 to 1832. Indicate which you think were most serious. **2.** Explain Thomas Jefferson's statement that the Missouri problem was "like a fire bell in the night." **3.** Compare John C. Calhoun's views on nullification with Thomas Jefferson's (page 138). Do you see any differences? If so, what are they?

ROUNDUP

Who?

Red Eagle
John C. Calhoun
John Quincy Adams
James Monroe
Robert Fulton
Henry Clay

What?

Creeks
Adams-Onís Treaty
Monroe Doctrine
turnpikes
commerce decisions
Democratic Party
Missouri Compromise
Tariff of Abominations
nullification
Force Bill
Compromise of 1833

Where?

East Florida
National Road
Cumberland Gap
Erie Canal
36° 30′ north latitude

KNOW THIS

Strengthening the Boundaries

1. How did the Creeks block national expansion?
2. What were the main provisions of the Adams-Onís Treaty?
3. How did events in Latin America affect the United States during James Monroe's administration?
4. How was Britain involved with the Monroe Doctrine?
5. Why did Monroe and Adams want the United States to go it alone in Latin America?

Transportation Opens the West

1. Why did the South vote against federal roads?
2. What were some of the developments in transportation before 1830?
3. What started the canal-building craze?
4. Why was the steamboat so important to the West?

John Marshall and Federal Power

1. Who was William Marbury?
2. What is the basis of the federal government's power to regulate business?
3. How did *McCulloch v. Maryland* uphold the Second Bank?
4. Why did Aaron Ogden lose his steamboat monopoly?

Politics in a Time of Change

1. What signs were there after 1815 that the Federalist Party was dying out?
2. Who were the candidates in 1824? What section did each represent?
3. What constitutional problem arose in the 1824 election? How was it decided?
4. How did the way Adams was elected hurt his administration?
5. What caused the heavy voter turnout in 1828?

Increasing Sectional Strife

1. What two protections for slavery were written into the United States Constitution?
2. Why did the South's attitude toward slavery harden in the 1830s?
3. What were the provisions of the Missouri Compromise?
4. How did the South hope to stop the Tariff of 1828?
5. How was the struggle over the tariff resolved?

DIG HERE!

Choose one of the following topics related to transportation for a detailed report: wagons, riverboats, roads, canals, or trails. You may want to pick a narrower topic within one of these broad areas and write about the Conestoga wagon, the flatboat, the turnpike, the Ohio Canal, the Natchez Trace, or some other special development.

For whatever topic you choose, describe it, explain its beginnings (when? where? by whom?), tell why it was needed, and how geography may have affected its introduction. Show how this development in transportation influenced people's lives socially, economically, politically. Was it more important to one part of the country than to another? Why? Is it still in use today? If not, why did it decline and disappear? For your conclusion you could deal with some of these questions:

1. Why were there so many new developments in transportation in the 1800s?
2. What general statements can you make about the way new methods of transportation affect society?
3. Would reviving some older method of travel help to protect the environment or conserve energy? Explain.

Here are some books that can give you the information you will need: Margaret Coit, *The Life History of the United States, Volume 3;* Frank Donovan, *River Boats of America;* Wilfred Owen, *Wheels;* Robert Payne, *Canal-Builders;* George Taylor, *The Transportation Revolution;* Time-Life Books.

THINK ABOUT IT

1. Did Jackson go beyond his orders when he invaded East Florida? Would he have been justified in doing so? Why, or why not?
2. Why do so many Americans fail to vote? Would changes in voting procedures cause more of them to turn out? What would the changes be? How would they help?

DO IT!

1. Write an article titled "Too Many Canals" for a business magazine published in 1834. Work in the reasons why so many canals were failing to make profits.
2. Create a series of posters, supposedly for display in local post offices, announcing each of the land acts passed between 1796 and 1841. To whom should the posters appeal? Poor farmers? Business people? Land speculators?
3. Look up the Voting Rights Acts of 1965, 1968, and 1970, and also the Twenty-sixth Amendment. Using the *Statistical Abstract of the United States* or an almanac, find out how each act affected the number of voters.

THEN AND NOW

Gibbons v. Ogden became an issue over 150 years later when New York State tried to prevent the Concorde supersonic transport from landing at one of its airports. How could *Gibbons v. Ogden* apply? Were there issues in the Concorde affair not found in the ferryboat case? Explain.

185

Andrew Jackson Represents a New Age

8

In the Age of Jackson torchlight parades, political slogans, and campaign songs heated up elections but cast no light on issues. However, conventions, party newspapers, and government jobs for loyal party members meant wider political knowledge and, in the long run, more democratic government.

1. POLITICS FOR A NEW PEOPLE

Andrew Jackson's lean face had the look of old hickory, a very tough wood. From that he got his nickname. In public Jackson behaved with genteel courtesy, and he insisted on a democratic plainness that showed him as a true man of the people. Yet some of his enemies denounced him as being ignorant of "law, history, politics, science, of everything which he who governs a country ought to know." Like Jefferson, he was a man of many contradictions.

"The people's day and the people's President." A new tone was set on March 4, 1829, Jackson's inauguration day. The weather was pleasant, and a crowd of almost 20,000 jammed around the Capitol to hear their hero take his presidential oath of office. All were intent on getting a first-hand glimpse of the white-haired, erect Jackson.

The democratic ideas of the new President were shown in a number of ways.

Previous inaugurations had been held inside the Capitol building; Jackson's took place outdoors. He walked to the ceremony and rode to the White House afterward on horseback. One observer recalled that he was followed by "countrymen, farmers, gentlemen mounted and dismounted, boys, women, children, black and white, carriages, wagons, and carts."

At the White House, Washington society could see the full effect of the change. A surging crowd, wanting to meet their President and share his refreshments, turned the affair into a shambles. "The President," as one woman reported, "after having been . . . nearly pressed to death and almost suffocated and torn to pieces by the people in their eagerness to shake hands with Old Hickory, had retreated through the back way . . . and had escaped to his lodgings." And she concluded, "It was the people's day, and the people's President, and the people would rule."

Plain republicanism. The new President spoke out for the common people. His belief was that "the great body of citizens . . . can never deliberately intend to do wrong." Left to their own instincts, the people would do what was right. To aid them in doing what was right, Jackson gave a new meaning to the Presidency. "The President," he said, "is the direct representative of the American people."

Read here of how

Jackson believed in democratic principles.
And in giving his followers government jobs.
The President got rid of his Cabinet.
But took his advice from old friends.

TIME CHART

1832	Nullification threatens the Union.
1832	Jackson vetoes the Second Bank charter.
1836	The Cherokee are moved to Oklahoma.
1836	Jackson issues the Specie Circular.
1836	Martin Van Buren is elected President.
1837	A business panic breaks out.
1840	William Henry Harrison is elected President.
1848	The Seneca Falls Convention meets.

Andrew Jackson never hesitated to wield the veto power, using it more often than all the Presidents before him. By using the veto the President, in a way, lets acts of Congress be appealed to the people.

Underlying Jacksonian democracy was a deep loyalty to Jackson himself. A self-made man, he appealed to the "real people" whose success depended "on their own industry and economy." So the true Jacksonian saw, in the old general's plain republicanism, the opportunity for every person to earn success through his or her own sweat and muscle.

Responsive officeholders. If Jackson and his followers had any theory about government, it was a belief that "the world is too much governed." Those words were the motto of their party's newspaper, and they were determined to bring government back to its barest essentials. Economy was their key word.

A popular view of Andrew Jackson. Old Hickory was a military hero before he was President.

As for other issues, Jackson's opposition to banks was well known; he dismissed them as agents of privilege. His view of public lands was that of most westerners: land should be sold cheaply to white settlers. He summed up his Indian policy in a very few words: get rid of Indians; make way for whites. Jackson was doubtful about internal improvements; he vetoed an extension of the National Road. He thought it benefited few people and was likely to increase the power of the central government. On one point he never varied: his complete devotion to the Union.

Jackson accepted it as a strict political rule that friends must be rewarded and enemies punished. This belief was summed up by a New York politician when he noted that "politicians in the United States see nothing wrong with the rule that to the victor belong the spoils." *Patronage,* as giving out government jobs was called, was the reward the victors wanted most. It kept the new state political organizations going.

In his two terms Jackson removed 1,500 out of about 10,000 officeholders. This disruption brought on deep criticism, but that didn't stop him. He energetically supported the "spoils system" as a sure way of making officeholders respond to the needs of the people. He disliked those with permanent positions because they were a privileged class. Furthermore, for the Jacksonians patronage was a way of expanding democracy. "No man," they said, "has any more right to official station than another."

A servant of the people. The system of removing officials for political reasons, once it was established, quickly spread. By the time of the Civil War, jobholders were being "hunted down like wild beasts." But whatever its faults, the system did make people aware that the government was their servant. Perhaps this was the most significant change under Jacksonian democracy. Before Jackson's time the citizen looked up to the politician; afterward it was the politician who listened respectfully to the citizen.

An idea then being promoted was that of holding national conventions to choose presidential candidates. Conventions had long been used for selecting state officeholders, but the first national organization to hold one was the Anti-Masonic Party in 1831. In May of the following year the Democrats met at Baltimore. When Jackson was nominated for a second term, he chose Martin Van Buren of New York to replace Calhoun as Vice President.

A shrewd politician. Van Buren's selection was one outcome of a scandal that had rocked Washington society. Peggy O'Neale was the daughter of a popular Washington tavernkeeper. Her first husband, a naval officer, had committed suicide; her second, John Eaton of Tennessee, was Secretary of War in Jackson's Cabinet. There were rumors that Peggy had been familiar with Eaton even before her husband's death. Because of the rumors, the aristocratic Mrs. John C. Calhoun, wife of the then Vice President, persuaded the Cabinet wives not to call upon Mrs. Eaton or receive her in their homes.

Jackson was furious. He was a friend of both Eaton and the O'Neales, and a firm believer in Peggy's good name. When his own niece sided with the Cabinet wives, he banished her from Washington, and he became more than ever an enemy of Calhoun.

The Secretary of State, Martin Van Buren, was clear of this uproar because he had no wife. Like Jackson, he was a widower. Being a shrewd politician, Van Buren suggested a way out of the tangle. He and Eaton would resign in protest. Jackson could then ask all other Cabinet members to do the same, thus ridding himself of Calhoun's supporters. The outcome made Van Buren Jackson's favorite and his chosen successor.

A Kitchen Cabinet. Jackson was able to get rid of his entire Cabinet in this offhand way because he paid so little attention to them anyway. Most were appointed in return for political favors or so that the government could represent all parts of the country. When Jackson wanted advice, he turned to a group of unofficial advisers who came to be called his Kitchen Cabinet. Its membership shifted from year to year. Sometimes it even included members of the regular Cabinet, such as Van Buren.

Other than Van Buren, the most influential member of the Kitchen Cabinet was Amos Kendall, a newspaper editor from Kentucky. He helped write a number of state papers, and as Jackson's last Postmaster General he overhauled the mail service. An English observer called him "the moving spring of the entire Administration; the thinker, planner, doer."

Almost as powerful as Amos Kendall was Francis Preston Blair of Kentucky. He edited the party newspaper, the Washington *Globe*. All loyal Jacksonians read the *Globe* with the greatest care to be sure they kept in step with the Administration.

189

Jackson's old friend Major William B. Lewis also remained near the President's side. Old Hickory never forgot that Lewis had worked harder than anyone to make him President. Others like the soon-to-be Chief Justice Roger Taney entered the magic circle for a time and then departed. But all while there made politics their sole business. And the aim of their business was to find votes for the Hero of New Orleans.

 **TRY THIS!**

1. Briefly explain Jackson's position on a) banks, b) public lands, c) Indians, d) internal improvements, e) patronage, f) the Union. **2.** Show how the method of choosing candidates for President changed in Jackson's time. **3.** Write out the conversation that might have taken place between Jackson and his niece over the Peggy Eaton affair.

2.   JACKSON IN THE WHITE HOUSE

There is no better example of Jackson's skill as a politician than the way he destroyed the Second Bank of the United States. Like many westerners, Jackson had lost money through bank failures. So he distrusted banks in general and the Second Bank of the United States in particular.

The Bank as the enemy. As we have seen, after the War of 1812 the followers of Thomas Jefferson adopted a number of Federalist ideas. Among these was the rechartering of the Bank of the United States in 1816. The First Bank had been allowed to go out of existence when its twenty-year charter expired in 1811 (page 158).

The Second Bank got off to a bumpy start. After the War of 1812 there was too much speculation in public lands. (That is, land was being bought and sold in the hope of profit, not for use.) This led to a business panic in 1819. A wave of bankruptcies, business failures, and bank closings washed over the country. The United States Bank was supposed to help in just such difficulties, but unfortunately its first two managers had not understood their jobs. They had made the problem worse by letting the Bank itself speculate in western lands and by putting out too much paper money in

the form of many bank notes. And some of the Bank's local branches fell into the hands of thieves. For example, the directors of the Baltimore branch robbed it of over three million dollars.

When the Panic of 1819 forced the Bank to call in its loans, the West was hurt most of all. In that section people were short of ready money, and the many land foreclosures convinced them that the Bank was their enemy. Not until 1823, when Nicholas Biddle became its president, did the Bank straighten out the money supply and bring lending under control.

"I will kill the Bank!" Like the Jeffersonians of earlier times, Jackson was absolutely convinced that Congress had no power to charter a bank. He believed as well that the Bank had given money to Adams's campaign against him in 1828.

Read here of how

Jackson distrusted the Second Bank.
In a mighty struggle he got rid of it.
Jackson disliked Indians, too.
And moved thousands of them to the West.

Jackson's attack on it began when he launched his campaign for re-election. The Bank's charter was to run out in 1836, and its supporters realized that once he was re-elected, Jackson would surely oppose giving it another.

Nicholas Biddle decided to try immediately for another charter. Leading members of Congress like Daniel Webster and Henry Clay assured him that his chances were excellent, as about a third of Jackson's own followers favored the Bank's cause. And the new charter answered some of Jackson's complaints. It limited the number of branches, gave the Bank more control of the money supply, and would run out in only fifteen years. Biddle had even appointed many Jackson Democrats to positions in the Bank and had worked hard for Jackson's policy of paying off the national debt.

When Congress voted for the charter by a thumping majority, this seemed to show the cleverness of Biddle's policy. In addition Pennsylvania, where the Bank had its main office, gave it strong support. If Jackson vetoed the charter, he would risk losing that state's large electoral vote.

But Biddle had overlooked one critical point. Jackson's fighting spirit had been roused. When Van Buren saw him after being some time away from Washington, he found the President gaunt and ill. Yet he was unyielding as he declared, "The Bank, Mr. Van Buren, is trying to kill me, *but I will kill it!*" And he did.

In a powerful veto message Jackson made his fight one between the privileges of the few and the welfare of the many. His struggle with the "monster" Bank was intended to preserve equal opportunity. "It is to be regretted," he said in his veto message, "that the rich and powerful too often

bend the acts of government to their selfish purpose." Jackson wanted none of this.

Total victory. The Bank's supporters fumbled badly. They even failed to defend its real achievements. The Bank received and paid out federal funds. It stabilized the nation's money supply. Furthermore, it shifted needed funds from the wealthy East to the underdeveloped West and South. As a central bank, it kept check on business growth and the loans of other banks.

The Bank's very success was its undoing. By acting effectively the Bank had shown how powerful it was—and roused jealousy on all sides. Biddle was just the kind of enemy Jackson liked. And once the Old Hero entered a battle, nothing short of total victory would satisfy him.

In the 1832 election, the Democrats took their stand behind Jackson and his Bank veto. It was all they had to do. Old Hickory won a smashing victory over Henry Clay and the National Republicans.

Instead of waiting for the controversy to die down, Biddle again pressed for a new charter. That was all Jackson needed to move in for the kill. He declared that government deposits in the Bank were unsafe. Meanwhile, banks in Boston, New York, Philadelphia, and Baltimore were eager to receive government funds.

Biddle's next move was a disaster. He stopped renewing loans, thus drastically reducing the amount of credit available in the country. A near depression struck the business community, and Jackson quickly blamed it on Biddle. Jackson's enemy had proved him right. The Bank of the United States *did* have too much power.

"John Marshall has made his opinion." In dealing with the Indians of the South, Jackson was just as ruthless as he was with the Bank. Well over 50,000 members of the

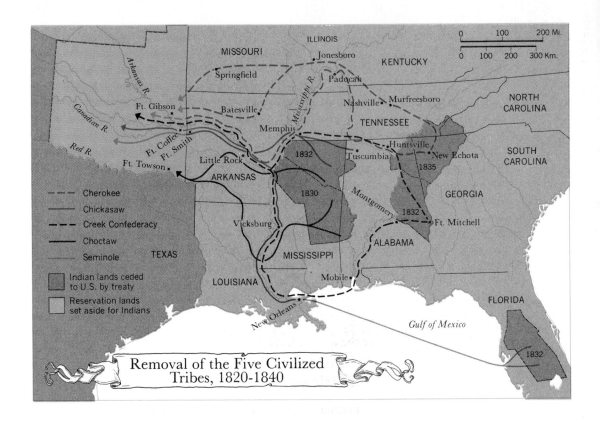

Removal of the Five Civilized
Tribes, 1820-1840

In the lands beyond the Mississippi River wood and water were scarce. Crops were poor. The Indians longed for the fertile fields, forests, and streams of their homeland.

Cherokee, Choctaw, Chickasaw, Creek, and Seminole tribes lived there on 33 million acres of land. After their defeat at the time of the War of 1812 (pages 156–157) most of them had settled down and become farmers. They adopted European crops and farming methods, and many accepted Christianity. The Cherokee invented a system of writing and lived under their own constitution, with their own officials and courts. The position of these tribes was secured by federal treaties, one of them signed by Andrew Jackson.

By any kind of justice the Five Civi-

lized Tribes (as they were called) should have been allowed to keep their lands, but they had drawn the envy of their white neighbors. Georgia broke the treaties and took over Creek and Cherokee lands.

The Jackson Administration met this lawless act by trying to persuade the Indians to remove themselves to the West. It gave them lands in what is now Oklahoma. Instead of moving, the Cherokee decided to sue the state of Georgia in the federal courts. In two cases the Supreme Court upheld their claims, but Georgia defied the decisions. Jackson himself is supposed to have said, "John Marshall has made his opinion; now let him enforce it."

The trail of tears. A delegation of Indians called on Jackson at his home in Ten-

192

nessee to protest. He told them that if they continued to oppose removal, it would lead to their destruction. Reluctantly the Indians gave way. They agreed to begin their migration in 1832.

The tragedy that followed was truly terrible. White settlers moved in and took over the lands before the Indians had left. Politicians and government agents combined to cheat them. Even the money to pay for their migration was stolen. The Choctaw were forced to leave Mississippi in bitter winter weather. The thinly clad, often barefoot, Indians endured such sufferings that their journey was called "the trail of tears." The same fate awaited the other tribes; the Creek Indians of Alabama were sent out of the state in chains. Only the Seminole fought back. For three years, under their remarkable leader Osceola, they held off federal troops.

Of the 60,000 Indians who were sent away, as many as 15,000 may have died. The removal policy disturbed the consciences of some Americans and turned large numbers against Jackson. Senator Frelinghuysen of New Jersey asked, "Do the obligations of justice change with the color of the skin?" May the white man, he wondered, "disregard . . . moral principles when an Indian shall be concerned?"

TRY THIS!

1. Write a speech that Nicholas Biddle might have delivered defending the Second Bank of the United States. 2. Compare the ways Jackson dealt with the Bank and with the Indians of the South. Did he show the same personal qualities in each case? Why do today's historians admire his methods in one case and disapprove of them in the other?

CAPTURED BY TREACHERY

As a child of about eleven, he fought against Andrew Jackson. Grown to manhood, Osceola tried to persuade the Seminole people of Florida to reject the "treaties" which took away their land.

Efforts to remove his people to the West led Osceola to start the Seminole War of 1835. First he hid the women, children, and old men in a great swamp; then he attacked the federal forces. One United States officer after another lost his way, his temper, his army, and finally his military reputation trying to conquer the wily young chief.

In the end, General Thomas S. Jesup seized Osceola under a flag of truce. People were shocked at such treachery. They had been demanding Osceola's scalp. Now they wanted Jesup's.

But Osceola remained a prisoner. In three years he was dead, not even forty years old.

3. MARTIN VAN BUREN AND THE WHIGS

The strong steps Andrew Jackson took as President led his enemies to the formation of a new party, the Whigs. They took the label "Whig" to remind Americans of their Revolutionary ancestors. In colonial times the Whigs had been against King George III; now Jackson was called "King Andrew" by those who saw him as a tyrant.

The Whig Party's chief issue was President Jackson himself. This was spelled out by the great orator Daniel Webster. "According to . . . the President," he said, "although Congress may have passed a law, and although the Supreme Court may have pronounced it constitutional, yet it is no law at all if he . . . sees fit . . . to repeal or annul it."

To the new Whig Party rallied not only people of property and high standing but a number of working people and small farmers as well. Generally the Whigs were more conservative than Jackson's followers, and they distrusted mass democracy. Furthermore, they felt that Congress ought to have greater power than the President.

Triumphant Democrats—formidable Whigs. The dream of Jefferson, and later of Jackson's followers, was that one day the debt of the United States government would be paid off. The dream came true in 1836, partly because of a boom in land sales. Between 1834 and 1836 the amount of land sold by the federal government increased from 4.5 million acres to over 20 million. For the first time federal income from land sales was greater than from tariff payments. Total government receipts ran far ahead of expenses. When the federal surplus totaled 36 million dollars, Congress passed a measure that would distribute most of it to the states.

Jackson was more concerned with providing a dependable money supply and putting an end to speculating in public land (pages 173-174) than with the surplus. In that same year, 1836, he issued the Specie Circular. According to this order the federal land offices were to accept only gold and silver, not paper bank notes, as payment for federal lands. The supply of gold was limited, so the President's action soon slowed down the speculation.

Jackson was also busy getting his Vice President, Martin Van Buren, nominated and elected President. To bring this about, he made use of federal jobs and of every other means available. Since the leaders of the new Whig Party were badly divided, they put up strong candidates in all parts of the country. Their purpose was to divide the electoral vote so that no one would have a majority, as had happened in 1824 (pages 178-179). Then the election would again go to the House of Representatives, where the Whigs believed they would win.

The plan backfired. When the returns were counted, Van Buren had carried the day. He had won by a sizable majority of electoral votes. However, his margin of the popular vote was only 25,688 out of more than a million and a half votes cast. (In the South Van Buren had run far behind the

---

Read here of how

Jackson's enemies started the Whig Party. But Jackson made Van Buren his successor. Then a depression rocked the country. And helped to elect Harrison.

---

totals cast for Jackson in two previous elections.) The Democrats seemed triumphant, but the Whigs had showed formidable strength.

Congressman Davy Crockett disgustedly wrote of the new President, "Van Buren is as opposite to General Jackson as dung is to a diamond. Jackson is open, bold, warmhearted, confiding, and passionate to a fault. Van Buren is secret, sly, selfish, cold, calculating, distrustful, treacherous, and if he could gain an object as well by openness as intrigue, he would choose the latter." This was not fair and not true, but it shows how the eighth President struck many of his fellow citizens. A smooth, clever man, he had earned a reputation for shrewdness in the rough-and-tumble of New York State politics. And he had been very wise in hitching his career to Jackson's star.

No more state bank notes. Andrew Jackson, it was said, left office with only two regrets: he hadn't been able to hang John C. Calhoun or shoot Henry Clay. President Van Buren faced greater problems. There were plenty of signs that business was in trouble, and that a first-rate financial crisis was brewing.

The Panic of 1837 had many causes, but the most important was the destruction of the Second Bank of the United States. It had controlled banking practices throughout the country, and no other agency had been set up to do this in its place. Government deposits had been placed in state banks. And as these banks were in the hands of President Jackson's friends, they were soon called "pet banks."

Some of the "pet banks" were well run, but others stretched their credit much too rapidly. This was especially true in the West. There the need for roads, bridges,

These are notes issued by state banks during the 1830s. The notes were used as money. People were willing to accept such notes at face value— even three dollar bills—if the bank had a good reputation for paying its debts.

and canals led to great increases in bank loans. From 1832 to 1836 state bank notes, which circulated as money, expanded from 59 million dollars to 140 million. The notes were backed by overpriced land or by public faith alone. In 1836 the government said it would no longer accept state bank notes in payment for public lands. Banks failed. Prices fell. People couldn't pay their debts. This brought on the Panic of 1837.

Food riots. A poor wheat crop at this time was forcing the United States to import grain from other countries. This had to be paid for in gold and silver, tightening the money supply even further. A wave of bankruptcies, bank failures, and business disruptions followed. Unemployment spread until there were food riots in the cities. Labor unions, which had just begun

195

A banner carried by Whigs in 1840. It assures voters that William Henry Harrison is "O.K." This catchy slang term was just coming into use. Why would a log cabin appeal to voters?

to grow, were shattered by the deepening depression.

The Whigs placed the blame for the general suffering on Jackson's money policies. Van Buren made it easier for them to do so because he would not let the federal government take any step to help the people. "All communities are apt to look to government too much," he warned Congress.

"Tippecanoe and Tyler too." In the bad times the country was undergoing, the Whigs looked better and better. Their promise to help the people by helping business contrasted sharply with Van Buren's do-nothing image. In addition the Whigs adopted the word *democracy*, which they could see had great appeal.

For their candidate in the 1840 election, the Whigs wanted a war hero like Jackson. William Henry Harrison, the victor of Tippecanoe (page 156), seemed to fill the bill. With an anti-Jackson Democrat, John Tyler, running for Vice President, their slogan became "Tippecanoe and Tyler too."

When a Democratic paper sneered that Harrison would be better off with a log cabin, a barrel of hard cider, and a pension, the Whigs had the theme of their campaign. Suddenly, all over the country Harrison's symbols became a log cabin, a barrel of hard cider, and a coonskin cap. Real issues were raised by both parties, but they were kept in the background. Instead, the Whig campaign concentrated on presenting the wealthy Harrison as a simple farmer whose opponent, Van Buren, dined

off gold plates in the White House. "Van, Van, the used-up man," chanted Harrison's followers.

The *Democratic Review* admitted, "We have taught them to conquer us." Indeed they had. When the votes were counted, Harrison had swept nineteen of the 26 states. He carried all of the North except Illinois and New Hampshire. Congress too fell to the Whigs. Most significant, 80 per cent of the eligible voters had turned out. Two parties were now firmly established. A revolution had taken place in American politics.

 TRY THIS!

1. Show how the Whigs were able to blame the Panic of 1837 on the Democrats. **2.** Explain what the *Democratic Review* meant when it said of the Whig Party, "We have taught them to conquer us." **3.** Compare the Whig campaign of 1840 with the "selling" of a political candidate in a modern election.

4. RELIGIOUS CHANGE IN AMERICA

The exciting Presidency of Andrew Jackson is sometimes called "an age of ferment." Change was sweeping the country, and its effects were felt in religion, education, business, and every other part of American life. Every social problem from the treatment of prisoners and the insane to the need for eliminating war was investigated, preached about, argued over. The political changes of those days were only the tip of an iceberg.

"There is always some protester." In all of this, Americans had not been content with just showing the world the way to democracy. They wanted to create a society in which things could be tried that everyone had thought were impossible.

Reform-minded people saw themselves as children of a successful revolution against British rule. To them revolution was natural. They welcomed it elsewhere in the world as an imitation of their own effort. And at home some of them were forever ready to demand the end of this or that abuse because it went against American beliefs. Ralph Waldo Emerson, the prophet of American reform, observed, "There is always . . . some protester against cruelty . . . some defender of the slave against the politician and the merchant, some champion of . . . humanity against the rich and luxurious . . . some pleader for

---

Read here of how

Religious groups changed in America.
And helped to change America.

---

peace . . . who will not stoop to infamy when all are gone mad."

American reformers have always tended to believe that however unpopular they might be at the moment, they had the power of right on their side. "One man more right than his neighbor is a majority of one already," said Henry David Thoreau, one of the most famous protesters of them all. In the mid-1800s, Americans firmly believed in progress. Their nation was rapidly expanding toward the Pacific, and the railroad and telegraph were drawing the states and sections together. This seemed to them convincing proof that everything was moving in an upward direction. Progress and expansion made reformers sure that they could conquer all social evils. With so much going for them, how could they fail?

Religions of the poor. Something like a religious revolution took place in the United States between 1790 and 1850. The first federal census, in 1790, showed the three largest churches to be the Anglican (Episcopalian), Presbyterian, and Congregational. But by the middle of the nineteenth century those groups had been displaced by the Roman Catholics, the Methodists, and the Baptists. All three of these churches had been persecuted in Great Britain. But in the United States they had flourished. They had one thing in common: they were the religions of the ordinary people and the poor.

Catholicism had flourished as German and Irish immigrants poured into the country after 1840. To be sure, Catholics often faced discrimination, but their large numbers soon gave them political influence. They had not enjoyed that in Britain.

Revival meetings were in the tradition of the Great Awakening a century earlier (page 63).

Before the 1840s American Catholics had been members of a small, highly regarded group. Heavy immigration changed this. Faced with opposition from the native-born, they became the strongest Catholic organization in the English-speaking world. Because they felt that the public schools were really Protestant institutions, they set about building their own school system. As millions of immigrants filled the cities, the Catholic Church tried very hard to give its members a sense of unity and of belonging.

Churches for an ever-moving society.
The Methodists were important in England, but they were still overshadowed by the Church of England. In the United States they became a well-organized group

with enormous social and political influence.

Baptist success was still more striking. A hundred years earlier they had been a minority, subject to all sorts of discrimination even in America (page 62). But Baptist preaching and teaching, like that of the Methodists, appealed to the ordinary working people of the day.

The Baptist message was usually carried by a "farmer preacher." Generally he settled on a tract of land, put his crops in, and then held religious services for his neighbors in his new home. Methodists were more highly organized. They had officials called bishops, but the bishops were not far away in great cathedrals. They "rode circuit" through the vast American countryside like the humblest of their clergy. Both Baptists and Methodists were struggling to meet the needs of an ever-moving, ever-changing society.

Revivals and reform. By the mid-1800s American Protestants were depending heavily on revivals to spread their message. Country people found release from the isolation of their lives by gathering in vast "camp meetings." These were highly emotional affairs where the emphasis was on the "old-time religion," energetic preaching and singing, and a lot of socializing.

Revival meetings were less dignified than some other religious gatherings. They were often criticized for crudeness and emotionalism. But defenders pointed to their heartwarming informality and compared it to the coldness of regular religious services. It might be said that the revivals had "soul."

The revivals were also criticized for failing to deal with the social problems of their day. But revivalist preachers expected those they converted to work for the abolition of slavery, the improvement of prisons, or against such social evils as heavy drinking. And most of the leaders in all these reform movements came from the popular churches.

New faiths for a new world. The older religions were changing too. Throughout New England, Congregational parishes switched to Unitarianism. They stressed the unity of God. And they accepted the teaching of William Ellery Channing that every human being possessed "an element truly divine and worthy of all reverence." For some New Englanders this was not enough. Men like Ralph Waldo Emerson embraced Transcendentalism, which preached that the seeds of eternal truth were buried within every human soul.

Both Unitarianism and Transcenden-

talism lent themselves to social reform. As an example, the Unitarian minister Theodore Parker preached freedom for the slave, and Emerson's friend Bronson Alcott went to live in a commune. Henry David Thoreau, Emerson's neighbor in Concord, Massachusetts, protested the Mexican War, calling for civil disobedience.

Meanwhile, other new faiths swept the backcountry of New England, upstate New York, and the shores of the Great Lakes. A wandering preacher, William Henry Miller, gathered his followers into the Adventist movement. They waited the second coming of Christ and the end of the world, which they expected at any moment. Equally striking was the appeal of the Spiritualists, who promised contact with the dead.

Few of the new faiths had a greater effect than that of the Mormons. The Church of Jesus Christ of Latter-Day Saints, as the Mormons called themselves, was founded by Joseph Smith in 1830. They followed their prophet from upstate New York to Ohio, Missouri, and then Nauvoo, Illinois. At each stop they were persecuted for their practice of plural marriage and their belief that new Scriptures had been revealed to them. Smith was lynched in 1844, and two years later Nauvoo was destroyed by a mob. Under the brilliant leadership of Brigham Young the Mormons struck out into the western wilderness. They settled in the valley of the Great Salt Lake. Later the Mormons founded the Territory of Utah.

The Mormons had a tight organization that still allowed for democratic participation. Under it they changed a desert into a green Eden. Their strength came in part from the belief in what they called the "United Order." This meant that security came from cooperation and not from the

199

Religion in America

Both "mainstream" churches like the Congregationalists (above) and such tiny sects as the Quakers (right) have influenced America. Quakers (the Society of Friends) opposed slavery in colonial times and war two hundred years later, in the 1960s. Many Congregationalist ministers were activists in the cause of American independence, as was Lemuel Haynes, shown here in the pulpit. Haynes fought at Concord and Ticonderoga. He was a black man, though he served only white congregations in New England.

200

fierce competition found elsewhere within the United States.

The new beliefs clearly showed how, in the United States, religious feeling could give birth to great varieties of faith. Older institutions and old ways were being made to point in new directions. The past was a fertile field in which hope for a better future could flourish.

 TRY THIS!

1. Account for the religious revolution in the United States between 1790 and 1850. **2.** Show how Catholics, Baptists, and Methodists tried to reach and serve the members of their congregations. **3.** List five new religious movements of the 1800s. Who were their leaders? What were their beliefs?

5.   THE STRUGGLE FOR SOCIAL REFORM

In popular religion, the excitement of revival campaigns was generally followed by a period of "backsliding." People's everyday lives did not seem much affected by a stirring religious experience. In the same way, nineteenth-century society was not changed as much as most reformers said it ought to be. Nevertheless, the accomplishments of the period were considerable.

Communal living. The decades before the Civil War saw a number of attempts to found new kinds of communities. Groups of men and women withdrew from cities and towns and attempted to live according to some ideal plan. Brook Farm, just outside Boston, was founded by writers and other intellectuals; it lasted only a few years. Robert Owen, an English manufacturer, established a socialist community at New Harmony, Indiana, which also failed. On the other hand, communes rooted in religious belief were more successful.

A few years after the Civil War a reporter from the New York *Herald* surveyed some of the religious communities that were still flourishing. The Amana Society in Iowa, the Oneida Community in New York State, and various Shaker settlements impressed him by their peacefulness and prosperity. Because of their prosperity, however, communes were often turned into ordinary corporations or cooperatives. Oneida took this route in 1880; Amana in 1932. Still, the number of communes planned and begun from the 1830s to the 1850s shows how widespread was the urge to change one's way of life.

Horace Mann and the one-room school. Educational reformers hoped to change society by giving schooling to all. There was wide public support for this movement, for many felt that democracy could work only if everybody was educated. Then, too, the "little old one-room schoolhouse" was often too hot in spring, too cold in winter, and closed most of the year. With its underpaid and poorly educated teacher, it badly needed modernization.

In the 1830s a large-scale effort to improve school buildings, courses of study,

---

Read here of how

New communities were founded.
Horace Mann reformed the schools.
Dorothea Dix helped the insane.
And Lyman Beecher fought against liquor.

---

and teacher training got under way. Its single most influential figure was Horace Mann, secretary of the Massachusetts State Board of Education. His yearly reports to the legislature contained a well-worked-out philosophy of education. Also a Whig Party politician, he understood that the voters might not be willing to pay the taxes for better schools. Against this feeling he argued that "a republican form of government without intelligence in the people must be on a vast scale what a madhouse without superintendent or keepers would be on a small one."

Mann's argument was responsible for increasing the Massachusetts school year to six months, doubling public spending on education, establishing fifty new high schools, and improving the professional training of teachers.

In Connecticut and Rhode Island, Henry Barnard fought for down-to-earth reforms in education. In 1840 Governor Seward of New York called for free schools where immigrant children would be taught in their native languages. The South was slow in providing public education for its people, but among the first state universities were those in North Carolina, Georgia, South Carolina, and Virginia.

Reforming the delinquent. In 1835 a French visitor wrote that in the United States "for the first time the idea of reforming as well as of punishing the delinquent formed a part of prison discipline." It was not really the first time, but New York and Pennsylvania early established workshops where a prisoner could learn a trade. At the Boston House of Refuge there was a system of self-government by which boy inmates were taught self-reliance, self-criticism, and responsibility. Many of those who led the prison reform movement were

ministers, and their interest came from a wish to save the criminal's soul.

The concern for social reform also launched campaigns to improve the lot of the mentally ill. No person argued more eloquently for better care of the insane than the gentle Dorothea Dix of Hamden, Maine. While teaching Sunday school at a jail near Boston, she stumbled upon a group of mental patients confined there in a bitterly cold, desolate room. There was, she was told, no other place for them.

"Beaten with rods, lashed into obedience." Once aroused, Dorothea Dix forced the Massachusetts legislature to listen to her charges. She told them that insane persons under their control were locked "in cages, closets, cellars, stalls, pens! Chained, naked, beaten with rods and lashed into obedience." Under pressure, the legislature voted funds to expand and improve the hospital for the insane at Worcester.

Miss Dix's success inspired her to push her campaign across the Massachusetts border into a dozen other states and the District of Columbia. She said, "I encounter nothing that a determined will does not enable me to vanquish."

The campaign against liquor. In 1810 over 14,000 distilleries were producing about three gallons of liquor a year for every man, woman, and child in the United States. With such production came ample evidence of excessive drinking. Whiskey and "corn squeezin's" were signs of hospitality regularly served at harvest suppers, barn raisings, quilting bees, christenings, and even ordinations. Liquor sometimes took the place of money in isolated regions and was often used "as a preventive of disease."

After 1825 the campaign against drinking flourished. Six of the Reverend Lyman

202

Education in America

Educational opportunities for American women were not exciting. They were usually taught such "polite" accomplishments as drawing and music. Opportunities for boys were limited too—by ill-trained, underpaid teachers. Which of these young rascals is *least* likely to win the "Reward for Industry"?

A Reward for Industry

Beecher's sermons against liquor were printed and circulated that year. In 1826 the American Society for the Promotion of Temperance was organized. From temperance presses poured grim stories of promising lives ruined by liquor. Ten years later the Society split into those who wanted to persuade individuals to drink less *(temperance)* and those who wanted to forbid all forms of alcohol by law *(prohibition)*. The prohibitionists soon became more prominent.

Prejudice against the foreign-born entered the prohibition campaign as German and Irish immigrants flowed into the country. Germans were used to gathering with their families on Sundays in beer halls and beer gardens. This practice outraged defenders of the strict Puritan sabbath. Older Americans also blamed the frequent poverty of the Irish immigrants on their drinking habits. Sharper restriction of the liquor trade soon followed. Numerous Massachusetts towns halted it altogether, and in 1851 Maine instituted statewide prohibition.

There was a wave of imitations of the Maine law, but the campaign for prohibition soon died out. After 1855 it was replaced by concern for the problem of slavery (pages 250–253 in Chapter 10).

 TRY THIS!

1. Trace the part played by organized religion in most of the reform movements of the early 1800s. 2. Show what Horace Mann did to improve education. Try writing a speech that he might have used to persuade a small town in Massachusetts to build a high school.

6.   A NEW ROLE FOR WOMEN

From colonial days women had worked side by side with men in building a new way of life in America. Abigail Adams had urged her husband, John, to "remember the ladies" as he and men from the other colonies met in Philadelphia to declare independence (page 81). But women were thought to be inferior to men both in physical strength and mental ability. They did not become full partners in the new democratic experience.

A man's world. In the mid-1800s the rights of all women were limited by law and custom. Married women had the fewest rights. According to the laws of most states, husband and wife were one, and that one was the husband. A married woman could not sign contracts. She had no claim to money she earned. And she could not control property even when it was her own. A father could make it part of his will that if he died, his children should be taken from their mother's control. Furthermore, as late as 1850 in most states a

---

Read here of how

Women won some basic human rights.
They produced inspired leaders.
And took up new careers.
But still had less than full equality.

---

husband had the right to beat his wife "with a reasonable instrument." (The reasonable instrument approved in one New York court was a horsewhip!)

Popular magazines and books promoted a "Cult of True Womanhood," which taught that woman's place was in the home and that the ideal womanly virtues included submissiveness, innocence, piety, and domesticity. Articles with such titles as "Woman, a Being to Come Home To" and "Woman, Man's Best Friend" appeared in women's magazines.

Dorothea Dix had singlehandedly shown what womanly strength and determination could do. An unmarried woman like her, or one with a cooperative husband, might carve out a meaningful career. One who did so was Phoebe Palmer, a lay

preacher of the Methodist Church, who pioneered social-welfare projects in the New York slums. Under her guidance religious services were introduced into the Tombs, the New York City prison. In 1850, she organized the Five Points Mission in New York's worst slum. This was long before settlement houses were established there and in other cities by later reformers. Equally far-reaching was Phoebe Palmer's creation in 1858 of the Ladies' Christian Association. From this idea grew the later YWCA.

The pioneer work of Phoebe Palmer showed a shift in the churches from spiritual concerns to social work. By the time of the Civil War it was accepted that churches ought to care about the physical good of the people, as well as their spiritual

Maria Mitchell won fame as an astronomer by discovering a comet in 1847.

205

needs. Since women were already expected to take part in church activities, this opened a new avenue for them. But too often they found themselves organized into "ladies' auxiliaries." In effect they did much of the work, while the men who ran the church got most of the credit. In the church as in the rest of society, a woman could make her mark, but it was against heavy odds. America was still distinctly a man's world.

A few determined women. Because there were immigrant women to work as servants, middle-class women were freed from housework. At the same time, however, there were few employment opportunities for middle-class women. In colonial times some women had served as doctors and had spoken for themselves in court. But medical schools and law schools had made these occupations more professional. As doctors and lawyers formed their own societies, they set up strict new rules for entry. Some of these limited the practice of medicine and law to men.

The teaching profession was open to women. But there were no schools where they could receive training equal to that of men teachers. A movement developed to improve educational opportunities for women. Catherine Beecher, Emma Willard, and Mary Lyon established seminaries for the education of girls. They hoped to train school teachers who would carry both learning and republican principles into every classroom.

The writer Margaret Fuller thought that the idea of natural superiority of males was nonsense. "We would have every path laid open to women as freely as to men," she wrote. And she was not afraid to suggest changes.

Margaret Fuller battled for women's admission to the professions. Here and

These book bindery workers earned much less than men doing the same jobs.

Though a qualified physician, Elizabeth Blackwell was barred from New York hospitals.

there, on a token basis, barriers began to fall. The Blackwell sisters, Elizabeth and Emily, qualified as medical doctors and went into practice. The admission of Antoinette Brown to Oberlin College in 1847 and her later ordination as a minister showed that a woman could sometimes unlock even the most unlikely doors.

"I wanted to work, but I wanted to choose my task." In 1848 the demand for equality between the sexes increased dramatically. That year Lucretia Mott and Elizabeth Cady Stanton called together the first women's rights convention. The meeting was held at Seneca Falls, New York, and issued a statement similar in language to the Declaration of Independence. This time the offender was "man," not King George. "Man" was accused of having tried "in every way he could, to destroy [woman's] confidence in her own powers,

to lessen her self-respect, and to make her willing to lead a dependent . . . life."

The assembly resolved that women must have "immediate admission to all the rights and privileges which belong to them as citizens of the United States." When Elizabeth Stanton wanted to include voting rights along with the convention's other demands, Lucretia Mott, a Quaker, warned against it. "Elizabeth," she said, "thee will make us ridiculous." The suffrage resolution was adopted and included in the Seneca Falls Declaration. But the battle for voting rights had only begun.

Susan B. Anthony, an educator and reformer, complained to a women's rights meeting, "Men like to see women . . . repair the damages of society! to claim that patching business is in 'woman's proper sphere,' but to be master of circumstances—that is man's sphere."

Such charges were the signs of a deep, burning resentment. Charlotte Woodward, a nineteen-year-old woman, was roused by the Seneca Falls Convention. Bitterly, she wrote, "For my own obscure self, I can say that every fiber of my being rebelled, although silently, all the hours that I sat and sewed gloves for a miserable pittance which after it was earned could never be mine. I wanted to work, but I wanted to choose my task and I wanted to collect my wages, not my father. That was my form of rebellion against the life into which I was born."

Women's work. The truth was that women played an enormous role in the everyday life of the United States. Men and women worked as partners in earning a living and rearing families. More than one planter's wife noted that she was expected to be manager, bookkeeper, nurse, and overseer in addition to her housekeeping duties on the plantation. A farm woman was up before dawn and working all the time until well after dusk. Her daughters learned early not only to cook and sew but also how to pitch hay and plow a field. Hard work was the everyday rule.

One young girl remembered how her family built a house on the frontier when they were left fatherless. "We held a family council after breakfast, and though I was only twelve, I took an eager and determined part," she recalled. "I loved work— it had always been my favorite form of recreation." In two weeks she, her mother, two sisters, and two brothers finished a sturdy house.

Young women also went to work in factories. The money they earned often went to help their families pay debts. Wages were low. By the mid-1830s women workers were prepared to strike against efforts to cut their wages. When members of the Massachusetts legislature urged them to trust their male employers to safeguard their rights, one woman had a blunt answer. "Bad as is the condition of so many women, it would be much worse if they had nothing but the boasted protection of men to rely upon," she declared, "but they have . . . learned . . . to look for help from the strong and resolute of their own sex."

The promise of equality. In one area, women's supremacy was unquestioned. They were the keepers of the nation's conscience. They filled the ranks of Sunday School teachers. They were responsible for training children in moral values. Women took part in the temperance movement. They supported public education. They urged more humane treatment for criminals and for the insane. And nowhere was their impact stronger than in the fight against slavery. Men might lead the abolitionist movement, but women were the foot soldiers who carried on the day-by-day struggle. They held meetings. They circulated petitions. And they demanded and won the right to speak in public. This was an important victory in the struggle for women's rights.

 TRY THIS!

1. Briefly show how each of these advanced the cause of women's rights: a) Catherine Beecher, b) Emma Willard, c) Mary Lyon, d) Margaret Fuller, e) Phoebe Palmer, f) Elizabeth and Emily Blackwell, g) Antoinette Brown, h) Elizabeth Cady Stanton, i) Lucretia Mott, j) Susan B. Anthony. **2.** Describe the role played by women in the economic growth of the United States. **3.** Explain how women were "the keepers of the nation's conscience."

ROUNDUP

Who?

Peggy Eaton
Martin Van Buren
William Henry
    Harrison
Ralph Waldo Emerson
Henry David Thoreau
William Ellery
    Channing
Brigham Young
Horace Mann
Dorothea Dix
Elizabeth Cady Stanton
Phoebe Palmer
Susan B. Anthony

What?

patronage
Kitchen Cabinet
Second Bank
Five Civilized Tribes
trail of tears
Whig Party
Specie Circular
pet banks
Panic of 1837
revival meetings
Mormons
Seneca Falls
    Convention

Where?

trail of tears
Seneca Falls
Oberlin

KNOW THIS

Politics for a New People

1. Why was Andrew Jackson called "the people's President"?
2. What motto sums up the Jacksonian idea of government? What does the motto mean?
3. How did Jackson justify his method of appointing people to government jobs? What effect did it have?

Jackson in the White House

1. What were some problems of the Second Bank of the United States in its early years?
2. List the Second Bank's accomplishments.
3. Why did Jackson oppose the Bank? How did he kill it?
4. What was Jackson's Indian policy?

Martin Van Buren and the Whigs

1. How did the Whig Party get its name? What did the Whigs stand for?
2. How was the government able to pay off its debt?
3. Why did Jackson issue the Specie Circular?
4. What was the strength of Democrats in 1836? of the Whigs?
5. How did the Whigs win the election of 1840?

Religious Change in America

1. What underlying beliefs gave American reformers confidence?
2. Why did American Catholicism grow rapidly after 1840?
3. What were revivals like? Why were they so popular?
4. Why were the Mormons so successful? Why were they persecuted? Where did they finally settle?

The Struggle for Social Reform

1. Which kind of ideal community succeeded best?
2. What was the goal of educational reform in the 1800s?
3. Why was there a drive to reform, not punish, criminals?
4. Who brought about better treatment of the insane?
5. What caused the early campaigns against drinking?

A New Role for Women

1. How would you describe the status of American women in the mid-1800s?
2. What progress did women make in the professions?
3. How did churches help to expand women's roles?

DIG HERE!

Look up one of the experiments in communal living begun in the mid-1800s. If possible, compare it with a similar group of the 1960s or 1970s. Consider questions like these:

1. On what principles or beliefs was the community based? What conditions or ideas of its own time did it reject?
2. What kind of people joined (age, background, interests)?
3. What were its operating rules?
4. Was anything in its rules or lifestyle hard for some members to accept? Explain.
5. Was there a single leader? What were his/her personal qualities?
6. How did other Americans react to this community or group?
7. Why did the group you examined succeed or fail?

Here are some religious and communal groups of the 1800s: Amana, Aurora, Bethel, Brook Farm, Millerites, Mormons, New Harmony, Oneida, Separatists, Seventh-Day Adventists, Shakers, Spiritualists. An interesting modern community is the Brotherhood of the Spirit in Warwick, Massachusetts.

Some helpful books are: Edward D. Andrews, *The People Called Shakers;* Doris Faber, *The Perfect Life: The Shakers in America;* Rosabeth Kanter, *Commitment and Community;* Marguerite Melcher, *The Shaker Adventure;* Robert Mullan, *The Latter-Day Saints;* Charles Nordhoff, *Communistic Societies of the United States;* Ron R. Roberts, *New Communes;* Bernard Weisberger, *They Gathered at the River.*

THINK ABOUT IT

1. Civil Service began around a hundred years ago. Merit, not political influence, was to be used in filling government jobs. Now public officials are sometimes called insensitive to the people's needs and wishes. Would the "spoils system" work today? Why, or why not? Can you describe a possible third method?
2. The American attitude toward reform movements is described in the fourth paragraph on page 197. Do you agree that this still applies? Why, or why not?

DO IT!

1. Organize a panel discussion in which students play the roles of a German Catholic priest, a Baptist farmer-preacher, and a Methodist bishop and tell why their churches have grown rapidly.
2. Report on one of the reformers or women's rights leaders in this chapter. Describe personal characteristics and circumstances, inspirations, goals, obstacles, and achievements.

THEN AND NOW

Presidential candidates are chosen today much as they were in Jackson's day. At national conventions party delegates draw up platforms and decide on candidates. Does the system still work well? Should all states hold primaries to select convention delegates? Should there be national primaries instead of conventions? Explain.

TEST YOUR HISTORY

1. What financial policies did Alexander Hamilton propose?
2. How did Jefferson's ideas on government differ from Hamilton's?
3. How did political parties begin?
4. How did the Alien and Sedition Acts threaten constitutional liberties?
5. What was nullification, as set out in the Virginia and Kentucky Resolutions?
6. Why is Jefferson's election called "the Revolution of 1800"?
7. How did the United States get the Louisiana Territory?
8. Why did the United States go to war in 1812? How did the war affect the nation?
9. What new foreign policy did the Monroe Doctrine set forth?
10. How did transportation encourage settlement of the West?
11. How did Marshall expand the power of the Supreme Court?
12. Why was Monroe's Presidency an "Era of Good Feelings"?
13. Distinguish between a protective tariff and a revenue tariff.
14. Why did Jefferson call the Missouri question "a fire bell in the night"?
15. Why did Jackson destroy the Second Bank of the United States?
16. What steps did Jackson take against the Indians?
17. In Jackson's day, what tied religion with reform?
18. How did people's lives improve in the mid-1800s?
19. What changes took place in the roles of women?

II
REVIEW

FURTHER READING

Bakeless, J., *Lewis and Clark.* Morrow, 1947.

Coit, M., *The Growing Years,* Vol. 3, *Life History of the United States.* Time, 1974.

Cunliffe, M. and R. Morris, *George Washington and the Making of a Nation.* Am. Heritage, 1966.

Cunliffe, M., ed., *American Heritage History of the Presidency.* Am. Heritage, 1968.

Josephy, A.M., Jr., ed., *American Heritage Book of Indians.* Am. Heritage, 1961.

Laing, A., ed., *American Ships.* Am. Heritage, 1971.

Lavender, D., *American Heritage History of the Great West.* Am. Heritage, 1965.

Scott, A.F., *Women in American Life.* Houghton, 1970.

Whitney, J., *Abigail Adams.* Atlantic-Little, Brown, 1947.

Wise, W., *Alexander Hamilton.* Putnam, 1963.

Oct 1861

III

A
TIME
OF
TRIAL

If there is no struggle, there is no progress. Those who profess to favor freedom and yet deprecate agitation . . . want crops without plowing up the ground, they want rain without thunder and lightning. . . . Power concedes nothing without a demand.

Frederick Douglass   213

An Industrial Giant Rises in the North

9

In the early 1800s, building and running railroads was the greatest feat of technology and engineering. More than anything else, railroads encouraged manufacturing and made the industrial Northeast and the agricultural Northwest one region—the North.

In the mid-1800s the northern part of the United States stretched from the pine forests of Maine in the Northeast to the fertile plains of Iowa and Minnesota in the Northwest (map on page 228). Nature had given this part of the country broad river valleys that opened the way from magnificent seaports into the interior. Roads, canals, and railroads also helped people and products move freely throughout the area. The Northeast and the Northwest had begun to take on a single character—they were the North.

People who traveled through the North found everywhere the hum of activity. Important changes were taking place. Those changes would make the United States a great industrial nation.

1. THE GROWTH OF MANUFACTURING

In 1815 most of the nation's manufactured goods were being produced in the home. This was true both of things to be sold and things to be used there. By 1860 a complete change had taken place. Fewer products were being made by the people who would actually be using them. The factory was now the center of manufacturing.

Mass production. Between 1815 and 1860, machinery was introduced on a wide scale. With it came the system of breaking all production into a series of small, simple tasks. Each could be learned quickly and then performed with ease, even by an inexperienced worker. It took years of apprenticeship to make a skilled craftsman; a factory "hand" could be trained in a few days. Mass production became the rule.

Once mass production and the factory system were brought into an industry, a process of natural growth began. Increasingly complicated and expensive machinery was introduced, and the work was further and further divided. At the same time, the cost of production became cheaper. Lower costs meant lower prices and higher profits. They did not, however, always mean higher wages.

The growth of manufacturing in the United States was further aided by a common American trait that a group of British manufacturers looking over American industry before the Civil War had noted: Americans seized upon and improved every new idea that came along. The result was an increase in patents. For example, 993 patents were issued in 1850 and 4,778 in 1860.

The Waltham system. Along with mechanical inventiveness went an equally im-

---

Read here of how

Manufacturing shifted to factories.
Lowell introduced a new kind of factory.
Kelly found a new way to refine iron.
Capital came from Europe and from public funds.

TIME CHART

1808–1815	Embargo and the war with England stimulate U.S. manufacturing.
1813	Francis Lowell organizes the Boston Manufacturing Company.
1842	*Commonwealth vs. Hunt* gives labor the right to organize.
1846	Elias Howe invents the sewing machine.
1851	William Kelly develops the blast furnace.
1853	Congress authorizes the mapping of transcontinental railroad routes.

---

portant characteristic. Americans were always ready to try out new ways of organizing production. A typical business leader was Francis Cabot Lowell of Boston. At college he had shown equal talent for mathematics and for mischief. (He was nearly expelled for starting a bonfire in Harvard Yard.) In 1810, before he was 35, Lowell had made a fortune in importing and exporting. He did it during the period of European wars when international trade was especially difficult (pages 153–154). In such times, extra talent and daring were needed for success.

Ill health caused Francis Lowell to spend some time in England. There he visited a number of cotton mills and was fascinated by the machines used in cloth making. When Lowell returned to the United States just before the War of 1812, he was determined to start manufacturing cloth in his own country.

Lowell died in 1817, so he never saw his plans worked out. However, the group of

Weaving and printing cloth in the same factory, as at Waltham.

businessmen he organized and a mechanical genius he hired, Paul Moody, set up the Boston Manufacturing Company at Waltham, Massachusetts. It brought together, for the first time in one factory, the two main steps in making cloth: spinning and weaving.

The Waltham system spread throughout New England. Textile factories concentrated on producing cheap, long-wearing cotton cloth, because it was most in demand. The same methods were soon being applied to wool manufacturing as well. By 1860 the United States textile industry was second only to Britain's. At that time the North was using one quarter of the South's cotton crop.

Michigan iron and Pennsylvania coal. New manufacturing methods in the iron industry were less spectacular. Neverthe-

less, by the late 1840s machinery and the division of labor had made changes there as well. The iron furnaces and mills of eastern Pennsylvania and New Jersey were true factories.

Iron ore was shipped across the Great Lakes from Michigan to be smelted with Pennsylvania coal in Pittsburgh. The industry got a tremendous boost in 1851. In that year William Kelly, a Kentucky iron-maker, discovered a way of purifying melted iron by blasting oxygen through it.

As iron-making expanded, other factories sprang up to turn the finished metal into bolts, screws, tools, firearms, locomotives, and farm equipment. The iron industry's best customers were the railroads. Their need was so great that they had to import some of their rails from Britain. So iron makers knew that if they expanded production, there would be buyers for all the rails they could turn out.

As the Civil War approached, other forms of manufacturing grew rapidly too. Furniture, wagons, and carriages had always been made by skilled craftsmen. Now, more and more, these products were made by power-driven woodworking machinery.

A French idea. In the first part of the 1800s Eli Whitney (page 99) and Simeon North introduced from France the idea of using interchangeable parts. Whitney used this method in making rifles for the United States Army. Stocks, barrels, and trigger mechanisms were made separately to exact measurements. Then the parts were put together. It was a much faster process than making each gun separately. Use of interchangeable parts was one more step in the process of mass production. Soon it was being used in the manufacture of clocks, watches, and tools.

There seemed to be no limits to American ingenuity. In 1846 Elias Howe patented the sewing machine. He thought of it as something for home use, but it soon revolutionized the manufacturing of clothing and shoes.

Free enterprise and government money. In the twenty years from 1840 to 1860 there was a fourfold increase in the value of United States manufactures. During the same years the work force did not even double. This shows that the average worker must have been producing more than twice as much. Such an increase was possible only through the use of labor-saving machinery. In the Northeast an economic revolution had begun.

Manufacturing and other forms of business can expand only if there is *capital* (investment money) available. Long before

WOMAN OF IRON

She was 31 when her husband died, the mother of four children—one newborn. The family business was in serious financial trouble.

In 1825 Rebecca Lukens took charge. She bought supplies, set prices, made contracts, dealt with customers. In nine years all debts were paid and the business was flourishing. It survived the Panic of 1837, when so many others failed.

Not an unusual story? Many a woman did as well at running the family shop or tavern or plantation?

True, but Rebecca Lukens was operating the big Brandywine Ironworks, in Pennsylvania. She ran it well until she died in 1854. Then her sons-in-law renamed the company in her memory. Today it survives and prospers as Lukens Steel.

any profit comes in, buildings must be constructed, machinery and materials must be bought, and help must be hired. In the United States a lot of the needed capital came from those like Francis Lowell (page 215) who had prospered as merchants. Or it came from people with savings who saw a chance of profit in the new ventures. Still, there was never enough from those sources; so some of the capital had to come from Europe.

There were also public funds. States, counties, cities, and towns used their money and credit, especially for railroad construction. It was widely believed that nothing would insure the prosperity and growth of a town or region better than a railroad. That seemed to justify using public money to build one. Earlier the same thing had been believed about canals.

Of 245 million dollars invested in southern railroads before the Civil War, 55 per cent came from state and local governments. In the North the state of Pennsylvania spent over 100 million dollars to encourage railroad- and canal-building.

The Union Glass Works is one example of small-scaled manufacturing common in the United States before the Civil War. Such industries were often built close to rivers. Why was this done?

Baltimore, Maryland, invested twenty million dollars in railroads; Charleston, South Carolina, over three million.

Some states followed the example of Virginia and put public money into any company chartered by the state. Others took the lead of Georgia, which built and ran the Western and Atlantic Railroad. It was 400 miles long and connected Savannah, on the Atlantic Coast, with Chattanooga, Tennessee.

But usually as soon as a state-financed project began to make money, it was sold to private investors. In the early years American free enterprise was greatly helped by government money.

 **TRY THIS!**

1. Write a letter that Francis Lowell might have sent from England to one of his wealthy friends in Boston, describing his idea for a new kind of textile mill.   **2.** Explain (with examples) how labor-saving machinery can make it possible for twice as many workers to turn out four times as much goods. **3.** Write an editorial that might have appeared in a local paper favoring the use of public money to build a railroad.

e greatest benefactors of mankind in all ages have been those by whose
ve genius discoveries have been made, whereby the labor and fatigue
nt upon every-day life has been lessened and ameliorated.

All hail! we come, as woman's friend we come,
To renovate the rubbing, scrubbing, washing world;
Upon our merits we alone depend;
Topmast to the breeze our banner is unfurled.

Boston Feby 4 1851

Mr P Curtis Jr

Bought of MOORE, COLLINS & CO

Sole Proprietors and Manufacturers of the justly celebrated

NORTH AMERICAN ELECTRIC WASHING FLUID,

Warranted perfectly harmless in its operations, and to possess double the power
of any thing of the kind ever discovered.

Office of the Laboratory, 67, 69 & 71 Ann, corner of Shoe & Leather St

Where all orders should be sent early to ensure a supply.

16 Gally Fluid 25 4,00
2 Doz 9h " 2/6 4,00
$ 8,00

2. WORKERS FOR AMERICA'S FACTORIES

Besides capital, the factory system needed workers. After the mid-1840s, immigration provided the great bulk of the factory hands. At the time, though, many Americans did not see the arrival of new people as a good thing for the country.

Flight from hunger. In 1847 a newspaper editor from New England reported, "I regret that the tide of immigration has thrown many of our [workers] out of employment . . . and they tell me that it is the cause of these hard times." Behind the editor's words was a startling fact. From 1845 to 1855, over 1,300,000 Irish and almost a million Germans poured into the country (graph on page 225).

The Irish immigrants were fleeing the horrors of a famine. Potatoes were a mainstay of the Irish diet. With the failure of the potato crop during the "hungry forties" the number of deaths from starvation and disease soared into the millions. Millions more bundled together their few belongings and fled to the United States, Britain, Canada, Australia, or anywhere else that they could go.

Many German immigrants to the United States were running away from famine too, for the 1840s were a time of crop failures in much of western Europe. But some Germans left home for political reasons. Most had a little money. They were able to provide themselves with a few small comforts, even in their flight from hunger. They were also able to travel beyond the eastern seaboard to the Old

Read here of how

Irish and Germans poured into America.
Their labor was needed.
And they worked under terrible conditions.
But they were not welcomed by all.

219

Northwest. There, some took up the "worn out" land American farmers had abandoned. Others were able to start small businesses.

Cheap labor. The Irish were almost without assets. For centuries English landlords had taken most of what Ireland produced. Now the Irish lacked even the necessities of life. In 1847 a Boston newspaper reported the arrival of Irish immigrants "so weak . . . that many of them could with difficulty crawl on shore." They carried with them terrible memories of what the famine had done to their homeland.

The Irish were truly desperate. Often the families they had left behind were depending on them for any help they could send back. So they poured into the cities of the eastern United States ready to take any job they were offered.

Many Americans were hostile to the Irish because of social problems. Crime and disease are always worst in the slums, and that was where Irish immigrants had to live. But if the Irish had to do the meanest jobs, these were nevertheless essential jobs. They dug the sewers, laid the rails, and carried burdens where even pack animals could not go. They were a huge reservoir of cheap labor ready to be exploited by profit-seeking businessmen. The booming factories drew them like magnets.

Low wages, long hours. Before the 1840s, American factory workers had generally been people born in this country. Usually they were driven into the factories by necessity. Many were young farm boys and girls who worked to add a few dollars to the family income.

In Massachusetts and Rhode Island

Fresh air on deck, a rare luxury on crowded immigrant ships.

factories about half of all textile workers were children. After the mid-1800s some changes were noticeable. The number of children dropped to about 8 per cent. At the same time the proportion of women rose to almost half the total. And more and more of the workers were immigrants.

The hours of factory work in the years before the Civil War remained long and the wages low. The average work week ran from sixty to 72 hours. In summer the work day was from sunrise to sunset. Winter work days lasted until nine o'clock. Wages were 25 cents a day for children and ninety cents a day for men. Women were paid forty cents daily.

"The oppressed in our midst." With the long hours and low pay went unbelievable working conditions. Children who fell asleep over their work were whipped. Factories were like prisons, and the workers were no better off than slaves. An editorial in one labor paper said, "Let us not stretch our ears to catch the sound of the lash on the flesh of the oppressed black while the oppressed in our midst are crying out in thunder tones."

In early factories there was little attention to health or safety. Workers had to eat their meals on the job, and few had any guarantee that they would receive the wages that they had earned. If an employer went bankrupt, creditors divided whatever he had, leaving nothing for the workers.

When workers tried to form unions to improve their lives, they were sometimes prosecuted. English common law under which American courts worked made any such activity a conspiracy against the employer. Only in 1842 did a Massachusetts case, *Commonwealth v. Hunt,* declare it legal to organize a union.

A shoe factory in 1854. Factory owners often had trouble getting workers. What was the advantage of hiring children?

When a depression struck, the hard life of the factory hand became considerably worse. The reformer Orestes Brownson said that then the worker had "to go days without food; to [remain idle for] weeks, seeking work and finding none." The brightest prospect for the worker's family was a trip to the poorhouse.

Respectable lives. Employers often did take a *paternalistic* interest in their workers. That is, they treated them like children. Their needs were taken care of, but they were given little independence or responsibility. Some employers built tenement houses for their workers.

221

Building reaping machines in McCormick's Chicago factory.

Large numbers of young women worked in the early textile mills. They came from New England farms where there was little for them to do, and they went into the factories to help their families or to save money for their education. In some early New England textile mills they were almost the entire work force.

Under the Waltham system (pages 215–216) women "operatives" were required to attend church services and generally lead respectable lives. The rules assured farm families that their daughters were living in a proper environment. In the earliest years "factory girls" were also encouraged to improve themselves. Even after a seventy-hour work week some managed to attend lectures, prepare literary journals, and learn French. But most fell into bed right after their evening meal to rest up for the next long day.

Knowing their rights. Many times in the years before 1860 workers struck to improve working conditions or to keep their wages from being reduced. At least once—in Lowell, Massachusetts, in 1834—they were successful. More often the strikes ended with firings and *blacklisting*. The latter meant that workers would have a hard time finding other jobs in the same community or industry. Their crime, as one labor paper said in 1848, was in knowing their rights and daring to assert them.

In 1828 the carpenters of Philadelphia, trying to win a ten-hour day, founded the first workingmen's party. The party organized its members to vote for Andrew Jackson. A National Trades' Union was formed in New York in 1834. The Union favored education, free land for farmers, and restrictions on child labor. Frequently the unions and workingmen's parties demanded higher wages and a ten-hour day. But prosecution in the courts and the Panic of 1837 (page 195) put an end to the early labor organizations.

The independent workingmen's parties attacked banks, corporations, and all forms of special privilege. They stressed the right of every person to follow his or her own self-interest as long as there was no interference with the rights of others.

Some middle-class people also tried to improve working conditions and provide educational opportunities for the poor. They believed that educated workers were less likely to disrupt society than ignorant ones. And they applied pressure to soften the laws against indebtedness. As many as 75,000 people were put in prison for debt in 1829.

"I don't know." Many of the workingmen's organizations were really unions of small independent businessmen. They feared that a strong government would give privileges to some citizens, and they wanted equal opportunities for all. Others tried to protect native labor from the rising tide of immigrant workers. The newcomers were accused of holding down wages by working for next to nothing. Immigrants were also used by employers to break strikes.

On the political front antiforeign and anti-Catholic feeling led to the formation of the American Party. It sought to keep foreigners and Catholics from holding public office and demanded a 21-year residency rule for citizenship. The American Party was a half-secret organization. Its members were supposed to answer, "I don't know," when questioned about it. That led to their being called "Know-Nothings." Know-Nothingism reached a peak in 1853 and 1854. For a time it controlled the state legislature of Massachusetts, and in 1856 the party put up a candidate for President. Thereafter, it rapidly faded.

Heavy immigration continued right into the first years of the twentieth century. Antiforeign feeling did not die out after the 1850s, but it no longer had an organized political voice.

 TRY THIS!

1. Explain why there was so much opposition to immigrants, even though the country needed them.   2. Write a letter explaining the feelings of a German immigrant family about their new home.   3. Tell how a farm boy or girl might have felt about working in a textile mill. What would one probably dislike about it? Was anything about mill work better than farm work? Explain.

3.   NEW CITIES LINKED WITH IRON

Read here of how

Cities grew by trade and manufacturing.
But developed slums, crime, and disease.
Early railroads gave a rough ride.
But drew the nation's sections together.

In their hearts most Americans believed that in every way country life was superior to life in the city. Even as their urban centers grew and flourished throughout the 1800s, they clung to the view that there was something unnatural about urban life. The unquestioned virtue of the farmer and the pioneer was self-reliance. The careful planning and interdependence needed to

223

keep a city functioning seemed the opposite of what was good and proper.

The best route to the heart of the country. The growth of cities has always been taken as a sign of progress. It is the mark of a society moving from underdevelopment to maturity. While city growth was slow in the South, it moved rapidly in the rest of the country (graph on page 174). The proportion of city dwellers increased by 800 per cent between 1820 and 1840. In 1820 there were only twelve cities with populations of more than 10,000. By 1860 there were 101. Eight of those had more than 100,000 people. One, New York City, was well over the million mark.

In the early 1800s most United States cities were on the seacoast, and their chief concern was trade. Merchants, who had been their leading citizens since colonial times, were mostly engaged in importing and exporting. But they also built their own ships and acted as their own bankers and insurance agents. In earlier times the merchant might operate a rum distillery, a rope factory, a flour mill, or a lumber-supply business.

After 1815, manufacturing operations grew larger and more complicated (pages 215–216). And the work of running them became more specialized. By 1860 trading had increased, but manufacturing was the chief activity in the older cities along the coast. For the newer ones of the interior, manufacturing was the main reason for their existence.

The growing wealth of the interior meant greater prosperity for New York, Philadelphia, and Boston as they competed for trade. In this rivalry New York's lead was unchallengeable. The Hudson and Mohawk valleys and the Great Lakes gave it the best route to the heart of the country (maps on pages 172 and 228). But the West and the South were soon creating enough business for all the coastal cities.

The worst slum. Cities could grow breathtakingly fast. Chicago had about 300 people in 1830. By 1860 it had 109,000. But such quick expansion caused deep problems. In 1820 a foreign visitor described New York as a city without "hovels . . . ruined garrets or dank and gloomy cellars filled with wretched victims." In other words, it was a city without slums. By the middle of the century New York's slums, packed with immigrants, were notorious throughout the world.

No district anywhere had as bad a reputation as the Five Points in New York City. It had been built on drained land to provide housing for the middle class. When the soft soil began to settle, its houses were abandoned and fell into disrepair. Then the poor moved in. Within a single building called The Brewery there was, on the average, a murder every single day. The New York police went into the Five Points only in platoon strength (ten to thirty men).

In 1844 a newspaper editor wrote that the streets of the Five Points were clogged "with offal and filth" thrown from neighboring buildings. All this was mixed with "the usual deposits of mud and manure." The area was a frightening view of the worst level to which a city could descend.

A rising death rate. Lack of sewers added to the unpleasantness of city life. On the eve of the Civil War only a third of New York City had sewers, and they were not in the slum districts. It is no surprise that there were frequent outbreaks of disease. Yellow fever struck often, especially in the slum sections. Even more common were cholera and malaria, which spared

224

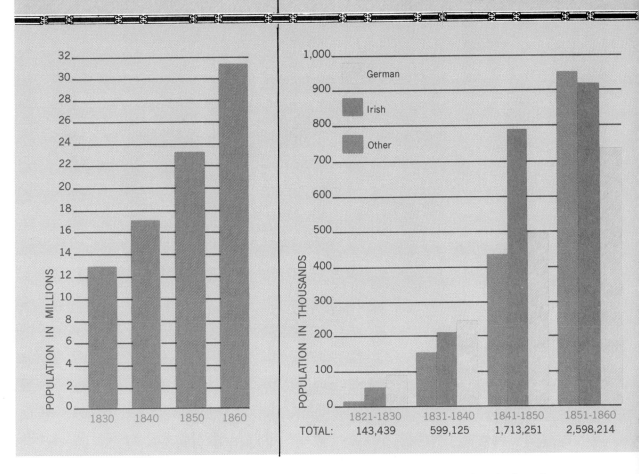

Between 1830 and 1860 the population of the United States more than doubled. Immigration, chiefly from Ireland and Germany, contributed to growth.

neither rich nor poor. Little was known about the causes of disease, and most cities had no health service.

From 1810 to 1859 the city death rate rose frighteningly. Voices were raised to demand reform and to improve the quality of city life. By the late 1830s people were insisting on improvements in tenement construction. Some laws were passed, but they applied only to new buildings. Little was done about existing structures. And immigrants kept arriving to fill these rick-

ety firetraps to overflowing. Just before the Civil War there were 29,000 New Yorkers living in the stinking cellars of old buildings.

Crime was a steady product of the slums, and most of the lawbreakers were assumed to be immigrants. In 1844 New York created the first publicly supported police force. Other eastern cities soon followed. In the 1850s old-fashioned volunteer fire companies were replaced by paid firefighters.

These were the first small efforts of cities to get rid of their worst conditions. Real reform would not come until the late 1800s.

225

Sea Links

Packets (sail or steam) carried passengers, mail, and freight on regular schedules. By the early 1800s they were making transatlantic travel more comfortable and convenient (upper left). But the glory of United States shipping in that period was the clipper ship (right). Its hull was designed for speed, not cargo space, and it carried more than the usual amount of sail. Sailors on a clipper had little time to carve amusing wooden figures like the one shown here (lower left). Captains drove their crews mercilessly to set new speed records. The clippers were "monuments carved from snow. For a brief time they flashed their splendor round the world then disappeared."

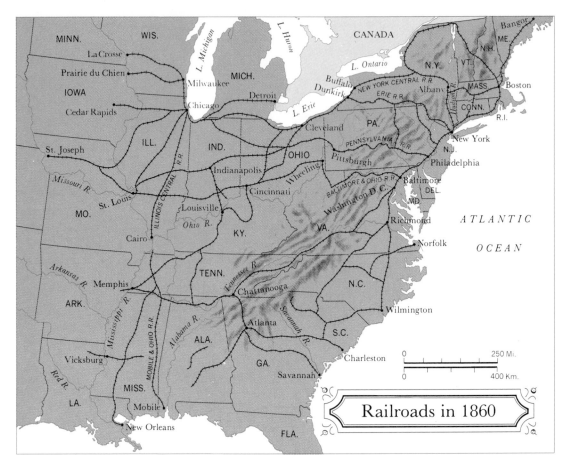

Railroads in 1860

By 1860 people and products could travel by rail from the Atlantic seacoast to the Mississippi Valley. Note that few railroads linked North and South. How were these sections joined?

EARLY RAILROADS

Nothing had a greater effect on the expansion of business and the growth of cities than the railroads. In 1830 they scarcely existed; by 1860 over 30,000 miles of track crisscrossed the nation.

The railroads were not laid out according to any central plan, and so their track gauges (the distances between rails) were a hodgepodge. Eleven different sizes were found in the North, though 4 feet 8½ inches (now the standard gauge) was most common. In the South most tracks were 5 feet apart. Not having one standard gauge meant that cars carrying freight or passengers could not move from one rail line to another. Constant loading and unloading was necessary. Throngs of passengers and wagonloads of freight making their way from one railroad station to another added to the burden of city traffic.

The pleasures of travel. No one who made a journey by railroad in the 1800s was ever likely to forget it. Travelers going from New York to the West had to leave the city by a ferryboat that landed them in Jersey City across the Hudson River. Once the travelers had landed, they had to unload their own luggage and carry it to the passenger cars.

The cars were made of wood. Their seats were stiffbacked, so that a passenger could sleep only in a sitting position. Heat in winter came from cast iron stoves at the ends of the cars. Newspapers often carried stories of trains set ablaze by coals spilling from the stoves or by sparks from the locomotive landing on the car roofs. The heat of summer could be relieved only by opening car windows. Soot from the engine came in the open windows.

Schedules were carelessly kept. A passenger often arrived at the station to find that the train either had left or would not depart for several hours. If they fell asleep, waiting travelers might have their baggage stolen. Aboard the trains no meals were served. Passengers had to bring their own food with them or dash off at a stop to buy some from a peddler.

Railroad disasters were frequent. They might be caused by a train's plunging into a stream where a bridge had been washed out. Or they might be the result of a collapsed rail. A two- or three-day journey left the traveler exhausted, dirty, hungry, and very much relieved. Unlike the stage-coaches, though, trains did not leave a passenger sore and bruised. Unless, of course, the trip ended in a wreck.

The great dream. Nevertheless, the railroads grew. And as they grew, they improved in safety and comfort. In 1850, about 318 million dollars had been invested in railroads. Ten years later the amount was well over a billion. By then the United States had almost half the world's railroad mileage. The South's share had grown fourfold, while the West's was eight times more in 1860 than in 1850.

A major step in railroad development was the formation of large systems. The New York Central, Erie, Pennsylvania, and Baltimore and Ohio roads tied together the Atlantic Coast, the Great Lakes, and the Ohio Valley. Even as the Civil War threatened, railroad managers were planning to push their tracks west to Chicago. Running south from Chicago to Mobile, Alabama, the Illinois Central and the Mobile and Ohio paralleled the Mississippi River.

The great dream was a transcontinental line to link the Atlantic and Pacific coasts. Chicago, Milwaukee, St. Louis, Memphis, Vicksburg, and New Orleans angled to be made the eastern end of this mighty railroad (map on page 228). In 1853 Congress put up the money to map

out four possible routes. That same year, Senator Jefferson Davis of Mississippi pushed through the Gadsden Purchase (map on page 270) to improve the chance of getting a southern route.

So railroads, like earlier "internal improvements" (page 168), stirred up rivalries between the sections of the country. At the same time, they changed old relationships. Where the bulk of the Northwest's produce had once gone southward down the Ohio and Mississippi rivers, it now moved eastward. Rails carried it to Great Lakes ports; then it was moved to the eastern seaboard by lake steamships and Erie Canal boats. The railroads were pulling Northwest and Northeast together. The Union was being bound by bands of iron.

 TRY THIS!

1. Using the map on page 228, show why New York had a better route to the interior than any other port city. 2. Explain why reform of city life was so slow before the Civil War. 3. Describe the modern improvements that eliminated each of the horrors of early railroad travel.

4. WESTERN FARMS TO FEED A NATION

In spite of the growth of cities and development of manufacturing, most people in the United States continued to earn their living by farming. But farms too were changing. In the years before the Civil War, agriculture, like manufacturing, became increasingly specialized. That is, farmers raised just one crop or a single type of crop. The price of wheat or corn in some distant city became their overriding concern.

In the early 1800s most farmers were outside this cash crop system, though that too was rapidly changing. Something that did not change was the view held by most Americans that farming was the ideal way of life. It was one based on Jefferson's conviction that those who worked the earth were God's favored children.

A wider distribution of wealth. The common unit of agriculture in the North was the family farm. That method of production gave the North a wider distribution of wealth than the plantation system gave the South. The owner of a family farm had two concerns. The first was growing the food needed by family members and livestock. The second was earning enough cash to pay taxes and debts and to buy whatever the farm did not produce.

The chief crop offered for sale by northern farmers was grain. By the mid-1800s their income was increasingly dependent on the millers who ground and processed the crop. Most milling operations were small, but those in Baltimore, in Buffalo,

———————— ➤◄•◄ ————————

Read here of how

Agriculture changed in the early 1800s.
Farmers shifted to cash crops.
Wheat production moved to the West.
Railroads brought about both changes.

———————— ➤◄•◄ ————————

and in Rochester, New York, had become true industrial operations.

One continuing grievance of farmers was the money they had to pay the miller. In New York State it was 10 to 22 per cent of the price farmers got for grain. Farmers were also concerned that a single miller so often got most of the business in a region. Competition was then reduced, and farmers had to pay whatever the miller asked.

A westward shift. With the settlement of the prairies, the center of grain production moved westward. The Erie Canal and the railroads made it possible for the western states, with their richer soil, to grow wheat and corn for East Coast cities and for sale abroad. In 1839 the chief wheat-growing states were Ohio, Pennsylvania, New York, and Virginia. Twenty years lat-er they were Illinois, Indiana, Wisconsin, and Ohio.

Western farmers relied heavily on machinery to make up for the shortage of hired help. Improved plows were everywhere, mowing machines reduced the work of cutting hay to a third, mechanical reapers replaced hand-held scythes. On large spreads seed drills and cultivators kept down the number of hands needed.

As railroads pushed into the developing parts of the country, the cost of shipping grain went down. From fifteen cents a ton-mile by wagon, it dropped to one and a half cents by rail. Grain production rose rapidly. In 1850 wheat had become as important to the West as cotton was to the South. The value of wheat and flour exports went from eleven and a half million

Rochester, N.Y., a flour milling center. Why?

dollars in 1851 to almost 63 million in 1861. By that time Chicago had become a world center of grain marketing.

Government controls and standards. When western wheat cut into the markets of eastern farmers, they shifted to other crops. They began supplying fresh fruits, vegetables, eggs, and dairy products to nearby cities. Dairy farming developed rapidly in upstate New York and in western New England. New Jersey, sitting on the doorstep of New York and Philadelphia, became "the Garden State." It shipped vegetables, fruits, and dairy products to both cities.

Again, the railroads made a big difference. They carried fresh fruits and vegetables to market in season, milk and other dairy products year round.

Eastern farmers tried to raise the quality of the products they sold. Disease-carrying milk had been blamed for the deaths of thousands of children in New York City alone. Public pressure brought government controls and standards to make milk more healthful.

"Embalmed" beef. Yet there were limits to agricultural growth. Lack of refrigeration meant that meat had to be slaughtered close to where it was consumed. Northerners were used to seeing herds of animals being driven to eastern cities to be killed and packed.

Salting and pickling meat helped. But some food preserved in this way had a bad reputation. Jokers referred to "embalmed" beef. One said that "a meal of 'embalmed' beef saved the undertaker the trouble of embalming the corpse." Not until the next century were there federal standards for pure foods.

The low incomes of city workers (page 221) kept them from buying the farmers' products. The average family had to make do with such vegetables as potatoes and turnips, grain products, the cheapest cuts of meat, and some fish. But eastern farmers were beginning to realize that their prosperity depended on thriving cities. The nation's farms were producing more food than its own people could consume. There was a clear need for bigger markets.

Little regard for the future. The high opinion of farmers and farming held by most Americans failed to take into account some serious shortcomings. Farming practices were often bad. Many farmers saw their land as something to be held briefly, used up quickly, and sold at a profit as soon as possible. Once they had gotten rid of their holdings, farmers expected to acquire new land farther west. They used up the soil with no regard to the future.

In addition, because farmers lacked cash, they operated on credit. Interest rates were anywhere from 12 to 50 per cent. As long as prices were high and sales good, farmers could carry such a burden. But when there was a bad crop, an unexpected blight, or a business depression in some far-off city, financial failure followed. One result of such extensive credit was a steady rise in *tenancy* (renting instead of owning land).

In newly settled regions everything was in short supply. The farmer had to depend on credit from the local storekeeper for tools, seed—even food. Often the storekeeper demanded the farmer's crop as security and charged a heavy interest on the credit advanced.

Hidden problems. Under tenancy or heavy debt, farmers had little interest in improving their output or livestock. But government and private organizations were urging them to adopt better practices. The

Horse-drawn machines greatly increased farm output. How?

experts wished to try European ideas of crop rotation and soil conservation. They also wanted agricultural schools.

None of these ideas made much headway with western farmers. They seemed not to realize how quickly manufacturing and trade were catching up with farming as the nation's chief occupations. For the time being, these problems seemed to farmers to be less important than the growing struggle between North and South.

 TRY THIS!

1. Compare the life on a western wheat farm with that on a New England dairy farm. Which would be larger? What would be the chief concern of each farmer? What machinery would you expect to find on each farm? What would be alike about the two operations? **2.** Using the map on page 228, trace three routes by which wheat might move from Chicago to the East Coast.

ROUNDUP

Who?
> Francis Lowell
> Paul Moody
> Eli Whitney
> Rebecca Lukens
> William Kelly

What?
> Boston Manufacturing
>   Company
> interchangeable parts
> *Commonwealth v. Hunt*
> Know-Nothings
> Five Points
> packet ship

Where?
> Mohawk Valley
> Gadsden Purchase
> Lowell, Massachusetts

KNOW THIS

The Growth of Manufacturing

1. Why did manufacturing move from homes to factories during the early 1800s?
2. How did the Waltham system of production revolutionize cloth manufacturing?
3. What did each of these contribute to industry: Francis Lowell; Eli Whitney; William Kelly?
4. Why is capital important in the development of industry?
5. Name three sources of capital for American industry.

Workers for America's Factories

1. Why did the Irish and German immigrants to the United States leave their European homelands?
2. Why did the Irish find it more difficult to get a start in the United States than did the Germans?
3. What were factory working conditions like in the mid-1800s? Consider wages, hours, and job security.
4. How did workers try to improve their employment conditions? Why were they generally unsuccessful?
5. Who were the Know-Nothings? What did their political party want?

New Cities Linked with Iron

1. What evidence shows that large numbers of people moved to cities in the 1800s?
2. How did the business life of cities change after 1815?
3. What efforts were made to improve the quality of city life in the mid-1800s?
4. What three serious problems were caused by the rapid growth of cities?
5. Explain why no one who made a journey by railroad in the mid-1800s "was ever likely to forget it."

Western Farms to Feed a Nation

1. What were two important changes in farming after 1800?
2. What was the chief difference between farming in the North and in the South?
3. Why did the center of grain production move westward in the mid-1800s?
4. What changes did eastern farmers make as a result of competition from western farmers?
5. What were the two major shortcomings of farm practices in the 1800s?

DIG HERE!

Research the life and career of an American inventor of the 1800s. Here are some you might investigate: James Bogardus, George Washington Carver, Samuel Colt, Peter Cooper, Phineas Davis, John Deere, Thomas Edison, Oliver Evans, Robert Fulton, Charles Goodyear, Joseph Henry, Herman Hollerith, Richard M. Hoe, Elias Howe, Cyrus McCormick, Elijah McCoy, Samuel F. B. Morse, George Pullman, Frederick E. Sickels, John Stevens, Gustavus Swift, George Westinghouse, Granville Woods.

Use these questions as a guide in gathering your information:

A. When and where was the inventor born? Were education and family life important to the inventor's career?

B. What was the inventor's occupation? Did it help in developing the invention?

C. What circumstances led to development of the invention? Did certain people or events encourage the work? Did any discourage it?

D. How did the invention affect or change American life? Is it still important today?

E. Was the invention important to America's Industrial Revolution?

These books should be useful to you: Breeden, *Those Inventive Americans,* National Geographic; Blow, *Men of Science and Invention,* American Heritage; Burlingame, *Machines That Built America,* Harcourt; Meyer, *World Book of Great Inventions,* World; Poole, *Men Who Pioneered Inventions,* Dodd; Usher, *History of Mechanical Inventions,* Harvard.

THINK ABOUT IT

1. When manufacturing moved from home to factory, it brought more and cheaper goods. What new problems did manufacturing create? Have these problems been solved? Why, or why not?

2. It is hard for us to imagine the shock early immigrants felt on leaving their homelands and coming to America. Explain this. Draw up a list of the adjustments immigrants would have had to make in the 1800s.

DO IT!

1. Imagine that you are one of the women who spent their early years working in the mills. Write about your experiences. Why did you leave your farm home? What is your work routine? What are your living conditions? How do you feel about your employer?

2. With classmates, research a community problem in your own or a nearby city (newspaper and magazine files will help). Define the problem; explain its cause; examine some solutions.

THEN AND NOW

The right to have unions was won by workers before the Civil War. Today, some states have "right-to-work" laws. In such states a person can be hired in a union-organized plant or store without joining the union. Does your state have a right-to-work law? How do local labor leaders and employers feel about right-to-work laws? What do you think about the issue?

The South Becomes a Cotton Kingdom

10

By 1860 the South's cotton exports were earning over 200 million dollars. Note that the hand holding this cotton plant is black. Sixty percent of all slaves were directly involved in planting, hoeing, picking, and transporting the South's "white gold."

South of the Pennsylvania-Maryland border and the Ohio River were the slave-holding states (map on page 238). Together they were sometimes called the Cotton Kingdom, but they were not as much alike as the name might suggest. The Cotton Kingdom was a vast territory extending southward to the Gulf of Mexico and the Rio Grande. Most of the people who lived in it were *subsistence* farmers; that is, they produced only what their own families used. The little extra they grew was exchanged for tools, weapons, gunpowder and other things they could not make or raise themselves. The vast majority of southerners grew no cotton and owned no slaves. But those who did were the region's real leaders.

1. COTTON AND THE PLANTATION SYSTEM

The South produced a wide range of crops. The most important of these, both in total value and number of acres used, was corn. In fact, the South's corn crop was more than half again as valuable as its cotton. Corn was easy to grow. It fed the farm families and their livestock, and it was the chief item in the diet of the slaves. In the South a failure of the corn crop was a real disaster. This was quite different from the situation in the North, where the variety of food was much greater.

However, the Deep South did not produce enough corn for its own needs. The great cotton planters of Georgia, Alabama, and Mississippi depended on the upper South and on the free farmers of the West for the corn and wheat they needed. Also, cotton planters bought some of the slaves needed to work their fields from Virginia and Maryland. Those two states of the upper South had more slaves than they needed. For many planters, the money they got for selling them made the difference between profit or loss on their whole operation. Economic ties like these kept the upper and lower South close to one another. (See the map on page 238.)

Wealth and poverty side by side. The importance given to cotton hid the fact that many Southern planters and farmers got their living from other crops. For instance, South Carolina and Georgia produced quantities of rice, while in Louisiana sugar was important. In the upper South, particularly in Virginia, Maryland, and North Carolina, tobacco was still a major crop, just as it had been in colonial times. But by 1860 Virginia's wheat was several

------

Read here of how

Cotton was the South's main cash crop.
But not its only one.
Cotton growing wore out the soil.
The plantation system benefited only the
    wealthy.
And it kept the South dependent.

TIME CHART

1775	Quakers start the first American antislavery society.
1816	American Colonization Society is founded.
1831	William Lloyd Garrison begins publishing the *Liberator.*
1831	Nat Turner leads a slave uprising.
1836	Congress adopts a "gag rule."
1857	Hinton R. Helper publishes *The Impending Crisis of the South.*

------

times more valuable than its tobacco. Hemp was important in Kentucky. This coarse fiber was used for the bags and rope needed in picking and baling cotton. Furthermore, herds of cattle roamed the grasslands of Florida and Texas.

So two very different kinds of farming existed together in the South. On the one hand were the great planters producing cotton, rice, sugar, or some other staple crop for sale. On the other were the ordinary small farmers growing food for their own use. This separation brought about a condition that all visitors to the South mentioned, the striking differences between the style of life enjoyed by planters and that of the poor farmers. In the Cotton Kingdom wealth and poverty existed side by side.

"One of the richest soils." In spite of the variety of southern farming, cotton overshadowed everything else. In 1860 about 75 per cent of the cotton crop was exported, and most of the rest was shipped to northern mills. Returns from the sale of raw cotton accounted for over half the foreign earnings of the United States. This fact convinced many southerners that the whole world depended on their "white gold." It also caused them to believe that a good part of the North's prosperity and growth was paid for by the South.

Cotton was extremely easy to grow, and this was its attraction for southern farmers. It could be produced with little work wherever the growing season was long enough and the land was well drained.

A great deal of cotton was grown on newly cleared land. Smaller planters took it for granted that they could always pull up stakes and push westward to better soil. Because they had to get a quick return from their new land, they soon used up the soil, which seemed so cheap and limitless. From the older southern states along the seaboard came many accounts of "red old hills, stripped of their native growth . . . washed into deep gullies, with here and there . . . stunted pine shrubs struggling for [existence] on what was once one of the richest soils in America."

The wealthy few. Misuse of the soil also helped to increase the power of the largest planters. These growers could afford to rotate their crops or rest their fields. But as an Alabama settler explained, the "small planters, after taking the cream off their lands . . . [go] farther west and south." There, he went on, they found other land to use up and ruin. Then the next step took place. The wealthier farmers bought out

This map shows the major cash crops of the South in the 1840s. (Various food crops were also grown for local use.) Which cash crops were grown mostly in the upper South? In the lower South? Where were cattle raised?

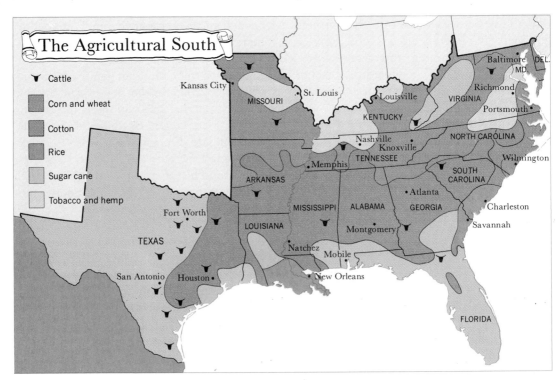

The Agricultural South

▼ Cattle

Corn and wheat

Cotton

Rice

Sugar cane

Tobacco and hemp

Steamboats took the South's "white gold"—bales of cotton—down the rivers to ocean ports.

their poorer neighbors, enlarging their own plantations and adding to their slave force. The wealthy few were able to offer their cotton at a lower price, and so they drove away those who were not so well off.

The life of a successful planter seemed truly enviable. Before the Civil War the average size of farms in the United States was shrinking, but in the cotton-growing South the opposite was true. In Alabama there were almost 700 plantations of over 1,000 acres and one of over 14,000. There were some 25,000-acre spreads in the rich country of the lower Mississippi. And one cotton and sugar grower of Natchez, Mississippi, had eight plantations and over 1,000 slaves. In 1850 his income from these holdings was almost 170,000 dollars. Similar amounts were earned in the rice regions. There it was not unusual for a single planter to own from 300 to 1,000 slaves.

Though the great planters were only a tiny part of the population, they dominated politics and everything else in southern life. They made very little effort to get along with their poorer neighbors; quite the reverse. As one small planter near Natchez reported, they bought up "every square inch of land" around the Mississippi town just to keep poor people out. The anger of poorer southerners swelled against the big planters. Only their fear and dislike of the slaves kept feelings of the poor whites in check. On one point all southern whites were in agreement—the blacks had to be kept under control.

The planter's businessman. The southern planter was far from the market in which his cotton, rice, or sugar was sold. Furthermore, the day-to-day work of running his plantation was more than enough to keep him busy. As a result, he depended

239

on an agent (sometimes called a *factor*) to manage his sales and other business affairs.

Agents, or factors, in interior towns were willing to buy cotton on the spot. In this way they relieved the small planter of further shipping costs. The planter did not usually take cash for his crop. Instead, he got credit for the supplies, household goods, or luxuries he might want. Large planters shipped their bales to the great cotton ports of New Orleans, Mobile, Pensacola, Savannah, or Charleston. There prices were better, but the factor system worked in much the same way.

Yankee bankers and merchants. Whether a planter was great or small, he had to depend on his agent, or factor, because he could not get credit in any other way. The factor, on the other hand, was able to do business with merchants in New York and Liverpool, the English port to which most American cotton was shipped.

Naturally, disputes between factor and planter were common. Factors often charged that the planters' bales were lighter or of poorer quality than claimed. Planters complained that they were overcharged for the factors' services or hadn't gotten the best price for their crop.

The business dealings of the two groups were more difficult because the planters were almost always in debt to their factors. Most planters borrowed against the next year's crop. And they were likely to count on a better growth and higher prices than the weather and market brought them. Furthermore, the factor system constantly reminded the planter that he was dependent on Yankee bankers and merchants.

 TRY THIS!

Explain why each of these statements is not completely true: **1.** The South, before the Civil War, was a land of slave owners. **2.** "Cotton Kingdom" is an accurate description of the South in the period covered by this chapter. **3.** The South before the Civil War was the richest and most prosperous part of the United States.

2. LIFE UNDER THE SLAVE SYSTEM

Southerners sometimes referred to slavery as their "peculiar institution." Certainly nothing about the region drew more attention—and criticism—than slavery. Before 1830, especially in Virginia, some of the

———————◆——————◆———————

Read here of how

The South defended the slave system.
There were good profits in slavery.
But it gave the slaves only a crude living.

criticism came from southerners themselves. One called slavery "a foul and deadly blot . . . in a nation boasting . . . of her principles." "Do unto all men as you would have them do unto you," said another. "This golden rule and slavery are hard to reconcile."

Slavery and southern life. But after 1830 there were very few southern critics of slavery. More and more, southerners saw it as not only "an institution which is profitable to [us], but . . . as an evil which does not affect [us]." Indeed, by the 1840s and 1850s such southern leaders as John C.

———————◆——————◆———————

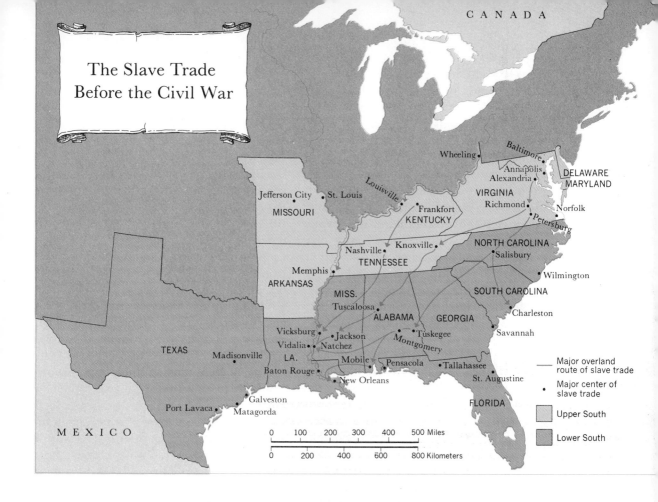

CANADA

Wheeling
Baltimore
Annapolis
Alexandria
DELAWARE
MARYLAND
Jefferson City • St. Louis • Louisville
MISSOURI • Frankfort
KENTUCKY
VIRGINIA
Richmond • Norfolk
Petersburg
Nashville • Knoxville
TENNESSEE
NORTH CAROLINA
Salisbury
Memphis •
ARKANSAS
SOUTH CAROLINA
Wilmington
MISS.
Tuscaloosa
ALABAMA GEORGIA
Charleston
Vicksburg • Jackson • Tuskegee
Vidalia • Natchez Montgomery
Savannah
TEXAS
Madisonville •
LA. Mobile • Pensacola • Tallahassee
Baton Rouge •
St. Augustine
Port Lavaca • Galveston
Matagorda
New Orleans
FLORIDA
MEXICO

0 100 200 300 400 500 Miles
0 200 400 600 800 Kilometers

— Major overland
route of slave trade
• Major center of
slave trade
Upper South
Lower South

Calhoun and the writer George Fitzhugh were arguing that slavery was the best labor system. Fitzhugh pointed out that slaves were cared for in old age and illness. Northern factory workers, on the other hand, might be sent off to the poorhouse or left to starve when they were of no further use to their employers. White workers would be better off, Fitzhugh said, if they too were slaves.

In 1860, out of eight million southern whites, fewer than 400,000 owned slaves. Of those, 200,000 owned five or fewer. But these figures hide an important fact. About 300 slaveholders had more than 200 slaves each, and 2,300 were masters of a hundred

On the cotton, rice, and sugar plantations of the West and the lower South, more slaves were needed. Some were transported by riverboat; others were marched overland, as in the picture on page 246. What cities were slave-trade centers?

or more. Altogether this group owned over half a million of their fellow human beings. Their slave property was valued at 250 million dollars.

On the average, only one out of every four whites in the whole South belonged to a slaveholding family. But this number varied from one part of the region to another. In parts of the upper South it dropped to one in every thirty whites, but in the lower South it rose to one out of two. It was even greater in some places. Issaquena County, Mississippi, for example, was part of the Black Belt—a region of deep rich topsoil. Here, at one time, 587 whites lived amid 7,244 slaves. (In a single year these slaves produced 41,170 bales of cotton worth close to 2 million dollars.)

Did slavery pay? Historians have disagreed for years about whether or not slavery was profitable. In the past many of them claimed that it was not, that slavery only dragged down the value and quality of free labor. These same people charged that slaves were inefficient, unskillful, and unable to learn new tasks quickly or easily.

Not all slaves worked in cotton fields. Some learned special skills, as shown in this picture of a gold-mining operation in the West.

Money used to buy slaves, it was said, could and should have been put into railroads, factories, machinery, and other useful investments. The South might then have enjoyed the same kind of prosperity that was found in the North.

But if slavery didn't pay, why did it continue to exist? Much of the argument that it didn't pay came from the idea that the real purpose of slavery was not just to make money. Rather, it was a means of keeping the black population under control. In other words it was a social system, not just an economic one.

Robbing the many. A number of modern historians take a different view. They point out that the money invested in slaves paid a profit of from 6 to 8 per cent. This was as much as most business opportunities available at the time. For large holders of slaves it meant a very good return indeed.

But did slavery have a bad effect on the South as a whole? Considering the way in which slave ownership was distributed (page 241), only a minority of whites could have benefited. Meanwhile, there was little money for railroads, factories, or even new farming methods. So a good part of the white population was able to produce little more than enough to keep itself alive. A North Carolinian who opposed slavery said, "Slavery *is* profitable to the few because it is simply a privilege of robbing the many."

A coarse, crude living. Whatever profits there were from slavery, none of them went to the slave. As Abraham Lincoln explained, the system let the master "sit in the shade with gloves on his hands and subsist on the bread that [the slave was] earning in the burning sun."

It cost less than 35 dollars a year to keep a slave. The slave's food was coarse and unchanging, though there was usually enough of it. Slave cabins, too, were crude, but they kept out the wind and rain. Each year the men got two cotton shirts, a pair of pants and a wool jacket, and heavy work shoes. Women were given twelve yards of cloth, thread, a needle, and work shoes. There was usually some kind of medical treatment available.

If a master took good care of the slaves, it was not out of kindness or charity. There was a lot of money tied up in each one. For the same reason, when dangerous work had to be done, planters often hired white laborers rather than risk their valuable property. A northern visitor once asked a Louisiana planter why some Irish workers were being used to drain a swamp. He was quickly told that there was malaria in the swamp and that it was too unhealthy for slaves.

A harsh system. A slave's work day was from sunrise to sunset, but at special times of the year it might run for sixteen hours. On the Louisiana sugar plantations, when the crop ripened, the work went on around the clock, seven days a week. Usually the slave was free on Sunday, and on many plantations Saturday was a half day. In their free time slaves could work in their own gardens. This of course helped the master, since it cut down the cost of feeding the slaves.

When the cotton was ripe, a full hand was expected to pick 150 pounds a day. A full hand was a grown man, in good health, between his late teens and fifty or sixty years old. Lesser amounts were expected of women, children, and older people. Slaves were divided into gangs and placed under a driver. Drivers were trusted slaves whose job it was to set the pace for their gangs. Drivers also kept order in the field and in the slave quarters, got their people out in the morning, and acted as assistants to the overseer.

The overseer was almost always a white man. He organized the work of the plantation, set the tasks for the slave gangs, and saw that they were carried out. He was also in final charge of slave discipline.

Not all slaves had to labor long hours in the fields. A small number worked as gardeners, coachmen, and house servants. They enjoyed better food and clothing than the field hands and sometimes could pick up a little education. Their work was easier too, partly because planters often kept more servants than they needed. In this way the planter could appear better off than he really was.

On a large plantation an even smaller number of slaves might be trained in carpentry, blacksmithing, and other highly skilled trades. Such training often cost the owner a great deal of money and made these slaves the most valuable of all. They could sometimes earn enough money on their own to buy their freedom.

But even the slave who was best off knew that failure to do what the master wished would be punished by the lash. A slave was expected to obey any order instantly and unquestioningly. It was a harsh system. It asked a lot of the slave and gave very little. One observer wrote, "You may talk of the lighthearted, merry slave as much as you will. It . . . has no foundation in fact."

Day-to-day resistance. Slave owners always insisted that the blacks were happy and content, but the facts say otherwise. The songs and spirituals of the slaves showed that they longed for freedom. They often sang of Moses leading the children of Israel out of bondage in Egypt, of Daniel

243

STATE OF VIRGINIA,
City of Petersburg, to wit: No. 3046

Eliza Scott (formerly Smith) a free Woman of color, who was heretofore registered in the Clerk's Office of the Hustings Court of the said City, this day delivered up to me, the former certificate of her registration, and applied for a renewal of the same, which is granted her; and she is now of the following discription, to wit: five feet 2½ inches high, about twenty five years of age, of a mulatto complexion, has a small dent near the centre of her forehead, a small scar on her left hand, one on each thumb two small moles on her chin, and was born free in Prince George County. Her mother was free before first May, 1806. This renewal is made in obedience to an order of the said Court made the 31st instant

In Testimony whereof, I DAVID M. BERNARD, Clerk of the said Hustings Court, have hereto set my hand and affixed the Seal of the said court, this 22 day of Nov A. D., 1856.

John Peterson
Master of Police   D M Bernard
                          by McMann

Slave Life

Slaves to do the hard work on Deep South plantations (right) sometimes came from the Upper South (below). Slaves feared being "sold down the river." Free blacks also lived in terror. Even with papers (left) they might be carried off.

NOTICE

NEGROES FOR SALE AT AUCTION THIS DAY AT 1 O'CLOCK

Arise! Arise! and weep no more
dry up your tears, we Shall part
no more. Come rose we go to
Tennessee,
that happy Shore to old virginia
never — never — return.

A band of Virginia slaves are transported to a new master in Tennessee. Some family groups can be seen here. But slaves feared that family members would be sold to different masters.

escaping from the lions' den, and of Noah riding out the flood. The words had a double meaning. They were religious songs but also a way of expressing the slaves' feelings about their condition.

In fact much of the slaves' religious activity—meetings and the like—took place at night without the master's knowing anything about it. Religion gave a much-needed change from the harshness of slavery, and it was a great source of strength.

Because whites outnumbered slaves in the total population and were better organized, the slaves had little chance to resist. But they did so whenever they could. For example, there was the day-to-day resistance—pretending to be ill, breaking tools, doing poor work, taking food from the smokehouse at night.

The Moses of her people. There were thousands of slaves who ran away. They

were mostly from the upper South, and they generally fled either to southern cities or to the North. Much has been said about the Underground Railroad. The Railroad, which was run by both blacks and whites, was a system of secret "stations" where fugitives could get help. But most runaway slaves who won their way to freedom did so on their own. If they got any help, it was from fellow slaves or from free blacks in the North.

Some of the fugitives became leaders in the antislavery movement. These included Frederick Douglass, Henry Bibb, Henry H. Garnet, and Harriet Tubman. Called "the Moses of her people," Harriet Tubman returned to the South many times to lead other slaves to freedom.

War between the races. Finally, there were the slave rebellions. These were threatening enough to terrify southern whites. In the 1800s the three most daring rebels were Gabriel Prosser, Denmark Vesey, and Nat Turner. Prosser was a slave blacksmith in Virginia. His plot, in 1800, was betrayed by fellow slaves. Denmark

Vesey was a free black of Charleston. In 1822 he organized a widespread uprising, but it was discovered by the Charleston authorities before it could get under way.

Nat Turner was a slave preacher in Virginia. He came to believe that God had chosen him to lead a war between the races. Turner had great influence among his fellow slaves, and in 1831 he led them in a bloody uprising. They killed Turner's master and about sixty other whites within 24 hours. Finally they were stopped by federal troops and state militia. Over a hundred slaves were killed in the course of putting down the revolt.

After all three rebellions the leaders and those suspected of taking part were hanged. In Turner's case thirteen slaves and three free blacks, besides the leader himself, were executed. But Turner's uprising had other effects. Much stricter rules were adopted to prevent slaves, and free blacks too, from moving around the countryside. Night patrols were organized, and laws were passed in some states making it harder for masters to free their slaves. Then, in January 1832, a few months after Nat Turner's rebellion, the Virginia legislature openly debated the merits of slavery. A proposal to free all of the state's slaves was defeated by a very close vote. It was the last time before the Civil War that such a discussion took place anywhere in the South.

 TRY THIS!

1. Answer the argument of George Fitzhugh that white workers in northern factories would have been better off as slaves.   **2.** Describe the life of a field hand on a large cotton plantation.   **3.** Show that slaves were not "happy and content."

3.   THE COMMON PEOPLE OF THE SOUTH

As we have seen, most southern whites owned only a few slaves or none at all. Those with fewer than ten slaves generally worked side by side with them in the fields or in the shop. A small planter could hope that one day he too would become a great

---

Read here of how

Slavery held back the South's development.
And kept poor whites from improving their lives.
The South's free blacks were severely restricted.
Yet some managed to earn good livings.

---

landholder living in a pillared mansion. But as the Civil War approached, the chance of its happening grew less and less.

A sign of stagnation. An English economist once said that all slave societies could be divided into three classes: the slaves, who did most of the work; the slaveowners, who enjoyed all of the benefits; and "an idle, lawless rabble who live . . . in a condition little removed from barbarism." The poor whites of the South were not "lawless" or "barbaric," but that was the way members of the planter class usually spoke of their poorer neighbors.

Certainly many southern whites lived in grinding poverty. In 1850 the governor of South Carolina said that at least 50,000 white people in his state could not make any kind of decent living. Yet among these poor whites were the free farmers Jefferson had called the backbone of the nation.

There is no doubt that the average white southern farm family was hardworking and self-reliant. Mostly they had to make do with second-rate land but still managed to produce grain, vegetables, and fruit and to raise cattle. Some families did very well, but most lived only a rough, homespun existence. They knew nothing of the world beyond their own county or district and they cared less. They needed very little from outside, so there was almost no trade. And lack of trade is generally taken as a sign of stagnation.

"We are accustomed to black labor." Lack of trade also meant fewer and smaller cities. This became especially noticeable after 1830, when cities in the North and West were rapidly expanding. Most of the important southern cities were seaports or river ports through which plantation crops were shipped. The city growth that did take place before the Civil War was mostly in the upper South. Richmond, Virginia, especially was becoming an industrial center.

One thing was clear about southern cities: their slave population was decreasing. There were three reasons for this: It was a lot harder to control slaves in a city environment, there was endless demand for slaves on the plantations, and white city workers tried in every way they could to get rid of slave competition. In this effort they were not always successful. Much factory and railroad work was done by slaves, and this meant fewer jobs for white workers. Southern planters were likely to claim, "We are accustomed to black labor, and it would create a revolution to drive it away."

Forever dependent. With the growing split between the sections of the country, southerners were more and more dismayed at how much they had to depend on the North. One writer who dealt with this subject was Hinton Rowan Helper of North Carolina.

In 1857, Helper attacked the whole slave system in his book *The Impending Crisis of the South: How to Meet It.* He had traveled in the North and in California. Helper claimed that this had opened his eyes to the evils of slavery. Of the effects of slavery on the South, he wrote:

It is a fact well known to every intelligent southerner that we are compelled to go to the North for almost every article . . . from matches and shoelaces to cotton mills, steamships, and statuary; that we have no foreign trade, no princely merchants, nor respectable artists; . . . that . . . the North becomes in one way or another the proprietor and dispenser of all our floating wealth, and that we are dependent on northern capitalists for the means necessary to build our railroads, canals, and other public improvements; . . . and that nearly all the profits arising from . . . insurance and shipping offices, and from the thousand and one industrial pursuits of the country, [go] to the North.

The South's cotton was the nation's leading money earner, yet it had enriched the people of the North more than those of the South. Southerners thought that with their cotton, sugar, rice, and tobacco they would need neither cities nor manufacturing nor trade. Instead, they could use their farm products to buy whatever they wanted. But of course, in that case they would remain forever dependent on the North or Europe.

Separate and unequal. There were a quarter of a million free blacks in the South before the Civil War. Though north-

Blacks in some parts of the South had to wear identification tags. A slave found away from his or her plantation would have to show the tag to any white challenger. Note that one tag identifies a free black.

Maine, New Hampshire, Vermont, and Massachusetts allowed them to vote. And New York had special property qualifications just for blacks. In the western states it was even worse. Illinois, Indiana, and Oregon barred blacks from entering their territory, and until 1849 Ohio denied them the right to attend public schools or serve on juries. Ohio then set up a separate school system for blacks but spent little money on it.

Northern blacks escaped the worst problem of their free brothers and sisters in the South. They didn't have to worry about keeping their liberty. Southern blacks who could not produce papers proving they were free might be clapped into chains. Even if they had such papers, they still might be carried off by kidnappers.

In spite of all these handicaps there were free blacks, even in the South, who made a good living. Most farmed the land or worked as laborers in the towns. But many of them had bought their freedom by working at various skilled trades such as blacksmithing, carpentry, or shoemaking, for which they had been trained when they were slaves. These blacks were able to earn good livings as high-grade workmen. At least one of them, Thomas Day, a cabinetmaker of North Carolina, employed a white assistant.

ern blacks were usually city-dwellers, free southern blacks might be found in either city or countryside. But in neither place were the lives of southern blacks very secure or very comfortable. Especially after Nat Turner's rebellion (page 247), harsh laws called black codes governed their lives. It was not easy for free blacks to own property, and their freedom of movement was severely restricted. In some places there even were laws forcing each free black to have a white guardian.

In many ways northern blacks were not much better off. In the Northeast only

 TRY THIS!

1. Show (a) some ways in which all white southerners benefited from slavery and (b) some ways in which all white southerners were hurt by it. **2.** Compare the lives of free blacks, before the Civil War, in the Northeast, the West, and the South. **3.** Explain how some free blacks managed to earn good livings.

249

4. THE ANTISLAVERY MOVEMENT

Outside the South and also among many southerners slavery caused deep soul-searching. Somehow it seemed contradictory for a country that prided itself on its democracy to deny some of its people their basic human rights.

"The rights of white men, not of all men." Agitation against the South's "peculiar institution" went back to colonial times (page 97). Then two Quakers, John Woolman and Anthony Benezet, had campaigned against it. Woolman flatly refused to accept the idea that whites were superior to blacks. When he visited other Quakers in the Chesapeake Bay area of Maryland, Woolman refused to allow slaves to clean his muddy boots. Furthermore, he insisted on sleeping in the stables rather than in beds made up by slaves. He warned his fellow Quakers that if they refused to free their slaves, they could expect "some extraordinary means to bring about their freedom." Woolman added, "God [will] answer us in this matter."

Woolman's friend Anthony Benezet called for the end of the slave trade. He was disgusted when he found that it would not be mentioned in the Declaration of Independence. It seemed that "these blessings [of freedom] were only meant to be the rights of white men, not of all men." He challenged Americans to explain how they could continue to support slavery while talking so much of freedom.

Five days before the Battle of Lexington started the American Revolution, members of the Society of Friends (the Quakers) and other Philadelphians organized "The Society for the Relief of Free Negroes Unlawfully Held in Bondage." The Revolution itself gave a push to the antislavery movement in the North and even to some degree in the South by focusing attention on freedom.

Only 12,000. The American Colonization Society was begun in 1816. Among its founders were President James Madison, Chief Justice John Marshall, congressional leaders Henry Clay and John Randolph, and Francis Scott Key, who wrote the words of "The Star-Spangled Banner." But these people had no intention of freeing slaves. Indeed, some of them owned slaves. The purpose of their society was to persuade free blacks to leave the United States and settle in Africa. Like Thomas Jefferson, they did not believe it was possible for whites and free blacks to live together in the same society (page 143).

A few black leaders, among them the wealthy New England shipowner Paul Cuffe, favored the idea of going to Africa. But most agreed with Peter Williams, a black Episcopal minister, who said, "It is certain that very few free people of color wish to go to that land. . . . The Colonization Society know this, and yet they do certainly calculate that in time they will have us all removed there."

No more than 12,000 blacks ever left the United States for Africa. They were

---

Read here of how

Antislavery feeling began in colonial times.
The abolition movement spread in the 1830s.
Abolition was opposed in the North and in the South.
But antislavery feeling kept growing.

---

heavily outnumbered by the natural increase in the black population of the United States. In time the Society founded the West African state of Liberia and named its capital, Monrovia, in honor of President James Monroe. Meanwhile, helped by the ferment of the Jackson period (page 197), a far more radical movement was getting under way.

"I will be heard." No one expressed the extreme antislavery viewpoint more strongly than William Lloyd Garrison. Starting in the 1830s, Garrison began demanding the immediate, complete end of slavery. He was not the least bit interested in any gradual methods or halfway schemes for getting rid of it. He was even willing to see the Union fall apart rather than continue to live with slavery. More than anything, he wanted to awaken the American people to the evils of slavery and to force political leaders and the two major parties to say where they stood. Those who shared this belief were called *abolitionists.*

In the first issue of his newspaper, the *Liberator,* which appeared in Boston in 1831, Garrison proclaimed, "On this subject I do not wish to think, speak, or write with moderation. . . . I am in earnest . . . and I will be heard." And he was. The *Liberator* made Garrison notorious. Southern newspapers reprinted his attacks on slavery so that they could show their readers how dangerous he was. But in doing so, of course, they built up his reputation and gave him a much larger audience than his small paper would otherwise have gotten.

"Immediate emancipation." In 1833 English abolitionists were able to outlaw slavery in all parts of the British Empire. This led American antislavery people to ask for "immediate *emancipation*" (freeing all slaves at once). The idea was in line with the religious thinking of the day. Re-

vivalist preachers (page 199) called for immediate repentance for sins. Abolitionists, seeing slavery as a sin and a crime, began insisting on immediate emancipation.

Abolitionists also borrowed the methods of revivalist preachers. They held mass meetings, they organized lectures, they printed and distributed pamphlets. In the 1830s Theodore Weld of Ohio sent out seventy workers to crisscross the northern part of the country. By 1837 they had set up over a thousand antislavery societies.

In the meantime William Lloyd Garrison was calling on people not to obey a government that supported slavery. He even favored civil war and a slave uprising. More moderate abolitionists argued that the slavery question was too complicated to be solved at once. They wished to see some step-by-step plan adopted, but Garrison answered, "He that is with the slaveholder is against the slave; he that is with the slave is against the slaveholder."

"Gentlemen of property." Garrison's views were unpopular with most white northerners. Many of them saw the antislavery crusade as a threat to the Union, to property rights, and to white supremacy. They mobbed abolitionist speakers, broke up their meetings, and destroyed their printing presses. In 1834 an anti-abolitionist mob attacked a New York meeting and then set fire to parts of the city's black section. The next year a lynch mob led William Lloyd Garrison through the streets of Boston with a rope around his neck. The police finally put him in jail for his own safety. (Both outbreaks were said to be led by "gentlemen of property and standing.") Then in 1837, Elijah Lovejoy, an abolitionist editor in Illinois, was killed by a mob while trying to protect his printing press.

But the abolitionists were not disheartened. They knew that the attacks on them

251

would win more followers for their cause. And many Americans became troubled by the violence and what they feared it might lead to. Abraham Lincoln, then a young politician in Illinois, warned that the government might be destroyed by such mob actions.

Freedom for black and white. The former President John Quincy Adams was serving as a congressman from Massachusetts. In 1836 some voters in Adams's district sent him a petition that called for ending the slave trade in Washington, D.C. Congress refused even to hear the petition. Adams and a small group of congressmen were shocked. They called the resolution that forbade such petitions a "gag rule" and claimed that it was against the First Amendment to the Constitution. That Amendment clearly states that Congress cannot interfere with "the right of the people . . . to petition the government."

In 1844 the gag rule was repealed. But by then the abolitionists had convinced tens of thousands of northerners that slavery endangered everyone's civil liberties. As one abolitionist put it, "The contest is fast becoming . . . one, not alone of freedom for the black, but of freedom for the white."

Two paths. Garrison always stayed clear of politics. He felt that abolitionists should stick to winning people over to their

Stormy debates took place in the House of Representatives as some northern congressmen angrily protested the "gagging" of citizens who wanted to petition the government to end slavery.

cause. Politics, he knew, meant compromise, and he wished always to stand firm on his principles. But in 1840 James G. Birney (once an Alabama slaveowner), Theodore Weld, and other moderates split with Garrison and his followers.

One reason the moderates left was that they did not want women taking part in their meetings. They feared that this might drive away some men whose support they needed. But mostly the moderates felt that slavery could be abolished only through political action; that is, by changing the laws. After 1840 abolitionists had two paths open to them. They might follow either Garrison's American Antislavery Society or James G. Birney's Liberty Party.

One escaped slave. Birney first ran for President in 1840, and he got only 7,000 votes. But in the 1844 election the total climbed to 62,000. After 1848, as we will see in the next two chapters, a series of events drew more and more northerners into the antislavery ranks.

For example, in 1854 something quite remarkable took place in Boston, where less than twenty years earlier the abolitionist Garrison was nearly lynched. One June day 50,000 people lined the streets to hiss and jeer more than a thousand U. S. Marines, militia, and police. The force had turned out—with a loaded cannon—to escort one captured runaway slave, Anthony Burns, to a ship that would carry him back to the South. The federal authorities feared that anything less might tempt the mob to seize the prisoner and set him free. Burns's own words are worth noting. "There was a lot of folks to see a colored man walk down the street," he told his captors.

A question of survival. Garrison's hard line on slavery made him very popular with northern blacks. From the beginning

black antislavery people had helped his work. James Forten, a wealthy sailmaker from Philadelphia, gave money to Garrison's paper, the *Liberator*. Forten and other blacks also served on the board of directors of the American Antislavery Society.

Nevertheless, many black abolitionists found it difficult to work with the white-dominated antislavery movement. They charged that they were never given positions of leadership. White abolitionists expected them to be workers and speakers but seldom took their advice on important matters. Many of the black abolitionists were runaway slaves like Frederick Douglass and Henry H. Garnet. They were usually strong-minded and able. Yet at different times they were severely criticized for calling on the slaves to rebel, for starting their own newspapers, and for taking up antislavery politics.

Douglass once said of Garrison and his followers, "They talk . . . just as if the antislavery cause belonged to them—as if all antislavery ideas originated with them and . . . no man has the right to peep or mutter on the subject who does not have [permission] from them." But black abolitionists felt—as no white could—that as long as slavery existed, their own freedom was in danger. For blacks abolitionism was more than a cause: it was a question of survival.

 TRY THIS!

1. Explain why Americans found it hard to defend the slave system. 2. State the positions of the American Antislavery Society and the Liberty Party. In what way did each believe that the other was doing the wrong thing? 3. Describe the part taken by blacks in the antislavery movement.

ROUNDUP

Who?

George Fitzhugh
Frederick Douglass
Harriet Tubman
Nat Turner
Hinton R. Helper
William Lloyd Garrison
Theodore Weld
James G. Birney

What?

"white gold"
factor
black codes
American Colonization
    Society
the *Liberator*
gag rule
Liberty Party

Where?

Cotton Kingdom

KNOW THIS

Cotton and the Plantation System

1. How does the name "Cotton Kingdom" give a mistaken impression of the South before the Civil War?
2. List six crops that the South grew for sale.
3. Why did southerners believe that the world depended on their "white gold"?
4. How did the South come under the control of wealthy planters?
5. Why did planters and their business agents quarrel?

Life Under the Slave System

1. How did early observers answer the question "Is slavery profitable?"
2. Describe the living conditions of the slaves.
3. How was slave labor organized for field work? What parts did the driver and the overseer play?
4. Describe some of the slaves' hidden methods of resistance.
5. What were some notable slave uprisings?

The Common People of the South

1. Describe the life-styles of those called poor whites.
2. Explain how cotton production and slavery slowed down the development of cities in the South.
3. How did southerners, before the Civil War, feel about the South's financial dealings with the North?
4. What were some of the laws restricting black Americans even when they were free?

The Antislavery Movement

1. What was the American Colonization Society? How did it propose to solve the problems of blacks?
2. What were the aims of the antislavery crusade? How did the abolitionists spread their message?
3. Compare the viewpoints of William Lloyd Garrison with those of more moderate abolitionists.
4. How did black Americans aid the abolitionists' cause?
5. How did many northerners at first react to abolition? What changed their views?

DIG HERE!

Investigate the general topic of slavery in the South from 1800 to 1861. As you use the books listed here, those on page 327, or others available in your school or public library, keep these questions in mind for your report.

A. How fast did the slave population grow? (You may wish to show this on a chart.) What accounted for the rapid growth? How many large-scale slaveholders were there?

B. Compare occupations and working conditions on plantations with those in cities. How did the overseer system affect working conditions? What were slave rentals?

C. Compare family life and living conditions on plantations and in cities. Consider food, shelter, clothing, health care, and educational opportunities.

D. Did attitudes and relationships between slaves and masters change in these years? How? Why?

E. What rebellions and slave-ship mutinies took place from 1800 to 1861? Who led them? What were their outcomes?

These are some useful books: Cuban, *The Negro in America*, Scott, Foresman; Franklin, *From Slavery to Freedom*, Knopf; *Historical Statistics of the United States*, U.S. Government Printing Office; Katz, *Eyewitness: The Negro in American History*, Pittman; Logan, Cohen, *The American Negro*, Houghton; Polski, Kaiser, *The Negro Almanac*, Bellwether; Stampp, *The Peculiar Institution*, Knopf.

THINK ABOUT IT

1. If you had been a free black with a skilled trade, before the Civil War, would you have wanted your family to settle in the North or in one of the slave states? Why? (Remember that in the North you might have found no other black family in your community.)

2. How much does geography influence history? From what you have read in this chapter and on page 99, weigh the effect of cotton-growing on the South. What might have happened to slavery if there had been no cotton plantations? Suppose cotton had flourished only in a northern climate. Would slavery have spread there? Explain.

DO IT!

1. Create a bulletin-board display, or make a model, of a southern plantation. Be sure to include the mills and workshops as well as the mansion. Explain the importance of all buildings.

2. Write a one-page essay defending or attacking this statement: "Slavery was a profitable institution for white southerners."

THEN AND NOW

There are countries today that sell a single crop or product to the rest of the world. Most are poor and feel that the industrial nations take advantage of them. If the South had broken away from the Union, would it now be one of these exploited countries? Or would it have become industrialized? Why?

255

The Nation Seeks Its Destiny

"Mountain men" were the first whites in the Far West. They hunted, trapped, and traded with the Indians. They lived among the Indians and adopted their lifestyle. These hats, once worn by "mountain men," combine buffalo skin and horn, trade beads, and feathers.

The United States Constitution was a compromise between the power of the states and that of the national government. Southerners generally favored stronger states; northerners, a more powerful federal Union. But the compromise was supposed to be broad enough to satisfy both nationalists and states' rightists. However, those on each side of the compromise sometimes shifted positions. Northerners defended states' rights when it suited them. (New Englanders had talked of leaving the Union over the Louisiana Purchase and the War of 1812.) Southerners urged vigorous federal action when it would help them (by protecting slavery, for instance).

But what would happen when a state tried to force the whole nation to accept its views? Could a state set aside an act passed by Congress? Could the federal government then use force to make the state obey? Was the United States "one nation, indivisible" or an association of states? People held opposite views on this question.

1. AN INDEPENDENT TEXAS

From its beginnings, the United States had been a self-confident nation bent on expansion. Most of its founders agreed with Jefferson that "conquest [was] not in our principles." Yet they still expected the country to grow "naturally."

Americans of the early 1800s could say that they conquered no one. (And when they tried, as in the War of 1812, they failed.) They dismissed their treatment of the Indians as a natural takeover of land that was not put to good use. Jefferson bought the first big piece of new territory, Louisiana, from France. John Quincy Adams used a little pressure to get Florida from Spain. Exploring and organizing these territories took about twenty-five years. And by the 1840s the United States was again ready to move.

A handy phrase. By 1845 the editor of the *Democratic Review,* John L. O'Sullivan, had made up the term *manifest destiny.* He used it to express the feeling of most Americans that it was their certain fate one day to rule North America from coast to coast—even to the North Pole.

The drive for more territory was considered right for a number of reasons, such as "natural rights" and "the will of God." And "manifest destiny" was a handy phrase. It covered everything: the peaceful wish to expand trade; the right to take land simply by putting it to good use. It even included the "right" to drive others (Spaniards, Mexicans, or Indians) from a territory because they were regarded as "inferior."

———— ◆ ————

Read here of how

Americans looked westward for new land.
Many of them settled in Texas.
The Texans won independence from Mexico.
The U.S. ended a disagreement with Britain.

———— ◆ ————

TIME CHART

1822	Americans begin settling in Texas.
1836	Texas wins independence from Mexico.
1841	John Tyler becomes President.
1842	The Webster-Ashburton Treaty is negotiated.
1845	A newspaper first uses the term "manifest destiny."
1845	The United States annexes Texas.
1846	The Oregon dispute is settled.
1846	War with Mexico is begun.
1848	Treaty of Guadalupe Hidalgo ends the war with Mexico.
1850	Millard Fillmore becomes President.
1850	Congress passes the Compromise of 1850.

———— ◆——◆ ————

In a time when the country was badly divided, "manifest destiny" gave a sense of national unity—for a while. To expand America's empire, northerners and westerners as well as southerners were willing to work—even to fight—together. The South had most to gain from expansion. The territory open to slavery under the Missouri Compromise had been pretty well filled by the 1840s (map on page 181). The best land in Alabama, Mississippi, Louisiana, and Arkansas had been taken up. Only the Indian Territory of present-day Oklahoma was left.

Americans in Texas. Cotton planters, ever in need of fresh soil for King Cotton (page 238), looked westward to the lands belonging to Mexico. Texas was the part they liked best. By the Adams-Onís Treaty

Opening Up the West

54°40'

OREGON COUNTRY

(to Britain in 1846)
49°

PACIFIC OCEAN

B R I T I S H

Astoria
Portland

Willamette Valley

OREGON TERRITORY 1848
42°

Columbia R.

ROCKY

Oregon Trail

Snake R.

UNORGANIZED TERRITORY

MINNESOTA TERRITORY

WISCONSIN

Missouri R.

Mormon Trail

Ft. Laramie

Platte R.

Oregon Trail

Mormon Trail

IOWA

Nauvoo

Independence

ILLINOIS

St. Louis

Sacramento R.

California Trail

Great Salt Lake

Salt Lake City

UTAH TERRITORY

Los Angeles Route

Sutter's Fort (Sacramento)

Donner Pass

San Francisco

Butterfield Overland Mail

Salt Lake – Los Angeles Route

Old Spanish Trail

Colorado R.

Santa Fe Trail

Lawrence

Arkansas R.

MISSOURI

TENN.

Memphis

CALIFORNIA

Los Angeles

San Diego

Santa Fe

NEW MEXICO TERRITORY

Ft. Smith – Santa Fe Route

INDIAN RESERVE

Ft. Smith

ARKANSAS

Gila R.

Tucson

Gila River Trail

El Paso

Rio Grande

Butterfield Overland Mail

TEXAS

LOUISIANA

MISS.

Mississippi R.

MEXICO

Gulf of Mexico

Sea route from eastern ports via Cape Horn, Isthmus of Panama, Nicaragua, or Mexico.

0 — 500 Mi
0 — 800 Km.

Note that trails follow rivers wherever they can. Why? Parties traveling west had to plan carefully to avoid being caught by the snows in the high mountain passes.

(page 167), the United States had given up a very shaky claim that Texas was part of the Louisiana Purchase. Nevertheless, Americans had been settling there since 1822. Moses Austin of Missouri had gotten permission from the government of Mexico to occupy lands along the Brazos River in central Texas. His son, Stephen, took up the grant after Moses died.

The Mexican government welcomed settlers, requiring only that they obey Mexican law and follow the Catholic faith. The American settlers eagerly sought land in Texas and soon found that the Mexican government bothered them very little. Before long 20,000 of them, along with 2,000 slaves, had settled in the region. Most of these ex-American citizens were from Alabama, Mississippi, Louisiana, and Tennessee. Presidents John Quincy Adams and Andrew Jackson both had wanted to buy Texas, but Mexico would not sell.

By 1830 the Mexican government began to worry about the large number of foreigners living within its borders. It shut off further entry from the United States and tried to enforce Mexican law and do away with slavery in Texas. The Texans wanted Mexico to let them have their own state government under Mexican rule. When Stephen Austin took this request to Mexico City, the Mexican President, Antonio Lopez de Santa Anna, kept him in prison for eight months. The people of Texas began organizing an army under Sam Houston. They also declared their complete independence.

"Remember the Alamo!" By the winter of 1836 Santa Anna had marched into Texas with a 6,000-man army. He threw 3,000 of his troops against the Alamo, a mission at San Antonio defended by 188 Texans. These included both ex-Americans and Mexicans. On March 6, after holding out for almost two weeks, the garrison fell. All of its defenders, among them the famous frontiersmen Davy Crockett and Jim Bowie, were killed. Later that month, 200 other Texas soldiers surrendered at Goliad and were massacred at Santa Anna's orders.

By the middle of April the Mexican army had cut its way through to Galveston Bay, where Sam Houston took it by surprise. At San Jacinto (SAN juh-SIN-toh) the Texans' battle cry was "Remember the Alamo!" In this final victory, they captured Santa Anna. The Treaty of San Jacinto, which he signed, recognized the independence of Texas. The Mexican Congress refused to accept the treaty, but it had no way to retake the territory. Sam Houston was elected president of Texas, the Lone Star Republic.

This farmhouse at Columbia, Texas, was the first permanent capitol of the republic.

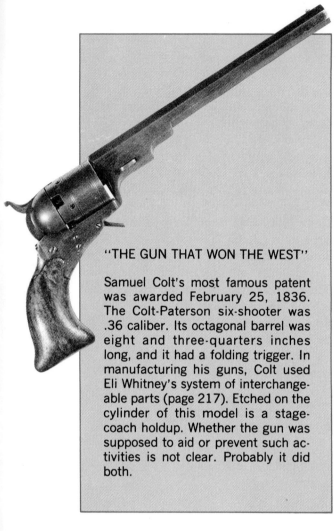

"THE GUN THAT WON THE WEST"

Samuel Colt's most famous patent was awarded February 25, 1836. The Colt-Paterson six-shooter was .36 caliber. Its octagonal barrel was eight and three-quarters inches long, and it had a folding trigger. In manufacturing his guns, Colt used Eli Whitney's system of interchangeable parts (page 217). Etched on the cylinder of this model is a stagecoach holdup. Whether the gun was supposed to aid or prevent such activities is not clear. Probably it did both.

More slave states. Many Americans wanted to annex Texas right away. Southerners were especially eager to do so. If four or five new slave states could be made out of Texas, the Senate would remain balanced, as it had been since the Missouri Compromise. In Congress resolutions for annexation were introduced.

But northerners had no wish for more slave states. Reluctantly, President Jackson sided with them, because he was sure that adding Texas to the Union would bring on

a war with Mexico. So for the time, Texas remained an independent republic. Nothing more was done about it until the election of 1844.

The shortest term. The Whigs had very little time to enjoy their triumph after the "log cabin and hard cider" campaign of 1840 (page 196). Their candidate, William Henry Harrison ("Old Tippecanoe"), caught a bad cold at his inauguration. In thirty days he was dead. His inaugural address was the longest in history (over an hour and a half), but his term of office was the shortest.

Harrison's Vice President, John Tyler, did not agree with the ideas of the Whig Party. In fact, he wasn't a Whig at all. He was a Democrat who hated Jackson for his stand on nullification (page 182). By putting him on the ticket, the Whigs had hoped to draw votes from other anti-Jackson southerners.

A peaceful settlement. As President, Tyler showed his true feelings by vetoing all the Whig measures that Henry Clay managed to put through Congress. A protective tariff, a plan to give to the states money from the sale of public lands, and two attempts to start a third United States Bank all went down in quick defeat. The entire Whig Cabinet, except Secretary of State Daniel Webster, resigned.

Webster stayed on because he was working out a settlement with the British. The Webster-Ashburton Treaty of 1842 ended a quarrel over the United States-Canadian boundary. The treaty redrew the line from Maine into what is now Minnesota (map on page 270). The two nations continued to settle their disputes peacefully as they had since the War of 1812.

President Tyler's new Cabinet were mostly southerners, and they were eager to see Texas become part of the United States. However, Texas was having great success as an independent nation and seemed uninterested in joining the Union. But that was before the annexation of Texas became an issue in the presidential campaign of 1844.

 TRY THIS!

Compare the movement for Texan independence in 1836 with that of the American colonies in 1776 (pages 73 to 86). What features were similar? Which were different? Draw up parallel lists.

2. IN OREGON: A PEACEFUL SOLUTION

There were enough issues in the presidential campaign of 1844 for four elections. The tariff, the Bank, and the President's use of the veto were hotly debated. But the issue that got most attention was territorial expansion.

A dark horse. Everyone thought that Martin Van Buren would be the Democratic candidate in 1844—including Van Buren himself. As for President Tyler, though he had been elected as a Whig, he did his best to win favor with the Democratic Party of Andrew Jackson. But neither of them got the nomination. Instead, it went to James K. Polk of Tennessee, the first "dark horse" candidate in American politics.

The expansionists in the Democratic Party would not accept Van Buren after he came out publicly against the annexation of Texas. And ex-President Jackson favored his fellow Tennesseean Polk over his old enemy Tyler. So when the front runner, Van Buren, could not get a two-thirds majority at the Democratic Convention in Baltimore, Polk was nominated.

"Fifty-four forty or fight!" The Democratic platform called for the "*re*occupation of Oregon" and the "*re*annexation of Texas." This gave the impression that in Texas and Oregon the United States would be taking back territory it had once owned. It also offered Oregon to those northerners who did not want to see Texas upsetting the balance of free and slave territory. Oregon promised them a region of

---

Read here of how

James K. Polk was successful as President. The United States did not fight for 54°40′. The nation adopted a new tariff policy.

 THE "DARK HORSE"

At country racetracks a dishonest trainer would sometimes disguise a well-known favorite by painting the horse a darker color. If the trick worked, local people could be counted on to bet heavily on the local entries. Then, as the race was run, the mysterious dark horse would emerge from the pack and romp home a winner.

The trainer's next trick was to get out of town before the truth was discovered.

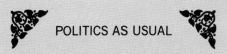

POLITICS AS USUAL

The 1844 Democratic Convention at Baltimore was the first to make use of the telegraph. Congress had voted its inventor, Samuel F. B. Morse, 30,000 dollars for an experimental line from Washington to Baltimore.

In May of 1844 the forty miles of wire had been strung. So when the convention nominated Senator Silas Wright of New York to run for Vice President, a message was telegraphed to him in Washington. Would he accept? Wright wired back that he would not. The convention leaders were dismayed. They were also distrustful of the newfangled device. They waited until a committee had traveled the forty miles to Washington and brought back Wright's refusal before choosing George Dallas of Pennsylvania in his place.

Congress didn't think much of the invention either. They refused to buy the telegraph. So Morse and his partner had to set up their own company.

It made them very rich indeed.

well-watered farmland like the Old Northwest (the present-day Midwest). It was a place where slavery could never exist.

The Party's boastful slogan was "Fifty-four forty or fight!" This meant that the nation would demand all of the Oregon Country up to 54°40′ north latitude: in other words, right up to the Alaska Panhandle (map on page 258).

A loss of respect—and votes. The Democrats' clever moves left the old compromiser Henry Clay in a difficult spot. As

the Whig candidate for President, he had joined Van Buren in saying that the annexation of Texas would be bad for the country, because it would bring on war with Mexico. Now he found himself opposing an expansion that many of his fellow countrymen seemed to want.

So Clay did what politicians are often tempted to do when a big election is at stake: he trimmed his position. Clay let it be known that he just might favor annexation after all. He also said, "I do not think the subject of slavery ought to affect [annexation] one way or the other." The seeming lack of principle cost Clay a lot of respect—and plenty of votes—throughout the North.

A chance to change history. The election of 1844 was very close. Of almost 2,700,000 votes cast, Polk won by only 38,000. James G. Birney, the antislavery Liberty Party candidate, got only 62,000 votes (page 253), but they were the key to the election. The Liberty Party took enough votes from Clay in New York to give the state's 36 electoral votes to Polk. With them, Clay would have won the Presidency by seven electoral votes.

If Clay had won the election of 1844, the history of the United States might have been very different. As it was, President Tyler, while still in office, claimed that "a controlling majority of the states" had spoken out in favor of annexing Texas. He then asked Congress to pass a joint resolution making the Lone Star Republic part of the Union. Normally, annexation would have been by a treaty and a two-thirds vote of the Senate. A joint resolution requires only a majority of both houses. The Senate passed the resolution by only two votes.

Before Polk even took office, an invitation to join the Union was on its way to

Texas. The aging ex-President John Quincy Adams called the annexation "the heaviest calamity that ever befell myself and my country."

A bad idea. If Presidents were measured by the success they had in carrying out their intentions, James K. Polk would be rated one of the greatest Presidents in the nation's history. He applied himself to a four-point program. He wished to extend the border of Texas to the Rio Grande (map, page 266). He also wanted to settle the Oregon question with Britain. He wished to reduce the tariff. And as a final point, he wanted to restore the independent treasury system.

The last of Polk's plans, the independent treasury system, meant that the federal government would store its money in its own vaults, not in central or state banks. The idea was much favored by Andrew Jackson's followers, who distrusted banks anyway. But it was probably a bad idea in a new country needing bank credit in order to expand.

By the end of his single four-year term of office, President Polk had done all four things he wanted to do. However, some of

Trading for furs at Fort Walla Walla in the Oregon Country (now Washington State).

his accomplishments seemed unwise at the time and turned out more so later on. It is never possible to be certain of such things, but with Clay as President, the pull of manifest destiny might have been overcome and war with Mexico avoided.

Forty-nine and no fight. In his inaugural address Polk said that the United States' right to the Oregon Country was "clear and unquestionable." However, in his dealings with Britain he was more restrained. "Fifty-four forty or fight!" was quietly laid to rest along with a lot of campaign oratory.

The Oregon Country was made up of the present-day states of Oregon, Washington, Idaho, part of Montana, and the Canadian province of British Columbia. Since 1818 it had been jointly occupied by Britain and the United States (page 167). That is, citizens of either country were free to live in any part. Reports of the lush farmland in the Willamette Valley had drawn settlers to the region, especially from New England and the Old Northwest. The magnificent harbors of Puget Sound would help the nation's growing Pacific trade. Finally, there was the rich fur-trapping business. John Jacob Astor's American Fur Company and the British Hudson's Bay Company were vigorously competing for it. In 1846, Congress voted to end joint occupation of Oregon, and the way was open for a final agreement.

Every American President since James Monroe had said he was willing to accept 49° north latitude as the boundary of Oregon. This was the line agreed to by Britain and the United States in 1818 (map on page 270). The British, like the Americans, had also made exaggerated claims to most of Oregon, so it was easy for the two nations to split the difference.

But Senate debate over the treaty was stormy. Some felt that the Administration's campaign pledge had been betrayed. Northerners loudly questioned why the nation was selling out in Oregon. They suspected that the South was trying to hold down the amount of free territory.

Free trade. In the middle of the U.S.-British negotiations over Oregon, Congress passed the Walker Tariff. It did so by a very close vote, with the Vice President breaking a tie in the Senate. The Walker Tariff was controversial because it reversed the policy of *protectionism* that the country had more or less followed since the Era of Good Feelings (page 177).

After the War of 1812 the country had accepted the idea that American goods, especially manufactured goods, should be protected from foreign competition (pages 127 and 182). The Walker Tariff, however, was intended only to raise money, not to keep out foreign goods. In other words, it was a *revenue* tariff. This new tariff policy meant that the United States would be a better market for British goods, especially if the two nations remained friendly.

The British were also becoming a *free trade* nation (the opposite of protectionist), and they hoped that other countries would do the same. United States free-trade policy lasted until the Civil War. After the war, as we will see, the country remained protectionist for over a hundred years.

 TRY THIS!

1. Outline both sides of a debate between a Polk supporter and someone who voted for Henry Clay—twenty years *after* the election.
2. Explain how the Oregon question was settled. **3.** Defend the Walker Tariff.

3. WITH MEXICO: A DIVISIVE WAR

Mexico had never recognized the independence of Texas. It still regarded the Lone Star Republic as a Mexican province that happened to be in the hands of rebels. Furthermore, Mexico considered the Nueces River, not the Rio Grande, the southern boundary of Texas (map on page 266).

In spite of this, President Polk believed that he could persuade the Mexicans to let Texas become part of the United States and to sell him California as well. When Mexico rejected Polk's offer and stationed 8,000 troops on the Rio Grande, Polk took more direct action. He ordered General Zachary Taylor to occupy the land between the two rivers.

The Bear Flag Republic. Polk did not wait for matters in California to take their own course. He told the consul at Monterey to stir up a revolt among the American settlers in California. Meanwhile, Polk sent secret orders to Captain John C. Frémont, an explorer who was in the region with a small military force. Frémont was told to help the uprising.

The result of this intrigue was the Bear Flag Republic, an effort to repeat what had happened in Texas. But the Spanish-speaking people rebelled against American rule, and the outbreak of war between the

THE BEAR FLAG

This drawing was made by a sixteen-year-old aboard the *U.S.S. Portsmouth* in San Francisco Bay. He sent it to his mother in a letter telling her about the California Republic.

Read here of how

The United States went to war with Mexico.
The slavery question took a new turn.
The nation fought three military campaigns.
And gained an empire.

United States and Mexico swept away the new California government.

"American blood upon American soil." We know what President Polk was up to in California because we can read about it in his diary. The diary also tells us how impatiently Polk waited for news of an incident on the Rio Grande that would be an excuse for a message to Congress. On May 9, 1846, he told his Cabinet that the country wanted a message on the Mexican question. If he failed to send one soon, he said, he would not be doing his duty. Should his message also ask for a declaration of war? All but the Secretary of the Navy thought so.

That same night the long-awaited dispatches arrived from Texas. A Mexican

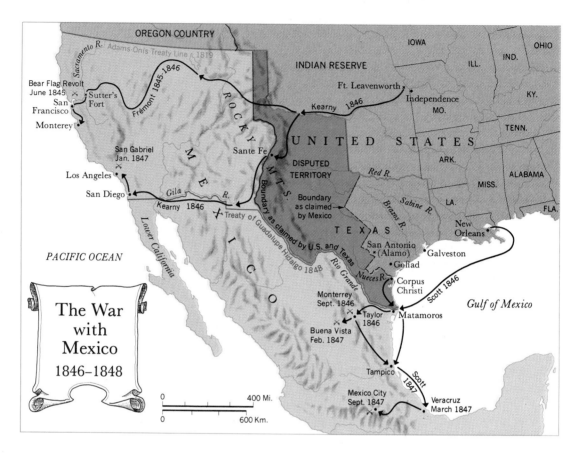

The War
with
Mexico
1846–1848

OREGON COUNTRY

Sacramento R.   Adams-Onis Treaty Line 1819

IOWA   OHIO
IND.
ILL.
INDIAN RESERVE
Ft. Leavenworth
KY.
Kearny 1846   Independence
MO.

Bear Flag Revolt
June 1845
San
Francisco
Monterey
Sutter's
Fort
Frémont 1845-1846

ROCKY MTS.

UNITED   STATES
TENN.

San Gabriel
Jan. 1847
Los Angeles
San Diego
Gila   R.
Kearny 1846
Sante Fe
DISPUTED
TERRITORY
ARK.

Red R.
ALABAMA
MISS.
Treaty of Guadalupe Hidalgo 1848
Boundary
as claimed
by Mexico
Boundary as claimed by U.S. and Texas
LA.
Sabine R.
Brazos R.
FLA.

PACIFIC OCEAN

Lower California

TEXAS
San Antonio
(Alamo)   Galveston
Goliad
Corpus
Christi
New
Orleans
Scott 1846

Gulf of Mexico

Monterrey
Sept. 1846
Taylor
1846   Matamoros
Buena Vista
Feb. 1847

Rio Grande
Nueces R.

Tampico
Scott
1847

Mexico City
Sept. 1847
Veracruz
March 1847

0   400 Mi.
0   600 Km.

Which of the overland trails was Kearny's force following (map on page 258)? How did his expedition enable the United States to "seize a million square miles of Mexican territory" (page 269)?

force had crossed the Rio Grande. There they had "attacked and killed and captured" two cavalry companies from General Taylor's army. In telling all this to his Cabinet, Polk failed to mention that Taylor had been blockading Matamoros, a town plainly on the Mexican side of the river.

Two days later, Polk told Congress that Mexico had "invaded our territory and shed American blood . . . upon American soil." Congress declared that a state of war existed "by act of the Republic of Mexico."

A momentous public issue. The vote in Congress was overwhelming, but the debate was long and bitter. Those opposed were mostly northern Whigs like Congressman Abraham Lincoln of Illinois. Lincoln kept calling on President Polk to point out the exact spot on American soil where American blood had been shed. But John C. Calhoun of South Carolina also doubted that war existed "according to the sense of our Constitution."

However, once the war began, those in Congress who had been against it willingly voted funds to keep it going. It probably made them feel better to attach the "Wilmot Proviso" to each one of these money bills. The motion of David Wilmot, a Congressman from Pennsylvania, said that

266

"neither slavery nor involuntary servitude" would ever exist in any territory acquired from Mexico.

It was antislavery Whigs and northern Democrats who pushed Wilmot's Proviso. The Democrats knew their voters were for expansion but opposed to any spread of slavery. President Polk condemned the Wilmot Proviso, but most people did not pay much attention to it—at the time.

So, quietly, almost absentmindedly, a momentous public issue was born. *Free soil,* as it came to be called, grew until fifteen years later it broke the country in two.

A slave-state conspiracy. Support of the war varied in different sections of the nation. The West favored it for patriotic reasons: America must grow and become great. The South desperately needed territory for future slave states. If it failed to get them, it would be outnumbered and outvoted. Moreover, the South needed new farmland because what it had was being worn out by cotton-growing. The Northeast liked the idea of having such a fine port as San Francisco for its China trade—but it was not in a hurry. Perhaps, in time, the United States could buy San Francisco.

Opposition to the war was strongest in the Northeast. The Massachusetts legislature passed a resolution against the war. It urged "all good citizens to join in efforts to arrest this gigantic crime." Young Henry David Thoreau was jailed when he refused to pay a two-dollar tax because it would help to support the war effort. Later, Thoreau made the incident part of his essay "Civil Disobedience." A century later, this had a deep influence on the Indian Mohandas Gandhi and the civil rights leader Martin Luther King, Jr.

Many northerners undoubtedly saw the war as a slave-state conspiracy to give the South control of the nation.

General Zachary Taylor ("Old Zach") looks very military on this embroidery.

A balance sheet. At the beginning of the war, Mexico had 32,000 men in its armed forces. The entire Mexican army may have reached 36,000 in the course of the fighting. They were not well trained or well led, and their artillery and other equipment were far out-of-date. But they were fighting on their own ground in a war that they regarded as a matter of honor.

The United States Army began the war with a little more than 7,000 men: fourteen regiments. In time marines and short-term volunteers brought this to over 100,000. Transportation, communication, and sanitation were poor. The telegraph was very

267

new and not yet adapted for military use. There was also jealousy between the two top commanders, Winfield Scott and Zachary Taylor. Politics were a problem too, since Scott and Taylor were both Whigs, while Polk's Administration was Democratic.

A great personal triumph. As soon as war was declared, General Stephen W. Kearny was ordered to lead his men (a regiment of cavalry and some Missouri volunteers) from Fort Leavenworth, Kansas, to New Mexico. There he was to capture the town of Santa Fe. He did so and then marched a thousand grueling miles to California, where he took Los Angeles. Eight months after the outbreak of the war, the United States had seized a million square miles of Mexican territory.

Meanwhile, the force on the Rio Grande under Zachary Taylor drove the Mexican army deep into their own country. Santa Anna, no longer President of Mexico, was living in exile in Cuba. He wanted to get back into power. President Polk was willing to help him, if once he got control of Mexico, Santa Anna would make peace with the United States.

The dictator accepted and returned to power with U. S. help. But instead of making peace, he launched an all-out attack on Taylor at Buena Vista. Zachary Taylor won a smashing victory in that battle, and as most of his troops had been sent to fight under Scott, it was a great personal triumph.

The halls of Montezuma. To finish off the war, General Winfield Scott led a land and sea force to Veracruz, a Mexican seaport on the Gulf of Mexico. From there, Scott and his troops marched to Mexico City, just as Cortés had done more than three hundred years earlier (page 29). When they reached the great Valley of Mexico, Scott and his troops engaged the Mexicans in a series of sharp, bloody battles until they had control of the city. A detachment of U.S. Marines occupied the National Palace, the "halls of Montezuma" mentioned in the Marine Hymn.

The climax of Scott's siege took place at Chapultepec (chuh-POOL-tuh-pek). This was a fortified hill guarding the entrance to the city. Part of the old structure was a military school. It was defended by about a hundred of its students, some of whom died rather than surrender. As most of these heroic youngsters were in their early teens, they are remembered in Mexico as *los niños héroes*, "the heroic young boys." Their place in Mexican history is like that of the defenders of the Alamo in ours.

The United States forces under Scott fought a brilliant campaign against heavy odds. As a professional soldier, Scott did far better than "Old Rough and Ready" Zachary Taylor. Furthermore, the Mexican War was a kind of on-the-job training for the graduates of West Point. Practically every commander of any importance on either side in the Civil War had fought as a junior officer in Mexico.

An unauthorized treaty. When the time came to make peace, President Polk already had a representative in Mexico, Nicholas P. Trist. But the President, dissatisfied with Trist, had ordered him to come home. Instead of obeying, Trist quickly negotiated a treaty with the Mexican government. The Treaty of Guadalupe Hidalgo (gwah-duh-LOO-pay ee-DAHL-goh)

In 1854, the United States paid Mexico 15 million dollars for the Gadsden Purchase (map on page 270). A southern route was now possible for the transcontinental railroad.

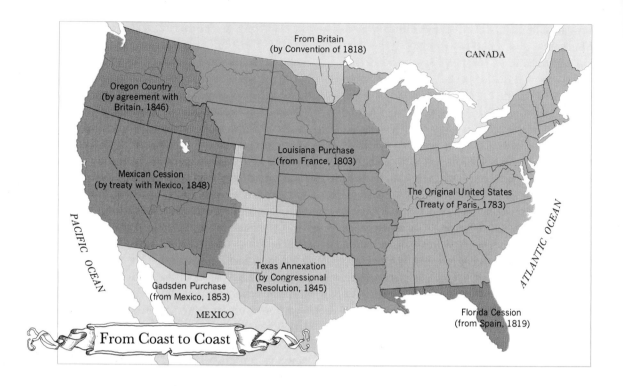

From Britain
(by Convention of 1818)

CANADA

Oregon Country
(by agreement with
Britain, 1846)

Louisiana Purchase
(from France, 1803)

Mexican Cession
(by treaty with Mexico, 1848)

The Original United States
(Treaty of Paris, 1783)

PACIFIC OCEAN

ATLANTIC OCEAN

Texas Annexation
(by Congressional
Resolution, 1845)

Gadsden Purchase
(from Mexico, 1853)

MEXICO

Florida Cession
(from Spain, 1819)

From Coast to Coast

made the Rio Grande the southern boundary of Texas. It also gave the United States all or most of Arizona, New Mexico, Utah, Nevada, Colorado, and Upper California. (Polk had wanted Lower California too.)

In return for all this, the United States agreed to recognize the land titles of the Mexicans in the area taken. The United States was also willing to pay Mexico 15 million dollars and to take over 3.25 million dollars in United States citizens' claims against Mexico. When various costs were deducted, Mexico actually got 8.5 million dollars (maps on pages 266 and 270).

President Polk was furious with Trist for having gone ahead on his own. Nevertheless, the war was becoming more unpopular all the time, so Polk decided to submit the unauthorized treaty to the Sen-

Which of these United States territories were taken in war? Which ones were bought from other nations? Which did the United States gain by negotiation? Can all of them be fitted into one of those three categories?

ate. There it was promptly approved by a vote of 38 to 14. Most of the opposition came from those, like Secretary of State Buchanan, who wanted all of Mexico.

 TRY THIS!

1. Compare Scott and Taylor as military leaders. What did each accomplish? **2.** Write a letter that one of the surviving Mexican cadets might have sent to his parents after the fighting at Chapultepec.

4. THE COMPROMISE OF 1850

"The United States will conquer Mexico," the philosopher Ralph Waldo Emerson had said, "but . . . Mexico will poison us." Indeed, the war with Mexico raised questions no peace treaty could settle.

Divisions in the ranks. The Whigs, who had opposed the war, stood to gain most from it. They had two military heroes, Scott and Taylor. Either might lead them to victory in the 1848 election. On the other hand, the Democrats, whose expansionist ideas had triumphed, seemed to be in the greatest trouble. Their membership was badly split over the Wilmot Proviso (pages 266–267), especially in the key state of New York.

David Wilmot's proposal to forbid slavery in the new territories had not died when the war ended. Eight northern state legislatures endorsed the Proviso. John C. Calhoun reacted by saying that the South would be "at the entire mercy of the non-slaveholding states." Wilmot charged that slaveholders were moving into the new territories even before they were annexed. The division among Democrats over the question of slavery in the new territories was too wide to be hidden.

But when American political parties are split in this way, they try to find a candidate who is acceptable to both sides. In Lewis Cass, a faithful party worker from Michigan, the Democrats thought they had one. When Polk refused a second term in 1848, Cass became the Democratic candidate.

Which would it hurt more? The Whigs chose Zachary Taylor, a southerner and a slave owner, to run for President. "Old Zach" was still angry with Polk for having given so many of his troops to Scott. Whig leaders expected him to forget issues and just run as the candidate of all the people, but this was not going to work. Slavery was too big an issue to be ignored. The Conscience Whigs (northern Whigs who opposed slavery and favored the Wilmot Proviso) left the party.

The issue of *free soil* (barring slavery from the new territories) had seriously divided both Democrats and Whigs. The only question was, which one would it hurt more?

During the summer of 1848 antislavery Whigs and Democrats met at Buffalo, New York, to form a new party. They drew, besides those two groups, Liberty Party people, abolitionists, those favoring internal improvements (page 170), small businessmen, and supporters of all kinds of reforms from women's rights to temperance. Calling themselves the Free Soil Party, they chose Martin Van Buren to run for President on a platform that called for "free soil, free speech, free labor, and free men." Among them were many of the same people who formed the Republican Party a few years later.

But the position of the Free Soil Party on slavery was not quite the same as that of

Read here of how

The election of 1848 solved nothing.
Henry Clay put a compromise together.
The compromise was rejected.
But each of its parts was accepted.

Before the Mexican War, Californians developed all the techniques and equipment of the American cowboy. The lariat, horned saddle (used in roping), high-heeled boot (helpful in bulldogging a calf or steer), and the fast, surefooted pony were used earlier by the *vaquero* (Spanish for cowboy).

the old Liberty Party or of the abolitionists. Both of these had attacked slavery as immoral. The Free Soilers, on the other hand, wanted to convince white working people that slavery would hurt them by keeping free workers out of the new territories. It was an appeal to self-interest, and it was just a little bit racist.

"The blood and treasure of the whole people." When the votes were counted in 1848, Taylor had won but with less than a majority. Van Buren and the Free Soilers, with 291,000 votes, had carried New York State and the city of Chicago. In Congress

they had enough members to hold the balance between Whigs and Democrats. It was a bad sign for the friends of slavery. Yet the vote settled nothing as far as slavery in the new territories was concerned.

One thing was certain. Extending the old Missouri Compromise line (page 181) into the lands gained from Mexico would not be acceptable to either side. Southerners demanded the right to hold slaves in all the new territories. These lands, they said, had been "purchased with the common blood and treasure of the whole people." Northerners wanted no slavery in California, even though most of it was below the old Compromise line.

At this point events were taking place that made the need for settlement more urgent than ever.

California, here we come! On January 29, 1848, a man named James Marshall was building a sawmill in the lower Sacramento Valley. While he was inspecting a channel that had just been dug, Marshall noticed something gleaming in the water. The shining substance was gold! News of its discovery spread, and soon people were pouring in from all over the world. In 1851, thirty-five million dollars worth of gold was produced in California.

The settlement of California was different from that of any other territory. Up to this time, people from northern and southern states had moved west along parallel lines. They had filled up whatever region was just to their west, taking their own way of life with them. In this way Ohio, Indiana, and Illinois had been settled by New Englanders and New Yorkers; Kentucky and Tennessee by Virginians and North Carolinians; Alabama, Mississippi, and Louisiana by South Carolinians and Georgians.

California had a small Spanish population in addition to its Indian population. The settlers from the East were almost all northerners. Many came by sea from the Northeast, sailing around the tip of South America or crossing the Isthmus of Panama. They were not about to let California enter the Union as a slave state. The fact that San Francisco was south of a line someone had drawn across a map thirty years earlier meant nothing to them.

Meanwhile, California was still under military rule. This gave President Zachary Taylor, as Commander-in-Chief, control of

"Gold fever." When this town's streets were paved, citizens looked for gold flakes in the gravel.

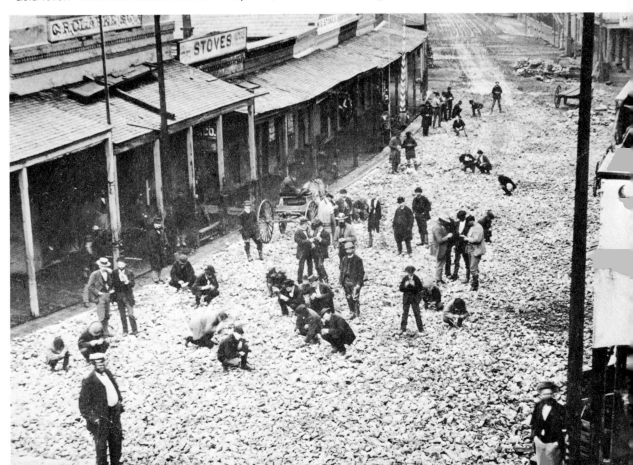

the political situation. He ordered the military officers in the area to start enrolling voters for a territorial convention. This was promptly done, and in September 1849 the convention met. It drew up a constitution barring slavery, organized a state government, appointed two senators, and demanded admission to the Union.

President Taylor told Congress that it must respect the wishes of the Californians. What they decided to do about slavery, he said, was their own business.

One more try. The next move was up to Congress. There the House was so divided it spent three weeks just trying to elect a Speaker. In the Senate things were changing very quickly. Henry Clay, Daniel Webster, and John C. Calhoun had been in Congress for almost forty years. These older leaders had worked carefully, within fixed rules, mindful that a bad mistake might tear the Union apart. They were great believers in compromise. The younger men taking their places, like William Seward of New York and Jefferson Davis of Mississippi, seemed to regard compromise as something shameful.

But Henry Clay, the expert compromiser, made one more try. In 1850, with the help of Stephen A. Douglas of Illinois, he put together the Omnibus Bill, which he hoped would give enough to everybody to restore harmony. Its provisions were:

1) California would immediately be admitted as a free state.

2) The rest of the territory gained from Mexico would be organized without provision for or against slavery. (It seemed unlikely that anyone would be able to grow cotton or rice in that dry, windswept country.)

3) A new western boundary would be adopted for Texas. (The state claimed parts of Oklahoma, Kansas, and Colorado, as well as most of New Mexico.) As compensation the federal government would take over the debts of the former Republic, which the state had agreed to pay.

4) The slave trade, but not slavery, would be abolished in the District of Columbia.

5) A new, effective fugitive slave law would be adopted.

The key to the success of the compromise was Daniel Webster of Massachusetts. He would be best able to "sell" the compromise package in the North, even with its fugitive slave law and its failure to ban slavery in the territories gained from Mexico. Webster tried to win support for the compromise in a speech that began, "I wish to speak today not as a Massachusetts man, nor as a northern man, but as an American." But Webster was roundly attacked for his speech by many northern leaders.

As the debate on the Omnibus Bill opened, a ghostlike Calhoun, plainly a dying man, appeared in the Senate. The Bill, he said in a speech that was read for him, was no compromise, but a surrender. The Union could regain its health, he went on, only if the North accepted the South's terms: equal rights for North and South in the territories and an end to agitation over slavery.

Different backing for each provision. President Taylor opposed some provisions of the compromise, and he objected to the way they were tied together. However, on July 9, 1850, Taylor died. This brought Vice President Millard Fillmore to the Presidency. He made it clear that he was willing to sign the compromise. So with the greatest skill, Stephen A. Douglas carved the Omnibus Bill into its separate parts.

274

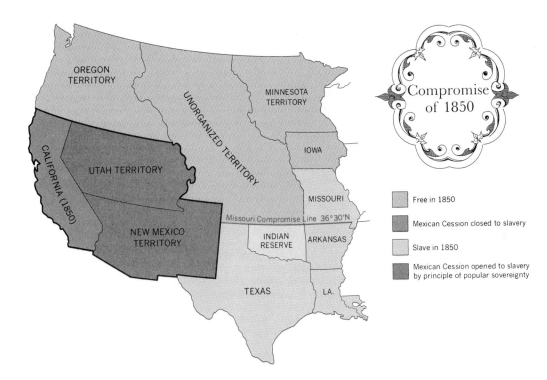

OREGON TERRITORY

MINNESOTA TERRITORY

UNORGANIZED TERRITORY

CALIFORNIA (1850)

UTAH TERRITORY

IOWA

MISSOURI

Missouri Compromise Line 36°30′N

NEW MEXICO TERRITORY

INDIAN RESERVE

ARKANSAS

TEXAS

LA.

Compromise of 1850

- Free in 1850
- Mexican Cession closed to slavery
- Slave in 1850
- Mexican Cession opened to slavery by principle of popular sovereignty

Was Emerson right when he said, "Mexico will poison us" (page 271)? In what way does the map show that he was? Is it possible that if there had been no Mexican War there would never have been an American Civil War?

Then he found a different set of members to back each individual piece of legislation. In this way he got the Compromise of 1850 passed into law. Everyone agreed that it was quite a performance.

An unreal dispute. The Compromise of 1850 might have lasted if it had not been for the Fugitive Slave Law. This gave federal marshals the power to order bystanders help them capture a runaway. The law also imposed a six-month jail sentence and a thousand-dollar fine for helping escapees.

In state after state throughout the North, personal liberty laws were passed or strengthened. This clearly placed state authority between a citizen (the accused black) and the power of the federal government (the Fugitive Slave Law). It was the same doctrine favored by the South in the case of nullification (page 182). By insisting on this harsh Fugitive Slave Law, the South may have done more than all the abolitionists together to turn northerners against slavery (page 253).

TRY THIS!

1. Compare the Compromise of 1850 with Henry Clay's earlier efforts: the Missouri Compromise (page 181) and the Compromise of 1833 (page 183). Which seemed to work best? Which was hardest to get accepted? Why? **2.** Explain how the provisions of the Fugitive Slave Law might have made people turn against slavery.

275

ROUNDUP

Who?
> Sam Houston
> John C. Frémont
> John Sutter
> Winfield Scott
> Zachary Taylor

What?
> manifest destiny
> "dark horse"
> protectionism
> free trade
> Lone Star Republic
> Wilmot Proviso
> free soil
> Compromise of 1850

Where?
> Alamo
> San Jacinto
> 54° 40'
> 49th parallel
> Veracruz
> Mexico City
> Sacramento Valley

KNOW THIS

An Independent Texas

1. What was "manifest destiny"? How did it affect westward expansion?
2. What did Stephen Austin and Sam Houston do for Texas?
3. What was the importance of the Alamo?
4. When and how did Texas win its independence?
5. Why didn't the United States annex Texas at once?

In Oregon: A Peaceful Solution

1. How did a Democrat happen to be President after the Whigs won the election of 1840?
2. Why was the "dark horse" James Polk nominated in 1844?
3. What successes did Polk have in carrying out the plans for his administration?
4. To what does the slogan "Fifty-four forty or fight!" refer? Why wasn't it acted upon?
5. Was the Walker Tariff of 1842 protectionist or free-trade? Explain.

With Mexico: A Divisive War

1. How much support was there in the United States for war with Mexico? Where was it strongest? Where weakest?
2. How did slavery become an issue in the Mexican War?
3. What events led to the outbreak of war with Mexico?
4. What part did former President Santa Anna play in the war?
5. What were the chief provisions of the Treaty of Guadalupe Hidalgo?

The Compromise of 1850

1. What were the political parties and candidates in the 1848 election? What was the outcome?
2. What was the connection between the discovery of gold in California and the Compromise of 1850?
3. List the chief points of the Compromise of 1850.
4. How was the Compromise finally adopted?
5. What were some results of the Fugitive Slave Law?

DIG HERE!

Choose one of the regions added to the U.S. in the 1840s (Texas, Oregon, California, the Southwest); then carry out *one* of these research projects:

1. Prepare a large-scale political and topographical map of the territory for the bulletin board. Include bodies of water, deserts, mountains, forts, and early towns. Show the routes used by early settlers. (Use the map on page 258 and the *American Heritage Pictorial Atlas of American History,* or another source.)
2. Describe the culture that existed when the first U.S. settlers arrived (homes, clothing, food, government, way of making a living, social life). Remember that you may build models, make sketches, prepare food, and so forth.
3. Look up the transportation routes used by settlers going to your region. Prepare a guidebook for them. Include maps, information about wagons, lists of clothing and equipment (illustrated?) which should be brought west, typical weather, and possible hazards.
4. Report on the daily life of the first settlers. Give attention to their relations with the earlier inhabitants. (It doesn't have to be just a *written* report.)
5. Select a famous "first citizen" of your region. Write a biography, draw a series of cartoons, or prepare a skit of some important event in the character's life. For all of these topics, you will find useful references on page 326.

THINK ABOUT IT

1. What five personal characteristics would you expect to find in the kind of people who took part in the westward migration? Do you think these characteristics were necessary for life in a wilderness? Are they the ones admired by Americans today? Why, or why not?
2. How much have the Mexican-American people of California and the Southwest influenced the language, customs, music, films, and lifestyles of the United States? How do you account for this?

DO IT!

1. Organize a debate or panel discussion on one of these topics: manifest destiny, the Mexican War, the Compromise of 1850.
2. Find out why early settlers struggled across some of the richest soil in the world to settle in Oregon. Why didn't they stop sooner? Report your findings to the class.

THEN AND NOW

What are the rights (and duties) of a citizen who feels that his or her country is doing something (fighting a war, for instance) that is wrong? Is the situation any different when the action seems morally wrong rather than just unwise? Thoreau went to jail to avoid supporting the Mexican War. Many Americans did the same because of Vietnam. How do you feel about these people?

277

12

The People Divide over Slavery

Civil wars are usually the most terrible. This was true of the fighting between proslavery and antislavery settlers in Kansas. Beginning in the 1850s, it continued during the much bigger Civil War of the 1860s. Here Union troops are forcibly evacuating southerners from a Kansas town.

1.   A NEW SECTIONAL QUARREL

Until the Civil War Americans had always settled differences between the sections of their country by compromise. The Constitution, the original great compromise, had given protection to southern slavery (page 110). In 1820 the Missouri Compromise (page 181) had ended a serious crisis between the sections. The tariff dispute of 1833 (page 182) had ended without fighting. Even the bad feelings stirred by the Mexican War seemed to be settled by the Compromise of 1850 (page 274). But beneath the surface were warning signs.

"I am bound to disobey this act." In 1848, the northern Whigs split into two factions. One, called the Conscience Whigs (page 271), found it difficult to cooperate with the slaveholding Whigs of the South. The other, the Cotton Whigs, had close business ties with the South. The Cotton Whigs struggled to maintain a nationwide Whig Party, but the Fugitive Slave Act deepened their division. Conscience Whigs flatly refused to support the measure.

A harsh note was now heard in public debate. Senator Charles Sumner of Massa-

278

chusetts expressed the feelings of many when he denounced the Fugitive Slave Act. "By the Supreme Law, which commands me to do no injustice; by the . . . Christian law of brotherhood; by the Constitution, which I have sworn to support," he declared, "I am bound to disobey this act." Many Americans now wondered if there would be a final crisis that would smash the Union.

Defeat and collapse of the Whigs. The election of 1852 was the last one until 1880 in which slavery or its results would not be the main issue. It was also one of the rare elections, before the Civil War, in which the winning candidate gained a majority of the popular vote. But the disorganized state of politics was clear at the party conventions. It took the Democrats 49 ballots to choose colorless Franklin Pierce. The Whigs used 53 ballots to decide on cantankerous General Winfield Scott.

Yet both parties endorsed the Compromise of 1850 and said there should be no further agitation over the slavery issue. Conscience Whigs tried to revive the Free Soil Party, but Pierce won an overwhelming popular victory.

The Whigs were in a bad way. On all sides the cry went up that their party had no future. In the South many declared that there was no longer a basis for relations

---

Read here of how

The Democrats won the election of 1852.
Douglas upset the Compromise of 1850.
And helped to start the Republican Party.

TIME CHART

1852	Franklin Pierce is elected President.
1854	Stephen A. Douglas introduces the Kansas-Nebraska Bill, and the Republican Party is born.
1856	James Buchanan is elected President.
1856	Civil war breaks out in Kansas.
1857	Chief Justice Roger Taney announces the Dred Scott decision.
1858	Lincoln and Douglas debate in Illinois.
1859	John Brown raids the arsenal at Harper's Ferry.
1860	Abraham Lincoln is elected President.
1861	Seven states secede and form the Confederate States of America.

---

with the northern Whigs. Charles Sumner and Charles Francis Adams, spokesmen for free soil, believed it was time to build a new party of freedom. Other northern Whigs traced their defeat to the swiftly growing immigrant vote. Soon thousands of them were joining the Know-Nothing movement (page 223). The Whig Party had run its course; it needed only a push for final collapse. Early in January 1854 that push came.

Slavery in every territory. The great novelist Nathaniel Hawthorne, long a friend of Franklin Pierce, described him as one who was "deep, deep, deep. . . . Nothing can ruin him." Hawthorne was wrong. Pierce tried to please everyone and managed only to stir up old rivalries.

279

In Congress the ambitious young senator from Illinois, Stephen A. Douglas (page 274), had his eye on the Presidency. Early in 1854 his committee introduced a bill that would divide the territory west of Iowa and Missouri into Kansas and Nebraska. It left the question of slavery up to the people living in the territories. This way of ducking the slavery issue was called *popular* or *"squatter" sovereignty*. But the most startling thing about the Kansas-Nebraska Bill was that it would repeal the Missouri Compromise. Suddenly it became possible to introduce slavery into any territory.

Douglas had said of this provision, "I know it will raise a hell of a storm." He was understating the problem. The senator from Illinois had just made slavery the chief public issue for the next 25 years. Because he did not care one way or the other about slavery, Douglas could not understand the fears his bill raised among abolitionists and free-soilers. They could see only that a vast territory, guaranteed freedom since 1820, might be opened to slavery.

Douglas was driven partly by political ambition and partly by desire to open the way for a transcontinental railroad across what was still Indian country. He also really thought he could get the slavery issue out of politics. But northerners and southerners took opposite views of his Kansas-Nebraska Bill. Instead of stabilizing political life, Douglas brought about two new forces. These were the strictly northern Republican Party and the solid Democratic South.

By opening to slavery territory north of 36°30′ within the Louisiana Purchase, the Kansas-Nebraska Act would repeal the Missouri Compromise. For free-soilers that was unthinkable.

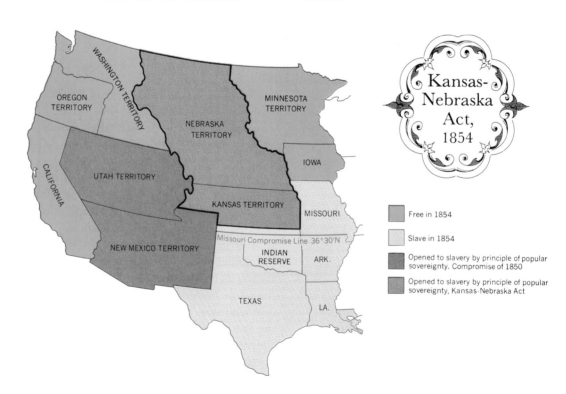

Kansas-Nebraska Act, 1854

Free in 1854

Slave in 1854

Opened to slavery by principle of popular sovereignty, Compromise of 1850

Opened to slavery by principle of popular sovereignty, Kansas-Nebraska Act

The Republican banner on the left shows two of the party's important principles. The one on the right makes fun of the Democratic candidates, Buchanan (Buck) and Breckenridge (Breck).

A mixed crew. The Kansas-Nebraska Bill stirred northerners to angry protests. They reacted with fierce charges that southerners were swindling them out of soil guaranteed to free farmers. There were so many spontaneous "anti-Nebraska" meetings that it is hard to tell which one really started the Republican Party. However, a session at Ripon, Wisconsin, in February 1854, called for a Republican state convention the following July. Many make this the beginning of the present-day party.

Once organized, the Republicans attracted a mixed crew. Former Free Soil Party members, abolitionists, discontented Democrats, temperance advocates, and many northern Whigs swelled their ranks. These people were not just antislavery. They also believed that the North's "free labor society" was in every way superior to the "slave society" of the South. Horace Greeley, editor of the New York *Tribune,* was among those who joined the new party. So was the shrewd New York politician William H. Seward, a man with presidential ambitions. The Republicans were attracting into their ranks many kinds of northern voters.

But nothing the "anti-Nebraska" people could do prevented Congress from adopting Stephen A. Douglas's fateful bill. Late in May 1854 the Kansas-Nebraska Act became law.

Solid South and almost solid North. The Republican Party became truly national in 1856 when it met at Philadelphia to choose a candidate. Delegates were surprised to find that the Presidency was almost in their grasp. Hoping to win it, they chose the colorful explorer John C. Frémont. (Someone described Frémont as a man who had all the marks of genius ex-

281

cept ability.) The Republicans' platform promised to bar both slavery and Mormon plural marriages from the territories. They were referring to the Mormon belief that a man should marry as many wives as he could provide for. As we saw in Chapter 8, Mormons were often persecuted by other Americans (page 199).

The Democrats chose as their candidate the easygoing James Buchanan of Pennsylvania. His chief qualification was that he had made no one angry. What was left of the Know-Nothing Party put up former President Millard Fillmore.

In the campaign that followed, Republicans preached "Free Soil, Free Labor, Free Speech, Free Men, and Frémont." Millard Fillmore stood by the Union, and James Buchanan warned that a Republi-

can victory would cause the South to break away.

Buchanan did well in the South and won, but he got less than half the total vote. Frémont carried most of the North, so both the Democrats and Republicans were now sectional parties. Democrats controlled a solid South, while the Republicans held an almost solid North. It did not promise well for the future of the Union.

 TRY THIS!

1. Explain how the collapse of the Whig Party was caused by a) the split of the northern Whigs, b) the election of 1852, c) the Kansas-Nebraska Act.   **2.** Tell how politics became sectional in the 1850s and why this was not good for the country.

2.   SLAVERY IN THE TERRITORIES

When President Buchanan took office in 1857, he expected that the Supreme Court would soon settle the dispute over slavery in the territories. This issue had been stirring up the country ever since the Kansas-Nebraska Act ended the Missouri Compromise. Now the new President in his inaugural address said that the Court would "speedily and finally" resolve it.

"Bleeding Kansas." To the people of Kansas, slavery was no dry legal question. Since the Kansas-Nebraska Act had set them on the road to statehood three years earlier, they found themselves part of a bitter struggle. Two streams of settlers had begun pouring into their territory. One, from Iowa, opposed the introduction of slavery; the other, from Missouri, wanted it. When Kansas voted in 1855 to elect a territorial

legislature, 5,000 Missourians crossed the border and cast ballots so that there would be a proslavery majority.

Of course outlaws soon seized upon the disorder in Kansas as an opportunity for horse-stealing and other forms of theft. A strong federal authority might have kept things from getting out of hand, but the territorial governor quickly gave in to proslavery threats. Outraged free-soilers re-

Read here of how

A civil war broke out in Kansas.
Dred Scott caused antislavery feeling.
Buchanan betrayed Governor Walker.

282

sponded by choosing their own officials. Kansas now had two governments.

President Pierce tried to restore order by appointing a new governor, but he too failed. Then, in 1856, events took a bloody turn. The nation learned that proslavery agents had attacked the antislavery center of Lawrence. This was no sooner reported than rumor filtered east of an even worse atrocity. A band of six men, led by an abolitionist named John Brown, had massacred five proslavery settlers at Pottawatomie.

Guerrilla warfare now blazed through the territory. "Border ruffians," as northerners called them, battled antislavery "jayhawkers" all summer in 1856.

A third governor, John W. Geary, took over next. He had an advantage over the two before him. He had lived on the frontier, and his experiences there had convinced him that peace depended on using force. Aided by federal troops, he broke up a small army of Missourians marching on Lawrence. An uneasy peace was restored to what the New York *Tribune* called "bleeding Kansas." But 200 had died, and millions of dollars in property had been destroyed.

Buchanan's mistake. Two days after Buchanan's inauguration, the Supreme Court handed down a ruling that shook the nation. It also made solving the Kansas problem even harder. A Missouri slave, Dred Scott, had been trying since 1846 to gain his freedom. His master had taken Scott for a time into territory from which slavery was barred by the Northwest Ordinance (page 102) and by the Missouri Compromise. This, Scott's lawyers claimed, made him a free man. The other side argued that slaves were property and that a person's property was protected by

the Constitution anywhere in the United States (Article Four, Section 2, paragraph a).

Scott's case was appealed to the Supreme Court in 1854, just as the Kansas-Nebraska Act was passed. Did Congress have the right to say whether a territory should be slave or free? Or should it be up to the people living there? That was what the uproar over the Kansas-Nebraska Act was about. Now it had become entangled with a Supreme Court case too. If Dred Scott's owner was right, neither Congress nor the people could keep slavery out of any territory. And if Buchanan really believed, as he said, that the country would "cheerfully submit" to the Supreme Court's ruling in this question, he was badly mistaken.

A storm of protest. On March 6, 1857, the aged Chief Justice Roger B. Taney, speaking softly, delivered the Court's decision. First, the Court denied that Dred Scott was a citizen. That meant Scott had no right to bring his case at all, so the Court could have stopped right there. Instead, Taney went on to say that neither Congress nor the people living in a territory could forbid slavery there. The Court then finished by pointing out that the Missouri Compromise had been unconstitutional.

In the Dred Scott decision the Supreme Court had agreed that a slave was to be treated as a piece of property. Further, it had refused to accept the Republican view that Congress could regulate slavery in the territories. A storm of protest swept the North. The New York *Tribune* dismissed the Court's ruling as "entitled to just so much moral weight as would be the judgment of a majority of those . . . in any . . . barroom." One abolitionist paper warned,

283

THE CRIME AGAINST KANSAS

In the 1850s, not all the blood that was shed over slavery fell on the soil of Kansas. In May 1856, Charles Sumner of Massachusetts rose in the Senate and delivered a truly blistering speech. It was titled "The Crime Against Kansas," and it attacked those Sumner held responsible for trying to introduce slavery into the territory. In it Sumner poured scorn on a number of senators, including Andrew Butler of South Carolina.

Two days later, Sumner was seated at his desk. The Senate had adjourned, and he was alone in the chamber. Hearing his name, Sumner looked up to face the tall, handsome Congressman Preston Brooks of South Carolina. Brooks said, "I have read your speech carefully. It is a libel on South Carolina and on Mr. Butler who is a relative of mine." With that Brooks raised his cane and beat Sumner unmercifully over the head and shoulders until the stick broke. Sumner tried to stand but fell to the floor in a pool of blood.

Three and a half years later, after several painful operations, Sumner was able to resume his place in the Senate. During that time, Massachusetts re-elected him almost unanimously, leaving his seat empty as a reproach to the attackers.

Meanwhile, Preston Brooks resigned from Congress and went home. He too was returned almost unanimously by the people of his district. In addition, Brooks received dozens of gold-headed canes from all over the South, with instructions to make good use of them. Brooks died a year later.

"If the people obey this decision, they disobey God."

Southerners were more certain than ever that the North was intent on overthrowing slavery.

No choice for Kansas. To solve the Kansas problem, Buchanan sent out yet another governor. After some persuasion Robert Walker, former Secretary of the Treasury, had accepted the post. Walker was a firm believer in popular sovereignty, and he wanted it to get a fair chance in Kansas. Furthermore, he had assurances from Buchanan that only actual residents of the territory would be allowed to vote on the question of slavery. Walker showed at once that he meant to have free elections. When proslavery forces tried to introduce some fake ballots, he removed them from the count.

The struggle over the state constitution with which Kansas would enter the Union was even angrier. It had been drawn up at Lecompton, Kansas, when free-soilers were boycotting elections. It would let the people choose between having slavery permanently and keeping only those slaves already in the territory. There was no way the people could vote to get rid of slavery altogether. Voters who wanted Kansas to be a free state stayed away from the polls, and the Lecompton constitution was accepted by a sizable majority.

Buchanan backed the admission of Kansas under the Lecompton constitution. He even argued that the Dred Scott decision made Kansas "as much a slave state as Georgia or South Carolina." The worst fears of the Republicans seemed to have come true. For Stephen A. Douglas the Dred Scott decision was even more dismaying. To support Buchanan would be to deny popular sovereignty. Douglas's political future was at stake. He spoke out against the President.

Governor Walker now felt betrayed by Buchanan. Because of Walker's strict fairness, the antislavery forces won the next territorial election. The election allowed the people to vote again on the proslavery constitution, and this time it was voted down. There had been over 6,000 votes to accept it; now there were more than 10,000 to reject it. Kansas entered the Union as a free state in 1861. Meanwhile, the fight over slavery had moved out of the Kansas Territory and into the halls of Congress.

 TRY THIS!

1. Trace the steps by which Kansas moved from an unorganized territory in 1854 to statehood in 1861. 2. Tell how the Dred Scott decision had an effect far beyond the fate of a single man.

3.   A RACE FOR THE SENATE

President Buchanan had taken a lead from Andrew Jackson and tried to crack the whip over Douglas. The senator from Illinois refused to be frightened, and their break split the Democratic Party. Many northern Democrats openly supported Douglas. For them popular sovereignty was a good answer to the Republican free-soilers. When Buchanan pressed Congress to accept the Lecompton constitution, which would have made Kansas a slave state, he was no longer speaking for a majority of his own party.

Two unlike politicians. Stephen A. Douglas never allowed principle to stand in the way of practical politics. He had struggled against the leaders of his own party to

---

Read here of how

Lincoln and Douglas ran for the Senate.
They debated over slavery in the territories.
Douglas was re-elected to the Senate.
But lost the support of the South.

---

block the Lecompton constitution (page 284), but this had been mainly to save his political neck. It had allowed him to restore his prestige in the North. It had even led some Republicans to think seriously of supporting this prominent Democrat for re-election to the Senate. That would have been bad news for Illinois Republicans and for their leader, Abraham Lincoln. But Douglas was playing for higher stakes—the Presidency.

Neither did Douglas sympathize with the strong antislavery bias held by many Republicans. In private he was willing to admit that slavery was a "curse," but publicly he said he was indifferent to whether it was voted in or out.

Abraham Lincoln was a different kind of man. He was a self-educated lawyer who had been born in a Kentucky cabin and had known harsh poverty in his youth. When asked about his family, he stated simply that they were poor. Possessed of a powerful ambition, Lincoln had all the hard-driving qualities of a self-made man. But Lincoln also viewed the less fortunate with real concern.

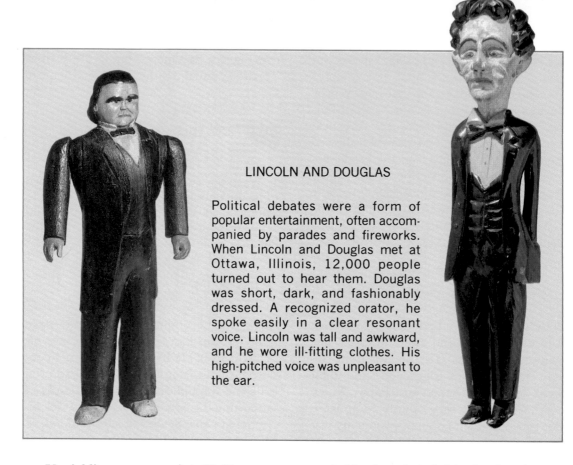

LINCOLN AND DOUGLAS

Political debates were a form of popular entertainment, often accompanied by parades and fireworks. When Lincoln and Douglas met at Ottawa, Illinois, 12,000 people turned out to hear them. Douglas was short, dark, and fashionably dressed. A recognized orator, he spoke easily in a clear resonant voice. Lincoln was tall and awkward, and he wore ill-fitting clothes. His high-pitched voice was unpleasant to the ear.

Unyielding on one point. Unlike most speakers of the time, Lincoln avoided flowery speeches. Instead, he preferred a simple, straightforward style. He had served a single term as a Whig congressman in the late 1840s, but otherwise his whole political career had been in Illinois. Although he had frequently run for higher office, he had never been elected. While in Congress Lincoln opposed the war with Mexico. Going against the opinion in his district, he denounced it as an unjust attack by the United States.

Lincoln was not prepared to think of blacks as his equals, but he detested slavery. He protested bitterly to a southern friend, "I confess I hate to see the poor creatures hunted down, and caught, and carried back to their [whippings] and unrewarded toils. But I bite my lip and keep quiet." He added pointedly, "It is hardly fair for you to assume that I have no interest in a thing that . . . continually exercises the power of making me miserable." He admitted that he did not know what to do about slavery, but often said that he did not expect the nation to remain half slave and half free. On one point he was unyielding: he insisted that slavery be kept out of the territories.

Victorious senator; future President. At this time, United States senators were chosen by state legislatures. Whichever party won a majority of the seats in the Illinois legislature would send its candidate to Washington. To help the Republicans win the 1858 state election, Lincoln set about making himself better known. He challenged Douglas to join him in addressing the same audiences. Douglas agreed, and they arranged to hold seven debates throughout the state of Illinois.

The two politicians made a vivid contrast on the platform. Douglas was short and thickset, with a massive head, dark complexion, and fierce, bulldog look. This had given him his nickname, "the Little Giant." He differed sharply from the tall, thin, homely Lincoln. Douglas had a nimble, quick-witted style, but Lincoln's calm explanation of the issues allowed his listeners to follow him easily. Audiences at the debates soon realized that both men were giants. When the contest was over, Douglas had been re-elected to the Senate by a narrow margin. Lincoln, on the other hand, by winning national attention, had made his own claim to the Presidency.

"All should have an equal chance." In the debates Douglas took the offensive right away. He accused Lincoln of being an abolitionist because he had said earlier, "This government cannot endure half slave and half free." He also charged Lincoln with believing in racial equality. When Lincoln protested that Douglas was twisting his words, Douglas claimed that Lincoln changed positions to suit his audience. "For my part," Douglas declared, "I do not regard the Negro as my equal."

It was true that in southern Illinois, where racial feelings were strong, Lincoln had said, "I am not . . . in favor of bringing about . . . social and political equality of white and black races." Further, he denied that he would ever interfere with slavery where it existed. But he also said that the black worker had "the right to eat the bread which his own hand earns." And he repeated that closing the territories to slavery would, in time, bring it to an end.

In the debates Lincoln seemed to be saying that blacks should not be slaves. At the same time, he was offering them very little hope except in the far-distant future.

But there was a difference between Lincoln's views and those of Douglas. Douglas said a slave had no rights that might interfere with those of whites. Lincoln, on the other hand, had always declared himself against the extension of slavery. "I hate it," he said, "because of the monstrous injustice of slavery itself. I hate it . . . because it forces so many . . . among us into open war with the very principles of civil liberty." Douglas accepted slavery as a permanent condition. Lincoln dreamed of the day when "all should have an equal chance."

"Let it offend them." The high point of the Lincoln-Douglas debates came at Freeport, Illinois. Lincoln was anxious not to upset the moderate voters in this central part of the state. He assured them that he would not interfere with slavery in the District of Columbia or with the slave trade within the United States. He insisted, however, that Congress could bar slavery from the territories.

Next, Lincoln pressed Douglas to explain how he could support both popular sovereignty and the Dred Scott decision. Douglas had an answer ready. If the people of a territory opposed slavery, he said, they would pass laws that were unfriendly to it, and they would fail to pass laws that would protect it. In this way slavery would be kept out of their territory. Of course this answer was offensive to the South, but Douglas did not care. "Let it offend them," he said. At that moment he wanted to hold on to his chances in Illinois.

287

On a rainy November day the Illinois voters went to the polls. They chose a legislature that assured Douglas's re-election to the Senate, but there was a swelling tide of Republican strength. In other states that day northern Democrats lost heavily.

Douglas was clearly the spokesman of the northern Democrats, but those in the South were determined to prevent his nomination. A southerner called the Illinois race a meaningless choice between a "pair of depraved, blustering, mischievous, lowdown demagogues." This view threatened to disrupt the coming 1860 presidential campaign.

 TRY THIS!

List the numbers of these sentences on a piece of paper. Beside each one write *D* if the sentence is more true of Stephen Douglas, *L* if it is more true of Abraham Lincoln, or *B* if it is true of both of them. **1.** He was a self-educated country lawyer. **2.** He was well known throughout the country. **3.** He was very ambitious. **4.** He disliked slavery but was unwilling to oppose it. **5.** He wanted to keep slavery out of the territories. **6.** He spoke in a simple, straightforward style. **7.** He accused his opponent of changing his views to suit his audience. **8.** He got something from the debates that he badly needed.

4.   THE ROAD TO DISUNION

In October 1859 an event took place that brought North and South to the breaking point. At its center was John Brown, already notorious for his activities in Kansas (page 283).

JOHN BROWN'S RAID

Most abolitionists believed in peace. John Brown, however, insisted that violence was justified in the crusade against slavery. In 1857 Brown enlisted a group of rich and powerful antislavery men who called themselves the Secret Committee of Six. These included the wealthy businessman Gerrit Smith, the widely known Unitarian minister Theodore Parker, the reformer Samuel Gridley Howe, and Thomas Wentworth Higginson of Harvard College. They opened the way, for Brown, to such important New Englanders as Ralph Waldo Emerson and Henry David Thoreau. Probably

none of these people knew what Brown really had in mind, but they raised money for him.

An army of liberation. In 1859 John Brown and a handful of followers began to gather guns and ammunition at a farm on the Potomac River. They chose the spot because it was just opposite Harper's Ferry, Virginia, where there was a federal arsenal and armory. On Sunday, October 16, 1859, Brown and 21 followers, including a few blacks, invaded the town and seized the powerhouse at the arsenal. They killed

Read here of how

John Brown tried to start a slave uprising.
And became a popular martyr in the North.
The Democratic Party split.
Lincoln was elected President.

288

one local citizen, a free black, and took others as hostages.

What was the point of Brown's attack? Apparently he expected that slaves on nearby plantations would rise up and join his force. He would then equip them with guns from the arsenal. This, he was sure, would encourage others until there would be a general slave revolt throughout the South. It never took place.

On Tuesday morning a force of U.S. Marines led by Colonel Robert E. Lee battered down the doors of the powerhouse and captured the rebels. Ten of Brown's followers and seven other people were killed in the fighting.

"For the furtherance of justice." A week after the raid, John Brown was tried for treason against the state of Virginia. At his trial he insisted that he had followed the teachings of the Bible. He had not intended, he said, to shed blood, but he was ready to give up his life "for the furtherance of justice." There were pleas that Brown's life be spared, but on December 2, 1859, he was hanged. In his final letter he wrote, "I, John Brown, am quite certain that the crimes of this guilty land will never be purged away but by blood."

Throughout the antislavery North, Brown was hailed as a martyr. The great abolitionist William Lloyd Garrison en-

John Brown rides to his execution.

289

dorsed his raid as one way to destroy slavery. Abraham Lincoln said that as long as slavery existed, there would be other John Browns.

The events at Harper's Ferry spread horror and panic throughout the South. The deepest southern fears of a slave uprising had been stirred. Southerners felt that a Republican administration in Washington would encourage future raids or at least do little to stop them. Radical southern leaders were soon asking, would continued union with the North mean suicide? They insisted that only secession was left.

THE ELECTION OF 1860

The people of the United States proudly claim that their political system is able to meet any emergency. In 1860, however, the system broke down. It was totally un-

able to solve the problems centering on slavery. The price of this failure was the terrible Civil War. It left wounds that are still not entirely healed over a hundred years later. Up to the very last moment many people believed that another compromise would be found. This, they felt, would buy time in which to find a permanent solution to the slavery question. But a majority of Americans discovered that they were northerners or southerners first. Their great experiment in democracy had reached a crisis.

Divisions too deep for solution. Charleston, South Carolina, was a hotbed

Of the states Lincoln won, he carried all but California and Oregon by absolute majorities. If all the votes against him had gone to one candidate, Lincoln would still have won—with 40 per cent of the popular vote! Add up his electoral vote in the Northeast and Midwest to see why.

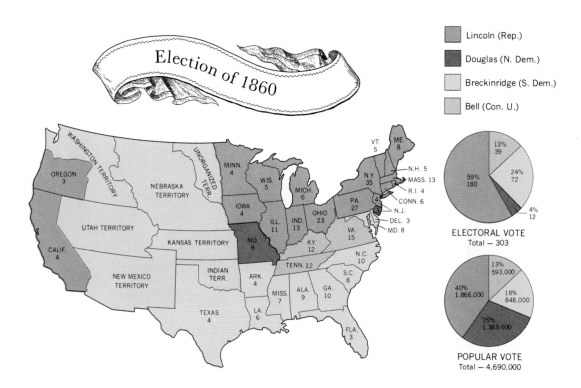

Election of 1860

Lincoln (Rep.)

Douglas (N. Dem.)

Breckinridge (S. Dem.)

Bell (Con. U.)

ELECTORAL VOTE
Total — 303

POPULAR VOTE
Total — 4,690,000

Buttons and funny hats are old campaign devices. Breckenridge and Bell flank Douglas. And the hat?

of secession. It was the very worst place the Democrats could have chosen for their 1860 convention. No sooner had the delegates gathered than a battle broke out. Southern delegates demanded that the party platform support their views on slavery. Neither Congress nor the territories themselves, they claimed, could bar slavery within their borders. Northern delegates, who were backing Douglas, refused to go along. They could win in their home states only by supporting popular sovereignty. The division among Democrats was too deep for any solution.

It was soon clear that Douglas's supporters had enough votes to nominate him. And so, to thunderous applause from the packed galleries, Alabama led the states of the Deep South out of the hall. The convention then adjourned, to meet the next month at Baltimore. There, amid angry bitterness, Stephen A. Douglas was nominated. He had won the empty honor of representing a hopelessly divided party.

Ten days later those who had walked out of the Charleston meeting also gathered at Baltimore. They nominated John C. Breckenridge of Kentucky on a platform supporting slavery in the territories. The Democratic Party, the last political link between the sections of the country, had been cut in two.

Three easy ballots. As the Democrats traded angry charges, Republican hopes soared. Their leaders gathered at Chicago with Senator William H. Seward of New York as the front runner. Yet he had a fatal weakness. Moderate northerners feared that his long antislavery record would hasten the end of the Union. Twelve years earlier he had said, "Slavery must be abolished, and you and I must do it."

With victory in their grasp the Republican delegates decided to choose a different candidate. The immediate gainer from this move was Abraham Lincoln. His manager had shrewdly worked to make him everybody's second choice. Lincoln's rise from poverty appealed to the deep American admiration for a self-made man. In secret meetings his manager promised plenty of government jobs to Indiana, New Jersey, and Pennsylvania. In case there were still any waverers, the galleries of the convention hall were packed with Lincoln's wildly enthusiastic supporters. (One of these, it

291

was said, could shout all the way across Lake Michigan.) In three easy ballots Lincoln carried the nomination.

Was the South bluffing? The breakup of American politics continued. Some Whigs, a group that was particularly strong in the upper South, put up John Bell of Tennessee for President. The Whigs were especially eager to hold the Union together. Yet of all the candidates, only Douglas campaigned in every part of the country. Even so, he knew he was doomed. He could see that he would run second to Breckenridge in the Deep South, second to Bell in the upper South, and second to Lincoln in the North.

Lincoln did not seem to understand that the South would really leave the Union if he were elected. Time and again, before the vote, he was asked to restate his views on the South. Lincoln would only say, "I'm certainly not of a temper . . . to embitter the feelings of the South." He had promised earlier that he would not interfere with slavery where it existed. When pressed to add to his statement, he would say no more than, "It would do no good." His election, he predicted, would not lead to any very strong effort to break the Union.

"Let the God of battles decide the issue." As the map on page 290 shows, Lincoln won a thumping electoral victory in 1860. Note also that it was a curious victory. His popular vote was almost a million less than that of his opponents. Yet it is clear that he would have won an electoral victory even if all the opposition votes had gone to a single candidate. The greater population of the northern states Lincoln carried made this outcome possible.

Five months still remained before war would break out, but many southerners agreed with one of their number who said, "Argument is exhausted . . . hesitation is dangerous, delay is submission, 'to your tents, O Israel, and let the God of battles decide the issue.' "

 TRY THIS!

1. Tell how differently John Brown was regarded in the North and in the South. 2. Explain why each of these political leaders was *not* elected President in 1860: a) Stephen A. Douglas, b) John Breckenridge, c) John Bell, d) William H. Seward. 3. Prove that in 1860 Lincoln would have won even if the Democrats had been united.

5.   THE SECESSION OF THE SOUTH

With the election of Lincoln the long-predicted moment came. The nation split in two. A southern newspaper said, "No claptrap about the Union, no detail of private conversations with northern men can alter it or weaken its force. It is here, a present, living, mischievous fact. The government of the Union is in the hands of the avowed enemies of one entire section."

Read here of how

Seven southern states left the Union.
They formed the Confederate States of America.
Buchanan failed to act.
Lincoln refused to compromise.

Not whether to secede, but how. On December 2, 1860, South Carolina formally cut its ties with the Union. South Carolina was the most discontented of the southern states (pages 181–182). It pointed the way for the rest of the Deep South. By February 1, 1861, Mississippi, Florida, Alabama, Georgia, Louisiana, and Texas had also withdrawn from the Union.

In all of these states the issue was not whether to secede, but how. Some leaders opposed immediate withdrawal. They favored holding off so that the whole South could leave at the same time. Others wanted to secede only if certain demands

Why was Fort Sumter a deciding factor for so many southern states? What step did Lincoln take in response to the attack on the fort? If Lincoln had not moved as he did, could war have been avoided? Did the President have a choice?

were not met. But in state after state those insisting on immediate withdrawal won out.

The Deep South believed that slavery would never be safe under a Republican Administration. It had long resented the North's influence over its business affairs, and it had complete confidence in the power of King Cotton (page 237). It looked forward to a great and prosperous slave empire, one that would take in Cuba, the West Indies, Mexico, and Central America.

A new government. Well before Lincoln's inauguration, delegates gathered at Montgomery, Alabama. Between February 4 and 10, in an atmosphere of glowing enthusiasm they formed the Confederate States of America. The constitution they drew up gave outright guarantees to maintain slavery and states' rights, and it made

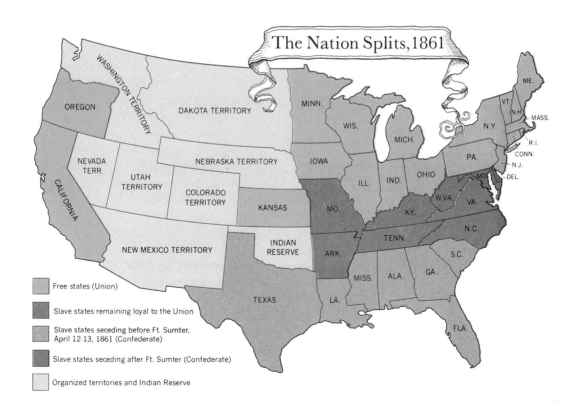

The Nation Splits, 1861

Free states (Union)

Slave states remaining loyal to the Union

Slave states seceding before Ft. Sumter, April 12-13, 1861 (Confederate)

Slave states seceding after Ft. Sumter (Confederate)

Organized territories and Indian Reserve

293

some small changes in government operation. Otherwise it was almost word-for-word the same as the Constitution of the United States.

The Confederate constitution required a two-thirds vote of both houses of Congress for the appropriation of money, and it allowed the President of the Confederacy to veto parts of spending bills. It also restricted him to a single six-year term. "The right of property in Negro slaves" was made final, and protective tariffs (page 127) were outlawed. The preamble to the new constitution declared that it was based on "the people of the Confederate States, each State acting in its sovereign and independent character."

The final business of the convention was the election of Jefferson Davis of Mississippi as acting president and Alexander Stephens of Georgia as acting vice president. Neither had been a strong supporter of secession, but once in office Davis worked hard to keep the South independent.

Buying time. The outgoing President Buchanan faced a terrible problem. He was surrounded by a Cabinet in which several members favored secession and did not know whom to trust. His party leadership had been undermined by his own betrayal of Governor Walker of Kansas and by his quarrel with Douglas (page 285). Furthermore, his Administration had been voted down in the last election.

Buchanan saw nothing in the Constitution that allowed a state to secede. Withdrawal, therefore, was unconstitutional. However, the federal government could act only if a state interfered with federal authority. In this, President Buchanan established an important point. War could only come as a result of an attack by the South.

Buchanan was also buying time. The total military force in 1860 was under 20,000, and many of its officers were sympathetic to the South. At the same time the President continued to look for possible compromises. None was found. The old give-and-take of North and South within the same Union was now impossible.

"The tug has to come." The House and Senate formed committees to seek ways out of the crisis. Senator Crittenden of Kentucky proposed a plan that looked promising. It consisted of six amendments to the Constitution. One of these would extend the Missouri Compromise line to the Pacific; another would guarantee the existence of slavery forever. Crittenden's plan seemed to meet the South's chief demands, but Lincoln, as President-to-be, would not agree to it. Extending a line to the Pacific would have meant the spread of slavery to the territories, which he flatly refused to accept.

In February 1861 a peace conference called by the state of Virginia failed for the same reason. All efforts at compromise sank on the rock of free soil. In far-off Springfield, Illinois, Lincoln gloomily concluded, "The tug has to come, and better now than any time hereafter." For him the struggle begun long ago by David Wilmot (pages 266-267) was over.

The risk of war. Lincoln believed that if he gave in to the South's demands, he might put future Presidents in an impossible situation. Every time some dissatisfied group threatened to disrupt the Union, it would be necessary to let them have whatever they wanted. "If we surrender," he warned Republican congressmen, "it will be the end of us and the government. They will repeat the experiment again and again. A year will not pass until we will have to take Cuba as a condition upon which they will spare the Union." Later he said, "When a chief magistrate is constitutionally elected, [if] he cannot be inaugurated until he betrays those who elected him . . . this government and all popular government is at an end."

If the price of peace was surrender to threats, Lincoln would accept the risk of war. He had already resolved to hold the federal forts and to collect federal taxes. Meanwhile, to reassure the South, he repeated his intention of enforcing the Constitution. This included the Fugitive Slave Law which the South had wanted so much, and which was so detested in the North (page 275).

In his inaugural address Lincoln spelled out his final stand. To the South he said, "You have no oath registered in heaven to destroy the government, while I shall have the most solemn one to 'preserve, protect, and defend' it."

The line of no retreat was drawn; the time for decision had been reached. Throughout both sections of the country there were people who agreed with one southerner that ". . . it is better to meet the crisis now than to defer it to our children." His final words were terrifying but true: "That all this will be ended in the bloodiest war that ever deluged any country, I have no doubt." The long night of the Civil War had begun.

 TRY THIS!

1. Trace the steps by which the Confederate States of America was formed.   2. Tell how each of these reacted to secession: a) President Buchanan, b) Senator Crittenden, c) Abraham Lincoln.

ROUNDUP

Who?

Franklin Pierce
William H. Seward
Jefferson Davis
Stephen A. Douglas
James Buchanan
John C. Frémont
John Brown
Dred Scott
Robert Walker
Abraham Lincoln

What?

Conscience Whigs
Cotton Whigs
Kansas-Nebraska Act
popular sovereignty
bleeding Kansas
Lecompton constitution

Where?

Ripon
Lawrence
Pottawatomie
Lecompton
Harper's Ferry
Montgomery

KNOW THIS

A New Sectional Quarrel

1. Why did the northern Whigs divide into two groups, and what was the result?
2. What were the three major provisions of the Kansas-Nebraska Act? What was the political effect of the Act?
3. When and where was the Republican Party "born"?
4. What groups of people became Republicans?
5. Who were the presidential candidates in 1856? What issues did each stress?

Slavery in the Territories

1. Why did Kansas have two territorial governments?
2. What was the role of John Brown in Kansas?
3. What were the issues in the Dred Scott case?
4. Why was the Dred Scott decision such a shock to people in the North?
5. How did the Lecompton constitution come to be first accepted, then voted down?

A Race for the Senate

1. What caused the Democratic Party to divide?
2. Why had Douglas opposed the Lecompton constitution?
3. What was Lincoln's position on slavery? On blacks?
4. How did Lincoln try to trap Douglas in their debates, and how did Douglas answer him?

The Road to Disunion

1. What was John Brown trying to do at Harper's Ferry?
2. From whom did John Brown get money and support?
3. Why was Douglas's nomination called "an empty honor"?
4. Why was William Seward *not* nominated by the Republicans in 1860? How was Lincoln chosen?
5. What did the election indicate about the condition of the country in 1860?

The Secession of the South

1. Why did the southern states secede?
2. Whom did the Confederate States choose as President and Vice President?
3. How did President Buchanan view the secession crisis and what important point did he establish?
4. Why did Lincoln turn down the Crittenden compromise? What steps did Lincoln plan to take?

DIG HERE!

For this research activity, you will look at an example of American writing, painting, sculpture or music from the period before the Civil War. Select a work by one of the following: *Writers:* Alcott (Louisa May), Bryant, Cooper, Emerson, Hawthorne, Irving, Longfellow, Melville, Poe, Whittier. *Painters and sculptors:* Allston, Audubon, Bingham, Catlin, Cole, Durand, Greenough, Morse, the Peales (Charles, Raphael, Rembrandt, Titian), Trumbull. *Musicians and composers:* Hopkinson (Joseph), Emmett, Foster, Gottschalk, Mason. Report on the work you have chosen, giving the following information:

A. What were the artist's childhood and early career like? Did this period influence his or her later work? What people or circumstances encouraged or discouraged the artist?

B. What is the theme of the story, poem, painting, sculpture, or musical selection you have chosen? What was the artist's purpose in creating it?

C. Can you see any connection between this work of art and the historic period in which it was created? Does that period suggest reasons why the theme of this work appealed to this artist?

Some books to help you are: Eliot, *Three Hundred Years of American Painting,* Time; Howard, *Our American Music,* Crowell; Larkin, *Art and Life in America,* Holt; Mendelowitz, *A History of American Art,* Holt; Myron, Sundell, *Art in America,* Collier; Rublowsky, *Music in America,* Collier; Spaeth, *A History of Popular Music in America,* Random.

THINK ABOUT IT

1. If you knew that right now the United States was heading into a time of crisis like the 1850s, what sort of leader would you want to see as President? Would you vote for a Franklin Pierce? a James Buchanan? a Robert Walker? a John Brown? a Stephen Douglas? an Abraham Lincoln? What good or bad qualities did each of these show? Which ones among them were chosen to lead the country? Which should not have been elected? Why?

2. Should political parties make compromises in their platforms in order to appeal to as many voters as possible? Or should they give voters a clear choice among different policies? Explain.

DO IT!

1. Write two "letters to the editor," or draw two cartoons, contrasting the feelings of North and South over John Brown's raid at Harper's Ferry.

2. Do some research on the South Carolina secession convention. Then write an eyewitness account of the proceedings.

THEN AND NOW

The Confederate constitution called for a single six-year term for the President and allowed him to veto separate items in a bill passed by Congress. Both of these changes have been suggested for the United States Constitution. What do you think of them? Would they be an improvement or not? Explain.

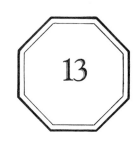

A Civil War Tests the Nation

13

Once a war begins, past problems become unimportant. Only victory seems to matter. In peacetime, politics are largely a matter of compromise. War changes that. Restraint gives way to the belief that the enemy must be destroyed. And the longer a war goes on, the more savage it becomes. Today's bloodshed avenges yesterday's and justifies tomorrow's.

All this is doubly true of civil wars. Then a single people with their common history, institutions, memories, and interests, divide against each other. The blood they shed is that of kin, and it falls on land that belongs to all.

1. NORTH AND SOUTH COMPARED

In the middle of Charleston Harbor stands Fort Sumter. In April 1861, it was the last federal stronghold in South Carolina. Behind its looming walls were eight officers, 68 soldiers, eight musicians, and 43 workmen. All were under the command of Major Robert Anderson.

"To maintain the national Union." Anderson was a southerner who had remained loyal to the Union. He planned to

The Civil War was the first modern war, the first in which industrial might counted as much as courage and leadership. But human beings still had to fight—and die. Some, like the drummer boys, were fourteen, or even younger.

abandon the fort on April 15, unless he was either reinforced or attacked. Meanwhile, the Confederate commander in Charleston, General P. G. T. Beauregard, had orders to attack the fort on April 12. At 4:50 A.M. that day, whitehaired Edmund Ruffin, a fierce secessionist, fired off the first cannon shot of the bombardment. It rose red against the dark sky, the first of numberless shells that would rock the land for the next four years.

During the following 34 hours the Confederates fired some 4,000 shells into Fort Sumter. A few times the Union garrison fired back, but it was no match for the bombarding force. The roofs of the city were jammed with residents cheering each time a Southern shell hit the fort. Anderson was hopelessly outnumbered. At noon on Sunday, April 14, he surrendered and was allowed to leave his position.

Only one soldier in Fort Sumter was killed. He died in an accidental explosion after the surrender. His was the first of what would be over 600,000 deaths before the shooting stopped.

President Lincoln now asked the governors of the states to send him 75,000 troops for three months "to maintain the honor, integrity, and the existence of the national Union." Throughout the land the news of the attack and Lincoln's call for troops had instant effect. In the North doubts van-

———————◆———————

Read here of how

The first shots of the war were fired.
The North had great advantages.
But the South had an easier task.

———————◆———————

TIME CHART

1861	Fort Sumter is fired upon. The Battle of Bull Run is fought.
1862	McClellan fails to take Richmond. The *Monitor* meets the *Merrimac (Virginia)*.
1863	The Emancipation Proclamation goes into effect.
1863	The South loses at Gettysburg and Vicksburg.
1864	Sherman marches to the sea.
1865	Lee surrenders to Grant. Lincoln is assassinated.

———————◆———————

ished. Everywhere, there was determination to save the Union. The poet Walt Whitman called the reaction "an earthquake." In the South, Lincoln's call sent Virginia, Arkansas, Tennessee, and North Carolina to join the other seven states of the Confederacy (page 293).

Lose the battles, win the war. Neither North nor South had a modern industrial system. Both were mostly agricultural. Yet, as can be seen from the chart on page 301, the North outstripped the South on every point. In addition, the North owned the bulk of the country's shipping and provided most of the navy's manpower. The loyalty of the army was divided, but this was not reflected in the navy. Control of the sea lanes made it possible for the North to blockade the South throughout the war.

On one point the two sides were on an equal footing. In the beginning both had to import arms from Europe. But before long each was producing what it needed.

There were sharp divisions in the border states. At Knoxville, Tennessee, rival meetings were held.

In spite of its advantages, it took the North two years to get its resources organized. Even then, the South often made better use of the little it had.

The South had some advantages too. Its population was smaller, but a higher proportion could be used for military service. The South's three million slaves did much of the necessary work. Furthermore, it was fighting on the defensive and so required fewer troops. To win, the North would have to invade and conquer the South. The South needed only to go on resisting. Like the American forces in the Revolution, the Confederacy could lose all the battles and still win the war (page 87).

"Virginia is my country." At least a third of the nation's regular army officers joined the Confederacy. They included such outstanding leaders as Robert E. Lee, Joseph Johnston, and Thomas "Stonewall" Jackson. Lee's reputation was so high that he probably could have had command of the Union forces. Instead, he accepted the motto of his father, "Virginia is my country. Her I will obey."

The loose, agricultural foundation of the South was also in its favor. The population was spread over a wide area and could be defeated only when the war was brought to its doorstep. As the fighting dragged on, the capital—Richmond, Virginia—became an important symbol. Otherwise, no city was truly vital to the Confederacy.

The South had a further advantage in its political leaders. Many of them had had long experience in government. President Jefferson Davis had been a senator from Mississippi and President Pierce's Secretary of War. He was precise, cold, and a dedicated public official. Unfortunately, as a West Point graduate, he also considered himself a superior soldier. This led him to interfere continually in military matters.

A flexible leader. From the beginning of the war, Lincoln gave the North superb political leadership. He was practical and could readily adjust his plans if they proved unworkable. But he never wavered in his determination to restore the Union. Holding on to the border states (Missouri, Kentucky, Maryland, and Delaware) and winning back the South were Lincoln's earliest aims. Yet he promised not to fight "a war of conquest" and to respect "the established institutions" of the South. (He was referring to slavery.)

But as the war went on, Lincoln's ideas changed. Freeing the slaves became a second (but important) Union aim. By then, too, the President had accepted the fact that the war would be a long one. He decided to invade the South, and if necessary, to devastate it. Lincoln would do what was necessary to save the Union.

 TRY THIS!

1. List the advantages of the North in what you consider the order of their importance to victory. 2. Explain the placement of the first and last items on your list.

NORTH AND SOUTH IN 1861

	NORTH (19 free and 4 loyal slave states)	SOUTH (11 seceding states)
Human Resources		
Population (total)	22,340,000	9,103,000
White	21,832,000	5,735,000
Black	508,000	3,368,000
Military (white males 17–35)	4,000,000	1,150,000
Enlistments (throughout war years)*	1,557,000	1,082,000
Black	200,000	—
Industrial workers	1,198,000	111,000
Industrial Resources		
Real estate and personal property (dollars)	11,000,000,000	5,000,000,000
Manufactures (dollars per year)	1,794,417,000	155,552,000
Number of factories and shops	111,000	21,000
Tons of pig iron produced	675,000	225,000
Improved farm land (acres)	105,831,000	56,832,000
Transportation Resources		
Miles of railroad track	21,846	8,947
Number of draft animals	4,550,000	245,000

* Some short-term enlistees signed up more than once.

2. TWO YEARS OF FRUITLESS STRUGGLE

In 1861 everyone expected a short war. Lincoln's first call for troops had been for only ninety days (page 299). The people of the North demanded a march on Richmond before the brief period of service was up. Those of the South pushed their government to attack Washington. Ignorant of the horrors of war, each side was looking for a fight—and a quick victory.

Saved by poor discipline. The commanding general of the Union forces, 75-year-old Winfield Scott, knew that the ninety-day volunteers were poorly trained. He objected to using them for any offensive

———————————◆———————————

Read here of how

The North made a poor beginning.
And could have lost its navy.
But found able generals in the West.
And opened the Mississippi River.

———————————◆———————————

In the early years, expecting a short war, soldiers' families sometimes accompanied them to camp.

operation. Lincoln overrode him. On July 25, 1861, a Union army was ordered to occupy an important railroad junction at Manassas, 25 miles from Washington (map on this page). A Confederate force, just as ill-trained and poorly led, marched north to stop it.

The two forces came together at a small stream called Bull Run. A confused, seesaw battle followed in which the two armies had trouble telling friend from foe. (Some Union militia had gray uniforms, while many Confederate units still wore blue. Red, white, and blue flags of both forces hung limp, and hard to tell apart, in the summer air.) In late afternoon the federal forces broke and ran. Only confusion and poor discipline kept the Confederate force from seizing Washington.

A "young Napoleon." The North was stunned and humiliated. It moved quickly to reorganize its forces. Now 300,000 men were enlisted for three years. There was talk of "hanging rebels" and burning their towns.

To head the newly organized Army of the Potomac, Lincoln chose General George B. McClellan. He was a 35-year-old West Point graduate who had gone into the railroad business. When the war began, he had staged a whirlwind campaign in West Virginia that led people in the North to hail him as "the young Napoleon."

McClellan was a genius at organization. In no time he had his force looking and acting like an army. The troops loved him.

The new commander's immediate objectives were to build an army that could crush anything the Confederates sent against it and to fortify Washington. But McClellan's failure to move swiftly against the enemy caused impatience. He also

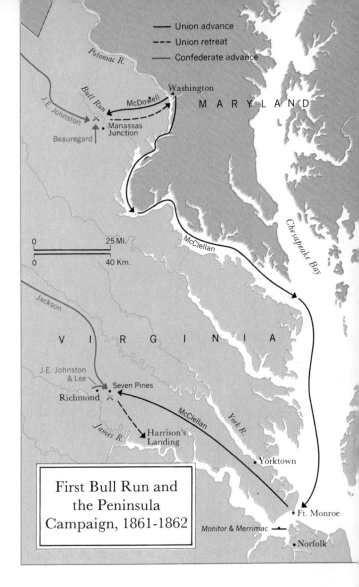

First Bull Run and the Peninsula Campaign, 1861-1862

Richmond was the goal. Twice the Union failed to take it. Lee dug trenches and earthworks, so some called him "King of Spades." They had a better opinion of him after McClellan's retreat.

made little effort to hide his contempt for the Lincoln Administration. In spite of this, the President defended the young commander and gave him whatever he asked for.

A triumphant retreat. In the spring of 1862 Lincoln and Edwin M. Stanton, the Secretary of War, pressed McClellan to use

303

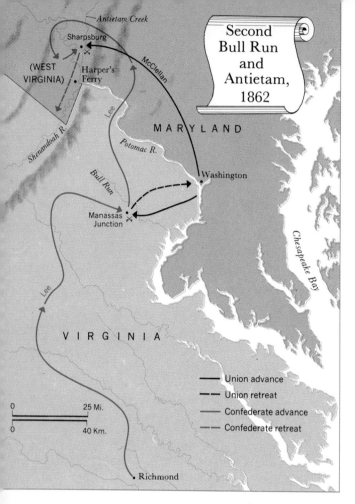

Second
Bull Run
and
Antietam,
1862

Antietam Creek

Sharpsburg

(WEST
VIRGINIA) Harper's
Ferry

McClellan

Shenandoah R.

Lee

M A R Y L A N D

Potomac R.

Bull Run

Washington

Manassas
Junction

Chesapeake Bay

Lee

V I R G I N I A

—— Union advance
- - - Union retreat
—— Confederate advance
- - - Confederate retreat

0   25 Mi.

0   40 Km.

Richmond

When the third Union move on Richmond failed,
Lee took the offensive. He lost at Antietam.

his magnificent force for an attack on Richmond. The young general proposed a seaborne assault from the southeast, using the
peninsula between the James and York rivers (map on page 303). McClellan spent
ten weeks, from mid-March to the end of
May, getting his army in position for an
attack on Richmond. Meanwhile, the
South's "Stonewall" Jackson threatened
Washington. To protect the nation's capital, Lincoln withheld some of the reinforcements McClellan wanted.

In a fierce battle just outside Seven
Pines, the Confederate general, Joseph

Johnston, was wounded, and Robert E.
Lee took over. Another month of maneuvering followed. Then through seven days
of heavy fighting McClellan kept his army
together and fought off a murderous assault
by Lee. He succeeded in withdrawing from
Richmond in good order.

"The young Napoleon" had carried out
a magnificent defense and saved his army.
But that wasn't the kind of news the North
ached to hear. Lincoln removed McClellan. His successor was overwhelmingly defeated at the Second Battle of Bull Run by
an outnumbered force under Lee. The
Confederate army now invaded Maryland.

Grass before the scythe. Lincoln had
no one else to turn to, so he brought Mc-
Clellan back. The Battle of Antietam (an-
TEE-tum) that followed was the bloodiest
single day's fighting of the war. When it
was over, a reporter wandered over the
field and then wrote: "The hillside was
dotted with the forms of men in blue, but
in the sunken road, what a ghastly spectacle! The Confederates had gone down as
the grass falls before the scythe. Where a
short time before they had been in the full
flush of young manhood, both Yankee and
Rebel were now corpses."

Antietam ended McClellan's military
career. He had never lost a battle, but he
had never quite won one either. Antietam
was typical. Lee was thrown back but not
defeated. McClellan's army was too weary
to follow and destroy the Southern force.

A surprise attack. The leadership that
finally brought victory to the Union came
from the West. In the western theater of
operations, Lincoln found generals who
knew what it took to win. Ulysses S. Grant,
William T. Sherman, Philip H. Sheridan,
and George H. Thomas all proved themselves in the Mississippi Valley fighting.

In February 1862 Grant moved south from Kentucky. He captured Forts Henry and Donelson and invaded Tennessee (map on this page). At Shiloh Landing on the Tennessee River, a Confederate force made a surprise attack. Only a desperate rally saved the federal troops from panic. Bitter hand-to-hand fighting followed until Grant ordered a counterattack, and the Confederates withdrew. The way was now open to take the Mississippi River and split the Confederacy in two. Grant pushed west, crossed the Mississippi River, and advanced toward Vicksburg.

Two strange-looking ships. Throughout the war the North blockaded the Confederate coast (page 299). Its control of the sea was seriously threatened for only a few days in March 1862. The South had captured the Union ship *Merrimac,* covered it with iron plates, and renamed it the *Virginia.* On March 8 the *Virginia* sailed out of Norfolk and sank some wooden navy vessels blockading the port.

Near panic followed, but the next day the *Virginia* was met by a Union ironclad called the *Monitor.* It was a sort of raft with a revolving turret gun. The two strange-looking ships bounced cannonballs off one another for five hours. Neither won, but the *Virginia* had to retreat for repairs. The fight marked the end of wooden naval craft.

Meanwhile, the old sailing vessels still had a role to play. Throughout the war they tightened the blockade. By 1865 the South was largely cut off from the rest of the world. The old ships also carried out a number of seaborne assaults.

General Grant's problem. In April 1862 a federal army-navy force ran past the forts guarding New Orleans. The great seaport fell to the Union. The naval com-

mander, David C. Farragut, then sailed up the Mississippi in an attempt to capture Vicksburg. But for another year Rebel forces managed to hold on to the river between Vicksburg and Port Hudson (map on this page). It gave them a two-hundred-mile corridor linking the eastern Confederacy with Texas and Arkansas.

Vicksburg was protected on one side by the river and on the other by a swamp. It was now General Grant's problem, and he worked at it for nine months. He finally had the city completely surrounded. For 47 days Grant sent an average of three shells a

Taking the Mississippi was a Northern aim from the beginning of the war. Why was it important to the South to keep the river open between Vicksburg and Port Hudson?

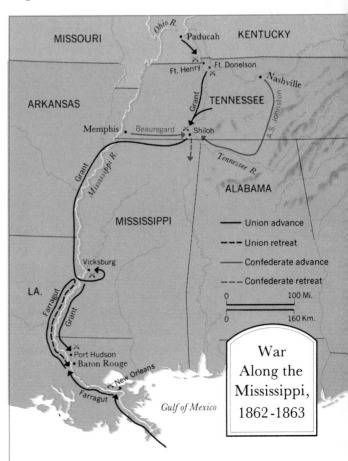

War Along the Mississippi, 1862-1863

Farragut's flagship, the *U.S.S. Hartford*. In 1862 sail still ruled the seas, but not for much longer.

minute smashing into its fortifications. Hungry, living in caves, without hope of relief, the Confederate garrison finally surrendered on July 4, 1863. Port Hudson followed five days later. These were two brutal victories. But they contrasted sharply with the bloody, discouraging struggle going on in the East.

 **TRY THIS!**

1. Compare the North's military operations in the East and the West. Can you account for the difference? **2.** Defend General McClellan as a military leader. **3.** Using the map on page 305, show why Vicksburg was an important position.

3.   EMANCIPATION, HOW AND WHY

From the beginning of the war, one group within the Republican Party had insisted that all the slaves should be freed. These people were known as the *Radical Republicans,* and they had considerable power in Congress. This was especially true after the southern Democrats left in 1861.

   Punishing the rebellion. Two military commanders, John C. Frémont in the St.

Read here of how

Lincoln resisted freeing the slaves.
But finally did, for many reasons.
The Confederates counted on foreign help.
But Europe disappointed them.

Louis area and David Hunter in the deep South, were especially admired by the Radicals. Each had emancipated (freed) the slaves in the area under his control. In both cases, Lincoln revoked these orders.

The President was determined to have the final say on emancipation. He was concerned about losing the loyal slave states of Missouri, Kentucky, Maryland, and Delaware. And in the early part of the war he still hoped to bring the Confederate states back into the Union. Making the war a crusade against slavery would not help.

But by 1862 the war had grown bloodier. There was increasing pressure in the North to end slavery. As a politician Lincoln was well aware of the change in public opinion. Congress too was insisting that the South be punished. It voted to fine, and take away the property of, any who supported the rebellion. Slave property was included. Congress also freed the slaves in the District of Columbia and in the territories.

Americans too. Lincoln knew that in Congress the Radical Republicans were the strongest supporters of the war. He had to satisfy them. First, he tried to persuade the people of the border states to free their slaves. He promised that the federal government would pay for them and that the slaves would be settled in Central America. The people of the border states refused the President's request. And blacks soon let him know that they were Americans too, and that they had no wish to leave the country.

By midsummer of 1862 Lincoln was thinking about some wider plan of emancipation. In August he told the Cabinet of his plans. Secretary of State Seward wisely suggested saving the announcement until Union troops had won a military victory. Otherwise, he said, it might look as though the North were desperate. Antietam (page 304) was no smashing triumph, but Lincoln used it anyway. On September 22, 1862, he issued a preliminary Emancipation Proclamation.

"Forever free." The President stated that as of January 1, 1863, all slaves in areas that were still in rebellion would be "forever free." Of course, no slave was actually freed on that date. Those living where the federal government was still in control would have to wait until the passage of the Thirteenth Amendment to the Constitution. Those living under the Confederacy would be freed only when Union troops occupied the areas where they lived.

Actually, emancipation was a threat that unless the South ended its rebellion by January 1, 1863, it would lose its slaves. Neither Lincoln nor his Cabinet claimed that they were undoing a great national injustice. Instead, they claimed emancipation was a measure to preserve the Union.

Yet no one really expected the South to surrender and end its struggle for independence. The first effects of emancipation were felt in the North and in foreign countries. Within the hearts of many Americans there was a feeling of genuine relief. No longer would they have to seem like hypocrites, preaching freedom while keeping slaves.

The dawn of January 1, 1863, was greeted as a new day by free blacks, especially the newly emancipated ones in the District of Columbia. They knew that freedom was far from complete. Nevertheless, the war was now an entirely different kind of struggle. The advancing Union army would be an army of liberation.

A swift, harsh answer. Emancipation also allowed the North to mobilize its black population. Until then, when blacks had tried to volunteer, they had been rejected. Now they were enlisted. In the end

307

A few of the North's black troops. They were in far greater danger if captured than white soldiers.

178,895 black soldiers served with the Union forces. And as the Northern armies pushed into the South, slaves left the plantations and headed for the Union lines. There they were welcomed and put to work.

The South's answer to the use of black troops against them was swift and harsh. The Confederate Congress authorized President Davis to have the officers of black regiments put to death. Black enlisted men were to be turned over to "the authorities of the state . . . in which they shall be captured to be dealt with according to the . . . laws of such state." The message was clear—slavery or death.

It was no empty threat. In April 1864 the Confederate raider Nathan B. Forrest captured Fort Pillow, Tennessee. Several dozen black troops were executed along with their white comrades-in-arms. It made Radical Republicans more resolved than ever to impose a harsh peace.

Lincoln never doubted that black troops made a critical difference in the war. Their conduct under fire helped to destroy the old racist view of blacks. In a very real sense, blacks helped to free themselves.

FOREIGN RELATIONS

Slavery and emancipation were closely tied to foreign affairs during the Civil War. From the beginning the South staked its hopes on aid from Europe. Southerners were sure that would save them, just as French assistance had helped the Americans to win their Revolution (page 90).

At the very least, the Confederacy hoped to be recognized as an independent country by Britain and France. But it was slavery as much as anything else that kept Britain from recognizing or helping the South. France would not move without Britain.

A high-handed act. Southern hopes soared in 1861 when a United States warship stopped and boarded the British

309

Blacks first hear the news of emancipation.

steamship *Trent*. The Confederate agents James Mason and John Slidell, bound for England and France, were taken off the *Trent* and held in Boston. The British threatened war and sent troops to Canada.

The United States had committed the same kind of high-handed act it had gone to war over in 1812. Lincoln and Secretary of State Seward recognized this (and the danger of British ill will). Mason and Slidell were released and an apology made. The war scare died.

Antislavery feeling. Thinking they could force the British to help them, Confederate leaders had forbidden the exporting of cotton at the beginning of the war. Their action fell especially hard on the English middle-class owners of the cotton mills, and on the workers who earned a living in them. Yet these were the people most strongly opposed to slavery and most sympathetic to the North. They continued to be against slavery, though the British upper classes expected a Confederate victory and would have welcomed one.

When Lincoln changed his views and issued the Emancipation Proclamation, he had the antislavery views of the British people in mind. Lee's failure to win a clear victory also helped to keep Britain neutral.

Going it alone. Throughout the war diplomatic relations with Britain were ably handled by Charles Francis Adams, son of the sixth President. In 1863 Adams protested bitterly because British authorities had allowed the commerce raiders *Alabama* and *Florida* to be built and fitted in their country. He pointed out that such an act was against international law, and the British stopped a third raider from leaving.

Adams also persuaded the British to stop delivery of some ironclads being built in Laird's shipyards. (France also stopped delivery of ironclads under construction in French yards.) The Confederates might have used these ships to break the Northern blockade.

By late in 1863 it was clear that the South would have to go it alone. There was no hope for foreign assistance.

 TRY THIS!

1. Write a speech, favoring emancipation, as it might have been delivered by a Radical Republican congressman. **2.** Write a letter from Abraham Lincoln replying to the congressman's arguments. **3.** Explain why Britain failed to aid the Confederacy.

4.   THE END OF THE FIGHTING

After Antietam and the second removal of McClellan (page 304), Ambrose Burnside took over the Army of the Potomac. He threw it against Lee's fortifications at Fredericksburg, Virginia. The result was a massacre of Union forces.

"Fighting Joe" Hooker was Lee and Jackson's next victim. At Chancellorsville, Virginia, the South again won easily, but it was a costly day. A Confederate sharp-

Read here of how

The South lost a decisive battle.
Grant pounded Lee's army into surrender.
And lost a lot of men.
General Sherman made military history.
And a bad name for himself.

shooter mistook Jackson for a Union officer and killed him. He was irreplaceable. Also, though Lee lost fewer men than Hooker at Chancellorsville, the South's casualties were harder to replace. The North's superior numbers were beginning to count.

Never to return. Lee gambled again. In June 1863 he made his final invasion of the North, getting as far as Gettysburg, Pennsylvania (map on this page). Lee hoped that this would relieve some of the pressure on the West and win a victory that would bring foreign recognition and aid. His campaign was the high point of Confederate hope and strength.

From July 1 to 3, 1863, Lee battled the new commander of the Union force, George Gordon Meade. On the final day, in a last desperate try to break the federal army, Lee hurled 15,000 men against its line. "Pickett's Charge," as it is called, was raked by rifle fire and was finally thrown back in hand-to-hand combat. The next day Lee turned southward never to return. As before, the battered Northern army was unable to follow him.

Lincoln was disappointed that Lee's army had again slipped away. But the two victories of Gettysburg and Vicksburg (pages 305-306), falling only a day apart, convinced him that victory was certain.

An unbeatable team. Throughout the rest of 1863 most of the fighting took place in Tennessee. A series of Union blunders almost gave the South a badly needed victory. Only General George Thomas, "the Rock of Chickamauga," holding off the Southern army, gave the Union force a chance to escape.

The Battle of Chickamauga was a clear Confederate victory. But it showed the South's growing weakness. The Confederates lacked the troops needed to launch an attack. They could only lay siege to the

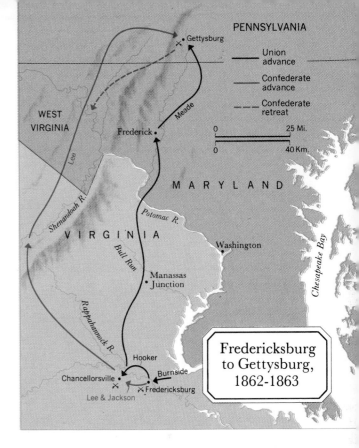

It was a grinding, disappointing war in the East. The Union was beaten in Virginia, but Lee was just as unsuccessful in Pennsylvania.

enemy. Grant and Sherman were able to break through the Southern lines in the Battle of Chattanooga. The way was now open for an invasion of Georgia.

Chattanooga showed Lincoln that in Grant he had a general who knew how to win. He was called east and put in command of the operations against Lee.

Grant in the East and Sherman in the West made an unbeatable team. In mid-March of 1864 they laid out a strategy to overwhelm the Confederacy. Both their armies would attack "all along the line" and keep at it. Grant would drive Lee back to Richmond and lock him in a death grip. Sherman would do the same to Johnston at Atlanta. The victory would be a bloody

311

Grant (lower left) leans over Meade's shoulder at a council of war in Virginia (May 1864).

one. But with Lincoln's full backing, they were prepared to pay the price.

A mighty roar. In a campaign from May 4 to June 3, 1864, Grant lost 50,000 men. But losses of 32,000 hurt Lee much more. At one point Grant brought the federal force to a halt. Lee expected the kind of lull he had known before in his struggle with the Northern army. Instead, Grant ordered his men to press southward again. When his command reached the Union troops, a mighty roar went up. They were ready to fight to the end.

At the Wilderness, Spotsylvania, and Cold Harbor (map on page 313), the casualties mounted. At the end of that terrible month, Grant admitted he was no nearer to Richmond than McClellan had been (page 304). But he dug in for a nine-month siege of Petersburg, the railroad center south of Richmond.

Utter destruction. Meanwhile, in the deep South, Sherman was pressing hard on Atlanta. With a smaller force, the opposing general, Joseph Johnston, had to keep falling back. This annoyed Jefferson Davis, who replaced Johnston with John B. Hood. Hood only made matters worse by attempting to attack the larger Union force.

Early in September 1864 the Confederates abandoned Atlanta.

Sherman now had a problem. He wanted to keep pushing southeast. But if he advanced from Atlanta, Hood might cut his supply line. Sherman finally decided on a plan of action that made military history—and made his name hated throughout the South.

First, he ordered the civilian population out of Atlanta; then he burned it to the ground. Next, he took off across Georgia, abandoning his own supply line, and living off the country. In doing so, he cut a path of destruction from Atlanta to Savannah on the coast.

The North's eastern and western armies are about to join. The struggle is all but over.

Sherman's "March to the Sea" lasted from November 15 to December 21. He destroyed everything of military value (and much else as well) in a sixty-mile-wide belt of territory. "The utter destruction [of] roads, houses, and people will cripple their military resources," he said.

The lost cause. In Virginia, Philip Sheridan waged the same kind of campaign in the Shenandoah Valley. He reported, "A crow would have had to carry its rations if it had flown across the valley." Never again could a Southern army use this route to threaten Washington.

Sherman swept northward into South Carolina, burning and destroying as he went. On April 1, 1865, Grant broke the lines protecting Richmond, and the Yankees entered the Confederate capital. In

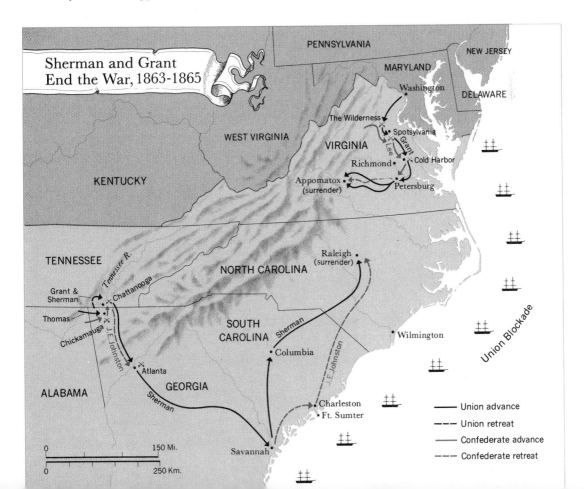

Sherman and Grant End the War, 1863-1865

PENNSYLVANIA
NEW JERSEY
MARYLAND
Washington
DELAWARE
The Wilderness
Spotsylvania
WEST VIRGINIA
VIRGINIA
Richmond
Cold Harbor
KENTUCKY
Appomatox (surrender)
Petersburg
TENNESSEE
Raleigh (surrender)
NORTH CAROLINA
Grant & Sherman
Chattanooga
Thomas
Chickamauga
J.E. Johnston
SOUTH CAROLINA
Sherman
Wilmington
Columbia
J.E. Johnston
Union Blockade
Atlanta
ALABAMA
GEORGIA
Sherman
Charleston
Ft. Sumter

0   150 Mi.
0   250 Km.

Savannah

——— Union advance
- - - Union retreat
——— Confederate advance
- - - Confederate retreat

313

hot pursuit Grant went after the weary, ragged remnant of Lee's army. He trapped it in a final battle at Appomattox Court House.

On April 9, Robert E. Lee surrendered. His army was allowed to return home with little but its memory of four years of warfare. The Confederacy had joined history's long list of lost causes.

 TRY THIS!

1. Show how the North's greater resources (chart on page 301) weighed upon the South in the last years of fighting. **2.** Be a war correspondent with the forces of Lee, Johnston, Grant, or Sherman at Atlanta or in the Wilderness campaign. Tell people at home what it's really like.

After a brave, four-year defense, the people of Richmond flee from their burning city.

ULYSSES S. GRANT REMEMBERS APPOMATTOX

General Lee was dressed in a full uniform which was entirely new and was wearing a sword of considerable value, very likely the sword which had been presented by the state of Virginia. . . . In my rough traveling suit, the uniform of a private with the straps of a lieutenant general, I must have contrasted very strangely with a man so handsomely dressed, six feet high, and of faultless form. But this was not a matter that I thought of until afterward.

We soon fell into a conversation about old army times. He remarked that he remembered me very well in the old army, and I told him that as a matter of course I remembered him perfectly, but from the difference in our rank and years (there being about sixteen years' difference in our ages), I had thought it very likely that I had not attracted his attention sufficiently to be remembered by him after such a long interval. Our conversation grew so pleasant that I almost forgot the object of our meeting. After the conversation had run on in this style for some time, General Lee called my attention to the object of our meeting and said that he had asked for this interview for the purpose of getting from me the terms I proposed to give his army. I said that I meant merely that his army should lay down their arms, not to take them up again during the continuance of the war unless duly and properly exchanged. He said that he had so understood my letter. . . .

I then said to him that I thought this would be about the last battle of the war—I sincerely hoped so; and I said further I took it that most of the men in the ranks were small farmers. The whole country had been so raided by the two armies that it was doubtful whether they would be able to put in a crop to carry themselves and their families through the next winter without the aid of the horses they were riding. The United States did not want them, and I would, therefore, instruct the officers I left behind to receive the paroles of his troops to let every man in the Confederate army who claimed to own a horse or mule take the animal to his home. Lee remarked again that this would have a happy effect.

Ulysses S. Grant, *Personal Memoirs*, 2 vols., New York, 1885–1886.

5. ACTION ON THE HOME FRONTS

As President Lincoln carried on the war, Republicans in Congress set to work on a program for their party. Their job was made easier by the departure of the southern Democrats in 1861 and by the death, that same year, of the Democratic leader Stephen A. Douglas (page 285). Congressmen like John Sherman of Ohio (younger brother of General Sherman), Thaddeus Stevens of Pennsylvania, Benjamin Wade of Ohio, and Henry Wilson of Massachusetts became the new leaders.

 ONE OF THE 400,000

Federal officials were in a state of shock. They had learned that the Confederates were building an iron-clad ship to use against the Union's wooden vessels.

No need for panic. John Ericsson, an ingenious Swede living in the United States, was already at work on the revolutionary *Monitor.*

Iron construction was just one remarkable feature of Ericsson's creation. It was fully steam-powered, needing no sails for reserve power. It had an underwater propeller in place of paddle wheels and it used one powerful gun, not a lot of smaller ones. War at sea has never been the same. But the greatest novelty was the *Monitor's* revolving gun turret, used ever after by all the navies of the world.

Over 400,000 foreign-born Americans served the Union in the Civil War. None made a greater contribution than John Ericsson.

A powerful lift. Very high on the list of what the Republicans wanted was a protective tariff (page 127). They could claim that additional revenues were needed to pay for the war. And the Morrill Tariffs of 1861 and 1862 did increase rates on tea, coffee, spices, and India rubber—articles produced outside the country.

But tariff rates were also raised on iron and other goods that could be made at home. Here the reason given was protection for United States manufacturers. It was needed, the argument went, because of the high wartime taxes paid by American industry. In all, rates were raised about 47 per cent.

Whatever the reasons for the Morrill Tariff, it gave a powerful lift to American business. Democrats and some westerners objected, but most people accepted the tariff as a patriotic sacrifice.

A banking system better than none. The severest problem facing Congress was raising money to pay for the war. Higher tariffs, an income tax, and special taxes on liquor, tobacco, and meat brought in only a small part of what was needed. This is not surprising. No government can finance a full-scale war on a "pay-as-you-go" basis. Only massive borrowing will raise enough money.

Read here of how

Both sides needed to raise money and men.
Northern tax policies helped business.
Nobody wanted the draft.
And politics went on—North and South.

The most direct way for a government to borrow money from its people is to sell them bonds. This is much easier when there is a central bank like the First or the Second Bank of the United States (page 190). In the 1860s there was no central bank, so a substitute had to be found.

A National Banking System was set up in 1863. Under it, a national bank gave the government gold equal to one third of its funds. The bank got government bonds in return. It could then lend to customers bank notes up to 90 per cent of the value of the bonds. The National Banking System continued for the next fifty years. Almost all United States banks with "national" in their titles were organized under it.

The National Banking System was better than what it replaced: uncontrolled state banks. But it had a lot of weaknesses. Instead of being spread around the country, about 60 per cent of the currency stayed in New York and New England. And any banking crisis in New York City made waves that were felt in every part of the country.

The second way that governments get the money they need is by printing it. In 1862 and 1863 Congress authorized the government to put out 450 million dollars in *greenbacks*. These were United States notes—paper money—without gold or silver backing. Greenbacks were supposed to be accepted as regular money. In fact, most people would take them only at a discount. During the worst days of the war it took two dollars and 64 cents in greenbacks to equal one dollar in silver or gold.

Riots and inflation. In the South the printing press was the chief means for raising money. Loans of fifteen million dollars came from abroad, and of a hundred million from the people of the South. Taxes

Collections of the Henry Ford Museum.

The GAR was the Union veterans' organization. It became politically powerful in the late 1800s.

brought in another hundred million or more, but the Confederacy had to print over a billion dollars in paper money to pay its bills.

The blockade tightened as the war went on, and goods became scarcer in the South. The result was runaway inflation. By the fall of 1864 butter was 25 dollars a pound in Richmond, Virginia, and eggs were six dollars a dozen. There were bread riots in Richmond and in other cities. Scores of women mobbed military warehouses demanding food. But in the countryside and in the army there was generally enough to eat throughout the war.

Unpopular drafts. Raising armies was as much a problem as raising money for the war. In the North most of the recruiting was done by the states. They increased their militia through enlistment campaigns

317

and by using federal, state, and local bounties—payment to those who signed up. But militia were often poorly trained and led. Their officers were political appointees or were elected by the men they commanded. And sometimes the terms of service were very short.

Starting in 1863 the Union made use of a draft. All men from 25 to 40 were eligible, but anyone called up could send a substitute or pay 300 dollars to avoid serving. The draft seemed unfair, and it was especially unpopular among the foreign-born Irish in New York and Germans in the West. There were draft riots in New York and in Wisconsin, but Irish and German units also served the Union with distinction throughout the war.

In fact, the continual flow of immigrants was among the many advantages of the North. Nearly 800,000 entered the country during the war. Some served in the army, others did the farm and factory work of those who fought.

The South started drafting men in 1862. However, there were a great many ways of getting out of serving—by holding political office or owning a few slaves, as well as by sending a substitute.

Desertions in both armies were about 10 per cent. Some of these were by "bounty jumpers": men who enlisted over and over again under different names in order to collect the bounties offered.

Women in the war. The Civil War brought women of the North and South out of their homes on a large scale. Medical and relief work was the area of greatest need and they rushed to fill it. Dorothea Dix was a national figure through her work for the insane (page 202). She was appointed superintendent of nurses for the Union army.

In the North, however, most women helped the war effort through the Sanitary Commission. It was a private organization like the Red Cross. The Commission's work was to help care for sick and wounded soldiers and their families. Women like Clara Barton, who later founded the American Red Cross, Mary Ann Bickerdyke, Mary Livermore, and Jane Hoge served with the Commission. So did hundreds of others who showed great organizing and administrative talent.

In the South there was no organization like the Sanitary Commission. But southern women ran farms and plantations and supervised hospitals. They helped the war

Members of the Sanitary Commission faced great dangers while reducing the hardships of the battlefield and the army camp.

April 11.—Mrs. Ogden tried to prepare me for the scenes which I should witness upon entering the wards. But alas! Nothing I had ever heard or read had given me the faintest idea of the horrors witnessed here. . . . Gray-haired men—men in the pride of manhood—beardless boys—Federals and all, mutilated in every imaginable way, lying on the floor, just as they were taken from the battlefield, so close together that it was almost impossible to walk without stepping on them. . . . What can be in the minds of our enemies, who are now arrayed against us, who have never harmed them in any way, but simply claim our own and nothing more! May God forgive them. . . .

This was no time for recrimination; there was work to do; so I went at it to do what I could. If I were to live a hundred years, I should never forget the poor sufferers' gratitude. . . . A little water to drink or the bathing of their wounds seemed to afford them the greatest relief.

The Federal prisoners are receiving the same attention as our men; they are lying side by side. . . . I went with a lady to give some Federal officers their supper. . . . Before I went in, I thought that I would be polite and say as little as possible to them. But when I saw them laughing and apparently indifferent to the woe which they had been instrumental in bringing upon us, I could not help being indignant. When one of them told me he was from Iowa, and that was generally called out of the world, I told him that was where I wished him, and all like him, so that they might not trouble us any more.

April 12.—I sat up all night bathing the men's wounds and giving them water. Everyone attending to them seemed completely worn out. . . .

Other ladies have their special patients, whom they never leave. One of them from Natchez, Mississippi, has been constantly by a young man, badly wounded, ever since she came here. The doctors say that she has been the means of saving his life. . . .

There seems to be no order. All do as they please. We have men for nurses, and the doctors complain very much at the manner in which they are appointed. They are detailed from the different regiments, like guards. We have a new set every few hours. I cannot see how it is possible for them to take proper care of the men, as nursing is a thing that has to be learned.

A CONFEDERATE NURSE
AFTER SHILOH

Kate Cummings
The Journal of a Confederate Nurse

effort by increasing food production and reviving home manufactures.

Rival candidates. The bloody fighting of 1864 (page 312) brought war weariness to a peak. There were a number of former southerners living in the northern states, especially those of the Northwest. Most of them disliked slavery, but they did not like making war on the South. After the Emancipation Proclamation racist feeling strengthened their opposition to the war.

Whatever its cause, antiwar feeling ran high in the presidential election year of 1864. Democrats had made large gains in Illinois and Indiana. A group of Radical Republicans believed that Lincoln hadn't pushed hard enough to win the war. They wanted John C. Frémont for their candidate. Moderates were unhappy with the President for the opposite reason.

But Lincoln's control of the Republican Party made his nomination sure. To widen his appeal the party made Governor Andrew Johnson of Tennessee his running mate. Johnson was a War Democrat, one who supported the Union. The Republican platform called for the use of black troops and for a constitutional amendment completely ending slavery. Still, Lincoln's chances did not seem bright.

A close contest. Two things saved the President. The Democrats put up General George B. McClellan (page 303) for President on a platform that called for a peace conference with the South. McClellan rejected the peace plank, but it still made the Democrats look as though they were ready to give up the Union. Republicans had to unite behind Lincoln. Then, in September, came the fall of Atlanta (page 313). New confidence swept through the North.

Lincoln won by 212 electoral votes to only 21 for McClellan. But in key states

In spite of the war, Lincoln voters held torchlight parades and carried lanterns with his picture.

like New York his lead was razor-thin. It had really been a close contest.

Against their principles. While Lincoln struggled to keep the Union together, Jefferson Davis faced worse problems. Northern armies steadily advanced into the South, and morale sagged. Davis did not have a strong political party to back him at the state and local level. Southern leaders, trying to maintain unity, had avoided forming parties.

The states' rights idea was strong in the South, and it made Southern leaders unwilling to approve the kind of strong measures needed to win the war. For instance, Georgia's governor insisted on controlling all the troops raised in his state. He believed that the draft was against "all the principles for . . . which Georgia . . . entered into this revolution." He tried to block its operation. The governor of North Carolina did much the same.

The poor white areas of western Virginia, eastern Tennessee, northwestern

Georgia, and northern Alabama and Mississippi, had opposed secession. Many people who lived in these areas remained loyal to the Union throughout the war. They had little in common with the great planters. They owned no slaves and just managed to make a living on their farms.

Before the war the feelings of poor southern whites had been hidden. The draft and the seizure of goods by the Confederate government brought their anger into the open. In some areas the Stars and Stripes flew throughout the war, and Confederate forces were occasionally attacked by angry farmers.

 TRY THIS!

Compare the North and South on the following points: **1.** Raising money for the war. **2.** Drafting men for the army. **3.** Using the talents of women. **4.** Having dissatisfied citizens.

6. RECONSTRUCTION DURING THE WAR

From the earliest days of the war, Republicans debated how the Southern states could be brought back into the Union; in other words, how *Reconstruction* should be handled. Lincoln's view was that the states had never really left the Union. There was no way, he said, that they could legally have seceded; therefore, they never had. That at least sounded logical.

However, many Radical Republicans (page 306) argued that by attempting to secede the Southern states had given up their statehood. Once conquered, the Radicals claimed, they could be ruled from Washington, like territories. With the problem of bringing the Southern states back into the Union, there was another question. Who should be in charge of Reconstruction: Congress or the President?

An easy plan. Lincoln wanted to keep the matter of Reconstruction open. He never set out a complete policy for dealing with it. But as Union armies overran the Southern states, some action had to be taken. During 1863 the President moved to organize state governments under the military commanders in Tennessee and Louisiana.

In December of 1863 Lincoln set out the rules for Reconstruction in all of the Confederacy. He offered a pardon to any Southerner who would take an oath of allegiance to the Constitution and the Union. Only Confederate leaders were excluded. If one tenth of the voters as of 1860 agreed upon a state government, Lincoln would recognize it as official. The only requirement was that the state had to abolish slavery within its borders.

Under the President's "ten-per-cent plan" state governments were organized for Tennessee, Virginia, Arkansas, and Louisiana. The whole business was as much a war measure as anything else. It was supposed to show that there was a lot of Union

Read here of how

Lincoln wanted Reconstruction to be easy. Radicals in Congress favored a hard peace. Hope for compromise was ended.

321

The work of an Illinois woodcarver. How does the artist seem to view Lincoln?

sentiment in the South. Waverers might then be drawn to the Union side. But if it was to work in that way, the plan had to be an easy one for the South.

Certain failure. Congress was not asked to vote on Lincoln's plan. But congressional leaders had their own ideas about Reconstruction. They wanted Southern states to be re-admitted only when more than 50 per cent of the voters as of 1860 took an oath of allegiance. Two Radical leaders,

Benjamin Wade of Ohio and Henry W. Davis of Maryland, introduced a bill that became the basis of Congress's plan of Reconstruction. Under the Wade-Davis Bill, former Confederate and state officeholders were excluded from organizing the new governments. So was anyone who had fought against the Union.

Voting under the Wade-Davis plan was further limited by an "ironclad" test oath. The oath was so strict that no one who had aided the Confederate cause in any way could take it. This meant, of course, that Congress's plan could work only if more than half the voters in the South had failed to support the Confederacy. Since this was obviously not true, the plan would be sure to fail. Apparently that was the way Congress wanted it.

Besides feeling that Lincoln's plan of Reconstruction was too easy, Republicans in Congress feared a revival of the Democratic Party in the South. Congressmen of both parties disapproved of the President expanding his powers in wartime.

In the summer of 1864 Lincoln killed the Wade-Davis Bill with a pocket veto (see the Constitution, Article One, Section 7, paragraph b). In doing so, the President said that he didn't want to set aside the governments already organized in Louisiana and Arkansas. (At this time Tennessee had not completed its new government.)

The last word. Radical Republican views about Reconstruction, however, could not be so easily brushed aside. Wade and Davis accused Lincoln of playing election-year politics. They also warned the President that although putting down the rebellion was his job, it was up to Congress to reorganize the states.

In one sense Congress had the last word. When the Arkansas and Louisiana senators and congressmen showed up at the Capitol later that year, they were not allowed to take their seats. Lincoln pushed for their admission, but Congress steadfastly refused. Radical leaders would not go along with governments drawn up by a few thousand voters.

The President did not help matters when he accepted the fact that in Louisiana no blacks were allowed to vote. He had asked the state at least to let blacks who had fought as Union soldiers cast ballots. Louisiana would not. But for him the question was, "Will it be wiser to take [the state] as it is and help improve it, or reject and disperse it?"

Most likely Lincoln would have continued working to keep the question open. He would never have gotten into a head-on fight with his own party in Congress. His successor, Andrew Johnson, was not nearly as good a politician as Lincoln.

A mad scheme. Whatever Lincoln's plans may have been, he didn't live to see them develop. On April 5, 1865, he went to Richmond, from which the Confederate armies had just departed. There he was surrounded by a surging mass of men, women, and children, both black and white. They shouted, cheered, and danced wildly. When the war ended a few days later, Mrs. Lincoln said, "I never saw him so supremely cheerful." It was as though an enormous weight had been lifted from him.

On Good Friday, April 14, Lincoln was still enjoying the fact that the nation's ordeal was over. That night he went with Mrs. Lincoln to see a play at Ford's Theater in Washington. About ten o'clock an actor, John Wilkes Booth, entered the theater box where Lincoln was seated and fired a bullet into the back of the President's head. Nine hours later Lincoln died in a house near the theater.

The assassination was part of a mad scheme to kill Lincoln, Vice President Andrew Johnson, Secretary of State William Seward, and others. Only Lincoln was killed. Seward was stabbed but survived. The rest were unharmed.

Some of those involved in the plot got away. Booth was shot by those sent to catch

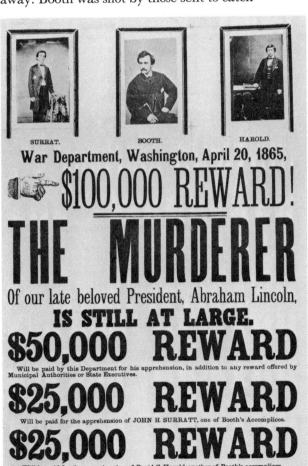

SURRAT.   BOOTH.   HAROLD.

War Department, Washington, April 20, 1865,

$100,000 REWARD!

THE MURDERER

Of our late beloved President, Abraham Lincoln,
IS STILL AT LARGE.

$50,000 REWARD
Will be paid by this Department for his apprehension, in addition to any reward offered by Municipal Authorities or State Executives.

$25,000 REWARD
Will be paid for the apprehension of JOHN H. SURRATT, one of Booth's Accomplices.

$25,000 REWARD
Will be paid for the apprehension of David C. Harold, another of Booth's accomplices.

LIBERAL REWARDS will be paid for any information that shall conduce to the arrest of either of the above-named criminals, or their accomplices.
All persons harboring or secreting the said persons, or either of them, or aiding or assisting their concealment or escape, will be treated as accomplices in the murder of the President and the attempted assassination of the Secretary of State, and shall be subject to trial before a Military Commission and the punishment of DEATH.
Let the stain of innocent blood be removed from the land by the arrest and punishment of the murderers.
All good citizens are exhorted to aid public justice on this occasion. Every man should consider his own conscience charged with this solemn duty, and rest neither night nor day until it be accomplished.

EDWIN M. STANTON, Secretary of War.

DESCRIPTIONS.—BOOTH is Five Feet 7 or 8 inches high, slender build, high forehead, black hair, black eyes, and wears a heavy black moustache.
JOHN H. SURRAT is about 5 feet, 9 inches. Hair rather thin and dark; eyes rather light; no beard. Would weigh 145 or 150 pounds. Complexion rather pale and clear, with color in his cheeks. Wore light clothes of fine quality. Shoulders square; cheek bones rather prominent; chin narrow; ears projecting at the top; forehead rather low and square, but broad. Parts his hair on the right side; neck rather long. His lips are firmly set. A slim man.
DAVID C. HAROLD is five feet six inches high, hair dark, eyes dark, eyebrows rather heavy, full face, nose short,

Surratt escaped. His mother (almost surely innocent) was hanged. Herold fled with Booth. He too was executed. (The two names are misspelled.)

him. Others were tried and hanged or imprisoned. Some were probably innocent.

In the North Lincoln was mourned as a martyr. In the South, suffering the agony of defeat, there was some rejoicing. One young girl wrote in her diary, "Hurrah! Old Abe Lincoln has been killed." More thoughtful Southerners, especially leaders like Jefferson Davis and Robert E. Lee, knew better. They were very much aware that the defeated Confederacy had lost a friend.

Lincoln had made the Union physically one, but years would pass before it was reunited in spirit. And ahead lay the trials of the Reconstruction era.

 TRY THIS!

1. Explain why Radical Republicans objected to Lincoln's plan of Reconstruction.
2. Show why the President objected to Congress's plan of Reconstruction.

At several cities, Lincoln's funeral train stopped so that local services could be held.

Roundup

Who?

Robert E. Lee
George B. McClellan
Edwin M. Stanton
Ulysses S. Grant
Charles Francis Adams
Andrew Johnson
John Wilkes Booth

What?

the *Virginia (Merrimac)*
the *Monitor*
Emancipation
    Proclamation
Sherman's March
National Banking
    System
greenbacks
Sanitary Commission
ten-per-cent plan
Ford's Theater

Where?

Fort Sumter
Richmond
Vicksburg
Appomattox

KNOW THIS

North and South Compared

1. When and where did the Civil War begin?
2. In the North, what was the effect of Lincoln's call for troops? In the South?
3. List three advantages of the North as the war began.
4. Why was the South's smaller population not a disadvantage at the beginning of the war?

Two Years of Fruitless Struggle

1. What was the outcome of the First Battle of Bull Run?
2. Who was General George B. McClellan? What was his chief strength as a military leader?
3. Why was Vicksburg important for the North?
4. Describe the encounter of the *Monitor* and *Merrimac*.
5. What part did the Union navy take in the Civil War?

Emancipation, How and Why

1. What did the Radical Republicans see as the chief purpose of war? Why did Lincoln oppose their view?
2. Why did Lincoln issue the Emancipation Proclamation?
3. What effect did Emancipation have on the South?
4. Why did Britain and France never assist the South?

The End of the Fighting

1. What was the outcome of the fighting at (a) Fredericksburg, (b) Chancellorsville, and (c) Gettysburg?
2. Why was the Battle of Gettysburg important?
3. What was Grant's strategy for winning the war?
4. What were the military and political reasons for Sherman's March to the Sea?

Action on the Home Fronts

1. Were the Morrill Tariffs for protection, or for revenue?
2. How did the North and the South raise money for the war?
3. How did women contribute during the Civil War?
4. Who were the candidates, and what were the issues, in the election of 1864? Why did Lincoln win?
5. Name four problems of President Jefferson Davis.

Reconstruction During the War

1. How did Lincoln's views on Reconstruction differ from those of the Radical Republicans?
2. What was Lincoln's plan for the Confederate states?
3. How did the Radicals try to change Lincoln's plan?
4. What were some reactions to Lincoln's death?

DIG HERE!

With a partner, choose one of the important campaigns or battles of the Civil War. Research and answer these questions about your topic. (One partner should concentrate on the Union leaders and strategy. Have the other partner take the Confederate side.)

A. Prepare a map showing the battle location and the surrounding countryside. Did geography affect the outcome? If so, how?
B. Who were the commanders? Look up their lives and previous careers. How effective was their leadership?
C. What were the strategies of North and South in this operation?
D. How do you account for the outcome of the fighting?
E. How important was this campaign or battle to the total war effort?

Here are some of the major engagements: First Bull Run, *Monitor* and *Merrimac*, Peninsular Campaign, Second Bull Run, Antietam, Fredericksburg, Chancellorsville, Gettysburg, Forts Henry and Donelson, Shiloh, New Orleans, Vicksburg, Chattanooga/Chickamauga Creek, Atlanta/Savannah, Wilderness.

Some good references would be these: Catton, *American Heritage Picture History of the Civil War,* American Heritage; Catton, *This Hallowed Ground,* Doubleday; Commager, *The Blue and the Gray,* Bobbs-Merrill; Dowdey, *The Land They Fought For,* Doubleday; Jordan, *The Civil War,* National Geographic; Williams, *Life History of the United States,* Volumes 5 and 6, Time-Life.

THINK ABOUT IT

1. "The Confederacy was not shot to death. It strangled to death." This statement was made about the North's naval blockade. Do you agree with the statement? Explain why or why not.
2. Early in the war Lincoln said his only purpose was to save the Union. He put off emancipation as long as possible. What do you think of his actions?
3. The Civil War was called "a rich man's war and a poor man's fight." Explain this. Do you agree or not? Why?

DO IT!

1. Select one of the excellent novels about the Civil War (Crane, *The Red Badge of Courage;* Dowdey, *Blow Bugles No More;* Mitchell, *Gone With the Wind;* Shaara, *The Killer Angels,* or another). If you enjoy it, make a report to the class that will persuade them to read it too.
2. Soldiers of both armies sang continually. Many recordings of Civil War songs are available. Report to the class about the songs. Play some of the recordings.
3. Design a poster illustrating flags and uniforms of both armies.

THEN AND NOW

Sherman vowed to "make Georgia howl" by his famous March to the Sea. Can such tactics be defended? Was the March aimed at ending the war, or was it an attack on helpless civilians? How does Sherman's March compare with bombing cities?

TEST YOUR HISTORY

1. What changes did the growth of manufacturing bring about?
2. How did railroads help the spread of industry? How did industry assist the railroads?
3. Why did the North replace the South as the West's best customer?
4. How widespread was the plantation system?
5. Describe the life of a slave.
6. How did the antislavery movement change in the 1800s?
7. Why did the idea of "manifest destiny" appeal to Americans?
8. Compare the ways Texas and Oregon were acquired.
9. What were the causes of the Mexican War? The results?
10. What were the chief provisions of the Compromise of 1850?
11. On what issue did the Compromise of 1850 break down?
12. How did Kansas become a battleground in the 1850s?
13. What issues were raised in the Lincoln-Douglas debates?
14. What was the most important result of the Democratic Party split of 1860?
15. By what steps did the South secede from the Union?
16. What were the strengths and weaknesses of each side in the Civil War?
17. How did Lincoln regard slavery at the beginning of the war? At the end?
18. Why were Vicksburg and Gettysburg important battles?
19. What part did Britain and France play in the Civil War?
20. What were Lincoln's views on Reconstruction?

III

REVIEW

FURTHER READING

Angle, P., *Pictorial History of the Civil War Years.* Doubleday, 1967.

Angle, P., and E. S. Miers, *The Tragic Years, 1860–1865.* Simon and Schuster, 1960.

Burlingame, R., *March of the Iron Men.* Grosset, 1960.

Catton, B., *American Heritage Picture History of the Civil War.* Am. Heritage, 1960.

Catton, B., *The Civil War.* McGraw, 1971.

Cohn, D. L., *The Life and Times of King Cotton.* Greenwood, 1974.

Donald, D., *Why the North Won the Civil War.* Macmillan, 1962.

Hansen, M. L., *The Atlantic Migration.* Howard, 1940.

Kouwenhoven, J. A., *Made in America.* Doubleday, 1948.

Nichols, R., *Franklin Pierce.* U. Penna., 1964.

Stampp, K., *And the War Came.* U. Chicago, 1964.

Wiley, B., *The Life of Billy Yank* and *The Life of Johnny Reb* (2 vols). Doubleday, 1971.

Williams, T. H., *The Union Sundered,* Vol. 5, *Life History of the United States.* Time, 1963.

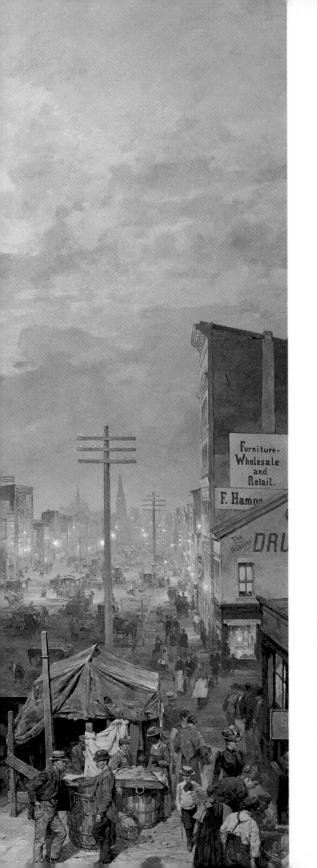

A TIME OF CHANGE

Members of the human race have a right to just one great boast: that they have an endless capacity to invent and learn. They can learn not merely as other mammals do, from imitation and from individual experience, but from experience passed down to a present generation from thousands of forebears now dead and gone.

Ruth Benedict
"The Growth of Culture"

329

Some "Other" Americans Lose Ground

14

Blacks, Indians, and Spanish-speaking Americans found themselves left out of the new United States that science and industry were creating in the late 1800s. Because black people were the largest of these groups, the chapter looks at them first.

Soon after General Lee's surrender at Appomattax Courthouse (page 314), all Confederate military activity ended. Within a month rebel forces in the Carolinas, Alabama, and Texas had laid down their arms, and peace returned to the United States. The North had won the war, leaving the South a conquered land.

1. POSTWAR RECONSTRUCTION

The cost of the Civil War was staggering. In the North over a million and a half men had been mobilized. Of those, more than 360,000 had died and 280,000 were wounded. The cost was over twenty billion dollars. In the last two years alone the federal government spent more than it had in all the years from 1789 to 1861.

But wartime spending gave a big push to northern industry. And military needs led the North to standardize its railroad gauges at four feet, eight and a half inches (page 228). The foundation was laid for a real network of rail transportation. In spite of all the sacrifices, veterans returning to the North found a prosperous and undamaged homeland.

Desperately poor. In the South more than 258,000 soldiers had died and 191,000 were permanently disabled. About half of all the South's cotton farmers were in one of these two groups.

Throughout the region there were no sheriffs, no courts, in fact, no government. Discharged Confederate soldiers roamed the countryside.

From 1860 to 1865 the South lost about 2.5 billion dollars in property. About 1.5 billion of that sum disappeared with the abolition of slavery. A third of all livestock was lost and half of all farm equipment destroyed. Property values dropped alarmingly. A Louisiana plantation bought for 100,000 dollars in 1857 was sold for 6,000 in 1865. The South was desperately poor.

"Black codes." Southern whites were not ready for emancipation. They were not prepared to accept blacks as equals. Most expected that some kind of forced labor system would have to continue, though under a new name and new legal arrangement. "All Negro labor," they said, "must be compulsory."

To get cotton production under way once more, *black codes* were adopted in most

---

Read here of how

North and South emerged from the war.
The South dealt with the freed slaves.
Johnson thought Reconstruction was over.
Congress thought otherwise.
And impeached the President.

TIME CHART

1865	President Andrew Johnson takes office.
1867	Congress passes the First Reconstruction Act.
1868	President Johnson is impeached.
1868	The Fourteenth Amendment is ratified.
1869	Ulysses S. Grant becomes President.
1876	The Sioux and Cheyenne defeat the Seventh U.S. Cavalry.
1876	The disputed Tilden-Hayes election is held.
1877	The last federal troops are withdrawn from the South.
1878	California ceases to be officially bilingual.
1887	The Dawes Allotment Act is passed.
1895	Booker T. Washington proposes the "Atlanta Compromise."
1896	The Supreme Court establishes the "separate but equal" doctrine.
1908	The NAACP is founded.

---

southern states. They gave freedmen some protection for themselves and their property. But mostly they were intended to keep blacks on a level lower than that of whites.

Under the black code of Mississippi, for example, blacks could not rent or lease land outside of the towns. (This, of course, would make it very hard for them to become independent farmers.) All freedmen had to have legal residences and regular jobs by January 1866. Any who left their

331

employers without a good reason could be returned by force—and at their own expense.

Homeless black children could be "apprenticed" by the courts. Vagrancy laws were strict. A homeless black who couldn't pay a fine might be made to work for any planter who paid it. But the greatest disadvantage of free blacks was their lack of land. Without land or any means of getting it, permanent poverty would surely be their fate.

A promise never kept. Meanwhile, blacks were not entirely without protection. In the last months of the war, Congress set up the Freedmen's Bureau under General O. O. Howard of Maine. The Bureau was to care for blacks and for white refugees in the South. Its job was to find work for them, protect their interests, educate them, and give them medical care.

According to the first Freedmen's Bureau Act, freedmen and white refugees were supposed to get the use of up to forty acres of land. The land was to come from estates that had been abandoned or taken over from Rebel leaders. After three years, the government would help them to buy the acres they were using. Here was the promise of a real social revolution. It would create, in the South, a large body of independent farmers, both black and white.

The promise was never kept. Instead, President Andrew Johnson gave the land back to its original owners, the former Rebels. Sometimes freedmen had to sign contracts to work for their former masters on land they had thought of as their own. More than once, the Freedmen's Bureau had the sad job of persuading them to sign.

Reconstruction completed? Turning the land back to its original owners was just one of the steps taken by Andrew Johnson on becoming President after the assassination of Lincoln (page 323). In May 1865, he declared a general *amnesty,* or pardon, for most southerners. Only high Confederate officials and officers, and some people having over 20,000 dollars worth of property were not included.

Otherwise, Lincoln's plan of Reconstruction (page 321) was allowed to stand. Johnson recognized the governments in Louisiana, Tennessee, Virginia, and Arkansas (page 321). And he accepted similar arrangements in the other seven states of the Confederacy. As far as the President was concerned, Reconstruction was practically complete.

Johnson made only two conditions for the re-admitted states. They had to abolish slavery and not repay any Confederate war debts. The President tried to get them to allow blacks who could read and had 250 dollars worth of property to vote. (He was frankly trying to keep the Radical Republicans in Congress from giving all blacks the vote.) The states refused his request.

A signal from Congress. Congress was not meeting when Johnson took office in April 1865. Representatives and senators returned to Washington in December, prepared to set their own course. Not only Radicals but moderates, too, felt that the President had given the South too much. Southerners were as stubborn as ever, they felt, and through the black codes they had taken away all of the freedmen's political and civil rights.

When the representatives of the reconstructed states showed up to take their seats in Congress, the trouble began. Among them were Rebel generals and colonels, members of the Confederate Congress— even Alexander Stephens, the Vice President of the Confederacy! Congress refused

Whistle-stop campaigns are not new in American politics. In 1866 President Johnson traveled through the East and Midwest urging people to support his plan of Reconstruction.

to seat any of the southern members. Clearly, it considered Reconstruction its business.

"The President is beyond hope." At first, moderate Republicans went along with Johnson, hoping that he would see things their way. Most of them gave up on him after April 1866. It was then that the President vetoed a civil rights bill aimed at "abolishing slavery not only in name, but in fact."

The Civil Rights Bill of 1866 gave the freedmen citizenship and the same legal and property rights as whites. In refusing to sign it, Johnson said that it was unconstitutional. He questioned the granting of citizenship to blacks. He further stated that it would allow the federal government to interfere with states' rights.

Clearly, the President would oppose any measure to secure the rights of freedmen. A moderate senator from Maine told a friend, "I have tried hard to save Johnson, but I am afraid he is beyond hope."

What Johnson saw as the views of a few Radicals in Congress represented wide public opinion in the North. Congress passed the Civil Rights Act over the President's veto.

A presidential disaster. The Thirteenth Amendment, ending all slavery, had become law a few months earlier, but neither it nor the Civil Rights Act gave blacks all the protection they needed. Northerners felt that only the right to vote would do that. Serious race riots in New Orleans and Memphis strengthened this feeling. The result was the Fourteenth Amendment.

The Fourteenth Amendment gave blacks federal and state citizenship and the protection of the Constitution. It also allowed a state to limit black voting, but it reduced some of the state's representation in Congress if it did so. It promised that the federal war debts would be paid but forbade payment of the Confederate debts. Acceptance of the Fourteenth Amendment was to be the test for a Confederate state's re-admission to the Union. (Congress had not accepted the "Johnson" governments—page 332.)

A conquered people. When the results of the congressional election of 1866 were

333

in, the Radicals had full control of Congress. Right away, they passed the First Reconstruction Act. It divided the South into five military districts and placed each one under a major general backed by federal troops and state militia. The military occupation in each state was to last until a convention, elected by black and white voters, had drawn up an acceptable state constitution. The new government would have to give the vote to black citizens and ratify the Fourteenth Amendment. Former Confederate leaders were not allowed to take part. Southerners knew now that they were a conquered people.

Setting the stage. Along with its program of Reconstruction, Congress also began to take away some of the President's power. It passed the Tenure of Office Act stating that the President could not remove an official appointed with the approval of the Senate unless the Senate agreed. In August 1867, President Andrew Johnson

did what Congress had hoped he would. He fired Secretary of War Edwin Stanton, a close friend of the Radicals. The stage was set for impeachment.

The Constitution states that the President, Vice President, and other civil officers can be impeached and removed from office for "treason, bribery, or other high crimes and misdemeanors" (Article Two, Section 4). It also states that the House of Representatives brings the impeachment, and the Senate tries the case. Many Presidents have been threatened with impeachment, but only Andrew Johnson has actually undergone it. (In 1974 Richard Nixon almost certainly would have been impeached and put on trial, but he resigned before the House could act.)

High crimes and misdemeanors. On February 4, 1868, a dark and snowy afternoon, the House voted 126 to 47 to impeach President Andrew Johnson. They charged him with violating the Tenure of

President Johnson's trial before the Senate was presided over by Chief Justice Salmon Chase.

334

Office Act and of trying "to bring into disgrace, ridicule, hatred, and contempt the Congress of the United States." Today these actions seem a long way from "high crimes and misdemeanors." But to many people at the time it looked like a good way to get rid of a President who they believed was hurting the country.

The President's lawyers were able to show that Johnson was being attacked for political, not legal, reasons. The Senate voted 35 guilty, 19 not guilty, one vote short of the two thirds needed for removal. Seven Republicans went against the leaders of their own party to vote not guilty.

Andrew Johnson remained President for nine more months. In 1868 the Republican Party elected General Ulysses S. Grant as Johnson's successor.

 TRY THIS!

1. Compare conditions in the North and South at war's end. **2.** Show how President Johnson reconstructed the South. **3.** Explain why Congress impeached Johnson.

2.   THE SOUTH UNDER RADICAL RULE

What took place in the South after the triumph of the Radicals in 1867 and 1868 is sometimes called Black Reconstruction. It was a time in which federal troops enforced the law, freedmen were given the vote, northerners were active throughout the South as businessmen and government officials, and some white southerners supported the Radical Republicans. These

---

Read here of how

New black voters gained many rights.
Many white northerners helped them.
So did some white southerners.
Southern Democrats called it "misrule."

---

white southerners worked with the blacks and northerners to change the South.

A look at the evidence. Southern Democrats called the whole period of Radical Republican power and congressional Reconstruction a "time of troubles." Everything bad that happened and anything that went wrong during that time was blamed on military occupation, northern interference, and "black misrule." A close look at the evidence indicates that this view is not correct.

Take the question of military occupation. The largest number of federal troops in the whole South during the years of Black Reconstruction was 25,000, and it was steadily reduced. By 1869 there were only 716 soldiers in all of Mississippi. Texas had a large number, but that was because

335

of developments in Mexico. Except for those living in the larger southern towns, few people ever saw a United States soldier.

As to "black misrule," no southern state was ever ruled by blacks. Only in South Carolina did blacks briefly control the legislature. Just two United States senators and fourteen congressmen out of hundreds of southern representatives sent to Washington from 1865 to 1877 were black. In character, education, and intelligence these sixteen were plainly equal to the other members of Congress at the time.

The idea that freedmen in general were ignorant and illiterate is also false. It is true that a majority of them had not been taught to read and write, but they clearly understood their own needs and best interests. They wanted land, education, and political and civil rights. They supported the Republican Party for the sound reason that the Republicans were more likely than the Democrats to supply those needs.

A body of skilled and educated blacks provided leadership for this group. Many of them came from the free blacks who had lived in the South before the war or former slaves who had had special privileges and opportunities. Others had come to the South as soldiers, Freedmen's Bureau agents, or missionaries.

The conquerors. Any northerner living in the South who spoke or acted in favor of Reconstruction was called a *carpetbagger*. The carpetbaggers were a mixed lot. Some came south looking for business opportunities. They brought with them much-needed capital for investment. They ran plantations, built railroads, operated coal and iron mines, and opened hotels. Often they were resented, even though their money was helping southern recovery.

Northerners who came to help the freedmen—as teachers, ministers, Freedmen's Bureau agents, and so forth—were equally unwelcome. So were the Treasury agents, tax collectors, customs officers, and other political appointees. All were regarded as representatives of the conquering federal government.

White "Union men" of the South were *scalawags*. Many had opposed secession and the war, so naturally other southerners saw them as traitors. Some were former Whigs who felt at home in the Republican Party. Most were poor whites. A few, like former Confederate General James Longstreet, who had been Lee's trusted lieutenant, were people of prominence.

Where the money went. The sight of blacks taking part in government was probably the hardest thing for southern whites to get used to. Any failings or shortcomings of this group were greatly exaggerated. There was corruption in the South Carolina legislature and in others under Republican control. But it was not nearly as great as charged. If anything, it was far less than what was taking place at the same time in New York and other northern cities.

Taxes and public debt climbed enormously in the Reconstruction period, but most of the money went to repair war damage, set up a system of public education, and build needed railroads. To help pay for these things, southern tax rates rose to four times what they had been before the war. But part of the rise came about because property values on which the rate was based had been cut in half (page 331).

Dedicated men and women. The foundation for a system of public education in the South was laid by the Freedmen's Bureau. It had almost 10,000 teachers, half of them from the North, staffing its schools.

336

HIRAM R. REVELS was a senator from Mississippi from 1870 to 1871. A free black, he had graduated from Knox College in Illinois. He served as a chaplain in the Union army, then entered politics and was elected to the seat formerly held by Jefferson Davis.

BLANCHE K. BRUCE was a senator from Mississippi from 1875 to 1881. He had been born a slave in Virginia but had run away. Bruce attended Oberlin College in Ohio, then settled in Mississippi and became a planter. As a senator, he worked hard for better treatment of Indians and poor southern whites. He especially wanted more money spent on schools, North and South.

ROBERT B. ELLIOTT was born in Boston, Massachusetts. He went to school in Jamaica and in London, then graduated from the famous school for boys at Eton. He was a newspaper editor and a member of the South Carolina Constitutional Convention before going to Congress (1871–1875).

ADELBERT AMES was the governor of Mississippi from 1874 to 1876. A West Point graduate, he had been a Union general with an excellent record. (He earned a Congressional Medal of Honor at Bull Run.) In all, he was a "carpetbagger" of the highest type.

JAMES ORR was a Confederate senator and governor of South Carolina under the Lincoln-Johnson Plan. He opposed the South Carolina black code and warned that it would bring trouble. Orr favored votes for blacks long before Radical Reconstruction.

A black teacher watches over students in a one-room school. Reconstruction legislatures provided public schools open to both black and white children. Schools soon became segregated.

While freedmen were taking an active part in politics, education was well supported. The New England common school system (page 202) was widely copied in the South's new state constitutions. However, southern schools were organized on county rather than town or village lines.

What the Declaration promised. Reconstruction was the time in which blacks first emerged from slavery. In spite of difficulties, they made important advances.

During Radical Reconstruction blacks organized a number of Methodist and Baptist churches. These offered not only religious services, but political and social guidance and educational help. At the same time, thousands of blacks were able to buy land and enter a number of businesses. Black schools and colleges were established, and local black leaders came forward to act as sheriffs, assessors, and Republican Party officials. Many of these gains, but not all of them, were wiped out with the end of Reconstruction.

Yet no result was more important than the fact that for a time black Americans were treated as the equals of whites. That was what the Declaration of Independence had promised.

 TRY THIS!

1. Describe two views of Radical Reconstruction as it might have been seen by a white southern Democrat and a black Republican official. **2.** Report on one of the persons mentioned on page 337.

The teachers worked under difficult conditions. Poor housing, bad food, and public contempt were their lot. Often, after regular school hours, these dedicated men and women ran classes for adults as well. Some planters saw that it was in their interest to have workers who could read and write. But hostility was deep.

338

3. THE TRIUMPH OF JIM CROW

The period during which southern blacks enjoyed some equality with whites was brief. By 1877 Democrats had control of all state governments in the former Confederacy. For another ten or fifteen years blacks continued to vote and hold office. Yet they had been unable to get a foothold in the South's economic system. The period of equality was too short for them to become landowners or acquire the advanced skills needed in business or the professions. Being

Read here of how

Sharecropping developed in the South.
Radical Republican rule was ended.
The Democrats lost a close election.
Blacks lost their Reconstruction gains.
And found an ''accommodating'' spokesman.

dependent on whites for their living, they soon lost their political and social rights.

A substitute for cash. In the earliest years of Reconstruction most freedmen worked on white-owned land as hired help. But planters, except for those with the largest farms, had no cash to pay wages. And workers had no way of buying or renting land. By the 1870s *sharecropping* had taken the place of cash.

Under the sharecropping system, a white landowner provided land, tools, seed, and a house. The black sharecropper did what he had learned to do as a slave; he grew cotton. When the crop had been harvested and sold, the money was divided between owner and worker. If the "cropper" had his own tools and seed, he got a two-thirds share. If the owner provided the tools and seed, the "cropper" got only one third.

Trapped in the system. Sharecropping grew up out of necessity. What made the

Poverty was the lot of most blacks who stayed on the land and became sharecroppers.

system so bad and so long-lasting was the way in which future cotton crops had to be pledged or mortgaged to pay for equipment, food, and other needs. Local bankers and storekeepers often charged enormous interest on loans and advances they made. And they were not above juggling the books to take advantage of the illiterate sharecroppers.

Between owners and storekeepers a sharecropper often found that even after handing over all of the year's cotton, there was still a debt outstanding. The next year's crop had to be pledged in advance so that the sharecropper could live until the growing season.

Sharecroppers were by no means all black. Every census from 1870 to 1940 showed a greater number of whites than blacks among them. But almost two thirds of all southern blacks were trapped in the sharecropping system. Though free, they still had to work land owned by whites.

With rifles showing. The Grant Administration (1869 to 1877) was firmly in Republican hands. But northerners had grown weary of the "southern problem." They were more and more willing to let the region work out its own problems. However, some problems were being worked out through secret terror organizations like the Ku Klux Klan, the Knights of the White Camellia, and the Red Shirts. All of them used threats and violence to drive blacks out of government.

Klan members might appear on the night before an election wherever blacks were gathered. Their weird disguises (often with rifles clearly showing under the robes) were usually enough to frighten the freedmen away from voting places. Blacks who resisted might be whipped or even killed.

Dressed in white robes and hoods, Klan members brutally attacked and even murdered people who advocated racial equality.

340

White men or women who refused to cooperate with the terrorists were treated in the same way.

The Ku Klux Klan was often closely linked to the Democratic Party in the South. The party's goal of making sure that only whites voted was no secret. The process of restoring white rule was called *redemption*.

Many charges, few convictions. President Grant declared martial law in some southern districts. Counties where Klan murders took place had to pay fines. Congress investigated the organization and passed laws against interfering with people's voting rights. Over a thousand cases were brought to court, but white juries did not want to punish the Klan too harshly. Few of the accused were found guilty.

None of this federal activity prevented white Republicans from being silenced or driven away. Not many blacks were able to resist without help. Between 1869 and 1875 white rule was restored in eight Confederate states. Only South Carolina, Florida, and Louisiana remained under Republican control.

A stolen election. The Republican Party was in poor shape going into the 1876 presidential election. The Grant Administration had been riddled with graft and scandal, so the Democrats could stand as the party of reform. Their candidate, Samuel Tilden, had cleaned up corruption in New York City while he was governor of the state.

The Republican Party chose Rutherford B. Hayes of Ohio. He had something for everyone. He had been a Civil War general and a party regular, he had supported Reconstruction but now favored southern home rule, he had been an able and honest governor, and he favored reform.

Early in the campaign the Republicans knew they were in trouble. A lot was going to depend on the black voters in South Carolina, Florida, and Louisiana. On election night, the Democrat, Tilden, was 250,000 votes ahead. A total of twenty electoral votes (from the three southern Republican states and Oregon) were in doubt, but Tilden needed only one of the twenty to win. Victory seemed certain.

Tilden never did get the one vote he needed. The Republicans claimed "irregularities." (In South Carolina more ballots had been cast than there were voters registered.) And the Republican-run Electoral Commission gave all the disputed votes to Hayes. That made him the winner—by *one* electoral vote. The Democrats had almost surely won honestly in Florida, so Tilden should have gotten its four electoral votes. The election of 1876 was a "steal."

The South had pinned great hopes on a Democratic victory. However, Hayes promised to withdraw federal troops from the last three southern states. This would enable them to return to white rule. Southern leaders decided not to oppose Hayes's election. Talk of another rebellion died away.

As part of the deal, the South would also get federal money to improve its rivers and harbors and to help with railroad construction. But the final reassurance may have been Hayes's statement that the rights of southern blacks would be safest in the hands of white leaders. They stayed there for almost a hundred years.

One of the "redeemers." Wade Hampton of South Carolina was typical of the white leaders Hayes had in mind. He was a successful planter, a political leader, and an ex-Confederate general. As an aristocrat he did not have the fear of blacks felt by many poorer whites.

When Hampton ran for governor of the state in 1876, it was as a trusted native son, with a paternal concern for all South Carolinians. He promised to be fair to the state's black citizens. To a great extent he kept his word. The state's civil rights laws stayed on the books, and the legal rights of blacks were respected. Governor Hampton appointed many blacks to minor offices.

Throughout the late 1800s a few black congressmen continued to serve in Washington. In heavily black counties the Democratic ticket often included black candidates for coroner, assessor, and justice of the peace. But as the Republican Party died out in the South, so did black participation in politics.

The laws by which blacks were prevented from voting after 1890 (tests of reading ability, advance payment of a two-dollar poll tax) worked against poor whites too. In Mississippi the number of white voters dropped from 120,000 in 1890 to half that number two years later. But when Louisiana adopted the same plan that was used in Mississippi, black voters there went from over 100,000 to fewer than 1,000.

"Separate but equal?" During the late 1800s southern blacks were also subject to many controls. Before the Civil War, legal *segregation* (separating people by race) had been much more common in the North than in the South. In the "free" states, railroads, streetcars, and public places were sometimes rigidly segregated. Even in 1878 a former abolitionist on a visit to Virginia found black and white people mingling more freely than in his own New England. A little later a black lawyer declared that in the South he could ride first-class on the railroads, and that he was waited on more politely there than in some parts of the North.

FREED HIMSELF

He was born a slave but managed to get some education. When the Civil War began, Robert Smalls was put on a Confederate dispatch boat stationed at Charleston.

Smalls was ready to lay down his life but not for Dixie. He waited his chance, smuggled his wife and children aboard, then seized the vessel. Sailing it to the Union squadron, he freed himself, his family, and twelve other crew members.

The government paid Robert Smalls for the boat, and President Lincoln made him a navy pilot. He did well at the capture of Charleston and was made a naval captain.

After the war, Smalls settled in South Carolina. He served as a state senator and a major general in the state militia, before going to Congress (1875–1879 and 1881–1887).

The worst blows to black equality came from the United States Supreme Court. Its justices, mostly northerners, took away much of the protection that blacks had been given by the Fourteenth Amendment (page 333) and the civil rights acts. In 1883 the Court threw out the Civil Rights Act of 1875, which had outlawed discrimination in restaurants, theaters, stores, and the like. In doing so, the Court said that the Fourteenth Amendment applied only to state actions, not those of individuals.

Then, in 1896, in the case of *Plessy v. Ferguson*, the Court upheld a Louisiana law requiring segregation in railroad cars. As with so many Supreme Court decisions, *Plessy v. Ferguson* went far beyond the case at hand. It set down the "separate but equal" doctrine. Separate facilities were perfectly legal, it said, as long as they were equal to those for whites. The so-called "Jim Crow laws" were soon applying the principle to all public facilities and to schools.

A national figure. The time from 1890 to 1910 has been called the lowest point of black life in America. The oppression of those years caused a black migration to southern cities, and to New York, Chicago, and Detroit as well. It also brought about a new kind of black leadership.

Booker T. Washington had been a slave in Virginia. After emancipation he worked his way through Hampton Institute, which trained blacks in agricultural, industrial, and mechanical skills. In 1881 he opened Tuskegee Institute, in Alabama, along the same lines as Hampton.

Washington became a national figure in 1895 with a speech that he made at Atlanta, Georgia. He called upon blacks to learn modern industrial skills and, for the time, to forget literature, philosophy and

Segregation even extended to such things as water fountains. A separate but *unequal* society developed in the South.

art. If whites would help blacks to get such training, he said in effect, blacks would stop agitating for social equality. It was a clear acceptance of second-class citizenship.

Washington's plan was called the "Atlanta Compromise." It went down very well with whites. In both the North and the South they were looking for easy solutions to the hard problems posed by black America. Washington was accepted as the leading spokesman for blacks everywhere. Presidents consulted him about their speeches; rich men invited him to their homes and aboard their yachts. They also gave him money, which he used to encourage other blacks who felt as he did.

343

A student concert at Tuskegee Institute in 1903.

A different voice. The years from 1890 to 1910 were also a time of political and social reform. The reforms did very little for blacks, but blacks did something for themselves. In 1908, with a group of interested whites, they organized the National Association for the Advancement of Colored People (the NAACP). It gathered facts about injustices to blacks and published them in its magazine. The NAACP also fought for the rights of blacks, in courts and lawmaking bodies.

The spirit behind the NAACP in its early years was W. E. B. Du Bois, a proud young northern-born black. Du Bois was a brilliant scholar who earned degrees from several universities. He seemed the opposite of all that Booker T. Washington wanted for black people, and he spoke out against the older man's views. Du Bois wanted full and immediate justice for black people so that they could develop all of their talents. The militant ideas of W. E. B. Du Bois are more in keeping with the thinking of today's blacks than the more accommodating ones of Booker T. Washington.

TRY THIS!

1. Explain why sharecropping continued for so long after Reconstruction. 2. Tell how the Republicans won the election of 1876. 3. Explain how Booker T. Washington *and* W. E. B. Du Bois might have regarded Wade Hampton.

4. THE PEOPLE OF THE WEST

The late 1800s were a bad time for American minorities. As we have seen, the states passed segregation, or "Jim Crow," laws that made black citizenship a mockery. In the same period the last organized resistance of Indian peoples was crushed, and they were penned in reservations. Finally, Mexican Americans of California and the Southwest lost lands they had held for a hundred years or more.

Read here of how

Plains Indians depended on the buffalo.
Their livelihood was destroyed.
The Dawes Act did not help the Indians.
Mexican Americans lost their lands.

All of these Americans were pushed to the edges of the nation's life. A prosperous society was developing in the United States, but they had little part in it. Instead, they continued and advanced their own black, Native American, or Spanish cultures. These gave each minority a hidden life that the white majority rarely noticed and rarely understood.

As long as the rivers flow. Before the Civil War, thousands of easterners made the long trek westward to California and Oregon. They passed as quickly as they could over the open territory between the Missouri River and the Rocky Mountains. To them the sea of grass that seemed to stretch to the end of the world looked all but empty. Only herds of buffalo and antelope and occasional bands of Indians occupied it.

A sea of grass. What challenges did the people who settled on the Great Plains face?

Something for Supper by Harvey Dunn; collection South Dakota Memorial Art Center, Brookings.

These Plains Indians were a mixture of tribes. Some had lived in the region since before the time of Columbus. Others were from the East like the Cherokee and the Creek (page 192), who had been forced to move west. From 1834 until the Civil War the western plains had been called Indian Territory, and that was supposed to be closed forever to white settlement.

But as early as 1840 the Mormons had found homes in Utah (page 199). In the 1850s wagon trains had pushed westward, and the United States government had talked of various routes for transcontinental railroads. The space open to the Indians had shrunk. Treaties that gave the region to the Indian people for "as long as the sun shall shine and the rivers flow" were broken more often than they were upheld.

Harsh terms. In 1862 the powerful Sioux of the northern Great Plains (map on page 20) exploded into action. For all of the people of the Plains the buffalo had provided food, clothing, shelter, fuel, and weapons. In 1850 there were fifteen million of the great shaggy beasts throughout the West. But white hunters shot more and more of them for their hides or just for sport.

Soon the buffalo had become so scarce that the people of the Plains could not find enough of them for their needs. They were forced to depend on government goods and food. In 1862 there was a cutback in supplies and credit; the Sioux went on the warpath.

In Minnesota, 700 white settlers were killed, and 30,000 had to flee from their homes. But federal and state forces defeated the Sioux and gave them the usual harsh terms. The chiefs and some of their followers were executed, and the Sioux had to give up their Minnesota lands.

A painted buffalo head decorates this Sioux medicine shield. Why were buffalo important to the Plains Indians?

Kill the buffalo! For the next fifteen years fighting continued throughout the West. In 1864 at Sand Creek, Colorado, militia attacked a few hundred Cheyenne and Arapaho who had already made a truce. Within a few hours almost 300 Cheyenne men, women, and children were massacred. The Cheyenne and Sioux fought back. They defeated an army unit at Platte Bridge, Wyoming (map on page 349), then withdrew to their hunting grounds.

When the Civil War ended, westward migrations increased. The Oglala Sioux and their leader, Red Cloud, for a time cut off the trail to Montana. But none of these gains were permanent. The government worked harder than ever to open the Plains for settlement. It even encouraged whites to kill off the buffalo so that greater numbers of Indians would have to move to reservations and live on government rations. In six years almost ten million animals were wiped out in the southern part of the Plains alone.

No longer independent. By the 1870s the government was looking forward to a time when all of the Indian tribes would be confined to reservations. Once a tribe accepted reservation life, the government no longer had to recognize it as an independent nation. Its members were expected to live under United States laws.

The laws were supposed to be upheld by government agents. However, the agents were political appointees. At best they were ignorant about the people they were supposed to protect and insensitive to their needs. At worst the agents cheated and stole from their charges. Mistreatment by the agents led to Indian resistance. Then the army had to be called in to restore order.

The Kansas Pacific Railroad used mounted buffalo heads to advertise hunting along its route to Denver. Passengers could open the car windows and shoot at buffalo as the train sped along.

A centennial happening. In the mid-1870s federal troops invaded the Black Hills (map on page 350), a region sacred to the Dakota Sioux. Led by Lieutenant Colonel George Armstrong Custer, these soldiers were looking for gold. They found it, and when the word got out, a gold rush followed. The Sioux refused to give up the Black Hills, the dwelling place of their ancestors' spirits. But the government could not keep gold prospectors out either, so it decided to take the Black Hills anyway. It ordered the tribes to a reservation.

Neither the Sioux nor their allies, the Northern Cheyenne, would obey the government's order. So in the spring of 1876, the War Department sent an expedition against them.

The Sioux and Cheyenne forces were led by Crazy Horse. In a series of brilliant moves he halted the army's advance at Rosebud Creek, Montana. Meanwhile, Custer did not realize that part of the federal troops had retreated. He decided to attack an Indian encampment on the Little Big Horn River. At once his Seventh Cavalry was caught between forces led by Crazy Horse, Sitting Bull, and a chief named Gall. Custer and more than two hundred of his men were killed at the Battle of Little Big Horn.

In the long run, the victory did the tribes no good. News of "Custer's Last Stand" reached the East in the midst of the July 4th, 1876, centennial celebrations. It caused a sensation, and the government redoubled its efforts to conquer the Sioux. Some, under Sitting Bull, escaped to Canada. Others, followers of Crazy Horse, fought desperately until they were starved into surrender. Crazy Horse was murdered after his capture, and Indian resistance crumbled.

348

White Bird, a Northern Cheyenne, made this painting of the Battle of Little Big Horn. As a boy, he had fought against Custer's troops.

The last Indian uprising occurred in 1890. It ended with a massacre at Wounded Knee in South Dakota. Federal troops slaughtered defenseless Sioux women and children by firing artillery into their tents.

Everyone's enemy. At the same time whites were moving into the Great Plains, they were also migrating to the Southwest. In this area lived many Indians who were farmers and herders rather than hunters. The people of the Pueblos had been farmers for 2,000 years. Their neighbors, the Navaho, had adopted the Spaniards' horses and sheep and had become successful herders. There were a few disputes with whites, but the way of life went on pretty much the same.

For a number of tribes, grouped together under the name Apache, the situation was quite different. Wanting only to be free, they were deeply suspicious of attempts to control them. The Spaniards and Mexicans had aroused Indian hostility when they enslaved Apache women and children. Apache raiders were a constant threat to Spanish and Mexican settlements. Even their Indian neighbors feared them.

Broken treaties, massacres, and removals soon turned the Apache against the *Anglos,* English-speaking people from the East. Because the Apache had a reputation for ferocity and often tortured captives, the government decided to kill them off rather than make peace. But the Apache used the experience they had gained from being everyone's enemy for 200 years. Led by outstanding men such as Cochise and Geronimo, small bands would attack and be gone before federal troops could engage them in battle. Finally the government chose General George Crook to bring the Apache to terms. A renowned Indian-fighter, Crook was unusual in his dealing with Indians. When he gave his word, he kept it. This honesty persuaded many Apache to make peace. Then they were used to bring other tribes under federal control. When Geronimo surrendered in 1886, the once-feared Apache became reservation Indians.

Another way of stealing land. By the end of the 1800s most American Indians were living on reservations. And these grew steadily smaller as the most valuable land was taken away by the government and private citizens using various legal tricks and by outright theft. The children of Indians on the reservations got very little education. It was poorly suited to their needs. In fact, the educational system seemed deliberately planned to break down family and tribal loyalties and make the Indian children ashamed of their own heritage.

In 1887 Congress passed the Dawes General Allotment Act. Like the reservations' school system, the intention of the Dawes Act was to wipe out the Indians' way of life. It called for dividing the land of each reservation among the people living there. Heads of families on reservations that accepted the government's plan got 160 acres, and single persons eighty.

One trouble was that on the inferior land belonging to most reservations, 160 acres was not enough to support a family. At the time the Dawes Act was passed, friends of the Indians said that it would become another way of stealing Indian land. They were right. Within 45 years almost two thirds of the reservation lands had passed into the hands of whites.   349

Little Big Horn
1876

Rosebud
1876

Sioux Battles
1862

Platte Bridge
1865

Wounded Knee
1890

Sand Creek
Massacre 1864

Reservations, 1875

Reservations, 1890

Present state boundaries

Indian Losses and Defeats, 1862–1890

By 1890 the Indians had been driven onto reservations and forced to give up lands they had once called their own. Why had this happened?

THE MEXICAN AMERICANS

In California and the Southwest, Anglos had been arriving. They came to seek gold or land, and at first most of them settled in the northern part of California. The Mexican government had welcomed settlers from the United States. And after the Mexican War, the *Californios* (Spanish-speaking settlers) were glad to have them too. The Anglos paid good prices for beef and other products of the local ranches and farms.

South of San Francisco, the land taken from Mexico remained Spanish-speaking and kept its Spanish culture. Both Mexican Americans and Anglos had helped to draw up California's constitution (page 274), and until 1878 the state was *bilingual* (that is, it had two official languages—Spanish and English).

Long court cases. As might be expected, the culture of California and the

Southwest was changed most by the coming of the railroads. The Anglo population grew rapidly, and state government became less sympathetic to Mexican American citizens. Sometimes they were treated like outsiders in their own country. There was occasional violence too, in which both sides took the law into their own hands.

By the Treaty of Guadalupe Hidalgo (pages 269-270) and the Gadsden Purchase (page 269), property rights of Mexican Americans were supposed to be respected. But often Anglo settlers were able to get the Mexican land deeds set aside. Sometimes the land in question had never been surveyed. Occasionally, too, the deeds dated back to the 1600s, and many records had been lost or destroyed.

An additional problem was that much of the land was held on a community basis.

Individual families used small plots to grow food, while their cattle grazed on large open areas. Communal landholding grew out of American Indian traditions; there was no basis for it in the law of the United States.

Mexican Americans could not usually prove ownership of the land they claimed except through long and expensive court cases. And the courts were those of the Anglo authorities. Once they had lost their land, Mexican Americans lost their standing, just as blacks and Indians had.

TRY THIS!

1. Describe the steps of United States policy by which the Indian people were driven to war. 2. Explain why the Dawes Act caused a decline in Indian landholding. 3. Tell how the railroads helped to change the character of California.

When this painting of Market Plaza in San Antonio, Texas was made in 1879, Mexican population was larger than that of Anglos.

ROUNDUP

Who?
    Andrew Johnson
    O.O. Howard
    Rutherford B. Hayes
    Wade Hampton
    Booker T. Washington
    W.E.B. DuBois
    Sitting Bull
    Crazy Horse

What?
    black codes
    Freedmen's Bureau
    Tenure of Office Act
    Black Reconstruction
    First Reconstruction
       Act
    carpetbaggers
    scalawags
    sharecropping
    Ku Klux Klan
    Plessy v. Ferguson
    Jim Crow
    Plains Indians
    Dawes Act
    Californios

Where?
    Little Big Horn
    Wounded Knee

KNOW THIS

Postwar Reconstruction
1. What did the Civil War cost, in dollars and in lives? How did wartime spending benefit the North?
2. Why were black codes adopted in most southern states? What provisions were found in the codes?
3. Was the Freedmen's Bureau successful in carrying out its mission? Why, or why not?
4. What was the Fourteenth Amendment expected to accomplish?
5. How did the Radical Republicans in Congress propose to deal with the South?
6. Why did the effort to remove President Johnson fail?

The South Under Radical Rule
1. What evidence challenges the claim about black "misrule" during Reconstruction?
2. Why did the carpetbaggers come to the South?
3. Why did taxes and public debt in the South increase during the Reconstruction period?
4. What did the Freedmen's Bureau do for public education in the South?

The Triumph of Jim Crow
1. How did sharecropping trap blacks and poor whites?
2. What means did the Ku Klux Klan use to drive blacks from government?
3. In what sense was the 1876 election "stolen"?
4. Should racial segregation be seen as a southern development? Explain your answer.
5. In the late 1800s, how did the Supreme Court hold back black equality?
6. What different views of black Americans were held by Booker T. Washington and W.E.B. DuBois?

The People of the West
1. Besides black Americans, what groups suffered injustices in the late 1800s?
2. What caused the Sioux to go to war in 1862?
3. How were the Indian reservations governed?
4. What brought on the battle at the Little Big Horn? What were its results?
5. What was the purpose of the Dawes Act?
6. What caused the relationship between Anglos and Californios to change in the late 1800s?

DIG HERE!

Choose one of the Indian peoples or tribal groups shown on the map on page 20. Find the information needed to answer these five questions about the group you have chosen.

A. Did this Indian people continue to live in the area shown on the map on page 20? Does the map show the land features of the region? If not, use an outline map to show this information.

B. Tell about the people's religion. What were their most important beliefs? What rituals and ceremonies were sacred to them? How did religion influence their activities?

C. Describe the people's a) dwellings, b) food and cooking, c) clothing, d) crafts, e) occupations. Were any of these related to the physical environment in which they lived? If so, explain how.

D. How did the people govern themselves? How were decisions made? What important rules did they have? How were their leaders chosen? Compare the government of the Indian people with that of the United States. Was the tribal government democratic? How well did it maintain order and promote the good of all?

E. Write a brief history of the people you have chosen. Show their dealings with whites.

To start your research, use the appropriate books from those listed on page 425.

THINK ABOUT IT

1. If Rebel lands had been redistributed among blacks and poor whites (page 332), how would this have influenced Reconstruction? How would it have affected the position of blacks today?

2. Explain why there was more prejudice against blacks among poor and middle-class southern whites than among the well-to-do.

3. One historian blames the failure of Reconstruction on both North and South—the South because it was unwilling to change, and the North because of "bungling idealism." Do you agree? Why, or why not?

DO IT!

1. Prepare a report on the origins and activities of the Ku Klux Klan. What did the white robes represent? The fiery crosses?

2. Read and report on *Bury My Heart at Wounded Knee,* by Dee Brown. An Indian has stated, "The whites told only one side. Told it to please themselves." Do conquerors always do that? Explain.

THEN AND NOW

What accounts for the intolerance of Americans during the late 1800s and early 1900s? The civil rights movement of the 1960s and 1970s has been called a "second Reconstruction." Why did it occur at this time? How successful was it?

New Problems Fill the Gilded Age

15

In the Gilded Age small businesses could become giant corporations by using labor-saving machinery. Rotary presses (above) were costly, but they could print daily newspapers by the hundreds of thousands. They also brought down the price of magazines and introduced mass advertising.

As the reunited nation tried to solve its problems after the Civil War, the North underwent a hectic period of industrial growth. Green valleys and rolling meadows were ripped apart. Factories and ugly tenement houses sprawled over them. People moved off the land, as well as from overseas, into the cities.

The frontier that had once seemed endless was rapidly filled. There was a ruthless pursuit of wealth. Names like Carnegie, Rockefeller, and Gould—unknown before the war—became household words. Change was everywhere. As people looked back to the time before the war, they recalled it as "the good old days." Life then had seemed simple, tranquil, innocent, and safe. In the New America, it was complicated, vulgar, gaudy, corrupt, and often dangerous.

1.   GREAT GENERAL—POOR PRESIDENT

Mark Twain and Charles Dudley Warner wrote a novel about the United States after the Civil War; they called their book *The Gilded Age*. Behind all the lavish wealth and prosperity, the authors saw poverty, suffering, and despair. The poet Walt Whitman observed that the nation was becoming as mighty as the Roman Empire but losing its

354

soul. However, once it set out after profit and power, there was no turning back. For better or for worse, the United States would influence the destiny of half the globe.

The first hundred years. The Gilded Age began in 1876 with the centennial, the anniversary of the first hundred years of United States history. Population was soaring; production boomed. Almost everyone felt that the second hundred years, carrying the nation to July 4, 1976, would be a time of tremendous growth.

But in the midst of the centennial celebrations, there was cause for worry. In 1868, millions of Americans had voted for Ulysses S. Grant as President. The scruffy-looking general with the stars of his rank pinned to the collar of a private's uniform had been a symbol of democracy. When the immaculately turned-out Robert E. Lee offered Grant his sword at Appomattox, it seemed a triumph over outdated aristocracy (pages 314-315).

Unfortunately, Grant turned out to be a man who was completely at home only in the wartime army. Everywhere else, he was a stranger. In the smoke of battle, under the greatest pressure, he could reduce a complicated military problem to its main points and come up with a plan. And he had the unconquerable will to see the plan through.

———————— •◆• ————————

Read here of how

Grant failed as President.
He was a victim of his "friends."
The *Alabama* claims were settled.

———————— •◆• ————————

TIME CHART

1869	The first transcontinental railroad is completed.
1871	The Treaty of Washington is signed.
1877	*Munn v. Illinois* upholds the Granger laws.
1882	Standard Oil is organized.
1886	*Wabash v. Illinois* reverses *Munn*.
1886	The Haymarket riot alarms the nation.
1886	The AFL is established.
1887	The Interstate Commerce Commission is formed.
1890	The Sherman Antitrust Act is passed.
1894	President Cleveland intervenes in the Pullman strike.
1895	*U.S. v. E. C. Knight* destroys the Sherman Act.

————— ▬◆◆◆▬ —————

However, faced with difficult situations in civilian life, Grant hadn't the least idea how to handle them. Before the war, he had failed at everything he tried, even the peacetime army. His business career had been a disaster. In 1861, he was working as a clerk in his father's store.

Like many who fail at business, Grant was in awe of those who had succeeded. Moreover, during his years in politics it apparently never occurred to him that people who gave him money, houses, or other gifts expected favors in return. In his last annual message to Congress, in December 1876, President Grant confessed that he had made "mistakes." Some of his appointments had been unwise, he said, "as all can see, and I admit."

Profits without risks. The period after any war is likely to be a time of political scandal. The Civil War was no exception. Still, Grant himself was not responsible for all the graft and corruption associated with his administration. The spoils system (page 188) had become the lifeblood of American politics. Party workers demanded rewards in the form of jobs. And officeholders were expected to pay some of their salaries to the party that appointed them. Presidents who tried to control this system soon found themselves in a fight with Congress over party patronage.

The biggest scandal of the Gilded Age was that surrounding the Crédit Mobilier. In 1860 the Republican platform had called for a transcontinental railroad. The Party's promise was kept by the Pacific Railway Acts of 1862 and 1864. The first gave the Union Pacific and Central Pacific railroads ten sections of public land for every mile of track they put down. The 1864 act increased this to twenty sections. The railroads could sell the sections (chart on page 102) to settlers or keep them for their minerals and timber.

Government backing set off a scramble among wealthy tycoons for railroad charters and for the land grants that went with them. Much of the struggle took place in Congress. Its members soon found ways to share in the profits of railroad-building while avoiding the risks.

Oakes Ames, a member of Congress who had grown wealthy manufacturing shovels, set up a company to build the Union Pacific Railroad. He called it the Crédit Mobilier. To prevent Congress from looking too closely at the company, and to keep the generous grants flowing, Ames let key members buy shares in the Crédit Mobilier at special rates. Within two years the stock had earned three and a half times its original value. Among those who benefited were both of Grant's Vice Presidents.

In time, Congress voted to *censure* (severely criticize or blame) Ames and a few others for their actions. But no one was expelled from Congress.

"Let no guilty man escape." In connection with the building of Washington, D.C., there were more scandals. Grant placed "Boss" Alexander Shepherd in charge of city development. Shepherd grasped the opportunity for plunder. A lot of his spending went into kickbacks and padded payrolls. But Shepherd also made possible the splendid capital city we know today. He revived the master plan dating back to George Washington's time. He paved miles of streets and sidewalks and lined them with trees. And he gave the city its first decent water and sewage systems.

It was in Grant's own Cabinet that corruption was most outrageous. The Secretary of the Navy deposited over 300,000 dollars in a personal bank account from 1869 to 1876. As this was many times his salary, he was almost surely taking payoffs from navy contractors. The United States minister to London used his position to push worthless mining stock on British investors. The Secretary of War was impeached by the Democratic House of Representatives for selling the right to trade on the Indian reservations. But the Republican Senate acquitted him.

In 1874 Grant appointed Benjamin H. Bristow Secretary of the Treasury, to clean up that department. Bristow soon found that the St. Louis, Missouri, Internal Revenue office was systematically cheating the government out of tax money. He brought charges against 203 people, including one of the President's private secretaries, General Babcock. Grant had said, "Let no guilty man escape," but he intervened to save the secretary. The President was unable to recognize dishonesty when he saw it; he was also blindly loyal to his friends.

Some good appointments. Not all Grant's friends were thieves. The scientist John Wesley Powell got help from the President for an expedition down the Colorado River. Though he had lost an arm at the Battle of Shiloh, Powell made a 900-mile canoe trip through the Grand Canyon. He gained much valuable scientific information, and in time he became the first director of the United States Geological Survey.

Grant's best Cabinet appointment was his Secretary of State, Hamilton Fish. Fish successfully settled the British-American disputes that had grown out of the Civil War. Furthermore, he did it in a way that broke new ground in the relations between the two countries.

British negligence. The British government had allowed the Confederacy to have the *Alabama, Florida, Shenandoah,* and other commerce raiders built in its shipyards (page 310). The vessels were manned by Confederate officers and sailors, plus a few British volunteers. Sailing from British ports, they had sunk and captured millions of dollars worth of United States shipping.

Under international law, the United States had a right to demand damages from Britain, though the actual amount was in doubt. Charles Sumner (page 284) was Chairman of the Senate Foreign Relations Committee. He wanted direct damages for the "*Alabama* claims," as the whole amount was called. Sumner also demanded two billion dollars more because, he said, the raiders had caused the war to be dragged out an extra two years.

Secretary of State Fish took a more reasonable line. He negotiated the Treaty of Washington (1872). Under the treaty, Britain agreed to submit the *Alabama* claims to a board of representatives from the United States, Britain, Italy, Switzerland, and Brazil. The board found that Britain had been "negligent" in allowing the commerce raiders to leave its ports. It awarded the United States direct damages of 15,500,000 dollars, but not the amount Sumner had wanted. It was an early and outstanding settlement by peaceful means of a quarrel between two nations.

In 1872 some reform-minded Republicans withdrew from the regular party and put up their own candidate to oppose Grant. They chose Horace Greeley, outspoken editor of the New York *Tribune*. In desperation the Democrats also named

Thomas Nast, cartoonist for *Harper's Weekly*, drew this stinging cartoon about corruption in Grant's Administration.

U. S. G. AS A RAG-PICKER.

U. S. G.—"*Why, here is Zach Chandler thrown out of the Senate Chamber as rubbish! But he may be worth something to me. I must pick him up and fling him into my basket.*"

Greeley, but it did them no good. At that time, the amount of government corruption was not generally known, and Grant was still popular. The Republicans won easily. The next election, in 1876, would be a different story.

 TRY THIS!

1. Compare Ulysses S. Grant as a soldier and as a politician. What qualities does each job require? Which did he have? 2. Describe the work of Grant's good appointees.

2. THE TRANSCONTINENTAL RAILROADS

Much of the nation's prosperity in the late 1800s was based on railroad construction. Generous land grants and other government aid (page 356) cleared the way for construction of the first transcontinental railroad. In 1863 the Central Pacific began laying track eastward from Sacramento. The problem of getting enough laborers to build the railroad was solved by bringing in workers from China.

The Union Pacific pushed westward from Omaha. Large numbers of Irish worked on the construction crews. In May 1869 the Union Pacific joined the Central Pacific at Promontory Point, Utah.

Other transcontinental lines were already being planned. The Southern Pacific was completed in 1882, and the Northern Pacific a year later (map on page 363).

THE GOLDEN SPIKE

A few well-aimed blows (California's Governor Stanford missed with the first swing of his sledge) drove in this gold spike and joined the Central Pacific with the Union Pacific.

The biggest businesses. The railroads were granted 131 million acres of land by the federal government and another 49 million acres by the states. This added up to more territory than the state of Texas. The roads sold most of the land they got, for a total of 435 million dollars. They kept more than 60 million dollars' worth for themselves.

The Great Northern Railroad from Lake Superior to Puget Sound (map on page 363) was built without government help. James J. Hill completed it in 1890.

But it's unlikely that the earlier roads would or could have been built without heavy government gifts. The lines, after all, had to cross hundreds of miles of plains and mountains where there was no one to buy tickets or receive freight.

Many objected to the size of the railroad companies. They were the biggest businesses the country—or the world—had ever seen. But they could not have been

———— ◆•◆ ————

Read here of how

The government helped the railroads.
Large rail systems came into existence.
They sometimes fought one another.
But the government tried to regulate them.

———— ◆•◆ ————

Promontory Point, May 10, 1869. "Facing on a single track. Half a world behind each back."

smaller and still built rail lines that spanned the continent. As the new roads were pushing westward, older ones in the East were being joined into giant systems.

More comfort, less danger. Cornelius Vanderbilt, a New York steamboat operator, put together the New York Central system. It connected New York, the nation's largest city, with Chicago, which promised to be the second largest. Vanderbilt shrewdly got control of the safest and cheapest route between the two cities (the Hudson and Mohawk valleys and the shore of Lake Erie—map on page 363). With smooth roadbeds and solid bridges, Vanderbilt cut New York-to-Chicago travel time to 24 hours.

The Pennsylvania Railroad tied together Philadelphia and Pittsburgh. It soon pushed east to the New Jersey side of the Hudson River, and westward to Chicago and St. Louis. In time, this railroad even tunneled under the Hudson River to invade New York City.

The powerful investment banker J. Pierpont Morgan often acted to end what he saw as destructive competition. In 1885 he stopped a disastrous rate war between the New York Central and Pennsylvania railroads. Eight years later he put together the Southern Railroad out of a number of competing lines.

More efficient locomotives and other mechanical improvements helped railroad

359

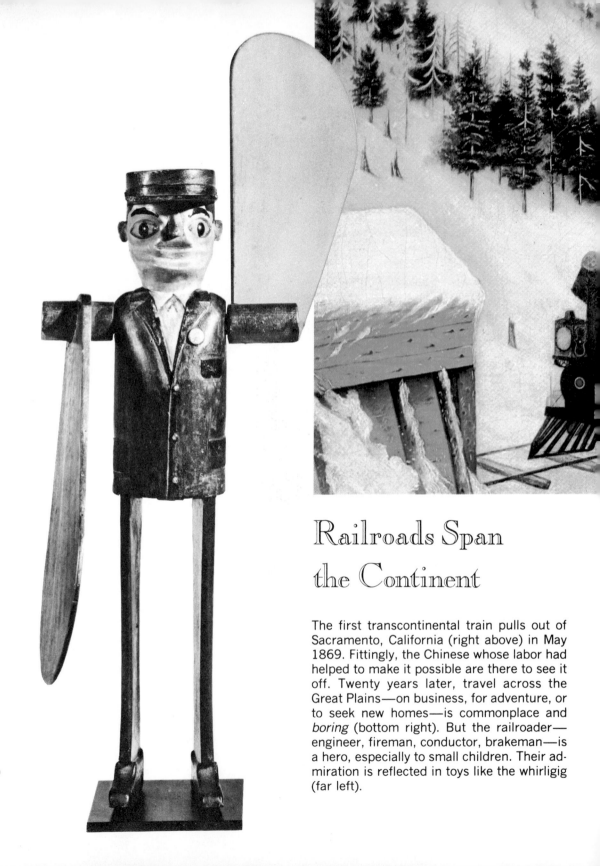

Railroads Span the Continent

The first transcontinental train pulls out of Sacramento, California (right above) in May 1869. Fittingly, the Chinese whose labor had helped to make it possible are there to see it off. Twenty years later, travel across the Great Plains—on business, for adventure, or to seek new homes—is commonplace and *boring* (bottom right). But the railroader—engineer, fireman, conductor, brakeman—is a hero, especially to small children. Their admiration is reflected in toys like the whirligig (far left).

growth. Use of a single, standard gauge meant that freight and passenger cars could move from one line to another without unloading. Westinghouse air brakes let the engineer bring a train to a swift, smooth halt. (There were no more bone-jarring stops or jackknife pileups.) Block signals made it possible for trains to move in opposite directions on a single track without danger of collision. And then there was the division of the country into standard time-zones, so that the railroads could maintain precise schedules (map on page 363).

Higher rates. What worried people most at the time was not the size of the railroad companies but their growing power. To obtain steady and dependable business, the lines offered *rebates* to the biggest customers. These were refunds on freight payments. The practice meant that though farmers and small manufacturers seemed to be paying the same rates as big shippers, they were really paying much higher ones. Small shippers were charged the same amount per ton for each mile, but they got no rebate. Rebates also helped the largest businesses to crush their smaller competitors.

Railroads also gave free passes to state legislators, allowing them unlimited travel. Sometimes the lawmakers' families and political friends got passes too. Of course, the representative was expected to vote as the railroad wished on any measure affecting it. In the United States Senate, the great lines had "railroad senators" who behaved in the same way. The railroad managers belonged to neither party. They used each as it suited their needs.

Wall Street pirates. Actually, the only real problems the railroads had came from each other, not from the government. Often there were fights to get control of additional lines. The combatants used any method that came to hand. In 1868 Cornelius Vanderbilt and his son tried to buy up stock of the Erie Railroad so that they could control it. The Erie's owners, Jay Gould, Jim Fisk, and Daniel Drew—true Wall Street pirates, simply printed shares as fast as the Vanderbilts could buy them. In no time the Vanderbilts found they had more stock than was supposed to exist—and they still had not gained control of the Erie Railroad!

Jay Gould also discovered the use of "blackmail" lines. These were railroads planned or built parallel to others that already existed. Gould found that established roads would pay handsomely for the charters of such lines just to keep them from being built. The discovery added to the 80 million dollars Gould made before he died in 1892.

It was the railroads' customers who suffered from these shenanigans. They had to pay higher rates. And the regular investors often lost money. Gould bribed the New York State legislature to legalize the shares he had sold to the Vanderbilts. That left the line's affairs in such a mess that it paid nothing to its shareholders from 1869 to 1942.

Angry farmers. The seemingly endless prosperity that followed the Civil War faltered in the early 1870s. Profits, production, and wholesale prices had continued to rise, but wages did not keep up with them. Twenty-five railroads failed to pay the interest on their bonds in 1873, and the banking house of Jay Cooke and Company went bankrupt. There was a business panic. The stock market fell, and other investment houses failed. The Panic of 1873 soon turned into a full-fledged depression.

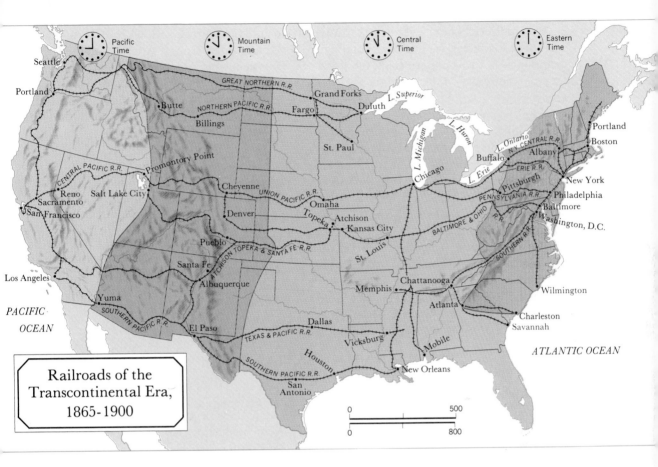

Railroads of the Transcontinental Era, 1865-1900

Railroad companies encouraged people to settle on the Great Plains. Farmers were willing to pay more for land along the routes of the transcontinental lines. Why was this so?

Hard times led to a demand for laws to control the railroads. For years, farmers of the Middle West (the Old Northwest) had been organizing for this very purpose. In 1873 they caused the Illinois Board of Railroad and Warehouse Commissioners to set freight rates. No line could charge more. Wisconsin, Iowa, Nebraska, Kansas, Minnesota, Missouri, Georgia, and California also passed Granger laws (the farm organizations were called Grangers).

The railroads fought the Granger laws until the Supreme Court upheld the laws in 1877. In *Munn v. Illinois* and other "Granger Cases," the Court found that the states had the power to set railroad and warehouse rates.

But the Supreme Court can change its views as new members are appointed and fresh arguments brought up. In 1886, two cases, *Santa Clara County v. Southern Pacific* and *Wabash v. Illinois,* reversed the earlier decisions. The Supreme Court now said that the states had no power to regulate railroad rates. Only the federal government could do so, under the commerce clause of the Constitution (page 109).

363

Sympathetic courts. The next move was up to Congress. In 1887 the Interstate Commerce Act was passed. It set up a five-member commission to regulate railroad affairs.

The Interstate Commerce Commission was the first attempt of the government to control the affairs of private business. Later it served as a model for government agencies that were supposed to assure pure food, fair business practices, good faith in labor bargaining, safe airlines, and control of radio and television broadcasting.

But in the short run the ICC did not amount to much. A railroad's rates were accepted as long as they were "reasonable and just." Their reasonableness was worked out in lengthy lawsuits. The courts usually sympathized with the railroads. One United States Attorney General assured a worried railroad official that the Commission merely "satisfied the popular clamor for government supervision of the railroads." At the same time, he admitted, it was supervision in name only.

TRY THIS!

1. Compare the railroads and the canals (pages 170–173). Which were bigger businesses? Which had greater power? Why? Which did more to help the country grow?
2. Explain how the government tried to control the railroads.

3. THE EXPANSION OF INDUSTRY

There was a great burst of inventive energy in the United States during the late 1880s. Not only new machines and devices but new processes too were introduced. As with Francis Lowell and the Boston Manufacturing Company (page 216) the spirit of inventiveness also led to new forms of business organization and new methods of production.

A better way to raise capital. The Boston Manufacturing Company was one of the first businesses organized as a corporation. However, corporations did not come into their own until after the Civil War. Before that, someone with an idea for a new company, but with little money or capital, would look for partners. Typically, these would be people with extra funds, looking for a way to increase their wealth. Partners might take an active role in the business or remain "silent." Either way, it was difficult for them to get their money out if they needed it. And if the business went bankrupt, partners could be sued for everything they owned.

The corporation, or joint-stock company, had great advantages over the partnership. An investor could buy shares in a corporation (or sell them) quite easily. While an investor held shares, he or she had one vote in running the corporation for each share owned. In addition, a corporation had only *limited liability*. If it went out of business, investors could lose all the money they had put in, but they could not personally be sued.

All this made it much easier for business people to start new companies. And corporations had another advantage. Not only could they be sued in court like individuals; they had ongoing lives of their own. A corporation's entire ownership might change, yet the corporation would still go on. Partnerships had to be dissolved and formed over again whenever one partner died or sold out.

Brand names. Some felt that it was the Civil War itself that had released so much energy in the late 1800s. The drive that had gone into mobilizing and equipping armies was now turned to developing the country's businesses. A New England manufacturer claimed that the war had made great things possible that otherwise would have been put off until the 1900s.

It is true that a number of important inventions date from this period. The first practical typewriter appeared just after the war; the first adding machine, in the 1880s. Together they revolutionized office work. The passenger elevator was in use before the Civil War. It made possible the "skyscrapers" (buildings more than ten stories high), which gave a new look to the cities of the late 1800s. The rotary press, air brake (page 362), and the telephone all date from the late 1860s or early 1870s.

Read here of how

There were new business organizations.
And new products appeared.
Fierce competition led to monopolies.
And the government couldn't control them.

These women are arriving for work at a shoe factory in Lynn, Massachusetts.

INVENTIONS

GOLF TEE

The golf tee hardly rates as one of the world's great labor-saving devices, but it does make life easier for golfers—and caddies. Without it, a small mound of dirt had to be piled up for each drive. Like many things used in industry, at home, and for recreation, the golf tee was patented by a black man. In this case, George F. Grant, in 1899.

BALLPOINT PEN

When it caught on in 1945, the ballpoint pen was called "atomic" and sold for $12.50. John J. Loud had patented it in 1888. He thought it would be useful for writing on wood and rough wrapping paper. Loud's pen had a spring that held the ball in place. As it moved over a writing surface, the ball pushed back, allowing ink to flow. Nobody liked it.

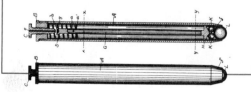

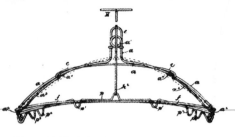

COAT HANGER

O. A. North made the first coat hanger in 1869. The dry-cleaning business simplified and popularized it in the 1930s. The cardboard tube that holds trousers and skirts without creasing was patented in 1935 by Elmer David Rogers.

RAZOR BLADE

"Invent something to be used once and thrown away," King C. Gillette was told in 1895. Why not a piece of steel that could be fitted to a handle and used for shaving? Finding a way to roll steel that was thin, hard, sharp, and *cheap* took nine years.

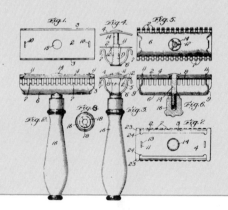

Can openers must have appeared very soon after cans did—about 1810. The record is not clear. Very early, some cans had a wire around the edge that could be pulled to release the lid. After 1866 the caps of many cans had tabs that could be twisted back, allowing the lid to be rolled off. By 1870 some thirty million cans a year were being sold. And many of them were being opened by Mr. Sprague's steel-cutting knife. The advertisement shown here appeared in an 1874 newspaper.

NAIL CLIPPER

Various devices have been used for cutting nails. One, patented in 1866, was a sliding knife, copied after the famous French guillotine. But nail clippers have been popular for hundreds of years. In most cases, manufacturers in the United States faithfully copied English and German designs. But sometime around 1900, they added an extra folding piece, with a point for cleaning and a rough side for filing.

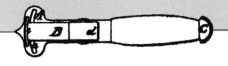

TYPEWRITER

When Christopher L. Sholes made the first one, it had no shift-key and printed only capital letters. But two businessmen saw the possibilities of the typewriter. In 1873 they talked the Remington Arms Company into manufacturing it, following the Sholes design. At the Centennial Exposition in 1876, it attracted no more attention than that other worthless gadget, the telephone. Since it couldn't sell the machines, Remington started lending them to business offices, free of charge. That worked, and in no time the customers were lined up. In spite of changes in appearance, much of the Sholes design remains—even the keyboard.

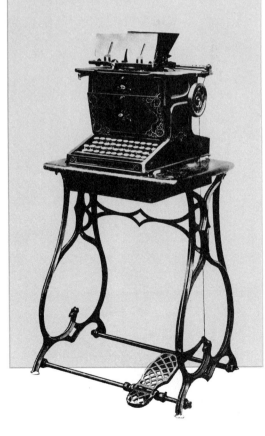

367

Blacks were contributing to the growing industrialization of the United States. Elijah McCoy patented inventions that made possible the automatic oiling of machinery. Jan E. Matzeliger invented a machine that shaped and fastened the leather over the sole of a shoe. This process led to mass production of shoes and greatly reduced their cost. And Granville T. Woods obtained some fifty patents during his lifetime. One of those patents was for an incubator which was the forerunner of present-day machines used to hatch eggs.

At this time familiar trade names also appeared for the first time, many of them associated with the new inventions: Standard Oil, Remington typewriters, Burroughs adding machines, Otis elevators, and Westinghouse air brakes. In 1880 the first practical roll film was patented by George Eastman (earlier photographs were made with glass plates). Shortly after, Eastman's film was being sold under the trade name "Kodak." The safety razor with disposable blades was invented by King C. Gillette (page 366).

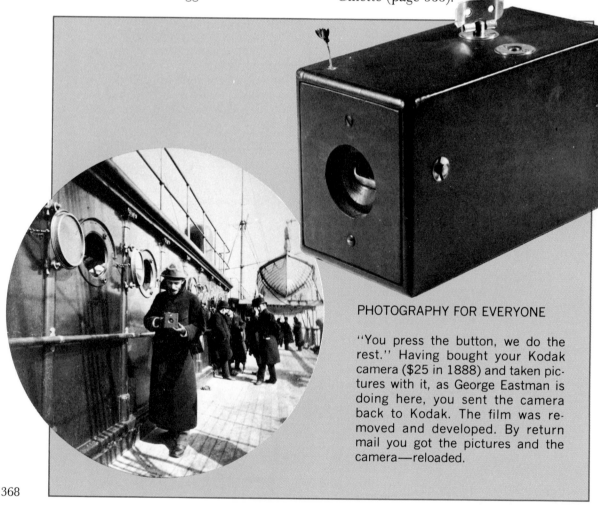

PHOTOGRAPHY FOR EVERYONE

"You press the button, we do the rest." Having bought your Kodak camera ($25 in 1888) and taken pictures with it, as George Eastman is doing here, you sent the camera back to Kodak. The film was removed and developed. By return mail you got the pictures and the camera—reloaded.

368

No more competition. The familiar names are another indication that if corporations survive their shaky early years, they can last for a very long time. They also show that this was a period when competition and individual drive often made a few giant organizations the leaders in a number of industries. The American Sugar Refining Company and American Tobacco were examples.

The public was often uneasy about the large enterprises. Workers, small-business owners, and professional people questioned the right of one person or group of persons to have this kind of power.

Especially alarming were the *trusts*. To form a trust, stockholders of a number of companies in the same industry (sugar, for example) turned over their shares to a board of "trustees." The trustees then ran the corporations as a single giant enterprise, dividing up the customers and doing away with competition.

A nine-year battle. The stockholders got "trust certificates" for their shares. The certificates assured stockholders a part of the profits (which usually were very large) but took away their voting powers. The trustees were in charge. The states, since they chartered most corporations, tried to control the trusts. But states ran into the same kind of trouble with trusts that they had had with the railroads (page 363).

The Standard Oil Company of Ohio was a typical case. It was organized by John D. Rockefeller in 1870. By making use of railroad rebates (page 362), Standard beat most other oil companies into submission. In 1882 it organized them as the Standard Oil Trust. In 1889 David K. Watson, a crusading young state attorney general, discovered that the Standard Trust violated Ohio law. He took it to court and won his case. But it was *nine years* later (1898) before the Ohio laws caught up with the illegal operation.

When that happened, Standard simply moved to New Jersey and reorganized as a *holding company*. This is a means by which one large company owns the stock in a number of smaller ones. It then issues its own stock. Standard's profits became astronomical. So did its power in the industry.

A showdown. Since state law was powerless, people expected Congress to "do something" about trusts. In 1890 it passed the Sherman Antitrust Act. The federal government now had the power to break up "combinations" or "trusts" that were "in restraint of trade."

The trouble was, the Sherman Act did not define *combination, trust,* or *restraint of trade.* The corporation lawyers went to work. In 1895 there was a showdown between the government and the sugar trust that controlled 95 per cent of all sugar refining (*U.S. v. E. C. Knight Co.*). The Supreme Court ruled 8 to 1 that "manufacturing" was not "commerce," so the government had no right to regulate it.

A billion-dollar corporation. Steel is the measure of a nation's industrial might. The United States became an industrial power because of the Mesabi iron ore deposits in Minnesota. Cheap water transportation on the Great Lakes brought this ore to the coal fields of Pennsylvania, West Virginia, and Illinois.

By the 1870s the area near the Great Lakes was dotted with steel plants. One among them belonged to Andrew Carnegie, a clever young Scots immigrant. Twenty years later the Carnegie Steel Company of Pittsburgh was producing more steel rails and plate than all the mills of Great Britain together.

J. PIERPONT MORGAN, UNLIKE ALEXANDER THE GREAT, HAS MORE WORLDS TO CONQUER.
This Stirring American, Having Gained Control of Our Railroads and Steel Business, is Reaching for the Shipping of the Universe.

Do you think the cartoonist approved of J. P. Morgan's business methods?

In 1900 the banker J. P. Morgan (page 359) formed a combination that bought out the Carnegie Steel Company for 492 million dollars. (Carnegie himself got 215 million in gold bonds.) With the Carnegie works as a base, Morgan put together the United States Steel Company, the first billion-dollar corporation. The public was staggered.

Some contradictions. The capitalist, free-enterprise system was supposed to be built on unrestricted competition. Yet its end result seemed to be consolidation and *monopoly* (a single company) or *oligopoly* (a small number of companies). Supporters of the new enterprises, and many business leaders, worried about this contradiction.

In addition, while business leaders objected to any control or regulation by government, they were quick to accept government aid. Land grants and cash payments were helping the railroads. Protective tariffs enabled the trusts to compete with foreign goods.

However, it must be kept in mind that trusts still have their defenders. These people point to the wasteful and murderous competition the trusts and monopolies replaced. And they note that before he died, Andrew Carnegie gave away most of his fortune to causes that still benefit from it.

 TRY THIS!

1. Compare the attempts of government in trying to control the railroads and the trusts. Were such attempts successful? Why, or why not? **2.** Explain how some of the inventions mentioned on pages 366-367 changed people's lives. **3.** Write brief interviews with David K. Watson and John D. Rockefeller about the Standard Oil case.

4. UNIONS, STRIKES, AND RIOTS

Abraham Lincoln had a very simple view of capital and labor. He said, "The prudent, penniless beginner in the world labors for wages awhile, saves a surplus with which to buy tools or land for himself, then labors on his own account another while, and at length hires another new beginner to help him." In other words, any American could become an independent capitalist.

Lincoln's idea was based on his own early years in the Middle West of pre-Civil War days. During that time, it would have been very difficult for an ordinary worker in a New England mill town to follow his advice. After the war, in one of the industrial cities springing up across the land, it would have clearly been impossible. By then the chance that a day laborer, earning a dollar a day or less, might become a factory owner was remote. Increasingly, workers turned to labor organizations to improve their position.

Nine survivors. Six *trade* or *craft unions* (uniting the workers who followed a particular occupation) had survived from before the Civil War. They were the printers, hatters, stonecutters, ironmolders, machinists, and blacksmiths—all highly skilled occupations.

Between 1864 and 1873 twenty more unions, with over 300,000 members, were formed. But the Panic of 1873 and the depression that followed (page 362) wiped out all but three of the newer organizations: the railway "brotherhoods."

Burning freight cars. To keep up the profits of shareholders during bad times, employers often cut workers' wages—sometimes as much as 25 per cent. (In such times, Lincoln's advice to save money and go into business for oneself must have sounded like a bad joke.)

In 1877 wage cuts led to strikes and rioting all along the Baltimore and Ohio Railroad (map on page 363). State militia were sent to Pittsburgh and arrived just as the day shift was getting out of the steel mills. Steelworkers joined the railroaders in attacking the soldiers. Fierce battles soon raged through the railroad station and machine shops. The sky glowed with the light of burning freight cars.

Finally, President Rutherford B. Hayes sent federal troops to crush the uprising. A new and terrible kind of civil war seemed about to begin. Middle-class Americans were truly frightened. Newspapers and politicians angrily brushed aside the workers' complaints—many of which were justified.

Something new for Mr. Gould. With the return of prosperity in the 1880s, a new labor organization appeared. The Knights of Labor was a secret society that had begun in Philadelphia in 1869. It now came out in the open as a *general labor union*. That is, it organized people into local associations without regard to trade, occupation, or industry.

Read here of how

The Knights of Labor won a great victory.
Yet it all but destroyed them.
The AFL became a strong force.
But helped only a small number of workers.

Employers fought the new movement with blacklists (page 222) and *yellow-dog contracts* (by which workers had to promise they would never join a union). But the Knights of Labor grew steadily. Then in 1885, the Grand Master Workman, Terence V. Powderly, called a strike against Jay Gould's Wabash Railroad. Gould (page 362) had tried to cut wages on the line; the Knights forced him to restore the cuts.

It was an astonishing development. No one had ever beaten Gould before at anything. The Knights' membership shot from 110,000 to 700,000 in a single year. In fact, it grew so fast that it soon got out of hand. Locals were calling unauthorized strikes that they couldn't possibly win and making the organization look bad.

In May 1886 workers held nationwide demonstrations to demand an eight-hour day. At the rally in Haymarket Square, Chicago, someone threw a bomb at the police, killing seven of them. To this day no one knows who did it, but the police arrested eight radicals who were in or near the square that day. On no more evidence than that, four of the accused were hanged and the others imprisoned.

Ahead of their time. The Knights of Labor were in favor of the eight-hour day, but they had nothing to do with the demonstrations or the bomb. Nevertheless, they suffered from the bad public reaction to what had happened. Their numbers declined, and by 1900 they had just about disappeared.

In many ways the Knights of Labor were ahead of their time. The late 1800s were a period of growing discrimination and segregation in North and South (page 339). Yet the Knights admitted blacks and women to full membership. They also took in and tried to help unskilled laborers. The older craft unions were interested only in those workers who were already the best off—and easiest to help.

The unions of skilled workers had the strength to hang on through bad times as well as good. Their members could not easily be replaced if they went on strike, so those unions controlled the labor supply in their trades. Also, their members could afford to pay high dues and build up healthy treasuries.

A conservative leader. The craft unions found a leader in Samuel Gompers, an

Frank Farrell, black member of the Knights of Labor, introduces Grand Master Workman Terence V. Powderly.

English-born cigar maker. Gompers regarded the "one big union" idea as hopeless. In 1886 he and his followers formed the American Federation of Labor.

The AFL, as it was usually called, was a loose federation of independent craft unions. Its president did not have the same power as a corporation president. But Samuel Gompers did exert a lot of influence.

Gompers believed passionately in the trade-union movement and in the rights of workers. In other ways, though, his thinking was much like that of the business leaders who opposed him. He was against having a social-security system, and he opposed any government interference in labor disputes—even to help a union.

The conservative ideas of Gompers didn't keep business from attacking his unions. In 1892 the AFL's Ironworkers struck the Carnegie Steel plant at Homestead, Pennsylvania. Carnegie's manager, Henry Clay Frick, brought armed strikebreakers into the plant by floating them down the Monongahela River on barges. Both the strike and the union were broken. It was almost fifty years before the steel industry was finally unionized.

"Restraint of trade?" A more radical leader than Gompers, Eugene V. Debs, headed the independent American Railway Union. In 1894 (during another depression) the manufacturer of Pullman cars cut the wages of his workers. Debs's union refused to work on any train having Pullman cars, and that soon tied up most of the rail traffic in the Midwest.

The strike affected United States mails, so the United States Attorney General used strikebreakers to get the trains moving. Violence followed, and President Grover Cleveland sent federal troops to protect the strikebreakers. A court order was issued

Striking workers often used force to prevent crews from operating trains.

against Debs, and he went to prison for refusing to obey it. It's worth noting that the court order was based on the Sherman Antitrust Act (page 369). For the first time the government won a case under this act, and it was against a labor union "in restraint of trade."

 TRY THIS!

1. Explain Lincoln's ideas on capital and labor. Why, do you think, did he hold such views? **2.** Compare the Knights of Labor and the AFL. Which would you have joined if you were a worker in the late 1800s?

ROUNDUP

Who?

Oakes Ames
John Wesley Powell
Cornelius Vanderbilt
Jay Gould
John D. Rockefeller
J. Pierpont Morgan
Terence V. Powderly
Samuel Gompers
Eugene V. Debs

What?

Crédit Mobilier
Alabama claims
Granger laws
Interstate Commerce
    Commission
corporation
Standard Oil
Panic of 1873
Knights of Labor
Haymarket riot
AFL
Pullman strike

Where?

Promontory Point

KNOW THIS

Great General—Poor President

1. Why did Mark Twain and Charles Dudley Warner call the period after the Civil War the "Gilded Age"?
2. What part did Oakes Ames play in the Crédit Mobilier? What did Congress do about that scandal?
3. What were some scandals involving Grant's Cabinet?
4. Who was Grant's best Cabinet appointee?
5. What settled the dispute with Britain over Civil War claims?

The Transcontinental Railroads

1. How did each of these contribute to the development of railroads: the federal government; Cornelius Vanderbilt; J.P. Morgan; new inventions and developments?
2. How did railroads use rebates to gain more power over business?
3. How did railroad managers gain political influence?
4. Why did the Supreme Court change its view on the Granger laws?
5. What were the short-run effects of the Interstate Commerce Act? The long-run effects?

The Expansion of Industry

1. What are the advantages of corporations as business organizations?
2. What new inventions and familiar brand names appeared in the 1880s?
3. What is a trust? How can a trust control an industry?
4. What laws were passed to get rid of trusts? How well did the laws work?
5. How did United States Steel become a billion-dollar corporation?
6. By the end of the 1800s, what contradictions appeared in the free enterprise system?

Unions, Strikes, and Riots

1. How were the Knights of Labor different from earlier craft unions?
2. How did employers fight the labor movement?
3. Why did the membership in the Knights of Labor first soar, then decline?
4. What were Samuel Gompers's views on labor organization? How did he become a power in the union movement?
5. In what ways was the Pullman strike a milestone?

DIG HERE!

Leaders of business and labor have sometimes changed America more than its politicians. Choose some man or woman who headed a great corporation or an important labor organization. Report the following information about him or her.

A. When and where was the business or labor leader born? Describe his or her childhood and early work experiences. Are these related to the leader's later role? Explain.

B. How did this individual get started? To what extent was the individual self-made? What people or circumstances aided his or her rise to prominence?

C. What goals guided the leader? Describe three episodes or incidents showing his or her ability to manage people and events for desired ends.

D. What were five characteristics or qualities of this leader? Which were essential in gaining wealth or power?

E. What values did he or she consider important? Would most Americans living at the same time have agreed with that view?

These books will help you: Chamberlain, J., *The Enterprising Americans,* Harper; Holbrook, S.H., *The Age of Moguls,* Doubleday; Josephson, M., *The Robber Barons,* Harcourt; Lens, S., *The Labor Wars,* Doubleday; Pelling, H., *American Labor,* U. of Chicago; Spence, C.C., *The Sinews of American Capitalism,* Hill & Wang.

THINK ABOUT IT

1. From 1860 to 1890 the value of manufactures in the United States rose by almost 500 per cent. At the same time, the poet Walt Whitman feared that the nation was "losing its soul." What did he mean? Do you think he was right? Explain.

2. The fortunes of the Rockefellers, Andrew Carnegie, and other wealthy people have paid for libraries, concert halls, universities, scholarships, medical research, and art galleries, all of which benefit the public. Does this kind of generosity make up for the low wages and miserable working conditions that made the fortunes possible? Why, or why not?

DO IT!

1. Design a bulletin board display comparing the Centennial Exposition of 1876 with any of the Bicentennial Celebrations in 1976. Can you point to any differences in people's attitudes toward each event?

2. Report to the class about the books of Horatio Alger. Who were the author's heroes? What lessons did the books teach? How can you account for their popularity?

THEN AND NOW

In the 1800s workers' complaints were generally ignored. Unions were unpopular with the press, the politicians, and the public. Has this attitude changed today? Defend your answer.

The Nation Faces New
Challenges at Century's End

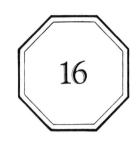

16

Finding a place for millions of new Americans, drawn to the nation's shores by Liberty's torch, was one of the challenges at century's end.

1. A NEW KIND OF IMMIGRATION

If American business was to grow, it would need more than money, machines, coal, and railroads. It would also need workers. These came from among the immigrants, millions of them, mostly from Europe, who poured into the country in the 1800s. This was the largest movement of people the world has ever seen. In those years, 35 million men, women, and children uprooted themselves and crossed the sea to the land of promise.

Huddled masses. Business leaders welcomed the newcomers. They provided a plentiful supply of labor for industry and lots of customers for its products. Union leaders such as Terence V. Powderly (page 372) and Samuel Gompers (page 372) were not so sure. They feared that the hordes of new workers were keeping down the wages of those already here.

In 1883 Emma Lazarus wrote a poem about the new Statue of Liberty in New York Harbor. (The enormous figure was a gift from the people of France for the nation's hundredth birthday.) Part of her poem reads:

Give me your tired, your poor,
Your huddled masses yearning to breathe free,
The wretched refuse of your teeming shore.
Send these, the homeless, tempest-tossed to me;
I lift my lamp beside the golden door!

But a growing number of Americans were beginning to think that much of the Old World's "refuse" was not good enough for the United States. In fact, by the time Emma Lazarus had written her poem, Congress had voted (in 1882) to bar criminals, insane people, and other "undesirables" from entry. And in the same year, it considered excluding one group of people, the Chinese.

A hard-working people. China had had a long and glorious history. Those Americans who knew the country best argued that its people were thrifty, hardworking, and law-abiding. In every way, they would make model citizens. But too many Americans preferred to see the Chinese as "a degraded race, ignorant of civilized life," as one magazine put it.

To some former abolitionists, the Chinese immigrants even appeared to be part of a new slave trade. Their willingness to work long and hard for very little was looked upon as a threat to the living standards of white laborers. Anti-Chinese riots broke out in California in the 1870s. Not

---

Read here of how

New immigrants flooded the nation.
They came from southern and eastern Europe.
And were prepared to work hard.
But some people wanted to keep them out.

TIME CHART

1862	The Homestead Act is passed.
1869	The American Woman Suffrage and the National Woman Suffrage Associations are founded.
1873	The Treasury stops buying silver.
1878	The Bland-Allison Silver Purchase Act is passed.
1882	Congress bars "undesirables" from immigration.
1887	Electric streetcars appear first in Richmond, Virginia.
1889	Jane Addams founds Hull House.
1890	The Sherman Silver Purchase Act is passed.
1892	The Populists adopt their Omaha Platform.
1893	The Sherman Silver Purchase Act is repealed.
1896	The "free silver" election is fought.
1902	Chinese exclusion is made permanent.

---

only conservative labor leaders like Samuel Gompers, but radical ones like Eugene Debs supported laws to keep the Chinese out. In 1882 Congress voted overwhelmingly to bar them for ten years. The law was renewed in 1892 and made permanent in 1902.

And still they came. Meanwhile, Europeans continued by the thousands to brave the miseries of the *steerage* (the cheapest part of an immigrant ship, the one nearest the rudder). They were treated as freight. Each got a berth six feet long, two feet wide, with two and a half feet above it. All

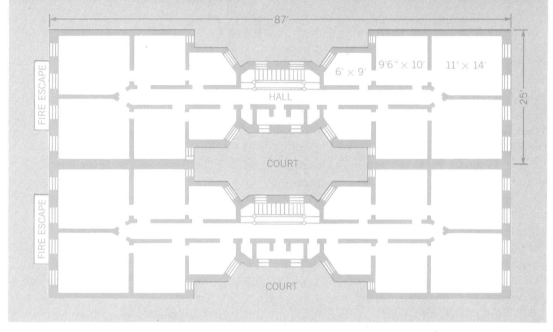

Sometimes a whole family was crowded into a single room.

other space had to be shared. The filth and stench of the cramped quarters was all but unendurable, especially in bad weather.

But the immigrants came, generally to be crowded into something almost as bad as the steerage, the *dumbbell tenement* (diagram above). These were designed to make use of every inch of space in a city block. Just as bad were the homes that had once belonged to the middle class and the rich. These downtown dwellings were divided into apartments, sometimes with one large family in every room.

In most cases, the newcomers were also drawn into some kind of grinding, underpaid work. Often they were introduced to it by fellow countrymen who had arrived earlier and learned the ropes.

And still they came. By the 1880s, over half a million a year came. In the 1900s

this number increased. From 1905 to 1914 it averaged a million a year.

A preferred group. Before 1890, each ten-year census had shown the location of the frontier line. The 1890 report declared that the line no longer existed. The frontier was officially closed. That fact would have been reason enough to begin limiting the number of immigrants. But at the time, debate on the issue was not over *how many* people were to be admitted. Instead, it was concerned with where those people were to come from.

Until the 1890s most immigrants came from the countries of northern and western Europe (Great Britain, Germany, Scandinavia). But in the 1880s a shift began. By 1890 most were from southern and eastern Europe (Italy, Austria-Hungary, Russia, the Balkans). Immigrants from northern and western Europe had seemed foreign enough when they made up practically all of the arrivals. And they had often been treated badly. Now they were preferred.

A bill to test immigrants for their ability to read and write was introduced in Congress in 1896. The sponsor of this literacy bill was Henry Cabot Lodge, a Massachusetts blueblood. He freely admitted that it was planned to "fall most heavily upon Italians, Russians, Poles, Hungarians, and Asiatics." Lodge referred to them as "races with which the English-speaking people have never hitherto assimilated, and who are most alien to the great body of the people of the United States."

The labor leader Samuel Gompers agreed. In 1897 he committed the AFL to supporting the literacy bill. He said that "the maintenance of the nation depended on the maintenance of racial purity and strength."

Only willingness to work. President Grover Cleveland disagreed with Gompers and Lodge and the demand that immigration be limited. He vetoed the literacy bill, with a strongly worded message: "A century's stupendous growth, largely due to the assimilation and thrift of sturdy and patriotic adopted citizens," he said, "attests to the success of this generous and free-handed policy [of unlimited entry] which [demands] from our immigrants only physical and moral soundness and a willingness and ability to work."

For the moment, the gates of the United States were open to all except the Chinese. But the victory was not permanent. This was only the first battle. Twenty years later, others too lost out.

An 1893 cartoon shows prosperous Americans—shadowed by their former immigrant and pioneer selves—rejecting a "new" immigrant.

NEW-YORK CENTRAL RAILROAD.

EMIGRANT.

NEW-YORK. 1 1 BUFFALO.

ONE PASSAGE

FROM

ALBANY to BUFFALO.

With ___ lbs Gross Luggage.

No. *260* *Weed & Bankes*

 TRY THIS!

1. Compare the experience of the "new" immigrants with that of the "old" ones (pages 219–223). Were the new immigrants better or worse off? Why? 2. Write a letter that might have been sent to the old country by a newly arrived immigrant. Tell about the voyage and about life in the New World.

2. CITY GROWTH AND CITY PROBLEMS

The immigrants who came to the United States in the late 1800s spread out over the land. Some became lumberjacks in northern Maine, or copper miners in Montana, or farmers on the prairie. But most went where so many others at that time were going—into the biggest cities.

In the late 1800s the total population of the earth increased by 37 per cent. The population of the world's cities went up over 200 per cent. In 1900 eleven cities in the world had over a million people. Three of them were in the United States: New York (five million), Chicago (two million), and Philadelphia (one and a half million). In 1910 less than 8 per cent of the rural population of the United States was born outside the country; in the eight largest cities, more than 30 per cent.

Stretching the radius. Creating livable conditions for millions of new city-dwellers was a staggering problem. In 1890 only 629 of Chicago's 2,048 miles of streets were paved. Street lighting, pure water, and sewage disposal had to be provided on a massive scale.

The city of the early 1800s was a "walking city." Laborers and business people lived within walking distance of the places where they worked. Few cities could expand beyond a radius of one or two miles.

In the late 1800s the modern "commuter city" had appeared. It began with the horse-drawn streetcar and the steam-powered "elevated railway." That noisy marvel was introduced in New York in 1870. Cable cars began moving up and down San Francisco's steep hills in 1873. Starting in Richmond, Virginia, in 1887, electric streetcars made their appearance almost everywhere during the next ten years. The first subway was opened in Boston in 1895. With all these improvements, cities could now spread out to a radius of five or ten miles.

Read here of how

Cities grew rapidly in the late 1800s.
Services and living space were problems.
A new kind of political leader appeared.
And religious groups took on new roles.

Plenty of corruption. It was mostly middle-class families that took advantage of the new streetcar and elevated lines. They could now move to the suburbs and build larger, more modern houses—and escape the hordes of immigrants filling the downtown neighborhoods. The population of the suburbs swelled with city people. Often, in this period, outlying communities voted to join their bigger neighbors, thus expanding the city limits.

Should the new city services (water, sewage, street lighting, and public transportation) be run by private business for profit? Or should they be owned by the city government? This became a burning political question. Some cities built their own gas and water works; others gave out *franchises.* These were licenses to run streetcar lines and install lighting. Either way, there was plenty of room for political corruption.

No melting pot. An ever-present problem in the new cities was how to keep them from breaking apart. In Chicago, Boston, New York, and—a little later—Detroit, there was a variety of people that could be found nowhere else in the world. German town-dwellers, Irish and Italian laborers, Portuguese sailors, migrants from the southern part of the United States, and Jewish refugees from the persecutions of the Russian Czar were all thrown together in American cities.

There was a theory that in time these people would blend into something new

The first elevated train in New York frightened horses and fascinated people. How did such rapid transit systems affect city life?

and unique—the American. It was the theory of the *melting pot,* but in practice it seemed not to work that way. For sheer survival in their new and frightening surroundings immigrants had to flock together with their own kind. Each nationality had its separate section of the city. Today the sections would be called "ethnic neighborhoods." They were the Little Italys and Little Russias, the Germantowns and Chinatowns, into which the cities divided.

From the days of Jefferson. No public welfare agencies and almost no private charities aided the newcomers. What help they got came from their churches or the local *political machine* and its head, the *political boss* or *ward boss.*

In New York City the local Democratic machine was Tammany Hall, a club dating back to the days of Thomas Jefferson. As early as the 1860s it was welcoming and helping—and using—the immigrants. When no one else would, the Tammany machine gave them jobs, handouts, legal advice, and friendship. All it asked in return was their votes. With those it was able to elect its candidates to local offices and use the city treasury as it pleased.

In one city after another, political machines grew up. In the larger places each neighborhood had its precinct leader and each district its ward boss. They traded the votes of their loyal followers for political favors for themselves and their friends.

In New York in the early 1870s, the system got badly out of hand. There the head of Tammany Hall, the boss of bosses, was William Marcy Tweed. He and his henchmen made up the Tweed Ring.

George Bellow's painting *Cliff Dwellers* shows a crowded street in the tenement district of **New York City. What caused these conditions?**

Among other pieces of skullduggery, they built a horrible-looking New York County Courthouse. No one knows for sure how much it cost. But one way or another, the Tweed Ring helped itself to millions of dollars.

Worse than Tweed. The business people of New York finally realized that it was their money the Tweed Ring was stealing. They backed Samuel Tilden, a shrewd and ruthless railroad lawyer. He prosecuted the members of the Tweed Ring and put it out of business.

Boss Tweed spent the rest of his life in court and prison or running away from the law. Samuel Tilden, a Democrat, went on to become the reform governor of New York and a candidate for President in 1876 (page 341).

Corruption in New York was by no means ended. There, and in every other city with a large immigrant population, the system went on. Boss Tweed was succeeded by "Honest John" Kelly in 1871. But Richard Croker re-established the Tammany system in 1886. Some thought he was far worse than Tweed.

In Chicago, Mayor Carter Harrison kept power by paying careful attention to the problems of immigrant voters. In Boston and other places, the bosses ran representatives of the immigrant population for office. Hugh O'Brien and Patrick Collins, both mayors of Boston, were such men.

A crude welfare state. One scene from the days of the political bosses has often been described. The ward boss sits, as he does every day, in his clubhouse headquarters. One poor man or woman after another comes forward haltingly to whisper some tale of family trouble. The boss listens sympathetically and asks a few shrewd questions. Then he passes something across

The "Tammany Bank." A politician is seated on a throne-like chair. When a coin is placed in his outstretched hand, he deposits it in his pocket.

the table. It may be a bit of money. Or it may be a note to some city foreman telling him to put the petitioner on the payroll, or an order for a bag of coal or a basket of groceries.

Who cares if the money was gotten by graft, the job already has three people doing the work of one, the coal is from the city yards, or the food was bought for the county hospital? Not the poor immigrant. He or she leaves the clubhouse, calling the blessings of heaven down upon the cigar-chewing boss.

By operating in this way, trying to please as many people as possible, bosses held the cities together. They gave the new citizens experience in politics and in working together for common goals. But they

383

gave the reformers fits. Those good people were shocked at the cost. Nevertheless, when Boss Tweed died in 1878, one of the papers confessed, "The bulk of the poor voters of this city revere his memory." The boss had run a crude welfare state.

The gap between rich and poor. The only other institutions that seemed to care at all for the urban poor were the churches. Protestants saw the city as a new mission field like the old frontier. They carried to it both a gospel message and direct material help. The help might be given through skid-row missions such as those of the Salvation Army or large settlement houses able to serve women and children. Jane Addams founded the first of these in Chicago in 1889.

At the same time, inner-city ministers were saying that it was not enough for Christian business people to lead upright lives and go to church. They must also pay their workers a living wage and allow them to join unions.

In 1885 the Central Conference of American Rabbis adopted a declaration of principles. It concluded that society must work to bridge the gap between rich and poor. This "Pittsburgh Platform" started the social justice movement of American Reform Judaism.

The heart of the people. At about the same time, Catholic Archbishop James Gibbons of Baltimore spoke up for the Knights of Labor (page 371). He told the leaders of the American Catholic Church that the Knights were working for the good of the city poor. If they were condemned, he said, "the Catholic Church might lose the heart of the people." A few years after Archbishop Gibbons made his statement, Pope Leo XIII spoke out in favor of labor and the right of workers to organize.

From all these movements and ideas came something called the *social gospel.* It stressed that religion and religious leaders must try to improve the living conditions of workers, not just prepare them for the next world. As the ordained minister and Socialist leader Norman Thomas said, "Man does not live by bread alone, but he does live by bread."

 TRY THIS!

1. Tell how a "walking city" differed from a "commuter city." What caused commuter cities to develop?   **2.** Write some questions you would want a political boss to answer if you were a newspaper reporter.   **3.** Explain the social gospel.

3.   THE WOMAN MOVEMENT

"I want new experiences," wrote Louisa May Alcott in her diary. The year was 1862, and the New England writer was about to start work as a nurse in a Washington, D.C., army hospital. She also wrote that her trip to the capital was "a most interesting journey into a new world full of stirring sights and sounds, new adventures,

and an ever-growing sense of the great task I have undertaken."

Many women were equally enthusiastic about occupations opened to them during the Civil War years (pages 318–320). With men going off to fight, some turned to nursing, teaching, charity work, even to businesses and jobs in offices.

Women's demands for equality have always drawn this kind of "joke." Must the rise of one group mean another's fall? Can't they be truly equal?

"Homes and families destroyed." With the rapid changes that took place after the Civil War, some women were unwilling to go back to their old lives. The had contributed to the war effort. They knew that they were half the population, and they wanted full rights of citizenship.

Women began to think about what they might do to change the situation. But they faced ridicule and scorn whenever they sought a voice in public affairs. The tradition that a woman's place was in the home was a powerful one. The argument was often heard that homes and families would be destroyed if women gained equality. Moreover, most men (and some women) truly believed that women were not as healthy or as intelligent as men.

Fighting their own battles. Even laws held women back. Before the Civil War, they had won some legal rights over their children and their property (pages 204–208). But they still could not vote. Growing numbers of women took up the

---

Read here of how

Women gained recognition in the Civil War.
They entered business and professions.
They sought the right to vote.
But they failed to win it at that time.

---

battle to win new opportunities in employment and education. But *suffrage* (the right to vote) became their major goal in the second half of the century.

If women must obey the laws, they asked, why shouldn't they share in choosing the people who make and enforce the laws? In fact, why shouldn't they serve as public officials? Political power, they knew, could be a tool for winning social reforms and equal opportunities.

Women had played an active part in the antislavery movement (page 253). After the Civil War many women abolitionists began to speak out on behalf of their own cause. The experience they had gained in writing, public speaking, and organizing was now put to use in the *woman movement* (the name generally given to their drive for equality).

In this new effort, women leaders found that they could not necessarily count on the support of the men who were their allies in the antislavery campaign. Freeing slaves was one thing; letting women vote was quite another. So the women leaders planned their own strategies and fought their own battles.

Twenty years later. Women had been admitted to a few colleges before the Civil War (page 207). But through the rest of the century, young women who wanted to study at the college level faced a struggle. State colleges and universities in the Middle West began accepting them first. In the East such colleges as Vassar, Wellesley, Smith, and Bryn Mawr were founded just for women. The teaching profession had been open to women for a number of years. Women college graduates now began to enter other fields of work.

Barriers still existed for women who hoped to get training in the professions.

Myra Bradwell of Illinois overcame the obstacles and emerged as an outstanding lawyer. She learned law from her husband and passed the required examination for the state of Illinois. But in 1870 she was refused admission to the profession. The Illinois Supreme Court questioned whether for a woman "to engage in the hot strifes of the bar in the presence of the public . . . would not tend to destroy the deference and delicacy with which it is the pride of our ruder sex to treat her."

This settlement house nurse is making her way over tenement rooftops to attend to the needs of people in the slums of New York.

Twenty years later, Mrs. Bradwell won admission. Meanwhile, she had founded and edited an influential law journal and campaigned successfully for reforms and improvements in court operations. Her efforts made the way a little smoother for later women lawyers, including her own daughter.

Nursing also attracted women seeking new fields of work. The Civil War had shown how valuable trained nurses could be (pages 318–319). During the 1870s several schools for women nurses opened. The first was the New England Hospital for Women and Children in Massachusetts. Elizabeth Blackwell's New York Infirmary (page 207) organized another. Among the New England Hospital's graduates was Mary Elizabeth Mahoney, the first black woman to become a professional nurse in the United States.

"Acceptable" activities. It was difficult for middle-class women to get professional training. But there were other opportunities for them to use their skills outside the home. Charitable institutions attracted many capable women organizers. They ran day nurseries for working mothers, set up social clubs for working girls, and assisted missionary activities.

The campaign for temperance in the use of alcohol was also an area of women's leadership. The Woman's Christian Temperance Union (WCTU) was founded in 1874 at a national convention in Cleveland, Ohio. As its membership grew, the WCTU became an active and forceful organization. Under Frances Willard, it probably worked as hard for woman suffrage and child-labor laws as for temperance.

Working women, though, had different problems. Getting an education or finding ways of using leisure time were remote concerns. Whether they labored on farms or in factories or as servants or scrubwomen in the houses of the middle class, their chief need was making enough to live on. As now, the demand for the same pay as males doing the same work was a serious issue. In the present day this effort is supported by laws, but in the 1800s women had no such backing.

Meanwhile, work in business offices and in stores was becoming socially acceptable for middle-class women. The new office equipment—typewriters, telephones, and adding machines—quickly became their specialties. But here too a wide difference in pay between men and women was the accepted rule.

"I restrained the impulse to hurl my manuscript." There were two nationwide organizations in the campaign for woman suffrage. One was Elizabeth Cady Stanton's and Susan B. Anthony's National Woman Suffrage Association, organized in 1869. The other was the American Woman Suffrage Association founded by Lucy Stone and her husband, Henry Blackwell.

The Stanton and Anthony group sought a Constitutional amendment that would give women in all states the vote. Lucy Stone's organization preferred to work for change on a state-by-state basis.

But the chief obstacle was the refusal of men to take the women's demand for voting rights seriously. The scorn heaped upon the suffragists can be seen from Elizabeth Cady Stanton's description of a Senate committee chairman hearing her arguments on a proposed woman suffrage bill: "He stretched, yawned, gazed at the ceiling, cut his nails, sharpened his pencil, changing his occupation and position every two minutes. . . . I restrained the impulse to hurl my manuscript at his head."

Sovereigns, not subjects. Despite the real gains made in other fields, women leaders failed to win the suffrage battle in the 1800s. They simply lacked political power to overcome prejudice and tradition. By the end of the century women could vote in only four states—Wyoming, Utah, Colorado, and Idaho.

In 1897 Susan B. Anthony summed up the suffragists' feeling: "If women could make the laws or elect those who make them, they would be in the position of sovereigns instead of subjects."

 TRY THIS!

1. Compare the gains made by women in the late 1800s with those before the Civil War (pages 204–208). Which were greater? What remained to be done? **2.** List some of the organizations by which women were able to help their own cause.

4.   FARMERS, POPULISTS, AND REFORM

As business prospered and cities grew, farmers did not share in the prosperity. Unlike the railroads, they got no government grants, and the protective tariff helped manufacturers but not farmers. Even workers' wages were kept above European levels by the tariff. (Or at least workers believed they were.) Yet farmers had to sell their crops in competition with cheaper foreign grain.

A generous law? The only thing farmers had gotten from the Republican Party was free land in the West, under the Homestead Act of 1862. But the Act had never worked the way it was supposed to. It was supposed to allow any citizen (man or woman) who was over twenty and the head of a family to claim 160 acres of public land. The person making the claim had to live on the land for five years, cultivate at least half of it, put up some kind of shelter, and pay a small fee.

On the surface, the Homestead Act made it seem that anyone could get a farm free in return for a little hard work. Not quite. Those using the Act had to have enough money to live on until their farms began to pay. Even then, farm machinery and tools had to be purchased. Few poor people had the kind of backing required to homestead. All but the hardiest, or luckiest, soon gave up.

The Homestead Act was supposed to end speculation in public land. But 131 million acres were given western railroads (page 358). Anyone wanting land near the tracks (the most valuable location) generally had to buy it from the railroad owners. The average price of railroad land was almost five dollars an acre. In addition, mining, timber, and cattle companies got vast acreage through fraud. They set up dummy claims under the Homestead Act, then transferred the land to themselves.

The Homestead Act allowed a quarter-section (160 acres) as a family-sized farm. That would have been a generous spread in the East or Middle West, where there was plenty of rainfall. But in the drier Plains region it was not nearly enough to give a family a decent living.

Sometimes people moved to the Plains during a period of wet weather. One oc-

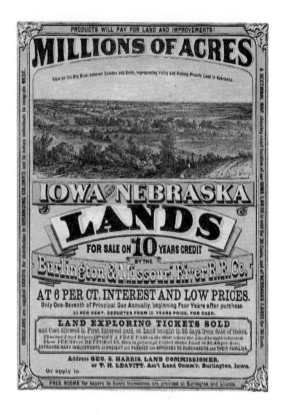

Read here of how

Farmers were part of a world market.
Their costs and debts kept rising.
But their needs were ignored.
So they formed a radical new political party.

---

curred every six or seven years, and usually looked like a permanent change. When the period ended, as it always did, settlers learned the harsh truth: they were in a land of blizzards, grasshoppers, and drought.

Part of a world market. Farmers in the older, long-settled agricultural areas had problems too. In some ways they were as much victims as the immigrant laborers. Not only railroads and milling companies, but dishonest seed merchants, quack veterinarians, and fake advertisers of all kinds took advantage of them. In the rising cities they were likely to be laughed at as "hicks," "hayseeds," and "rubes."

Changes taking place in the life of the nation through the growth of industry left 389 farmers bewildered, anxious, and uncertain about what to believe. They were only beginning to understand that there was such a thing as a world grain market. Yet railroads, fast steamships, and transatlantic telegraph cables had already made them part of it. A dealer in Chicago could instantly learn the price of wheat in London. Growers in Russia, Argentina, Canada, and the western plains of the United States were all competing with one another and keeping the world price down.

Forty per cent interest. Machinery might help American farmers to meet the lower prices, but it was terribly expensive.

A giant steam thresher or a McCormick harvester, successor to the McCormick reaper that had appeared in 1834 (page 231), would put the purchaser deeply in debt. And interest rates alone on farm debts sometimes ran as high as 40 per cent a year!

By 1900 the North Central States (map in Appendix) were the richest farm region in the country. Even there, though, less than 44 per cent of all persons working on farms owned their own land. Another 19 per cent were tenants or managers for absent owners. All the rest were day laborers, earning an average of 117 dollars a year

(equal to about 500 dollars at present-day prices).

Plenty of villains. Trapped by falling prices and sky-high interest, farmers looked for someone to blame for their troubles. There were plenty of villains around, but banks and railroads led the list.

The Grangers had focused farmers' reform efforts during the 1860s (page 363). Grain elevators and railroads had been their targets. But rising prices in the early 1880s and Supreme Court decisions against the Granger laws took a lot of the fight out of the movement. Today the Granges continue as social clubs in the Middle West and the farm regions of the Northeast.

The next groups to become nationwide representatives of agriculture were the Farmers' Alliances and the Agricultural Wheel. The first local Alliances were organized in 1880. They called upon the operators of family-sized farms to work together. In no other way, they told farmers, could they match the power of the banks, railroads, and large corporations.

All prices declined steadily after 1885. Western wheat farmers and southern cotton growers were particularly hard hit. Between 1887 and 1889 more than two million white farmers joined Alliances in the South. A separate organization, the National Colored Farmers' Alliance, had one and a quarter million black members. The line between the races remained, but white farmers were beginning to accept the fact that they would have to work with black farmers if they were ever going to solve the problems.

The new farm movement quickly spread into the wheat belt of the Middle West. But there, many immigrant farmers stayed out, and the Alliances tended to be made up of white Protestants of British stock.

"In Kansas We Busted." Together, the Alliances gave birth to the People's Party, generally called the Populists. It was a political movement such as the nation hadn't seen since the rise of the Republican Party in the 1850s.

In Kansas, between 1889 and 1893, some 11,000 mortgages were foreclosed. Thousands of settlers fled the state. (Sometimes their wagons bore the slogan "In God We Trusted, in Kansas We Busted.") The Populists put up their own slates for the 1890 elections. They captured five of the state's seats in Congress and got control of the state legislature.

There were Populist candidates in a number of midwestern and southern states that year. In Nebraska, they won both houses of the legislature, and a Democratic candidate who agreed with their views became governor.

The Democrats suffered too. In the South, Alabama, Florida, North Carolina, and Tennessee elected legislatures that were either Populist or sympathetic to the goals of the Alliances. But what most alarmed conservative southern Democrats was a meeting in December 1890, at Ocala, Florida. There the white Southern Alliance and the Colored Farmers' Alliance came together to plan combined political action.

A nation brought to the verge of ruin. In 1892, a presidential election year, representatives of all Alliance groups met at Omaha, Nebraska, to launch the Populist Party. It was a different kind of political gathering. Some of the poorer delegates had to steal rides on freight cars to get to

Genuine horsepower! How did machines such as this affect farm production?

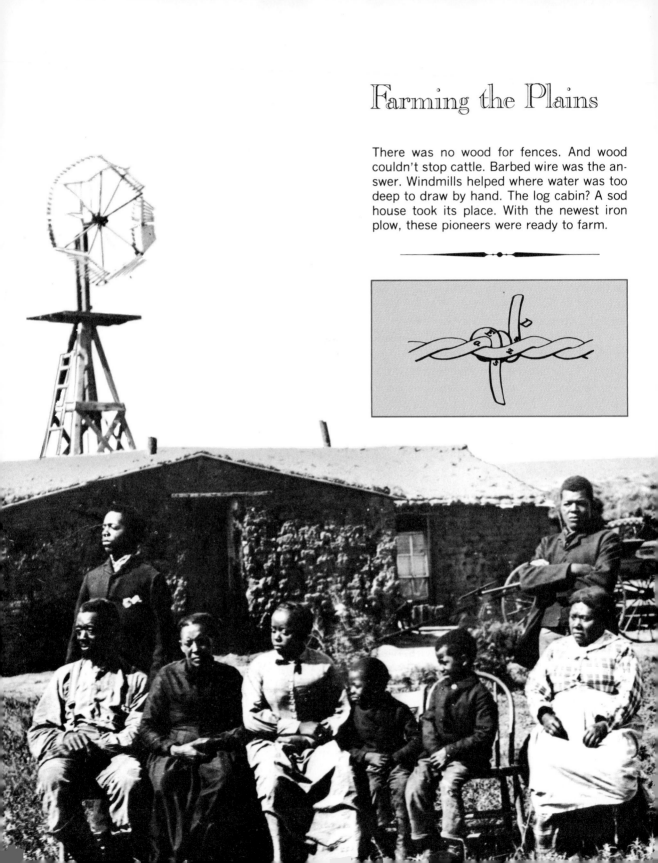

Farming the Plains

There was no wood for fences. And wood couldn't stop cattle. Barbed wire was the answer. Windmills helped where water was too deep to draw by hand. The log cabin? A sod house took its place. With the newest iron plow, these pioneers were ready to farm.

Omaha. They chose James B. Weaver, a respectable, bewhiskered Civil War general, as their candidate for President. His running mate was a Confederate veteran, James G. Field of Virginia.

This was a pretty tame slate for people who were talking about rebellion and having "a second Independence Day." But they made up for it in their platform. It began:

We meet in the midst of a nation brought to the verge of moral, political, and material ruin. Corruption dominates the ballot-box, the state legislatures, the Congress, and touches even the ermine of the bench. . . . The newspapers are largely subsidized or muzzled, public opinion silenced, business prostrated, homes covered with mortgages, labor impoverished, and the land concentrated in the hands of capitalists.

After running on in this way at some length, the platform got down to exact recommendations. It called for government ownership of the railroads, a money supply that was not tied to the price of gold, an income tax, the secret ballot, restricted immigration, the eight-hour work day, and popular election of United States senators.

The Populist program was wide-ranging and was meant to appeal to urban workers as well as to farmers. Practically all of it has by now been adopted in one way or another, so it's hard to think of it as very radical. But in 1892 it sounded like pure socialism—and that was about as radical as anyone could be. However, four years later, in the election of 1896, the whole Populist program became bogged down on one issue: the use of silver to back the money supply.

 TRY THIS!

1. Show how a protective tariff (page 127) could help an American shoe manufacturer, but not a wheat farmer. (Recall who the customers of each were likely to be.) 2. Explain why farmers thought the government had not paid attention to their needs. 3. Report what a leader of the AFL might have said about the Populist platform of 1892.

5.   A CHOICE BETWEEN GOLD AND SILVER

The Populist platform of 1892 may have looked a lot like socialism, but the Populists really didn't want to remake the business and political systems of the country. They wanted only to make them work better, especially in the area of money and banking.

A shortage of money. The National Banking System set up during the Civil War (page 317) had many faults. The worst of them was that it served the needs of the Northeast far better than those of any other section of the country. For instance, Connecticut had more bank notes in circulation than Michigan, Wisconsin, Minnesota, Iowa, Missouri, Kansas, Kentucky, and Tennessee combined. Rhode Is-

---

Read here of how

The money system was not working well.
Some called for more paper money.
While others wanted to coin silver.
The 1896 election put an end to both ideas.

---

land had an average of 77 dollars for every man, woman, and child in the state; Arkansas had 13 cents!

According to the banking act of 1863, western states should have been able to start their own banks. But in that part of the country it was hard to raise the many thousands of dollars needed to do so.

To make the situation worse, in the years after the Civil War the government was taking in more money from land sales and the tariff than it was spending. The extra funds were used to reduce the national debt. But the number of bank notes in circulation depended on the number of government bonds (that is, on what the government owed). Paying off the debt dried up the money in circulation.

The demand for silver. When less money circulates, what there is of it becomes more valuable, and prices go down. Keeping prices from going even lower in those years was about 350 million dollars' worth of greenbacks still circulating from Civil War days (page 317).

As long as the greenbacks had no gold or silver behind them, some bankers and business people wanted them withdrawn. As this would have driven prices down, farmers and other people who owed money opposed the measure. In fact, during the bad times of the 1870s they wanted the government to issue more greenbacks. Populist candidate James B. Weaver (page 393) was a leader in this movement.

The greenback movement had some success. The notes continued to circulate, though after 1879 they were backed by gold like other United States money. By 1890 the greenback movement had given way to demand for the use of silver.

Sixteen to one. Using both gold and silver to back the money supply has a great weakness. The value of one metal in terms of the other keeps changing. An ounce of gold is always worth more than an ounce of silver, but how much more depends on a lot of things.

Let's say it takes sixteen ounces of silver to buy one ounce of gold. Then imagine that new gold mines are discovered. Gold will be worth less, because there is more of it. An ounce of gold may be bought for as little as fourteen ounces of silver. But if the supply of silver increases, the opposite will happen. Then it may take eighteen ounces of silver to buy one of gold.

Something like this happened in the United States during the 1800s. When the nation began, both gold and silver were used as money, and an ounce of gold was valued at sixteen ounces of silver. Discoveries of gold in California and Australia before the Civil War drove the world price of gold down. So in 1873, the United States Treasury stopped buying silver for its money supply. It did so because for years the mine owners had not been selling it at the official price—sixteen ounces of silver for one ounce of gold. The real price of silver had become much higher than that. Hardly anyone paid attention to the Treasury's action at that time.

In a few years there were "silver rushes" in Nevada, Colorado, and other parts of the West. In 1878 alone, Nevada's Comstock Lode produced 45 million dollars' worth of silver. The value of that metal dropped to eighteen ounces of silver for one of gold. And miners learned that the government was not buying any. Dark suspicions arose that "eastern bankers" were responsible. People started talking about "the crime of 1873."

A veto overridden. A depression and falling prices in the late 1880s led to de-

394

mands that silver once more be made part of the nation's money supply. This would bring on inflation and cause prices to go up again.

The silver-mining state of Colorado joined the Union in 1876. Congressman Richard Bland of Missouri pushed a silver purchase bill through Congress in 1878. When President Rutherford B. Hayes vetoed it, his veto was overridden. The West and South voted overwhelmingly for Bland's bill, which allowed a limited amount of silver to be purchased and coined each year.

At this time, Britain and the European nations were adopting a gold standard for their money supplies. United States bankers and business people interested in trade wanted the United States to do the same. They opposed making silver again part of the money supply, because it might interfere with trade.

Farmers saw it differently. They had borrowed money when farm prices were high and dollars were cheap. Now they were being asked to pay back expensive gold dollars—dollars worth far more in wheat and cotton than the ones they had

SOME PRESIDENTS IN THE GILDED AGE

President	Served	Party	Opponent	Points of Interest
James A. Garfield	1881	Republican	W. S. Hancock	A compromise between Republican factions. Assassinated.
Chester A. Arthur	1881–1885	Republican	No one. Succeeded Garfield.	A surprise. A "spoilsman," he signed the Civil Service Reform Act.
Grover Cleveland	1885–1889	Democrat	J. G. Blaine	Honest, hardworking, not imaginative. Introduced tariff reforms and cut back spending.
Benjamin Harrison	1889–1893	Republican	G. Cleveland	Not a strong President. Followed the advice of Republican leaders in Congress. Took positions opposite to Cleveland on tariffs, spending, and overseas expansion.
Grover Cleveland	1893–1897	Democrat	B. Harrison	Adopted views of bankers and business leaders on money and unions. Opposed overseas expansion.

borrowed. Again, behind this price squeeze, farmers thought they could see J. P. Morgan or some other Wall Street banker.

An endless chain. In 1890 the "silverites" gained much more: the Sherman Silver Purchase Act was passed. The Treasury was now forced to buy 450 million ounces of silver a month and use it to back a new supply of one-, two-, and five-dollar bills called silver certificates.

Meanwhile, former President Grover Cleveland won the election of 1892 (chart on page 395). He was the only President to serve a split term. But it brought him back to office just in time for the Panic of 1893 and the business depression that followed it. Government tax collections had been falling for some time; and as Cleveland was inaugurated, the gold reserve backing the nation's money supply fell below 100 million dollars. Bankers considered this dangerously low.

Cleveland was determined to maintain the gold supply at all costs. He called a special session of Congress and applied all the pressure he could to get the Sherman Silver Purchase Act repealed. On November 1, 1893, he was successful.

But the gold reserves kept falling. The Secretary of the Treasury tried to get more by selling government bonds for gold, but this didn't work. The trouble was that bond buyers were getting their gold from the Treasury's own reserves! It was an endless chain. Reserves fell to 41 million dollars.

To break the endless chain, Cleveland had to go to the Wall Street bankers. A group headed by J. P. Morgan and August Belmont raised 62 million dollars in gold, half of it from outside the country. The gold reserves were safe. But the Morgan

group made a profit of seven million dollars on the deal. Populists—and many Democrats—concluded that Cleveland had sold out to the "international bankers."

Silverites and goldbugs. When the parties met to choose their candidates for the election of 1896, the lines were sharply drawn between "silverites" and "goldbugs." The second group was in firm control of the Republican convention. They made Congressman William McKinley of Ohio their candidate.

Cleveland would have liked the Democrats to nominate someone who favored a gold standard. But western and southern silverites were too strong.

William Jennings Bryan was a two-term Congressman from Nebraska. At the Democratic convention he delivered a rousing speech calling upon the party not to "crucify mankind upon a cross of gold." He was asking them not to favor the gold standard in their platform.

Bryan's speech swept him to the nomination. The Democrats adopted a platform for "free, unlimited coinage of silver at 16 to 1." Populists and Democrats joined forces against the "eastern bankers."

To the nation's business interests Bryan seemed a wild-eyed radical. The Republican campaign manager, Mark Hanna, had no trouble getting fat contributions from big corporations. "Free silver" terrified them. Yet Bryan was not trying to set the poor against the business class. He wished instead to win for them some of the favors being given to business.

An instrument of change. Bryan traveled up and down the land, delivering his "cross of gold" speech to enthusiastic Democrats and Populists. McKinley stayed home and met with groups of businessmen, veterans, and prosperous farmers, carefully

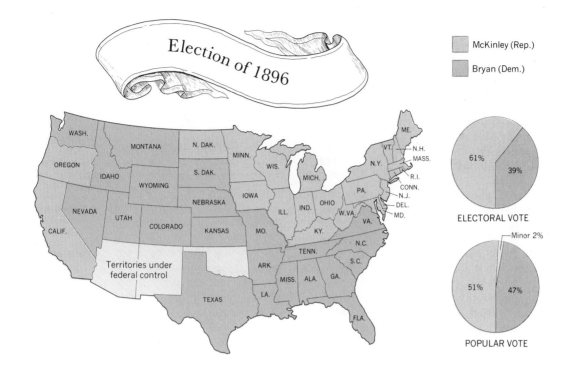

Election of 1896

■ McKinley (Rep.)

■ Bryan (Dem.)

WASH. MONTANA N. DAK. MINN. WIS. MICH. ME. VT. N.H. MASS. N.Y. R.I. CONN. N.J. PA. DEL. MD. OHIO IND. ILL. W.VA. VA. KY. N.C. TENN. S.C. MO. KANSAS COLORADO UTAH NEVADA IDAHO WYOMING S. DAK. NEBRASKA IOWA OREGON CALIF.

Territories under federal control

TEXAS LA. MISS. ALA. GA. ARK. FLA.

61% 39%

ELECTORAL VOTE

Minor 2%

51% 47%

POPULAR VOTE

Why did Bryan carry the South and West?

selected by Mark Hanna. Newspaper reporters wrote down the visitors' "questions" and McKinley's thoughtful "answers."

As can be seen from the map on page 290 and the one above, the 1896 election split the country along sectional lines much as the election of 1860 had. This time, however, instead of North against South, it was Far West and South against Northeast and Middle West.

Some saw the 1896 election as the triumph of the new manufacturing interests over those of agriculture. It was much more complicated than that. However, one thing is certain. A shift had taken place in American politics. Though McKinley won by a narrow margin of the popular vote, the Republicans had caught the spirit of the country. They continued to be the ma-

jority party until the depression years of the 1930s.

Meanwhile, prosperity returned, and new gold discoveries in Alaska ended, for the time, demands for "free silver." As the new century began, the middle class was stirring with ideas to meet the challenges of industrial America.

 TRY THIS!

1. Explain why those who owe money like to see prices going up, while those who lend it would rather see them fall. **2.** Explain the relationship between the gold rush of 1849, the Crime of 1873, the silver strikes in the later 1870s, and the Silver Purchase Act of 1878. **3.** Compare the goals of the greenbackers and the silverites.

ROUNDUP

Who?

"Boss" Tweed
Louisa May Alcott
Frances Willard
William Jennings
   Bryan
Mark Hanna
William McKinley

What?

dumbbell tenement
literacy test
walking city
commuter city
social gospel
Woman's Christian
   Temperance Union
woman suffrage
Homestead Act
Alliances
Omaha platform
free silver
"endless chain"
"cross of gold"

KNOW THIS

A New Kind of Immigration
1. Why did industry welcome the waves of immigrants?
2. What nationality was excluded first? Why?
3. What hardships did immigrants face in their crossing? In the New World?
4. How did the 1890 census support the need to limit immigration?
5. Who favored the literacy test? Who opposed it?

City Growth and City Problems
1. How did a "commuter city" differ from a "walking city"?
2. What is the "melting pot"? Why didn't it work?
3. How were political machines organized? Explain why they were "a crude kind of welfare state."
4. Describe the New York machine at this time. What was it called? Who ran it? What happened to him?
5. What did religious leaders do for the urban poor?

The Woman Movement
1. What was the woman movement's chief goal after 1850?
2. What traditions held women back from full citizenship? What laws?
3. How did the antislavery movement and the Civil War help women?
4. What were some "acceptable activities" for women?
5. What was the chief demand of working women?

Farmers, Populists, and Reform
1. How did the Homestead Act fail?
2. Why were farmers in financial trouble in the 1800s?
3. How did farmers try to protect their interests?
4. When and how was the Populist Party formed? Where was it strongest?
5. What reforms were demanded by the 1892 Populist Party platform?

A Choice Between Gold and Silver
1. List weaknesses of the National Banking System.
2. What was the goal of the greenback movement?
3. What happens if both gold and silver are used to back the currency?
4. What was the gold-reserve crisis? How did President Cleveland solve it?
5. Who ran for President in 1896? What were the issues and the outcome of the election?

DIG HERE!

In the late 1800s and early 1900s immigrants came to the United States in waves. What made them come? How were they received when they arrived? Select one national group for your research. Use the suggestions below to guide your investigation.

A. On an outline map, trace these people's journey to America. Shade and label their native country, and the regions where they settled in the United States.
B. Discuss the difficulties faced in the new land. Describe immediate problems of language, jobs, and housing, as well as longer-term challenges of gaining political power and social status.
C. What people or organizations helped these immigrants adjust to their new life? What services did each provide?
D. Did Americans generally welcome this group? How do you explain the public reaction?
E. Did the "melting pot" theory apply to the experiences of these people? Explain your answer.

These books should be helpful: Handlin, O., *The Uprooted,* Little; Higham, J., *Strangers in Our Land,* Rutgers; Jones, M.A., *American Immigration,* Chicago; Kennedy, J.F., *A Nation of Immigrants,* Harper; Mann, A., *Immigrants in American Life,* Houghton; Weisberger, B.A., *Reaching for Empire,* Vol. 8, *Life History of the United States,* Time; Wittke, C.F., *We Who Built America,* Prentice Hall.

THINK ABOUT IT

1. In the later 1800s cities were growing, industry was expanding, and farms were using more machinery. What connections do you see among these three developments? How did each element help the others?
2. Writing in 1897, Susan B. Anthony called suffrage a "pivotal right," one that could have brought other advances much earlier. Do you agree? How important has political power been to women in gaining equal standing and opportunity?

DO IT!

1. Draw up a proposal for improving urban conditions that might have been submitted to a city council in the 1890s.
2. Design a poster showing the differences between a walking city and a commuter city.
3. Investigate and report on one of these colorful Populist leaders: The "Kansas Pythoness" Mary Lease, "Pitchfork Ben" Tillman, or "Sockless Jerry" Simpson.

THEN AND NOW

Independent and third-party candidates have played important parts in presidential elections. What do they contribute? Do they hurt the major parties? Explain. Should independent and third-party candidates receive federal campaign funds? Should they be included with the major-party candidates in nationwide TV debates? Why, or why not?

399

A Progressive Era Opens the Twentieth Century

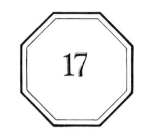

17

A "full dinner bucket" (lunch pail) meant jobs and good pay for all. In 1900 McKinley (left) and Roosevelt (right) gave William Jennings Bryan (page 396) his second defeat. McKinley prosperity carried the day, but it was Roosevelt who put his stamp on the Progressive Era.

1.   WHO WERE THE PROGRESSIVES?

Thursday, September 6, 1901, was a blazing hot day in Buffalo, New York. But the crowds swarming into the music hall at the Pan-American Exposition didn't seem to mind. Inside the building a public reception was being held for William McKinley, twenty-fifth President of the United States. Any person willing to wait in line might greet the President and shake his hand.

A great pipe organ filled the music hall with melody. Standing amid palms and other greenery on a platform at one end of the hall, McKinley reached out for hand after hand. Unnoticed among the waiting throng stood Leon Czolgosz (CHOL-gosh).

He was a small man with a dark mustache and a heavily bandaged right hand. At seven minutes past four, he came face-to-face with the President. McKinley offered his hand, but Czolgosz thrust it aside. There was a sudden flash, then two loud reports. With a .32 caliber pistol concealed in his bandaged hand, Czolgosz had shot the President of the United States.

A cowboy President. It seemed for a time that McKinley would recover. His doctors insisted that their patient was on the mend. To reassure an anxious nation, Vice President Theodore Roosevelt went vacationing with his family in the remote

400

Adirondack Mountains of upstate New York. However, on September 13, the President took a turn for the worse. When word of his hopeless condition reached Roosevelt, the Vice President began a headlong dash by buckboard and private train for Buffalo. But even as Roosevelt was recklessly racing down treacherous mountain roads, McKinley murmured, "It's God's way," sank into a coma, and died.

Six weeks short of his forty-third birthday, Roosevelt became the youngest President in history. Mark Hanna, the undisputed boss of the Republican Party, was grief-stricken. He was heard to mutter, "Now that cowboy is President of the United States." Hanna was speaking of Roosevelt's days as a cattle rancher.

Solid accomplishments. In September, 1901, few people realized that a conservative period of American history had come to an end. Even fewer thought that the new administration would be a time of change and reform. Yet the years following the tragic afternoon in Buffalo are known as the Progressive Era. They recall a time like that of Andrew Jackson (page 186), when demand for change shook the nation.

In the Progressive Era, government finally faced up to the problems caused by the growth of industry. It was an age that produced new leaders and questioned old values. A young progressive wrote that the

---

Read here of how

The nation got a new President.
And felt a new desire for reform.
Roosevelt moved cautiously.
But caught the spirit of the times.

TIME CHART

1901	McKinley is assassinated; Theodore Roosevelt becomes President.
1902	The Northern Securities Case is filed.
1902	The Newlands Act is passed.
1902	The anthracite coal strike is settled.
1906	The Hepburn Act is passed.
1906	The Pure Food and Drug Act and the Meat Inspection Act are passed.
1908	Taft is elected President.
1909	The Payne-Aldrich Tariff is adopted.
1912	Wilson is elected President.
1913	The Income Tax and Senate Election Amendments are ratified.
1913	The Federal Reserve Act is passed.
1914	The Clayton Antitrust Act is passed.
1919	The Prohibition Amendment is ratified.
1920	The Woman's Suffrage Amendment is ratified.

---

movement was "a revolt of youth against age." He also said, "My generation was spoiling for a fight with the ancient enemies of progress. . . . It was sick and tired of potbellied politicians, tired of bankers and businessmen preaching a one-day-in-seven version of the golden rule."

Progressivism was more than enthusiasm and youthful spirit. It had solid accomplishments. There were victories over corrupt political machines (page 405). For the first time since Reconstruction, the federal Constitution was amended, providing for direct popular election of senators and

401

HE WHO SOWS WIND WILL REAP STORM —
BUT FROM GOOD SEED SPRINGS PROSPERITY!

STRIFE
T.R.

PROSPERITY

AGRICULTURE
FORESTRY.
MINING.

INDUSTRY ARBITRATION LITERATURE
COMMERCE. JUSTICE. SCIENCE.
NAVIGATION. LAW. ART.

TAKE SPADE AND HOE THYSELF; DIG ON —
GREAT SHALT THOU BE THROUGH PEASANT TOIL.

GOETHE'S FAUST II PART.

To what groups of Americans did this poster appeal?

for a national income tax. New laws were passed to regulate trusts and monopolies. Old laws were enforced; the Sherman Antitrust Act was actually used against big business (page 373). And when a President of the United States intervened in a labor dispute in 1902, only eight years after the Pullman strike (page 373), he did so on the side of labor.

A respectable reformer. In many ways, Theodore Roosevelt perfectly suited the times. "He is not an American, you know," someone said of him, "he *is* America." Throughout his life, Roosevelt reflected the shifts in what the American people were thinking and doing. More than anything else, he showed that reform could be respectable. This was because Roosevelt and most other progressives were not radicals.

They had no wish to do away with the social and economic system of the United States. Nor were they like the angry and desperate farmers who flocked to the Populist banner a decade earlier (page 391). Instead they were the well-dressed men and women who could be seen strolling along the sidewalks of any prosperous neighborhood.

Theodore Roosevelt himself came from a wealthy, prominent New York family. His decision to enter politics showed a public spirit not often found at that time among the upper classes, but his ideas were conservative. In fact, as late as 1896 he bellowed that Bryan and the Democrats represented "the spirit of lawless mob violence." Like other progressives, Roosevelt was bothered by the disorder of the 1890s.

Shocking conditions. Much of Roosevelt's caution came from the fact that he was a politician. He was also ambitious and clever, and he could see changes in the way people were thinking. The most noticeable change was in the attitudes of prosperous farmers, small businessmen, professional people, and city dwellers of the middle class—all staunch Republicans. These solid citizens sensed that everything was not right in the land. The ship of state had lost its way.

The growth of industry and the emergence of great corporations had undermined the foundations of the government. Here were private organizations exercising immense power over individuals and entire communities. Yet, because of the law's failure to keep pace with changing conditions, they were beyond the control of the public. With growing fervor, thoughtful people called upon government to give up the old idea of *laissez-faire* (LES-ay FAIR), the policy of no government regulation of business. They wanted the government to support the interest of the public, not mainly those of private individuals.

Along with this concern over wrongdoing by the rich and powerful was the anxiety over the condition of the poor. A new kind of journalist—the *muckraker*—had brought to the attention of the country the shocking conditions under which the poor lived and worked. Day after day, Americans read in their newspapers and magazines of overcrowded, disease-ridden tenements, of children working twelve hours at a time for pitifully low wages, and of corrupt city governments. A prominent feature of progressivism was a rising demand that something be done about the condition of the cities.

A more orderly and efficient society. Both government and private organiza-tions, it was believed, should reach into the slums and raise up the poor. But often there were strings attached to these noble efforts. Some progressives were more interested in teaching middle-class values than in eliminating poverty. Prohibition, patriotic indoctrination, compulsory school attendance, and an end to unlimited immigration were among the reforms advocated by many upright progressives.

But the heart of progressivism was the desire for a more orderly and efficient society. In the previous generation the middle class had grown powerful through the industrial development of the nation. Now that same middle class wished to prevent a recurrence of the crisis of the 1890s. It seemed to progressive men and women that the depression, strikes, and class warfare of those years had been caused by the uncontrolled growth of industry. Progressives reasoned that such dangerous developments could be prevented. What was chiefly needed, they claimed, was improvement in the living and working conditions of the poor. State and federal governments, if made stronger, could limit the power of the trusts and monopolies. This, in turn, would bring about a safe and rational economic order.

 TRY THIS!

Tell which of the following Americans would have been likely to support the progressives, and which would not. In each case give a reason for your answer: **1.** A Populist farmer. **2.** The owner of a small business. **3.** A woman college professor. **4.** A political boss. **5.** A well-to-do farmer. **6.** The head of a large corporation. **7.** A recent immigrant from Europe. **8.** A woman in charge of a settlement house.

THE MUCKRAKERS

JACOB RIIS (1849–1914) was born in Denmark, where he was apprenticed to a carpenter. Riis (REESS) came to New York in 1870, and chance made him a police reporter. His books *How the Other Half Lives* and *Children of the Poor* brought him great fame. He worked all his life to help the needy, especially children, but he never liked to be called a reformer. What the poor needed, he often said, was not a change but a chance.

IDA TARBELL (1857–1944) grew up near the Pennsylvania oil fields. Her father was a manufacturer of the wooden oil tanks. After attending college in France, Miss Tarbell became an editor for *McClure's Magazine.* There she wrote about business problems and women's rights. She is most famous for the *History of the Standard Oil Company.* It was an attack on John D. Rockefeller, who, she felt, had ruined her father and many like him in the oil business.

LINCOLN STEFFENS (1866–1936) was born and educated in California. As a newspaperman, he wrote articles on police corruption, which brought him a lot of attention. He became an editor of *McClure's Magazine,* where his *The Shame of the Cities* first appeared as a series of articles on city politics. Unlike most reformers, Steffens became more radical as the years went by. He found much to praise in the Russian Revolution and the Soviet Union.

RAY STANNARD BAKER (1870–1946) wrote "The Railroads on Trial," for *McClure's Magazine.* Later he became the friend and biographer of President Wilson.

UPTON SINCLAIR (1878–1968) was the most famous novelist among the muckrakers. He wanted *The Jungle,* his story of an immigrant family in Chicago, to expose working conditions in the stockyards. But his readers became far more interested in the dreadful conditions under which their meat was prepared. The federal Meat Inspection Act was a direct result. Said Sinclair, "I aimed at the nation's heart, and I hit it in the stomach." A Socialist from his early twenties, he ran for office many times but was never elected.

2. PROGRESSIVISM IN CITY AND STATE

Progressivism first appeared not on the national scene but in the government of states and cities. Most of the reforms associated with progressivism were first tried out at these levels, and for good reason. Not until the 1930s was it thought proper for the federal government to deal directly with social problems. The welfare of the poor, the working conditions of labor, the safety of women and children in industry were questions normally seen to by state and local authorities. The rising band of progressives was concerned with just such issues. They transformed many a city hall and state capitol into a battleground of reform.

A double life. The greatest problems facing the progressives were those of the cities. In the cities were concentrated all the bad effects of industrialism. There, political corruption seemed to be destroying democracy. There, the free-enterprise system seemed a joke because of widespread poverty and unemployment. Furthermore, in the city, new values and a new culture were developing. These threatened to replace the age-old principles on which American life had been built.

At the turn of the century, city politics seemed to have a double life. On the one hand, there was the legal, elected government of mayor and city council, supposedly controlled by the people. But beneath the surface, corrupt political machines (page 382) were running things. Crooked politicians and dishonest businessmen regularly made deals with each other. The situation outraged the progressives. In a series of exposés, reporters like Lincoln Steffens (page 404) attacked this relationship. The center of their charges was the tie between city government and "the interests." One reporter wrote:

Underneath the surface . . . the activity of privilege appears, the privileges of the street railways, the gas, the water, the telephone, and the electric-lighting companies. The connection of these industries with politics explains the power of the boss and the machine. . . .

Progressive journalists—the ones called muckrakers—showed how city officials were often in the pay of the interests. For bribes and jobs and other benefits, certain mayors, city councils, and political bosses gladly helped out private utility companies. Low tax assessments and the right to operate as monopolies were some of the favors they granted.

Home rule. The progressives attacked corruption in local government first. In Toledo, Ohio, they rallied around Samuel M. "Golden Rule" Jones. In 1897, they made him mayor, and Jones said, "I don't want to rule anybody. Each individual must rule himself." Elected four times, Jones was a model progressive. During his time in office he started a system of free kindergartens and night schools, constructed new public playgrounds, saw to it that city workers were given higher pay, and provided free

---

Read here of how

Reforms were made in local government.
Direct democracy was introduced.
City bosses were tamed.
And state governments were improved.

---

lodging for the unemployed and homeless. In 1901, Cleveland, Ohio, elected Tom Johnson as mayor. For eight years his administration fought Cleveland's public utility companies and the state legislature.

In addition to electing reformers, the progressives tried to change the very nature of city government. Far from being independent, cities were under the control of the state legislatures. These were usually dominated by rural politicians who hated and feared cities, and by business groups with little interest in the affairs of any particular urban center. In 1900 the National Municipal League demanded a program of home rule for cities and towns. They should, the League said, be able to change their governments without approval from the state. By 1917 twelve states had passed such legislation. A city might experiment with a city manager or with a commission form of government. The efficiency of such systems appealed to the mind of the progressives.

More attention to the people. A constant demand of the progressives was for *direct democracy.* The way to strengthen democratic government, they said, was to make it even more democratic. One part of many new city charters, for instance, was provision for the *short ballot.* Instead of having to choose among candidates for a host of minor offices, voters might select only a mayor, city council, and school board. It was up to these officeholders to appoint minor officials and answer to the people if any of the officials failed.

Another popular demand was for *initiative, referendum,* and *recall.* By the first procedure, the people themselves could force a state legislature to hear a particular bill. By the second, they could make their own laws. The third procedure, recall, enabled

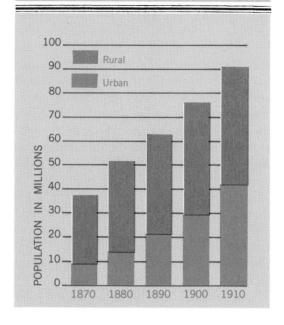

What caused the sharp increase in urban population between 1870 and 1910?

them to get rid of an elected official by a petition and a new election.

But the most widely adopted reform was the *direct primary.* Every state now selects its candidates for governor and other high offices by vote of the people in a primary election. No longer are they chosen by machine-controlled caucuses (page 145) and conventions.

No single change accomplished everything that its promoters hoped, but each brought some improvement. Even when party bosses ousted the progressives and returned to power, as they sometimes did, they behaved better. The recall, direct primary, and other reforms forced these old-line leaders to pay much closer attention to the people's wishes.

Reformers and the poor. Sometimes the work of the progressives backfired. For instance, in Pittsburgh, Pennsylvania, there were fewer people taking part in city government after reform measures were adopted than before. In the name of clean and efficient government, the progressives took a number of undemocratic steps. They did away with the old neighborhood wards in which clerks and manual laborers could hold positions of leadership. In their place the reformers then set up a city-wide system run by businessmen, leaders of "society," and a few carefully chosen "labor representatives." Clearly, they had copied not the town meeting, but the business corporation. Decision-making by a few, not direct democracy, was the model for this kind of reform.

Progressives also failed to appreciate the many good things done by the political boss and his machine (page 383). Even though he was corrupt, he gave the poor a means of getting the attention of the government. New citizens thoroughly understood this direct, personal approach.

Above all, the political boss respected the cultural differences found among immigrants. The progressive reformer was likely to think of these folkways as un-American. So when a progressive attacked the boss and the machine, he met with anger from those he was supposed to be helping. Indeed, the foreign-born were often suspicious of the reformers. The progressives' tight budgets, strict rules, and air of superiority kept them and the city poor far apart.

The best-governed state in the union. Bosses and political machines flourished statewide as well as in cities. For generations, one of the most powerful machines was to be found in Wisconsin. According to one reporter, that state belonged to the railways, lumber companies, and utilities. Through the state machine they nominated and elected governors, United States senators, and congressmen. These officials then used their power to enrich the state's business interests. The ambitious became politicians only when they were approved by the state machine.

Reform sentiment had reached Wisconsin by the turn of the century. The dynamic Robert M. LaFollette broke the machine and made Wisconsin the best-governed state in the nation.

Short, with a booming voice and a shock of steel-gray hair, LaFollette was a born leader. Throughout the 1890s he crisscrossed the state campaigning for the Republican nomination for governor. Three times the boss-run state convention dashed his hopes. But in 1900 he was not to be denied. He won both the nomination and the election.

The Wisconsin Idea. For the next quarter century, LaFollette dominated Wisconsin politics. He had more Populist in him than most progressives. That is, his activity as governor and later as senator was more radical and antibusiness than that of others, such as Theodore Roosevelt.

The LaFollette program came to be known as the "Wisconsin Idea." He extended democracy through the initiative, referendum, and recall of officials. His state administration took firm steps to control the power of big business. Impartial commissions regulated railway and public utility rates. The railroads and timber companies were forced to pay higher taxes. So were prosperous citizens, through a state income tax. LaFollette moved to protect workers with laws to cover injuries on the job, and to prohibit child labor. Finally, he set up a system of state insurance to protect personal savings-bank deposits.

In putting together these ideas, LaFollette began a lasting relationship between

407

This woman in New York is carrying work to be sewn at home. Why wasn't the work done at a factory?

Often victories over the "interests" were temporary, but much social legislation was lasting and really worked.

Wage-and-hour laws, protection for striking labor unions, special laws controlling the employment of women and children, measures making employers responsible in cases of accident, were major progressive accomplishments. New national leaders besides LaFollette emerged from the states: Hiram Johnson in California, Charles Evans Hughes in New York, and Woodrow Wilson in New Jersey.

LaFollette himself summed up the hopes of many of these state leaders:

It has been a fight supremely worth making, and I want to be judged . . . by results actually attained. If it can be shown that Wisconsin is a happier and a better state to live in, that its institutions are more democratic, that the opportunities of all its people are more equal, that social justice more nearly prevails, that human life is safer and sweeter—then I shall rest content in the feeling that the progressive movement has been successful.

 TRY THIS!

List these numbers on a piece of paper. Beside each write a *C* if the sentence would be truer of United States cities in the 1900s, an *S* if it would be truer of the states, or a *B* if it would be true of both. **1.** Sometimes they adopted a manager or commission form of government. **2.** Often they were controlled by railroads or other large corporations. **3.** Robert LaFollette first made his mark in one of them. **4.** They adopted primaries for choosing candidates. **5.** They wanted to have more independence.

the University of Wisconsin and the state legislature. He used the state's academic leaders to help solve current problems. Professors from the university wrote some of the new reform legislation, and faculty members served on a number of state commissions. So advanced was LaFollette's leadership that it took more than thirty years for most of the nation to catch up with the "Wisconsin Idea."

"A fight worth making." Other states followed Wisconsin's leadership. In Iowa, North and South Dakota, and Minnesota; in Oregon, Utah, and Arizona; in Oklahoma, Arkansas, Mississippi, Georgia, and the Carolinas the tide of reform ran strong.

3. THEODORE ROOSEVELT AS PRESIDENT

The great Supreme Court Justice Oliver Wendell Holmes described President Theodore Roosevelt as "very likable, a big figure, a rather ordinary intellect, with extraordinary gifts, a shrewd and I think pretty unscrupulous politician."

"The President is about six." Holmes might have added that Roosevelt was also a lot of fun. And this part of his nature captivated the American people. They were delighted when they learned that members of his Administration, and even foreign ambassadors, sometimes had to hike or ride horseback with him in Washington's Rock Creek Park, or play tennis or football on the White House lawn.

It was well known that pillow fights with the President's four lively young children sometimes interrupted official business (page 411). Once he even went a few rounds with heavyweight champion John L. Sullivan in the White House gym. All this led the British ambassador to say, "You must always remember that the President is about six." But it also made Theodore Roosevelt the most popular Chief Executive since Andrew Jackson.

As Holmes noted, there was another, less likable, side to Roosevelt. He was very ambitious, and he often sacrificed principle for political advantage. Seldom did his acts

as President live up to the progressive promises made in his public statements. He compromised so often that Robert LaFollette spent a whole chapter of his autobiography explaining why Roosevelt was not really a progressive at all. But Roosevelt did much for the progressive movement. He strengthened the Presidency after a long time of weak Chief Executives. He used the White House to advertise progressive ideas. He dramatized issues. And he made reform politics seem exciting and important.

The trustbuster. The greatest problem facing the new President in 1901 was the

Read here of how

Roosevelt was a different kind of President.
He took action against the trusts.
And he moved against the railroads.
But he did best in the field of conservation.

---

increasing strength of the trusts (page 369). The drive that so often ended with a single giant company's dominating each industry seemed unstoppable. It had led to 1200 mergers of manufacturing firms in 1899. Then, in 1901, the United States Steel Corporation was formed, the first billion-dollar company (page 370). The vast organization dwarfed other corporations. An awestruck observer noted: "[U.S. Steel] receives and expends more money every year than all but the very greatest of the world's national governments. . . . It absolutely controls the destinies of a population nearly as large as that of Maryland or Nebraska, and directly influences twice that number."

Roosevelt decided that limits must be placed on the trusts. Some of them had to be broken up and replaced with smaller, more competitive corporations. Armed with the Sherman Antitrust Act of 1890 (page 369), he began to take action.

"We don't want to fix it up." One evening in February 1902, J. P. Morgan, the most powerful banker in the United States (page 396), was entertaining some business associates. During dinner Morgan excused himself to take an important telephone call. He returned to the dining room visibly shaken. Slowly and calmly he told his guests that a friendly newspaperman had called with some bad news. Using the Sherman Act as his tool, President Roosevelt had decided to force the breakup of the Northern Securities Company.

Northern Securities was a huge railroad corporation that Morgan had recently put together. Now he learned that the government was preparing to go to court against it. Morgan feared that this might be the signal for a wholesale assault on all the nation's trusts.

The worried Morgan hurried to Washington for a meeting with the President. There, in the White House, he told Roosevelt, "If we have done anything wrong, send your man to my man and they can fix it up." Morgan's "man" was his lawyer; by the President's "man," he meant the Attorney General of the United States! This time the Attorney General said, "We don't want to fix it up; we want to stop it."

Morgan was not used to hearing such talk from political leaders. He asked the President if all his interests, including U.S. Steel, were under attack. "Certainly not," Roosevelt replied, "unless we find out that in any case they have done something we regard as wrong." After Morgan departed, the President said, "Mr. Morgan could not help regarding me as a rival operator."

"Good" and "bad" trusts. Roosevelt's remarks to Morgan showed his policy on the trusts. The President understood that large-scale production could be more efficient than small-scale. As a result, he had nothing against trusts as such, only against "bad" trusts. Bad trusts were those that in some way hurt the public.

Roosevelt's distinction between good and bad trusts meant that not all of them were illegal. In fact, there were more trusts when he left office than when he arrived. He even winked at consolidations when he thought they served the public good. For example, in 1907 he allowed U.S. Steel to take over the valuable Tennessee Coal and Iron Company because this prevented a stock-market panic.

Many reformers were demanding that the growth of big business be slowed down. Roosevelt's policy seemed instead to warn big business that it must reform itself.

Enthusiastic response. It is easy to overlook Roosevelt's solid achievements

A WHITE HOUSE SERVANT ON THE ROOSEVELTS

The life of [White House] employees who took their responsibilities too seriously was made miserable. The children (picture above) left no nook or corner unexplored. From the basement to the flagpole on the roof, every channel and cubbyhole was thoroughly investigated. Places that had not seen a human being for years were now made alive with the howls and laughter of these newcomers. The house became one general playground for them and their associates. Nothing was too sacred to be used for their amusement and no place too good for a playroom. . . .

One of the favorite stunts of the children was to crawl through the space between ceilings and floors where no living being but rats and ferrets had been for years. They took delight also in roller-skating and bicycle-riding all over the house, especially on the smooth hardwood floors. Practically every member of the family, with the exception of the President and Mrs. Roosevelt, had a pair of wooden stilts, and no stairs were too

well carpeted or too steep for their climbing, no tree too high to scramble to the top, nor fountain too deep to take a dip, no furniture too good or too high to use for leapfrog and horseplay; no bed was too expensive or chair too elegantly upholstered to be used as a resting place for the various pets. . . .

Giving the pony a ride in the elevator was but one of many stunts. This little fellow, spotted and handsome, had free access to any of the children's bedrooms. By means of the elevator he would be conveyed to the bedroom floor from the basement. . . .

As the President was heard to remark just before finally leaving, ''Perhaps others have lived longer in the place and enjoyed it quite as much; but none have ever really had more fun out of it than we have.''

From *42 Years in the White House*, by Irwin Hood (Ike) Hoover (Boston: Houghton Mifflin, 1934), pp. 27–30, 110. Copyright 1934 by James Osborne Hoover and Mildred Hoover Stewart. Copyright renewed 1952 by James Osborne Hoover. Reprinted by permission.

THE WESTERN UNION TELEGRAPH COMPANY.
INCORPORATED
23,000 OFFICES IN AMERICA.   CABLE SERVICE TO ALL THE WORLD.
ROBERT C. CLOWRY, President and General Manager.

RECEIVED at   170

176 C KA CS 33 Paid.   via Norfolk Va

Kitty Hawk N C Dec 17

Bishop M Wright

          7 Hawthorne St

Success four flights thursday morning all against twenty one mile

wind started from Level with engine power alone average speed

through air thirty one miles longest 57 seconds inform Press

home #### Christmas .   Orevelle Wright   525P

One momentous event of 1903 was so little noted that a clerk misspelled Orville Wright's name. TR became a vigorous supporter of aviation.

and make him seem more conservative than he was. The case against the Northern Securities railroad corporation showed that the government would no longer treat big business as a pampered child. In 1904 the Supreme Court upheld the Attorney General and forced the breakup of Northern Securities.

The public responded enthusiastically to Roosevelt's "trustbusting," so he moved against the Beef Trust. Again the Supreme Court upheld the government's case. During its last two years, the Roosevelt Administration brought suit against the American Tobacco Company and John D. Rockefeller's mammoth Standard Oil Company. In all, TR, as the newspapers now called him, began 25 cases against the trusts. He also pressured Congress to set up a Bureau of Corporations to regulate business.

Compromise or betrayal? Roosevelt's kind of Presidency proved popular with the voters. In the 1904 election he easily de-

feated the unexciting Democratic candidate, Alton B. Parker of New York. He could now feel that he had won his own way to the White House.

TR viewed his smashing victory as a signal to step up reform programs. Just as the Sherman Act had been little used against trusts, the Interstate Commerce Commission (page 364) had seldom regulated the railroads. During the first two years of his second term, Roosevelt worked to expand the power of the ICC over freight rates. What finally came out of his efforts was the Hepburn Act of 1906.

The Hepburn Act was really a compromise between the demands of the progressives and the fears of conservatives. It gave the ICC new powers but allowed the federal courts to review its actions. Because the courts were so conservative, progressives like LaFollette shouted "betrayal" and denounced Roosevelt. Nevertheless, the Hepburn Act did strengthen federal control of railroads.

A muckraking novel. Of more interest to the average citizen in 1906 were the laws relating to food and medicines. The story of sickening conditions in the meat-packing industry had been brought home to the consumer by Upton Sinclair's muckraking novel, *The Jungle* (page 404).

Congress reacted to pressure from Roosevelt and an outraged public by passing the Pure Food and Drug Act and the Meat Inspection Act. But these were tame laws, and they did not greatly inconvenience the meat-packing industry. Once again Roosevelt came under fire for not having insisted on tougher controls.

Forest and water problems. In one area, though, no one questioned TR's dedication or sincerity. The Roosevelt-led crusade to save the nation's natural resources stands as his most lasting achievement. In his first message to Congress, he said, "Forest and water problems are perhaps the most vital internal problems of the United States."

Roosevelt knew that for generations profit-seeking miners, ranchers, and lumbermen had helped themselves to the country's natural resources. By the turn of the century, 80 per cent of the forests was gone. Backed by imaginative and well-trained conservationists like Gifford Pinchot, who headed the Bureau of Forestry, Roosevelt acted firmly. Using laws that had been long neglected, he set aside 150 million acres of forest and 75 million acres of mineral deposits from public lands.

In addition, the Newlands Act of 1902 called for federal projects to reclaim and irrigate lands in sixteen western states. It also led to the construction of the great Roosevelt Dam in Arizona. During Roosevelt's time in office, the number of national parks doubled, and 51 wildlife refuges were created. Even his severe critic Robert LaFollette cheered TR's conservation efforts.

A first for organized labor. Roosevelt used presidential power against business in the field of labor relations too. He did so most dramatically during the great coal strike of 1902. In May of that year 50,000 members of the United Mine Workers union walked out of the pits, demanding more wages, shorter hours, and better working conditions. The mine operators refused to recognize the union or to talk with the miners about the issues.

With the lines drawn between miners and owners, the nation faced the grim prospect of a winter without fuel. Worried about the results, Roosevelt stepped in and threatened to take over the mines and run them with soldiers if the mine owners did not agree to *arbitration*. (A question under arbitration is referred to a third party. Both sides agree in advance to accept the third party's decision.)

TR's bluster worked. A federal arbitration board was set up, and the miners won a partial victory. For the first time, the government had stepped in not to break a strike, but to bring it to arbitration. Also for the first time, a President had threatened to seize a struck industry.

Uneasy about unions. Roosevelt's interference in the coal strike was not because of sympathy for working people. Rather, it was his conservatism that influenced him. When the mine owners prepared to use force to break the strike, Roosevelt became fearful of class violence. If other unions joined in a general sympathetic strike, he warned, it would surely mean a crisis "only less serious than the Civil War."

413

Like many middle-class progressives, Roosevelt was uneasy about labor unions. At the same time, he knew they probably could not be avoided in an industrialized America. If employers such as the mine owners did not come to terms with unions, TR believed, revolutionary violence and socialism would result. Then the progressive plan for an orderly capitalist society would be lost forever.

 TRY THIS!

1. Write what a Roosevelt supporter might have replied to the question "Why do you like TR?" **2.** Explain why Roosevelt did not attack all trusts. **3.** Describe the way in which each of the following involved the federal government in a new kind of activity: the Newlands Act, the Hepburn Act, and the Pure Food and Drug Act.

4.   THE UNHAPPY TAFT ADMINISTRATION

Theodore Roosevelt could probably have had another four years in the White House for the asking. But after his victory of 1904, he promised not to seek re-election. Instead, as a noncandidate, he set about handpicking the Republican presidential nominee. TR decided his successor should be Secretary of War William Howard Taft.

The Democrats for the third time turned to their silver-throated war horse, William Jennings Bryan (page 396). The "Boy Orator of the Platte" found Roosevelt's enthusiastic support of Taft too much to overcome. The Republicans breezed to an easy victory.

The wrong man. Taft became President on March 4, 1909, and Roosevelt at once hurried off to Africa for a round of big-game hunting. Some conservatives were glad to be rid of him. When told of the ex-President's travel plans, Nelson Aldrich, the conservative kingpin of the Senate, muttered, "Let every lion do his duty."

Roosevelt's was a hard act to follow, especially for William Howard Taft. The new President lacked TR's enthusiasm for public battles. While he believed in the theory of progressivism, he was by temperament and training a conservative. Taft

tipped the scales at well over 300 pounds, and he had a genial and easygoing nature. But he was not a politician.

During a lifetime of public service Taft held only one elective office, the Presidency. He found his greatest satisfaction in the law. His main goal in life was to be Chief Justice of the United States. In less troubled times, Taft's good qualities might have made him an excellent President. Because he lacked political experience, he was the wrong man to head a Republican party torn between progressives and conservatives.

"Uncle Joe" and the Insurgents. In some ways Taft proved a worthy successor to Roosevelt. He continued TR's policies in railroad regulation. For instance, in 1910 he signed the Mann-Elkins Act, which fur-

---

Read here of how

Taft tried to follow in TR's footsteps.
But lacked the talent for it.
Roosevelt challenged him in 1912.
But succeeded only in electing Wilson.

---

ther strengthened the authority of the ICC. Most of all, Taft's Administration actually prosecuted and "busted" twice as many trusts in one term as Roosevelt's had in two.

Such activity helped create the climate for the Supreme Court's landmark rulings against Standard Oil and American Tobacco. These cases, which were decided in 1911, seemed at last to bring the Court into line with the intent of the Sherman Antitrust Act of 1890.

Despite these efforts, Taft's position on other questions made enemies for him among the progressives. In the end it even placed him in line with the conservative wing of the Republican Party.

One fight came in the House of Representatives. There, a group of Republican progressives known as the *Insurgents* greatly resented the strict rule of Speaker "Uncle Joe" Cannon. Taft was caught in this quar-

rel. He needed Cannon's help in getting laws passed. But if he supported "Uncle Joe" against the progressive Republicans, it would destroy his reputation as a reform President. Taft sided with Cannon. The next year, when the revolt against Cannon succeeded, Taft was in an awkward position.

The best tariff. The Payne-Aldrich Tariff further widened the split between the President and the progressives. In 1908, Taft promised to reduce tariff rates. Once in office, he called Congress into special session for that reason. The result was a sorry mess. The House version of the tariff bill showed some progressive influence. Rates were very much lower. But in the Senate the measure fell into deep trouble. There, Senator Nelson Aldrich of Rhode Island saw to it that hundreds of changes were made—all of them favorable to the business community.

A determined band of Insurgents fought Aldrich and the old guard tooth and nail. But on each crucial point, President

TR worries because Taft allows Congress and the Cabinet to tangle the "strings" of government.

Taft supported Aldrich and the conservatives.

An open rebuke. On the heels of the tariff uproar, Taft again outraged the progressives. This time he seemed to tamper with Roosevelt's beloved conservation program. He named as Secretary of the Interior, Richard Ballinger, a conservative lawyer from Seattle. Ballinger soon began reversing some of TR's policies, in favor of private interests. In doing so he ran head-on into the fury of Chief Forester Gifford Pinchot, a holdover from the Roosevelt Administration.

As it turned out, Ballinger was not guilty of any dishonesty, but that hardly mattered. The Ballinger-Pinchot affair added fuel to an already raging fire. By 1910 the Republican Party was split wide open. In the elections of that year, the country voted overwhelmingly for the Democrats, and the Democratic Party won control of the House of Representatives. It was an open rebuke to Taft.

"My hat is in the ring." As the election of 1912 approached, angry progressives talked of challenging Taft for the Republican nomination. First into the field was Robert LaFollette, who announced his candidacy early. But everything was held up until Roosevelt could be heard from. For fifteen months he had been abroad, first in Africa and then triumphantly touring Europe. His supporters pleaded with him to come home and take on Taft.

TR believed his old friend Bill Taft had betrayed him. When LaFollette appeared lacking in wide support, Roosevelt declared, "My hat is in the ring." The "cowboy" then saddled up to pursue the Republican nomination.

The party steamroller. What followed was a bitter personal struggle. Taft had no taste for political gut-fighting. On the other hand, he thought Roosevelt's election would shatter the Republican Party. He even felt that it threatened the Constitution.

Taft used every means at his disposal to win renomination. He could not compete with Roosevelt's enormous popularity and took a beating in the presidential primaries. Most convention delegates, however, were chosen not by popular vote but by machine-run party caucuses. Here Taft had Roosevelt beaten. The President was in firm control of the Republican organization. At the Chicago convention the well-oiled party machine flattened TR's candidacy like a steamroller. There were fist-fights on the convention floor and taunting shouts from Roosevelt's followers, but Taft won renomination.

"We battle for the Lord." Knowing he had no chance to be the Republican candidate, Roosevelt decided to play for bigger stakes. Before the convention balloting, he addressed a throng of hysterical supporters in Chicago: "We fight in honorable fashion for the good of mankind, unheeding of our individual fates. With unflinching hearts and undimmed eyes, we stand at Armageddon and we battle for the Lord." The campaign against Taft had become a glorious crusade.

The progressives refused to play by the rules and throw in the towel when Taft won. Instead, Roosevelt and most of his delegates walked out of the convention and pledged themselves to form a new political party. In August a broad cross-section of reformers returned to Chicago. There they nominated Roosevelt for President. Officially they called themselves the Progressive Party. But because TR often said he felt "strong as a bull moose," they became better known by that name. The Bull Moose Party was born.

From the sidelines, the Democrats watched these wars with unconcealed joy. Thanks to this Republican split, they stood an excellent chance of winning their first presidential election in twenty years. But the Democrats too were divided. At the Baltimore convention, liberals were behind Governor Woodrow Wilson of New Jersey, a newcomer to politics.

Most of Wilson's life had been spent on college campuses. As president of Princeton University, he had gained national attention when he attempted to make student life more democratic. In addition, the professor proved to be a shrewd politician. He gained the powerful aid of William Jennings Bryan, and after 44 ballots, won the nomination.

Roosevelt's toughest foe. The election boiled down to a contest between Wilson and Roosevelt. Taft all but accepted a third-place finish in November. As one might have expected, Roosevelt threw himself into the campaign with his usual reckless energy. On one occasion he even stared death in the face. Three weeks before the balloting, TR emerged from a Milwaukee hotel on the way to a rally. A fanatic shot him in the chest. Pale and bleeding, the ex-President refused to be examined, shouting, "I'll make this speech or die!" Only after his hour-and-a-half address was finished did he let a doctor examine him. The bullet had broken a rib and barely missed his heart. The nation was awed by his magnificent, though foolhardy, display of courage.

In Woodrow Wilson, Roosevelt met his toughest foe. Gradually the voters came to respect the "Princeton schoolmaster" and admire his campaign lectures. He later

The election of 1912. Why is the Bull Moose nipping the elephant, not the donkey?

took over large parts of TR's program, but in 1912 Wilson was shocked by it. He claimed that TR's position would destroy free enterprise. Wilson offered a different brand of progressivism, which he called the New Freedom. Wilson wanted a return to the freer business methods of an earlier time. He said the proper role of government was to guarantee free competition. He did not think it was right to wait for business to grow too large and *then* try to police it. Wilson hoped to smash all the monopolies and special interests that interfered with individual rights. Roosevelt summoned the nation to an active program borrowed from Alexander Hamilton. Wilson looked to Thomas Jefferson for an answer to the country's problems—and such a

417

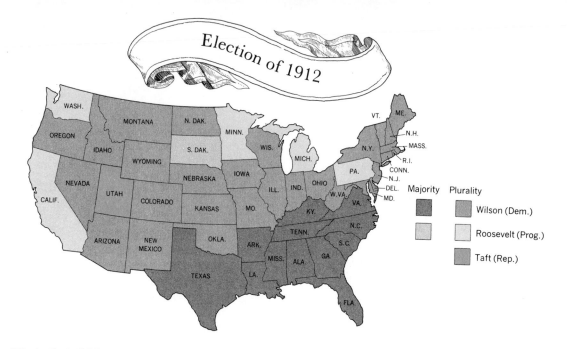

Election of 1912

Majority | Plurality
Wilson (Dem.)
Roosevelt (Prog.)
Taft (Rep.)

What effect did Roosevelt's candidacy have on the outcome of the election?

platform had a great deal of appeal to voters throughout the nation.

In the election, Wilson held on to the states that had always voted Democratic. In other places he took advantage of the Republican split and so won the election. On March 4, 1913, Woodrow Wilson became the twenty-eighth President of the United States.

TRY THIS!

Explain how President Taft might have avoided trouble if he had acted differently on each of these issues: **1.** The revolt against Speaker Cannon. **2.** The Payne-Aldrich Tariff. **3.** The Ballinger-Pinchot disagreement. **4.** The conservative-progressive split in the Republican Party.

5.   WILSON AND THE NEW FREEDOM

Woodrow Wilson was a remarkable figure. His rise in politics had been spectacular. Hardly three years before entering the White House, he looked like a man with no political ambitions. Who would expect a scholar from Princeton to survive in the rough-and-tumble world of cigar-chomping ward bosses and machine politicians?

But the things that set Wilson apart from other politicians made him a success.

Read here of how

Wilson reformed the tariff and banking.
And tried to control the trusts.
Four new amendments were adopted.
And war ended the Progressive Era.

He was a man of deep Christian faith and an idealist. His speeches were surpassed only by those of Abraham Lincoln. But there was also a less attractive side to the new President. Believing absolutely in the rightness of his cause, he became stubborn and cold-blooded when crossed. He was unwilling, and probably unable, to forgive those who did not measure up to his own lofty standards. Within Woodrow Wilson were the elements for a tale of greatness—and for a drama of tragedy.

The first since John Adams. Though he had been elected with only 42 per cent of the popular vote, Wilson set out to make the Democrats the country's majority party. He prepared to form this majority by giving the nation effective new programs in three fields that still badly needed reform. These were the tariff, money and banking, and government regulation of the trusts. As a result of the Republican/Progressive split, Wilson had a majority in Congress, though it was a narrow one. Committee chairmanships were in the hands of southern Democrats. But Wilson was able to get along with these men because he himself was of southern birth and upbringing. So immediately following his inauguration, he called Congress into special session and set it to work.

Wilson appeared before Congress to give his first message in person—the first President to do so since John Adams over a hundred years earlier. In his address the new President backed the Underwood Tariff bill, which would lower duties by as much as 10 per cent. This reduction meant less money from the customs, so the Underwood Bill also put a small graduated tax on income. An income tax was possible in 1913 because the Sixteenth Amendment had been adopted (see Appendix).

When the Underwood Bill ran into opposition in the Senate, Wilson applied the pressure of the Presidency to force his opponents into line. In this he may have been helped by the Seventeenth Amendment to the Constitution, also adopted in 1913 (see Appendix). Under this amendment, United States senators were elected by popular vote instead of by their state legislatures. A senator who knew he had to go before the people for re-election might think twice before defying the President on a popular measure. At any rate, the schoolmaster's methods worked; the Underwood Tariff was adopted.

Public and private banking. American banking was badly in need of an overhaul. Bankers and conservative Republicans wanted a powerful institution like the Bank of England—a central bank under private control. Conservative Democrats feared both the money power in New York City and the federal government. They wanted private banks to be independent of both. Progressives and socialists demanded a banking system owned and controlled by the people. What came out of all these different views was a compromise. Unlike some political bargains, this one worked.

The Owens-Glass Federal Reserve Act, which Wilson signed in December 1913, divided the country into twelve districts. Each district had its own Federal Reserve Bank. These twelve banks served the needs of member banks in the district. They loaned them money which the banks, in turn, could lend to their customers. Federal Reserve Banks also supplied member banks with cash in the form of Federal Reserve notes backed by the government.

A board of directors for each Reserve Bank set the policy within its district. In this it was supervised by a Federal Reserve

419

Workers in a cotton mill, too small to reach the machines without climbing onto the frames.

Board in Washington, appointed by the President. The result was an organization that controlled lending. It also gave the country a money supply that could be increased or decreased as needed.

The Federal Reserve System restored the balance between public and private banking. That was what Alexander Hamilton had wanted when he started the Bank of the United States. The country had not had such a system since Andrew Jackson had destroyed the Second Bank of the United States (page 191). Weaknesses remained, but it was a major improvement over the National Banking System. The leadership of President Wilson had been decisive in steering the Federal Reserve Act through Congress.

A victory for labor. With the tariff and banking questions out of the way, Wilson turned to the problem of the trusts. First, his Administration helped to set up the Federal Trade Commission. This new agency was to be a watchdog of big business. It had the power to issue a "cease and desist" order whenever it discovered that a business, large or small, was making use of unfair operating practices.

But a month after the birth of the FTC, Wilson maneuvered through Congress the Clayton Antitrust Act. It enlarged the old Sherman Act by listing a number of illegal business practices. Among these were cutting prices just to drive a competitor out of business, buying stock in another company to create a monopoly, spying on another company to learn its business secrets, and having the same directors for more than one large company in the same industry.

The Clayton Act was also a victory for organized labor. It declared that neither labor unions nor farm organizations could be taken to court for restraining trade. This had been done in the Pullman strike (page 373).

In the last two years of his first term Wilson sponsored a host of progressive measures. In doing so he drew to his own side many who had voted for TR in 1912.

During this period Wilson won approval of a federal child-labor statute, a workmen's compensation law, an eight-hour day for railroad employees, federal funds for vocational and agricultural training, and farm loan banks to supply cheap long-term credit to needy farmers.

Bone dry. Two Amendments were added to the Constitution in 1913: the Sixteenth (income tax) and the Seventeenth (for the popular election of United States senators). Two other amendments very much in keeping with progressivism were added during the Wilson Administration. These were the Eighteenth or Prohibition Amendment and the Nineteenth, which gave the vote to women (see Appendix).

Attempts to control or stop the sale of liquor had begun during Andrew Jackson's Administration (pages 202–204). However, little headway was made until after the Civil War. Then, in 1874, a group of church women founded the Woman's Christian Temperance Union, hoping to prove to the public that drinking liquor was morally wrong.

In 1893, the WCTU helped to start the Anti-Saloon League, a more active and militant group. The leaders of the Anti-Saloon League quickly spread a number of ideas that gained a ready hearing from progressives. One was that the liquor trade and "liquor money" played a large part in corrupting politicians. Another blamed liquor for adding immeasurably to crime and poverty. In this way, the Anti-Saloon League maintained, liquor greatly increased the tax burden of all citizens.

By 1905, four states were "dry": Kansas, Nebraska, Maine, and North Dakota. A few years later, at the beginning of World War I, 26 states had some laws restricting the sale of liquor, and thirteen states were "bone dry." The First World War added patriotism to the other arguments against liquor. Some also feared what the returned soldiers, "trained to kill," might do if drunk. So in December 1917, a Prohibition Amendment passed Congress. In little over a year (January 29, 1919), it was ratified by three fourths of the states. The Eighteenth Amendment made the "manufacture, sale, or transportation" of liquor illegal.

To the poorest parts. The woman's suffrage amendment had a history much like that of prohibition. Women began demanding their legal and civil rights in the early 1800s but won only limited victories (pages 204 and 384).

Then in 1869, the Territory of Wyoming granted them the vote on the same terms as men. Twenty years later, the constitution of the state of Wyoming affirmed this—first in the nation to do so. Other states followed: Colorado in 1893, Utah and Idaho in 1896. During the Progressive Era, six other western states joined the parade. In 1917, New York fell in line.

Many things fed the growing movement. In ever larger numbers, women had been going to college. Middle-class women had also been leaving their homes to work in schools, hospitals, settlement houses, child welfare centers, and consumers' leagues. Jane Addams and Florence Kelley

INEZ MILHOLLAND

Riding her horse down Fifth Avenue in a suffragist parade, she was a sensation. She was so beautiful that audiences gasped when she rose to speak.

Inez Milholland's father, a wealthy man, encouraged her to make full use of her talents. She became a lawyer—not easy for a woman in those days. The practice of law strengthened her attachment to labor unions, socialism, and women's rights. She was an editor for *McClure's Magazine,* as well as a war correspondent and peace worker early in World War I.

The last adventure of Inez Milholland was a successful race by automobile to win a stay of execution for a client. He was a labor leader wrongly convicted of murder. But Inez Milholland never saw the women's victory for which she worked. In 1916, aged thirty, she was dead of a blood disease.

422

were pioneers of the settlement-house movement, Julia Lathrop headed the federal Children's Bureau, and Lillian Wald began the public-health nursing service. The work of these women and thousands of others took them into the poorest parts of the cities. The poverty, crime, and suffering they found there helped to convince them that men had done a poor job of running the world.

Political prisoners. In the progressive years, women also carried on a campaign of public education through parades and the picketing of public buildings. Some of these activities were illegal, and members of the militant Woman's Party gladly went to jail to dramatize their cause. When they did so, they insisted like later radicals that they were political prisoners, not criminals.

Other feminists preferred the methods of the American Woman's Suffrage Association (page 388). This organization worked to change state laws and gain President Wilson's support for its cause. Wilson at first opposed a constitutional amendment. He felt that the question of votes for women should be left to the states. However, in 1918, he changed his stand, and the next year Congress adopted the Nineteenth Amendment. It was ratified by the states on August 26, 1920, in time for women to take part in the presidential election of that year.

 TRY THIS!

1. List some examples that show Wilson had a great gift for politics. **2.** Tell how the Eighteenth and Nineteenth Amendments were results of the progressive movement. **3.** Explain why Wilson adopted so much of TR's program.

ROUNDUP

Who?
Theodore Roosevelt
Robert M. LaFollette
J. Pierpont Morgan
William Howard Taft
Woodrow Wilson
Julia Lathrop
Lillian Wald

What?
Wisconsin Idea
Northern Securities
Company
Pure Food and Drug
Act
Federal Reserve Act
Clayton Antitrust Act
Woman's Christian
Temperance
Union
National Woman's
Suffrage
Association

KNOW THIS

Who Were the Progressives?
1. Describe the events that made Theodore Roosevelt President of the United States.
2. Around 1900 how were people changing their views on business, politics, and the poor?
3. Why did Roosevelt support progressive reforms?
4. Name five things the progressives accomplished.
5. Who were the muckrakers? Name five of them and identify one activity of each.

Progressivism in City and State
1. Why did progressive reform begin in state and local government, rather than national?
2. What was the "double life" of city politics?
3. Briefly explain these: home rule; the short ballot; the direct primary; initiative, referendum, and recall.
4. What was good, and bad, in progressive reforms?
5. What reforms were part of the "Wisconsin Idea"?

Theodore Roosevelt as President
1. Why was TR such a popular President?
2. Who were the chief actors in the Northern Securities Case? What role did each play?
3. Was Roosevelt against big business? Explain.
4. What did Roosevelt accomplish in these areas: railroad regulation, consumer protection, aid to labor unions, conservation?
5. Why did LaFollette feel that TR was not a progressive?

The Unhappy Taft Administration
1. Why was Taft wrong for the Presidency in 1909?
2. Which things that Taft did were in line with the progressives' ideas?
3. Why was the Republican Party so badly split in 1910?
4. What was the difference between Roosevelt's program and Wilson's?
5. How was Wilson able to win the election of 1912?

Wilson and the New Freedom
1. What experiences and personal qualities made Wilson a successful President?
2. How was Wilson able to get a lower tariff bill passed?
3. Why did the nation need a new banking system?
4. How did the Wilson Administration try to prevent business from becoming too large?
5. How and why were the Eighteenth and Nineteenth Amendments adopted?

423

DIG HERE!

The topics below all relate to popular culture. Examine one of them in depth for the years 1870–1920. You can choose either a main topic or one of the subtopics. (On page 425 is a list of books to help you.)

Fashions in dress (men's, women's, or children's); houses; home furnishings; handicrafts; dating, courtship, and marriage; manners and morals; popular music and dances; the theater; national holidays; festivals and celebrations (Valentine's Day, Hallowe'en, Winter Carnivals, World's Fairs); sports (baseball, football, basketball, boxing); entertainment (Chautauqua, motion pictures, vaudeville, circuses, amusement parks); popular literature (best sellers, magazines, dime novels, comic strips); women's and men's clubs and lodges; mail order catalogs.

A. Describe the development of your subject from 1870 to 1920. If possible, prepare illustrated charts or models to accompany your written descriptions.
B. Did your subject change in any way from 1870 to 1920?
C. Was your subject found in all parts of the country and in all social classes? Did it vary from one region or class to another? How?
D. Are the changes in your subject related to other developments in American life? For example, do they reflect economic or social changes? Describe or explain.

THINK ABOUT IT

1. Do you know what features of the "Wisconsin Idea" are now part of your state government? Describe the feature you think is best for the people of your state.
2. Compare TR with three strong Presidents of the 1800s: Jefferson, Jackson, and Lincoln. Did these leaders ever compromise for political reasons? Give one or more definite examples.

DO IT!

1. Write a thirty-second TV commercial promoting one of the progressive reforms. Divide your paper into two columns, one for the spoken lines and one for the camera shots.
2. From your local library or historical society find out what went on politically, in your community, between 1900 and 1910. Who were the leaders? What were the social conditions? Was the progressive movement having any effect?

THEN AND NOW

Is muckraking a thing of the past? Are present-day reporters investigating any issue the way Steffens looked at city government, and Ida Tarbell at Standard Oil? If so, tell about it; if not, explain.

TEST YOUR HISTORY

1. What was Congress's plan for the reconstruction of the South?
2. What were some features of Radical Reconstruction?
3. What ended Radical Reconstruction?
4. How did southern blacks fare after Reconstruction?
5. What new injustices were suffered by American Indians in the late 1800s?
6. How would you describe the Presidency of Ulysses S. Grant?
7. How were transcontinental railroads made possible?
8. What were some new products and new business methods in the late 1850s?
9. What type of labor organization did workers find best in that period?
10. How did immigration change in the late 1800s?
11. What problems arose because of the sudden growth of cities?
12. What progress did women make? What disappointments did they encounter?
13. What severe financial problems did farmers face? How did they try to solve them?
14. Who is helped when more money is put into circulation? Who is likely to be hurt?
15. How was the progressive movement a result of earlier reforms?
16. What important changes did the progressive movement bring?
17. What were Roosevelt's chief abilities as President?
18. Why was Taft so unsuccessful? Compare him with Roosevelt.
19. How did Wilson reform tariffs, banking, and business?

IV
REVIEW

FURTHER READING

Allen, F. L., *The Great Pierpont Morgan.* Harper, 1948.

Bergamini, J. D., *The Hundredth Year.* Putnam, 1976.

Billard, J. B., ed., *The World of the American Indian.* National Geographic, 1974.

Burner, D., ed., *America Through the Looking Glass: A Historical Reader in Popular Culture* (2 vols). Prentice, 1974.

Denisoff, R. S., and R. A. Peterson, *Sounds of Social Change: Studies in Popular Culture.* Rand, 1972.

Dick, E., *The Sod-House Frontier.* Johnsen, 1954.

Garraty, J. A., *A New Commonwealth.* Harper, 1968.

Marquis, A., *A Guide to America's Indians.* U. Okla., 1974.

Stampp, K., *Era of Reconstruction.* Random, 1967.

Weisberger, B., *Life History of the United States, Volume 7, The Age of Steel and Steam.* Time, 1974.

Williams, T. H., *The Union Restored, Vol. 6, Life History of the United States.* Time, 1974.

V

A
WORLD
POWER

Power may be compared to a great river which while kept within its due bounds is both beautiful and useful; but when it overflows its banks . . . brings destruction and desolation wherever it comes.

Andrew Hamilton, 1735   427

The United States Rises to World Power

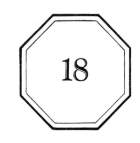

18

Americans swelled with pride as the country moved onto the international stage. Let Columbia rule!

*We don't want to fight, but by jingo if we do,
We've got the ships, we've got the men, we've
got the money too.*

These words are from a song that was very popular in England at the end of the 1800s. It added a new word, *jingoism*, to the language. Jingoism was a newer and noisier form of something much older: *imperialism*—the urge to conquer and rule over other people. Britain was the great imperialist nation of the day. By the late 1800s other countries were trying to imitate it. Soon the United States too was caught up in the race for overseas possessions. The nation that had begun by rebelling against colonial rule became the master of a colonial empire.

1. THE ROAD TO IMPERIALISM

In the years just after the Civil War, the United States seemed completely taken up with affairs at home. Reconstruction, the growth of industry, and the spread of cities provided more than enough problems for everyone. Actually, even in those years, Americans were also interested in overseas expansion. As early as 1867, Secretary of State William Seward arranged to buy Alaska from the Russians for 7,200,000 dollars.

Some called the vast new territory "Seward's Folly" and "Seward's Icebox." But at least one observer saw it as the "drawbridge between America and Asia." (And Secretary Seward himself clearly had Hawaii next on his shopping list.)

Manifest destiny again. One of the clearest voices in favor of expansion was raised by Navy Captain Alfred Thayer Mahan. Mahan was a teacher of history at the War College in Newport, Rhode Island. His book *The Influence of Sea Power on History* appeared in 1890 and stirred enormous interest.

Mahan argued that all the great empires from ancient Rome's to Britain's were based on naval supremacy. His prescription for the United States was plain. It must have a large navy, a strong merchant marine, and colonial possessions as well as naval bases to protect them. Mahan was listened to not only in the United States but also in Germany. Rapid expansion of the German navy in the early 1900s helped to bring on World War I.

Partly because of Mahan, from 1883 onward, Congress provided the money to build a fleet of steel warships. These ships made the United States a naval power. A

Read here of how

Manifest destiny took on a new look.
Alaska and Hawaii became U.S. possessions.
The United States used the Monroe Doctrine.

TIME CHART

1867	Alaska is purchased.
1898	The Spanish-American War is fought.
1898	Hawaii is annexed.
1898	The U.S. acquires Puerto Rico, Guam, and the Philippines.
1899	The Open Door Policy is announced.
1902	The Philippine Insurrection is ended.
1903	The Panama Canal Treaties are signed.
1904	The Roosevelt Corollary is stated.
1905	The Treaty of Portsmouth is negotiated.
1906	The Algeciras Conference is held.
1906	The "Gentlemen's Agreement" is reached.
1907	Work is begun on the Panama Canal.
1916	Pancho Villa raids New Mexico.

---

strong navy, it was agreed, was essential for the protection of foreign trade. And by 1898 the United States could point with pride to a volume of overseas business that approached two billion dollars. The promise of further profits led to new talk of "manifest destiny" (page 257).

This time there was a powerful new argument for America's manifest destiny: survival of the fittest. For instance, some believed that the British must be "fitter" than other nations because they ruled over so many of them.

Some Americans also believed that the dawning twentieth century would belong to the "Anglo-Saxon race." They thought that in the coming century the United States would replace Britain as a world leader. The older nation might then become a sort of junior partner. Meanwhile, the great American republic, said one prophet, would "move down upon . . . Central and South America, out upon the islands of the sea, over Africa and beyond." The man who said this went on to ask, "Can anyone doubt that the result of this competition will be the 'survival of the fittest'?"

"The Hawaiian pear is now fully ripe." The first islands of the sea that the United States moved down upon were the Midways, in 1867. A few years earlier an American sea captain had found these uninhabited rocks about 1200 miles northwest of Hawaii (map on page 442).

But much greater interest was stirred by the Hawaiian (Sandwich) Islands. Missionaries, merchants, and whalers had been stopping there since the days of clipper ships. As early as 1842, five sixths of the vessels anchored at Pearl Harbor were flying the United States flag.

By 1887 a handful of white families, mostly descended from American missionaries, were in firm control of the islands. In that year, they overthrew the native government and made King Kalakaua (kah-LAH-kah-oo-ah) a figurehead. At the same time, the United States government demanded and got exclusive rights to maintain a naval base at Pearl Harbor.

The prosperity of the Hawaiian whites was largely based on sugar, which could be shipped to United States markets duty-free. The McKinley Tariff of 1890 changed that. Whites saw that they would now be better off inside the United States protective tariff wall.

The very next year Queen Liliuokalani (lee-LEE-oo-oh-kah-LAH-nee) came to the throne. She hoped to restore the power enjoyed by her ancestors. And the queen's 80,000 native subjects fully backed her against the 2,000 whites. In 1893 both sides were prepared for a showdown. On January 16, sailors from the United States heavy cruiser *Boston* landed at Honolulu "to protect American property."

Queen Liliuokalani had little choice. She gave up her throne, not to the white settlers, but to the superior force of the United States Navy. The United States minister to Hawaii had arranged for the landing, telling the State Department, "The Hawaiian pear is now fully ripe, and this is the golden hour for the United States to pluck it." A treaty of annexation was quickly arranged with President Benjamin Harrison.

A pineapple king. Incoming President Grover Cleveland had other ideas. He was beginning his second term and had a deepening business depression to worry about (page 396). He was also much disturbed by news of the part the United States had played in overthrowing the Hawaiian queen. Furthermore, he and his Secretary of State disliked the idea of obtaining overseas possessions which, they thought, could never become states.

In his usual forthright manner Cleveland withdrew the annexation treaty that President Harrison had sent to the Senate. But a settlement with the Hawaiian queen was impossible. She insisted on nothing less than the heads of her American opponents! So for four years a Republic of Hawaii flourished under the presidency of Sanford B. Dole, the pineapple king.

A foreign people. Meanwhile, the population of the islands was changing. Boatloads of Japanese laborers were coming in to work the sugar and pineapple plantations. By 1898 the islands were one fourth Japanese. The Japanese government, which had just won a victory over China, stated that the rights of its people must be respected. In 1897 it sent a cruiser to Honolulu to underscore this point.

Possibly the United States would have annexed Hawaii even if there had been no Spanish-American War. But in the midst of that conflict, President William McKinley signed an act of Congress that made the Hawaiian Islands United States territory. For the first time in its history, the country reached overseas to acquire new territory and govern a foreign people.

An unthinkable conflict. In 1895, nearer home, Cleveland showed that he could be as warlike as any other President. A crisis arose in the Caribbean, and for the last time in history there was serious talk of war between England and the United States.

For some years Venezuela and British Guiana had disagreed over the boundary between them. When gold was discovered in the disputed territory, the London government was less willing than ever to yield. Twice it refused American offers to arbitrate. This led Secretary of State Richard Olney to say that the Monroe Doctrine forbade Britain to take the land in question; the British denied that the Doctrine applied. There was a brief threat of war, but both sides stated that a conflict between them would be unthinkable. The British accepted arbitration and were given most of the disputed territory.

TRY THIS!

1. "Should the United States build a fleet of steel warships?" Write out some of the testimony that Captain Alfred Thayer Mahan might have given to Congress in the 1880s on this question. 2. Draw up a message that President Harrison might have sent to the Senate with the Hawaiian annexation treaty. 3. Prepare a message that President Cleveland might have sent withdrawing the Hawaiian treaty.

2. THE SPANISH-AMERICAN WAR

In 1895, for the second time in thirty years, revolution broke out in Cuba. The United States government was under powerful pressure to become involved, but President Cleveland resisted. Meanwhile, Cuban exiles in New York skillfully worked on the sympathies of the American people. And newspapers belonging to Joseph Pulitzer and William Randolph Hearst printed horrifying stories of Spanish "atrocities." ·

The papers were struggling to build circulation, so each tried to outdo the other in sensational disclosures. When the Spanish commander sent people to concentration

Read here of how

The U.S. backed Cuban independence.
Two incidents led to war with Spain.
The nation won an easy victory in Cuba.
But found the Philippines a problem.

camps to break the power of the rebel guerrillas, the American papers began calling him "Butcher" Weyler.

Outrage and apology. President McKinley, who took office in 1897 (page 397), pushed Spain to settle the Cuban problem. After a long delay, the Spanish government gave in on a few important points. It agreed to recall General Weyler, to give Cuba some self-government, and to reform the concentration camps. All this satisfied no one. The rebels would accept nothing less than full independence; the loyalists feared that any amount of self-government would be a threat to their property. On top of this, the Spanish soldiers in Cuba felt betrayed because the government in Spain was giving in to the rebels.

Then two events a few days apart put the Cuban problem on a completely new footing. In February, 1898, a letter from the Spanish minister in Washington was somehow stolen from the Havana post office and printed in Hearst's New York *Journal*. In his letter the minister, Dupuy de Lôme, called President McKinley a cheap politician who would stoop to anything to remain popular. Public opinion in the United States was outraged; the Spanish government immmediately apologized and fired its minister.

"Remember the *Maine!*" But the fuss over de Lôme's letter was soon drowned out by the roar of an explosion in Havana Harbor. The battleship *Maine* had anchored there to "protect American lives and property." On the night of February 15 the *Maine* blew up with the loss of 260 lives. No explanation was found for the disaster, but that made no difference to sensational newspapers in the United States. They blamed the explosion on the Spanish government and demanded war, calling upon the nation to "Remember the *Maine!*"

It would be hard to think of anyone with more to lose from blowing up the *Maine* than the Spanish government, but McKinley could hold out no longer against the war fever. He asked Congress for the right to use military force in Cuba, and on April 20, 1898, he got it.

What advantages did the United States have in fighting Spain in the Caribbean?

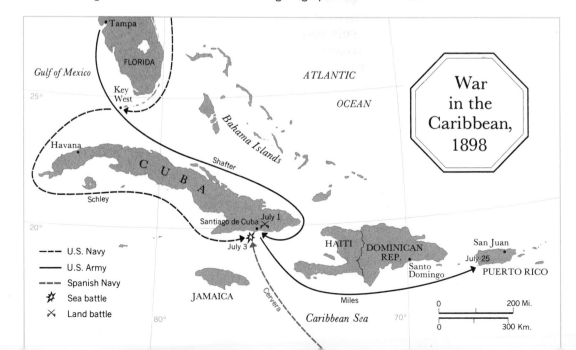

There is strong evidence that an internal explosion sank the *Maine*.

Secretary of State John Hay called the clash that followed "a splendid little war." From the United States viewpoint, it certainly was. Actual fighting lasted only fifteen weeks and ended in complete defeat for Spain. The treaty of peace, signed in December, gave Cuba its freedom and ceded Puerto Rico, Guam, and the Philippines to the United States. The United States paid Spain twenty million dollars for the Philippines.

The splendid little war. In the spring and summer of 1898, the United States had won a series of smashing victories. The very day war was declared, the Asiatic Squadron under Commodore George Dewey sailed to the Philippines (map on page 442). In Manila Bay, Dewey attacked the Spanish fleet, blowing it out of the water without the loss of a single American life. Filipino guerrillas who, like those in Cuba, had been struggling for independence, immediately took heart.

Half a world away another Spanish fleet, under Admiral Cervera (sur-VAY-ruh), slipped into the harbor at Santiago on Cuba's south coast (map on page 432). There shore guns protected the Spanish fleet from a United States squadron that had hunted it down.

Black troops of the 24th and 25th United States Infantry Regiments and the Rough Riders in Cuba.

It now became the job of the United States Army to land at Santiago, capture the shore forts, and force Cervera to surrender. In June 17,000 men under General William Shafter went ashore without opposition and began their march on Santiago. Among them was the First U.S. Volunteer Cavalry, the "Rough Riders," with its lieutenant colonel, Theodore Roosevelt.

A single day of fighting was enough to capture the forts at San Juan Hill (San-HWAHN) and El Caney (el KAY-nee). Except at San Juan Hill, the Spanish were too discouraged to resist.

The American land victory left Admiral Cervera in a very bad position. But he had been ordered not to surrender, so he determined to fight his way out of the harbor. It was a brave choice but not a wise one. The United States had spent a great deal of money modernizing its navy (page 429). Spain had not. At Santiago superior firepower and better-trained gun crews overwhelmed the Spaniards, just as they had at Manila.

In a four-hour running battle along Cuba's south coast, on July 3, Admiral Schley sank or drove aground all six of Cervera's ships. Only one American was killed and one wounded.

Deadly disease. Two weeks later, all Spanish forces in Cuba surrendered. Then, on July 25, Puerto Rico fell after slight resistance. The United States had won complete control of the Caribbean at a cost of fewer than 400 deaths in battle.

But ten times as many troops were killed by yellow fever and dysentery as by Spanish guns. Unlike the Navy, the United States Army had been very badly prepared for the war. It lacked the medical supplies, training, and even the uniforms needed to fight in the tropics.

A longer and dirtier war. Meanwhile, at Manila, Commodore Dewey had been waiting for land troops that could take the city. In July they arrived, and in mid-August 10,000 Americans, supported by a force of Filipino guerrillas, landed and seized the capital of the Philippines.

Trouble broke out almost at once. Emilio Aguinaldo (ahg-ee-NAHL-doh), the Filipino leader, believed the Americans had promised his people independence. The United States commander denied this. When Spain signed the Treaty of Paris, giving most of what was left of her empire to the United States, the Philippines were part of the package. Aguinaldo cried that he had been betrayed, and in May 1899 again raised the flag of revolt. This time it was not against the Spaniards but against the American liberators.

The people of the United States thought their forces had been fighting a splendid little war to free the Cubans. Quite unexpectedly, they found their army bogged down in a longer and dirtier war to conquer the Filipinos.

The road to empire. In the two years of bitter fighting that followed, 400 Americans and over 200,000 Filipinos lost their lives. Sixty thousand United States troops seemed unable to control more than the cities. The countryside belonged to Aguinaldo's forces and their supporters. As usually happens in guerrilla warfare, both sides committed atrocities. Each one led to a savage response. Men, women, and children were slaughtered, and soon the United States was operating concentration camps like those of "Butcher" Weyler.

Slowly the army beat down resistance. It shot one prisoner for every American killed, executed any Filipino thought to be helping the guerrillas, destroyed homes and crops. Finally, Aguinaldo was captured in March 1901. The Philippine Insurrection ended the next year.

"The white man's burden." Back home some Americans were bewildered by the takeover of these distant islands. It seemed to be against everything the United States had stood for. Others, however, were more than willing to follow the English imperialist style described by poet Rudyard Kipling and "take up the white man's burden" of ruling over "lesser breeds."

Theodore Roosevelt, the hero of San Juan Hill, told the American people that they must accept the burden. The Filipinos, he said, were not ready for self-government. In 1900 Roosevelt ran for Vice President with McKinley, on a Republican ticket supporting imperialism. Against them was William Jennings Bryan, who gambled on the country's turning its back on the overseas adventurers. But Bryan was beaten by a bigger margin than in 1896 (page 397).

Even the arguments of those against imperialism sounded racist. They talked of the Filipinos as "our little brown brothers." The liberal Republican—and immigrant—Carl Schurz proclaimed, "As first-class citizens with full civil rights Filipinos

435

and Puerto Ricans would corrupt the whole American system." Soon, he said, people could stop worrying about "a few thousand immigrants from Italy, Russia, and Hungary." We would be faced instead with "Malays and other unspeakable Asiatics." Similarly, the labor leader Samuel Gompers—also an immigrant—asked, "If the Philippines are annexed, what is to prevent the Chinese, Negritos, and Malays from coming to our country?"

A few anti-imperialists would ask if a people who had taken advantage of the black, almost wiped out the Indian, and conquered the Filipino could believe they were qualified to rule over other people. George F. Hoar, a grumpy old Republican senator from Massachusetts, had this contradiction in mind when he declared, "The Indian problem is not chiefly how to teach the Indian to be less savage in his treatment of the [white], but the [white] to be less savage in his treatment of the Indian." He also maintained, "The Negro question will be settled when the education of the white man is complete."

 TRY THIS!

1. Compare the performances of the U.S. Army and the U.S. Navy in the Spanish-American War. **2.** Tell why the guerrilla fighting in the Philippines was *not* a "splendid little war." **3.** Write on U.S. policy in the Philippines as it might have been described by Roosevelt or one of these men: Samuel Gompers, George Hoar.

Aboard the flagship *Olympia* in 1899, Roosevelt greeted Dewey, the hero of the Battle of Manilla Bay. The telegram below had been sent before the war with Spain began.

February 25, 1898.

Dewey, Hong Kong .

~~Secret and Confidential~~

Order the Squadron except Monocacy to Hong Kong. Keep full of coal. In the event of declaration war Spain, your duty will be to see that the Spanish squadron does not leave the Asiatic coast and then offensive operations in Philippine Islands. Keep Olympia until further orders.

Roosevelt

3. ROOSEVELT WIELDS A BIG STICK

During the Progressive Era the United States took on a new role in the world. Throughout most of the 1800s, its interests and energies had been taken up with filling the continent. Yet, as we have seen, in the late 1800s it thrust out to Alaska, Hawaii, and beyond.

The big stick. It was Theodore Roosevelt, as Assistant Secretary of the Navy, who gave the order sending Dewey's Asiatic Squadron to the Philippines. Then as President he set the nation's policy for dealing with all of the island territories taken from Spain. He also placed the United States on a new course by making it one of the great powers.

Roosevelt's most dramatic moves were made in Latin American affairs. There he openly behaved like an imperialist. Elsewhere his policies were more cautious, and his goals appeared to be peace through international order and military strength. He summed up this part of his policy with the old saying "Speak softly and carry a big stick."

Troops to Cuba. Cuba was the first Latin American country to feel TR's heavy hand. An amendment to the declaration of war with Spain (the Teller Amendment) had guaranteed Cuba's independence. Imperialists were not happy with such a re-

---

Read here of how

The nation faced imperialist problems.
It gave the Monroe Doctrine a new twist.
And built a canal through Panama.

---

striction, so in 1901 they passed the Platt Amendment. This measure, attached to an army appropriation bill and accepted by President McKinley, made Cuba practically a United States protectorate. It forbade the Cuban government to take any foreign loans without the permission of the United States. It gave the United States the right to interfere in Cuban affairs at any time to restore law and order. And it required Cuba to lease land to the United States for naval bases.

The United States had cleared Cuba of yellow fever and had built roads, railroads, schools, and hospitals there. However, the Platt Amendment wiped out much of the good will inspired by these actions.

The Platt Amendment had been a policy of the McKinley Administration, but Roosevelt was willing to use it. In 1906 he sent troops to the island following some trouble over an election.

"Does the Constitution follow the flag?" An important issue between McKinley and Bryan in the election of 1900 had been a legal one. Were the people of Puerto Rico, the Philippines, and the other new territories taken from Spain, American citizens or not?

And what about tariffs? The Constitution said there could be no duties on goods moving from one part of the United States to another. If Puerto Rico was now part of the United States, couldn't sugar be shipped from there to the mainland without tariffs? The argument was summed up in the question "Does the Constitution follow the flag?"

During the election campaign of 1900 (page 400), the imperialists McKinley and

Roosevelt claimed that the Constitution did *not* follow the flag, that Congress could make whatever rules it wished for the new possessions. Bryan and those who opposed imperialism took the opposite view, that there could be only one Constitution for the United States and all its possessions.

Congress agreed with McKinley and Roosevelt. Even before the election it passed the Foraker Act, making Puerto Ricans citizens of the island but not of the United States. (Puerto Ricans became United States citizens in 1917.) The Foraker Act also put a tariff on Puerto Rican sugar. In the election of 1900 the voters seemed to side with Congress, since they chose McKinley and Roosevelt by a wide margin.

In time, the Supreme Court also took the imperialist view. During the next few years it decided a series of disputes called the Insular (Island) Cases. The conclusion of these court actions was that Puerto Rico and the other new territories were not fully part of the United States. It was up to Congress, the Court said, to decide what kind of citizenship their people had or what rights they were entitled to. Congress could also levy tariffs on them if it wished.

The Court's willingness to go along with the imperialists on all these matters led one observer to say, "Whether the Constitution follows the flag or not, the Supreme Court follows the election returns."

International police power. Events in Venezuela and the Dominican Republic led TR to lay down a new policy for Latin America. Actually, he was following the lead of Richard Olney, Cleveland's Secretary of State. In 1905 Olney had said, "Today the United States is practically sovereign on [the South American] continent." Whenever it chose to speak, he went on, its word was law.

In 1902 Italy, Britain, and Germany blockaded Venezuela's coast and bombarded her ports. Venezuela had refused to pay debts owed to these countries, and the naval action was intended to force it to do so. By threatening to send the United States warships to Venezuela, Roosevelt forced both sides to accept arbitration. The dispute was settled by the international court—the Hague Tribunal— that met in Holland in 1904.

A little later the Dominican Republic had a similar experience. It too refused to pay its foreign debts and was threatened with intervention. In 1905 the Dominican government allowed the United States to take over its customhouses and collect all duties until the debt was paid.

The two incidents led TR in December 1904 to propose the Roosevelt Corollary to the Monroe Doctrine (page 168). "Chronic wrongdoing" by Latin American republics, he said, might invite European nations to interfere in the Western Hemisphere. Therefore the Monroe Doctrine would force the United States, "however reluctantly," to exercise "an international police power." In other words, the United States could take action to prevent an international incident from taking place.

A shift in power. In the 1800s the United States had often lacked the ability to uphold the Monroe Doctrine. Most of its enforcement had been supplied by the British. For reasons of trade, they too wanted the Latin American countries to remain independent of Europe. But the rise of Germany as a world power caused

Giant steam shovels were used to dig the Panama Canal.

Britain to withdraw some of its naval strength from the Caribbean. Equipped with the Roosevelt Corollary and a naval base in Cuba, the United States was stepping into Britain's place as keeper of the peace in that part of the world.

The British government was also willing to set aside the Clayton-Bulwer Treaty of 1850. Under that agreement, Great Britain and the United States had promised that neither would build a canal across Central America without the cooperation of the other. The Hay-Pauncefote Treaties of 1900 and 1901 gave the United States a free hand to build and fortify an Atlantic-Pacific Canal.

A spontaneous revolution? The Isthmus of Panama was chosen as the best site for the canal. A French company had tried to build one there but had gone bankrupt. The company was now willing to sell its rights and machinery for 40 million dollars. This looked like a bargain.

Of course it was also necessary to obtain the permission of Colombia, of which Panama was a part. In 1903 the United States arranged the Hay-Herran Treaty with Colombia. Under it that country was to receive ten million dollars for the land on which the canal would be built, plus 250,000 dollars a year as rent. But the Colombian Senate refused to ratify the treaty. It wanted at least 25 million as the first payment. TR was furious. But a representative of the bankrupt French canal company, Philippe Bunau-Varilla, was on hand. This fast-moving operator soon took over.

On November 3, 1903, there was a "spontaneous" revolution against the Colombian government in Panama City. The uprising was greatly helped by the United States cruiser *Nashville,* which arrived just in time to prevent Colombian troops from putting down the revolt. Within three days the United States recognized the new Republic of Panama. A week later it negotiated a treaty with the Panamanian minister—none other than Señor Bunau-Varilla! The Hay-Bunau-Varilla Treaty gave the United States, forever, a ten-mile-wide zone. Payment to Panama was to be the same sum that Colombia had turned down.

An engineering marvel. Work on the canal got off to a slow start due to yellow fever and various engineering problems. But army medics all but wiped out yellow fever in Panama. Meanwhile, Colonel George W. Goethals of the Army Corps of Engineers resolved the engineering problems, and under his direction work began in 1907.

Across the Isthmus of Panama, a canal with a series of locks was cheaper and easier to build than a sea-level canal. For seven years men toiled in the jungle, using dynamite to blast rock and steam shovels and trains to move dirt.

The canal was finished at a cost of almost 380 million dollars and opened to traffic August 15, 1914. In its day it was rightly regarded as an engineering marvel. It carried ships over fifty miles from Cristobal on the Atlantic side of Panama to Balboa on the Pacific.

 TRY THIS!

1. Explain the difference between the Teller Amendment and the Platt Amendment.
2. Explain how the United States was taking over Britain's role in the Caribbean.   3. Give some reasons why the United States has not been popular in Latin America.

4.   POWER POLITICS IN THE FAR EAST

Owning the Philippine Islands made the United States one of the nations with an interest in Asia. But in the Far East its opponents were not small Latin American nations. They were the empires of Britain, France, Germany, Russia, and fast-rising Japan. Among them the big stick was not nearly as fearsome as in the Caribbean.

A showcase for imperialism. By the time TR became President, fighting in the Philippines was almost finished. He was able to end military government there and appoint William Howard Taft head of a civilian Philippine Commission. This was in line with the Philippine Government Act of 1902 making the islands an unorganized territory. It declared the Filipinos citizens of the islands, but not of the United States.

Taft's on-the-spot administration was a showcase for imperialism. Filipinos were brought into the civil service as quickly as possible. At the same time, the territorial legislature came under complete Filipino control. It was hoped that in time the islands would be Americanized but also entirely independent. In 1921, after only twenty years of United States rule, President Wilson urged self-government for the Philippines. They did not achieve it, however, until after World War II.

Read here of how

The U.S. became involved in Asia.
It tried to help China.
And settled a war for Japan and Russia.
But made few friends in the Far East.

Afraid to quarrel. In 1895 the modernized armed forces of Japan had overwhelmed China. Japan's victory touched off a scramble by European colonizers for pieces of the ancient Chinese empire. If the Europeans had succeeded in their designs, the United States would have lost its freedom to trade with China's ports and interior cities. In 1899 the American Secretary of State John Hay proposed an "Open Door" policy, which the major European and Asiatic powers accepted.

The Open Door Policy was aimed at the European *spheres of influence* in China. A sphere of influence was a province or section of some country where one or another imperialist government had special privileges. The United States (and Britain too) wanted to be sure that the European imperialists and Japan did not stop other countries from doing business within the imperialists' spheres of influence. American trade with China was small, but the hope for the future was very great.

Britain, Germany, France, Japan, and Russia accepted the United States proposal, but not because they feared United States strength in Asia. At that time there was almost none. Probably the great powers drew back because they were afraid of what might happen if they quarreled seriously among themselves. They did quarrel in Europe a few years later. The horror of World War I was the result of their failure to reach an agreement.

A reasonable settlement. From the beginning the Philippines were a source of worry to the United States. They lay right in the path of the world's newly imperialist nation, Japan. When war broke out in   441

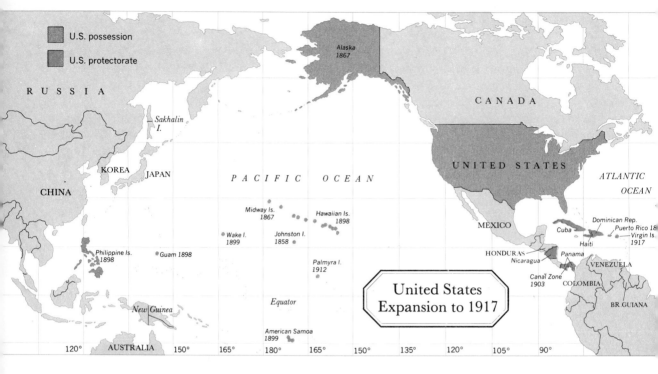

Of what value to the United States were the island possessions in the Pacific?

1904 between the Japanese and the Russians, it was of special concern to the United States. If either side in the war overwhelmed the other, the victor could threaten the Philippines.

To the surprise of everyone little Japan won a series of quick victories over the ill-supplied, poorly led forces of giant Russia. "Backward" Asians supposedly could not defeat great European industrial nations. Yet the Japanese sank a good part of the Russian navy in the straits between Japan and Korea. However, the effort drained Japan's strength. The Asian nation asked President Roosevelt to help settle the conflict with Russia.

The peace conference met in August 1905 at the Navy Yard in Portsmouth, New Hampshire. The Treaty of Ports-

mouth was the first, between any world powers, in which an American President played a part. Under it, the Japanese got one half of Sakhalin Island off the coast of Asia, a sphere of influence in Korea, and some of Russia's rights in China. Japan wanted a cash payment too, but TR blocked that. By doing so, he did not make himself very popular with the Japanese people. All things considered, the settlement was a reasonable one. Russia's ambition was checked by its losses. Yet Japan was not made strong enough to upset the balance in Asia.

A secret meeting. That same summer of 1905, William Howard Taft, now Secretary of War, met secretly in the Philippines with the Japanese Minister Taro Katsura. The two men worked out an agreement by

442

which Japan promised not to interfere in the Philippines, and the United States recognized that Japan had special interests in Korea. Since Korea had long been attached to China, the agreement was clearly against the Open Door Policy.

But TR realized that the Open Door was mostly bluff. Privately he told his good friend Senator Henry Cabot Lodge of Massachusetts that the policy completely disappeared "as soon as any powerful nation determined to disregard it. . . ."

A Gentlemen's Agreement. Besides the Treaty of Portsmouth, Japan had another reason for being upset with the United States. Since the 1890s, America's West Coast had been attracting Japanese laborers. Whites in California became alarmed, as they had been a generation earlier by Chinese immigrants. Then, following the San Francisco earthquake of 1906, the city school board set up a separate, segregated school for Oriental children. Of course, this was a local matter over which the federal government had no control. But public opinion in Japan was outraged, and the Japanese government soon let Washington know it.

President Roosevelt moved into the muddle with his usual vigor. First, he persuaded the San Francisco school board to withdraw its plan to segregate Oriental children. Second, he got the Japanese government to promise that it would no longer allow its people to emigrate to the United States as laborers. Since nothing was formally signed by the two governments, the arrangement was called the "Gentlemen's Agreement."

For a time the crisis was eased. The following year a "great white fleet" of American warships made a round-the-world cruise. On arriving in Japan, the fleet was greeted with friendly enthusiasm. Such a display of America's might was typical Theodore Roosevelt showmanship. He wanted others to accept the United States as a leader among the nations of the world.

"When we shake hands, we shake the world." United States interests in Europe were not as pressing as those in Asia. Nevertheless, TR made important diplomatic moves there too. In 1905 a crisis rose between France and Germany over Morocco. Germany's ruler, Kaiser Wilhelm II, called for an international conference at Algeciras (al-juh-SEE-ras), a Spanish town on the Strait of Gibraltar. The Kaiser asked the American President to persuade the French to attend. Because a general European war would be dangerous for the United States, Roosevelt agreed. United States representatives also helped to work out a solution and convinced the Germans to accept it. The United States role was not a large one, but it was a change for the United States to concern itself with strictly European affairs.

A few years later, when TR finished his term of office, he went on a grand tour of Europe (page 414). While he was visiting Germany, the ex-President and the Kaiser were photographed on horseback at a military review. Across one of the prints Wilhelm scrawled, "Roosevelt, when we shake hands, we shake the world." He may have been right.

 TRY THIS!

Explain why the United States behaved differently in all of these circumstances: **1.** In the Caribbean and the Far East.   **2.** Towards China and Japan.   **3.** With Europe and with Latin America.

5. DOLLAR DIPLOMACY IN THE AMERICAS

In the early 1900s the term *Dollar Diplomacy* was supposed to stand for peaceful support of trade and encouragement of American businessmen overseas. The Taft Administration used it in that sense to describe the policy it was following throughout the world. However, in Latin America, Dollar Diplomacy occasionally amounted to something quite dangerous. There, the United States sometimes backed dictators and other national leaders, even when they were opposed by their own people.

Trouble in the Caribbean. We have seen that in Theodore Roosevelt's time some Latin American governments got into debt to European bankers. When these governments failed to meet the payments on their loans, European nations had an excuse for sending warships and threatening to use force to collect. This had happened in Venezuela and the Dominican Republic (page 438). In Taft's time Haiti and Honduras had to be bailed out by loans from United States bankers. Taft arranged these loans to limit the influence of European nations in the Caribbean.

In 1911 it was Nicaragua's turn. The United States was especially concerned about Nicaragua because it offered a possible route for a second canal across Central America. Taft tried to straighten out Nicaragua's finances with American loans, but the Nicaraguans rebelled against the government that accepted Taft's plan.

The American President responded by sending in the Marines. This was supposedly for the protection of United States life and property, but actually it was to put down the rebellion. Marines remained in Nicaragua until 1933. Others, sent to Haiti for a similar reason, were not withdrawn

Mexican artists supported the revolution. They adopted Aztec styles and forms and painted murals on public buildings and factories. Diego Rivera's *Impassioned Documentary* presents the issues and leaders of the revolution.

Read here of how

Taft and Wilson had problems with Latin American countries.
Taft used the Marines.
Wilson tried diplomacy as well.
But neither method helped the U.S.

until 1928, when President Herbert Hoover brought them home.

Bad luck. Taft's record in foreign affairs was not good. He seemed to have nothing but bad luck. He tried to make up for the Payne-Aldrich Tariff disaster (page 415) by a trade treaty with Canada. Under it the United States was to admit certain Canadian farm products without duties. For its part, the Canadian government would allow some United States manufactures to enter Canada free of tariffs. This kind of arrangement is called *reciprocity* (ress-uh-PROSS-uh-tee). Today the United States has a number of such treaties with other nations.

There was opposition to the 1911 Canadian Reciprocity Treaty in the United States, especially among midwestern farmers, but that wasn't what caused it to fail. General elections in Canada threw the Liberal Party out of office and brought in the Conservatives. The Conservatives did not believe in free trade. So the Canadian government rejected the Reciprocity Treaty. Canadians felt they had acted wisely in not tying their country more closely to the giant south of the border.

A mission of democracy? The followers of President Woodrow Wilson claimed that his foreign policy was very different from that of Roosevelt and Taft. The facts do

445

Pancho Villa (second from the right) rose to command because of ability to handle men and supplies.

not bear this out. Wilson spoke against Dollar Diplomacy, yet from time to time made use of it. For instance, he called the United States role in the world "the mission of democracy," but in his hands it sometimes looked very much like Theodore Roosevelt's big stick.

For one thing, Wilson continued the military occupation of Nicaragua. He also moved naval forces onto the island of Santo Domingo to prevent revolutions in Haiti (1915) and the Dominican Republic (1916). In effect, he made all three countries military protectorates of the United States.

A new diplomacy. In one way the Wilson Administration added something new to United States foreign policy. For years there had been just two reasons for *recognizing* (having diplomatic dealings with) another country. One was that a government really controlled the country it claimed to head; the other was that it appeared willing to carry out its obligations to other countries. No one thought that sending or

not sending ambassadors meant approval or disapproval of a government.

Nevertheless, by withholding recognition of the Mexican government, Woodrow Wilson tried to influence events in that country. This approach only made him disliked and resented by Mexicans of all parties.

A Mexican refusal. The Mexican problem arose in this way: Porfirio Díaz was dictator of Mexico for thirty years. In 1910 his government was overthrown by Francisco Madero, who promised a sweeping political and social revolution. President Taft recognized the Madero government in the usual way. Just before Wilson's 1913 inauguration, Madero was murdered and Victoriano Huerta (HWAYR-tah) took control.

To everyone's surprise Wilson announced he would withhold recognition of Huerta's government until it behaved in a manner that he found acceptable. When yet another rebel, Venustiano Carranza, rose in the north, Wilson offered to support

446

him in place of Huerta. Carranza turned down the offer.

Matters were at a standstill the following year, 1914. Then the United States warship *Dolphin* put a small boat ashore at Tampico, Mexico, for supplies. An over-eager Mexican officer, a follower of Huerta, arrested the unarmed sailors. The Mexican commander at Tampico apologized at once for the officer's action, but Wilson decided to use the incident as an excuse for intervening in Mexico. Meanwhile, Admiral Mayo, the American naval commander on the scene, made several demands. Among them, he insisted that the Mexicans raise a United States flag on shore and give it a 21-gun salute. The Mexicans refused.

The next development was the American seizure of the Mexican port of Veracruz. This was to prevent a German cargo ship from landing munitions there. Naturally, the action united Mexicans against the United States as nothing else could have.

Border raids. In spite of these acts, Wilson did not want all-out war with Mexico. When Argentina, Brazil, and Chile (they were called the ABC powers) offered to help settle his dispute with Mexico, the American President accepted. However, the effort came to nothing. In August 1914, just as the First World War was getting under way in Europe, the revolutionary leader Carranza entered Mexico City in triumph. Wilson then withdrew the United States forces from Veracruz, and a year later he gave Carranza limited recognition as head of the Mexican government.

Meanwhile, there had been a serious falling out between Carranza and some of his military chiefs. One of these, Pancho Villa, kidnapped and then executed some American engineers Carranza had invited into Mexico. Villa followed up this outrage with a raid across the United States border into Columbus, New Mexico. This time nineteen more American citizens were killed. President Wilson reacted by ordering General John J. Pershing to enter Mexico and capture Pancho Villa.

Villa had deliberately provoked the United States because he wanted to make trouble between Wilson and Carranza. Now he retreated into the barren, mountainous country of northern Mexico. There he easily avoided capture, while leading Pershing farther and farther south.

A poor performance. By the summer of 1916 the United States and Mexico were at the point of going to war with one another. But by January 1917 the war in Europe and difficulties with Germany made it impossible for the United States to fight Mexico. Wilson agreed to withdraw Pershing's force and grant Carranza full recognition.

Wilson's action came much too late to keep the Mexican people from being resentful and suspicious of the United States. It was also a poor performance for a President who, the next year, would try to apply American standards and ideals to the rest of the world.

 TRY THIS!

1. Tell how Taft applied Dollar Diplomacy in Haiti and Nicaragua. 2. When Wilson reported the Tampico incident to Congress, he said he had backed the demand for a salute to the United States flag "to attract the attention of the whole population." How might a Mexican have answered this? 3. Describe the part played by the ABC countries in the United States dispute with Mexico.

ROUNDUP

Who?
> Alfred T. Mahan
> Liliuokalani
> George Dewey
> Emilio Aguinaldo
> Victoriano Huerta
> Pancho Villa

What?
> Imperialism
> *U.S.S. Maine*
> big stick
> Platt Amendment
> Insular Cases
> Roosevelt Corollary
> Open Door Policy
> "Gentlemen's
>   Agreement"

Where?
> Havana
> Philippines
> Manila
> Puerto Rico
> Panama
> Nicaragua
> Haiti
> Honduras

KNOW THIS

The Road to Imperialism

1. What were the first overseas possessions of the United States? How were they obtained?
2. How did Mahan influence the United States?
3. Why did whites who lived in Hawaii want the islands to be taken over by the United States?
4. How did Hawaii become part of the United States?

The Spanish-American War

1. In what sense was the United States conflict with Spain called a "splendid little war"?
2. How did the Philippine Islands become involved in the Spanish-American War?
3. Why did U.S. forces have to capture San Juan Hill?
4. How did most Americans seem to feel about taking over the Philippines? How do you know?
5. In what way did the public debate over the Philippines sound "racist"? Give some examples.

Roosevelt Wields a Big Stick

1. How was TR's policy in the Caribbean unlike the one he followed in other parts of the world?
2. What power did the United States hold over Cuba?
3. What two questions were settled by the Insular Cases?
4. List the steps the United States had to take before building the Panama Canal.
5. What problems delayed work on the Panama Canal?

Power Politics in the Far East

1. How was United States rule in the Philippines unlike the methods of other imperialist nations?
2. Why did Roosevelt see Japan as a threat to United States interests?
3. How did TR try to meet the Japanese problem?
4. In what way was the Open Door Policy a bluff?
5. How did the United States first become involved in Europe's affairs?

Dollar Diplomacy in the Americas

1. What are the two meanings of "Dollar Diplomacy"?
2. How was Canadian Reciprocity embarrassing to Taft?
3. How was Wilson's foreign policy like that of TR and Taft? How was it unlike theirs?
4. Trace President Wilson's dealings with Mexico.
5. What caused Wilson to give up his efforts in regard to Mexico? Why is his performance there called poor?

DIG HERE!

Look closely at United States relations with one of these areas of the world:

Hawaii
the Philippines
Cuba
Puerto Rico
Panama

For whichever one you choose, consider the following:

A. Briefly, what happened in the area from 1870 to the present?
B. What developments in the United States caused it to become involved with the area?
C. What benefits have the area and the United States exchanged?
D. What problems have the area and the United States created for one another?
E. What is the present status of the area, and how was this achieved?
F. What appear to be the present attitudes toward the United States in this area?
G. What are some possible future developments in the relations of the area with the United States?

To get the information you need, use recent encyclopedias, American histories, or similar books you find in the subject catalog of your school or local library.

THINK ABOUT IT

1. Why was the United States able to defeat Spain in fifteen weeks, while it took two years to subdue the Filipino rebels? Did the United States ever fight another war in the tropics against an enemy who used guerrilla tactics? Where? Was the outcome different? Can you explain this?
2. Should the United States withhold recognition of a country because it disapproves of that country's government? What has the United States expected to accomplish by this? Was anything gained by the twenty-year delay in recognizing the People's Republic of China? What was lost?

DO IT!

1. Make a time line of events in the history of Hawaii from 1887 to 1898. What differences would there be if Queen Liliuokalani or Sanford B. Dole commented on these events? Discuss.
2. Role-play a series of interviews conducted in 1916 with the foreign ministers of Colombia, the Dominican Republic, Venezuela, Haiti, Nicaragua, Cuba, and Mexico. Ask each "minister" to report on relations with the U.S. during the years since 1900.

THEN AND NOW

How important is the Panama Canal today for United States defense and trade? Should Panama have control of the canal? Why, or why not? Should the United States try to find a route for a second canal? Explain.

The United States and the First World War

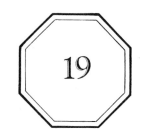

19

Foot soldiers suffered most in World War I. They lived—and died—in mud and dirt. Few believed their sacrifices had accomplished much. Twenty years later a second, bigger war broke out.

1. THE NATION ON THE ROAD TO WAR

June 28, 1914, was a day that changed the history of the world. In the town of Sarajevo, in what is now Yugoslavia (map on page 452), a nineteen-year-old high-school student assassinated the Archduke Franz Ferdinand and his wife. The Archduke was the heir to the throne of Austria-Hungary, and the student was a Serbian nationalist. Serbia was a small country on the Balkan peninsula of Europe.

The most terrible war. The Archduke hadn't been a popular figure. Even his uncle, the Emperor Franz Josef, didn't like him. But the leaders of Austria-Hungary saw in his murder an excuse for crushing the small country of Serbia.

For years the European powers had been building rival systems of defense treaties and alliances. By early August 1914, Austria-Hungary and Germany (the Central Powers) were lined up against Britain, France, and Russia (the Allies). In the first days of the conflict, German armies roared through Belgium. "The most terrible of all wars," as Wilson would soon call it, had begun. Within two years almost every European country had joined one side or the other (map on page 452).

450

Impartial in thought and action. As soon as the fighting began, President Woodrow Wilson took firm control of United States foreign policy. At once he proclaimed the country's neutrality and determination to stay out of the war. This course had the near-total backing of the American people. Wilson instructed them to be "impartial in thought as well as in action." He even requested that moviegoers not cheer newsreel battle scenes.

Being neutral in thought was easier said than done. One third of the nation's 92 million residents were either foreign-born or the children of European immigrants. Ties to the Old World ran deep.

But sympathy for the Allies outweighed the opposition. A majority of Americans traced their ancestry to Great Britain. There were close economic and cultural ties between the two nations. France, too, had many friends in the United States, and the war reawakened the memory of French aid during the American Revolution.

In addition, the Allies conducted a skillful propaganda campaign painting a gruesome picture of the German war machine. Some of their tales of German atrocities were real and some were invented. Supposedly, German soldiers had destroyed the countryside, bayoneted babies, and murdered innocent civilians.

Read here of how

A vast and terrible war began in Europe.
For a time, Wilson kept the peace.
And won a second term.
Then Germany tried a desperate gamble.

TIME CHART

1914	World War I begins.
1915	The *Lusitania* is sunk.
1916	Germany makes its *Sussex* pledge.
1916	Wilson is re-elected.
1917	Germany resumes unrestricted submarine warfare.
1917	The Zimmermann telegram is revealed.
1917	The United States declares war.
1918	The AEF goes into battle.
1918	The Armistice is signed.
1919	The Paris Conference meets.
1920	The Senate rejects the Versailles Treaty for the last time.
1921	The Washington Armament Conference meets.
1928	The Kellogg-Briand Pact is signed.
1928	The United States announces the end of the Roosevelt Corollary.

A booming trade. The Wilson Administration faced other, more important, obstacles to a policy of strict neutrality. It was accepted practice for private businesses in neutral nations to sell war materials to countries at war. In 1914 the United States was struggling through a recession. Business welcomed orders for war supplies.

But almost all of the war production flowed to the Allies. Early in the conflict, the British navy blockaded German ports and prevented most neutral ships from entering. Trade with the Allies soared from 824 million dollars in 1914 to over 3 billion in 1916. During the same period, trade

451

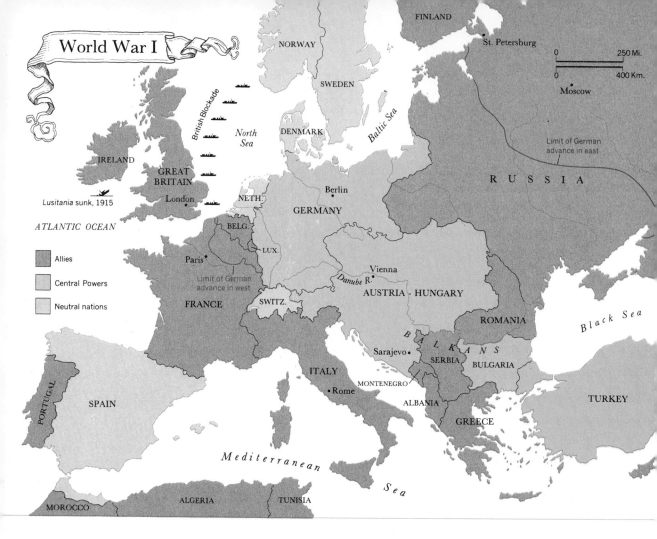

World War I

NORWAY

FINLAND

SWEDEN

St. Petersburg

Moscow

0 — 250 Mi.

0 — 400 Km.

Limit of German advance in east

R U S S I A

British Blockade

North Sea

DENMARK

Baltic Sea

IRELAND

GREAT BRITAIN

Berlin

Lusitania sunk, 1915

London

NETH.

GERMANY

BELG.

LUX.

Paris

Limit of German advance in west

Vienna

Danube R.

AUSTRIA - HUNGARY

ATLANTIC OCEAN

Allies

Central Powers

Neutral nations

FRANCE

SWITZ.

ROMANIA

Black Sea

B A L K A N S

Sarajevo

SERBIA

ITALY

BULGARIA

Rome

MONTENEGRO

PORTUGAL

SPAIN

ALBANIA

TURKEY

GREECE

Mediterranean

Sea

MOROCCO

ALGERIA

TUNISIA

In an effort to defeat France before Russia could mobilize, German armies crossed Belgium.

with the Central Powers declined from 169 million dollars to just over one million.

"Unneutral" loans. Britain and France soon ran out of money. Only loans to the Allies would permit the trade to continue. Wilson's Secretary of State, William Jennings Bryan, protested that loans and credits violated "the true spirit of neutrality."

For a short time Wilson sided with Bryan. But beginning in the fall of 1914, the President allowed United States banks to lend money to warring nations. By 1917,

loans to the Allies had reached 2.25 billion dollars. This dwarfed the amount loaned to Germany—only 27 million dollars. Under international law there was nothing illegal about these loans. They were "unneutral," however, in that the Allies were favored far more often than the Central Powers.

The one-sided blockade. Naturally, the German government was upset by the steady flow of war supplies to Britain and France. In August 1914 the Allies had stopped the German invasion of France.

452

The opposing armies then dug in along a line that stretched from the English Channel to the Swiss border (map on page 452). Hope for a quick victory faded as neither side was able to break the other's line. Instead, each tried to wear the other down. In a struggle of that kind, the best supplied force is sure to win out.

On February 4, 1915, the German government attempted a naval blockade of the British Isles. All Allied ships would be targeted for destruction. The German authorities claimed that the British often tried to disguise their ships by flying the flags of neutral countries. Consequently, the German navy would also consider neutral vessels fair game. President Wilson replied that Germany would be held "strictly accountable" for any loss of United States life or property. It was clear from this message that Wilson intended to protect the rights of United States ships in the war zone.

Surprise the only advantage. To enforce its blockade, Germany was depending on a new weapon—the submarine. The German government proclaimed a policy of unrestricted submarine warfare. That is, Germany said it would torpedo, without warning, enemy merchant ships carrying war supplies to England. The British protested. Traditionally, a warship that sighted an enemy merchant ship would stop it, determine its identity, and provide safety for its passengers and crew. Only then would the shelling begin.

It was not possible for submarines to follow this procedure. The submarine (U-boat, the Germans called it) was a hit-and-run weapon. World War I submarines were small and frail and much slower than surface ships. If a U-boat surfaced to give warning, a faster merchant ship could ei-

 INNOCENTS ABROAD

In 1906 William Jennings Bryan went on a world tour. In Turkey a U.S. embassy official assured him that he would enjoy visiting the Balkans.

"What," asked the man who would be Secretary of State when World War I broke out, "are the Balkans?"

Writing years later, the United States minister to Belgium when the war began said, "I had never heard of Sarajevo. I had not the least idea where it was in this world, if it was in this world."

During August 1914, Secretary of State Bryan, the minister to Belgium, and all other Americans got a crash course in world geography and recent European history. They would never again be so innocent.

ther escape or ram and sink its attacker. Furthermore, many merchant ships were armed and had the firepower to blow a surfaced submarine out of the water.

The U-boat's only real advantage was surprise, and the Germans were prepared to make use of it. The effect of this decision came home to the United States in the spring of 1915. The giant British liner *Lusitania* was torpedoed and sunk off the coast of Ireland. Among the 1,198 passengers drowned, there were 128 Americans.

Stiff language. A storm of protest was unleashed in the United States. Former President Theodore Roosevelt exclaimed, "That's murder!" and urged action "for . . . our own national self-respect."

453

Wilson sent a series of stern messages to the German government. His notes condemned the sinking and demanded that Germany stop attacking unarmed merchant ships. Secretary of State Bryan thought the stiff language might push the country into war. He felt that instead, the President should forbid Americans to travel on ships of warring nations.

In Bryan's view the British had also been at fault. The Secretary believed that the *Lusitania* was secretly carrying arms, which would have made it a proper target for attack.

Bryan had a point: the *Lusitania* had been transporting ammunition. But Wilson decided not to take Bryan's advice and the Secretary resigned from the Cabinet. The President replaced him with Robert Lansing, who had once taken speech lessons in the hope of acquiring a British accent. With Wilson's personal adviser, Colonel Edward M. House, the new Secretary moved the President to a position more favorable to the Allies.

Too proud to fight. Most Americans did not want to go to war over the *Lusitania*; they did not wish to give up their neutral rights either. Wilson spoke for most of the nation when he insisted that the United States would remain at peace. America, the President said, had to set an example for the rest of the war-torn world. "There is such a thing as a man being too proud to fight," he declared.

As the months went by, there were other sinkings and stiffer protests. Finally, in August 1915, after torpedoing the *Arabic* with the loss of two American lives, Germany promised not to sink ships without warning, unless they tried to escape. The promise was kept for only a few months. In March 1916, without warning, a German

submarine in the English Channel sank the unarmed French passenger ship *Sussex*. Two Americans were badly wounded. This time the President's note threatened severe action. Unless Germany ended its unrestricted submarine warfare and lived up to its earlier promise, the United States would break off diplomatic relations. This was a serious step, one just short of war. In May

The warning notice at left appeared in New York newspapers the day the *Lusitania* sailed. On May 7, German Submarine 20 sent a torpedo through the ship's hull. The *Lusitania* went down in eigh-teen minutes. A German official later wrote: "The death of Americans might have been avoided if our warning had been heeded . . . anybody can commit suicide."

1916, the Germans gave in and issued the *Sussex* pledge which generally met Wilson's demands.

A narrow victory. The lull after the *Sussex* pledge did not ease the fears of many Americans. Theodore Roosevelt was concerned about American defenses. He called Wilson a "peace prattler" and "that infernal skunk in the White House."

Wilson got Roosevelt's message and backed military preparedness. The President realized that the Republicans had a good issue to use in the 1916 election. Over the opposition of Congress, he got the legislation he wanted. The regular army doubled in size to nearly 220,000. The National Guard of 400,000 became part of the federal defense establishment. And a huge naval appropriation authorized construction of 137 new ships.

Woodrow Wilson was optimistic about his chances for re-election in 1916. The Democrats' campaign slogan was "He kept us out of war!" Many progressives like Bryan disliked Wilson's strong notes to Germany and his preparedness legislation. But they lined up in the President's camp. Nevertheless, the Republican candidate, Charles Evans Hughes, proved a tough opponent. The party had patched up its 1912 split and was united behind Hughes. But Wilson profited by the desire for peace and squeezed through to a narrow victory in November.

A peace built on quicksand. Wilson rightly saw from his victory at the polls that the people of the United States wanted peace. In a speech before the United States Senate in January 1917, Wilson spoke to "the people of the countries now at war." He talked of building a lasting peace, a "peace without victory." It was to be based on the equality of nations, disarmament, the right of all peoples to live under governments of their own choosing, and freedom of the seas.

A new international organization, the President said, must be created to prevent future wars. But above all, peace terms must not be forced on defeated countries. Such a settlement would be made "as upon quicksand." He argued that only a peace between equals could last.

Wilson's words excited idealists throughout the world. But his was a voice in the wilderness. Even as he spoke, Germany was planning to strike again.

A calculated risk. On January 31, 1917, the German Ambassador in Washington handed Secretary of State Robert Lansing a message which announced the resumption the next day of "unlimited submarine warfare." Why did Germany set aside its *Sussex* pledge? The Germans knew they were risking the wrath of the United States. But they decided on an all-out naval offensive. By unleashing their fleet of 100 U-boats on all merchant ships carrying supplies to England, they hoped to starve out the enemy. The German military planners estimated that in six months Britain would be crushed.

Even after diplomatic relations were broken, Wilson hoped for peace. But on February 25 he received an explosive piece of information. The British had picked up a secret message sent to Mexico by the German Foreign Secretary. They passed it along to the United States. The Zimmermann telegram proposed a German-Mexican alliance. If the Mexicans would attack the United States, Germany would help Mexico regain territory lost in the Mexican war of the 1840s—parts of Texas, New Mexico, and Arizona.

A world safe for democracy. On March 18, German U-boats sank three American merchant ships. The loss of life was heavy. After several sleepless nights, the President decided that the United States would have to fight. His doubts about the Allied cause were eased when the tyrannical Russian government was overthrown by what seemed to be a democratic revolution. Now it was a clear case of good against evil, the democratic nations of the world against the militaristic Central Powers.

On the evening of April 2, 1917, President Wilson rode down rainswept Pennsylvania Avenue to the Capitol. There he asked Congress for a declaration of war. It would be the war, he said, to make the world "safe for democracy."

 TRY THIS!

1. Using the map on page 452, show why it was easier for Britain to blockade the Central Powers than for Germany to blockade the Allies. **2.** Compare United States efforts to defend its neutral rights in World War I with its experiences in the wars of Napoleon (pages 152–155). a) What earlier event was most like the sinking of the *Lusitania*? b) Could the United States have used an embargo in World War I? How might an embargo have affected the fighting? c) In each case, why did the United States finally go to war?

2.   THE HOME FRONT IN WARTIME

United States entry into World War I provided critical help to the struggling Allies. Germany's all-out submarine offensive in early 1917 sank 900,000 tons of Allied shipping in April alone. United States warships at once began patrolling the Western Atlantic. Furthermore, the United States Navy convinced the British that they should adopt the convoy system. Merchant ships now moved in fleets, protected by screens of anti-submarine destroyers. By December, shipping losses dropped to almost a third of the April figure. The Germans had lost their gamble to win the war in six months.

Radical measures. The United States also tried to throw its enormous industrial weight behind the Allies. American goods and money began flowing to Europe. Altogether, the United States spent 33.5 billion dollars to fight the war. About a third of this was in the form of loans to the Allies.

———

Read here of how

United States industry aided the Allies.
Blacks and women helped the war effort.
But were not given full equality.
And the government limited personal liberty.

———

Most of the Allied loans were spent in the United States for supplies.

With the loans a dramatic shift took place. Before World War I the United States had been a debtor nation. Much of the money for its mines, factories, and railroads had been borrowed from Europe. But with wartime loans, Europe owed more money to the United States than the U.S. owed Europe. The United States became the world's greatest financial power.

To mobilize industry for war, President Wilson took some bold steps. A War Industries Board was to distribute national resources, oversee military purchases, set prices, and step up production. A brilliant businessman-engineer, Herbert Hoover, headed the Food Administration, which exercised strong controls over United States agriculture. A Fuel Administration set standards for the production and use of coal, gas, and oil.

In the most extreme measure of all, the federal government took over the railroads. For the duration of the war they were run by the Railroad Administration.

Bigness encouraged. The powerful government agencies operated with the help and approval of big business. Price controls by the War Industries Board assured business sizable profits. And in some cases, anti-trust laws were set aside as the government

457

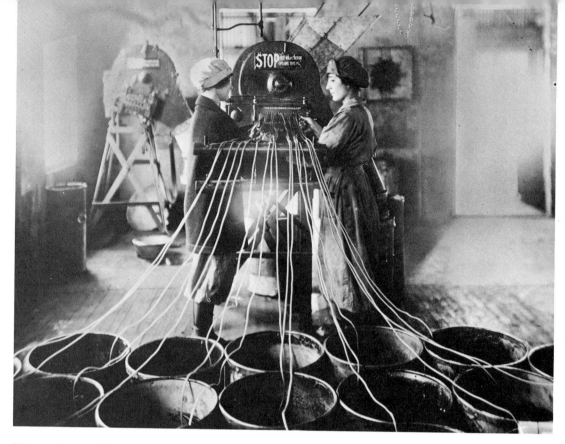

Women in a munitions plant. Twenty people worked in industry to supply one soldier in combat.

gave corporations the go-ahead to merge and expand. In fact, the government was encouraging bigness in business and agriculture.

Labor unions as well as business gained during the war. In exchange for a "no strike" pledge, unions got some long-sought goals—the right to organize and to bargain for their members, the eight-hour working day, decent wages, and equal pay for women workers. With the support of another agency, the War Labor Board, union membership doubled. By 1920, five million workers were union members. The new strength of unions and the booming wartime business caused wages to go up. Although inflation cut into pay envelopes, the real income of workers in 1918 was 20 per cent higher than it had been before the war.

New workers. The expansion of industry brought new job opportunities. However, the war in Europe had cut off immigration. And millions of young men had been drafted into the armed forces. To fill the gap, industry began recruiting women and blacks.

Women had made some progress during the Civil War. They hoped to do even better during World War I. Leadership opportunities and administrative duties, normally reserved for men, fell open to women, in the armed forces, the Red Cross, and the Liberty Bond drive. Jeannette Rankin, who had been active in neutrality efforts and woman suffrage organizations, became the first woman elected to Congress. She attracted nationwide attention when she voted against the declaration of war. But perhaps the most important development was that the women's role in the war effort built enough popular support to win ratification of the Nineteenth Amendment, which gave women the vote in 1920 (page 421).

As in the Civil War, women began to fill the jobs formerly closed to them. They worked in airplane factories and even put down railroad track. Yet to a great extent the gains were only temporary. In fact, by 1920 only 800,000 more women were at work than in 1910.

And many of the jobs women kept after the war were not the kind that paid well. For example, many became elevator operators and theater ushers. On the other hand, openings doubled and tripled in some occupations in which women had already gained a foothold before the war—library and social work, for example, and college teaching.

Population shifts. Many blacks had left the South before the war. They had hoped to escape discrimination and find worthwhile employment. The demand for labor during World War I speeded black migration northward. Between 1916 and 1920 an estimated 500,000 blacks moved North, settling in the big cities, close to the factories. Chicago's black population grew by 50,000 between 1916 and 1920; Detroit's, by 600 per cent from 1910 to 1920.

The black migration brought changes in race relations in the North. As blacks competed with whites for jobs and housing, racial tensions increased. Soon, the tensions exploded into ugly race riots. The bloodiest took place in East St. Louis, Illinois. There, one day in 1917, a rumor started that a black man had killed a white; and 3,000 whites stormed into the black community. The mob beat every black person in sight. White men set a group of rundown houses on fire and shot the black residents as they ran from the flames.

The National Guard was called in but it failed to restore order. Many of the guardsmen had no sympathy for the blacks. Some 6,000 terrified blacks were forced to flee the city. And when the sickening affair ended, no one was sure how many had been killed. A Congressional committee put the figure at 39; the NAACP estimated that it was between 100 and 200.

Black soldiers earned respect on the battlefield; at home they met prejudice and discrimination.

A stone wall of discrimination. Although the East St. Louis riot was the worst, it was by no means the only episode of violence. In all, 39 major race riots took place during World War I. Blacks coming North did find jobs and better pay. They did not escape prejudice and persecution.

Blacks served with distinction in the military. Eventually, 367,000 entered the armed forces, and by the war's end 100,000 were overseas. But a stone wall of discrimination ran through the military. The Marine Corps barred blacks entirely. The navy accepted them only as cooks and stewards.

At first the army refused to make blacks officers. Eventually, it dropped this rule, and in October 1917 over six hundred black captains and lieutenants were commissioned.

Still, blacks enthusiastically supported the war. An article in a black newspaper was entitled "Close Ranks." It appealed for united support of the war effort and argued that black patriotism would help to end segregation after the war. For all their exclusions from "white America," black citizens were ready to come to its defense in Wilson's war.

"Liberty cabbage." Popular backing for the war was a question which deeply concerned Wilson. Less than a week after war was declared, he set up the Committee on Public Information headed by George Creel. Creel's committee sponsored lectures, motion pictures, pamphlets, and posters with rousing, patriotic themes. Film stars and public figures staged rallies to encourage the public to buy *Liberty Bonds,* the chief means of financing the war. The Committee's campaign picked up the themes of the earlier Allied propaganda (page 451). The German enemy was portrayed as a savage beast ready to demolish civilization.

The Creel Committee did its job well—too well, in fact. A wave of intolerance swept the country. Those citizens not totally behind the war effort became the targets of "superpatriots." Individuals who did not buy Liberty Bonds were insulted and sometimes attacked. Some cities passed ordinances forbidding anyone to say anything bad about the United States. Many German-Americans were suspected of being disloyal to the cause or of being spies. Schools forbade the teaching of the German language. Sauerkraut was renamed "liberty cabbage," the dachshund became the "liberty pup," and hamburger was referred to as Salisbury steak.

The bounds ovestepped. Creel reported that Wilson had told him that freedom of speech in wartime was "insanity," and the move to silence dissent began. Under the Espionage Law of 1917 and the Sedition Law of 1918, people were jailed for criticizing the government, and many newspapers and magazines were banned from the mails.

The government, clearly, overstepped the bounds of common sense. Unfortunately, much of the damage could not be undone. Even after the war Americans sometimes hesitated before exercising their constitutional right to criticize government actions and policies.

 TRY THIS!

Compare the part played by each of these in World War I and the American Civil War: **1.** Industry (page 301). **2.** Naval power (page 305). **3.** Black Americans (pages 307–309). **4.** Women (pages 318–319).

3. WINNING THE WAR IN EUROPE

The war that United States troops were joining, in the spring of 1918, was unlike any fought before. It seemed like the worst war in human history.

Shell craters and barbed wire. In August 1914, the first month of fighting, the German drive had been stopped less than a hundred miles from Paris. German and Allied forces then struggled fiercely to outflank each other—that is, to get around the other side's lines. The huge numbers of soldiers on both sides prevented this.

To block one another's maneuvers, the armies stretched their lines east and west. Soon the lines extended hundreds of miles across northern France. The opposing forces hastily dug trenches, mounted machine guns, and paused to regroup. The arrangement turned into the Western Front. For four and a half years the fighting went on. The system of trenches grew more and more elaborate, with firing steps, dugouts, communications trenches, and machine-gun nests.

During those long years, the two armies faced each other across a no-man's-land of shell craters and barbed wire. Fighting

---

Read here of how

World War I brought a new kind of fighting.
The United States entered late.
But American forces fought well.
And they tipped the balance to the Allies.

Trench warfare gave World War I a special horror.

The contrast between the open skies and the muddy trenches gave aviation a romantic image.

consisted of offensives in which each side tried to push the other back, always hoping for the breakthrough that never came. Thousands of men died capturing or defending a few hundred yards of ground. In one terrible year—1916—a million lives were thrown away.

Rapid-firing machine guns were responsible for this deadlock. They gave each side an almost perfect defense against the other. Tanks and planes could have broken the deadlock, but they were not highly developed, and neither side had enough of

them. Poison gas might have worked. The Germans first used gas on a small scale, but gas masks, along with shifting winds, soon canceled it out as a weapon.

Poor planning. When the United States first entered the war, President Wilson had not expected to send a big army across the Atlantic. He hoped that the United States contribution would be mostly supplies and naval forces, and that no more than 500,000 soldiers would be needed.

But the condition of the Allies in 1918 changed Wilson's mind. Trench warfare had used up the manpower of Britain. Furthermore, events in Russia had helped the

FOUR MEN ON A HORSE

"Tanks" got their peculiar name for reasons of security. When they were first built, they were shipped through England to France. Soldiers guarding them were ordered to tell curious civilians that they were water tanks.

In a way, the armored tank brought the history of warfare full circle. In the early Middle Ages, the most effective fighters were knights in armor on armored war-horses. When knights charged, foot soldiers hadn't a chance.

But the infantry learned to cope. With the longbow, then with the crossbow, and finally with muskets and rifles, foot soldiers could stand up to the most ferocious cavalry charge. By the time of the American Civil War, horses were being used only for scouting or raiding—or to carry troops to the fighting. In World War I, infantry was supreme.

Tanks tipped the balance once more. Even a nest of machine guns couldn't stop them. In the opening battles of World War II, German tank units cut French and British infantry to pieces. In fact, you could think of a tank as three or four men, in a single suit of armor, propelled by an engine instead of a horse.

Germans. Late in 1917, six months after Czar Nicholas II was overthrown, Communists led by Nikolai Lenin seized power. At once they withdrew from the war and made peace with Germany. Therefore, German troops that had been battling the Russians could be sent to fight in France.

Because of poor prewar planning, it took a year for the United States to prepare an army for overseas combat. But the draft raised a force of nearly five million men. Between March and October 1918, 1.8 million United States soldiers arrived in France. This offset any German infantry advantage. By November 1918, Allied forces outnumbered the enemy by 600,000.

An American offensive. In the spring of 1918 the Germans began their last great offensive. Their drive featured a monster gun, "Big Bertha," the largest ever cast. It could hurl 260-pound shells into Paris from a distance of eighty miles. The newly arrived Americans went into battle to stop the German drive.

On May 28, 1918, the AEF (American Expeditionary Force) under General John J. Pershing won its first victory, at Cantigny (kahn-TEEN-yee). A few days later, Marines held off the Germans at Belleau Wood (map on page 464).

From mid-July to early August, in a battle on the Marne River, an army of

463

Western Front, 1918

Millions dead. American victories between the Meuse River and the Argonne Forest, coupled with French and British successes, totally demoralized German troops. Revolution had broken out in Berlin; civilians were starving; sailors mutinied. On November 3, Germany notified President Wilson that they would surrender. On November 11, 1918, an armistice was signed. The United States had tipped the scales in favor of the Allies.

The casualties of World War I staggered the world. In little more than four years, Britain lost 947,000 men; France, 1,400,000; Germany, 1,800,000; Russia, 1,700,000; Austria-Hungary, 1,200,000. Even the United States, entering late, saw 48,000 of its soldiers killed in action and 56,000 dead from disease.

What enabled the Allies to assume the offensive?

 TRY THIS!

85,000 United States troops helped to halt the German advance on Paris. As part of the counterdrive, 270,000 Americans fought in and around Chateau-Thierry (sha-TOE tee-AIR-ee). The first wholly American offensive took place in September at St. Mihiel (san mee-YEL). In 24 hours 550,000 soldiers of the AEF, with British air support, wiped out an advanced position long held by the Germans.

1. Trace the experiences of an American soldier who landed in France in April 1918 and was present at the Armistice on November 11. What battles could he have been in? What kind of fighting might he have seen? What could have been his thoughts about the United States' part in the war? **2.** Compare the fighting in the American Civil War with that in World War I. Trench warfare, for example, occurred only for short times in the Civil War. Why?

4. LOSING THE PEACE AT HOME

On January 8, 1918, President Wilson delivered one of the most important speeches of his life. Addressing Congress, the President outlined his ideas on the peace settlement that should follow the war. He spelled out a program along the lines of his earlier call for "peace without victory." The Fourteen Points the President set forth that day fired the imagination of the world.

An association of nations. The Fourteen Points included definite recommendations for changing the map of Europe.

464

They also listed some reforms Wilson said would prevent future wars. He called for an end to secret agreements among nations, for freedom of the seas, for a reduction in arms, for the right of nations to have the kind of governments they wanted, for the removal of barriers to trade among countries, and for adjustment of claims to colonial territories, with attention to the wishes of the colonists. Most important of all was the fourteenth point. Here Wilson advocated the establishment of a "general association of nations" to keep the peace. He was speaking of a League of Nations.

The Fourteen Points established Wilson as the most respected of world leaders—a man of noble ideals. The Fourteen Points were also a powerful weapon for ending the war. By holding them out to the German people as the basis for peace, Wilson encouraged a rebellion that led to the overthrow of the German emperor. All over Europe, people sick of war responded to the President's peace plan.

A minor contradiction. It was difficult to put the Fourteen Points into operation. Even the United States did not seem to live up to them. For instance, one point promised Russia "freedom to choose its own political future." However, when a civil war broke out between Communist and non-Communist forces in Russia (page 463), the President sent American troops there.

Read here of how

Wilson caught the world's imagination.
But could not win over Europe's leaders.
The President's enemies offered a deal.
When he rejected it, the League was lost.

Wilson claimed he was trying to keep Russian war supplies out of German hands. But on occasion United States troops took part in the fighting operations against the Communists. And the last Americans did not leave Russia until 1920, long after the German threat had passed.

Such a contradiction was a minor thing to Wilson—a detail that could be worked out later. Uppermost in the President's mind was getting the Fourteen Points written into the peace treaties officially ending the war.

Wilson attended the peace conference at Paris in January 1919. When the President and the American delegation arrived in Europe, shouting throngs tossed flowers in his path and hailed Wilson as the "Prince of Peace."

No peace among equals. At the conference the reception was colder. Wilson came face-to-face with the hardheaded leaders of Europe. Representing France was Premier Georges Clemenceau. Seventy-eight years old, the "Tiger," as he was called, came to the conference with one concern: he wished to make sure that Germany would never be able to wage war again. He insisted that the country be divided and that the Germans pay the Allies huge sums of money as *reparations* (payments for war damages and costs).

The British representative, Prime Minister David Lloyd George, also wanted to see Germany severely punished. Like Clemenceau, he insisted that the Germans pay for the war through reparations. He told the British people that Germany would be squeezed "until the pips squeak." Lloyd George was also doubtful about the Fourteen Points. In particular, he wanted no part of freedom of the seas. Such a rule might injure Great Britain, the world's greatest sea power.

Against such tough-minded men, Wilson's task was impossible. The Fourteen Points were not accepted. Instead, a compromise settlement was worked out. Wilson surrendered the "peace among equals" idea and permitted the Allies to punish the defeated enemy.

The Versailles (vair-SIGH) Treaty, which the Germans signed in May 1919, included a "war guilt" clause. It forced the Germans to accept total blame for starting the war. The treaty also required the Germans to pay for all the wartime damage to civilian property and for a host of indirect war costs. When finally added up, these reparation payments amounted to a staggering 33 billion dollars, far above what Germany could possibly pay. Furthermore, the treaty said nothing about freedom of the seas, disarmament, or the reduction of tariffs—all parts of the Fourteen Points.

A new organization. Wilson did score some victories. The map of Europe was redrawn. The new nations of Poland, Czechoslovakia, and Yugoslavia were carved out of the old empires. To a large degree, the creation of these countries fulfilled the promise to let people choose their own governments. The English statesman Winston Churchill calculated that under the boundary lines of 1919 only about 3 per cent of the European people lived in a country they would not have chosen as their own.

Wilson's greatest triumph was the establishment of the League of Nations. The charter of the League was written into the Treaty of Versailles. Any Allied nation that signed it became a member.

The League, Wilson believed, would settle all future international disputes through negotiation. The countries joining the League agreed to respect and preserve the independence of all members of the League. This pledge, in Article Ten of the charter, was the heart of the organization. The League would take action against a country that broke the peace. The League could ask member nations to provide peace-keeping military forces.

Wilson emphasized that no powerful country had to provide these forces and go to war against its will. But he firmly stated that members had a moral obligation to follow the decisions of the League.

Ties with the Old World. For the United States to become a League member, the Versailles Treaty had to win the approval of the Senate by a two-thirds vote (Article Two, Section 2, paragraph b of the Constitution). Not everyone in the Senate liked the idea of a League of Nations. A small group of senators opposed the Treaty and the League under any circumstances. They feared that the League would require permanent American involvement in Europe. All ties with the Old World, they said, should be avoided.

By themselves, the opposition did not have enough votes to block passage of the treaty. At least four fifths of the senators favored some sort of international organization. But a large part of this four fifths would not go along with the League of Nations as it stood in the Versailles Treaty.

The "strong reservationists," as they were called, had as their leader Senator Henry Cabot Lodge of Massachusetts. Lodge and his supporters would vote for the treaty only if changes were made. One would forbid the League to use American

The peace treaty is signed in the elegant Hall of Mirrors at Versailles, France. Wilson, Clemenceau, and Lloyd George (seated center, left to right) look on as the Germans sign.

troops without approval of Congress. The Lodge group said that if the change were not made, they would join the opposition and vote against the treaty.

Henry Cabot Lodge was a gentleman of the old school, but he was also a fierce Republican. Like his good friend Theodore Roosevelt, he detested Woodrow Wilson. He was also a clever politician and knew he was in the driver's seat. If Wilson compromised and accepted his reservations, then Senator Lodge and the Republicans could take much of the credit for getting the Senate behind the League. If the President refused to compromise, the treaty would be voted down and Wilson would suffer a defeat.

"A knife thrust at the heart of the treaty." Wilson refused to compromise. Some of the President's advisors urged him to meet Lodge halfway. They pointed out that it was the only hope for getting the country into the League. Wilson felt he had already given in enough at the Paris peace conference. He would yield nothing to the Senate. He said that the Lodge reservation about United States troops was "a knife thrust at the heart of the treaty." Yet none of the other Allied countries seriously objected to Lodge's reservations. The French and British wanted the United States in the League even if compromises were made.

Wilson hoped to outflank Lodge by appealing to the people. Once the public heard his side of the story, he was sure, they would come to his aid.

The last speech. To drum up popular support, the President planned a strenuous speaking campaign to the West Coast and back. His doctors were alarmed. They told him that his health could not stand such a strain. The pleas did no good.

At first all went well. Great crowds greeted Wilson at every stop and cheered his defense of the League and the Treaty. In 22 days he traveled 8,000 miles and delivered 36 speeches. The pace pushed his endurance to the limit.

In Pueblo, Colorado, Wilson gave the most moving speech of his entire tour. With tears streaming down his face, the President pleaded for the League of Nations. It was the last speech Wilson ever gave. As his train headed for Wichita, the President was struck by a terrible pain. His doctor could do nothing for him. With its blinds drawn the train raced back to Washington.

Back at the White House, Wilson seemed better. But several days later, Mrs. Wilson found her husband sprawled on the floor of his bathroom. The President was paralyzed, the victim of a stroke.

For several days Wilson hovered between life and death. Eventually, he regained some of his strength, but he remained an invalid for the last seventeen months of his term. The government pretty much ran itself.

But Wilson had given clear instruction to his loyal Democratic supporters in the Senate. No compromise with Lodge on the Treaty. In November 1919 and again in March 1920 the Wilson Democrats voted down the Treaty with Senator Lodge's amendment. The League of Nations was a dead issue.

 TRY THIS!

1. Show how Wilson hoped to prevent future wars. **2.** Explain why the people of Europe gave Wilson such an enthusiastic reception. **3.** Tell how the Versailles Treaty was voted down by its "friends."

468

5. FOREIGN RELATIONS AFTER THE WAR

Six months after the Senate took its final vote on the League of Nations and the Treaty of Versailles (page 468), the United States held its 1920 presidential election. Warren G. Harding, a Republican senator from Ohio, defeated Democrat James M. Cox, a former Democratic governor from the same state.

A period of isolationism? President Wilson had wanted the election to be a vote for the League. The Democratic candidate had promised that he would try to bring the United States into the League as soon as possible after election. But the Republicans were divided between pro- and anti-League forces, so Harding took no clear stand on the question. Once elected, he dropped the matter entirely. The United States seemed to have cut itself off from other nations, to have begun a period of *isolationism*.

Yet during the 1920s the nation continued to work for peace. It tried to protect China from the imperialist powers; and it tried a policy somewhat like the dollar diplomacy of the Taft years (page 444), but with greater skill and success.

An impossible race. The world's most powerful countries began a race for naval

---

Read here of how

The United States started a disarmament program.
But kept out of the League and the Court.
It tried to protect China.
And got on better with Latin America.

---

leadership immediately after World War I. The United States wanted a larger and more modern navy. The British strove to keep up with it. And Japan alarmed Britain, the United States, and other nations with an ambitious shipbuilding program. To halt the armament race, the United States took the lead and invited all important countries (except Russia) to a naval conference.

From November 1921 to February 1922 the conference met in Washington with Secretary of State Charles Evans Hughes as chairman. Hughes startled the delegates and world opinion when he proposed cutting back planned ship construction and also scrapping some ships already being built. The United States offered to destroy almost a million tons of partly completed shipping. The purpose of the conference was to keep a balance between the navies of the world, so that none would be able to overpower the others, and so that the governments of the world would not ruin themselves in an impossible race to build the biggest navy.

Nine treaties. The Washington conference finally reached an agreement that gave the United States and Britain equal tonnage (the total weight in larger ships, not the number of ships). Japan was allowed three fifths of what the United States and Britain each had. This was expressed as a 5:5:3 ratio.

The ratio upset Japan. They wished to be considered a full-fledged naval power, one on a par with the United States and Britain.

The agreement applied only to *capital* ships (battleships and heavy cruisers). Destroyers and submarines were not included.

However, the conference did make some rules about the way in which submarines would be used. It also settled some problems over the ownership of various Pacific islands. Finally, the conference tried to give some protection to China, which was being ruled by its generals and their separate armies. In all, nine separate treaties and agreements were made as a result of the Washington Armament Conference.

Once again, the Japanese felt cheated, just as they had after the Treaty of Portsmouth in 1906 (page 442). And again they blamed the United States.

Anti-United States feeling. No problem caused more bad feeling in the 1920s than the Allied war debts. The United States had advanced over ten billion dollars to various European nations during and just after the war. Most of the money had gone to Britain, France, and Italy.

Britain, in addition to borrowing over four billion dollars from the United States, had loaned ten billion to the other Allies. Britain first proposed that all the debts should be canceled. Many people in the United States agreed with this solution. After all, the borrowed money had been used to defeat a common enemy, and much of it had been spent in the United States. But the United States government insisted that the Allies pay what they owed.

At the same time, the United States wanted the Allies to cancel the reparation debts owed by Germany (page 466). The Allies would cancel the reparations only if the United States would wipe out its war debts.

Conferences were held during the 1920s at which the United States agreed to accept greatly reduced sums for settlement of the debt. Some interest payments were made, but Europe's finances were in terri-

ble shape following the war. The chief result of the negotiations was an increase in anti-United States feeling in Europe.

Some American efforts. Neither President Harding nor President Calvin Coolidge, who succeeded him in 1923, took any steps to bring the United States into the League of Nations. Nevertheless, all through the 1920s the United States cooperated with the League. It took part in conferences on drug traffic and other world problems. And throughout the period there were five permanent United States officials at the League headquarters in Geneva, Switzerland, looking out for the nation's interests.

Presidents Harding and Coolidge did make efforts to have the United States join the Court of International Justice at The Hague, a capital of the Netherlands. The United States had first called for such a world court to settle disputes between nations in 1899. Several United States lawyers, including Charles Evans Hughes, served as justices on the Court. It was separate from the League and could hear cases between nations only when the countries involved agreed to its doing so. But the Senate never took final action on United States membership.

In 1927, French Foreign Minister Aristide Briand proposed a treaty, between his country and the United States, promising that neither one would use war to advance its interests. Secretary of State Frank B. Kellogg agreed with the idea behind the treaty, and the United States invited other nations to sign. In all, 62 did so. However, the only "enforcement" available for the agreement would be world opinion. Some Americans had faith in the Kellogg-Briand Pact as a way of outlawing war, but the pact had no lasting influence.

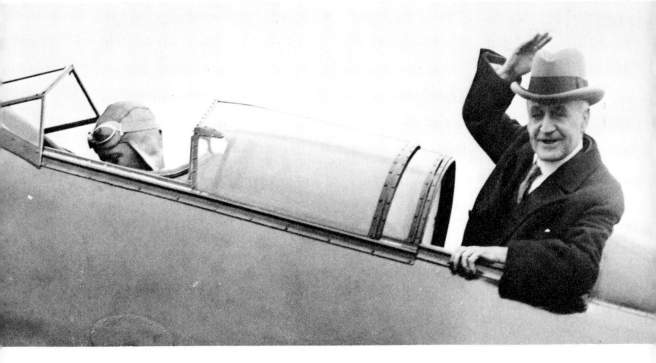

Ambassador Dwight W. Morrow in a plane flown by Charles A. Lindbergh.

A skilled negotiator. The United States did better in Latin America than it did in Europe during the 1920s. A revolutionary government in Mexico (page 446) had seized the oil fields owned by United States companies. Threats from the United States government did not move Mexico to return or pay for the lands. In fact, the threats seemed to make the revolutionaries' government more determined than ever to keep them.

Finally, President Coolidge sent his friend Dwight W. Morrow, a Wall Street banker, as ambassador to Mexico. Morrow proved to be a skilled negotiator. He won the trust and good will of the Mexican leaders, and the United States companies got back the lands they had held before 1917.

As the 1920s drew to a close, the United States had greatly improved its relations with the Dominican Republic and Nicaragua (pages 438 and 444). At the end of 1928, it officially set aside the Roosevelt Corollary to the Monroe Doctrine (page 438). The Monroe Doctrine, the United States said, applied to Europe, not Latin America.

 TRY THIS!

1. Compare the 1921 Washington Conference with the 1817 Rush-Bagot Agreement (page 167). Were both agreements "self-enforcing"? **2.** Write an editorial for a 1922 Japanese newspaper attacking the naval armament treaty.

Roundup

Who?

Robert Lansing
Charles Evans Hughes
George Creel
Nikolai Lenin
John J. Pershing
Henry Cabot Lodge
Georges Clemenceau
David Lloyd George
Dwight W. Morrow

What?

Central Powers
Allies
U-boat
Lusitania
Sussex pledge
Zimmermann telegram
War Industries Board
War Labor Board
Committee on Public
    Information
AEF
Fourteen Points
Versailles Treaty
Washington Armament
    Conference
International Court of
    Justice

Where?

Sarajevo
Balkans
Marne River
Meuse River
Argonne Forest

KNOW THIS

The Nation on the Road to War

1. What was the event that started World War I?
2. Before 1917, how did the United States aid the Allies?
3. How did Germany enforce its blockade?
4. When the *Lusitania* was torpedoed, how did a) former President Roosevelt and b) Secretary of State Bryan want the U.S. to respond?
5. What brought the U.S. into World War I?

The Home Front in Wartime

1. What did Wilson do to mobilize industry for the war?
2. How did the war help a) big business, b) labor unions, c) workers, and d) women?
3. What part did blacks take in World War I?
4. What was the work of the Creel Committee?
5. How did government restrict Americans' freedom during World War I?

Winning the War in Europe

1. What was trench warfare? How did it develop?
2. Why did trench warfare make unusual demands on men and equipment?
3. Why did the American Expeditionary Force take so long to enter the fighting?
4. In what important battles did the U.S. take part?
5. How was the war ended? What were some of its costs?

Losing the Peace at Home

1. What were some points of Wilson's peace plan?
2. What contradictions were there in Wilson's plan?
3. Which of Wilson's proposals did the Allies accept? Which did they not accept? In each case tell why.
4. What was the purpose of the League of Nations? What restrictions were placed on its power? Why?
5. Who in the United States opposed joining the League of Nations?

Foreign Relations After the War

1. Which countries led the naval armaments race?
2. How did the U.S. and Allies disagree on war debts?
3. In the 1920s, what role did the United States play in a) the League of Nations and b) the International Court of Justice?
4. How did the United States improve relations with Latin America in the 1920s?

DIG HERE!

For more than half the U.S. population, 1920 was a most important year. The Nineteenth Amendment was adopted, and women had equal voting rights with men. But plainly, "getting the vote" was not enough. Even today, over half a century later, women's rights are still big political (and personal) issues. "Women's work" and "women's place" are still being written about. Think about the work, and the place in American history, of a woman whose contribution seems especially interesting. Find out more about what she accomplished. Consider these questions:

A. What was your subject's upbringing like? Did she have much formal education? Did she marry? Have children? If so, what help did she have with home responsibilities?

B. What did she accomplish? Were her contributions recognized in her lifetime?

C. What were her personal characteristics? Did they help or hold back her career?

D. What frustrations did she meet, because of what others expected of women? How did she work out such problems? Did she ever offer any special advice for other gifted women?

E. Did she take part in any women's rights programs? How much did other women help her career?

There are books listed on page 537 that will help you. Note especially those by Flexner, Scott, and Smith as well as the *Life* special report.

THINK ABOUT IT

1. Could the Creel Committee have built support for the war effort *without* encouraging intolerance?

2. To what extent was Wilson's own attitude responsible for the United States' not joining the League of Nations? Should national leaders always hold firm to principles, or should they sometimes compromise? In what circumstances? Explain.

DO IT!

1. Create a bulletin-board display of World War I recruiting and propaganda posters.

2. Prepare a series of maps that will tell the story of World War I.

3. Write a script for a radio interview with the flying ace Captain Eddie Rickenbacker. Present the interview "live" for the class.

THEN AND NOW

After World War I some leaders argued for United States isolationism. To what extent should we become involved in the affairs of other nations? Do we have an obligation to help in their needs or disputes, or should we avoid "playing policeman"?

473

Prosperity and Change
Mark the 1920s

20

The 1920s were a time of change, and most of it involved the automobile. Cars like this and Ford's Model T set new patterns in industry, employment, recreation, manners, and morals.

Senator Warren G. Harding of Ohio, soon to be President, caught the postwar condition of the country in his statement that it needed "not heroism, but healing; not nostrums [cure-all formulas], but normalcy." The 1920s did not develop into an age of normalcy. They were a time of tremendous change. Workers, for example, no longer made things; they tended machines that made things. Leisure for working people was becoming less of a daydream and more of a reality.

The shift to a more modern society was marked by conflicts and contradictions. The 1920s looked more and more like a time of prosperity; yet farmers, women, and laborers were missing out on many benefits. Prohibition (page 421) was part of the law of the land, but a new figure had appeared: the *bootlegger*, who sold liquor illegally. "Old-time religion" seemed to be flourishing, but many young people challenged and rejected their parents' beliefs. American society was being remade.

1. THE POSTWAR RED SCARE

National wartime patriotism had gone to some extremes. These had led to abuse of people's civil liberties (page 460). That kind of hysteria did not end with the Ar-

mistice. Instead, it was directed just after the war at political radicals, people urging extreme kinds of change in the country's social and economic structure.

The second Russian Revolution of 1917 (page 463) and Communist uprisings in eastern European countries stirred up fear that communism was on the march. So did a Soviet propaganda campaign directed at other nations of the world. And a number of Socialists and other radicals in the United States were inspired by the successful Russian Revolution. They joined together to form the American Communist Party. All this alarmed the country's political conservatives—persons who distrusted abrupt change and who tended toward preserving traditional ways. They thought that a revolution was about to break out and that the government might soon be overthrown by violent means.

Real grievances ignored. A wave of strikes swept the country in 1919. Many thought it meant the approach of an uprising. Steelworkers, paid 28 dollars for a seven-day work week, left the mills. In Seattle, Washington, a general strike all but closed down the city. Coal miners— 394,000 of them—climbed out of the pits. Policemen in Boston, Massachusetts, refused to go on duty.

None of this labor activity was the result of secret orders from Moscow. The strikes occurred because in industry after industry wages were low and hours of work were long. Since 1914, prices had soared by

---

Read here of how

The nation failed to help its workers.
It even deported some of them.
And executed two Italian immigrants.

TIME CHART

1915	The Ku Klux Klan is reorganized.
1917	A literacy test for immigrants is adopted.
1919	Race riots break out in northern cities.
1920	Marcus Garvey's Universal Negro Improvement Association meets in New York.
1920	Warren Harding is elected President.
1923	Harding dies. Calvin Coolidge becomes President.
1924	The Teapot Dome scandal erupts.
1924	The National Origins Act is adopted.

---

102 per cent and workers could not keep pace. But many Americans chose to ignore the real grievances of labor. Instead, they were convinced, as one newspaper wrote, Socialists, Communists, and labor leaders were "joining together with the object of overthrowing the American government and establishing a Bolshevist republic."

In the same year of 1919, terrorist bombings fanned the fires of what had become a Red Scare. The postman handed a maid at a Georgia senator's home a small package; it exploded, destroying both her hands. Next day the New York Post Office discovered sixteen similar packages containing bombs; they had been addressed to such well-known people as J. P. Morgan and John D. Rockefeller of Standard Oil fame (page 369). One bomb went off outside the home of the United States Attorney General, A. Mitchell Palmer. Others exploded in front of public buildings. None of the terrorists was ever caught.

Without warrants. Even sensible, levelheaded people thought that action should be taken to rid the nation of the "Red menace." Many radicals were immigrants, they pointed out. Why not deport them; send them back home or to Russia? Some government officials responded eagerly. Attorney General Palmer swooped down on the supposed radical conspiracy, setting up a special division in the Justice Department, with young J. Edgar Hoover in charge.

On November 7, 1919, "Palmer raids" rounded up suspected radicals. Four days before Christmas an old army transport ship left New York, carrying 249 deported aliens toward Soviet Russia. On the night of January 2, 1920, over 4,000 alleged radicals in 23 states were arrested, many without warrants.

Gradually the Red Scare died. Some conservatives voiced opposition to the heavy-handed tactics of the government. When the New York legislature refused to seat five properly elected Socialist members, the noted Charles Evans Hughes offered to defend them. Justice Department predictions that a radical uprising was due on May Day, 1920 came to nothing, and people began to sense that in spite of all the smoke, there was not much fire.

Within Wilson's Cabinet, opposition to the witch hunt broke into the open. Convinced that the accused radicals had been denied their basic legal rights, Secretary of Labor William B. Wilson and his assistant Louis F. Post managed to undo some of the damage Palmer had done. Even the newspapers became tired of the scare stories.

"Indeed I am a radical." One incident from the Red Scare lingered on. In April 1920 a guard and a paymaster were shot and killed during a daylight robbery of a

476

Poet Edna St. Vincent Millay protests the execution of Sacco and Vanzetti in Boston in 1927.

shoe factory in South Braintree, Massachusetts. A month later, two immigrants, Nicola Sacco and Bartolomeo Vanzetti, were picked up in Brockton, Massachusetts, and charged with the murder. Both men admitted to being *anarchists*; that is, opposed to all government. In court they were convicted of the crime and sentenced to death.

Some of the evidence on which Sacco and Vanzetti were convicted was doubtful. Many people felt that the state had not proved its case beyond a reasonable doubt. It seemed that the jury had been influenced as much by the radicalism of the accused and by their foreign accents as by the evidence.

Among liberals and radicals throughout the world Sacco and Vanzetti became a mighty cause. Countless appeals for a new trial or for a reduction of their sentences poured in upon the governor of Massachusetts. But neither was granted. In August 1927 the two men were electrocuted.

Vanzetti's last public statement has been looked on as stating the case for many Red Scare victims. "I am not only innocent . . . I have struggled all my life, since I began to reason, to eliminate crime from the earth," he began. And as he finished his speech, he stated, "I am suffering . . . because I am a radical, and indeed I am a radical . . . because I was an Italian, and indeed I am an Italian. . . ."

 TRY THIS!

1. Trace the connection between World War I and the kinds of trouble at home that followed it. 2. Compare Attorney General Palmer's witch hunt with the one in colonial Salem (page 62)—the ways each began, grew, and died out. 3. Show what constitutional rights were denied the victims of the Red Scare.

2. THE HARDING AND COOLIDGE YEARS

Warren G. Harding was a first-term senator from Ohio when he won the Republican nomination. The 1920 convention was deadlocked, the story goes, and so the party leaders met in a "smoke-filled room" of the Blackstone Hotel in Chicago and agreed upon the inoffensive, easygoing Harding.

Since he was certain to defeat the Democratic candidates (James M. Cox and Franklin D. Roosevelt), Harding waged an old-fashioned "front-porch" campaign (page 396) from his home in Marion, Ohio. And after eight Democratic years, a Republican wound up in the White House.

Read here of how

The nation voted for normalcy in 1920.
But got plenty of political scandals.
Then tried to "keep cool with Coolidge."

Some excellent choices. In some respects Harding was a good Chief Executive. He suited the mood of the country perfectly. A tall, handsome man with silvery hair and distinguished bearing, he looked like Hollywood's version of an American President. His kindly nature and "just folks" appeal calmed a troubled nation. It was no mere coincidence that the Red Scare withered away after he took office. He pardoned Eugene V. Debs, the Socialist leader who was in jail for speaking out against World War I. It was an excellent way to bind up the wounds left from wartime dissent and reaction.

In the day-to-day chores of running the government there was considerable achievement. Some of Harding's choices for Cabinet officers were first-rate. Men like Secretary of State Charles Evans Hughes, Secretary of Commerce Herbert Hoover, and Secretary of the Treasury Andrew Mellon took firm hold of their respective departments. For instance, with Harding's

"Smoke-filled room" became a part of political language from the time of Harding's candidacy.

support, Hoover bargained with the tough-minded leaders of the steel industry and got an eight-hour day for steelworkers.

During Harding's Presidency the economy headed from postwar depression toward booming prosperity. Despite Wilson's failure with the League of Nations, foreign relations were soon being carried on successfully through regular channels. Harding did not promote progressive changes; nevertheless, the nation was better off in 1923 than in 1920.

Harding is not remembered for his successes. The corruption of his Administration outweighed his accomplishments. Along with his good appointments, he picked incompetent friends for Cabinet positions. His campaign manager, Harry Daugherty, became Attorney General. His Secretary of the Interior, Albert B. Fall, was the first Cabinet officer sent to prison

478

for corrupt use of his post. Government appointments, paroles and pardons, veterans' benefits—all were turned into opportunities for graft by the "Ohio Gang." Even the government's medical supplies were sold to private interests at a fraction of their true cost, then bought back, at much higher prices, for use in veterans' hospitals.

"I am not fit for this office." Discovering such carryings-on left Harding a visibly shaken man. When the famous Kansas editor William Allen White visited the White House, the President nearly broke down. "My friends, White," Harding complained, "they're the ones that keep me walking the floor nights!" To another supporter he confided, "I am not fit for this office and should never have been here."

In search of peace the President took a long journey. In San Francisco, on August 2, 1923, he died of a heart attack.

Montana bulldog. Shortly after Harding's death the Teapot Dome scandal was front-page news. Teapot Dome, in Wyoming, and Elk Hills in California, were government oil reserves being held for the navy. It was learned that both had been leased to private oil companies. The transfer was arranged by the Secretary of the Interior, Albert B. Fall, without competitive bidding.

At first the only question was whether such a natural resource ought to be "conserved" or "developed." But the sudden wealth that Albert Fall began to display led to an investigation. It was headed by a determined and bulldog-like senator from Montana, Thomas J. Walsh. The Secretary of the Interior, it turned out, had received a 100,000-dollar interest-free loan, 85,000 dollars in cash, 233,000 dollars in wartime Liberty Bonds, and a sprucing-up of his New Mexico ranch. All this came from the same oil companies that held the Teapot Dome and Elk Hills leases. In time the Supreme Court canceled the leases and forced full repayment to the government. Albert Fall was prosecuted, fined 100,000 dollars, and sentenced to a year in prison.

A President for the times. In the early morning hours of August 3, 1923, a notary public in Plymouth, Vermont, had administered the presidential oath to his son, Calvin Coolidge. During the Teapot Dome scandal, the memory of that homely scene reassured Americans that they had the right man for President. It even led them to forgive the Republican Party for activities of Harding's friends. In 1924, when Coolidge ran for President in his own right, he won an easy victory.

People called President Coolidge "Silent Cal." He was a small, tight-lipped, sour-looking man. Content to let the country run itself, Coolidge worked four hours a day, and killed time watching the traffic on Pennsylvania Avenue and playing tricks on the Secret Service men.

The writer H.L. Mencken complained that Coolidge "had no ideas" and was "only a nuisance." Others replied, "So what? Business is booming." Business people felt that Coolidge's "do-nothing" Presidency was the key to a prosperous economy. When Silent Cal ventured to speak, it

This cartoon poked fun at Coolidge's providing a friendly atmosphere for business.

was to pat business on the back. "The man who builds a factory builds a temple. The man who works there worships there," the President said. Or another time, "The business of America is business." For an increasingly affluent society, there seemed to be good reason to "keep cool with Coolidge."

 TRY THIS!

1. Write an editorial defending the record of President Harding.   **2.** Show why the Harding administration is often linked with Grant's as a time of corruption.   **3.** Explain why Coolidge was the President the United States thought it needed in 1924.

3.   A TIME OF NATIONAL PROSPERITY

A distinguished French writer, André Siegfried, visited America in the late 1920s and was astounded. The United States, he wrote, "has again become a new world. . . . The American people are now creating on a vast scale an entirely new social structure. . . . It may even be a new age."

The new age was one of apparently boundless prosperity. No matter where you looked, there were signs of good times: soaring production, shorter work hours, rising wages, and booming profits.

Happiness and success. At the core of this prosperity was technology. Mass production meant that by 1929 the average worker could produce 67 per cent more than in 1920. Scientific discoveries and inventions gave birth to new industries. Companies manufacturing cigarettes, wristwatches, rayon stockings, antifreeze, linoleum, and spray paint sprang up during the decade. Drawing upon the pioneer work of George Washington Carver, a botanist and former slave, manufacturers for the first time made shoe polish out of sweet potatoes and shaving cream from peanuts. By the end of the decade, the average work week was five hours shorter, and real wages had climbed by 11 per cent.

From the combination of stepped-up production, new industries, and additional spending power a consumer economy emerged. Items that a decade earlier either didn't exist, or were looked on as playthings for the rich, were now available to large numbers of people.

A revolution in selling enabled chain stores, through big-scale purchases and centralized management, to reduce prices. This, of course, encouraged greater spending. The whole economy began a steady shift away from heavy industry, which turned out such products as locomotives and railroad ties. Manufacturers moved instead to consumer goods, placing a car in the garage, a radio in the living room, a camera on the shelf, and a pack of cigarettes in the pocket.

Manufacturers of consumer goods found new ways of creating demand for their wares. Advertising itself became big business. Colorful, aggressive, and psycho-

Read here of how

Prosperity came to the United States.
Mass production fed it.
Consumer spending helped it.
But it was not shared by all Americans.

Sound effects gave a sense of reality to radio dramas.

logically keyed advertisements showed the consumer the way to happiness and social success.

A dread disease. Before 1920, people seldom worried about things like bad breath, and there was no common word for it in the English language. But in 1922 the maker of a little-known antiseptic called Listerine, anxious to increase sales, decided to market it as a cure for "halitosis." Advertising agencies were called in. A promotional campaign was mapped out. Suddenly newspapers and magazines blossomed with the Listerine message:

Nice people, fastidious people, people who consider others, recognize the constant risk of offending this way and keep themselves on the popular and polite side by using Listerine. Every morning. Every night.

Sales skyrocketed as halitosis became a feared affliction.

Other advertising slogans became etched on the public's mind. Lucky Strike cigarette ads counseled, "Reach for a Lucky instead of a sweet." (The candy business suffered.) Lux soap pledged the look of wealth: "No longer need a woman's hands say, 'I have no maid.'"

"Buy now, pay later." In the 1920s, for the first time, the messages of advertisers were heard as well as seen and read. With astonishing speed Americans took to a new gadget called the radio. In November 1920 station KDKA in East Pittsburgh, Pennsylvania, transmitted the first commercial broadcast. A few years later, seven hundred radio stations blanketed the United States with news broadcasts, drama, music, comedy—and commercials. By 1929 five

481

million radios a year were being sold, and nearly 40 per cent of all families owned one. Though a radio cost over 150 dollars, sales boomed.

Radios and other products had become easier to purchase. Businesses promoted a system of time payments and offered easy credit terms. Three out of every four radios, and 60 per cent of all automobiles and furniture, were bought on the installment plan. The volume of time purchases grew from slightly more than a billion dollars in 1920 to over six billion dollars in 1929. In a silent revolution, Ben Franklin's encouragement to "save for a rainy day" had been replaced by the advice to "buy now and pay later."

The chief symbol of the twenties was the automobile. Without it, there would have been no new age of prosperity. In 1900 only 4,000 automobiles had been built, and there was not one gas station in the entire country. In 1929 over 26 million cars and trucks crowded the highways, and nearly five million new ones rolled off the assembly lines. One out of every five Americans owned a car. In some towns, cars outnumbered bathtubs and homes with indoor plumbing.

The auto industry dominated the economy. Of all steel production, 15 per cent was consumed by the auto manufacturers. To fuel the Fords, Packards, and Chevys, the petroleum industry expanded. There was an unheard-of demand for rubber, plate glass, nickel, and lead.

Public funds built a network of highways. And along the roadside, the motorist began to notice hamburger stands, tourist cabins, billboards, and gas stations. Most important, the auto let people live farther from their places of work. Around most cities, suburbs grew.

"Get the prices down." The individual most responsible for putting America on wheels was Henry Ford. Although given to such strange habits as eating grass sandwiches, Ford had a rare genius. Early in his career, he hit on a double-barreled idea that not only affected the automobile business but actually changed the nation. First, he said, "Get the prices down to the buying power." In other words, lower the cost of a car so that an ordinary person could afford it. Second, he urged, bring wages up to increase the worker's purchasing power.

Gas stations, such as this one in the Bronx, New York, marked the end of the days when motorists had to store their own fuel.

Ford tested these ideas in 1908 when he designed the Model T. It was a simple, functional car with no frills. By introducing the assembly-line method of production, Ford's factories turned out these "Tin Lizzies" quickly and cheaply. As sales increased, he lowered the price, and even more customers walked into Ford showrooms.

The first Model T sold for 850 dollars. By 1916 the price had dropped to 360 dollars, and in 1924 one could be had for 290 dollars. Eventually there were 15 million Model T's on the streets. At the same time, Ford increased his employees' earning power. In 1914 he astounded the business world by offering a wage of five dollars a day, two dollars more than the usual rate. Not only did it make up for the dreary boredom of assembly-line work; it enabled more people than ever to buy Fords. By the mid-1920s Henry Ford, sole owner of the Ford Motor Company, was making 25,000 dollars a day.

Coolidge and the farmers. Not everyone in the 1920s shared equally in the prosperity of the times. Throughout the postwar period the farmer was the "sick man" of the economy. The share of the entire national income going to agriculture went down by almost 7 per cent between 1919 and 1929.

The farmer's problem was overproduction. Using newly developed insecticides and improved seeds, the farmer harvested more than ever before. Too much, in fact. Farm produce glutted the market as the supply of foodstuffs far outweighed the consumer's demand. Automatically, the prices of farm products fell and rural areas suffered.

As farm conditions grew worse, rural members of Congress from both parties formed a "farm bloc" to support relief measures. Twice they managed to ram through Congress the McNary-Haugen Bill. It would have set up a government marketing system for farm products and kept farm prices steady. On both occasions, though, President Coolidge vetoed the legislation. He had constitutional reasons for doing so, but he also said, "Farmers have never made much money. I don't believe we can do much about that."

A rugged road. During the time of Coolidge prosperity, more women than ever before were employed outside the home—ten million of them in 1929.

However, women ran into a solid wall of discrimination when they went to look

483

for jobs. By far the greatest number of them were domestic servants and unskilled workers. For those seeking white-collar and professional careers, the road was rugged. At times during the 1920s, the Harvard and Columbia law schools refused to admit any women at all. Medical schools established a quota system whereby only 5 per cent of their enrollments could be women. In every field women occupied positions with lower pay and less prestige than those of men.

A bad time for unions. Things were not good for factory workers, either. Although incomes were up, unskilled laborers were the last to benefit. Trying to improve matters by organizing into labor unions was almost hopeless. Encouraged by the conservative government in Washington, employers felt free to ignore workers' demands.

Despite his belief in better pay, Henry Ford terrorized his workers. He steadfastly refused to deal with any union. Furthermore, he hired spies and iron-fisted thugs to maintain discipline in his plant. And whenever Ford discovered one of his workers driving any car but a Ford, that worker was instantly fired. One setback after another plagued the labor movement. In 1930 only about 7 per cent of the work force were union members.

None of these discontents boiled over in the 1920s, but they were brewing. Few observers were troubled by the uneven distribution of income and the overproduction of consumer goods. The next decade—the 1930s—would be the one that would pay.

TRY THIS!

1. Write an advertisement that will persuade people to buy something they don't yet know they want. Have you ever bought such a product? **2.** Explain the place of wages and prices in bringing prosperity. **3.** Explain why some groups did not share in the prosperity of the 1920s.

4. NEW VALUES AGAINST OLD

In 1910 Alice Roosevelt Longworth, the daughter of President Theodore Roosevelt, was ordered out of a Chicago hotel because she lit up a cigarette in the lobby. Less than two decades later, women not only smoked in public; they ordered cocktails in *speakeasies* (illegal bars), cut their hair short, and wore their skirts above the kneecap. Any of these things would have been unthinkable before World War I. Together, they showed the changing standards in the United States. The "flaming youth" of the 1920s were out to challenge the morality of their parents. A group of movie stars, writers, intellectuals, and those who had made

————————— • —————————

Read here of how

Novels, poems, and plays reflected change.
Prohibition proved to be unenforceable.
The Ku Klux Klan reappeared.
And immigration was severely restricted.

————————— • —————————

People really kicked up their heels when they did the Charleston, the most popular dance of the 1920s.

or inherited great wealth led the way. But the spirit of change found its way into the lives of the less famous as well.

A bootlegger as hero. The effect of the First World War had been enormous. According to one author, young Americans had emerged from the experience to find "all gods dead, all wars fought, all faith in man shaken." How could anyone have faith in a civilization that sent millions to be slaughtered on the battlefield? For many, the war to remake the world, and the kind of idealism Woodrow Wilson had practiced, were bad jokes.

Drawing upon the new attitudes, a generation of writers created a body of remarkable fiction. The first to achieve fame was F. Scott Fitzgerald. Both his novels and his personal life represent the pleasure-seeking ways of the 1920s. In his most thoughtful work, *The Great Gatsby*, Fitzgerald examined the life of a millionaire bootlegger seeking high social position. The hero, Jay Gatsby, lives an extravagant and glamorous existence. But the corrupting influence of wealth dooms him to a tragic love affair and a violent death. Fitzgerald himself roamed a world not unlike Gatsby's—one of wild, all-night parties, trips abroad, and free spending. For Fitzgerald, too, success was poison. He died in Hollywood in 1940—an alcoholic scriptwriter.

There were others. Ernest Hemingway vividly described the horrors and futility of war in *A Farewell to Arms*. Sinclair Lewis and H.L. Mencken made fun of the value structure of middle-class Americans. William Faulkner brilliantly wrote of life in

485

Bootleggers didn't always hide liquor in their boots. How many other ways can you find?

A nation of lawbreakers? One of the easiest ways to rebel against the old values was not to write a book, but to take a drink. Since 1919 Prohibition had been in effect (page 421). In rural areas most people accepted it, but it was a different story in the cities. There the Prohibition Amendment was constantly violated. Gangsters like Al Capone of Chicago became millionaires by stocking speakeasies with bootleg whiskey and beer. In many middle-class homes gin was regularly manufactured in the upstairs bathtub.

Prohibition was practically unenforceable in the larger cities. Bootleggers bribed city officials and police departments. Federal agents were few and hopelessly underpaid. President Herbert Hoover, who tried to enforce the measure, grimly concluded that 250,000 federal police would be needed to crack down on the illegal liquor traffic. Congressman Fiorello LaGuardia added that an equal number would be needed in New York City alone. He also noted that it would take another 200,000 to police the police. Never in United States history had so many people so freely broken a law.

An alien element. Believers in Prohibition and the old morality fought back. Many defenders of an earlier, simpler nation were shocked by what was happening in the cities. Some gave way to prejudice and denounced newer Americans as inferior creatures plotting the overthrow of a white, Anglo-Saxon, Protestant civilization.

The ugliest example of intolerance was the revived Ku Klux Klan. By the light of a burning cross, the Klan was reorganized

the American South. Carl Sandburg, Robert Frost, Marianne Moore, and Ezra Pound brought new forms to poetry. The plays of Eugene O'Neill explored the fears and anxieties of the age.

The novels of Hemingway and Fitzgerald set many readers rethinking old truths. But most social change in the United States was brought about by modern technology. The automobile gave people the ability to move around and the chance to escape. Instead of staying home with the family on the front porch at night, young people went joyriding with their friends. The motion pictures opened new and exciting doors.

in 1915 by William J. Simmons on Stone Mountain in Georgia. Like the Klan of Reconstruction times (page 340), the members wore hooded sheets and called themselves protectors of white supremacy. But the new Klan had other goals as well. It attacked Jews as business manipulators, Catholics as a threat to Protestantism, the "Wets" (opponents of Prohibition) as lawbreakers, and immigrants as an "alien" element in American society.

By 1920 the Klan was using modern advertising techniques, and its membership was mushrooming across the country. Between four and five million joined up and wore the white robe. Why did so many people become Klansmen? The frustration with modern life was one answer. People with rural or small-town backgrounds

sensed that their way of life was disappearing. Somehow, they imagined, the Klan would stem the tide of change. It would protect them from the sin and foreign faces of the city.

In the early 1920s the Klan had a powerful influence. Rallies and marches were commonplace. Catholic churches were burned. A Klansman murdered a priest and went scot-free. The Democrats' 1924 convention swarmed with Klansmen. In Indiana, Klan leader D.C. Stephenson controlled state politics, ran the legislature, and told the governor what to do.

The Klan declined as quickly as it had erupted. When, in 1925, Indiana leader Stephenson was convicted of murdering a young secretary, members felt betrayed and left the organization in droves. By

John Steuart Curry, *Baptism in Kansas*. In a time of change, everyone did not adopt the new morality.

1930 only 9,000 Klansmen were left and in 1944 the Klan was formally disbanded.

Slamming the door. Though the Klan dwindled, the fear of foreigners did not. During the 1920s severe restrictions were placed on immigration. In 1917 a literacy test act (page 397) had been passed over President Wilson's veto. It required immigrants to prove that they could read English or another language before being admitted. Then, during the 1920s, further restrictions were adopted. President Harding signed the Emergency Quota Act of 1921. It was followed by the National Origins Act of 1924.

The intent of both laws was the same. They strictly limited the number of immigrants to be admitted each year (150,000 finally). And they gave each European nation a quota. The quotas were based on the number of people in the United States who could trace their origins to the particular country. As this worked out, the Act gave generous allowances to the countries of northern and western Europe. Those in eastern and southern Europe got very small quotas. People from the Western Hemisphere were admitted in large numbers, but Asiatics were barred altogether.

The effect was immediate. The "Golden Door" was slammed shut, and immigration fell to a trickle. It was an act of racism, reflecting the belief that Italians, Greeks, Russian Jews, and all Orientals were unworthy of becoming Americans.

 TRY THIS!

1. Tell how *The Great Gatsby* reflected the attitudes of the 1920s.   **2.** Write a conversation between two Klan members, one from Reconstruction days and one from the 1920s. Would they approve of one another's activities?   **3.** Explain how the National Origins Act was "racist."

5.   THE BLACK EXPERIENCE IN THE 1920s

While farmers and immigrants felt left out of American life in the 1920s, blacks continued to be as cut off as they had always been. By the 1920s every major northern city had a black ghetto.

Last hired, first fired. The largest and best-known black community in the United States was New York's Harlem. It had been a quiet middle-class area until the turn of the century. Then overbuilding caused real estate values to collapse. Enterprising black business people leased empty buildings from white owners and re-leased them to black tenants.

Slums grew up in Harlem and other black sections. As surrounding white neighborhoods resisted black expansion, and as southern blacks continued to move north, the population grew ever denser. Rents rose, and because most blacks were poorly paid, they took in lodgers to make ends meet. By the mid-1920s the majority of urban blacks lived in neighborhoods marked

Read here of how

Blacks moved into northern cities.
And found more militant leaders.
Black artists gained recognition.

488

Black artist Jacob Lawrence's painting depicts the migration of blacks to the North.

by poor housing, high crime and disease rates, and inferior incomes.

Those moving from the South earned higher wages than they could have at home. But they were tied to unskilled and semiskilled labor. When business was bad, they were the last to be hired and the first to be fired.

A touch of home. To help rural blacks adjust to city life, new institutions were formed and old ones were modernized. The National Urban League, an interracial group, helped the migrants to find jobs and housing. By the 1920s it had branches in every northern city.

The churches were always centers of social life for the black community. In the 1920s they began serving as employment offices, recreation centers, and welfare agencies. But some blacks found the large congregations cold and forbidding. They flocked instead to storefront churches. They found the preaching and singing of these smaller gatherings more like what they had known in the rural South.

New militancy. There was at this time, too, a rising tide of black nationalism. If blacks had believed that World War I would bring any greater democracy at home, they were severely disappointed. Black soldiers, returning from the war, met with abuse and prejudice. The rise of the new Ku Klux Klan (page 486) was just one part of it. There was also a series of particularly vicious race riots in 1919 and an increase in the number of lynchings. Ten of those lynched in that year were soldiers—in uniform.

But the war had also spurred a new black militancy. Black soldiers and veterans fought back in the race riots. Black leaders increasingly urged self-defense. The NAACP (page 344) took a bolder tone in its fight against lynching. New spokesmen, like A. Philip Randolph and Chandler Owen, urged blacks to adopt socialism and radical trade-unionism.

A world organization. The black leader who expressed the new feeling most effectively was Marcus Garvey. Born in Jamaica in 1887, he entered the United States in 1915 and organized a branch of his Universal Negro Improvement Association. By the early 1920s it had a membership in the tens of thousands. Its newspaper had a circulation of over 100,000.

Marcus Garvey (middle) was a forerunner of the Black Power movement of the 1960s.

In 1920 delegates from around the world came to New York for the first international black convention. Madison Square Garden was packed with 25,000 of Garvey's supporters. He established such groups as the Black Cross Nurses, the Knights of the Nile, and the African Legion. At the same time, he launched the Black Star Line, an all-black steamship company by which Garvey hoped to tie together blacks throughout the world.

Black pride. Thousands of black people bought stock in Garvey's company, but the Black Star Line failed and led to his downfall. Garvey and his associates were cheated and overcharged by white shipowners. Ambitious and controversial, Garvey made enemies—white and black—who sought to destroy him. Although he was sincere and honest, he was convicted on a technical charge of using the mails to defraud and was sentenced to prison. President Coolidge later reduced his sentence, but Garvey was deported to Jamaica as an undesirable alien. From there he went to London where he died in 1940.

Marcus Garvey succeeded at first because he had appealed to black pride. He told his followers that a black skin should be treasured. Garvey condemned blacks who tried to straighten their hair or make their skins lighter.

Garvey even told his followers that he agreed with the Ku Klux Klan when it demanded separation of the races. Integration, he insisted, was race suicide. Furthermore, Garvey condemned the NAACP for cooperating with and imitating whites. He urged blacks to study African history and told them, "Black men, you were once great; you shall be great again." He urged American blacks to help reclaim Africa and remove it from European control.

Black artists brought gospel singing into the mainstream of American music.

In his poem "Heritage," Countee Cullen drew a portrait of the Africa from which his ancestors had been taken three hundred years earlier. Cullen wrote of the "great pulsing tide" of African blood flowing in his veins.

Claude McKay, in his angry poem "If We Must Die," was speaking of the race riots of 1919:

> If we must die, let it not be like hogs
> Hunted and penned in an inglorious spot,
> While round us bark the mad and hungry
> dogs, . . .
> Like men we'll face the murderous, cowardly
> pack,
> Pressed to the wall, dying, but fighting back.

There was also a lighter side to the Harlem Renaissance, a glorification of the life of the ghetto. McKay's exciting novel *Home to Harlem* has as its hero a soldier, wandering through the exotic night-life of Harlem cabarets, gambling dens, and dance halls, searching for a woman he once knew. And titles of poems by Langston Hughes reveal his concern with the same theme: "The Weary Blues," "Midnight Nan at Leroy's," "Black Dancer at the Little Savoy."

THE HARLEM RENAISSANCE

Marcus Garvey was not alone in promoting the new militancy. Increasingly, during the 1920s, black literature focused black protest. Harlem in those years became the capital of black America, attracting young black artists from all over the country. Both in Harlem and on Broadway, the black theater flourished, bringing fame to actors and entertainers such as Paul Robeson, Florence Mills, and Ethel Waters. Within Harlem, "New Negro" writers emerged: young blacks determined to assert their racial pride and identity.

A "great pulsing tide." In many ways this "Harlem Renaissance," as it was called, was part of a larger trend in American culture. White writers and critics, who were questioning middle-class values, came to admire the freedom of the black culture and to feel less bound by their own.

 TRY THIS!

1. Explain the part played by churches and other institutions in the lives of northern blacks. **2.** Explain how each of these helped to change black attitudes: (a) World War I, (b) Marcus Garvey, (c) the Harlem Renaissance.

491

ROUNDUP

Who?

A. Mitchell Palmer
Sacco and Vanzetti
Warren G. Harding
Harry Daugherty
Albert B. Fall
Calvin Coolidge
F. Scott Fitzgerald
Ernest Hemingway
Henry Ford
A. Philip Randolph
Marcus Garvey
Langston Hughes

What?

Palmer raids
Teapot Dome
Model T
McNary-Haugen Bill
bootleggers
Wets
National Origins Act
Urban League
Harlem Renaissance

KNOW THIS

The Postwar Red Scare

1. What were some "contradictions" in American society of the 1920s?
2. Why did conservatives fear a revolution after the war?
3. What caused the wave of strikes in 1919? What did people *think* was causing them?
4. Who were the targets of the Palmer raids? Why did the Red Scare die out?
5. Why did the Sacco-Vanzetti case become an important cause?

The Harding and Coolidge Years

1. In what ways was Harding a good President?
2. What were some of the scandals of the Harding administration?
3. How did the Teapot Dome affair develop?
4. How did Calvin Coolidge become President? Why was he popular?
5. What was Coolidge's attitude towards business?

A Time of National Prosperity

1. In the 1920s, how did technology and mass production change workers' lives?
2. How did the following affect consumers: a) the revolution in selling, b) advertising, c) credit plans?
3. Why was the automobile so important in the 1920s?
4. Why did farmers not share in the 1920s' prosperity?
5. In what areas did women still face discrimination?

New Values Against Old

1. What were some of the changes in Americans' lifestyles after the First World War?
2. What books and plays reflected the life of the 1920s?
3. Why was Prohibition impossible to enforce?
4. What was the revived Ku Klux Klan?
5. How was immigration restricted in the 1920s?

The Black Experience in the 1920s

1. How did parts of Harlem become segregated?
2. What organizations helped rural blacks adjust to city life?
3. How did blacks react to the prejudice they encountered after World War I?
4. What were the ideas of Marcus Garvey on relations between blacks and whites in the United States?
5. Who were some artists of the Harlem Renaissance?

DIG HERE!

The United States has had not only its heroes and heroines, but also its share of bank robbers, gunslingers, gangsters, and assorted other outlaws. Choose one bad character from the books listed here, and answer the following questions about him or her:

A. What sort of childhood did he or she have? From his or her background, could you have predicted a life of crime?

B. What personal characteristics of your subject did you learn about? Are they the kind you would expect of a criminal?

C. How did this outlaw become involved in crime? What role did he or she play? Were others involved? Who suffered as a result of the crime or crimes? How did this life of crime end?

These books may help you: Drago, *Outlaws on Horseback*, Bramhall; Drago, *Wild, Woolly, and Wicked*, Potter; Horan, *Desperate Men* and *Desperate Women*, Putnam; Lyon, *The Wild, Wild West*, Funk; Sann, *The Lawless Decade*, Bonanza; Tyler, ed., *Organized Crime in America*, Ann Arbor Paperbacks.

THINK ABOUT IT

1. Coolidge said, "The business of America is business." What do you think he meant?
2. Prohibition was widely and openly disobeyed. When a law is treated in this way, what usually happens? Suppose you decided that some law today should be repealed, as Prohibition was. How would you go about getting it changed?

DO IT!

1. With a classmate prepare an illustrated magazine article on fads of the 1920s: flagpole-sitting, crossword puzzles, mah jong, dance marathons.
2. Stage or read aloud some scenes from the play *Inherit the Wind*, based on the Scopes trial. How does the play reflect changing values in America in the 1920s?

THEN AND NOW

In 1920 young John J. Carter wrote in the *Atlantic Monthly*, "The older generation has pretty well ruined the world before passing it on to us. . . . And then they are surprised that we won't accept it with the same enthusiasm with which they received it." Would a young person be likely to write a statement like that today? If so, would a great many others agree with it? Do you think a lot of young people in the 1920s agreed with John J. Carter? Explain why—or why not.

493

A Great Depression Begins

21

The 1930s. Lines of unemployed, seeking work, seeking food, seeking hope, finding none.

Herbert Hoover, thirty-first President, was not an exciting or dramatic figure. Yet in 1928 he was probably the most respected man in America. All his life he had been a model of unselfish public service. To millions he seemed to be the perfect individual to lead the country. As President, he was expected to continue the golden prosperity of the 1920s.

Within two years the hope for continued prosperity vanished. The economy was coming apart at the seams. For the next ten years, Americans lived through a nightmare called the "Great Depression."

1. THE 1929 STOCK MARKET CRASH

In the late 1920s many people turned to the stock market in an effort to "get rich quick." The prices of stocks were reaching new heights, and some people did become wealthy overnight. For those watching the stock market, the temptation to invest their savings was almost irresistible. Watching a stock such as Radio Corporation of America (RCA) go from less than 100 dollars a share to 400 dollars a share between March and November of 1928 made it very hard for anyone not to want to cash in on this booming market. By September 1929, RCA stock had jumped to 500 dollars a share. Not all stocks rose in value so dramatically, but nearly all were going up.

Those who had never owned stocks before wanted to be part of the action.

Fifty for ten. Buying stocks was made easy, too, which encouraged even more people to jump in. Like everything else, stocks could be bought on credit, or in the language of the stock market, *on margin.* Buying on margin means that an investor needs to put up only a small portion of the total price of the stock. The rest of the cost can be borrowed from the stockbroker, a member of the stock exchange who acts as a go-between from the buyer to the seller. In the 1920s a customer needed to put up only 10 per cent of the total price. The broker would supply the other 90 per cent. If a share of stock cost 100 dollars, for example, the customer paid 10 dollars and the broker loaned the remaining 90 dollars. Assuming that the stock rose to 150 dollars in a few months, the customer could sell, pay the broker the 90 dollars along with a small fee and interest and still have a profit of almost 50 dollars on a ten-dollar investment. To many people it seemed stupid not to invest in the stock market.

The stock market of the 1920s was in no way as safe as it seemed. Prices just could not keep going up. Sooner or later the value of stocks would have to drop. If the price of RCA stock, for example, had risen 500 per cent in a short time the Radio

---

Read here of how

The stock market boomed in the 1920s.
But it fell with a crash in 1929.
Too few people could buy consumer goods.
And banks were being poorly run.

TIME CHART

1927	The stock market boom begins.
1928	Herbert Hoover is elected President.
1929	The stock market crashes.
1931	Hoover declares a war-debt moratorium.
1932	The Norris-LaGuardia Act is signed.
1932	Bonus Marchers reach Washington.
1932	Franklin D. Roosevelt is elected President.
1933	The New Deal begins.

Corporation had not necessarily grown five times larger.

The value of a share of stock was supposed to reflect the company's earnings or a large increase in its product line. But by 1929 a kind of "stock fever" swept the country. People were convinced that stock prices would go on rising forever. They were willing to pay any sum for their shares, keep them for a time, and sell when they went higher.

The bottom fell out. In the fall of 1929, prices started to drop and panic struck the New York Stock Exchange. People rushed to sell their shares before prices dropped further, and this only made matters worse. Prices really started to go down until the bottom fell out of the market. On "Black Tuesday," October 29, 1929, investors tried to get anything they could for their stocks. The big gains the stock market had made during the 1920s were wiped out in hours. By November 1929 prices were half

OCT 29 · DIES IRAE

Wall Street didn't really look like this the day the crash came. It only seemed to after years of rising stock prices.

what they had been in September, and by the end of the year billions of dollars had been lost.

The stock market crash stunned the country. As the prices of stocks went down, people who had bought on margin did not have money to cover the loans from their brokers. They had counted on prices continuing to rise, and many had invested all

the money they had. Entire fortunes were completely wiped out. With the stock-market crash, people lost confidence in the age of prosperity that President Hoover had promised would continue.

Fool's paradise. Immediately, business leaders tried to make the situation look as good as they could. In a few months, they said, everything would be back to normal. President Hoover agreed. "The fundamental business of this country is on a sound and prosperous basis," he said.

Hoover and the business leaders were wrong. The stock market crash touched off the worst economic depression in American history. To be sure, the crash did not *cause* the depression. If the American business system had been sound, then recovery from the crash would have been fairly fast. But there were many weaknesses in the system—so many, in fact, that full recovery took ten years. For all the talk about a new era of prosperity, the 1920s were only a fool's paradise.

The rich get richer. What were the weaknesses in the business system? Probably the most important was the way income was distributed in the United States. Too much money was going to the rich and not enough to the middle- and low-income people. Business boomed during the twenties, but who benefited?

To some extent, low-income workers shared in the prosperous times. The average wage was higher in 1929 than it had been in 1920. But the big winners were the few who owned the corporations. While wages rose only slightly, the profits of corporations more than tripled during the 1920s. In 1929 a third of the national income went to the wealthiest 5 per cent of the population. The 36,000 richest families (less than 1 per cent of the population) earned more than the 12 million families at the bottom of the economic ladder.

This unbalanced distribution of income led to serious trouble. The prosperity of the twenties was based on the growth of new industries that produced such items as automobiles and washing machines. These businesses depended on the great majority of people having enough money to buy those cars or washing machines. But with so much of the national income going to the wealthy, too few people were able to buy consumer goods.

Thin ice. Even before the stock market crash, it was apparent that people did not have unlimited buying power. After 1925, auto sales stopped going up and the building of new houses dropped off by 40 per cent. If business leaders had raised wages or lowered prices, the economy might have been better than it was. But they were not willing to give up their high profits. Since labor unions at the time were weak and disorganized, workers had little chance of pressuring their employers for more money.

By 1929 industries were producing more goods than people could afford to buy. Because their products were not selling, business owners had to lay off workers, and many factories were forced to close. The economy stopped growing; times were bad; the stock market crash made them even worse.

Not only industry was on thin ice at this time, banks, too, were very shaky. Many bankers got caught up in the "stock fever" of the 1920s and made unsound investments with depositors' money. Many small, rural banks—not regulated by the government—were very badly managed. Even before the stock market crash, about seven thousand banks, mostly in small towns, were forced to close.

When the crash came, many other banks found that they were in serious trouble. Since savings accounts were not then

To earn interest, banks must put depositors' money out in mortgages and loans. Sudden demand for cash can destroy any bank.

497

insured by the federal government, depositors became nervous about their money and began withdrawing it from the banks. Unable to meet these sudden "runs," thousands more shut down. Their customers' savings accounts were wiped out.

Few takers. Some banks tried to stay alive by making people who had borrowed money pay it back immediately. Many farmers and home owners simply did not have the money to pay off their loans, so the banks took over the property.

By the end of 1933, the United States was in deep trouble. A third of the country's banks either had closed or had stopped operations for a while. Many factories had shut down, and a quarter of the workforce was jobless. Prices collapsed. Corn sold for five cents a bushel, and that famous RCA stock, once 500 dollars a share, could be had for two dollars and fifty cents. Even at those prices, there were very few takers. Money seemed to have vanished. The total national income, which stood at 88 billion dollars in 1929, plunged to 40 billion dollars by 1933. For all practical purposes, the American economy had come to a halt.

 TRY THIS!

1. Explain how people could double and triple their money through buying stocks on margin.   2. Explain how the poor distribution of income slowed the nation's prosperity.   3. Tell the story of one small investor in the late 1920s. What stocks might he or she have bought? How were they paid for? What happened to them after 1929?

2.   HOOVER AND THE GREAT DEPRESSION

Shortly before the 1920 presidential campaign got under way, a prominent young Democrat, Franklin D. Roosevelt, studied a list of possible candidates. In his mind one man stood head and shoulders above the rest—Herbert Hoover. "He is certainly a wonder," Roosevelt exclaimed, "and I wish we could make him President of the United States. There could not be a better one."

Food, clothing, and medical supplies. In some ways, Hoover was a wonder. Born in 1874 in the little Iowa village of West Branch, he was the son of a Quaker blacksmith. After being orphaned at the age of eight, Hoover was sent to live with relatives in Oregon. Eventually, he worked his way through Stanford University and became a mining engineer. In such distant places as Australia and China, Hoover rapidly reached the top of his profession. By 1914 he had become a millionaire.

When World War I broke out in August 1914, Hoover was living in London. The war, he wrote, struck "like an earthquake. The substance and bottom seemed to go out of everything." Hoover organized a committee in London to take care of

———————

Read here of how

Hoover ran wartime food supplies.
And he won the admiration of all.
As President, he tried to reform business.
But he could not end the depression.

———————

United States tourists stranded in Europe. In all, the committee arranged safe passage home for over 100,000 Americans. Soon after, Hoover became chairman of the Commission for Relief in Belgium, an organization providing food, clothing, and medical supplies to the Belgian people.

A Republican who didn't fit. When the United States entered the war in 1917, President Wilson called Hoover home to head the Food Administration (page 457). In this post, Hoover's name became a household word. To "Hooverize" meant to save food for war needs. The Food Administration shipped eighteen and a half million tons of food to the people in Europe.

At the war's end Hoover returned to Europe and directed efforts aimed at preventing mass starvation in Russia, Germany, and Austria. Hoover's wartime work was applauded by Americans and Europeans alike.

However, Roosevelt's wish that Hoover become President did not come true for some years. In 1920 Warren G. Harding was elected (page 477) and appointed Hoover to his Republican Cabinet as Secretary of Commerce. Hoover's main responsibility in this job was dealing with the business community. He did not wholly fit into the Republican Party of the 1920s. He was unwilling to let business run free and uncontrolled.

A full tide of prosperity. Secretary Hoover saw himself as a progressive in his approach to big business. He advised business leaders to reform their industries. He hoped to see American industry become more efficient and more responsive to the needs of the people. On one occasion, he even proposed breaking up the plantation system in the South. Under his plan, poor sharecroppers (page 339)—both white and

In wartime, Hoover's voluntary programs worked. Why didn't they work in a depression?

black—would have received land of their own. Ideas such as this were usually not much like those of President Coolidge.

When Coolidge decided not to run for re-election in 1928, Hoover became the 499

Do you think these people expected to find jobs? Why did they keep looking?

Republican candidate. The Democrats nominated Alfred E. Smith, the Governor of New York. "Al" Smith never had a chance. The first Catholic to be nominated by a major party, he came up against a wall of prejudice, but not all of it was due to his religion. Some voters could not accept Smith's views on Prohibition (he was against it), nor his big-city ways. Furthermore, in 1928 the golden prosperity of the 1920s was in full tide, and there seemed no good reason to turn the Republicans out of office.

Individualism the spark. As President, Herbert Hoover worked very hard. He sometimes stayed at his desk for sixteen hours at a time. At seven every morning, he played a round of medicine ball on the White House lawn or in the gym. At breakfast he talked with his advisers. Hoover was the first President to have a telephone installed in the Oval Office. Unlike Coolidge, President Hoover insisted on being in touch with what his administration was doing.

Hoover brought to the White House not only an enormous appetite for work but a definite set of ideas. He was committed to personal independence. To Hoover, *individualism* was the "divine spark" within each person. He defined it as the desire for self-expression and the freedom to chart one's own course.

Hoover recognized that individualism was difficult to maintain in a modern and industrialized nation. Industrialization could provide a high standard of living. Machines could reduce human drudgery and allow men and women to do more creative work. But industrialization could also destroy individualism. Modern capitalism, he thought, often allowed a few rich and powerful people to determine the welfare of great numbers of people. "The only trouble with capitalism," he once said, "is capitalists. They're too greedy."

Faith in the people. Hoover was against a powerful, centralized government that could control big business. Like Woodrow Wilson, he thought that big government was as much a threat as big business. Big government, he felt, was too far removed from the average citizen and would soon be ordering people around.

Hoover wanted less centralization and more self-government. He felt that everyone could be represented by such voluntary associations as labor unions, trade associations, cooperatives, and consumer groups. Hoover's outlook was based on faith in the American people. He could not imagine selfishness and narrowness as part of their character.

If the prosperity of the twenties had continued, Hoover might have put his plan into action. But in the face of the Great Depression, his beliefs seemed worthless.

Every imaginable pressure. Looking for a solution to the depression, Hoover first tried to use the spirit of willing cooperation. He met with prominent industrialists and business people, urging them to reduce their own profits but not to cut wages or lay off workers. The executives followed the President's advice for a while, but when the depression continued to get worse, they began cutting wages and laying people off.

President Hoover did not want to interfere with the nation's economy, but by 1932 he had no choice. He approved the establishment of the Reconstruction Finance Corporation (RFC), which loaned two billion dollars to banks and businesses that were on the verge of bankruptcy. The

RFC helped bolster the economy. Without it, the nation's whole system of credit might have collapsed. The RFC was the federal government's first peacetime attempt to help the free enterprise system operate.

In other ways, too, Hoover took action as President. His Administration sponsored some public-works programs such as Boulder Dam (later Hoover Dam) to give jobs to the unemployed. In 1932 Hoover signed the Norris-LaGuardia Act. This measure was an important step forward for organized labor. It forbade "yellow dog" contracts (page 372) and limited judges' power to halt strikes by court order.

Hoover thought much of the depression had been caused by weaknesses in international trade. In 1931 he gave the country's World War I Allies an extra year to pay their war debts to the United States (page 470). This, the President hoped, would strengthen foreign trade by helping the financial condition of the European nations.

With these measures the President drew the line. Despite every imaginable pressure, Hoover would not approve direct federal relief for the unemployed and poverty-stricken.

A ruined image. As the depression deepened, more and more people saw their jobs and savings vanish. In the winter of 1931–1932, there were a million unemployed in Pennsylvania alone. Some were actually starving.

Hoover wanted private charities to take care of the starving people. But by 1932 the charities had no money. Still Hoover would not provide federal relief to individuals. He refused to allow people to become dependent on the government. Hoover, who had rescued millions of Europeans from starvation during World War I, refused to provide relief for his fellow Americans.

501

This refusal ruined Hoover's image. The people who had supported him turned on him now. He became a target of comedians, and his name was used to describe the down-and-out. The shantytowns outside major cities, where the poor and homeless lived, were called Hoovervilles. Broken-down cars pulled by horses and mules were Hoover carts. An empty pocket turned inside out was a Hoover flag, and a newspaper, a Hoover blanket.

The President was stubborn. When urged to go to the people to win support for his policies, he replied, "This is not a showman's job. I will not step out of character."

But Hoover felt the sting of the public's rejection. At the end of his term he moaned, "All the money in the world could not induce me to live over the last nine months. The conditions we have experienced make this office a compound hell."

 TRY THIS!

1. Trace the public career of Herbert Hoover. 2. Compare Hoover's views of government and business with those of Wilson. 3. Explain why Hoover's ideas made it hard for him to deal with depression problems.

3. A MARCH ON WASHINGTON

One victim of the depression was Walter W. Waters of Portland, Oregon. Waters had served with distinction in World War I. By the late 1920s he had a steady job with a cannery in Portland. He and his wife had saved a thousand dollars, and they owned a car and a house.

But the Waterses' good fortune did not last. In 1930 Waters was laid off at the cannery. He, his wife, and two daughters were forced out of their home and into a run-down, two-room apartment. Desperately, Waters looked for work, but he had no luck. By 1932 the savings were gone and only charities and friends kept the Waters family from starvation.

But Waters and other former soldiers were not without hope. In 1924 Congress had promised them a bonus. Every veteran of World War I was to receive a cash payment in twenty years. A veteran could expect to collect about a thousand dollars in 1945. As the depression worsened, many began to demand immediate payment of

this bonus. Some members of Congress agreed and sponsored the legislation.

On to Washington. As Congress was considering legislation in March 1932, Waters suggested to other unemployed veterans that they travel to Washington. There they could present their demands for a bonus to Congress and to President Hoover. Few paid much attention. They expected the bill to be passed soon.

But in May a congressional committee stalled the bonus bill. The veterans were angry and were ready to take action. A few days later, back in Portland, 250 men de-

Read here of how

Veterans tried to collect their bonuses.
They marched to Washington.
But were turned down by Congress.
And driven out of town by the army.

502

The Bonus Army waits as the Senate argues over its demands. MacArthur called it a "bad looking mob." What do you think?

cided to go to Washington. They chose Waters as their leader. Among them, the 250 veterans could scrape together only thirty dollars. They decided to go all the way across country by freight train.

Under a banner that read "Portland Bonus March—On to Washington," the men rode eastward in empty cattle cars. On the way they picked up others, some wearing their old uniforms. Waters and his aides were strict about how the men should behave. They passed the word: "No pan-handling, no drinking, no radicalism." Each man had to pledge "to uphold the Constitution of the United States to the best of my ability" and swear an unswerving allegiance to the flag.

No White House visit. In East St. Louis, Illinois, the group ran into trouble. The Baltimore and Ohio Railroad refused to let them get on its trains. The veterans set up camp in the freight yards and refused to budge. The story hit the newspapers, and soon the men were being called the "Bonus Army." Across the country, former soldiers—hungry and unemployed—decided to join the movement and hopped freights to Washington.

503

Fourteen years earlier, the bonus marchers had worn the uniforms of their attackers.

Waters and his Bonus Army were rescued by the Illinois National Guard, which transported them to the Indiana border by car and truck. In Indiana other vehicles were waiting to drive them across that state. The governors were worried about the rapidly growing movement and wanted the men out of their states as quickly as possible.

Some 30,000 veterans managed to get to Washington. In parks, abandoned buildings, and dumps, they set up camps. The biggest was in Anacostia Flats, a marshy area near the Capitol. There some veterans were joined by their families. They lived in tarpaper shacks, lean-tos, tents, and wrecked cars.

In June the Bonus Army paraded to press its case for immediate payment of the bonus. Marching in military formation, the veterans passed the White House. They hoped to send a few men inside to meet President Hoover, but the gates were locked. The President ignored them.

A "temporary" setback. A few days later, the hopes of the Bonus Army soared. The House of Representatives voted to pay the bonus immediately. The bill went to the Senate.

The men gathered at the Capitol. Hoover was strongly against the bonus. He felt that it would unbalance the federal budget, so he put extreme pressure on the Senate to reject the bill. Furthermore, the Senators did not like giving in to a band of protesters camped on their doorstep. By a vote of 62 to 18 the bill was defeated.

Upon hearing of the defeat, Walter Waters told the crowd in front of the Capitol, "This is only a temporary setback. We are going to stay here until we change the minds of these guys."

Gallantry against the enemy. Any realistic chance for a bonus had vanished. Many of the men understood this and took advantage of the free railroad tickets home offered by the government. But others stayed. They paraded to the Capitol again, staged hunger marches, and wandered about the city. Rumors spread through Washington that the Bonus Army was filled with Communists planning a revolution to take over the government.

In late July, President Hoover decided that the veterans had to go. Police were ordered to evict a group of them from some abandoned government buildings on Pennsylvania Avenue. The veterans, armed with only bricks and bottles, fought the police. The police fired, and two of the bonus marchers fell dead. One of them was William Hrushka. He wore the Distinguished Service Cross for gallantry in 1918.

"A bad-looking mob." When the veterans refused to leave the buildings, Hoover made the biggest mistake of his Presidency. He called in the Army to evict the bonus marchers. Taking command of the operation was Chief of Staff General Douglas MacArthur. With his aide, Major Dwight D. Eisenhower, MacArthur put together a strong force of tanks, cavalry, and infantry.

The infantry descended on the buildings, firing volley after volley of tear gas. Choking and stumbling, the bonus marchers staggered out of the buildings and retreated to the camp at Anacostia Flats. Those who resisted were roughed up by the cavalry. Bystanders were shocked.

Hoover issued a clear command: under no circumstances should the soldiers follow the Bonus Army into Anacostia Flats. But there was no stopping MacArthur. He disobeyed the order. With fixed bayonets, the soldiers charged into the camp. The air turned a sickening blue from tear gas. The son of a bonus marcher tried to save a pet rabbit from his family's shack. A soldier shouted, "Get out of here!" and ran a bayonet into the child's leg. Two babies died from tear gas. Ambulances raced hundreds of wounded to the hospitals.

With the marchers fleeing to Maryland, MacArthur ordered his troops to set fire to the camp. At the White House, President Hoover saw the glow from the fire and wondered what had happened.

MacArthur thought it a great victory. According to him, he had taken care of a

  A WORLD WAR I SOUVENIR

At 11:15 P.M. on the day the army drove the Bonus Marchers out of Anacostia Flats, Major George S. Patton, Jr., led a cavalry charge through the camp's smoldering ruins. One of the shacks he finished off belonged to Joseph Angelino, an unemployed riveter from Camden, New Jersey.

Angelino escaped by running up a nearby hill. On his chest, he was wearing his Distinguished Service Cross.

He had won the decoration September 26, 1918, for saving the life of an officer in the Argonne Forest. The officer he had saved was George S. Patton, Jr.

"bad-looking mob . . . animated by the essence of revolution." Had the Bonus Army been permitted to stay, the General said, "the institutions of our government would have been severely threatened." President Hoover took full responsibility for what happened, never revealing that MacArthur had violated orders.

No evidence has ever been uncovered that the bonus marchers had revolution or radicalism on their minds. They were what they said they were: hungry, unemployed, and desperate veterans.

 TRY THIS!

Write the diary of a bonus marcher from Portland, Oregon. Could he be the same soldier whose career you traced in Chapter 19 (page 464)?

4. HARD TIMES THROUGHOUT THE LAND

In September 1932 a Los Angeles grocery store advertised these prices in a local newspaper:

Bread, 1 lb. loaf	5¢
Lettuce, per head	1¢
Oranges, 3 doz.	10¢
Sliced bacon, per lb.	10¢
Spring lamb chops, per lb.	12½¢

The items were not on sale. The prices were typical at the time. With prices so ridiculously low, some farmers did not even try to sell their crops. Instead, they slaughtered livestock, dumped milk, destroyed fruit and vegetables, and used corn as fuel for their stoves. It often seemed pointless to harvest crops at all. A whole wagonload of oats would not bring in enough money for a farmer to buy a pair of shoes—at four dollars a pair.

"My sister's day to eat." Even with low prices, many people could not afford to buy food. In 1932 those lucky enough to have jobs earned, on the average, $16.21 a week. A quarter of the workforce could not claim even this meager amount—they were unemployed. Private and public charities tried to meet the crisis by setting up free soup kitchens and bread lines. But there was simply not enough soup and bread to go around. It was not uncommon to see desperate men and women searching for scraps of food in garbage cans and city dumps.

Children were perhaps the most tragic victims of the depression. Twenty per cent of the students in the New York City school system suffered from malnutrition in 1932. In another town, a teacher told a sick-looking girl to go home and get something to eat. "I can't," the girl replied. "This is my sister's day to eat."

Cutbacks. The depression was felt in nearly every home in the United States. Millions of people had to change their way of living. People saved money in every way they could. They reused razorblades, returned pop bottles for the two cent deposit, and bought day-old bread. Parents' clothes were cut down to fit children. Through it all, those who had once belonged to the prosperous middle class struggled to "keep up appearances." But for blacks, Mexican Americans, other minorities, and many women, survival itself was the problem.

In 1934 there were 75,000 homeless, single women in New York City alone. They spent their days looking for work and their nights riding the subways. It was a rough life. If they were over 35, it was even rougher, as many companies would not even consider hiring them. Throughout the 1930s, 20 per cent of the female workforce was unemployed.

Blacks and Mexicans need not apply. During the prosperous 1920s, large numbers of Mexicans crossed the border hoping to find better-paying jobs in the United States. When the depression set in, those

Read here of how

Prices fell so low that farmers destroyed crops.
At the same time, people were starving.
Films and radio offered escape.
But some novels attacked capitalism.

Mexicans were hit hard. The few jobs open usually went to native-born Anglos. United States border officials tried to keep the Mexicans out, often by violence. During the depression, an estimated 500,000 Mexicans were deported for illegal entry. Even some who had become United States citizens were thrown out of the country. But the Mexicans continued to enter until, by 1940, there were two and a half million living in the United States. This was a half million more than in 1930.

For blacks the struggle against racism and poverty continued. Those who left the rural South to look for work in cities found the few jobs there going to whites. Sometimes, blacks could expect nothing from the local charities. One relief agency in Houston, Texas, posted a sign that read: "Applications are not being taken from unemployed Mexican or colored families. They are being asked to shift for themselves."

Happy endings. Oddly enough, some businesses boomed during the depression. Promoters of cheap family entertainment, such as miniature golf, made fortunes in the thirties. The biggest moneymaker was the motion picture industry. With the price of admission seldom more than thirty cents, even the unemployed could afford a few hours in the local "picture palace." To meet the enormous demand, studios were churning out one film after another. For Hollywood, it was a golden age.

Occasionally, the movies of the thirties showed the hardship of the depression. In *I Am a Fugitive from a Chain Gang*, actor Paul Muni played an ex-soldier crushed by an uncaring and corrupt society. Unlike almost all other movies of the 1930s, it did not have a happy ending. The ex-soldier remained a fugitive, unable to live a normal life.

Food was dumped as people starved. Was something wrong with "the system"?

507

The Movies

During the depression, twenty-five cents (until 1 P.M.) let anyone walk across marble floors and through ankle-deep carpeting (far right) to see the latest movie. The money sometimes came from the food budget, but the dreams for sale inside were solid gold. Characters played by Clark Gable or Vivien Leigh (above), Shirley Temple (left), and dancer Fred Astaire (right) had problems, but poverty and unemployment were seldom among them.

Once it was a prosperous family farm on the Great Plains. Now it looks like part of the desert.

Most films, though, had little to do with reality. The film industry set up rigid standards: evildoers always had to suffer. And as one actress complained, "We weren't even allowed to wiggle when we sang."

Filmmakers felt that people went to the movies to forget about their problems. Films, therefore, largely ignored the depression or at least tried to present a rosy future. The singing and dancing of lavish musicals encouraged people to be optimistic. Actress Ginger Rogers passed the word as she sang the popular tune, "We're in the Money."

Panic in New Jersey. Radio also gave people an escape from reality. The most popular shows like the "Green Hornet," "The Lone Ranger," "Amos 'n Andy," and the "Jack Benny Program," hardly ever dealt with the depression.

Perhaps the extreme of "escapist" entertainment occurred on the night before Halloween in 1938. Actor Orson Welles presented a science fiction fantasy, *The War of the Worlds*, about a Martian invasion of New Jersey. In the matter-of-fact fashion of news broadcasts, Welles reported pitched battles between Martians and state militia.

Welles presented the story with such realism that vast numbers of listeners believed that Martians had actually arrived. Panic gripped New Jersey, and when Welles announced that the creatures were wading across the Hudson River, thousands of terrified New Yorkers tried to flee the city. Fearing death, people as far away as California clutched one another in a last farewell. Welles nearly was arrested for terrifying so many people. But no law had been violated by the broadcast.

Radical writers. Although the movies and radio largely ignored the depression, many writers were deeply influenced by it. Angered by the weaknesses in the American economic system, major authors of the 1930s criticized its capitalist economy. John Dos Passos completed his three-volume *U.S.A.* with *The Big Money* in 1936. This novel is sympathetic to the common man and to radical causes.

James T. Farrell wrote the "Studs Lonigan" novels about a Chicago youth and the breakdown of the society in which he lived. Another novel set in Chicago was *Native Son.* Dealing with life in the black slums, author Richard Wright denounced racism and capitalism. Erskine Caldwell gave readers a moving description of the illiterate, poverty-ridden tenant farmers of the South in *Tobacco Road.*

John Steinbeck's *The Grapes of Wrath* is the story of the Joad family—Oklahomans forced off the land by hard times and by drought. Like other "Okies," they pack up their few belongings and head for California. Against all odds, the Joads fight to keep the family together.

"My hungry babies must be fed." For poor families like the Joads, the 1930s were a nightmare. Not only did the depression strike, but widespread drought ravaged the Great Plains. It rained so seldom that millions of acres of farmland were destroyed. Swirling dust storms blackened the sun as precious topsoil blew away. Even a thousand miles away, in eastern cities, yellow clouds of dust could be seen in the sky. The desperate people of the region known as the Dust Bowl had no choice but to get out. In a brief period, the population of a county in the Texas Panhandle dropped from 40,000 to less than 1,000.

Coming from Oklahoma was singer Woody Guthrie, the Bob Dylan of his generation. He summed up as well as anyone the fears and hardships of the depression when he sang:

> *I don't want your millions, mister;*
> *I don't want your diamond ring.*
> *All I want is the right to live, mister;*
> *Give me back my job again.*
>
> *Think me dumb if you wish, mister;*
> *Call me green or blue or red.*
> *This one thing I sure know, mister;*
> *My hungry babies must be fed.*

"I Don't Want Your Millions Mister," by Jim Garland © Copyright 1947 by Stormking Music Inc., all rights reserved. Used by permission.

TRY THIS!

1. Compare the problems of living in times of inflation (rising prices) and deflation (falling prices). Which are most people likely to find worse? Why? **2.** Explain why each of the businesses mentioned on page 507 and 510 prospered during the depression.

5.   THE 1932 PRESIDENTIAL ELECTION

Read here of how

A governor lost his admiration for Hoover.
Hoover lost a not-very-close election.
The United States won a New Deal.

In 1920 Franklin Roosevelt had thought Herbert Hoover the ideal man to be President (page 498). In 1932, as Governor of New York, Roosevelt completely changed his thinking. Hoover had been a great disappointment. In particular, Roosevelt thought that the way he had handled the Bonus Army was a disgrace. "There is

511

nothing inside the man but jelly," Roosevelt said of Hoover. "Maybe there was never anything else."

Roosevelt realized that Hoover was under enormous pressure, but he refused to feel sorry for the President. "I won't feel sorry for Hoover, even on Election Day," he said. These were not just idle words by a governor about a President. The Democrats had chosen Roosevelt to be their candidate to run against Hoover in 1932.

A bright political future? Roosevelt and Hoover were men of totally different character and background. Unlike Hoover, Roosevelt had come up the easy way. Born in 1882 to wealth and social position, young Franklin grew up on his father's estate overlooking the Hudson River, at Hyde Park, New York. Pleasant and handsome, he had the advantages of private schools, trips to Europe, and eventually Harvard University. In 1905 he married his fifth cousin, Eleanor, the favorite niece of President Theodore Roosevelt.

"FDR" served a term in the New York State Senate before joining the Wilson Administration in 1913 as Assistant Secretary of the Navy. In 1920 the Democrats nominated him for Vice President. He and his running mate, James M. Cox, took a beating from the Harding-Coolidge ticket (page 477). Still the future was bright for the vigorous 39-year-old Roosevelt.

In 1921 he was stricken with polio and never walked unassisted again. But with help from Eleanor Roosevelt, FDR kept his name before the public throughout the 1920s. In 1928 he won a narrow victory to become Governor of New York. After breezing to re-election in 1930, he was a contender for the Presidency.

"We are at the end of our string." In Chicago, in the worst year of the depression, the Democrats nominated Roosevelt for President. In his acceptance speech he attacked President Hoover and promised, "I pledge you, I pledge myself, to a new deal for the American people."

The Democratic platform called for unemployment and old-age insurance run by the states, lower tariffs, sound money, repeal of Prohibition, and some aid to veterans. It also called for helping the farmers by "every constitutional measure"—and promised a balanced budget.

Roosevelt carried out a shrewd campaign. He realized that nearly any Democrat would beat Hoover at the polls. After the Bonus March, and with the depression getting worse, Hoover was hated by millions. So FDR traveled about the country smiling, waving, and speaking—about jobs, security, and ending the depression. He seldom talked about issues, and he promised few new programs. Often he criticized Hoover for spending too much money.

FDR's campaign strategy worked brilliantly. In November 1932 he swept to a landslide victory over a tired and unhappy Herbert Hoover. Roosevelt won almost 58 per cent of the popular vote and 472 out of 531 electoral votes. The Democrats also gained overwhelming majorities in the House and Senate.

Inauguration Day, March 4, 1933, dawned cold and gray in Washington. Virtually alone in the White House, Herbert Hoover sighed, "We are at the end of our string. There is nothing more we can do."

It had been a most miserable time. The country seemed to have hit rock bottom. Nearly a quarter of the workforce were in unemployment lines. Thirty million people barely got by on charity and rapidly decreasing savings. The financial system of the country was collapsing.

On Inauguration Day, no bank in the United States opened for business. Worst of all, nobody seemed to have any solutions. Even Eleanor Roosevelt wondered whether anyone could "save America now."

"The only thing we have to fear." With the help of steel braces, Franklin Roosevelt stood to take the oath of office. Then, turning to the thousands of people before him and to the radio microphones that would carry his voice to a huge unseen audience, the new President began his inaugural address. In firm, clear tones he attempted to rebuild the shattered confidence of the American people: "Let me assert my firm belief that the only thing we have to fear is fear itself—nameless, unreasoning, unjustified terror which paralyzes needed efforts to convert retreat into advance."

Roosevelt went on to demand extraordinary power to fight the depression. "I shall ask the Congress for the one remaining instrument to meet this crisis—broad executive power to wage a war against the emergency, as great as the power that would be given me if we were in fact invaded by a foreign foe."

A new hold upon life. These bold words struck a deep chord in FDR's listeners. In the next few days 450,000 people wrote the new Chief Executive to promise support and express newfound confidence. One person wrote that the speech "seemed to give the people, as well as myself, a new hold upon life." All across the country, Americans were desperate for leadership.

Drawing upon this enormous public encouragement, Roosevelt launched his New Deal. The federal government soon took a leading position in nearly every phase of American life. Where once state and local government had been of primary impor-

Does Franklin D. Roosevelt look like a leader who could inspire confidence? Why?

tance, the average citizen now looked to Washington for direction and for aid. Social welfare and a measure of control over the economy became a duty of the federal government. Roosevelt and his New Dealers set out to rescue and improve the American system.

 TRY THIS!

Tell how you might have felt about the 1932 election and FDR's inaugural address if you were then (a) an unemployed factory worker, (b) a wealthy manufacturer, (c) a returned Bonus Marcher, (d) a banker, (e) a farmer in the wheat belt.

ROUNDUP

Who?

Franklin D. Roosevelt
Alfred E. Smith
John Dos Passos
James T. Farrell
Richard Wright
John Steinbeck
Eleanor Roosevelt

What?

"stock fever"
Black Tuesday
the Great Depression
Reconstruction Finance
   Corporation (RFC)
Norris-LaGuardia Act
Hoovervilles
Bonus Army
New Deal

KNOW THIS

The 1929 Stock Market Crash

1. Explain the method of buying stocks "on margin."
2. Describe what happened on Black Tuesday, October 29, 1929.
3. How did Hoover and business leaders interpret the stock market crash? Why were they wrong?
4. What were some major weaknesses of American business in the 1920s? What could have corrected them?
5. How did banks help cause the national crisis?

Hoover and the Great Depression

1. What offices did Hoover hold before 1928?
2. Who was the Democratic presidential candidate in 1928? Why wasn't he elected?
3. How were Hoover's ideas different from those of other Republicans? How did he feel about individualism? About big government?
4. How did Hoover try to cope with the depression?
5. How did people show that they rejected Hoover's leadership?

A March on Washington

1. What government action did war veterans urge?
2. How did the veterans react when Congress stalled?
3. What problems did the Bonus Army encounter on the way to Washington? How was it received there?
4. What part did Douglas MacArthur take in the way the Bonus Army was treated?
5. What showed that the Bonus Army was not a dangerous, subversive force?

Hard Times Throughout the Land

1. By 1932, what was the average weekly wage? How did school children suffer during the depression?
2. How did the depression affect women? Mexican Americans? Blacks?
3. What businesses boomed in the depression years?
4. What themes were most popular with filmmakers and radio entertainers in the 1930s? Why?
5. What disaster struck the Great Plains in the 1930s?

The 1932 Presidential Election

1. What background did Franklin Roosevelt have?
2. How did Roosevelt's having polio affect his career?
3. What tactics did he use in his campaign?
4. Who was elected President in 1932? By how much?
5. How did people react to the President's inaugural?

DIG HERE!

The phonograph, the motion-picture camera, the radio, and the television receiver made mass entertainment a big part of the American way of life. Research one of these forms of entertainment: music (live and recorded), films, radio, or television. Then answer these four questions, for each ten-year period from the 1920s through the 1970s.

A. List the best-known songs, recordings, films, radio, or TV programs for each decade.
B. Describe the themes favored, in each decade, by creators of the entertainment form you chose.
C. Name three important personalities (or performing groups) in each decade. Write a brief account of each person's or group's career. What seems to account for their fame and popularity?
D. Does the entertainment that Americans enjoyed reflect the social, economic, or political history of the decade? Think about it, and give reasons for your opinion.

To find the information you need, use these books: Baxter, *Hollywood in the Thirties,* Barnes; Blum, *A New Pictorial History of the Talkies,* Putnam; Feather, *Encyclopedia of Jazz,* Horizon; Griffith and Meyer, *The Movies,* Simon & Schuster; Halliwell, *The Filmgoer's Companion,* Hill & Wang; Higham and Greenberg, *Hollywood in the Forties,* Barnes; Settel, *A Pictorial History of Radio,* Grosset; Simon, *The Big Bands,* Macmillan; *This Fabulous Century* (Series), Time-Life.

THINK ABOUT IT

1. Hoover refused to allow the federal government to give individual persons relief, because he thought it would make them too dependent. Do you agree? Should there be a different policy for normal and for depression times? Explain.
2. How important is it for a President to be an inspiring speaker, like Franklin Roosevelt? Is it more important today? Why?
3. The Great Depression was triggered, in part, by credit purchases. What purpose does credit serve in today's economy? Should it be discouraged or controlled?

DO IT!

1. Read Frederick Lewis Allen's account of the depression in *Since Yesterday,* or Studs Terkel's in *Hard Times.* Write a radio script on life in the 1930s for a class presentation.
2. Ask a stockbroker to visit the class and describe present-day investing. Ask him or her about measures to prevent another crash.

THEN AND NOW

Were Americans right in holding Hoover responsible for the depression? Are political leaders often given credit or blame for events over which they have little control? Can you think of some recent examples?

A New Deal Gives Hope to the Nation

22

Symbol of hope in the depression years, the eagle of the NRA stood for both the successes and failures of the New Deal. The NRA was declared unconstitutional, but the Wagner Act and Fair Labor Standards Act carried on its best features.

After Roosevelt's inauguration the chief of the Secret Service traveled to California with Herbert Hoover. When he returned to Washington, he found it "full of people who oozed confidence."

This new atmosphere came from able, high-spirited individuals. To staff his Administration, Roosevelt brought to Washington large numbers of creative, dedicated people. They included young lawyers, professors, and social workers—not the sort of people usually found in government.

Roosevelt wasted no time getting the New Deal under way. The first hundred days of his administration were a period of government activity unequaled in United States history. Between March and June of 1933 the New Deal drew up a mass of legislation to combat the depression. Congress was delighted with anything that might cure the nation's woes. It shouted approval and passed the legislation without delay.

1. FDR'S FIRST HUNDRED DAYS

When Roosevelt took office, the banking system was near ruin. Since 1900 the United States had been on the gold standard (page 374). All paper money could be turned in for its value in gold. As long as there were large reserves of the precious metal on hand, there was no problem. But the European market for United States goods had dropped sharply. More gold was flowing out of the country than in.

Many banks had lost huge sums in the stock-market crash (page 495). They were forced to call in loans to stay in business. But individuals and companies had no money with which to repay them, so some banks had to close.

A banking guarantee. Roosevelt chose to strengthen the existing banking system instead of remaking it. On March 6, 1933, he stopped the exporting of gold and closed all the nation's banks. In the record time of eight hours Congress passed a law calling for federal examiners to check the books of all banks in the United States. Those that were hopelessly shaky would stay closed. Sound banks were issued licenses to reopen, and they received loans to increase their reserves.

Most of the larger banks reopened in a few days. Later in the year Congress set up the Federal Deposit Insurance Corporation (FDIC) to protect individual bank accounts. With their savings insured by the federal government, depositors could be sure of getting their money back even if a bank failed. The FDIC, which continues to guarantee individual bank accounts, made banking panics a thing of the past.

An end to the great experiment. Next, the President honored some campaign promises. He proposed, and Congress ap-

Read here of how

The New Deal ended bank panics.
It helped farmers and the unemployed.
And it changed the Tennessee Valley.
But it failed to regulate business.

TIME CHART

1933	The Bank Holiday is declared.
1933	The NRA, AAA, and other emergency New Deal legislation is passed.
1934	Huey Long founds Share Our Wealth.
1934	The WPA, the Wagner Act, and the Social Security Act are passed.
1935	The NRA is declared unconstitutional.
1936	The AAA is declared unconstitutional.
1936	FDR is re-elected.
1937	Roosevelt fails to change the Supreme Court.
1938	The Fair Labor Standards Act is passed.

proved, the Economy Act. This cut veterans' payments and government payrolls. The act was in keeping with the Democrats' 1932 attack on Hoover's "spendthrift" administration, but it certainly did nothing to cure the depression. In fact, most of the cuts in veterans' payments were restored a year later.

A more popular measure was the President's call to make the sale of beer and wine legal. This would give the government badly needed tax revenues. Prohibition had been unpopular (page 486), and Congress swiftly passed the bill on March 22, 1933. Later that year the Twenty-first Amendment to the Constitution (Appendix) quietly ended the great experiment. 517

Relief for the down-and-out. The first steps of the New Deal pleased conservatives; nothing dramatic or radical had been attempted. But FDR, as the newspapers called him, had some less traditional moves up his sleeve. At the end of March 1933 Congress approved his scheme to establish the Civilian Conservation Corps. In its lifetime the CCC would put more than two million unemployed young men to work conserving the nation's natural resources. Across the nation unemployed youths planted trees, cleaned up beaches, built park shelters and reservoirs, and dug irrigation ditches. By giving them work, the CCC restored their self-respect.

For the millions of other citizens who were hungry and unemployed, Roosevelt proposed the Federal Emergency Relief Act. The FERA, passed by Congress in May 1933, gave money to the states so that they could aid the unemployed. To head the agency, FDR picked Harry Hopkins, a former New York social worker. Hopkins followed in the footsteps of Jane Addams (page 384) and other women who urged social welfare programs. His social work had made him acutely aware of the need to help the down-and-out.

Hopkins instantly became one of the New Deal's most powerful figures. In his first two *hours* in office he spent five million dollars on relief. Because it helped them directly, when they needed it most, the FERA made thousands lifelong supporters of Roosevelt and of the Democratic Party.

Hopkins convinced Roosevelt that the FERA was not enough. The Civil Works Administration was set up to take people off relief and give them jobs building schools, airports, and roads. By January 1934 the CWA was employing 4,330,000 people.

A good taste. Perhaps the most lasting creation of Roosevelt's first Hundred Days was the Tennessee Valley Authority. The TVA harnessed the Tennessee River by building a vast network of dams. These provided flood control and low-cost electric power to an entire section of the South.

The government's entrance into the power industry—traditionally restricted to private business—met with immediate attack. The New Deal was accused of promoting *socialism* (government ownership of the means of production). Private power companies complained that the TVA's low rates would drive them out of business. Roosevelt replied that the TVA was neither capitalism nor socialism, but merely something that would "taste awfully good to the people of the Tennessee Valley."

FDR was right. The TVA saved three million acres of farm land. It also manufactured fertilizer for the valley's farmers. More important, its cheap electricity encouraged industry to move into the valley. This led to a dramatic rise in the average income of those living in the region.

Help for farmers. By 1933 prices for farm products had dropped to less than half of what they'd been before the 1929 crash (page 495). One farm spokesman warned, "Unless something is done for the American farmer, we will have a revolution in the countryside within less than twelve months."

The New Deal responded to the crisis with a new farm policy, the Agricultural Adjustment Act. Passed by Congress in May 1933, the AAA was partly an outgrowth of the populist movement of the 1890s (page 388). It sought to raise farm prices so that farmers would have the buying power they had before World War I. The New Dealers argued that this could be

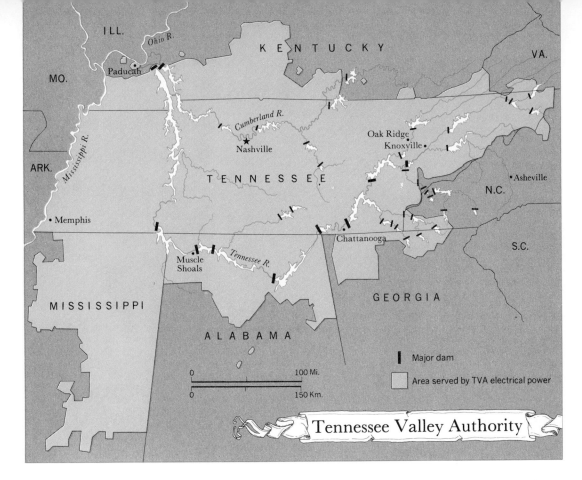

TVA brought prosperity to a depressed region. Could these states have done this by themselves?

Map labels:
ILL. / MO. / ARK. / MISSISSIPPI / Ohio R. / Paducah / KENTUCKY / Cumberland R. / Nashville / TENNESSEE / Memphis / Muscle Shoals / Tennessee R. / ALABAMA / VA. / Oak Ridge / Knoxville / Asheville / N.C. / Chattanooga / S.C. / GEORGIA

0   100 Mi.   0   150 Km.

Major dam
Area served by TVA electrical power

Tennessee Valley Authority

done by cutting farm production. Instead of growing as much as he could and selling it, a farmer would be paid to grow less. The payments were to be financed by a tax on such food processors as meat-packers, flour-millers, and cereal-makers.

To some observers the AAA seemed to create as many problems as it solved. Food processors passed the AAA tax on to consumers by raising prices. In a nation where millions were desperate for food, it seemed senseless to cut down on farm production. Southern sharecroppers and tenant farmers were hit especially hard. Plantation owners who cut production often turned tenants off

the land or refused to share the AAA payments with them.

Though the Supreme Court later declared the AAA unconstitutional, the measure introduced a policy that has shaped all farm programs since the 1930s. The AAA accomplished much of what it set out to do. Farm income doubled between 1933 and 1936. By the late 1930s most of the radical discontent of farmers had vanished.

A giant construction agency. Helping the nation's farmers was fine. But by 1933 the United States was an overwhelmingly industrial nation. The National Industrial Recovery Act was the New Deal's first attempt to help industry, business, and labor. It set up the Public Works Administration (PWA) to give jobs to the unemployed.

519

Under its leader, Harold L. Ickes, a Republican turned New Dealer, the PWA was a giant construction agency. It built a new sewage system for Chicago, a municipal auditorium for Kansas City, Missouri, the Triborough Bridge in New York City, and a water system for Denver, Colorado. It also installed electrical systems, built schools, and put up other public buildings.

"Where the blue eagle flies." The National Industrial Recovery Act also gave birth to the National Recovery Administration. The NRA was colossal both in its extent and in its final failure. It set up *codes,* or sets of rules, for each industry. Each industry code set the amount of goods to be produced and the price to be charged. This was supposed to keep prices from falling, end cutthroat competition, and provide organized labor with certain guarantees.

At first business and industry were enthusiastic about the NRA. The fixed prices insured a profit and set aside the troublesome antitrust laws (page 369). The NRA also helped organized labor get a foot in the door. It fixed minimum wages, limited the hours of work, and encouraged employers to recognize and deal with their workers' unions. Sweatshop working conditions and child labor were outlawed.

As head of the NRA, Roosevelt named General Hugh Johnson, a crusty, outspoken man. Johnson was determined to make the codes work. Asked what would happen to business leaders who refused to sign up, Johnson replied, "They'll get a sock right on the nose."

NRA codes eventually covered two and a half million firms and 22 million workers. A blue eagle and the slogan "We Do Our

This mural is typical of the art created for public buildings by the WPA (page 522).

Part" became the NRA's symbol. James M. Curley, the colorful Mayor of Boston, spoke for many: "I promise as a good American citizen to do my part for the NRA. I will buy only where the blue eagle flies."

On our way. New Dealers soon had second thoughts. Old-line progressives attacked the NRA for encouraging monopolistic practices. And it was hard to enforce the codes. Many big industrialists ignored them. Owners of small businesses complained that they had to give too much to labor and got nothing in return. Organized labor replied that manufacturers were not living up to wage and hour agreements. And consumers balked at having to pay the higher prices set by NRA codes. Worst of all, the NRA did little to help recovery. Limiting production and raising prices in the middle of a depression was no solution. When the Supreme Court declared the NRA unconstitutional in 1935, few tears were shed.

The Hundred Days came to an end in June 1933. A remarkable body of legislation had been enacted in that short time. Although the depression was far from over, people had regained some of their hope and confidence. When FDR collected his statements on the Hundred Days for publication, he had every reason to call them *On Our Way.*

TRY THIS!

1. Compare the relief efforts of FDR with those of Herbert Hoover (page 501). **2.** Tell how the New Deal sometimes copied and sometimes changed the ideas of the populists (page 388). **3.** Describe the way people felt about FDR in the first Hundred Days of the New Deal.

2.   THE SECOND NEW DEAL PROGRAMS

In the 1934 congressional elections, New Deal Democrats won a huge victory. Roosevelt sensed that the time had come for some far-reaching legislation. Harry Hopkins (page 518) told his associates, "Boys, this is our hour. We've got to get everything we want—a works program, Social Security, wages and hours, everything—now or never!"

WPA artists identified with working people and showed it in their paintings.

A blessing for the unemployed. Roosevelt had never liked the idea of just giving money, food, or clothing to the poor. He felt this undermined their self-respect. In April 1935 Congress approved his proposal for a government job program. It provided 4.8 billion dollars—the largest peacetime appropriation in American history—for the creation of the Works Progress Administration. For the next six years the WPA, with Hopkins as its chief, was at the center of all New Deal relief efforts.

The WPA had many critics. Even at its height it provided jobs for only 40 per cent of the unemployed. The average wage—52 dollars a month—was not enough for most households. And one skeptic complained that some WPA jobs were "about as sensible as hiring grown men to chase tumbleweeds on a windy day."

In spite of the low pay, to those on its payroll the WPA was a blessing. WPA projects did meet a variety of social and cultural needs. They led to the building of 2,500 hospitals; 5,900 schools; 13,000 playgrounds. Actors and musicians went on tour with outstanding plays and concerts. Writers turned out hundreds of publications, including state guidebooks that are still in use. By pumping eleven billion dollars into the economy, the WPA signifi-

Read here of how

The New Deal set up long-term relief.
And it established Social Security.
It encouraged workers to organize.
So the labor movement split but also grew.

Social Security was such a new idea it had to be "sold" to workers through posters like this one.

cantly eased the burden of the depression.

Help for the aged and unemployed.
One of Roosevelt's pet ideas was a system that would make life more secure. In 1935 Congress passed the Social Security Act, a sweeping three-part bill. Much of this social legislation was based on recommendations made by FDR's Secretary of Labor, Frances Perkins. The first woman to sit on the Cabinet, she was one of the many women who gave the New Deal a spirit of social concern.

Social Security provided benefits for the elderly. If they had worked long enough, they would receive pension payments on retirement at age 65. To get funds, the federal government taxed an employee's pay and collected an equal amount from his or her employer.

The second Social Security measure provided aid for the unemployed. People who lost their jobs received a certain percentage of their wages until they found work. Though set up by the federal government, unemployment compensation was administered by the states. Taxes on employers provided the necessary funds.

The third Social Security measure was designed to help the helpless. Disabled or blind people, regardless of age, would receive disability benefits. Social Security payments would also be made to children under eighteen who lacked parental support. Like unemployment compensation, public assistance was administered by the states and financed by federal funds.

Flawed legislation. The Social Security Act has been amended and expanded many times since 1935. It was a groundbreaking piece of legislation, and it remains the basis for most government assistance in the United States. It accepted, as no earlier program had, the idea that government had a continuing responsibility for the welfare of its citizens. The Act brought the United States into line with other industrial nations. They had long had similar social insurance plans.

523

I graduated college in '35. I went down to Washington and started to work in the spring of '36. The New Deal was a young man's world. Young people, if they showed any ability, got an opportunity. I was a kid, 22 or 23. In a few months I was made head of the department. We had a meeting with hotshots. What's to be done? I pointed out some problems; let's define what we're looking for. They immediately had me take over. I had to set up the organization and hire 75 people. Given a chance as a youngster to try out ideas, I learned a fantastic amount. The challenge itself was great. . . .

Ordinarily, I might have had a job at the university, marking papers or helping a professor. All of a sudden, I'm doing original research and asking basic questions about how our society works. What makes a depression? What makes for pulling out of it? Once you start thinking in these terms, you're in a different ball game. . . .

The idea of being involved close to the center of political life was unthinkable just two or three years before all this happened. Unthinkable for someone like me, of lower middle-class, close to ghetto, Jewish life. Suddenly you were a significant member of society. It was not the kind of closed society you had lived in before.

You weren't in the situation kids are in today, where you're confronted with . . . hopelessness . . . unless you just break things up. You were really part of something. Changes could be made. Bringing *immediate* results to people who were starving. You could do something about it. That was the most important thing. This you felt. A feeling that if you had something to say, it would get to the top. . . . The biggest thrill of my life was hearing a speech of Roosevelt's, using a selection from a memorandum I had written.

AN ECONOMIST RECALLS THE EARLY NEW DEAL

From *Hard Times: An Oral History of the Great Depression*, by Studs Terkel, Copyright © 1970 by Pantheon Books, a division of Random House, Inc. Reprinted by permission.

Though it was a breakthrough in social reform, the Social Security Act had some shortcomings. No other nation taxed an employee's pay to get pension funds. And the original act left out many groups—farm workers, domestic servants, and government employees, among others. Then, too, unemployment payments and the length of time they were paid differed from state to state. So did public-assistance pay-

ments. For example, people in Mississippi might receive less than New Yorkers.

A first for labor. When the Supreme Court declared the NRA unconstitutional, labor lost its right to organize. Congress quickly pressed for passage of a plan suggested by Senator Robert F. Wagner of New York. Frances Perkins, long a supporter of labor's right to organize, said that the President "never lifted a finger" in support of the bill. But FDR did sign it into law in July 1935. In time he came to view it as an enormous step forward for the labor movement.

The Wagner Act (officially, the National Labor Relations Act) made it clear that the federal government was on labor's side. It gave workers the right to form unions. Once a majority of a firm's workers voted for a union, it became their *bargaining agent.* The union had the right to act for all the workers in that firm. This is called *collective bargaining*—negotiating agreements with employers for employees' wages, hours, and working conditions.

The Wagner Act also prohibited employers from interfering with union formation, from firing workers for joining a union, and from forming company-controlled unions. The National Labor Relations Board was set up to conduct the elections for bargaining agents and to hear complaints of unfair practices.

Anti-union pressure. Many employers were upset because the Wagner Act restricted their activities while giving unions a free hand. Some tried to keep unions from forming. One large grocer in Cleveland, for example, closed his store and subtracted the time lost from his employees' pay. Instead of scaring workers off, such tactics tended to strengthen their determination to organize.

Sometimes employers called upon the police or the National Guard to drive striking employees back to work. At one auto-supply plant in Ohio there were pitched battles between National Guardsmen and strikers. The fights led a correspondent to write: "Toledo is in the grip of civil war." Minneapolis witnessed battles between supporters of management and the Teamsters Union, which was organizing drivers.

In one clash 67 strikers were wounded; two of them later died. A general strike in San Francisco paralyzed the city for four days.

A new kind of union. Once industrial workers started to organize, it became clear that the American Federation of Labor (page 373) could not meet their needs. Most AFL leaders continued to cling to the idea of organizing skilled workers by trades or occupations. This left the semiskilled and skilled industrial workers out in the cold.

Miners in the coal fields owned by U. S. Steel won an early victory for John L. Lewis (page 526).

The head of the United Mine Workers, John L. Lewis, went all out for industry-wide organization. This fiery, six-foot-three Welsh American was given both to quoting the Bible and to fistfighting in public. Lewis declared, "The American Federation of Labor is standing still with its face toward the dead past."

When the 1935 AFL convention opposed Lewis's proposals, he walked out. With other progressive labor leaders, he formed the Congress of Industrial Organizations. The CIO took the fullest advantage of the Wagner Act and the NLRB. By 1940 nearly nine million workers—twice the 1930 number—were union members. The most active were in the Steelworkers, Auto Workers, Electrical Workers, and other CIO unions.

Bound in affection. The Hundred Days and the Second New Deal had lessened the hardships of the depression. They also helped win Roosevelt the lifelong support of millions.

But there was more to FDR's enduring popularity than that. When he spoke to the nation on the radio, as he often did in what were called "Fireside Chats," his warm and reassuring voice entered the living rooms of ordinary people. Frances Perkins reported that during broadcasts, "His face would smile and light up as though he were actually sitting on the front porch or in the parlor with them. People felt this, and it bound them to him in affection."

TRY THIS!

1. Write two editorials, one attacking and one defending the WPA. **2.** Tell how Social Security is "flawed" legislation. **3.** Compare John L. Lewis and Samuel Gompers (page 372) as labor leaders. Could either one have filled the other's shoes? Why, or why not?

3. THE NEW DEAL COMES UNDER FIRE

Though very popular during his term in office, President Roosevelt still made enemies. Conservatives denounced the New Deal as a threat to American values. Some of the wealthiest people in the country angrily termed FDR "a traitor to his class." Others referred to the President as "Frankenstein Roosevelt" and the New Deal as "the road from democracy to communism."

This was certainly news to American Communists, who saw the New Deal as a plot of the wealthy. Their newspaper, *The Daily Worker*, protested that "every action of the Roosevelt regime strengthens the powerful lever of the exploiters, crushing the masses to the ground."

But FDR's greatest challenge came from other popular leaders. All of them charged that the New Deal was not doing enough to fight the depression. Since eight to nine million people were still unemployed by 1935, the charge made some sense.

Read here of how

FDR made enemies as well as friends. His foes said the New Deal did too little. Huey Long promised to "Share Our Wealth." But Roosevelt still won big in 1936.

Bitter vinegar. The Roosevelt foe with the biggest audience was a Canadian-born priest, Father Charles E. Coughlin. The local Ku Klux Klan (page 486) burned his Detroit church in 1926. Father Coughlin turned to radio broadcasts to denounce them. The "Radio Priest" was an instant success. By 1930 he had a national audience and was mixing politics with religion.

Coughlin attacked both capitalists and Communists. He claimed that the depression had been caused by the "politics of greed" pursued by bankers, brokers, and industrialists. He also warned that the Communists were waiting in the wings to pick up the pieces.

Coughlin called for support from men and women "weary of drinking the bitter

A cartoonist attacks FDR's programs. Gulliver (Uncle Sam) is tied down by the Lilliputians (New Dealers).

vinegar of sordid capitalism" and "fearsome of being nailed to the cross of communism." By the second year of the New Deal he was getting more mail than President Roosevelt and was taking in twenty thousand dollars a week in contributions.

Originally a supporter of Roosevelt, Coughlin became an outspoken critic of the New Deal. He was especially scornful of the AAA and its subsidy program (page 518). On the radio he thundered that there could be no surplus of either cotton or wheat "until every naked back has been clothed, every empty stomach filled." Many agreed with this attack. When Coughlin formed the National Union of Social Justice, he attracted millions of members.

Farm and small-town America. Another critic of the New Deal was a physician, Dr. Francis Townsend. He performed an important service by focusing attention on the elderly. Townsend lost his public health job during the depression and was left with only a hundred dollars in savings. But one morning in 1933 he realized that he was better off than many. That morning, amid the garbage cans in the alley below his window, he saw "three haggard, very old women, stooped with great age, bending over the barrels, clawing into the contents." He decided then that something had to be done for the elderly.

Townsend's proposal was a pension plan that would pay two hundred dollars a month to every American over sixty years old. On receiving the pension, an individual had to promise to retire from all gainful work, to spend the entire two hundred within one month, and to spend it inside the United States. Economists ridiculed this proposal. They pointed out that it would cost 24 billion dollars a year—nearly half the national income.

This did not stop Townsend. He teamed up with a sharp real estate promoter and began pushing his plan. By 1934 there were 1,200 Townsend clubs of spirited senior citizens. Townsend described his followers as those "who believe in the Bible, believe in God, cheer when the flag passes by, the Bible Belt solid Americans." By and large it was true. The Townsend movement represented a last battle for the old America of farms and small towns. Townsendites felt left out by modern trends and crippled by the depression.

Roosevelt recognized the need for helping the elderly. Old-age pensions became part of the Social Security Act of 1935 (page 523). But Townsend protested that the pensions were too small and that too many people were left out. This made sense to many, and the Townsend movement reached its peak after the new law went on the books.

The Townsend movement posed a serious threat to the New Deal. But then it was discovered that the movement's leaders (though not Townsend himself) had tampered with the organization's treasury. By the late 1930s the movement was but a shadow of its former self.

A model state? Roosevelt's major challenge came not from Father Coughlin or Doctor Townsend but from Senator Huey P. Long of Louisiana. A showy and shrewd politician, Long was a true populist. He hailed from the northern section of Louisiana, which had been a hotbed of populism in the 1890s (page 388). His rural background made him genuinely concerned for the plight of the poor.

Long was convinced that big business and the rich took advantage of common people and made poverty unavoidable. The Louisianans had for years been the victims of corrupt misgovernment. They threw their support to Long and elected him governor in 1928.

Huey Long lost no time making changes. By increasing taxes on corporations, he got funds for a better educational system, new roads, hospitals, and mental institutions. Unlike other southern politicians of the time, he did not denounce blacks. He even attacked the Ku Klux Klan and prevented its leaders from entering Louisiana. The nation watched with interest; Long seemed to be building a model state.

"Nuts Running America." But what Louisiana gained in public services, it lost in civil liberties. Long, popularly called "the Kingfish," ran the state with an iron hand. He proudly boasted that the Louisiana legislature was "the best legislature that money can buy." But the many services he provided kept him popular, and in 1930 the Kingfish was elected to the United States Senate.

Like Coughlin, Long was originally on friendly terms with Roosevelt. But the New Deal was too tame for him. He said that the NRA (page 521) stood for "Nuts Running America."

After meeting with Roosevelt, Long likened FDR to a Louisiana "scrootch" owl— one that "slips into the roost and scrootches up to the hen and talks softly to her. And the hen just falls in love with him, and the first thing you know, there ain't no hen!"

In the 1930s Huey Long was one politician who used radio effectively. Who was another?

He told his fellow senators that the New Deal would not satisfy the discontented and unemployed. "Men, it will not be long before there will be a mob assembling here to hang senators from the rafters of the Senate. I have to determine whether I will stay here and be hung with you or go out and lead the mob."

Long decided to lead the mob. Early in 1934 he founded an organization called "Share Our Wealth." It proposed limiting all private fortunes to no more than three million dollars. The government would take over anything above that amount and give the people a whole range of benefits. Everyone in the country would receive 5,000 dollars, a radio, a washing machine, a college education, an old-age pension, and best of all, an annual income of 2,000 dollars. Share Our Wealth soon counted its followers in the millions.

"I have so much to do." When Long and his supporters started planning to form a third party for the 1936 presidential campaign, Roosevelt was truly worried. The White House commissioned a secret poll and discovered that at least four million voters would probably support the new party. This would be enough to throw the election to the Republicans.

The challenge never came. In September 1935 Long went to Louisiana to ram some bills down the throat of the state legislature. As he jauntily strolled through the capitol building, a young man walked up to him, shoved a pistol against the senator's stomach, and fired. Thirty-one hours later Huey Long was dead. His last words were, "O God, don't let me die. I have so much to do."

No world-beaters. It was hardly surprising that Roosevelt won re-election in 1936. His left-wing opponents—Coughlinites, Townsendites, and a scattering of others—gathered behind Congressman William Lemke of North Dakota in the Union Party. Some of their critics pointed out that their symbol, the Liberty Bell, had been cracked for a long time. The Republicans furnished the main opposition to Roosevelt but they too provided little challenge. Their nominee, Governor Alfred Landon of Kansas, was a good-natured moderate. Even his supporters admitted that he was no "world-beater."

For the first time blacks left the party of Lincoln and voted Democratic. Although left out of many New Deal programs, blacks had been employed by the CCC, WPA, and PWA. FDR had several black advisers, called the "Black Cabinet." Headed by Mary McLeod Bethune, founder-president of Bethune-Cookman College, it included economist Robert C. Weaver; Robert L. Vann, editor of the *Pittsburgh Courier;* and William H. Hastie, Dean of Howard University Law School. Blacks responded to this recognition by voting for FDR. In 1932 he had received only 21 per cent of the black vote; in 1936 he got 75 per cent.

Roosevelt's majority in the 1936 election was spectacular—over 60 per cent of the popular vote. Every state except Maine and Vermont gave him its electoral votes. Shown the figures of his amazing triumph, the President took a long drag on his cigarette, smiled, and uttered one word: "Wow!"

 TRY THIS!

1. Tell how critics of the New Deal affected its programs. **2.** Write a brief newspaper account of Huey Long's career. **3.** Explain why *two* forces opposed FDR in 1936.

4. THE END OF THE NEW DEAL

On January 20, 1937, Roosevelt once again took the oath of office. Chief Justice Charles Evans Hughes read the words slowly. Roosevelt repeated them with emphasis, especially the final phrase, "preserve, protect, and defend the Constitution of the United States." At this point, FDR later said, he wanted to shout at Hughes, "Yes, but it's the Constitution as *I* understand it, flexible enough to meet any new problem of democracy—not the kind of Constitution your Court has raised up as a barrier to progress and democracy."

A horse-and-buggy Court. Roosevelt had reason to complain. The Supreme Court had taken much of the New Deal legislation off the books. Most of the nine justices believed that the powers of the federal government were quite limited. To them, agencies like the AAA and the NRA went too far. Both were declared unconstitutional.

FDR decided to attack the "horse-and-buggy-age view" of the Court. He proposed appointing a new Supreme Court justice for every one who did not retire at the age of seventy. Six of the justices were already over seventy. Roosevelt's proposal would let him add six new members to the Court. This would give New Deal legislation clear

---

Read here of how

FDR tried to change the Supreme Court.
And ran into a storm of opposition.
He cut back on relief programs too soon.
And had trouble with Congress.
But when he died, millions wept.

---

sailing. FDR pretended that the reform would make the Court more efficient.

This "court-packing" measure met with an angry reaction. John W. Davis, the 1924 Democratic nominee and a leading constitutional lawyer, considered the proposal "the gravest attack on our system of government that has occurred in my lifetime, or perhaps, in the history of the Republic." To conservatives like Davis, Roosevelt was tampering with the Constitution by interfering with the separation of powers in government (page 111).

Stinging defeat. Much to his surprise, the President discovered that many of his followers agreed with the conservatives. He had also underestimated public support for the Court. Many Americans disliked its decisions. But they held the Court itself in high regard. For them a solemn and changeless Supreme Court should be above political maneuvering.

The fatal blows to the President's plan came from the Supreme Court itself. Chief Justice Hughes explained that adding justices "would not promote the efficiency of the court. . . . There would be more judges to confer, more judges to discuss, more judges to be convinced and to decide." Next, a series of 5-4 votes showed that the Court was not as conservative as everybody thought. It upheld several pieces of progressive legislation, including the Wagner Act and the Social Security Act.

Then one of the most conservative justices resigned, leaving a seat open for a Roosevelt appointee. The President eventually gave up. He had suffered the most stinging defeat of his career.

In a sense Roosevelt lost the battle but won the war. After the spring of 1937 the

Does this cartoonist seem to support FDR's "nine old men" view of the Supreme Court?

Supreme Court upheld every piece of New Deal legislation that came before it. Eventually other conservative justices retired, and Roosevelt appointed younger, more liberal Supreme Court justices. Among them were Hugo L. Black, William O. Douglas, and Felix Frankfurter.

Division in the ranks. What Roosevelt gained in support from the Court he lost in Congress. Many of those who broke with the New Deal on the court-packing question never returned to the fold. Southern Democrats, once Roosevelt backers, increasingly voted with the Republican minority to block new reform measures.

The division in the Democratic ranks became worse in 1938. Liberal candidates, backed by Roosevelt, failed to defeat the conservative Democrats seeking re-election. Once again, the President had suffered defeat.

Heavy-handed methods. The New Deal was running into trouble on other fronts. The middle class, from which Roosevelt drew much support, became frightened by labor's methods. Striking to win recognition from the auto industry, the United Auto Workers Union (UAW) used the *sit-down strike.* Instead of leaving the plant, the workers seized control of it and stayed inside.

For conservatives and many moderates this takeover of private property looked too much like Communist tactics. By a vote of 75–3 the Senate condemned sit-down strikes. But FDR rejected pleas to call out the National Guard and dislodge the strikers. Though the auto industry eventually recognized the UAW, the strike had shaken the confidence of nonunion people.

The end of the road. Then the economy took a turn for the worse. Early in

1937 there was a mild burst of prosperity. But the President, anxious to cut government spending, made some bad decisions. Like Hoover, Roosevelt wanted to balance the federal budget (page 512). He cut back funds for relief and public works projects. At the same time, the Federal Reserve Board (page 419) tightened the money supply. With less money in circulation, the modest boom collapsed. In less than a year nearly four million people were thrown out of work, and the unemployment figures soared to 11.5 million.

The Fair Labor Standards Act, passed by Congress in 1938, helped a bit. It established a national minimum wage of twenty-five cents an hour. (Later it became forty cents.) The maximum work week was to start at forty-four hours and be reduced in time to forty. But the damage had been done. Instead of recovery, the nation suffered two more years of depression. Eight million people were still searching for jobs in 1939.

The Republicans capitalized on the growing public dismay. Their success in the congressional elections of 1938 spelled the end of the road for the New Deal. Although Roosevelt continued to promote further reform, he ran into a solid wall of opposition in Congress.

A patchwork of experiments. What had the New Deal accomplished? For the first time in American history, the federal government set up public works projects to help unemployment and took direct responsibility for relief. Through the FDIC (page 517) and Social Security, Americans were given a measure of security which they had not had before. Labor won the right to organize, workers got a minimum wage, and some of the worst employer abuses were ended.

But the New Deal often made as many problems as it solved. It created a mushrooming federal *bureaucracy* (rule by government officials) that lacked central control. New agencies tended to be poorly organized and easily sidetracked from their purpose. Besides, Roosevelt was not a good administrator. He was maddeningly inconsistent in his policies.

Neither FDR nor his advisers seemed to have really thought out the programs they were pushing. The New Deal was a patchwork of experiments, some of them miserable failures. Conservatives denounced it for undermining individualism. They were upset by the growing power of the federal government. Radicals took the New Deal to task for not seizing a golden opportunity to get rid of capitalism.

"Negroes Ruined Again." The New Deal also failed to come to grips with some especially critical problems. It certainly did not bring back prosperity. Many of the neediest citizens were overlooked by the Roosevelt Administration. And nothing in particular was done for blacks or other minorities. In fact, New Deal programs often practiced discrimination. The CCC placed blacks in separate units. A TVA town in Tennessee barred blacks altogether. And the NRA codes (page 521) accepted unequal hiring and wage practices without question. One black sadly suggested that the agency's initials must stand for "Negroes Ruined Again."

Though Roosevelt sometimes spoke up for black rights, he took no firm steps to fight discrimination. Eleanor Roosevelt was a far more outspoken champion of civil rights than her husband. An incident in 1936 revealed her concern. The Daughters of the American Revolution refused to let the world-famous black singer Marian

533

Anderson give a concert in their hall in Washington. The First Lady arranged for Anderson to sing at the Lincoln Memorial. A close friend of Mary McLeod Bethune (page 530), Eleanor Roosevelt played an important part in getting FDR to include blacks and women in his New Deal Administration. Throughout her life she remained a tireless defender of civil rights. Unfortunately, she was never able to convince her husband that he ought to take a more aggressive stand against racism.

"Because of Mr. Roosevelt." Millions of Americans overlooked the many faults of Franklin Roosevelt. When he died in 1945, at the outset of his fourth term as President, there was a massive and genuine outpouring of grief. As a funeral train returned his body to Hyde Park, New York, the nation wept.

On the evening of FDR's death a young congressman from Texas, Lyndon B. Johnson, fought back tears and said of him: "He was just like a daddy to me always. He was the one person I ever knew—anywhere—who was never afraid. . . . The people who are going to be crushed by his death are the little guys—the little guy down in my district, say, who makes $21.50 a week driving a truck and has a decent house to live in now, cheap, because of Mr. Roosevelt."

 TRY THIS!

Compare (a) FDR's efforts to change the Supreme Court with those of Thomas Jefferson (page 146), and (b) Roosevelt's attempt to defeat some members of Congress (page 532) with that of Andrew Johnson (page 334). Why, do you think, were none of these presidential attempts successful?

A much larger crowd heard Marian Anderson at the Lincoln Memorial than could have gotten into the DAR's Constitutional Hall.

ROUNDUP

Who?

Harry Hopkins
Harold L. Ickes
Hugh Johnson
John L. Lewis
Frances Perkins
Charles E. Coughlin
Francis Townsend
Huey P. Long

What?

Federal Deposit
Insurance
Corporation (FDIC)
Civilian Conservation
Corps (CCC)
Tennessee Valley
Authority (TVA)
Agricultural
Adjustment Act
(AAA)
Public Works
Administration
(PWA)
National Recovery
Administration
(NRA)
the Blue Eagle
Works Progress
Administration
(WPA)
Social Security
Wagner Act
National Labor
Relations Board
(NLRB)
Fireside Chats
Share Our Wealth
court-packing measure
Fair Labor Standards
Act

KNOW THIS

FDR's First Hundred Days

1. How were the early New Dealers different from regular government workers?
2. How did Roosevelt try to strengthen the bank system?
3. What steps did the New Deal take to assist the unemployed?
4. How was the Agricultural Adjustment Act supposed to help farmers? What problems did it create?
5. Under the National Industrial Recovery Act, what agencies were set up? What programs did each of them sponsor?

The Second New Deal's Programs

1. How successful was the New Deal in providing jobs for the unemployed?
2. What were some shortcomings of the Social Security Act?
3. What were the chief provisions of the Wagner Act? How did employers try to resist it?
4. What labor union did John L. Lewis organize?
5. Aside from his New Deal legislation, what explains Franklin Roosevelt's great popularity?

The New Deal Comes Under Fire

1. Who were some of the critics of FDR's programs? What were their programs?
2. Why was Huey Long called the "Kingfish"? What organization did he sponsor?
3. How were FDR's critics—such as Long—a political threat to him?
4. Why didn't Huey Long figure in the 1936 presidential election?
5. Who were Roosevelt's opponents in the 1936 election? What was its outcome?

The End of the New Deal

1. How and why did Roosevelt try to change the Supreme Court?
2. In what sense did Roosevelt "lose the battle but win the war" over the Supreme Court?
3. Why did southern Democrats and the middle class stop supporting the New Deal?
4. What were the major accomplishments of the New Deal? What were its failings?
5. How good was the New Deal's record on racial discrimination?

DIG HERE!

The story of the depression is best told by those who lived through it. Interview one person (a relative or older friend) who remembers the 1930s. Here are some questions you might ask:

A. What was your life like before the depression? Were you still in school, or were you working? Were you married? Did you have children to support?
B. Where did you live?
C. Do you remember the stock market crash? When did you first know there was a depression?
D. What did the depression do to you and your family? What hardships did your friends have?
E. What do you remember about the New Deal programs (WPA, NRA, CCC, AAA)? Which did people back then think were successful? Were you critical of some programs? Why?
F. What do you remember about Roosevelt? Did you admire him then? How do you feel about him now?
G. Can you remember any good things about the depression years? What is the best thing you remember happening in the 1930s?

THINK ABOUT IT

1. With the New Deal, government began playing a much larger part in the nation's business life. Does it play too large or too small a part today? Consider wages, prices, unemployment rates, health and safety regulations.
2. Coughlin, Townsend, and Long offered certain simple "cures" for the nation's ills. How do you account for their large followings?
3. Suppose FDR had succeeded in changing the Supreme Court. Would the government system of checks and balances have been seriously weakened? Why?

DO IT!

1. Research and report to the class on the financial problems of the Social Security system. What ways have been proposed to keep it from "going broke"?
2. Prepare an exhibit on comic-strip characters of the 1930s. Include Little Orphan Annie, Flash Gordon, Dick Tracy, Jack Armstrong, Buck Rogers, and Tarzan.

THEN AND NOW

Unions grew steadily during the depression, reaching almost 36 per cent of the work force by 1945. Today they have slipped nearer to 25 per cent. How could each of these factors help to explain the decline: a) a larger, better-off middle class, b) fewer workers in manufacturing, more in services, c) women and minority groups seeking employment?

TEST YOUR HISTORY

1. What was "imperialism"? Why did so many nations practice it?
2. Why did the United States take an interest in the Caribbean?
3. How was the U.S. position in the Far East different from its position in Latin America?
4. How did the United States become involved in World War I?
5. What steps were taken to mobilize people and resources?
6. Why did the United States refuse to join the League of Nations?
7. What effects of World War I influenced Americans in the 1920s?
8. What caused the great prosperity of the Coolidge years?
9. What groups did *not* share in the Coolidge-era prosperity?
10. What new ideas and new values were adopted at this time?
11. What advances did black Americans make in the 1920s?
12. What were Hoover's good and bad points as President?
13. What did Hoover do to end the depression? What major step did he refuse to take?
14. Describe ways in which the depression affected most people's everyday lives.
15. What political shift occurred in the 1932 election?
16. What did FDR give to the nation in his first days as President?
17. Name some of the lasting New Deal programs and reforms.
18. What groups opposed FDR and the New Deal?
19. Did Roosevelt succeed in changing the Supreme Court? Explain.

V

REVIEW

FURTHER READING

Burner, D., ed., *The Diversity of Modern America: Essays in History Since World War One.* Irvington, 1970.

Flexner, E., *Century of Struggle.* Harvard, 1975.

Graham, O., ed., *From Roosevelt to Roosevelt, 1901–1941.* Irvington, 1971.

Johnson, E. A., *A History of Negro Soldiers in the Spanish American War.* Johnson, 1970.

Lash, J., *Eleanor and Franklin.* Norton, 1971.

Life Special Report on Remarkable American Women. Time, 1976.

Lord, W., *The Good Years: From Nineteen Hundred to the First World War.* Harper, 1960.

May, E. R., *Boom and Bust,* Vol. 10, *Life History of the United States.* Time, 1974.

Scott, A. F., ed., *The American Woman.* Prentice, 1971.

Smith, P., *Daughters of the Promised Land.* Little, 1970.

Weisberger, B., *Reaching for Empire,* Vol. 8, *Life History of the United States.* Time, 1974.

VI

A WORLD LEADER

We have learned that we cannot live alone, at peace; that our own well-being is dependent on the well-being of other nations far away. . . . We have learned to be citizens of the world, members of the human community.

Franklin Delano Roosevelt,
Fourth Inaugural Address, 1945

The Nation Moves into a Second World War

23

In the 1930s Hitler (front, center) deceived many by promising peace in return for territory. Those who met his terms by giving in to him soon regretted it. Led by FDR, the American people realized that he must be stopped.

1. DICTATORS AND THEIR NEIGHBORS

Secretary of State Henry Stimson arrived in his office early on September 18, 1931. There he read with dismay that Japanese troops were rapidly moving into the Chinese province of Manchuria. It was an area as large as Texas and New Mexico combined, and it had a population of over 30 million. In 1922 Japan and the rest of the world's important nations had agreed at the Washington Conference (page 469) to respect China's independence. But now Japan was openly violating that agreement. It seemed to Stimson that Japan's aggression had to be stopped.

"Sticking pins in tigers." The League of Nations invited the United States to help in curbing Japanese expansion. But Stimson was quick to emphasize that he did not want this problem "dumped" into America's lap. The world powers, he thought, should work together in dealing with the problem.

Through the last months of 1931, Stimson tried to build up public opinion against Japan. He considered calling for economic sanctions against the Japanese; that is, stopping American trade with them. Then, in January 1932, Japanese troops and planes attacked the Chinese city of Shanghai. Japanese bombs killed thousands of Chinese people and turned vast areas of the city into flaming ruins.

A few weeks earlier, Stimson had sent notes to all the nations that had met at the Washington Conference. The notes stated that the United States would not "recognize any situation, treaty, or agreement brought about by the use of force." In other words, the United States did not intend to recognize any Japanese takeover of Chinese territory. This stand became known as the Stimson Doctrine. After the attack on Shanghai, the League of Nations assembly adopted the Stimson Doctrine and called for an end to Japanese attacks on China.

Stimson's idea for using economic sanctions against Japan ran into opposition from President Hoover. The President doubted that sanctions would be useful. Unless the United States was prepared to back up sanctions with force, they would, he said, be little more than "sticking pins in tigers."

Seeds of a future showdown. Stimson argued that Japanese aggression in China might well grow into a world war. He also pointed out that United States abandonment of China might destroy U.S. prestige in Asia. But Hoover was more concerned with the worsening economic crisis at home. Moreover, he doubted that the pub-

---

Read here of how

Japan invaded China.
The United States did little about it.
European dictators grew powerful.
But Americans were busy at home.

TIME CHART

1931	Japan invades Manchuria.
1933	The United States adopts the Good Neighbor Policy toward other American nations.
1935	Italy conquers Ethiopia.
1935	The first Neutrality Act is passed.
1936	Germany and Italy give aid to Franco.
1937	Japan launches full-scale war on China.
1937	A "cash and carry" policy is adopted.
1938	Hitler invades Austria and Czechoslovakia.
1939	World War II begins in Poland.
1940	France surrenders to Germany.
1940	The United States adopts a peacetime draft.
1940	Roosevelt wins a third term.

---

lic would support Stimson's suggested policy. Hoover reassured Japan that the United States would not use economic sanctions.

Shortly after that, faced with stiff Chinese resistance, Japan eased its pressure on Shanghai. But Manchuria remained under Japanese control with a new name, Manchukuo. And the Japanese warned that any United States effort to interfere with their "destiny" in Asia would be grounds for war. The seeds were there for a future Japanese-American showdown.

A Good Neighbor Policy. As the United States became less active in the Pacific, it continued to improve its relations

Ethiopians swearing allegiance to their conqueror. What does their attitude appear to be?

with Latin America (page 444). In his first inaugural address, Franklin Delano Roosevelt pledged that the nation would follow "the policy of the good neighbor—the neighbor who . . . respects himself and, because he does so, respects the rights of others." In this policy, Roosevelt picked up where Herbert Hoover left off. During his Presidency, Hoover had continually worked to improve United States relations with Latin America.

At a Pan-American Conference in 1933, Secretary of State Cordell Hull

promised that the United States would no longer interfere in the affairs of other countries. His promise was shown to be sincere in 1934, when the United States gave up its long-claimed right to intervene in Cuba (page 437). In that same year, American marines were withdrawn from Haiti, as they had been the year before from Nicaragua (page 444).

The Good Neighbor Policy met a real test in 1938. Mexico that year nationalized all foreign-owned oil holdings in its territory (page 471). United States oil companies protested, but President Roosevelt refused to interfere. Instead, he requested that Mexico pay for the seized property. And, after some pressure, Mexico agreed to do so.

Just as important to the Good Neighbor Policy were trade agreements made between the United States and its neighbors to the south. These agreements gave Latin American countries advantages, for their exports, in United States markets. Cooperation rather than pressure marked the United States' relations with its Latin American neighbors in the 1930s.

A mission to "civilize." As the Far East slid toward war, peace in Europe also grew more uncertain. In Italy the dictator Benito Mussolini proclaimed that it was time to rebuild the ancient Roman Empire. Mussolini had developed the theory of government called *fascism*, an extreme, nationalistic, right-wing movement. Fascists claimed that they could save the world from socialism and communism.

Fascist publications began speaking of Italy's mission to "civilize the black continent." Clearly, the target of this campaign was Ethiopia (map on page 525). At this time Ethiopia and Liberia were the only two independent nations in Africa.

In October 1935 Mussolini invaded Ethiopia. In spite of protests from the League of Nations, Italian troops soon occupied the entire country. Black Americans had regarded Ethiopia as a major symbol of black dignity. Outraged by Italy's actions, they held protest meetings and sought in various ways to aid Ethiopia.

But protests had no effect. Again the world powers had allowed an aggressor to attack another country and get away with it.

Undoing the Versailles Treaty. More ominous was the coming to power in Germany of Adolf Hitler and the Nazi Party (the German fascist movement) early in 1933. A corporal in the German army during World War I, Hitler had sworn to avenge Germany's defeat. His opportunity came when a depression swept Germany in the 1930s. For millions of Germans, this was the final blow. Behind them lay the memory of their humiliation at Versailles (page 466) and crushing inflation in the postwar years. Then it had taken a wheelbarrow of money to buy a loaf of bread. Now unemployment hit Germany on a massive scale.

Hitler was a spellbinding orator. He pledged to tear up the Treaty of Versailles and restore Germany to its "place in the sun." But there would be a price. Germans would have to accept the loss of individual freedom. A more frightening prospect awaited the Jewish citizens of Germany. Hitler meant to destroy them.

By 1936 the Nazis were well on their way to undoing the Treaty of Versailles. German troops reoccupied the Rhineland region. (Under the Treaty, they should not have been there.)

The uncomfortable truth was that aggression seemed to pay off. In fact, many people in western Europe and the United

Hitler presides at a Nazi Party meeting. His medal was awarded for bravery in World War I.

543

States saw no reason to oppose Hitler. They believed that Germany had real grievances. They failed to see that Hitler was threatening all democratic values. Their misunderstanding of the Nazi movement was to prove costly in the years just ahead.

Merchants of death. When Franklin D. Roosevelt entered the White House, outgoing Secretary of State Stimson tried to persuade the new President to take a stand against Japanese aggression. But President Roosevelt was busy with the problems of the depression. In New Deal planning, the nation's economic recovery came first.

Congress agreed with the new President about foreign problems. One senator said it was "the policy of the United States of America to keep out of European controversies, European wars, and European difficulties." National feeling in support of neutrality grew even stronger as a Senate committee investigated the arms industry and trade. This committee became known as the Nye Committee, after its chairman, Senator Gerald Nye of North Dakota.

Reporting on the hearings of the Nye Committee, newspapers carried headlines about the "merchants of death." And books and magazines pressed the argument that arms makers were a major cause of war. Many agreed with Nye that the United States should find a way to isolate itself from foreign wars.

 TRY THIS!

1. Compare the Good Neighbor Policy with the one set out in the Monroe Doctrine. Why did the United States' attitude change?
2. Explain the United States' unwillingness to oppose the aggressive moves of (a) Japan, (b) Italy, and (c) Germany.

2.   UNITED STATES NEUTRALITY

In the mid-1930s many Americans thought that cutting off the arms trade would be a good way to stay out of the wars heating up in several parts of the world. From 1935 to 1937 Congress passed several so-called neutrality laws.

Flexibility of action. In 1935 Gerald Nye and another senator introduced the first neutrality bill in Congress. After some revision, it was passed into law. The Neutrality Act of 1935 gave the President power to cut off arms shipments to any nation at war. It also empowered him to forbid United States citizens to travel on the ships of any warring nation.

At the time Congress passed the law, Italy was invading Ethiopia (page 543).

Critics pointed out that the Neutrality Act would probably hurt the victim of aggression more than the aggressor. The Italian soldiers invading Ethiopia were far better equipped than the African army that was trying to defend its homeland.

This first Neutrality Act lasted only six months. Congress passed another act in

----◆----◆----

Read here of how

War raged in Spain and China.
The United States tried to stay neutral.
FDR demanded a quarantine on aggression.

----◆----◆----

544

1936. It extended the provisions of the first act but added something new. United States citizens were forbidden to lend money to nations at war. This new law was to last for fifteen months.

Neither Roosevelt nor Secretary of State Hull thought the embargo on trade with warring nations should be made permanent. Roosevelt explained, when he signed the Neutrality Act of 1935: "It is the policy of this government to avoid being drawn into wars between other nations, but . . . no Congress and no [President] can foresee all possible future situations. History is filled with unforeseeable situations that call for some flexibility of action." He even warned that a hard-and-fast position "might drag us into war instead of keeping us out."

War by popular demand. In the increasingly dangerous world of the 1930s the problem of staying neutral had no easy solution. Some critics pointed out that protection of United States interests might require intervention on the side of one nation against another. For example, if Canada were invaded, would the United States refuse to help its neighbor? Would the United States be ready to defend itself against aggression? One member of Congress proposed a constitutional amendment that would have taken away Congress's

Those sympathetic to the Spanish Republic send a message to FDR.

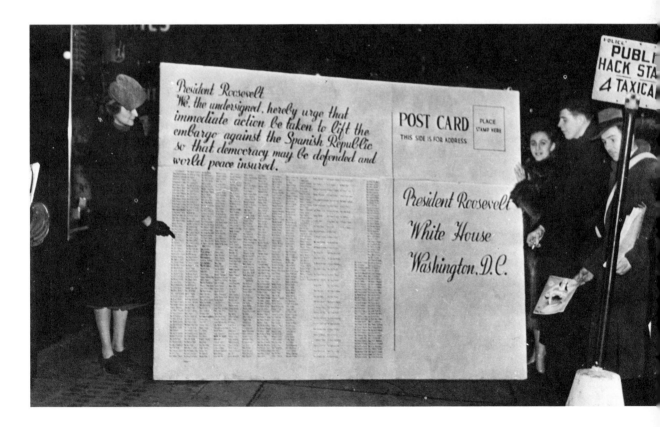

warmaking power. It would have required any declaration of war to be approved by a nationwide vote. The only exception would have been in case of an invasion of the United States itself.

The amendment was defeated after a long debate in Congress. One senator commented that "it would be as sensible to require a town meeting before permitting the fire department to put out the blaze."

A friendly gesture to an aggressor? In the summer of 1936 civil war broke out in Spain. People in the United States were far more interested in their presidential campaign that year than in another country's troubles. In fact, neither political party even referred to foreign issues during the campaign. In his second inaugural address FDR did not mention foreign affairs.

But by early 1937 the nation's businesses were ready to trade with the opposing sides in the Spanish Civil War. Roosevelt and Congress then adopted an embargo forbidding arms shipments to Spain. Only one member of Congress voted against the measure. He protested that it failed to distinguish between aggressors and their victims.

In the Spanish Civil War the aggressor was Francisco Franco, who was attacking the republican government. Nazi Germany and Fascist Italy openly aided Franco's forces. The republican government of Spain was getting help from the Soviet Union. Anti-Communists in the United States argued that any aid to the Spanish government would mean helping Communists. Others pointed out that the Spanish government had little choice, if the Soviet Union was its only source of aid.

Former Secretary of State Stimson rejected the idea that the Spanish government was "Communist." He argued that the United States "should furnish arms to the government that had been recognized as legal and no other." The one-sidedness of United States neutrality became clear when Franco praised U.S. policy as a gesture friendly to him.

Divided sympathies. American public opinion was divided on the Spanish Civil War. Many Catholics in the United States sided with Franco. They denounced the Madrid government for actions taken against the Catholic Church in Spain. Roosevelt privately admitted to a Cabinet official that he was afraid giving aid to Spanish government forces would mean the loss of Catholic votes.

An American member of the Abraham Lincoln Brigade, defending Madrid against Franco.

On the other hand, some Americans vigorously supported the Spanish government because it was anti-Fascist. Among them was Ernest Hemingway (page 485), who wrote the novel *For Whom the Bell Tolls* after visits to besieged Madrid. In addition, several thousand young Americans volunteered to fight for the Spanish government as part of an International Brigade.

"At their own risk." The need to give the United States government greater freedom in foreign policy became more apparent in 1937. Any hope that Japan would be satisfied with having seized Manchuria ended in July 1937. On an 800-year-old bridge named for Marco Polo, outside the Chinese capital of Peking, there was a skirmish between Japanese and Chinese troops. An all-out war now began. Its full horror appeared daily in newspaper pictures. The most famous showed a crying baby sitting in the middle of a war-smashed street.

President Roosevelt sympathized with the government of the Chinese leader, Chiang Kai-shek. The President knew that the United States neutrality laws would hardly help the Chinese war effort. So the Roosevelt Administration did not call for an embargo on shipments to Japan and China. Yet U.S. policy on the Asian war was uncertain. This was shown in the fall of 1937, when Roosevelt announced that privately owned American vessels would carry war goods to Japan or China "at their own risk."

In December 1937, Japanese planes sank the United States gunboat *Panay* on China's Yangtze River. Two sailors were killed and forty-eight others wounded. There was no doubt that the act was deliberate, since both the *Panay* and the ships it was escorting were clearly identified as American. The Japanese government apologized, however, and agreed to pay damages. Roosevelt's military authorities advised him that the United States lacked the military muscle to go to war.

Cash and carry. With war raging in Spain and China, the United States began to reconsider its neutrality policy. Some in the United States wondered whether an embargo on the shipment of war goods was enough. Should it be extended to all goods? But if all goods were embargoed, the national economy would be hurt. Roosevelt declared, "If we face the choice of profits or peace, the nation will answer—must answer, 'We choose peace.' " But most Americans wanted both peace *and* profits.

Out of this desire came a compromise called the "cash-and-carry" plan. The idea was to allow warring nations to buy non-military goods if they paid cash and transported the goods in their own ships. This Neutrality Act was adopted in May 1937. It also forbade United States citizens to travel on ships of warring nations and prohibited the arming of United States merchant ships. This provision of the law was designed to prevent incidents like the *Lusitania* sinking (page 453), which helped drag the United States into World War I.

But this act had an important difference from previous neutrality acts. The final decision on when and how it would be imposed was left up to the President.

Roosevelt knew that the "cash-and-carry" plan would work to the benefit of Great Britain and France. In any war with the Fascist countries, Britain and France would control the seas and so be able to buy United States goods and raw materials. One German newspaper claimed that "cash-and-carry" was in effect an Anglo-American alliance.

Not safe. Through the summer of 1937 the Roosevelt Administration remained silent about the crisis in Asia. In early October, Roosevelt dramatically broke his silence. In a speech in Chicago, he said, "It seems to be unfortunately true that the epidemic of world lawlessness is spreading." The President added that the "epidemic" was not likely to end unless the nations of the world combined to halt further attacks. Then, in words that everyone could understand, Roosevelt drew a simple comparison: "When an epidemic of physical disease starts to spread, the community . . . joins in a quarantine of the patients in order to protect the health of the community against the spread of the disease. . . . War is a contagion, whether it be declared or undeclared." Thus the President called for a quarantine on the aggressor nations.

The speech puzzled many people. Exactly how did a country quarantine an aggressor nation? Roosevelt had made no specific proposals. But the speech showed his feeling that something had to be done before the world was swept into another war. In a private letter, he admitted his intention: "I . . . believe that as time goes on we can slowly but surely make people realize that war will be a greater danger to us if we close all the doors and windows than if we go out in the street and use our influence to curb the riot."

The President had decided that neutrality was not a safe policy for the country. The United States would have to prepare to stop the aggressors. Without anyone's quite realizing it, the nation had set itself on the road to World War II.

 TRY THIS!

1. Explain how the Neutrality Acts of 1935 and 1936 were supposed to keep the United States out of foreign wars. 2. Show how the 1937 Neutrality Act was different from those of 1935 and 1936. 3. Compare FDR's efforts to remain neutral with those of Wilson (page 450) and Jefferson (page 152).

3. THE BEGINNING OF WAR IN EUROPE

Adolf Hitler had promised that he would tear up the Treaty of Versailles—and he did. Early in 1938 his army invaded and occupied a helpless Austria. Hitler then turned his attention to Czechoslovakia. Through the summer of 1938 he pressed the Czech government to give up a region called the Sudetenland. This was a part of Czechoslovakia that had large numbers of German-speaking people. War seemed likely.

In September the prime ministers of Britain and France flew to Munich, Germany, to meet with Hitler and his Axis partner, Mussolini. (The German and Italian leaders had formed an alliance called the Rome-Berlin *Axis* in 1936.) The British and French prime ministers gave in to Hitler. The Nazi leader got the Sudetenland but promised to leave the rest of Czechoslo-

Read here of how

Hitler persecuted the Jews.
He seized parts of Eastern Europe.
And made a deal with Soviet Russia.
Then he unleashed a blitzkrieg.

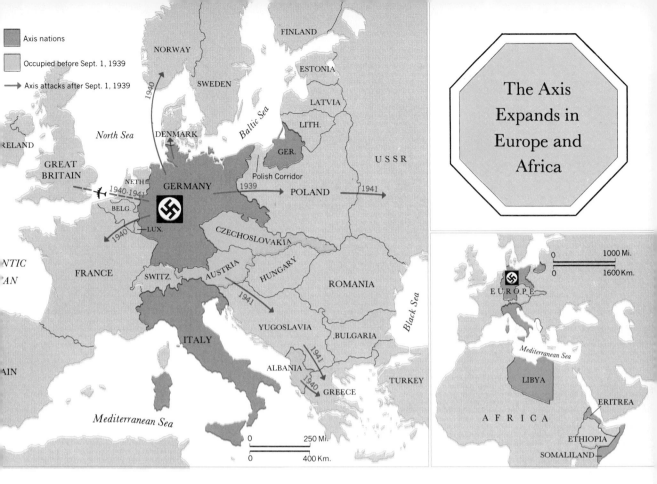

Axis nations

Occupied before Sept. 1, 1939

→ Axis attacks after Sept. 1, 1939

The German army did not bog down in trenches, as in World War I. At first, it was unbeatable.

vakia alone. This agreement was hailed by many Europeans as having prevented war.

A night of broken glass. With the Munich settlement, the United States too hoped that war had been avoided. But Hitler's anti-Jewish policies caused many Americans to feel deep concern.

Among the first acts of Hitler after he came to power in 1933 was the passage of laws denying German Jews police and legal protection. The Nazi intention was to drive the Jews out of Germany. Any who did leave the country had to give up all their property.

The situation of the Jews took a sharp turn for the worse in November 1938. A young German Jewish refugee shot a German diplomat in Paris. In revenge, Hitler authorized a savage attack on the Jews still living in Germany. Thousands were arrested, while in one night organized rioters burned and wrecked Jewish synagogues, homes, and businesses. The climax of what became known as the "night of broken glass" was a fine of 400 million dollars levied against the Jews of Germany.

People in the United States were shocked. But the nation continued to apply the quota system to Jewish immigrants (page 488). As a result, only 75,000 German Jews were able to enter the United States between 1933 and 1941.

549

Herschel Gryszpan, assassin of a German diplomat, being led from a Paris police station.

A broken promise. Six months after the Munich settlement, Hitler broke his part of the agreement. German troops occupied the rest of Czechoslovakia in March 1939. This put an end to hopes that Hitler's demands could ever be satisfied. Moreover, within a month Franco triumphed in Spain, and Italy occupied Albania.

Hitler then began demanding the Polish Corridor, a strip of territory that connected Poland with the Baltic Sea. It had been given to the new Polish state (page 466) by the Treaty of Versailles. Britain and France pledged their support to the Polish government. President Roosevelt appealed to the Axis powers not to attack or invade any more independent nations. "An atmosphere of peace," said Roosevelt's message, "cannot exist if negotiations are overshadowed by the threat of force or by the fear of war." Roosevelt offered to ar-

550

range international conferences on trade and disarmament. Hitler and Mussolini treated Roosevelt's proposal with contempt and refused to consider it.

The President was now convinced that the arms embargo had to be repealed. He also called upon Congress to strengthen the armed forces to meet any threat to the Western Hemisphere. But his first efforts to get Congress to revise the Neutrality Act of 1937 failed. *Isolationists,* as the antiwar group was called, insisted that there would be no conflict in the near future. Their prediction was totally wrong.

War! Throughout the spring and summer of 1939, Germany increased its pressure on Poland. In Europe, diplomats worked overtime. The United States showed its pro-British feelings by inviting the British king and queen to visit the New York World's Fair.

Any lingering hope of peace finally ended late in August. Germany and the Soviet Union announced that they had signed a friendship treaty. Hitler, now free from the threat of a two-front war, invaded Poland on September 1, 1939. Two days later, Britain and France declared war on Germany. World War II had begun.

President Roosevelt spoke on the radio to the people of the United States. "When peace has been broken anywhere," he said, "the peace of all countries everywhere is in danger." He also declared, "This nation must remain a neutral nation, but I cannot ask that every American remain neutral in thought as well. . . . Even a neutral cannot be asked to close his mind or his conscience." Privately Roosevelt believed it was in our national interest to aid Britain and France.

Survival. At the outbreak of the war, a poll indicated that 84 per cent of all

Americans wanted the Allies to win. But in keeping with the country's officially neutral stand, Roosevelt issued two proclamations of neutrality. One barred the export of arms. The other forbade United States citizens to give illegal aid to any nation at war.

Actually, Roosevelt was determined to repeal the Neutrality Act. He was well aware that ending the arms embargo would give a lift to Britain and France. He also agreed with the prediction of the United States ambassador to Britain: "I am entirely certain that if France and England should be unable to defeat Hitler in Europe, American soldiers will have to fight him in America." Roosevelt was certain that the fate of United States democracy depended on the survival of the European democracies.

Good news for Hitler. Three weeks after the invasion of Poland, the President asked Congress to repeal the arms embargo. He made the safety of the Western Hemisphere the central issue. "The peace, the integrity, and the safety of the Americas—these must be kept firm and serene," declared Roosevelt. After a long debate, Congress passed a revised Neutrality Act in November 1939.

This new Neutrality Act extended the idea of "cash and carry" (page 547) to the sale of military goods. Warring nations could now buy United States arms if they were paid for in cash and transported in ships other than United States vessels.

But the new law also forbade United States ships to sail into combat zones. The aim was to keep them from being sunk. Roosevelt defined the "combat zones" as

Mass ceremonies like this one frightened Germany's enemies—and helped to hypnotize its people.

The Camera's Eye

Some of World War II's most moving photographs are not what they seem. In war torn Shanghai (below) the cameraman snatched a baby from its mother and sat it amidst the rubble, causing it to cry and make a most effective picture (page 547). A Frenchman (top, left) appears filled with patriotic despair as German troops enter Paris. He was later charged with being a Nazi sympathizer whose tears were those of pride and joy. Hitler (bottom, left) was filmed as the French army surrendered in 1940. In one shot he stamped his foot. Repeating those frames made him perform a triumphant jig. (The trick is used also in TV commercials.)

552

the Baltic Sea and the Atlantic Ocean from Norway to Spain. This part of the Neutrality Act of 1939 was good news for Hitler. In launching a submarine war against Britain, he did not have to be concerned about sinking United States ships.

Even so, Britain welcomed the Neutrality Act. The British prime minister pointed out that it reopened for the Allies "the doors of the greatest storehouse of supplies in the world." The new act clearly showed that even though the United States was neutral, it was neutral in favor of Britain and France.

A phony war. Meanwhile, Poland had been crushed by the Nazi invasion. And Soviet troops had invaded it from the east. Within a few weeks Poland was divided by Germany and the Soviet Union. Then the war settled down into a curiously quiet period. Some even called it a "phony" war.

At home, the Roosevelt Administration concentrated on building up the defenses of the Western Hemisphere. In October 1939 an Inter-American Conference, meeting in Panama City, issued the Declaration of Panama. This established a "war-free" zone in the Atlantic Ocean around the American continents south of Canada. The warring nations were told not to fight in that zone. As it turned out, the declaration could not keep the oceans of the Western Hemisphere free of naval warfare.

In the spring of 1940 the phony war suddenly ended. On April 9 German troops swept into the neutral countries of Denmark and Norway. In a few hours Denmark was overrun, and in little more than six weeks Norway was occupied. These attacks made clear to the United States how little a nation's "neutrality" mattered to the Nazis. An alarmed world realized that Hitler would use the German war machine in any way he wanted.

Collapse. Worse was to come. On May 10 the mighty German army launched a *blitzkrieg* ("lightning war") against the Netherlands, Luxembourg, and Belgium. The first two countries fell to the German forces within a few days. And the Belgian King Leopold ordered his soldiers to surrender on May 28. Already, German forces were driving rapidly through northern France. Millions of French civilians clogged the highways as they fled to the interior and south.

At the French port of Dunkirk on the English Channel a huge rescue operation got under way. The British managed to ship some 300,000 Allied troops across the Channel, thus saving them from German capture. But this was the only bright spot in the disaster overtaking Western Europe.

On June 10 the French government abandoned Paris. Four days later, German troops marched triumphantly through the French capital. The same day, Mussolini, the Italian dictator, declared war on Britain and France. The French leaders surrendered on June 22. In July they set up a new government in the town of Vichy.

A stunned United States faced the fact that only Britain remained to resist the triumphant Nazis. Americans were moved by the eloquent words of Winston Churchill, who had become British Prime Minister a few weeks before the fall of France. Churchill pledged that the British would fight on the beaches, landing fields, and streets, or from abroad if the British Isles were overrun, "until, in God's good time, the New World, with its power and might, steps forth to the rescue and liberation of the Old."

President Roosevelt now viewed Britain as America's first line of defense. His aim was to keep Britain fighting until the United States could mobilize.

1. Using the map on page 549 (a) show what areas Germany and Italy took over before World War II began and which areas were attacked afterwards. Then (b) explain how Hitler's pact with the Soviet Union made it safe for him to attack Poland. **2.** Show how the Neutrality Act of 1939 brought the United States closer to war. **3.** Write the script for a radio broadcast describing the fall of France. Include eyewitness accounts of refugees fleeing southward.

4.   THE ARSENAL OF DEMOCRACY

Americans in the 1930s were not used to seeing people in military uniforms. Traditionally, the United States kept only a small army in peacetime. Except for the powerful Pacific fleet based at Pearl Harbor in Hawaii, United States military power was not impressive. The army had only one armored unit and no up-to-date combat planes. There was no separate air force.

The first change in this policy came in 1938 when Congress voted over a billion dollars to build up the navy. Hitler's attack on Western Europe in 1940 persuaded Congress to do even more. Roosevelt asked for money to modernize the army and buy tanks and planes. Within the year Congress voted over a billion dollars to expand the army and build a two-ocean navy.

A two-party war policy. Roosevelt was well aware that Woodrow Wilson had made a mistake in World War I when he refused to give Republicans a part in the war or peacemaking efforts. To avoid this kind of error, FDR appointed Republicans to serve as Secretary of War and Secretary of the Navy.

The new Secretary of War was Henry L. Stimson. He was the man who as Secretary of State had wanted to take a strong stand against Japanese aggression in Manchuria (page 540). Now he was responsible for mobilizing United States military strength. Stimson had testified before a Senate committee: "We shall [not] be safe from invasion if we sit down and wait for the enemy to attack our shores."

The new Navy Secretary was Frank Knox, a Chicago newspaper publisher. Knox was ready to push for direct naval aid to the hard-pressed British. On the eve of the 1940 election, Roosevelt could speak of preparation for war as a policy supported by leaders in both political parties.

Never in United States history had the country drafted men in a time of peace. But Stimson believed that only a draft would provide the manpower needed in the developing emergency. The issue was given a major boost by Wendell Willkie, the 1940 Republican presidential candidate. Willkie declared that "some sort of selective service is the only democratic way

Read here of how

The nation moved farther from neutrality.
It drafted men in peacetime.
And it broke the two-term tradition.
But kept a two-party war policy.

Morale of British civilians was not shattered by bombing. Neither was that of Germans and Japanese when their turn came a few years later.

in which to secure the . . . manpower we need for national defense."

A high school team. After the fall of France, Congress too realized that a draft was needed. A one-year draft law was passed in September 1940. The Selective Service Act required all men between the ages of 21 and 35 to sign up for possible military duty. Not everyone liked the idea. One senator said: "A [drafted] army made up of youths trained for a year or two, compared to Hitler's army, is like a high school football team going up against the professional teams."

Under the 1940 draft law, more than a million men were taken into the military service. A year later the Selective Service Act was extended, but only after a hard battle in Congress. The issue was not over the draft itself but over the extension of the new inductees' service for another eighteen months. Faced with the problems of building up the army, the military were reluctant to discharge trained men. On a very close vote, Congress agreed not only to continue the draft but to extend the service as requested by the army. The foundation of a huge wartime military establishment had been laid.

Two friends in danger. The British situation in 1940 was desperate. At Dunkirk (page 553) Britain had saved its army but was forced to leave most of its military equipment in France. After the French surrender, Britain was fighting Hitler alone. Dependent on the outside world for food and raw materials, the island nation had to use its navy both to protect merchant vessels and to defend itself against invasion. Meanwhile, British cities suffered a devastating bombing attack from German planes through the summer and fall of 1940. It seemed that Hitler must be getting ready to invade.

Prime Minister Winston Churchill asked Roosevelt for all possible aid, even pleading for destroyers. These small, fast warships would be especially useful against German submarines. Churchill promised to pay for such help as long as Britain could. But he added: "I should like to feel reasonably sure that when we can pay no more, you will give us the stuff all the same."

WENDELL WILLKIE

AMERICA
NEEDS HIM
in the
HOUSE

WE THE PEOPLE
WANT WILLKIE

Roosevelt, as usual, was cautious. He did not feel he could give all-out aid until he was sure of popular support. But he was prepared to give some help. Taking his authority from a 1917 law, Roosevelt shipped rifles, machine guns, artillery, planes, and tons of ammunition to Britain. It was the beginning of what was to become a flood of aid.

Through the summer of 1940 British and United States officials hammered out a deal for additional help. By early September an agreement was reached. Britain would give the United States military bases in Newfoundland and Bermuda. In exchange for bases on British islands in the Caribbean, the United States sent to Britain fifty destroyers left over from World War I. Churchill described the trade as "two friends in danger helping each other as far as [they] can." As Churchill happily admitted, it was *not* a neutral act.

A "drafted" candidate? As the United States moved away from neutrality, it also prepared for a presidential election. The Republican Party gave the country a surprise by its choice of Wendell Willkie. He was a Wall Street lawyer and corporation president who four years earlier had been a Democrat. He generally favored Roosevelt's foreign policy, including the aid to Great Britain. His nomination showed that the Republican Party was not totally controlled by isolationists.

The Democrats met in Chicago to choose their candidate. The chief question was whether FDR would run again. While there was no law against a third term, there was a tradition dating back to Washington and Jefferson that Presidents served no more than eight years.

Roosevelt had indicated that he was not interested in running. But the worsening international crisis changed his mind. In a carefully controlled convention, a "draft" of Roosevelt was maneuvered. It allowed him to come forth as a candidate who had not asked for a third term but had to bow to popular demand. The Secretary of Agriculture, Henry Wallace, was chosen as the vice presidential candidate.

"Their liberty and our security." Willkie launched a hard-hitting campaign. He criticized the New Deal for failure to solve the economic problems of the depression. But the real issue was the frightening international situation. Roosevelt emphasized that United States forces would not fight "foreign wars" in "foreign lands," unless attacked. He also pledged that "no combination of dictator countries in Europe and Asia will stop the help we are giving to almost the last free people now fighting to hold them at bay."

Willkie answered: "If his promise to keep our boys out of foreign wars is no better than his promise to balance the budget, they're already almost on the transports." Roosevelt responded, in Boston, "I have said this before, but I will say it again and again: Your boys are not going to be sent into any foreign wars."

Willkie found it almost impossible to outmaneuver the President. After all, Willkie himself supported the draft, the destroyers-for-bases deal, and other aid to Britain. In the voting on November 5, 1940, Roosevelt swept to a third term. The American people in an insecure world had chosen to stick with the leader they knew.

As the year ended, Roosevelt, in a "fireside chat" (page 526), warned the nation that Nazi Germany would settle for nothing less than world domination. If Britain fell, it would open the Western Hemisphere to assault. The President said

that the United States had to "take risks now for peace in the future." Arms and munitions had to be given to the British to preserve "their liberty and our security." Roosevelt defined a new role for the nation when he declared that "America must be the great arsenal of democracy." Thus the United States abandoned its stand of neutrality.

 TRY THIS!

1. Show why FDR needed Republican support for aid to Britain. **2.** Explain the football-team comparison between the United States army and Hitler's. **3.** Write out a brief campaign statement for Wendell Willkie, showing where he agreed and disagreed with FDR.

557

Roundup

Who?

> Henry L. Stimson
> Cordell Hull
> Benito Mussolini
> Adolf Hitler
> Gerald Nye
> Francisco Franco
> Chiang Kai-shek
> Winston Churchill
> Wendell Willkie

What?

> Stimson Doctrine
> Good Neighbor Policy
> Nazi Party
> Neutrality Act of 1935
> *Panay* incident
> cash-and-carry
> Rome-Berlin Axis
> night of broken glass
> Polish Corridor
> Neutrality Act of 1937
> Neutrality Act of 1939
> blitzkrieg
> Selective Service

Where?

> Manchuria
> Shanghai
> Ethiopia

KNOW THIS

Dictators and Their Neighbors

1. How did the League of Nations respond to Japanese aggression in Manchuria?
2. What action did Secretary of State Stimson want the United States to take? Why did President Hoover reject this idea?
3. How did the U.S. carry out the Good Neighbor Policy in its dealings with Latin America?
4. What was Mussolini's theory of government? What program of conquest did he launch?
5. In the 1930s, what was the general feeling in the United States about foreign wars?

United States Neutrality

1. What was the Nye Committee? What policy did it want adopted?
2. What were the opposing sides in the Spanish Civil War? How did the United States respond to the conflict?
3. When full-scale war broke out between Japan and China, which side did the U.S. favor? What action did it take?
4. How was ''cash-and-carry'' different from earlier United States neutrality measures?

The Beginning of War in Europe

1. What triumph did Hitler win in 1938?
2. How did Hitler first attempt to drive the Jews out of Germany? In what other ways did he attack them?
3. How did World War II begin in Europe?
4. Why did Roosevelt wish to repeal the Neutrality Act of 1937?
5. When did the ''phony war'' end? What countries had fallen to Hitler by June 1940?

The Arsenal of Democracy

1. How did the Roosevelt Administration strengthen the United States in the face of World War II?
2. How did Congress arrange to supply needed manpower?
3. What aid did FDR give Britain? What did the United States receive in return?
4. How did Roosevelt win nomination for a third term?
5. Who was FDR's opponent in the 1940 election? What were the issues?

DIG HERE!

Despite being a time of economic depression, with an increasing threat of war, the 1930s were a period of artistic activity in painting, photography, sculpture, architecture, and interior design. Choose one of these art forms, and examine it in detail for each of three time periods: 1900–1930, 1930–1945, 1945–present. For whatever art form you choose, work with these topics:

A. What main styles emerged in each period? Were there particular kinds of line, form, material, shape, or color that artists favored?

B. Do the styles reflect what was happening during the period? For example, did a war or an economic depression influence artists' work? How?

C. Were any of the artists reacting *against* what was happening during the period? What in their work suggests this to you?

D. Select one artist and research his or her work. If possible, prepare an exhibit about the artist's work. (It may be reproduced in low-priced photos, or on slides.)

Use these books for a start: Bour, *New Art in America: Fifteen Painters of the Twentieth Century*, Praeger; Cole, *From Tipi to Skyscraper*, Braziller; Faulkner, *Inside Today's Home*, Holt; Mendelowitz, *A History of American Art*, Holt; Rhodes, *American Art Since 1900: A Critical History*, Praeger; Solomon, *New York: The Art Scene*, Holt.

THINK ABOUT IT

1. Should President Hoover have agreed to economic sanctions against Japan? Would the Japanese have withdrawn from Manchuria? Why, or why not? When else has the U.S. used economic sanctions instead of going to war? Did they work?

2. Most Americans were isolationists during the 1930s. Why? Public opinion soon changed. Why?

3. Before the 1970s most Americans would not have considered dealing with Communist China. They thought it would appear to be encouraging dictatorship. Were they mistaken? Explain.

DO IT!

1. Organize the kind of radio debate between FDR and Wendell Willkie that could have been held during the 1940 campaign.

2. Research the outbreak of the Spanish Civil War. File the kind of "background" piece a U.S. correspondent in Madrid might have sent to his editor.

THEN AND NOW

If it seemed all right in the 1940s for the United States to sell arms to its friends, is it therefore all right now? Do arms sales benefit the United States economically? Politically? Does this make the arms race more intense? Are there reasons why the U.S. should *not* sell arms to other nations?

The United States In World War II

24

In World War I he was called a doughboy, in World War II a G. I. or dogface, in Vietnam he was a grunt. By whatever name, the infantryman was the final key to victory. After Presidents and generals had made their decisions, he went forward to take and hold the battleground.

1. AN UNDECLARED WAR WITH THE AXIS

Within a month of President Roosevelt's election to a third term (page 557), Prime Minister Churchill reviewed the war situation with FDR. He pointed out that the British had taken a savage mauling from German bombers and had withstood the worst the Nazis could deliver. In spite of these attacks, they had built and equipped an army of over fifty divisions. Plane production far outstripped losses; in fact, it exceeded that of Germany. Alone, Britain could meet any German invasion.

But Churchill made it clear that there were still serious problems. German sub-

marine warfare was causing heavy shipping losses. And Britain was running out of money to buy war supplies. He concluded with the request that the United States supply Britain, either as a gift or a loan, 2,000 bombers a month, as well as destroyers, tools, and arms.

Like lending chewing gum? Roosevelt wanted to provide aid to Britain. He also remembered the struggle after World War I to collect debts the Allies owed to the United States. At a press conference the President stated his intention to "get rid of the silly, foolish old dollar sign" by asking that debts be paid in goods or services.

Roosevelt used a homely example to illustrate his position: "Suppose my neighbor's home catches on fire, and I have a length of garden hose four or five hundred feet away. If he can take my garden hose and connect it up with his hydrant, I may help him put out his fire. . . . If it goes through the fire all right, . . . he gives it back to me, and thanks me . . . for its use. And if not, he replaces it."

Roosevelt was attempting to win support for a policy called *Lend-Lease.* If approved by Congress, that policy would give the President the power to make or obtain war goods for any country whose defense he believed important to the nation's security. Roosevelt wanted American farms, mines, and factories to produce the supplies needed to defeat Germany and its Axis partners.

The Lend-Lease Bill was introduced in Congress in January 1941. The proposal drew heavy fire from isolationists in both parties. Senator Burton K. Wheeler, a Montana Democrat, feared that by supplying Britain, the United States would be drawn into the war. Other isolationists sounded the same note.

Many Americans opposed any move that might entangle the United States in Europe's war. A well-financed organiza-

---

Read here of how

Britain asked for massive aid.
FDR got it for them.
The U.S. edged nearer to war.
The Japanese decided to climb a mountain.

TIME CHART

1941	The Lend-Lease Act is passed.
1941	Germany invades the USSR.
1941	Japan attacks Pearl Harbor.
1942	The Allies stop retreating in the Pacific, Africa, and the USSR.
1943	Italy falls.
1944	The Allies invade Normandy.
1944	Roosevelt wins a fourth term.
1944	The Philippines are retaken.
1945	The Yalta Conference is held.
1945	FDR dies. Harry Truman becomes President.
1945	World War II ends.

---

tion, America First, sponsored antiwar rallies and worked against Roosevelt's foreign policy. Charles A. Lindbergh, the hero of the 1920s, frequently spoke at America First gatherings. The Socialist leader Norman Thomas, former President Herbert Hoover, labor leader John L. Lewis, and architect Frank Lloyd Wright were all isolationists, or as they preferred to be called, noninterventionists. Their argument was simple: The war is none of America's business. Even if Britain falls, they said, a well-armed United States cannot be threatened by Hitler.

The isolationists offered strong opposition. But Congress overrode their objections. On March 11, 1941, Lend-Lease became law. Roosevelt could now supply vast amounts of weapons to the nations fighting Hitler. The new law also let the President decide how these goods could be paid for. He could agree to lend or lease war goods. Countries receiving them would not, there-

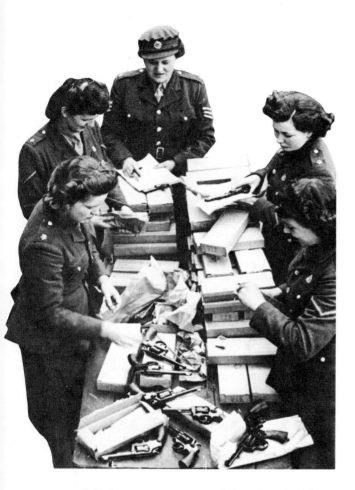

British army women unpack American lend-lease revolvers at an arms supply center.

fore, owe money to the United States. Senator Taft of Ohio snorted that "lending war equipment is a good deal like lending chewing gum. You don't want it back."

The chief danger. In the spring of 1941 Germany launched an invasion of Yugoslavia and Greece. The two countries were soon overrun. And in Africa, the "Desert Fox," German Field Marshal Erwin Rommel, drove the British forces out of Libya and back into Egypt.

On June 22, 1941, Hitler's legions poured into the Soviet Union on a thousand-mile front stretching from the Baltic to the Black Sea (map on page 549). Without hesitation Britain pledged aid to the Russians. Roosevelt, after stating that he found the Communist dictatorship of the Soviet Union unattractive, added that nonetheless "Hitler's armies are today the chief danger." By early November, the United States had extended a billion dollars in Lend-Lease aid to the USSR.

All but in it. As the war changed from a European war into a world war, the United States became an undeclared enemy of Germany and Italy. American authorities seized German and Italian ships in U.S. ports. Over protests from Berlin and Rome they imprisoned more than a thousand Axis seamen. United States troops occupied Greenland and Iceland as a defensive measure. The United States Navy began to alert the British to the presence of submarines in the western Atlantic. And United States shipyards were used to repair British merchant and war ships.

Matters heated up further when the United States merchant ship *Robin Moor* was sunk in the South Atlantic. Roosevelt responded by declaring an "unlimited national emergency" and freezing all Axis-held property in the United States. Shortly afterwards, German and Italian consulates throughout the country were closed. Increasingly, U.S. naval craft escorted merchant vessels as far as Iceland.

When a German submarine fired two torpedoes at the U.S. destroyer *Greer*, Roosevelt likened submarines to a "rattlesnake poised to strike," and ordered naval craft to fire at them on sight. In addition, the nation's warships began to convoy British shipping in the western two thirds of the

Atlantic, greatly reducing the strain on the British fleet. Understandably, the Chief of Naval Operations observed about the war, "We are all but, if not actually, in it."

Freedom from fear and want. In early October, the Administration asked Congress to repeal the 1939 Neutrality Act, which forbade the arming of merchant ships or their sailing into waters near Britain. Even as Congress debated the request, two incidents further deepened the crisis in the Atlantic. A German submarine torpedoed and damaged the U.S. destroyer *Kearny,* killing eleven seamen. Two weeks later, another destroyer, the *Reuben James,* was sunk six hundred miles west of Iceland. This time the loss was 76 officers and seamen. An angry Congress repealed the Neutrality Act.

Ties between British and Americans were further strengthened in early August 1941 when Churchill, Roosevelt, and their chiefs of staff met aboard United States and British warships off Newfoundland. They agreed to join in patrolling the Atlantic Ocean. And they drew up what came to be called the Atlantic Charter. It pledged both countries to work for a peace guaranteeing "that all men in all lands may live out their lives in freedom from fear and want."

In Berlin, German navy officers pressed Hitler for permission to strike United States ships anywhere in the Atlantic. Hitler refused but promised that in time he would "fight the naval war against the Anglo-Saxons to the end." The United States and Germany stood on the brink of war.

A double-barreled shotgun. The German conquest of France and the Netherlands in Western Europe (page 553) caused problems in Southeast Asia. Suddenly, French Indochina (Vietnam, Cambodia, and Laos) and the Dutch East Indies (Indonesia) were defenseless. And Britain was in no position to protect Hong Kong and Burma, its colonial possessions. Even the vast subcontinent of India seemed in danger.

Japanese leaders spoke openly of establishing a Greater East Asia Co-prosperity Sphere in East Asia. Control of this region would give Japan vital oil, rubber, tin, and other resources. It would also enable Japan to complete its takeover of China. By 1941

Freedom of speech and worship, freedom from fear and want became important Allied war aims.

the Japanese military had gained control of all of eastern China. The government of Chiang Kai-shek (page 547) fled into the far western regions and set up a capital in the remote city of Chungking. There it remained throughout the war years and beyond.

To United States authorities, it seemed that Japan was bent upon the conquest of East Asia. The United States reacted by moving the main Pacific fleet from San Diego, California, to Pearl Harbor, in Hawaii. Secretary of State Hull admitted that it was an action designed to serve as a "double-barreled shotgun" in future talks with the Japanese.

"Climb Mount Niitaka." The United States also took other steps to stop Japanese aggression. It forbade the sale to Japan of oil, scrap metals, and aviation gasoline without prior governmental approval. The Japanese reacted by entering an alliance with the Germans and Italians. Japan agreed to go to war with any power, other than the USSR, that might attack them.

There was now a Rome-Berlin-Tokyo Axis. Its obvious target was the United States. But in Washington the Japanese ambassador and Secretary of State Hull continued to talk about ways to maintain peace.

United States forces in the Pacific were put on the alert when these talks bogged down. A year before, the Japanese secret code had been broken. The United States was well aware that Japan had decided on war. But they expected any attack to come in the Far East. No one in Washington knew that a Japanese fleet had received instructions to "Climb Mount Niitaka." The order to attack Pearl Harbor had been issued.

 TRY THIS!

1. Record the thoughts that might have gone through the mind of an American isolationist watching the events of 1941. **2.** Explain FDR's "garden hose" comparison. Would it have persuaded you? Why, or why not?

2. WORLD WAR II IN THE UNITED STATES

December 7, 1941, dawned bright and sunny in Hawaii. On the naval base at Pearl Harbor, sailors were busy with peacetime duties. Beyond the gates of the base, the citizens of Honolulu were heading for church or sitting down to breakfast. Shortly after 7:00 A.M. two army privates manning a radar station on one of the northern islands noted a large number of blips on their screen. They notified the radar center and were assured that the blips were either naval planes or a flight of B17's arriving from the West Coast. The two privates then continued to watch the blips

"for fun" until the hills around blocked them from view.

A crippling blow. At 7:55 A.M. Japanese planes began their bombing run over

Read here of how

Japan all but wiped out U.S. sea power.
U.S. war plants roared into production.
Unemployment was finally cured.
And FDR won a fourth term.

The U. S. S. *West Virginia,* one of the great battleships damaged or sunk December 7, 1941.

the battleships of the Pacific fleet anchored in Pearl Harbor. The *Arizona* exploded with a deafening roar. The *Oklahoma* capsized. The *Nevada* made a desperate run for open water but, struck by bombs and torpedoes, went aground. The *West Virginia* and *California,* hit by torpedoes, sank. Both the *Tennessee* and the *Maryland* were badly damaged, as was the *Pennsylvania,* in drydock. A number of lesser vessels were also sunk or damaged.

Other Japanese dive bombers smashed United States planes before they could take off. The planes had been lined up, wing tip to wing tip, as a protection from sabotage. Within two hours, the bulk of the Pacific fleet was destroyed or disabled, as was most of the United States air strength in the region. The toll was 2,335 soldiers and sailors and 68 civilians killed, 1,178 wounded. Eight hours later, Japanese planes destroyed the United States bomber fleet at Clark Field in the Philippines.

Out of the Pearl Harbor disaster came one piece of good fortune; the fleet's aircraft carriers had been at sea. They were safe. But the United States had suffered a crippling blow. For the moment, the Japanese had won near naval supremacy in the Pacific Ocean.

"This is no drill!" December 7 was bitter cold in Washington. At 1:50 P.M. the Navy Department was notified: "Air raid Pearl Harbor. This is no drill." An angry Cordell Hull denounced the action to the Japanese diplomats who had been conducting peace talks in the nation's capital. They were shocked. Neither had known of the planned attack.

At Carnegie Hall in New York, the Philharmonic was preparing for its Sunday performance. When the audience was told that war had begun, there was a moment of stunned silence. The audience then joined in singing as the orchestra played "The Star-Spangled Banner."

The next day a unified nation listened as the President called for war against Japan and described December 7 as "a date that will live in infamy." By a lopsided 82-0 in the Senate and 388 to 1 in the House, war was declared. (The one negative vote was cast by Congresswoman Jeannette Rankin of Montana. She had also voted against World War I.)

On December 11, Hitler denounced Roosevelt as being "mad, just as Wilson was," and declared war on the United States. Immediately afterwards Mussolini added Italy's declaration of war. That afternoon, Congress, without debate, declared war on Germany and Italy. The struggle which had begun 27 months earlier on the plains of Poland had spread around the world. And Americans believed that the very existence of their republic was at stake.

An unending demand. Once at war, the United States turned to the task of crushing its enemies. A near-total mobilization of manpower was ordered. In the next four years 15,050,000 men between the ages of 17 and 38 entered the armed forces.

They were joined by more than 200,000 women in auxiliary services—WAACS (Army), WAVES (Navy), SPARS (Coast Guard), and women Marines.

Mobilization was not restricted to the armed forces. The need for workers in such places as the Willow Run bomber plant, designed to employ 100,000, sent millions of women into war work. By war's end they made up more than 36 per cent of the labor force. "Rosie the Riveter" became a folk heroine.

High school students, too, became part-time workers, as did millions of retired persons. Throughout the country, children collected scrap metal and other materials for the war effort. In the harvest season, they were recruited to work the fields. Many

566

black workers came north from the agricultural South to add their labor to what seemed an unending demand.

Profits for business. Hitler had gleefully predicted, "It will be a simple matter for me to produce unrest and revolt in the United States. . . . Our strategy is to destroy the enemy from within, to conquer him through himself." He was wrong. The vast United States industrial plant went into production as federal money poured out for defense contracts.

To assure a regular flow of goods, a nine-member War Production Board headed by Donald Nelson, former Sears Roebuck executive, supervised production. The result was a flood of war material. Within twelve months after war was declared, 49,000 planes a year were being produced; by 1944 the figure was over 96,000. Almost 300,000 bombers and fighters had come off production lines by war's end.

To meet the challenge of German submarines and the Japanese navy, 55 million tons of shipping were built. The loss to the Japanese of the natural rubber supplies of Malaya and Indonesia caused the United States to construct industrial plants capable of producing 762,000 tons of synthetic rubber. Steel production had been barely 47 million tons in 1939. It reached 80 million in 1944. In 1942 United States production equalled that of Germany, Japan, and Italy combined; by 1944, it more than doubled.

Large profits were one result of booming production. As Secretary of War Stimson explained, "If you are going to . . . go to war . . . in a capitalist country, you have to let business make money out of the process or business won't work." No development was more striking than the concentration of defense contracts in a few large corporations. One hundred of the nation's 175,000 manufacturing companies received more than 70 per cent of all war and civilian contracts. Probably this was because they were most reliable. However, without anyone's quite realizing it, industrial production was passing into the control of a few major corporations.

Fewer farmers, more food. Production records were set on the land as well as in the factories. Wheat production increased by 300 million bushels between 1939 and 1944. Corn production soared to more than 600 million bushels, and beef and pork production went up by almost a third.

United States farms were the breadbasket of democracy. The nation's farmers increased production while using about the same amount of land and fewer farm workers. New kinds of seed and fertilizers vastly improved the yield per acre. And more power-driven machinery was used. Tractors increased by more than a million. In fact, the farm population declined by 17 per cent, but production per farm laborer increased by 25 per cent.

Forced savings. To keep prices from rising too high and to assure a fair distribution of limited supplies, the Office of Price Administration (OPA) established price controls and rationing. People learned to accept the need for coupons as well as cash for meat, cheese, bacon, fats, many canned goods, sugar, butter, coffee, gasoline, clothing, and shoes. The production of automobiles and other consumer goods ceased, so people had to make do with equipment that had been repaired. In coastal cities dimmed lighting, called a "brownout," lessened the danger of ships being silhouetted against the glowing sky as they moved along the coast.

Between 1941 and 1945, the federal government spent more than 320 billion dollars to finance the war. The money was obtained through the sale of war bonds to banks, corporations, public institutions, and private citizens, and through heavy taxation. To keep citizens up to date in their tax payments, a payroll withholding plan was adopted. Beginning on July 1, 1943, income taxes were deducted from the wage earners' pay before they received it.

A spending spree. The war effort touched nearly every aspect of life and finally solved the problem of the depression. Vast federal expenditures brought full employment at last. Incomes rose throughout the country. Job opportunities drew people to the booming industries of the North and East and to the new manufacturing centers of California and the Southwest.

Whether Americans thought about the future or not, their bank accounts steadily grew. Between 1941 and the end of 1944, individual savings increased from 50 billion dollars to an unheard-of 140 billion. The makings of a vast postwar spending spree existed. The war had revealed how much the United States economy could produce. People would expect a high level of production when peace came.

A loyal party member. One of the more remarkable aspects of United States politics has been the people's determination to let nothing interfere with elections for Congress and the Presidency. In the elections of 1942, Republicans gained enough seats in Congress to give them, with conservative southern Democrats (page

After Pearl Harbor, Japanese-Americans march to internment camps under armed guard. They were held until 1945. On the West Coast 126,000 of them lost homes, farms, and businesses.

532), control of Congress. They supported the war effort but would have nothing to do with further New Deal experiments.

In the 1944 presidential election, the Republicans named New York governor Thomas E. Dewey. The Democrats renominated Franklin Roosevelt but replaced Vice President Henry Wallace with Senator Harry S. Truman of Missouri. Truman had made a reputation by heading a Senate committee that exposed frauds in war contracts. But he was also a loyal party member. Although the public was not aware of it, there was mounting evidence that President Roosevelt's health was failing. Those close to him doubted that he would live through another term.

FDR won the 1944 election by a margin of 3 million votes out of almost 46 million cast. The electoral count was a thumping 432 to 99. Roosevelt had twice broken the two-term tradition. He was elected to the Presidency four times. But support for a limited term was strong. Less than six years after Roosevelt's death, the Twenty-second Amendment limited a President to a maximum of two elected terms.

 TRY THIS!

1. Explain how the United States was taken by surprise at Pearl Harbor. What lucky break did the nation receive? 2. Compare United States home-front activity in World War I (page 457) and World War II. How were the troops, money, and goods raised in each war?

3.   FIGHTING ON TWO FRONTS

From the outset the United States was faced with a two-front war. A choice had to be made. Which enemy should be defeated first? The decision was to concentrate on destroying Germany, while steadily increasing pressure on Japan. After Germany fell, United States forces would be ready for the final assault on the Japanese home islands. But for the time being, Germany and Japan were on the offensive. The

---

Read here of how

The Allies fell back in early 1942.
But that year was a turning point.
The U.S. and Britain won in Africa.
And Italy was the first Axis power to fall.

United States and its allies had little choice but to fight a defensive war.

A death march. Six months after the attack on Pearl Harbor, the Japanese flag flew over the Dutch East Indies, Burma, Singapore, New Guinea, the Solomon Islands, Wake Island, the western Aleutians, Guam, Malaya, and the Philippines (map on page 577). As the spring of 1942 faded into summer, Japanese forces threatened India, Australia, and Hawaii.

The Japanese takeover of the Philippines had riveted American attention. After a bitter struggle, first under General Douglas MacArthur and then under Major General Jonathan Wainwright, about 15,000 American and 40,000 Philippine troops abandoned Manila and took up positions on Bataan Peninsula and Corregidor, a fortress in Manila Bay. There, for

569

three months, the combined force held off 200,000 Japanese troops. Reduced to rations of a thousand calories a day, suffering from malaria and other diseases, they fought a hopeless fight.

On April 8, resistance ended on Bataan, and a month later, on Corregidor. The survivors of this ordeal now faced the horrors of the "Bataan Death March," during which more than 30,000 sick and starving captives died as their captors denied them food and water. In distant Australia, MacArthur, who had made a hazardous escape from Bataan in early March, pledged to return to the islands. It would be almost thirty months before he could make good his promise.

A turning tide. Hidden by the tragedy of Bataan, the United States Navy began operations that would finally bring Japan to its knees. In May 1942, the day after Corregidor surrendered, Admiral Chester Nimitz used aircraft carriers to smash a Japanese fleet in the Battle of the Coral Sea. Australia was now safe from attack.

A month later United States aircraft carriers destroyed a Japanese force threatening Midway Island, thus putting Hawaii out of danger. A bitter battle raged on Guadalcanal in the Solomon Islands. The United States Army and Marine forces won a victory there and destroyed a Japanese invasion force during the Battle of the Bismarck Sea. This was the turning point. The Japanese advance was halted.

Japan resolved to fight a defensive battle on every island it had seized. The Japanese believed that the United States would decide the war was hopeless and accept a negotiated settlement. But the nation's determination had been clearly shown when a fleet of B25 bombers, launched from U.S. aircraft carriers, hit Tokyo on April 18, 1942.

Huff-duff and escort carriers. German submarines hovered off the east coast of the United States. In the first eight months of the war they sank more than 360 merchant ships. People standing on the shores of New Jersey, Long Island, and Florida watched as helpless vessels were sunk. The beaches in the New York area were coated with oil, and bodies of seamen from the sunken vessels washed ashore.

The United States had not been completely prepared for war. But new techniques to counter the submarine were soon developed. Sonar enabled destroyers to locate submerged submarines; radar spotted them on the surface; and "huff-duff" allowed operators to find submarines by picking up their radio transmissions. The United States and Britain built escort carriers to provide air cover for convoys.

By mid-1943 German submarine losses reached forty-one in a single month. German U-boats avoided the heavily traveled North Atlantic routes. Allied shipping moved with growing ease to replenish Britain. United States troops were also sent overseas. By the end of 1942, almost 200,000 Americans were stationed in Britain.

A second front. The Russians bore the brunt of the German assault through 1942. During the spring and summer of that year, German troops swept into western and southern parts of the Soviet Union. By late summer their troops had penetrated to the outskirts of Stalingrad. The Red Army was ordered to defend the city—block by block, street by street, house by house. The battle raged until the end of January, when the German commander and 250,000 troops surrendered. The tide had turned in Russia, too.

In the year that they were taking the full weight of Hitler's army, the Russians were urging the Western Allies to attack the Axis powers. This would force Germany to fight on two fronts. The pressure on the Russian armies would not be so great. So in 1942, plans were made to open a second front.

Desert rats and a desert fox. Winston Churchill called the Mediterranean Basin the "soft underbelly" of Hitler's Europe. Rather than attack across the English Channel and through France, he proposed that the Allies strike at Germany through the Balkans and Italy. From 1940 to 1942 a seesaw battle was fought in Libya, with the British and the Axis forces pushing one another back and forth across the desert.

From the late winter of 1941, the key forces in Africa were the British Eighth Army (the "Desert Rats") and the German *Afrika Korps,* commanded by the tank ex-

pert Erwin Rommel, "the Desert Fox" (page 562). In the summer of 1942, Rommel opened an assault that brought his forces to within sixty miles of Alexandria, Egypt, and almost to the Suez Canal. It was the high-water mark of the German advance in Africa.

A new British general, Bernard L. Montgomery, took command of the Eighth Army. On October 23 he began a full-scale attack that broke the German lines. Montgomery was helped by Allied air superiority over the Mediterranean and by the British intelligence service, which had broken the German codes. The Eighth Army smashed forward to rid Libya of the Germans.

A question of when. While the fighting was going on in Libya, plans were completed for Operation Torch, the invasion of French North Africa (Morocco, Algeria, and Tunisia). In November 1942, 34,000 men under the command of General George S. Patton, Jr., landed in Morocco.

In this Cuban cartoon, FDR and Churchill are winning the game of dominoes. Who are their opponents? The onlookers?

571

World War II in Europe and Africa

Map labels:

- ICELAND
- ATLANTIC OCEAN
- United States supply line to USSR
- Murmansk
- NORWAY
- SWEDEN
- FINLAND
- North Sea
- Leningrad
- EST.
- LAT.
- LITH.
- Moscow
- U S S R
- IRELAND
- GREAT BRITAIN
- DENMARK
- Baltic Sea
- London
- NETH.
- Hamburg
- Berlin May 1945
- Warsaw
- Russian counteroffensives beginning July 1943
- June 1944 Normandy
- Dunkirk
- BELG.
- GERMANY
- POLAND
- Stalingrad
- LUX.
- CZECHOSLOVAKIA
- UKRAINE
- Paris August 1944
- Munich
- AUSTRIA
- HUNGARY
- ROMANIA
- CRIMEA
- CAUCASUS
- FRANCE
- SWITZ.
- Vichy
- Southern France August 1944
- Milan
- ITALY
- YUGOSLAVIA
- Yalta
- Black Sea
- PORTUGAL
- SPAIN
- June 1944 Rome
- Anzio Jan. 1944
- Sept. 1943 Salerno
- BULGARIA
- TURKEY
- ALBANIA
- GREECE
- May 1943 Tunis
- Palermo
- Sicily July 1943
- Casablanca
- Oran
- Algiers
- North Africa, November 1942
- TUNISIA
- SYRIA
- MOROCCO
- ALGERIA
- Mediterranean Sea
- LEBANON
- PALESTINE
- TRANS-JORDAN
- Alexandria
- Suez Canal
- LIBYA
- Cairo
- EGYPT

Legend:
- Allied advance
- Axis nations
- Axis-occupied area in 1942
- Vichy France and Vichy-controlled area
- Allied nations
- Neutral nations

Scale: 0 — 500 Mi. / 0 — 800 Km.

If Western Europe was the key to victory, why did the Allies invade Africa and Italy first?

They had come directly from the United States. It was the largest amphibious operation ever carried out so far from its base. The remainder of the force that ultimately totaled 290,000 came ashore in Algeria. They were commanded by Dwight D. Eisenhower. This army had been assembled in Britain. Within two days all of North Africa except Tunisia was in Allied hands.

The remnants of the *Afrika Korps* had retreated from Libya into Tunisia. It was their base, so they had large numbers of troops and plenty of supplies. But in early May 1943 the Axis force, ordered by Hitler to fight to the death, chose instead to surrender. More than a quarter of a million German and Italian troops were taken prisoner. It was a defeat on the scale of Stalingrad.

Everywhere evidence piled up to indicate that the fortunes of war had shifted to the Allied side. No longer was the question *whether* the Axis powers would be defeated, but *when*.

Italy defeated. The weakest link in the Axis defense was Italy. On July 22, 1943, an Anglo-American invasion force captured the port of Palermo, on the coast of Sicily. Within less than six weeks, the island fell to the Allied powers.

In Italy a political upheaval swept Mussolini from power. On September 3, 1943, the new Italian government asked for and received an armistice. The British Eighth Army landed on the "toe" of the Italian "boot." Five days later the United States Fifth Army, commanded by General Mark Clark, went ashore at Salerno, near Naples, and soon captured the city.

The Germans reacted swiftly. In a daring commando operation, they freed Mussolini from captivity and restored him to power, in Milan. Then they stubbornly resisted the Allied advance. A United States effort to outflank the Germans by landing at Anzio, north of Naples, proved a costly failure. However, in late May the German lines finally broke. The Allies moved into Rome. But the Germans re-established their lines north of that city. Not until the collapse of Germany in the spring of 1945 was northern Italy liberated.

 TRY THIS!

1. Show that 1942 was a decisive year in the Pacific, in the USSR, and in Africa. **2.** Explain what Churchill meant by "the soft underbelly of Europe." Could British experiences in World War I (pages 461–463) have caused him to think that way? Why? **3.** Using a relief map of Italy, show why the Germans were able to hold back the Allied advance in that country.

4.   VICTORY IN A GLOBAL STRUGGLE

Where once British cities had reeled under the bombings of the German *Luftwaffe* (LOOFT-vah-fuh), British and United States air fleets ranged over Germany from Hamburg and Berlin in the north to Munich in the south. The Allies seemed intent on returning every ton of German bombs

———— •◆• ————

Read here of how

The Allies invaded Hitler's Europe.
Western and Soviet Allies crushed Germany.
The U.S. island-hopped the Pacific.
And dropped two atom bombs on Japan.

———— •◆• ————

tenfold. Meanwhile, the Russians were advancing into Poland and the Balkans.

But everyone knew that the route to final victory over Germany could only be through France and the Low Countries. As the submarine menace in the North Atlantic lessened, United States supplies and manpower poured into Great Britain. Newspaper correspondents joked that the island might sink under their weight.

Preparations were being made for an attack across the English Channel. On June 6, 1944, United States, British, Canadian, and Free French forces went ashore on the beaches of Normandy. It was the largest military operation in all history. Dwight D. Eisenhower, the Supreme Al-

573

lied Commander in Western Europe, was in charge.

A breakout. In the first six weeks after the invasion, the Allies steadily expanded their beachheads against bitter German opposition. Finally, on July 25, after a massive air assault, United States forces broke out of St. Lô and swept eastward through central France. British and Canadian forces moved northward. And on August 25, 1944, Paris was liberated by a Free French force commanded by Charles De Gaulle.

A few days earlier, the U.S. Seventh Army had landed in southern France, forcing the Germans to retreat toward their frontier. By late 1944 the Allies had pushed into Germany itself. In the east, the Axis governments of Romania and Bulgaria surrendered to Russia's onrushing Red Army. Through the fall and winter, the Soviet forces continued to advance.

"Nuts!" Hitler tightened his control over Germany. After an unsuccessful attempt on his life in July 1944, he ordered all suspected participants executed, including Field Marshal Rommel. Instead, the Desert Fox (page 571) was allowed to commit suicide. All through Nazi Germany, concentration camps daily killed thousands of Jews and other supposed undesirables.

In the west, Hitler launched a final offensive. It opened in December 1944, when bad weather was likely to cancel out Allied air superiority. Some 250,000 Germans attacked the lightly held United States lines in Belgium and Luxembourg. For a brief moment, it seemed that the Germans might repeat their triumphs of 1940. But with the lifting of the winter clouds, Allied air fleets came back into operation, striking the Germans. And on the ground the 101st Airborne Division under Brigadier General

Anthony C. McAuliffe held off the attack at Bastogne. When the Germans demanded the 101st's surrender, McAuliffe answered with a simple but expressive "Nuts!"

A swift end. As the New Year dawned, the German attack had ended; by the end of January, it had been broken. In the "Battle of the Bulge," as the six-week operation was called, over 8,000 U.S. troops had been killed, and nearly 70,000 were wounded or missing. But German losses reached 120,000 in dead, wounded, and captured. After that, Germany no longer had the strength for a counterattack.

The Soviet army now approached Berlin. Allied forces swept across the Rhine River. From east and west, a Soviet and Allied steamroller overran the German heartland. Hitler, trapped in an air raid bunker, surrounded by the ruins of Berlin, committed suicide in late April.

War's end came swiftly. On May 7, 1945, General Alfred Jodl ordered all German forces to cease fighting. The next day, May 8, was V-E Day (for victory in Europe). After almost six years the war in Europe was over. Vast areas of Europe, stretching from the English Channel to the Volga River and from the Arctic Ocean to the Mediterranean Sea, lay in ruins. A horror-struck world learned that six million Jews and at least as many other Europeans had perished in Nazi death camps. But the business of war was not finished. Japan had still to be beaten.

The Republic continues. Even as the war in Europe swept toward its end, the nation received stunning news. On April 12, 1945, Franklin D. Roosevelt died of a stroke in Warm Springs, Georgia. The man who for twelve years had led the nation through depression and war was gone.

Senator Robert A. Taft of Ohio, never a supporter of Roosevelt, spoke for most when he said, "He dies a hero of the war, for he literally worked himself to death in the service of the American people."

Sitting in the Oval Office was Harry S. Truman who less than six months earlier had been a senator from Missouri. The nation mourned, but the United States and Allied armies swept on to victory. The old truth was repeated: Presidents come and go, but the Republic continues.

Cities in ashes. From 1943 onward, United States forces in the Pacific settled on a strategy called "island hopping." Developed by Admiral Nimitz and General MacArthur, the strategy did not aim to take every Japanese base. Instead, U.S. forces struck at the major points of strength, cutting the less important ones off from supplies or reinforcements. Tens and then hundreds of thousands of Japanese soldiers were isolated and left behind by the Pacific War (map on page 577).

Between June 1943 and April 1944, United States forces drove the Japanese army from the Solomon Islands and New Guinea and pushed ahead in the Central Pacific. A steady stream of U.S. bombers took off from bases in the Marianas and reduced a number of Japanese cities to ashes. In October 1944, MacArthur made good his pledge to return to the Philippines. At Leyte Gulf, in the greatest naval battle of history, the Japanese fleet lost two battleships, four aircraft carriers, nine cruisers, and dozens of smaller ships. Pearl Harbor had been avenged. In February, after two months of street-to-street fighting, Manila was liberated.

Kamikaze defense. In February 1945, the war drew nearer to the Japanese home islands. A U.S. Marine force took Iwo

Aircraft carrier gun crews defend their ship against the suicide attacks of *kamikaze* planes.

Jima, a small island only 750 miles from Tokyo. Six weeks later, an invasion force landed on Okinawa, the largest island of the Ryukyu chain stretching south from Japan. Its defenders fought with determination as *kamikaze* (kam-uh-KAHZ-ee) pilots deliberately crashed their planes into United States vessels.

When the battle ended in June, there were 49,151 American casualties. Of those, 12,520 had been killed or were missing.

Thirty-six ships had been sunk, and ten times that number were damaged. The Japanese lost more than 110,000 men and almost 8,000 planes. The stage was now set for an all-out assault upon Japan itself.

"Japan will be finished." As the fighting neared its end, there were a number of new technical developments. Adolf Hitler's long-promised secret weapons were unveiled shortly after the Allied invasion of France. Unmanned rocket missiles (called V1's and V2's) bombarded Britain and Belgium. And in the last weeks of the war, German pilots took to the air with the first jet planes. Had the Germans been able to produce these weapons in quantity earlier

in the struggle, they might have won the war. But the missiles and jet planes came too late. Nonetheless, both the United States and the Soviets were eager to capture German rocket experts. Both nations wanted to develop similar weapons.

The Germans were not alone in finding new ways to fight a war. The British had developed radar. The British and Americans together discovered how to produce penicillin in quantity. And the first atom bomb was made.

Of all the weapons developed during World War II, the atom bomb was the most destructive. Late in 1939 Roosevelt had received a letter from the physicist Albert Einstein warning that the Nazis might be developing a bomb capable of destroying a whole city. The President agreed to support work on ways to release the power of the atom.

Through the war years, a team of scientists—J. Robert Oppenheimer, Nils Bohr, Edward Teller, Enrico Fermi, and others—took part in the top-secret "Manhattan Project." At Oak Ridge, Tennessee, and at Los Alamos, New Mexico, they worked to build an atomic bomb. On July 16, 1945, at Alamogardo, New Mexico, the bomb was successfully exploded. Observing the event, General Leslie R. Groves, head of the "Manhattan Project," simply concluded, "The war's over. One or two of those things, and Japan will be finished."

This one was different. Early in the morning of August 6, 1945, the residents of Hiroshima were starting another day of work. Some noticed that high above them three bombers were moving across the sky. No one paid much attention. They were accustomed to daily observation runs by United States bombers. But this one was different. In one of the planes, the *Enola*

 MIRROR IMAGES

Atlantic and Pacific naval operations in World War II were like mirror images of one another. From Germany's viewpoint, the sea lanes of the Atlantic Allies were their chief weakness. Only by water could reinforcements and supplies be moved from North America to Britain, then from Britain to the Continent. Against the United States and Britain, submarines were an ideal weapon. Hitler used them desperately in an effort to cripple Allied shipping.

In the Pacific, Japan's island empire also depended heavily on sea communication. Here the United States used submarines against the Japanese just as Germany was using them against the United States in the Atlantic. However, while Allied shipping managed to stay ahead of Hitler's submarines, Japan fell behind its attacker. In the end it faced defeat.

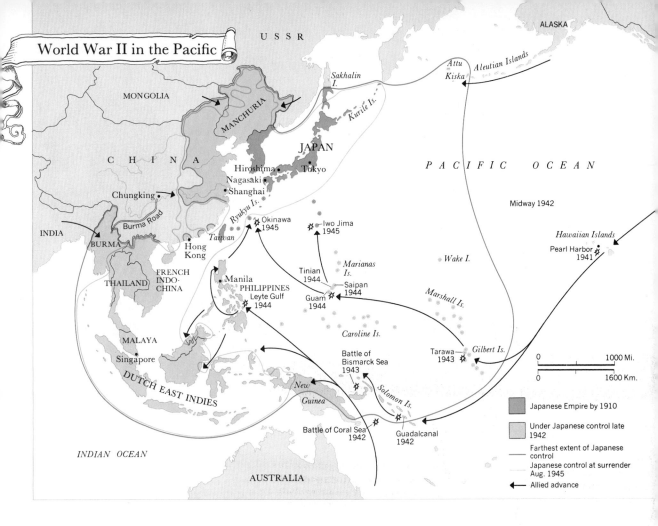

World War II in the Pacific

USSR

ALASKA

MONGOLIA

Attu *Aleutian Islands*

Kiska

Sakhalin I.

MANCHURIA

Kurile Is.

CHINA

JAPAN

PACIFIC OCEAN

Hiroshima•

•Tokyo

Nagasaki•

•Shanghai

Chungking•

Burma Road

Ryukyu Is.

Midway 1942

INDIA

Taiwan

Okinawa 1945

Iwo Jima 1945

Hawaiian Islands

BURMA

Hong Kong

Pearl Harbor 1941

FRENCH INDO-CHINA

Tinian 1944

Marianas Is.

Wake I.

THAILAND

•Manila

PHILIPPINES

Leyte Gulf 1944

Saipan 1944

Guam 1944

Marshall Is.

Caroline Is.

MALAYA

•Singapore

Tarawa 1943

Gilbert Is.

DUTCH EAST INDIES

Battle of Bismarck Sea 1943

| 0 | | 1000 Mi. |

| 0 | | 1600 Km. |

New Guinea

Solomon Is.

Battle of Coral Sea 1942

Guadalcanal 1942

INDIAN OCEAN

Japanese Empire by 1910

Under Japanese control late 1942

Farthest extent of Japanese control

Japanese control at surrender Aug. 1945

◄— Allied advance

AUSTRALIA

Which Japanese bases did the United States bypass in the strategy of island hopping?

Gay, there was a bomb code-named "The Thin Man."

The crew knew that an atom bomb had the destructive force of 20,000 tons of TNT. Yet they were not prepared for what happened when it was dropped on Hiroshima. A seething, boiling mass of fire a half-mile wide swept skyward into a mushroom cloud that the crew could still see when they were 270 miles away from the explosion.

The power of the sun. In Hiroshima, communication with the rest of Japan ceased. Only slowly did Japanese authorities learn that in a single explosion 78,150 people had been killed, 37,425 were injured, and 13,500 were missing. Three days later a second bomb laid waste the port city of Nagasaki, killing 38,500 of its residents. The world listened astonished as President Truman announced, "The force from which the sun draws its power has been loosed against those who brought war to the Far East."

It was Emperor Hirohito who decided that Japan must lay down its arms. The

577

navy knew that it was beaten, but the army held out for a last-ditch defense. Following the Hiroshima and Nagasaki bombings, Hirohito called together his war council and ordered it to surrender. On August 15, 1945 (V-J Day), the stunned Japanese people heard the voice of their emperor directing them to accept defeat and occupation.

September 2, 1945, aboard the battleship *Missouri* in Tokyo Bay, General MacArthur and Admiral Nimitz watched as the Japanese signed the document ending World War II. It was six years and one day since Hitler's armies had invaded Poland.

 TRY THIS!

1. Trace the course of the fighting across Europe, from the Normandy invasion to the surrender of Germany, as a United States infantryman might have described it. **2.** Explain the advantages of "island-hopping." From the map on page 577, tell what areas were left untouched.

An injured woman and child move through shattered Nagasaki, clutching pieces of bread.

5.   DIPLOMACY IN WARTIME

The war with the Axis powers was fought by a Grand Alliance of Great Britain, the Soviet Union, and the United States. Its task was to crush the war machines of Germany and Japan. Later it had the larger task of establishing the peace that would follow the war. Would there be another long armistice, ending in World War III, or would there be a secure peace? That would depend on the future relationships among the great powers. The men who conducted the diplomatic negotiations

were Franklin Roosevelt, Winston Churchill, and Joseph Stalin.

Read here of how

Roosevelt, Churchill, and Stalin formed a Grand Alliance.
The Alliance succeeded in winning the war.
But it had problems with the peace.

Little choice for Stalin. Roosevelt and Churchill shared values, a common language, and similar political institutions. Both were responsible to voters who could remove them from power. FDR was not enthusiastic about keeping the British Empire intact. But Churchill and he assumed that the future relationship between their countries would be close.

Between the Western Allies and the Soviet Union no such close relationship existed. Many westerners believed that the final object of the USSR was to destroy democracy and replace it with Communist dictatorship. The center of these suspicions was Joseph Stalin, dictator of the Soviet Union. He was a brutal tyrant who had caused the deaths of millions of real and imagined opponents. Stalin had cemented his control of the Soviet Union in the years just before the war. He had tried to keep peace with Hitler, even joining him in the conquest of Poland (page 553). But once the Nazis had invaded the Soviet Union, he was determined to stand and fight. Because they seemed intent upon destroying the Russian people, the Germans left Stalin little choice.

Once war engulfed Russia, Stalin's main concern in dealing with the West was to get needed supplies and a second front (page 571). But at the same time, he probably saw the alliance with the western countries as something temporary. Once the war was over, Stalin expected, the struggle between capitalism and communism would be resumed. Churchill thought so too. He favored strengthening the position of the western countries for that struggle against communism. Roosevelt was more concerned with the immediate task of winning the war. For that, both knew the Soviet effort was vital.

Unconditional surrender. The intentions of the Western Allies toward their Axis foes was made clear in January 1943. Churchill and Roosevelt met at Casablanca, Morocco. Roosevelt flatly stated, "The elimination of German, Japanese, and Italian war power means the unconditional surrender of Germany, Italy, and Japan." Nothing short of the total overthrow of Nazism, Fascism, and Japanese militarism would be acceptable.

But only in the case of Hitler and Germany was the demand for "unconditional surrender" carried through. Once Italy had withdrawn from the war in 1943, the Allies allowed that country to join them as a junior partner in the war against Hitler. Japan was allowed to retain her emperor, because the United States felt that keeping Hirohito on the throne would make it easier to control the Japanese people.

"Complete agreement." In the fall of 1943, Churchill and Roosevelt twice met with Chiang Kai-shek in Cairo, Egypt. At these conferences it was agreed that Japan's territory would be reduced to the home islands and that China would regain Taiwan and Manchuria. Korea was promised its independence. The Chinese were also told that victory in Europe must come before victory in the Pacific. The Russians were not present at these conferences, since they were not at war with Japan.

When Churchill, Roosevelt, and Chiang Kai-shek met at Teheran, Iran, late in 1943, Stalin joined them. He was told that the USSR would regain the southern half of Sakhalin Island, which it had lost to Japan in 1905. More important, they agreed upon the strategy to defeat Hitler. Roosevelt and Churchill told Stalin of their plans to open a second front, in France, in 1944.

579

Following the Teheran Conference, a Persian artist shows Stalin, Churchill, Roosevelt, and Chiang hunting down Mussolini, Hitler, and Hirohito.

Roosevelt was particularly interested in laying the foundations for a permanent peace-keeping body, the United Nations. These plans were more fully developed the following year at the Dumbarton Oaks Conference, in the United States.

Vital concerns. Once again, in early February 1945, Stalin, Roosevelt, and Churchill met at Yalta in the Russian Crimea. The war with Germany was about over; decisions about the coming peace had to be made. The United States also wanted Soviet help in the war with Japan.

As yet the atom bomb was a well-kept secret. No one was sure that it would work

or knew that Japan would surrender so readily. Roosevelt and other United States leaders were anxious to save American lives and thought that the Soviet's declaring war on Japan would help.

No less vital for the USSR was the future of Eastern and Central Europe. A new Polish-Soviet border was established by giving the USSR part of eastern Poland. To make up for its losses, Poland was to receive a sizable chunk of Germany. But no one openly favored dividing Germany permanently.

Less on agreements, more on armies. The USSR pledged that the Poles would have free elections to choose their own government. Similar promises were made to cover Romania, Hungary, Bulgaria, and Yugoslavia. Without its being said outright, the Soviet sphere of influence in Eastern Europe and the Balkans was acknowledged, while that of Britain in Greece was confirmed.

The Yalta Conference kept up talk of continuing unity among the Allies. But the real situation was put bluntly by Russian Foreign Minister V. M. Molotov when he observed, "It was not necessary for the Soviet Union to conclude an armistice with Hungary, since the Red Army was practically the master of that country. It could do what it wished." Future boundary lines and future politics depended less on diplomatic agreements and more on where the armies were when the war ended.

The uncertain peace. The Yalta agreement contained a number of secret provisions. The Soviets promised to enter the war against Japan three months after the war with Germany ended. They kept that promise, on August 8, 1945. In return, Soviet rights to ports and railroads in Manchuria were affirmed. The independence of Outer Mongolia (between China and the Soviet Union) was acknowledged. (In effect, the interests of China were traded off without its consent.)

As it turned out, this in time gave the Chinese Communists control of Manchuria. That was hardly to the advantage of the USSR. A more damaging arrangement allowed the Soviet Union to occupy North Korea, dividing that country. Finally, to get Soviet support for the United Nations, it was agreed that the USSR would receive three seats in the UN General Assembly— one for the Soviet Union itself and the others for two large Soviet Republics. (The USSR had originally demanded a seat for each of sixteen Republics.)

Roosevelt believed that the United Nations was a vital instrument "under which the peace of the world would be preserved and the forces of aggression permanently outlawed." It was a high hope and one that would not be fully met. As the guns fell silent, a longer struggle began to determine whether western-style democracy or Communist dictatorship would prevail.

 TRY THIS!

1. Compare the peace after World War II with the one that followed World War I. Which has lasted longer? Why? 2. Write two editorials—one attacking and one defending the Yalta agreement.

Stalin, FDR, and Churchill, with their staffs, dine together at Yalta in February 1945.

ROUNDUP

Who?

Erwin Rommel
Donald Nelson
Harry S. Truman
Douglas MacArthur
Chester W. Nimitz
Bernard L.
    Montgomery
George S. Patton
Dwight D. Eisenhower
Mark Clark
J. Robert Oppenheimer
Hirohito
Joseph Stalin

What?

Lend-Lease
Atlantic Charter
Desert Rats
Afrika Korps
Luftwaffe
Battle of the Bulge
Red Army
kamikaze
Manhattan Project
Grand Alliance
Big Three
Yalta Conference

Where?

Pearl Harbor
Bataan
Corregidor
Coral Sea
Midway Island
Anzio
Normandy
Bastogne
Leyte Gulf
Hiroshima

KNOW THIS

An Undeclared War with the Axis

1. Why did Britain badly need United States aid in 1941?
2. What other nations received Lend-Lease assistance?
3. How had the Axis powers brought the U.S. to the brink of war in 1941?
4. What principles did the Atlantic Charter lay down?
5. How did European developments affect Southeast Asia?

World War II in the United States

1. When did the United States finally enter World War II?
2. What steps did the United States take to mobilize industry for the war effort?
3. How did war production affect a) industry itself, b) agriculture, c) workers, d) the economy?
4. How did the government finance the war?
5. Why did FDR choose Truman for his Vice President in 1944? What was the outcome of that year's election?

Fighting on Two Fronts

1. What strategy did the Allies adopt against the Axis?
2. Where did the U.S. Navy halt the Japanese advance?
3. What tactics were used against German submarines?
4. What strategy did Winston Churchill favor for southern European countries?
5. Why had the balance shifted from the Axis to the Allies by mid-1943?

Victory in a Global Struggle

1. Why did the Allies have to invade Europe? Who was their commander in chief?
2. Describe the final German offensive of World War II.
3. What strategy did the U.S. follow in the Pacific? Why?
4. What new weapons were developed in World War II? What was the Manhattan Project?
5. How was the war with Japan ended?

Diplomacy in Wartime

1. Why were relations with Stalin different from those with Churchill?
2. When did the Allies first demand unconditional surrender? Did they follow through? Explain.
3. What agreements were made at Teheran? At Yalta?
4. Why was Yalta the most controversial wartime conference?
5. What made the USSR decide to support the UN?

DIG HERE!

World War II produced a number of outstanding military leaders. Women and black Americans were included in the conferring of high military rank. Research the life and career of one wartime leader, and try to determine what qualities brought military success.

A. When and where was the leader born? What was his or her childhood like? What influenced the person's choice of a military career?
B. At what age did he or she enter the military? In which branch? Describe his or her training.
C. When did the leader become an officer?
D. What specialized skills did the leader acquire? How did the skills contribute to success?
E. What was this person's outstanding strength as a leader?
F. Describe one critical operation or situation in which the person played an important part.

Here are some books that can get you started: Bradley, *A Soldier's Story,* Holt; Eisenhower, *Crusade in Europe,* Doubleday; Motley, ed., *The Invisible Soldier,* Wayne State (the black soldiers' story); Nimitz, *Triumph in the Atlantic,* Prentice; Snyder, *The War: A Concise History, 1939–1945,* Dell; Sulzberger, *American Heritage Picture History of World War II,* Am. Heritage.

THINK ABOUT IT

1. Churchill had wanted to invade southeastern Europe, partly to keep the Russians out of the region. The U.S. refused. Who was right? If the U.S. had agreed, might United States-Soviet relations be very different now?
2. Truman decided that using the atomic bomb would shorten the war and save American lives. If you had been the President faced with that decision, what would you have done?

DO IT!

1. Organize and direct a series of "man-in-the-street" interviews, supposedly on the day after Pearl Harbor. How are people reacting? What do they expect to happen next?
2. Tell the story of World War II using maps and time lines, identifying important battles.
3. Assemble an exhibit of Bill Mauldin's wartime cartoons. What do they tell about the nature of war?

THEN AND NOW

It has been said that armies often train and organize for the last war instead of the next one. Is the United States making such a mistake now, do you think? What would you say was a chief lesson of World War II?

The Postwar World Presents New Problems

25

The United States and the Soviet Union came out of World War II as superpowers. Conflicting interests in Europe and Asia ended their former alliance and started the Cold War. The divided city of Berlin was a particular danger point.

On August 15, 1945, wild celebrations broke out in the United States. Japan had been defeated. World War II was over. Crowds clogged Times Square in New York City, cheering and honking car horns. Many of those whooping it up on V-J Day could remember nothing but depression and war. Now the threats from Hitler's Nazis and the Japanese had been broken.

After fifteen years of fear, grief, and hardship, the country was at peace—and prosperous. Wartime production had put millions back to work, paychecks were bigger than ever before, and the spirit of hope was strong.

By the spring of 1947, however, the businessman-statesman Bernard Baruch was warning, "We are in the midst of a cold war." The United States and Soviet Russia maneuvered for postwar supremacy. The Soviets soon had their own nuclear bomb. Clearly, another world war could mean the end of civilization.

1. AFTER THE WAR

On April 13, 1945, one day after becoming President, Harry S. Truman told reporters, "Boys, if you ever pray, pray for me now." He was nearly 61 years old, and he had been Vice President for not quite three months. During that time, Franklin Roosevelt had met with him only twice. Truman had not taken any part in major decision-making.

Harry Truman had a very ordinary background. He grew up and went to high school in small towns in Missouri. His family could not afford to send him to college. As an army captain in World War I, he made a distinguished record for bravery.

After the war, Truman and a partner started a men's clothing store; it failed. Deeply in debt, he took a chance on a political career. He signed up with the political machine of "Boss" Pendergast in Kansas City, "stayed clean," became an elected county official, and in 1934 won a seat in the United States Senate.

Acceptable to all factions. During World War II, Senator Truman headed a "watchdog" committee investigating the national defense program. This Truman Committee saved the government billions of dollars, and its chairman became a national figure. In 1944 Roosevelt chose the man from Missouri as his running mate. This was because the Democratic Party was divided into liberal and conservative wings. Harry Truman was acceptable to all "sides," or factions.

Read here of how

The nation was uncertain about Truman.
The President fumbled inflation.
He got some important bills passed.
But the Democrats lost heavily in 1946.

TIME CHART

1945	The Potsdam Conference divides Germany.
1945	The United Nations is established.
1946	The Employment Act is passed.
1947	Congress passes the Taft-Hartley Act.
1947	The United States undertakes a policy of containment.
1947	The Truman Doctrine is announced.
1947	The Marshall Plan is launched.
1948	The Soviets blockade Berlin. An airlift is undertaken.
1948	Truman wins a second term.
1949	The NATO Treaty is signed.
1948–1954	Anti-Communist investigations lead to the Army-McCarthy hearings.

But even as Vice President, Truman was not a member of FDR's inner circle. The President had not told him about the atom bomb. In general, Harry Truman had little experience with foreign affairs and diplomacy.

Accustomed to Roosevelt's upper-class, polished manner, many saw Truman as too down-to-earth to be President. There were complaints of his peppery temper and salty language; even about the flashy sport shirts he sometimes wore.

"He does the big things right." Harry Truman became an effective chief of state. Above all, he knew how to make hard decisions. In his own brisk way he followed Roosevelt's path in both domestic and foreign affairs. On any question of national or global significance, the President usually

585

Truman's piano-playing delighted cartoonists. Artist Ben Shahn shows him performing.

was thoughtful, patient, and determined. One Washington reporter observed: "There are two Trumans—the White House Truman and the [county] courthouse Truman. He does the big things right, and the little things wrong."

Favorable views of the President came, for the most part, late in his Presidency or after he had left the White House. During the first year and a half of his administration, Truman appeared especially un-

steady in domestic matters. Yet as President he faced enormous problems. Switching from a wartime to a peacetime economy was not the least of them.

Shortages and inflation. The country's basic postwar difficulty came from inflation and shortages. During the war, people had made more money than ever before but had far fewer places to spend it. Consumer items were not being manufactured when all the nation's resources were going into the production of war materials. Workers had no choice but to save. When the war was over, these savings amounted to billions of dollars.

Interest rates were low and credit loose. With so much money available, everything pointed to a nationwide buying spree: new homes, cars, clothing, and good cuts of meat. However, postwar demand outran supply. Industry was unable to produce goods fast enough to satisfy consumers.

The most critical shortage was in housing. Marriages—wartime and postwar—led to an enormous need for apartments and houses. The price of housing and of everything else shot up. Inflation (the unusual rise in price levels) threatened to wipe out wartime economic gains. Prices rose nearly 25 per cent in the first year and a half of peace.

A toothless bill. Truman's handling of inflation was especially unfortunate. During the war, prices had been controlled by agencies such as the OPA (Office of Price Administration), which had the power to freeze them. In peacetime, business bitterly protested the continued price controls.

There was much bickering in the Truman Administration between those who wanted an end to controls and those who thought controls would keep a lid on inflation. Congress finally passed a toothless bill authorizing a much weaker price-control system. Truman vetoed it as not strong enough. Without controls, prices zoomed to record levels. Almost immediately Congress passed another bill—nearly a carbon copy of the first. Truman gave in and signed it. The bill had so many loopholes that inflation still plagued the country.

"A bulge in the line." Inflation cut deeply into pay envelopes. Workers had to spend more, even at the grocery store. The pay from overtime jobs that many had held in wartime was no longer available. Unions struck to win raises. In November 1945, the United Auto Workers walked out. So, in quick succession, did the steelworkers, coal miners, and railway employees. By spring of 1946, strikes had tied up the economy.

To help settle strikes, the Truman Administration developed the technique called "a bulge in the line." This permitted both wage increases for labor, and price increases for business. In other words, if an industry's profits dipped because of greater worker benefits, it could raise prices to make up the difference. The policy was acceptable to both labor and management. But it added to the inflation.

Draft the strikers? During one strike, Truman seemed to lose his head. In May 1946, when the railway unions went out, an angry President went before Congress and asked for drastic legislation. Even though the strike was settled as he spoke, Truman insisted on being given authority to draft strikers into the army. As Commander-in-Chief, he then could order them back to work.

The anti-union proposal failed; it was not approved by the Senate. And it wrecked Truman's reputation in the labor movement, something very important for a Democratic politician. (One union conference labeled him "Number One Strikebreaker" of the United States.)

Confronted by inflation and the labor unrest, Truman was unable to push programs for social reforms. In September 1945 he had spelled out a 21-point proposal for better housing legislation, greater Social Security and unemployment benefits, a higher minimum wage, advances in civil rights, and a national health insurance program. Congress ignored his requests.

"To Err Is Truman." Truman managed to win approval for the Employment Act of 1946, which set up the Council of

Postwar price rises forced families to stretch their dollars. Which was worse: inflation, or the falling prices of the Great Depression?

Economic Advisers. The Act proclaimed that the federal government should help to bring about full employment and prevent depressions. In the aftermath of the New Deal and World War II, most politicians were practical-minded. They were no longer sympathetic to old-fashioned laissez-faire economics (page 403).

A minor triumph like the Employment Act did little to help the President's popularity or the sagging fortunes of the Democratic Party. The Republicans smelled victory as the congressional elections of 1946 rolled around. Using slogans such as "Had Enough? Vote Republican" and "To Err Is Truman," the GOP capitalized on the dis-

THE G. I. BILL OF RIGHTS

G. I. (government issue) was the World War II term for an ordinary soldier. In 1944 a G. I. Bill of Rights was passed. It greatly eased the return of veterans to civilian life. It allowed a veteran tuition payments, living expenses, books, and supplies, while attending school or college or working as a trainee. The bill also made it easier for veterans to purchase homes or start businesses. And it allowed them unemployment benefits for one year. Money paid out was to be deducted from any future bonus.

may over inflation, shortages, and price controls.

Discouraged and dismayed, the Democratic candidates shunned the President and tried to run on the record of the late FDR. No use: in November the Republicans won control of the new 80th Congress.

 TRY THIS!

Write the thoughts of a returning World War II veteran. What does he think about a) the condition of the country, b) the new President, c) his chance of finding a job, d) inflation, e) price controls?

2. COLLAPSE OF THE GRAND ALLIANCE

Domestic problems in the Truman years were often overshadowed by international events. The immediate postwar years, 1945–1949, were a time of rising tensions between the United States and the Soviet Union. The successful wartime alliance between the western nations and the USSR collapsed. For almost a quarter century the Cold War was to dominate foreign affairs and prevent cooperation.

The early Cold War was a time of mistrust and suspicion. In Washington, United States policymakers insisted that the Soviet Union would force communism on one part of the world after another. In the name of peace and democracy, therefore, the United States challenged the USSR.

In Moscow the Russians, led by Joseph Stalin, took an equally unfriendly view of the United States. They accused it of wanting to run the world's economy through the power of its large corporations. Further-

more, the Soviets feared that the United States wanted them to feel threatened by further attack. They believed, too, that the Americans wished to undermine their experiment with socialism in which all the means of production were controlled by the state.

Bad memories. Ill will between the United States and the Soviet Union was nothing new. The recent wartime cooperation between the two nations had been an exception. The Russian Revolution of October 1917 had triggered, in the United States, a near-hysterical reaction called the Great Red Scare (page 475). It was thought then too that Russian Communists were bent on world conquest. The United States did not establish diplomatic relations with Moscow until 1933.

The Soviets also had some bad memories. They remembered how American forces had entered their country shortly after the Communist takeover (page 465).

Keeping the peace. When President Truman took office in the spring of 1945, rivalry between the United States and the USSR had not yet boiled over. In late April representatives from fifty countries met in San Francisco to establish the United Nations as a new world organization. There was some quarreling between the Russians and the western governments.

Read here of how

The U.S. and the USSR feared one another.
They joined to found the United Nations.
But split over the fate of Eastern Europe.
And an "iron curtain" fell between them.

589

This imaginary group portrait shows the 27 men and women who headed the nations at war with Germany, Italy, and Japan. In 1945 they set up the United Nations organization. Can you name them? Start with first row, center.

But at long last, Woodrow Wilson's dream of a peacekeeping "concert of nations" was to be realized.

In the General Assembly of the United Nations, every member nation has a seat and the right to be heard. But the real power of the organization rests with the Security Council, which includes as permanent members the five Great Powers (the United States, the Soviet Union, Great Britain, China, and France), plus ten smaller nations. The smaller nations are elected for two-year terms by the General Assembly. The Security Council can impose economic penalties or authorize the use of military force.

However, a clause in the United Nations Charter severely limits the effectiveness of the Council. Any of the five Great Powers can veto any proposed action. This means that the UN cannot easily resolve a dispute involving permanent members. As the Cold War developed, the Soviet Union used the veto power over and over again. This possibility was not foreseen, of course, in 1945.

Nevertheless, if the United States had not been assured, itself, of having veto power over UN action, the Senate might not have ratified the United Nations Charter. It was ratified, however, by an enthusiastic vote of 89 to 2.

Divisions and disagreement. In July 1945, not long after the San Francisco Conference concluded its business, Truman, Churchill, and Stalin held a conference at Potsdam, outside Berlin. In many respects, this last conference of the "Big Three" was friendly, and important agreements were hammered out.

The Allies decided to have Nazi leaders tried as war criminals for "outrages against humanity." (The trials were held at Nuremberg, Germany, in late 1945 and 1946.) The Big Three also made plans for dividing Germany into four zones, each to be occupied by forces of either Britain, the United States, the USSR, or France. Berlin, which was in the Soviet zone, was also split into four sectors. And while at Potsdam, Truman told Stalin that in the United States, scientists had succeeded in building an atom bomb.

There still was an entire range of problems unresolved. The Big Three came to no agreement on such important questions as the eventual future of Germany, the boundaries of Poland, or the nature of the governments in Eastern Europe.

For the sake of security. Probably no meeting of minds could have taken place on these touchy subjects. Eastern Europe, in particular, was a point of conflict. In its massive push against Nazi Germany, the Red Army had occupied most of the countries just beyond the Soviet border. After the war, the USSR was in no mood to withdraw either its troops or its influence. For Russian security, Stalin wanted to keep both.

In 1812, 1914, and 1941 invading armies had passed through Eastern European countries and entered Russia. Therefore, following World War II, Moscow either imposed or encouraged pro-Soviet governments in Poland, Romania, Bulgaria, Hungary, and Albania. The Soviets also set up a Communist regime in their German zone of occupation. (Yugoslavia, led by Marshal Tito, was a Communist nation, but it avoided both Russian and United States influences.)

Challenging the Russians. At the Yalta Conference in February 1945, Stalin had agreed to free elections in Eastern Europe (page 580). The Soviet dictator didn't keep that promise. Truman was upset, but short of going to war, there was little the United States could do to enforce the Yalta pledge.

Nevertheless, the President called in the Russian Foreign Minister, V. M. Molotov, and in strong, blunt terms told him the Russians must live up to their promises. "I have never been talked to like that in my life," Molotov replied. "Carry out your agreements, and you won't get talked to like that," Truman shot back.

Truman had decided it was a mistake to continue Roosevelt's flexible policy toward the USSR. His Administration began responding with firmness to any threatening behavior by the Soviet Union. The new United States attitude hardened the reality of the Cold War.

An iron curtain. The United States abandoned the spirit of cooperation with the Soviets. Immediately after the surrender of Germany, for instance, Truman abruptly cut off all lend-lease assistance to the USSR. When Stalin asked for a one-billion-dollar loan from the United States, United States officials "lost" his request. For the war-ravaged Soviet Union, this was most serious: they needed all possible help in rebuilding their nation.

By early 1946 the Grand Alliance no longer existed. In March Winston Churchill, no longer Prime Minister, came to the

Winston Churchill and Harry Truman at Fulton, Missouri, for Churchill's "iron curtain" speech.

United States and delivered an important speech at Westminster College in Fulton, Missouri. He bitterly denounced the Soviet Union. With Truman sitting approvingly on the platform, Churchill claimed that the Russians had lowered an "iron curtain" across Europe.

 TRY THIS!

1. Explain how the wartime alliance was an exception in U.S.-Soviet relations. **2.** Using the map on page 572, show why the USSR wanted to control Eastern Europe. **3.** Trace the steps by which the Cold War began.

3. EARLY COLD-WAR DECISIONS

Some in the United States disliked the firm new approach to the Soviet Union. Secretary of Commerce and former Vice President Henry A. Wallace (page 557), openly criticized Truman in a speech at Madison Square Garden. Wallace felt that the United States should stop protesting the Soviet takeover of Eastern Europe. "We should recognize," Wallace argued, "that we have no more business in the political

Read here of how

The United States tried to contain communism.
It intervened in Greece and Turkey.
The Marshall Plan offered Europe aid.
And an airlift broke Berlin's blockade.

affairs of Eastern Europe than Russia has in the political affairs of Latin America, Western Europe, and the United States."

Wallace thought the Soviets wished only to establish a sphere of influence (page 581) in Eastern Europe. He did not believe they would extend their power elsewhere. If the U.S. accepted this Soviet wish, he maintained, nothing would stand in the way of friendlier relations. The general reaction against Wallace's speech was very strong. The immediate result of the complaints was that Truman asked him to resign from the Cabinet.

A policy of containment. Hardly anyone in the Truman Administration agreed with Henry Wallace. Most United States policymakers thought that the USSR would force its way into any area where non-Communist forces were not strong.

Out of this anti-Soviet thinking came a policy called *containment*. It was a strategy of limiting, or holding, communism to Soviet Russia and Eastern Europe. From 1947 on, the United States generally followed the containment policy and intervened in countries that seemed threatened by communism.

Containment was first tested in the eastern Mediterranean. Following World War II, Greece was in political turmoil and seemed a likely spot for a Communist takeover. The Greek economy had been shattered by long years of Nazi occupation. Cruel poverty was a way of life for most of the Greeks. A strong guerrilla movement threatened to take over the government. Only support from Great Britain kept the royalists, who favored the Greek king's government, in power.

Greece gave this ancient vase to the American people in gratitude for the Truman Doctrine.

The strong, leftist, guerrilla movement was headed by Communists who Washington assumed were under the control of the Soviets. In February 1947 the British, almost bankrupt themselves, informed the United States that they could no longer continue aiding the Greek and Turkish governments.

A stark picture. Truman and his new Secretary of State, General George C. Marshall, decided that the United States must act. On March 12, 1947, the President went before Congress and asked for 350 million dollars for aid to the Greek government.

At the same time, President Truman asked for fifty million dollars' worth of assistance for Turkey. A neighbor of Greece, Turkey bordered on the USSR.

593

"We shall not realize our objectives," Truman said, "unless we are willing to help free peoples to maintain their free institutions and their national integrity against aggressive movements that seek to impose on them totalitarian regimes." (Totalitarian governments are the kind that keep all individuals, and whatever they produce, under the strict control of the state.) The principle of helping anti-Communist governments became known as the Truman Doctrine.

Truman's speech had painted a stark picture: Soviet-sponsored Communists on one side battling free governments on the other. Actually, the Greek situation was a good deal more complicated. The rebels had widespread popular backing and were receiving little encouragement from Moscow. Furthermore, the postwar Greek government was undemocratic.

Nevertheless, it seemed clear that Truman was concerned because Communist nations already existed on Greece's very borders. He was convincing. The House and Senate voted strongly in favor of the aid. American funds helped improve the Greek economy. And neither Greece nor Turkey "went Communist."

Against hunger and poverty. Both Truman and Marshall looked upon the assistance to Greece as a temporary measure. The Administration had in the works a far broader plan to help non-Communist governments. In June 1947 Secretary Marshall unveiled a massive United States offer to help rebuild the war-ravaged nations of Europe.

Europe was suffering terribly. Six years of all-out war had left cities in ruins, leveled factories, and destroyed farms. Hunger, unemployment, and frustration gripped millions of Europeans. The thought of a paralyzed continent alarmed Truman, Marshall, and other Americans. Already, the Communist parties of France and Italy had made dramatic gains. If these nations' economies were not rebuilt, the Truman Administration reasoned, communism could not be contained. It might sweep through Western Europe. Furthermore, United States industry needed a prosperous Europe as a trading partner.

The Administration's solution was the European Recovery Program, or the Marshall Plan, a massive outpouring of aid. Marshall explained that the plan was directed "not against any country or doctrine, but against hunger, poverty, desperation, and chaos." Accordingly, the Soviet Union and other Communist nations were invited to share its benefits. Realizing that the program would bring United States influence into Eastern Europe, the Soviets denounced it as imperialist and refused to accept the aid.

Not long after, the Soviets carried out a brutal Communist takeover in Czechoslovakia (February 1948). A worried Congress approved the Marshall Plan, and assistance began flowing to Western Europe's non-Communist countries.

In all, the United States spent thirteen billion dollars on reconstruction throughout the world. It had remarkable results. And as the economic picture brightened, the followings of the Communist parties in France and Italy dwindled.

A new and independent nation. The Marshall Plan was the keystone of the containment policy. But the United States sponsored other efforts to strengthen Western Europe. One of the most important came in Germany. West Berlin was controlled by the United States, Britain, and

France; East Berlin belonged to the Russians. West Berlin was like an island, surrounded by Soviet-dominated territory (page 591).

In 1948 the three western Allies, led by the United States, began to unite their three German occupation sectors into a single zone. They also revealed plans to form a new, independent nation—West Germany. The Russians were appalled at the thought of a redeveloped and re-armed German state. It was, after all, only seven years since German troops had invaded the Soviet Union.

Five thousand tons a day. Stalin reacted quickly. In June 1948 the Soviets announced a blockade of West Berlin. All ground transportation to the city's western zones was cut off. Briefly, West Berlin was stranded.

President Truman was unwilling to give up. Instead, he decided to make use of United States superiority in the air. He would fly in supplies. With a cargo plane landing every three minutes, the "Berlin Airlift" brought in nearly 5,000 tons a day. For nearly a year the planes shuttled food, fuel—including coal, and other necessary goods to two million West Berliners. The Soviets' challenge had been met. And United States generosity and technical superiority had been dramatically demonstrated. Certainly, Stalin was not about to start World War III by shooting down the aircraft. In May 1949 the USSR admitted defeat. It lifted its blockade and opened the roads to West Berlin.

"An attack against them all." Meanwhile, the three western Allies went ahead with plans for the new West German state. In September 1949 the Federal Republic of Germany, with its capital at Bonn, came into being. The Soviets responded by estab-

Marshall Plan aid helped Europe to rise from the ruins and kept it from becoming Communist.

lishing the German Democratic Republic (East Germany) in their former occupation zone. Thus Germany became two nations, a symbol of the Cold War and of a divided Europe.

The continuing menace from the Soviet Union, plus the great success of the Berlin Airlift, helped to convince western nations that a permanent military alliance was

595

necessary. On April 4, 1949, twelve non-Communist countries signed an agreement that produced the North Atlantic Treaty Organization (NATO).

The twelve NATO countries were the United States, Great Britain, Canada, France, Belgium, Luxembourg, the Netherlands, Norway, Denmark, Iceland, Italy, and Portugal. The treaty provided that they would maintain a joint military force and stated that an armed attack against one member country in Europe or North America "shall be considered an attack against them all."

By a vote of 82–13, the Senate approved American participation in NATO. The alliance represented a deep break with traditional United States policy. In fact, it was the nation's first formal alliance

with a foreign power since the one with France during the American Revolution (page 90). No longer was the country trying to keep clear of European affairs. Instead, in the 1945–1949 period the United States assumed leadership of the "free world," regularly confronted the Soviet Union, and carried on the Cold War.

 TRY THIS!

1. Compare United States policies after World War I (pages 469–471) and World War II. Deal with a) war debts and payments (page 470), b) involvement in European affairs, and c) world leadership. **2.** Explain why policies and attitudes after the Second World War were different from those after the First.

Berlin Airlift Christmas gifts included food, clothing, and toys donated by private citizens.

4. A DEMOCRATIC VICTORY IN 1948

The galleries of the Senate and the House were packed on January 3, 1947. The curious streamed into the Capitol building in order to see something unusual—the opening session of a Republican Congress. Having won the 1946 congressional elections, for the first time in sixteen years the GOP controlled both House and Senate.

A figure commanding the attention of nearly everyone present was Senator Robert A. Taft of Ohio, son of the twenty-seventh President. Honest and very able, Taft had the informal title "Mr. Republican."

Conservative Republicans liked Taft's viewpoints, which reflected the attitudes of most members of the new 80th Congress. They were fed up with the New Deal. They feared the growing power of labor unions, and they opposed big federal budgets, high taxes, and price controls.

No strikebreaker. The first item on the Republicans' long list was curbing the power of organized labor. On the first day the 80th Congress was in session, seventeen antilabor bills were introduced. Out of them came the Taft-Hartley Act, outlawing the "closed shop" (by which only union members could be hired). It also provided for federal supervision of union affairs, and empowered the President to halt for eighty days any strike that threatened national security.

Read here of how

Republicans controlled the 80th Congress.
And Democrats were split three ways.
Dewey ran a "dignified" campaign.
But Harry Truman beat him.

"Mr. Republican," Robert A. Taft, addressing one of the delegations at a national convention.

Labor leaders feared that the Taft-Hartley Act would undo what they had gained through the New Deal; they called it a "slave labor law." But the power of big unions did not significantly decline. However, the law made it more difficult for workers to unionize.

Truman vetoed the Taft-Hartley Bill, and that helped re-establish his popularity with labor. Congress overrode his veto by a large majority, but the President was no longer called a strikebreaker (page 587). Union labor now viewed Truman as a

597

friend and stood ready to help him in the 1948 election.

Progressive legislation. The conservative Republican Congress also put the ax to Truman's domestic program. Administration requests for such things as public housing and federal aid to education went down to defeat. Still, the President continued to promote progressive legislation and took up a cause that Roosevelt had not— civil rights for black Americans.

In late 1946, after a series of racial murders, Truman appointed a President's Committee on Civil Rights to investigate the situation. Less than a year later, the commission issued a report titled *To Secure These Rights*. The document condemned all forms of discrimination and proposed laws to end segregation.

In February 1948 Truman urged Congress to enact a wide-ranging program of civil rights laws. The Republicans in Congress ignored the proposal, and southern Democrats almost unanimously denounced it.

"The loneliest campaign." The approaching 1948 election looked bleak for Harry Truman. The Democratic Party seemed to be falling apart. On one side, Henry Wallace continued his attacks on Truman's foreign policy (page 593). In late 1947 Wallace announced his own candidacy for President. Running as a reform independent, Wallace stumped the country, drawing enthusiastic crowds. Some analysts predicted that Wallace would take as many as five million liberal votes away from the Democrats.

On the other side, southerners, upset by Truman's going over to the civil rights cause, were threatening to desert the Democratic Party. Disheartened, party leaders urged Truman not to run. The

598

Very few political slogans have been as effective as "Tippecanoe and Tyler too" (page 196).

President shrugged off the suggestions. He set out to win his own term in the White House.

One columnist noted, "If Truman is nominated, he will be forced to wage the loneliest campaign in history." The Democratic Convention became a stormy affair. Truman got the nomination, but a floor fight erupted over civil rights.

The civil rights group was led by the youthful mayor of Minneapolis, Hubert H. Humphrey. They succeeded in putting a strong civil rights plank into the party platform. Their victory angered southern Democrats. Waving Confederate flags and singing "Dixie," Mississippi delegates and some from Alabama marched out of the convention hall.

A few days later in Birmingham, Alabama, disgruntled southern Democrats formed the States' Rights, or "Dixiecrat," Party and nominated Governor J. Strom Thurmond of South Carolina for President. On election day Thurmond would carry four southern states. The "solid South" was no more.

Pollsters' predictions. Meanwhile, the Republicans were bursting with optimism. No longer would they have to run against champion vote-getter Franklin D. Roosevelt. Instead, the GOP was facing Harry Truman and the splintered Democratic Party. At their national convention the Republicans passed over Robert Taft, and once again nominated Governor Thomas E. Dewey of New York, the 1944 candidate.

Dewey, a moderate, was not like the rigid conservatives of the Republican past.

His record in New York was a model of efficient administration and prudent liberalism. As a campaigner, he lacked appeal, for he seemed distant and colorless. Nevertheless, every political expert and pollster in the country was predicting a landslide Dewey victory.

In contrast to his opponent's bland style, President Truman took to the campaign trail with a desperate fighting spirit. Traveling around the country by train, speaking at hundreds of small towns, Truman constantly attacked that "good-for-nothing 80th Congress."

Embarrassed experts. On election day Harry Truman scored the greatest upset in United States political history. By a margin of two million votes, the tough little

President Truman faced a hostile crowd at the 1948 Democratic Convention. Some delegates didn't like what he had done. Few of them thought he could win the election.

A personal triumph for Truman. An unfriendly paper had declared his opponent the winner.

man from Missouri humbled Dewey and the Republicans. The embarrassed "experts" tried to explain what had happened. In looking over the returns, they found that black voters had responded to Truman's civil rights appeal and had poured to the polls in record numbers. The cities of the North provided a cushion for victory.

Unions, too, felt they had a stake in the 1948 campaign. The Taft-Hartley Act was on the books (page 597), and a number of states were threatening to adopt similar restrictive laws. Organized labor had worked hard to get its membership to vote. They did not vote Republican.

In the Midwest and the Far West, farmers were angry about some policies of the Republican Congress, and in protest they flocked to Truman's banner. But the plain fact remained that in the aftermath of the New Deal, most Americans still were Democrats.

 TRY THIS!

1. Explain how the Democratic Party was split in 1948.   2. Write two editorials on the 1948 presidential campaign, one for a Republican and one for a Democratic paper. 3. Show how special-interest groups accounted for Truman's victory in 1948.

5.   ANOTHER POSTWAR RED SCARE

Read here of how

Growing Communist power alarmed many.
A State Department official went to jail.
And a senator from Wisconsin "had a list."
But the senator overreached himself.

Harry Truman's victory in 1948 did not set off a wave of new reform legislation. Plans for his new "Fair Deal" legislation took second place to a more explosive issue. Charges had been made that Communists were working their way into United States institutions.

In some respects the country's anti-Communist crusade of the 1940s and 1950s resembled the Great Red Scare that had followed the First World War. By the late 1940s many Americans were genuinely afraid that agents of international communism had worked their way into the government. For roughly a half-dozen years the country was rocked by well publicized investigations, spectacular trials, and the rise of Senator Joseph R. McCarthy of Wisconsin.

A sellout? Events abroad had fueled the controversy in the United States. The victory of Mao Tse-tung's Communist forces in China (page 608) suggested to some that perhaps there were Communist sympathizers in our State Department who had "sold out" China. If this were so, the United States, not Chiang Kai-shek, had "lost China." When the Soviets developed an atom bomb, many alarmed Americans concluded that a spy ring must have given away atomic secrets.

The anti-Communist crusade of the 1940s got under way with a congressional investigation in 1948. The House Un-American Activities Committee started questioning Alger Hiss, a lawyer who had held high positions in the State Department. The key witness against Hiss was a former Communist, Whittaker Chambers. The House Committee was spearheaded by a young California congressman named Richard M. Nixon. Chambers was charging Hiss with spying for the Soviet Union during the 1930s.

In December 1948 Chambers led investigators to a hollowed-out pumpkin on his Maryland farm. Inside were microfilms of State Department documents. Chambers claimed that Hiss had passed them to him during the 1930s while both worked for the Soviet Union. Chambers had made sure, he said, that the papers were delivered to Moscow.

The episode ended with Hiss going to prison for two years, for lying under oath. Ever after, Hiss maintained that he was not guilty, that he was a victim of Nixon and Chambers. The Hiss case made Richard Nixon a national figure and helped the

In 1975 Alger Hiss and his attorney (left) seek to reopen his case. Who else is in the photo?

Senator McCarthy tries to show extent of Communist influence in the United States.

Un-American Activities Committee gain support for further investigations.

Internment without trial. Because of the nation's militantly anti-Communist mood, President Truman in March 1947 established the Federal Employee Loyalty Program. This required an FBI check on backgrounds of all federal employees from the letter carriers on up. Three years later the Congress went even further. Over Truman's veto, the government was given power to arrest anyone it had "reason to believe" might commit acts of sabotage or spying for a foreign power. These suspects could be put into detention camps, without trial, for unlimited periods of time.

Such feeling had not died out easily. Only in 1971 was the "internment" (detention) power repealed.

"I have a list of names." On February 9, 1950, a little-known junior senator from Wisconsin made a speech in Wheeling, West Virginia. Within a few days the speech was front-page news. That night in Wheeling, Joseph McCarthy had waved sheets of paper at his audience and declared, "I have here in my hand a list of two hundred five—a list of names that were made known to the Secretary of State as being members of the Communist Party and who nevertheless are still working and shaping policy in the State Department."

No such "list of names" was ever produced. McCarthy, indeed, never offered evidence to back up his charges. Instead, he stepped up his attacks. He needed publicity for his re-election campaign in 1952, and he swung wildly. The Democratic Party, according to McCarthy, was being led by those "who had bent to the whispered pleas from the lips of traitors. . . ."

McCarthy went so far as to accuse the deeply respected General George C. Marshall, Army Chief of Staff in World War II and Truman's former Secretary of State. He called Marshall "a man steeped in falsehood," and involved in "a conspiracy so immense and an infamy so black as to dwarf any previous such venture in the history of man."

"No sense of decency?" McCarthy gained a wide, enthusiastic public following. When Senator Millard Tydings of Maryland called McCarthy's charges "the most [evil and vicious] campaign of half-truths and untruth in the history of the Republic," McCarthy wrecked the senator's career. He went to Maryland to speak against Tydings. He circulated a photo showing Tydings talking with Earl Browder, chairman of the American Communist Party. The picture was faked. Two separate photos had been printed to look like one.

McCarthy didn't turn up any secret Communists in the diplomatic service. Yet the State Department gave in before his accusations. Many persons suffered, their careers and reputations seriously affected.

But Americans had been shocked at events in Communist countries. Even John F. Kennedy, then a rising young Massachusetts Democrat, hesitated to attack the senator.

One of the few who did speak out against McCarthy was Senator Margaret Chase Smith of Maine. As early as June 1950, in her first major speech, she said he had made the Senate "a forum of hate and character assassination."

McCarthy finally destroyed his own career. He charged the military with being under Communist influence. The 1954 Army-McCarthy hearings that followed were televised. Millions saw the senator in action. His bullying manner and disregard for constitutional rights were demonstrated on-screen in living rooms throughout the United States. The viewing audience also saw and heard the firm, elderly, special counsel for the Army, Boston attorney Joseph N. Welch. Reacting to McCarthy, Welch finally exclaimed, "Have you no sense of decency, sir?"

The feeling in Welch's outburst was shared by many. Almost as quickly as it had developed, McCarthy's career began to slide. The latest Red Scare was dead by the mid-1950s, and the language had a new word, *McCarthyism.* One dictionary defines it as "the political practice of publicizing accusations of disloyalty or subversion with insufficient regard to evidence."

 TRY THIS!

1. Explain the Red Scare that followed World War II. What were the scare's origins? After World War II, was the threat of communism more real than after World War I? **2.** Show how McCarthy's attack on the Army destroyed him.

ROUNDUP

Who?

George C. Marshall
Henry A. Wallace
Robert A. Taft
J. Strom Thurmond
Joseph R. McCarthy
Alger Hiss
Richard M. Nixon

What?

Council of Economic
   Advisers
General Assembly
Security Council
veto power
iron curtain
containment
Truman Doctrine
Marshall Plan
Berlin Airlift
NATO
Taft-Hartley Act
Dixiecrats
House Un-American
   Activities Committee
McCarthyism

KNOW THIS

The United States After the War

1. Why were people unhappy with Truman as FDR's successor?
2. How had Truman been chosen for Vice President?
3. How did Truman handle postwar inflation?
4. What problems did the President have with organized labor?
5. Why was the Administration unsuccessful with social reforms?

Collapse of the Grand Alliance

1. Why was the United States suspicious of the USSR after World War II?
2. What caused the Soviets to distrust the United States?
3. Describe the two chief bodies of the UN. Why did the great powers insist on having a veto in the UN?
4. What issues were settled at Potsdam?
5. Why didn't Truman, as President, continue FDR's Russian policy?

Early Cold War Decisions

1. What policy toward the USSR did Henry Wallace favor?
2. What international crisis led to the Truman Doctrine?
3. Why was the Marshall Plan adopted?
4. When the western powers began to unite their German zones, what did Stalin do?
5. What was the purpose of NATO?

A Democratic Victory in 1948

1. Why did the 80th Congress pass the Taft-Hartley Act?
2. Why was Truman unable to get his civil rights proposals through Congress?
3. Explain the divisions within the Democratic Party in 1948.
4. Who were the candidates, and what were the issues, in the 1948 Presidentiai election?
5. Why did Truman win the election of 1948?

Another Postwar Red Scare

1. What started the Red Scare of the late 1940s?
2. What was the Hiss case about? What part did Richard Nixon play in it?
3. How did Senator Joseph McCarthy become a national figure?
4. What techniques did McCarthy use in his charges of communism? What ended his political career?

DIG HERE!

Since World War II, United States foreign policy has affected most parts of the world. Choose one of these regions or nations: Latin America, Southeast Asia, China, India, the Soviet Union, Western Europe, Africa. Research its recent history. Outline the U.S. role there, using these questions as a guide.

A. Is the U.S. a partner in any treaty involving the nation or region? If so, what are the treaty's major provisions?

B. What have been the main problems of the nation or region? Has U.S. aid played any part in the solving of these problems? Has the aid created difficulties?

C. How are political decisions generally made in the nation or region? Does it have a democratic government, or is it a dictatorship? Who are the leaders? Has the U.S. generally agreed with the government's policies? Has it tried to influence them? Explain.

D. What recent conflicts has the nation or region been involved in? Has the U.S. taken part in them?

E. Does the nation or region trade with the U.S.? If so, what trade agreements are there?

These books will be helpful: Fulbright, *Crippled Giant*, Random; Hanke, *Contemporary Latin America*, Van Nostrand; Hunter and Reilly, *Development Today*, Praeger; Kublin, World Regional Studies Series: *Africa, China, India, Japan, The Middle East, The Soviet Union*, Houghton; *U.S. Foreign Policy*, an annual publication of the U.S. Department of State.

THINK ABOUT IT

1. Some historians now place more blame for the Cold War on Truman and Acheson and less on Stalin. They say that the United States was too distrustful and rigid in dealing with the USSR. Which way do you feel about this? Defend your answer.

2. What do the Red Scares after the two World Wars suggest about people's right to express unpopular views? About ways of protecting national security? Can you justify what the government did to those suspected of disloyalty? Explain.

DO IT!

1. Organize a 1945 radio panel to discuss the topic of postwar readjustment. Have as panel members a wounded veteran, an employer, a married couple, a former war worker, and a member of Congress.

2. Design a bulletin-board display on the work of the UN.

THEN AND NOW

High hopes surrounded the founding of the UN. Some have been realized; others have not. What has been the UN's most recent success or failure? Was it partly the result of the way the UN is organized? Explain. Do you favor changing its organization now? Why, or why not?

605

A Cold War Engages the Nation

26

In the 1950s Americans learned to live with the threat of World War III and an atom bomb attack. These dangers influenced many government ac-

tions. They also led this cartoonist to question how much civilization had advanced—from cave dwelling to atom bomb shelter.

In Europe the containment policy (page 593) worked pretty much as the United States had hoped it would, holding communism to Soviet Russia and Eastern Europe. The Marshall Plan and NATO (pages 594 and 596) strengthened the non-

Communist governments of Western Europe and kept Soviet power from spreading. Asia was a different story. China became a Communist country in 1949, and Korea turned into a battleground where 33,000 American soldiers were killed.

1. SUCCESS AND FAILURE IN ASIA

For the United States there was one bright spot in the Pacific—Japan. After being defeated in World War II, Japan was occupied by United States troops. The head of the occupation force, General Douglas MacArthur, set about transforming Japanese society. The old imperialism and militarism were wiped out. Emperor Hirohito publicly proclaimed that he was not a divine being as his people had been taught to believe.

An industrial power. The emperor became a constitutional ruler, a symbolic head of state. A democratic political system replaced the old wartime dictatorship. All adult men and women were allowed to vote. A system of land reform was begun, giving Japanese farmers ownership of the land they worked. Previously the peasants had been sharecroppers (page 339), sometimes turning over to the landowners as much as 70 per cent of what they raised.

To assure that Japanese society would remain open and free, the secret police were abolished, individual rights were guaranteed, political prisoners were released, and schools were made more democratic. Labor unions were also set up and given the right to strike. However, when unions used the right too enthusiastically, the government and the occupation forces tried to limit it.

Under United States occupation, Japan received massive aid from its conquerors. Though Japan had nearly been demolished in the war, it recovered; slowly at first, then with startling speed. By the 1960s it had become an industrial power of the first order. And the former enemy was by then a firm and trustworthy ally of the United States. These developments were all the more reassuring because of what was happening on the mainland of Asia.

"Vinegar Joe." Compared with the success story in Japan, the situation in China was a tangled mess. During the war the United States supplied large amounts of military and financial assistance to China's leader, Generalissimo Chiang Kai-shek (page 547). The money and arms did little good. Chiang presided over a corrupt government. His armies, though well equipped, were poorly led and ineffective in battle. Chiang seemed more interested in fighting the Chinese Communist follow-

---

Read here of how

Containment did not work well in Asia.
MacArthur helped make Japan democratic.
But China was too big a problem.
Some Americans lost faith in the future.

TIME CHART

1949   Communist forces take over China.
1949   The Soviets explode an atomic bomb.
1950   North Korea invades South Korea. The United States sends troops.
1952   Dwight D. Eisenhower is elected President.
1953   The Korean conflict is ended.
1955   A "Big Four" conference is held at Geneva.
1956   "Peaceful coexistence" is attempted.
1959   Nikita Khrushchev visits the United States.

---

ers of Mao Tse-tung than in battling the Japanese.

The United States commander in China during World War II, General Joseph "Vinegar Joe" Stilwell, realized that China was in trouble. He observed how inefficiently the government was being run. Furthermore, Stilwell hated Chiang Kai-shek. It delighted Stilwell to see Chiang squirm, as he did once during the war, when Stilwell brought him a message from President Roosevelt. The message insisted that Chiang reform the Chinese army and begin to fight the Japanese more aggressively.

Down the drain. By the end of World War II the Nationalist government of Chiang Kai-shek was in deep trouble. The Communists controlled large sections of northern China and ruled about a quarter of the population. In their area the Communists began a sweeping program of land

607

Mao Tse-tung with the commander of the People's Army. Chou En-lai is at the far right.

reform (something Chiang refused to do) and won the support of millions. The United States wanted the Communists and the Nationalists to settle their differences.

In 1946 President Truman sent General George C. Marshall to China. Marshall managed to get Chiang and Mao together, but a settlement proved impossible. Both looked forward to complete victory. When Marshall returned home in 1947, a full-scale civil war erupted in China.

In an effort to contain communism, Truman sent $570 million to aid Chiang's Nationalists. Much of this support went down the drain as corrupt army officers pocketed the money. Chiang suffered a series of terrible battlefield defeats. By 1949 Mao Tse-tung was triumphant and controlled all of China. Chiang fled to Taiwan (the island of Formosa), where he set up a Nationalist government.

Incompetent and corrupt. Dean Acheson, who had become Secretary of State in 1947, tried to explain just what had gone wrong in China. In August 1949 he put out a State Department document of over a thousand pages. This "White Paper," as it was called, told of the unsuccessful efforts to make Chiang clean house and announced the end of all U.S. aid to his government. Acheson also totaled up the billion dollars in aid that the Nationalists had received after the war. Much of it, the Secretary said, had fallen into the hands of the Red Chinese.

Acheson told the American people that Chiang's government had been both incompetent and corrupt. His conclusion was that the fall of China was "the product of internal Chinese forces, forces which this country tried to influence but could not."

Groundless charges. If Truman and Acheson thought the people of the United States would calmly accept this lengthy and detailed explanation, they were wrong. During the war Chiang had been held up to Americans as a hero. Thanks to wartime propaganda, they had seen him as a worthy ally of Roosevelt and Churchill in the struggle against the Axis—a much more reliable one than the wily Stalin. Stilwell's opinion of Chiang had, of course, been hidden by the wartime need for military security. People found it hard to accept this new view.

So it was Truman and Acheson who were blamed for the Communist take-over in China. Anti-Communist crusaders, such as Senator Joseph McCarthy (pages 602-603), accused the President of losing China by failing to give Chiang Kai-shek enough support. They were also sure that the loss of China to the free world had been engineered by Communist sympathizers in the State Department.

These charges proved to be groundless. Since the Chinese people were dissatisfied with Chiang's government, there was not much the United States could have done to keep the Nationalists in power.

Too soon. Before the people of the United States could recover from the "loss" of China, their self-assurance took another hard knock. In September 1949 it was announced that the Russians possessed an atom bomb. Unmistakable evidence of a nuclear explosion had been picked up over Asia by United States planes carrying sensitive detection equipment.

United States officials had expected the Soviets to work out the technical problems and build a nuclear device by the end of the 1950s. Instead it had come ten years early.

It was in this atmosphere of dismay and confusion that Senator McCarthy made his 1950 address at Wheeling (page 602).

 TRY THIS!

1. Write the letter that a Japanese might have sent in 1948 to a friend in the United States. Assume that they have not heard from one another since before World War II. The Japanese tells how the country has changed since that time.   2. Explain why so many were upset by the triumph of communism in China.

2.   THE CONFLICT IN KOREA

On the heels of the Communist victory in China, a crisis in Korea took center stage.

———————————— • ————————————

Read here of how

The U.S. seemed to disregard South Korea.
But it soon changed its view.
The Communist Chinese took a hand.
And an old soldier "faded away."

———————————— • ————————————

At the end of World War II, Korea had been divided into two occupation zones along the line of 38° north latitude (map on page 611). North of this 38th parallel, the Russians established a Communist regime under the leadership of Kim Il Sung. In the South, a pro-United States government was led by Syngman Rhee.

A change of thinking. Kim Il Sung and Syngman Rhee each wanted to destroy the other and unify Korea. Kim made the first move. With Soviet encouragement, the

North Korean army swept across the 38th parallel on June 25, 1950.

The United States had a hard decision to make. As early as 1947, American policymakers had decided that South Korea would be too difficult to protect. In January 1950 Secretary of State Dean Acheson, listing places where the United States would fight to prevent a Communist takeover, did not include South Korea. Presumably it would be up to the South Koreans and the United Nations to do the fighting if attacked.

Within days of the North Korean invasion, President Truman reversed this

This South Korean Soldier is being trained to use United States arms, equipment, and tactics.

thinking. He later wrote, "I felt certain that if South Korea was allowed to fall, Communist leaders would be emboldened to override nations closer to our own shores."

Hurried retreat. Truman got the immediate support of the United Nations for military intervention to stop North Korea. The Soviet Union was boycotting Security Council meetings and was not present to veto the proposal. With UN support, Truman ordered planes and ground troops to Korea, and put General MacArthur in command. Eventually, sixteen nations took some part in the Korean fighting, but 90 per cent of it was done by the United States.

UN intervention came in the nick of time. The well-equipped North Koreans had overrun most of the South. But General MacArthur carried out a brilliant and daring plan. On September 15, 1950, UN forces landed at Inchon on the west coast of Korea, a point far behind enemy lines (map on page 611).

The Inchon landings took the North Koreans completely by surprise, and they began a hurried retreat. Within two weeks MacArthur's troops had occupied all of South Korea, captured or killed half of the enemy, and pushed the rest north of the 38th parallel. The United Nations goal had been achieved.

Home by Christmas? But MacArthur was not satisfied. He wanted to go north, totally defeat the Communists, and unify Korea under Syngman Rhee's leadership. Truman agreed and got UN approval for an expanded war. In early October, MacArthur's troops crossed the 38th parallel and began an advance northward. Their objective was the Yalu (YAH-loo) River, the border between Korea and China.

The new Communist government in China saw the advancing UN forces as a threat to their own security. Chinese Foreign Minister Chou En-lai warned that his country would not "tolerate seeing their neighbors being savagely invaded by imperialists." China began massing troops to help the North Koreans.

Alarmed at these developments, President Truman flew to Wake Island, in the Pacific, to confer with MacArthur. The General convinced Truman that there was little danger of Chinese intervention. And even if the Chinese did come into the war, MacArthur said, his troops would "slaughter" them. MacArthur boasted that the war was almost over and that American soldiers would be home by Christmas.

A costly mistake. Seldom had a military commander been so mistaken. On November 26, 1950, thirty-three Chinese divisions swept southward and halted MacArthur's advance. Suddenly, it was the UN armies that were in retreat. In the bitter Korean winter of sub-zero temperatures and frozen terrain, MacArthur's forces fled southward. The General feared that UN troops might have to evacuate Korea altogether.

Finally, in early 1951, the Chinese were stopped. The United States Eighth Army fought its way back to the 38th parallel. A bitter struggle continued along that line for two more years.

Truman realized that crossing the 38th parallel had been a blunder and would not allow MacArthur to invade North Korea again. Instead, the President wanted only to protect South Korea by keeping the Communists north of the 38th parallel. He wanted to get the United States out of the war by reaching a settlement with North Korea.

Why did the Chinese see the advance of United Nations troops as a threat to their territory?

"No substitute for victory." MacArthur saw things in a different light. He violently disagreed with Truman's orders not to invade North Korea. The General wanted to widen the conflict by bombing Chinese territory, blockading China's ports, and "unleashing" Chiang for military action in Korea or South China.

Truman gave MacArthur a firm no to each of these requests. The General refused to accept this decision silently, and began openly criticizing Truman's handling of the war. He wrote a letter in March 1951 to Joseph W. Martin, Jr., the Republican

611

leader in the House of Representatives. In strong language MacArthur condemned the President's limited aims in Korea: "If we lose the war to communism in Asia the fall of Europe is inevitable . . . there is no substitute for victory."

An old soldier. Truman was faced with a clear challenge to his constitutional role as Commander-in-Chief of the Armed Forces. On April 11, 1951, he fired MacArthur. "I could do nothing else," Truman said, "and still be President of the United States."

Truman's firing of MacArthur set off a wave of protest in the United States. Americans were used to winning wars. And they were frustrated with the situation in Korea. To many, MacArthur had shown that the way to defeat communism was by full-scale attack and total victory in Korea. When the General returned home, he was greeted with wild acclaim, partly a tribute to his World War II service. In New York the largest crowd the city had ever seen, an estimated 7,500,000 people, cheered his motorcade.

In Washington, MacArthur addressed a joint session of Congress. Weeping, he spoke of his days as a West Point cadet and concluded his speech:

I still remember the refrain of one of the most popular barracks ballads of that day which proclaimed most proudly that "Old soldiers never die; they just fade away." And like the old soldier of that ballad, I now close my military career and just fade away—an old soldier who tried to do his duty as God gave him the light to see that duty. Goodbye.

Angry telegrams and letters began pouring into Washington, most aimed at Truman.

The wrong war. The President quietly waited out the storm. When much of the

Police and Secret Service had trouble keeping back the enthusiastic crowds greeting MacArthur.

emotion had died away, the Democratic Congress conducted a series of hearings on the Korean conflict. All the top military leaders supported Truman and criticized MacArthur's plans for an expanded war. They argued that attacks against the Chinese would drain United States strength elsewhere, particularly in Europe. Such attacks might even lead to World War III. General Omar Bradley, Army Chief of Staff, summed up the case by saying that MacArthur's plans would have involved the United States in "the wrong war, at the wrong place, at the wrong time, and with the wrong enemy."

Although MacArthur did indeed fade away, the war did not. MacArthur's replacement, General Matthew B. Ridgway, accepted the orders from Washington and fought a limited war. The fighting stayed close to the 38th parallel.

Cease-fire. In July 1951, truce talks got under way. They frequently stalled on the prisoner-of-war issue. Almost 46,000 captured Chinese and North Korean soldiers did not want to be returned to Communist rule. When the United States refused to turn them over, the Communists walked out of the truce talks. They returned, but negotiations were extremely difficult. The final settlement gave prisoners the freedom not to return home if they declared their intentions before a neutral commission.

Truman left office in January 1953 with the war still going on and the peace negotiators still arguing. The combination of a new President, World War II General Dwight D. Eisenhower, and the death of Soviet dictator Joseph Stalin in March 1953, finally got the talks off dead center. On July 27, 1953, a cease-fire was signed. Both sides agreed to honor the boundary of the 38th parallel. The cost of keeping South Korea out of Communist hands had been sizable for the United States. American casualties totaled 33,629 dead and 103,284 wounded. In dollars, the war had cost nearly 22 billion.

TRY THIS!

1. Use the map on page 611 to show MacArthur's greatest triumph and his worst mistake in the Korean War. 2. Explain Truman's statement about firing MacArthur: "I could do nothing else and still be President of the United States." 3. Tell why the storm of protest over MacArthur quickly died down.

3. A NEW REPUBLICAN ADMINISTRATION

Read here of how

"Ike" Eisenhower became a politician.
He was a popular President.
He kept down military spending.
But the country slid into a recession.

In July 1952 the Republican Convention opened in Chicago. There was something new in the convention hall—television cameras. For the first time, the networks beamed the convention coast-to-coast, to an audience of seventy million viewers.

Rough-and-tumble politics. The main event of the convention was a closely fought battle for the presidential nomination between Senator Robert A. Taft of

613

Ohio (page 597) and General Dwight D. Eisenhower. Taft, making his third try for the Presidency, commanded the respect and loyalty of most Republicans. But many eastern Republicans feared that Taft was too conservative, that they needed a candidate who would appeal to independent voters and to some Democrats.

Taft might have won the nomination had not the more moderate wing of the party landed the biggest catch in United States politics—General Dwight D. "Ike" Eisenhower. The victorious commander of allied armies in Western Europe during World War II was the most popular living American. Although he did not especially want to be President, Eisenhower entered the race because he feared what Taft, as President, might do to the foreign policy of the United States.

Taft was not solidly in favor of a heavy military commitment to Europe, something Eisenhower strongly believed in. Furthermore, Taft had become identified with the anti-Communist crusade of Senator Mc-Carthy. "Ike," as headline writers called him, thought the danger of internal Communist subversion was greatly exaggerated.

Despite his tremendous popularity, Eisenhower's first-ballot victory over Taft came by a very narrow margin. Taft had a lot of influence in the party, and he had been the favorite when the convention began. Only Eisenhower could have beaten him.

If Eisenhower presented the image of a man above the rough-and-tumble world of politics, his vice presidential running mate, Richard M. Nixon of California, had a different reputation. He was known as an ambitious, hard-hitting young senator, dedicated to stamping out communism in the United States (page 601).

In 1952 even Democrats found it hard not to "Like Ike." He was not attacked in the way that Truman had been in the 1948 election campaign (page 598).

"I shall go to Korea." By 1952 polls showed that only a quarter of the country thought Truman was doing a good job as President. The conflict in Korea had dragged on and on with no end in sight. Stories of corruption and finagling in the Truman Administration made their way into print. Senator McCarthy was in his heyday and millions swallowed his charge that Communists infested Truman's government (page 603).

The President toyed briefly with the idea of running for another term. But when a crusading senator from Tennessee, Estes

614

Kefauver (KEE-faw-vur), beat him in the New Hampshire primary, Truman wisely dropped out of the race and planned for his retirement.

When Truman decided not to run for re-election, the Democrats chose as their presidential candidate the Governor of Illinois, Adlai E. Stevenson. Witty and sophisticated, Stevenson was an immediate hit with intellectuals and literary figures. One columnist thought the Governor to be "the first figure of stature to have emerged since Roosevelt." But Stevenson's highbrow style may have done him more harm than good. Too many people could not take in what he was saying. And like Taft, Stevenson found it impossible to combat Eisenhower's popularity.

If there was ever any doubt about an Eisenhower victory, it was removed when, twelve days before the election, the General pledged, "I shall go to Korea." The promise of a visit to the area of combat by the most respected military man of the time, brought many undecided voters into the Republican camp. "Ike will end the war," people told each other. On election day Eisenhower swamped Stevenson by over six and a half million votes.

"You trust him at once." Eisenhower was the first military career man to become President since Ulysses S. Grant. But most Americans did not think of Ike as a military type. Open, seemingly relaxed, and honest, Eisenhower inspired both respect and friendship. The British general Bernard Montgomery wrote of him: "He has the power of drawing the hearts of men towards him as a magnet attracts bits of metal. He merely has to smile at you, and you trust him at once."

Born in 1890, Eisenhower grew up in Abilene, Kansas, where his father worked

615

公自慢
（ミサイル之
1957.8
同君）

良

A Japanese cartoonist sees Khrushchev and Eisenhower boasting of their missiles. Why would the Japanese be especially concerned about the use of atomic weapons?

for a local creamery. Lacking the money for a college education, Ike secured an appointment to the Military Academy at West Point. A mediocre student, he ranked far down in the class of 1915. During the next twenty-five years, promotions in rank were few and far between.

But this changed with World War II. General Marshall spotted Eisenhower's talents and helped push him ahead. He responded brilliantly to the responsibilities of wartime. As Supreme Allied Commander, he skillfully resolved the conflicting interests of the nations trying to defeat Hitler. Eisenhower also had a talent for strategy and tactics. He planned four major invasions, including the Normandy landings in 1944.

A bigger bang. Eisenhower had the potential to be a strong, progressive President. Indeed, in foreign affairs, he often took firm control of troublesome situations. But on the domestic front, he seemed to let things drift. Basically, Eisenhower believed in less government and a less active Presidency. He seldom demanded that Congress pass important pieces of legislation, explaining, "I don't feel like I should nag them." The President said he stood for "dynamic conservatism—conservative when it comes to money and liberal when it comes to human beings."

Eisenhower claimed his Administration was "truly interested in the *little* fellow." He hoped to make prosperity a reality for all, by increasing the nation's economic growth. To accomplish this, the President favored reduced spending and a balanced federal budget. As a means of helping the economy, he suggested cuts in military spending.

Every gun that is made, every warship launched, every rocket fired signifies—in the final sense—a theft from those who hunger and are not fed, those who are cold and are not clothed.

This world in arms is not spending money alone.

Following up on the President's ideas, the Eisenhower Administration restructured the nation's military and defense strategy. To provide both security and economy, Eisenhower emphasized nuclear weapons and cut back on conventional land forces. Nuclear weapons were cheaper to build and maintain than ordinary ones, so the Administration hoped to get a "bigger bang for the buck." Between 1954 and 1957, expenses for the armed forces dropped from 50 billion dollars a year to 35 billion dollars.

Leap in unemployment. Eisenhower wanted to keep the lid on government spending. During Eisenhower's eight years as President, the federal budget increased by only 8 billion dollars (11 per cent), even though the United States population went up by 18 per cent.

Although Eisenhower was cost-conscious, he did not always say no to new government programs. He approved extensions in Social Security, which brought coverage to ten million additional people. He supported creation of the St. Lawrence Seaway, a project that opened the Great Lakes to oceangoing ships. The President enthusiastically signed the Federal Highways Act of 1956. This called for the construction of 42,000 miles of expressways (map on page 630).

Programs such as these were about as much as Eisenhower was willing to approve. He warned against "going too far to fool around with our economy." Using his veto power, Eisenhower axed public housing measures, public works bills, and anti-pollution legislation.

Partly because of Ike's refusal to spend government money, the country fell into a recession during the late 1950s. Not surprisingly, Democrats rolled to big wins in the Congressional election that year.

The only question. Perhaps the greatest criticism of the Republican regime of the fifties is that it did almost nothing to meet pressing social problems. The poor were ignored, even though a fifth of the population lived in poverty. The President failed to provide strong moral leadership in civil rights for blacks. He privately opposed a Supreme Court decision in 1954 that ordered the desegregation of all school systems. His silence encouraged southern resistance to integration and harmed the civil rights movement (page 631).

Throughout the 1950s, Eisenhower received much criticism for his conservative approach to government. But despite this, he held on to his enormous popularity. The only doubt about the 1956 election was whether Ike would run for another term. In the summer of 1955, he suffered a massive heart attack, which threw his political future into question. But when his doctors gave him a clean bill of health, Eisenhower stood for re-election, once again swamping Adlai Stevenson at the polls.

 TRY THIS!

Explain these seeming contradictions: a) A general who didn't want to be President decided to run. b) Americans chose as their political leader someone who was not a politician. c) A soldier-President kept down military spending.

4. A POLICY OF MASSIVE RETALIATION

Before sunrise one cold day in November 1952, President-elect Dwight D. Eisenhower left his New York home. With a Secret Service agent, he hurried to a black limousine that sped him through deserted streets. At an airfield outside the city, a plane awaited its passenger. Shortly the President-elect was airborne, about to keep his promise "I shall go to Korea."

To protect Eisenhower, the trip was kept top secret. His staff handed out fake schedules and convinced reporters that the General was still in New York, hard at work planning for his new Administration. Not until early December did the nation learn that Ike had been to the war zone.

New people with new ideas. Eisenhower spent seventy-two hours in Korea. He accomplished little beyond boosting the spirits of United Nations troops. But seeing the front lines up close strengthened the General's belief that somehow the war had to be ended. After his inauguration on January 20, 1953, peace in Korea was his primary goal.

It was not easy to get the many nations involved to agree on terms. Then, on March 5, 1953, Joseph Stalin, the Soviet dictator, died. The new Russian leaders, faced with many problems at home, did not want the Korean War to continue. They put pressure on the North Koreans to reach a settlement. At the same time, the Eisenhower Administration was threatening to use nuclear weapons against Communist China. New people with new ideas, in Washington and Moscow, all saw advantage in ending the struggle, and a cease-fire was signed on July 27, 1953.

Peaceful coexistence. For the next seven and a half years, President Eisenhower kept the country at peace. At times, there even seemed to be a thaw in the Cold War. In 1955 American and Soviet leaders met at Geneva, Switzerland. It was the first such gathering since Potsdam (page 591). Later that year they had a conference on the peaceful uses of nuclear energy. And in 1959 Nikita Khrushchev (KROOSH-choff), the new Soviet leader, toured the United States. His friendly, backslapping manner impressed onlookers.

Unfortunately, the moments of U.S.–Soviet goodwill were shortlived. Crises in world affairs continued. When Eisenhower left office in 1961, the Cold War was as much a fact of life as it had been in 1953.

Soon after coming to power, the Soviet leader declared an era of *peaceful coexistence.* This might be translated as: "I'll mind my business if you mind yours." The United States, weary of war, welcomed a lessening of tension. But the Eisenhower Administration believed that once the Communists became strong enough to compete with the United States on equal terms, there would be no more talk of peaceful coexistence.

"Liberation" instead of containment. If Eisenhower had believed Khrushchev, he would probably have named a different Secretary of State. John Foster Dulles, one

Read here of how

Eisenhower ended the Korean War.
His Administration called for liberation.
But it practiced containment.
Eastern Europe remained under Soviet rule.

of the United States' most unbending anti-Communists, headed the State Department for most of Eisenhower's term. He was a stern man who took a moralistic view of the Cold War. He frequently referred to "atheistic communism," "Soviet enslavement," and Russian "banditry."

One associate wrote of Dulles, "His face . . . was permanently lined with an expression of unhappiness mingled with faint distaste—the kind of face that . . . when it was drawn into a smile, looked as though it ached in every muscle to get back into its normal shape." The Secretary's abrasive, humorless manner even offended allies.

Dulles seemed to promise a new, more aggressive type of foreign policy than that of the Truman Administration. The 1952 Republican platform, which Dulles helped to write, denounced containment (page 593) as "negative, futile, and immoral." Dulles claimed that merely preventing the further spread of communism was not enough. Instead, he argued, the United States should work for the "liberation" of Eastern Europe from Soviet control (page 580). He angrily condemned the Communist takeover of mainland China (page 608) and spoke of using Chiang Kai-shek and the Chinese Nationalists for an attack on the People's Republic of China.

Going to the brink. The new Secretary saw little point in limited wars like the one in Korea. He felt they solved nothing. In his view the United States should boldly threaten nuclear attack if the Communists took the offensive. He believed that the threat of a nuclear strike—or "massive retaliatory power"—would discourage attempts to spread communism.

Dulles's schemes for "massive retaliation" fitted in well with the "new look" policy of the Defense Department. It em-

President-elect Eisenhower eats from a mess hall tray during his inspection tour of Korea.

phasized the use of nuclear weapons rather than conventional arms (page 577). It also resulted in the diplomacy known as *brinkmanship.* Dulles defined his strategy as "the ability to get to the verge without getting into . . . war. . . . If you try to run away from it, if you are scared to go to the brink, you are lost."

Brinkmanship was a policy filled with danger. By the 1950s the Soviet Union had developed an arsenal of nuclear weapons that were nearly as sophisticated as those of the United States. Each country had the power to devastate the other. As Winston Churchill said, the world lived in a "balance of terror."

619

For all their talk of "liberation" and "brinkmanship," Eisenhower and Dulles did not really change United States foreign policy. Instead they continued and expanded Truman's policy of containment. During the 1950s Dulles tried to build organizations like Europe's NATO in the Middle East, Southeast Asia, and the Pacific. The new groups looked impressive on paper, but none proved very effective. Some said the Secretary was suffering from "pactomania."

Not worth a war. Shadowed by the danger of nuclear war, Eisenhower tried to avoid all-or-nothing showdowns with the Communists. In Asia, he insisted that brinkmanship be used cautiously. However, he continued to support Chiang Kai-shek's Nationalist government on Taiwan against the Communists on the Chinese mainland.

In 1954 Dulles negotiated a treaty promising United States defense of Taiwan in case of attack. The Chinese Communists responded by shelling two Nationalist-held islands, Quemoy and Matsu. Eisenhower went before Congress and won approval of a sweeping resolution. It gave the President authority to use whatever force he thought necessary to protect Taiwan. This was as close to the brink as the Chief Executive went; he did not think the islands were worth a war. Apparently the Chinese Communists felt the same—for the time being they stopped shelling the islands.

Cheers from the free world. Events during the 1950s proved that "liberation" was an empty phrase. The death of Stalin in 1953 made Eastern Europeans hope for an end to the harsh Communist rule. In June 1953 thousands of East Germans took to the streets to protest their Communist

Khrushchev visited a Hollywood set in 1959. He found it "decadent." Who are the stars?

government. Soviet control was loosened a bit, but East Germany remained a Soviet satellite.

In 1956 there was another chance to liberate Eastern Europe. In February the Soviet premier, Nikita Khrushchev, formally denounced Stalin's policies. Eastern Europeans were soon demanding their freedom. Riots broke out in Poland in June, and by October the Soviet Union had agreed to loosen its controls there.

The Soviets had a very different reaction when the Hungarians revolted later in that month. On October 23, Hungarian "freedom fighters" stormed government buildings, shot members of the Hungarian secret police, and tore down symbols of Soviet rule.

Within four days the freedom fighters had driven the Russians from Budapest to the border. The free world cheered, but the rejoicing was short-lived. On November 1, reinforced Soviet troops and tanks moved back into Hungary and surrounded Budapest. The Hungarian premier's appeal to the United Nations went unanswered. On November 4 the Soviets took the city and ruthlessly stamped out the uprising. Some 30,000 Hungarians were killed; 160,000 more fled to the United States and other western countries.

To many, the Hungarian revolution had seemed a golden chance to liberate an Eastern European country. In spite of the Hungarians' pleas for help and a UN vote against the Soviet Union, the United States took no action. Eisenhower and Dulles felt that any American interference so close to the Soviet Union might result in World War III. "Liberation" was an effective slogan for political campaigns at home, but it had no place in the grim world of international politics.

A giant statue of Stalin loomed over Budapest until the Hungarians pulled it down.

 TRY THIS!

1. Compare the policies of containment and massive retaliation. What are the advantages of each? The dangers? 2. Show whether containment or massive retaliation was applied in a) Quemoy and Matsu, b) East Germany, c) Poland, and d) Hungary. 3. Write a short editorial defending Dulles's foreign policy.

621

ROUNDUP

Who?

Joseph Stilwell
Mao Tse-tung
Dean Acheson
Kim Il Sung
Syngman Rhee
Adlai Stevenson
Nikita Khrushchev
John Foster Dulles

What?

China White Paper
38th parallel
peaceful coexistence
massive retaliation
brinkmanship
Hungarian uprising
freedom fighters

Where?

Taiwan
Inchon
Yalu River
St. Lawrence Seaway

KNOW THIS

Success and Failure in Asia

1. What changes did the U.S. occupation forces make in Japan's government? In the lives of its people?
2. Why did General Stilwell dislike and distrust Chiang Kai-shek?
3. How did the United States hope to see the China problem settled?
4. What position did the Truman Administration take in the China White Paper?
5. Why were the American people unwilling to accept what was in the White Paper?

The Conflict in Korea

1. How did Korea become a divided country? What governments controlled each part?
2. When and why did the United States change its stand about defending Korea?
3. What was the principle aim of the United States in the Korean War?
4. Why did President Truman relieve MacArthur of his command?
5. How did the Korean fighting end?

A New Republican Administration

1. Why did General Eisenhower run for President in 1952?
2. What sort of campaign did Adlai Stevenson conduct? Why did it fail?
3. What attitude did President Eisenhower have towards Congress?
4. How did Eisenhower regard government spending?
5. What were some failures of the Eisenhower Administration?

A Policy of Massive Retaliation

1. How did the death of Stalin in 1953 affect United States-Soviet relations?
2. What sort of man was John Foster Dulles? How did he regard the Communist nations?
3. What policy did Eisenhower and Dulles favor in place of containment?
4. Why didn't the United States follow through on its statements about a) liberation and b) massive retaliation?
5. What seemed to be behind the uprisings in Europe in the late 1950s?

DIG HERE!

Since World War II, leisure time, affluence, and television have increased the interest of many, both as spectators and as players. Research the history of one sport, following this outline.

A. When did the sport first appear in the United States? When has it been most popular?
B. How have the sport and its rules changed? Have minority-group players found, in this sport, good chances for getting ahead?
C. Choose two champions or outstanding performers, one from the past and one from recent years. Write up their careers. Do you find any things that seem alike in their stories? Do you notice any big differences?
D. Does the sport attract mainly players or mainly spectators? How popular is the sport today?

You can start your research with some of these books: Allan, *The American League Story* and *The National League Story,* Hill & Wang; Bowen, *The Book of American Skiing,* Lippincott; Clerici, *The Ultimate Tennis Book,* tr. Weizell, Follett; Fox, *The Great Racing Cars and Drivers,* Grosset; Gerber, *American Women in Sports,* Addison; Grumsley, *Golf, Its History, People and Events,* Prentice; Jones, *Black Champions Challenge American Sports,* McKay; McCallum and Pearson, *College Football, U.S.A., 1869–1971,* McGraw; Mence, *Encyclopedia of Sports,* Barnes; Nelson, *Track and Field: The Great Ones,* Pelham; Wiebusch, ed., *More Than a Game: National Football,* Prentice; Woollett, *Racing Motorcycles,* Hamly.

THINK ABOUT IT

1. Massive United States aid helped make Japan and West Germany stronger and more prosperous than some of the nations that overcame them in World War II. Was this sensible? What might have happened if, after the war, the two losing countries had been punished instead?
2. Nothing Truman did roused as much opposition as his firing of MacArthur. Was Truman justified? Look up President Lincoln's firing of General John C. Frémont for a similar offense. Was Lincoln right? Explain.

DO IT!

1. Interview one of the Korean War veterans in your community about his experiences. If possible, invite him to speak to your class.
2. Make a display of political cartoons of the 1950s, attacking or supporting the Eisenhower policies.

THEN AND NOW

Should the United States have a small, inexpensive armed force, enough to handle a nuclear war? Or should there be, instead, a big armed force that could fight the conventional kind of conflict? The argument is still going on. Which would the ordinary citizen and taxpayer vote for, would you say? Why?

The 1950s Are An Age of Affluence

27

The automobile changed the nation in the 1950s just as it had in the 1920s. Personal cars became more necessary for work and recreation than family cars had been. Superhighways stretched past new industrial parks and shopping centers to distant suburbs, as businesses and people left the cities.

1. AN AFFLUENT, MOBILE SOCIETY

When the Second World War came to an end, Americans braced themselves for a return to hard times. Without heavy wartime spending, they reasoned, production would drop. The economy would plunge into another depression. It never happened. Instead, the country started on a period of prosperity that dwarfed the boom of the 1920s.

The affluent society. In the 1950s the growing middle class had fat pay envelopes, new cars, new homes, television, and vacation travel. They regarded the United States as the most *affluent* (wealthy) nation in the world. And indeed it was. By the end of the 1950s the average worker was earning 29 per cent more than in 1947. The Gross National Product (GNP)—the country's total output of goods and services—climbed to 500 billion dollars in 1960. That same year, 66.5 million Americans had jobs, an all-time high.

More jobs brought more money to spend. Before the war, the average American ate fifty pounds of meat a year. A decade later the typical citizen was eating 150 pounds yearly. For generations, hand-me-down clothes had been a part of growing up. In the 1950s this changed. Each year girls between fourteen and sixteen spent 773 million dollars on clothes. And "everyone" seemed to be buying cars. The number of automobiles registered increased by 135 per cent between 1945 and 1960.

Americans were only 6 per cent of the globe's population. But they were producing and consuming over a third of all the world's goods and services.

The not-so-affluent. In the 1950s those who worked hard and did their jobs well had every chance of getting ahead—if they were white. Most blacks, Mexican Americans, and American Indians were left out of the affluent society. They seldom got the education they needed for good jobs. Those who did found that few employers would hire them. Forty to fifty million Americans were stuck in the misery of the slums.

By 1960 a full 40 per cent of the women in the United States—more than ever before—had jobs. Often looked upon as temporary workers, they were seldom promoted to positions of responsibility. And they received lower wages than men. For most women, a career just didn't pay.

Read here of how

People feared a return of the depression.
But experienced unheard-of prosperity.
Cities lost population to suburbia.
And thousands moved west and southwest.

TIME CHART

1954	The Supreme Court hands down the *Brown* decision.
1955	The Montgomery bus boycott is launched.
1956	The Highway Act is passed.
1956	A crisis occurs over the Suez Canal.
1956	The Hungarians revolt against Soviet rule.
1957	The Eisenhower Doctrine is announced.
1957	Little Rock Central High School is integrated by federal order.
1957	The Soviets send Sputnik I into orbit.
1958	U.S. Marines land in Lebanon.
1959	Castro takes over in Cuba.
1960	The USSR shoots down a United States spy plane.

The birth of suburbia. In the 1950s the two-car family became commonplace, and roadbuilding boomed. The 1956 Highway Act gave the nation a network of superhighways (map on page 630), and nearly 74 million vehicles crowded the roads. Drive-in movies, restaurants, banks, and even churches indicated the new *mobility* (freedom of movement) enjoyed by Americans. So did the growth of suburbs, the "bedroom" communities on the outskirts of large cities. The automobile and the high-speed highway made it possible for people to live twenty or thirty miles from a city and still get to work easily. By 1950, 37 million people lived in suburbia. Two decades later this figure had doubled.

625

A housing boom encouraged suburban growth. When the war ended, there was a tremendous demand for housing. During the Depression and World War II, few new homes had been built. Making matters more pressing was the dramatic increase in the population. The postwar "baby boom" added 29 million new citizens during the 1950s.

William Levitt, a New York builder, saw the demand for homes and bought a 1500-acre potato field on Long Island. There he mass-produced housing the same way Henry Ford had built cars—on an assembly-line (page 482). The interchangeable parts could be put together on a tiny lot in a matter of hours—and at a low cost. Soon a town of 17,500 houses, with paved streets, schools, and a community swimming pool, stood on the old potato field. In March 1949 Levittown was opened to buyers. The reaction was amazing. Thousands eagerly paid the purchase price—6,900 dollars for a basic four-room house.

"Little boxes all the same." Other builders snatched up Levitt's idea and laid out developments of their own. Levitt himself bought up an eight-square-mile plot along the Delaware River in Pennsylvania and launched Levittown II. In a few years it had a population of 70,000 and had become the tenth largest town in the state.

There was no shortage of buyers for the suburban dwellings. The homes were generally inexpensive and the federal government made it easy to finance them. The G.I. Bill (page 588) and the Federal Housing Administration (FHA) guaranteed

For the good life in suburbia a family might need three cars—and a power mower.

mortgages. This meant that banks were willing to accept down payments of as little as 5 or 10 per cent of the total cost.

But some observers expressed alarm. They worried about what living crammed together in identical little houses would do to people. Folk singer Malvina Reynolds echoed their worries:

Little boxes on the hillside
Little boxes made of ticky-tacky
Little boxes on the hillside.
Little boxes all the same.

There's a green one and a pink one
And a blue one and a yellow one
and they're all made out of ticky-tacky
And they all look the same.

From the song "Little Boxes," words and music by Malvina Reynolds, © Copyright Schroder Music Co. (ASCAP) 1962. Used by permission.

Others were concerned by the way suburbs gobbled up the open spaces of the countryside. They had nightmares of a nation covered with Levittowns. Many also denounced the newness of suburbia. They wondered how a family could sink its roots in a community where a supermarket and a gas station were the most permanent institutions.

Black cities, white suburbs. The rush to suburbia dramatically changed the character of many cities. The old area inside the city limits, the central city, stopped growing or lost population as white families moved out. At the same time, large numbers of blacks from the South migrated to northern cities. Discrimination in the suburbs kept out even the few who could afford homes there. Black families had no choice but to move into the central city.

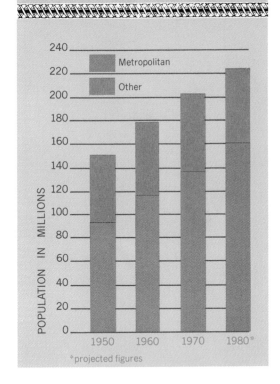

GROWTH OF METROPOLITAN-AREA POPULATION 1950-1980

*projected figures

Metropolitan Areas include central cities and suburbs. They have grown rapidly since 1950.

Many whites left for the suburbs to "escape" the incoming blacks. During the 1950s the twelve largest cities in the United States lost two million white residents and gained 1.8 million blacks. In 1940, Washington, D.C., had been 72 per cent white; twenty years later it was over 50 per cent black. Cities like Newark, New Jersey, Atlanta, Georgia, and Gary, Indiana, were about 35 per cent black by the 1960s.

The postwar migration of blacks to northern cities was caused by the introduction of machines on southern farms. By the 1960s only about half of the nation's black population remained in the South. But low incomes and discrimination forced them to live in city slums in the north. The suburbs were still 95 per cent white in 1970.

627

Youth in the 1950s

To the generation that had lived through a depression and a World War, young people in the 1950s seemed to lack convictions and to be altogether too "cool." Millions of them hurried home from high school to watch other people dance on TV shows like Dick Clark's *American Bandstand* (left). A carwash for some good cause (new outfits for the high school cheerleaders?) was a popular social activity (above). As always, there were fads. Telephone booth stuffing created as much excitement at colleges as goldfish swallowing had in the 1930s. (There are 22 students in this one.)

629

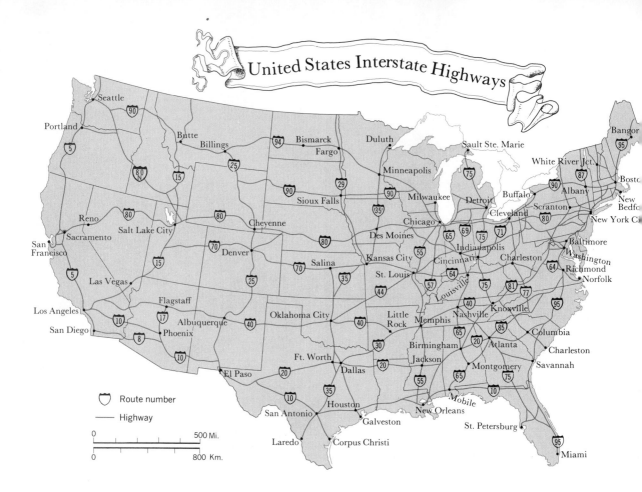

United States Interstate Highways

Route number
Highway

0 — 500 Mi.
0 — 800 Km.

The Interstate Highway system changed travel and commuting patterns throughout the United States.

"Westward Ho!" New cars and new highways encouraged another form of migration during the postwar era—the movement westward. Restless people saw the West and Southwest as the land of opportunity. New industries centered around aerospace programs, computer sciences, and plastics set up shop in Texas, New Mexico, Arizona, and California. Thousands upon thousands of workers flocked to these glamorous new jobs. The sunny climate of California, the Southwest, and Florida was an added attraction to northerners tired of shoveling snow. The resort business boomed. And thousands of retired Americans fled from the cold northern winters to the year-round sunshine of the south and west.

Between 1940 and 1960 the population of the Pacific Coast states zoomed by 110 per cent. Phoenix, Arizona, mushroomed from a desert town of 65,000 in 1940 to a metropolis of 439,000 in 1960. Fully half the residents of the Far West were newcomers who had moved from other sections of the country. The extent of the population shift became clear in 1963. That year California passed New York as the state with the largest population.

Even the world of sports was touched

630

by the "Westward Ho!" spirit. In 1958 New York's two National League baseball teams moved to California. The Brooklyn Dodgers left rickety old Ebbets Field for sunny Los Angeles, and the New York Giants fled the Polo Grounds for San Francisco's Candlestick Park. Californians, not New Yorkers, now cheered Willie Mays, Duke Snider, and Gil Hodges. It wasn't long before teams in other sports also sought greener pastures in the West.

 TRY THIS!

1. Compare the shift of population after World War II with the one that followed the Civil War (pages 380–381). How was each affected by a) opportunities to earn a better living, b) technology, c) methods of transportation? 2. Write a pair of letters that might have been exchanged between someone who had moved to California and a friend still living in a central city in the North.

2. CIVIL RIGHTS IN THE 1950s

When the Supreme Court assembled on May 17, 1954, few people realized how much its decision would change American social practices. Until 1954, segregation of the races was common throughout the land. For the most part blacks had separate housing, public facilities, employment opportunities, and schools. The 1954 decision was the beginning of the end for many kinds of segregation.

"With all deliberate speed." A black man, Oliver Brown of Topeka, Kansas, was disturbed because his ten-year-old daughter, Linda, had to travel across town to an all-black elementary school. With the help of the NAACP (page 344), Brown began legal action against the Board of Education of Topeka to let his daughter at-

---

Read here of how

The Supreme Court made a great decision.
A black girl went to school nearer home.
A woman refused to stand on the bus.
And the country began to change.

---

tend an all-white public school near home.

In 1953 *Brown v. Board of Education* was argued before the Supreme Court. Chief Justice Earl Warren delivered a unanimous court decision that concluded, "To separate [black children] from others of similar age and qualifications solely because of their race generates a feeling of inferiority . . . that may affect their hearts and minds in a way unlikely ever to be undone. . . . We conclude that in the field of public education the doctrine of 'separate but equal' has no place. Separate educational facilities are inherently unequal."

Segregation in education had been declared unconstitutional. The court ordered that black children be admitted to all public schools "with all deliberate speed." It was a complete reversal of the *Plessy v. Ferguson* decision of 1896.

"Feelings are deep on this." The court order angered many white southerners. The state of Alabama passed a nullification ordinance, which meant the state would use its power to block desegregation (page 139). Virginia decided to ignore the decision. South Carolina amended its state constitution to allow for the closing of the pub-

631

The nine justices of the Supreme Court who unanimously decided the *Brown* case.

lic school system. The governor of Georgia said his state intended to "map a program to insure continued and permanent segregation of the races."

The most dramatic reaction occurred in the United States Congress when 19 of the 22 southern senators and 81 southern representatives issued the Southern Manifesto. They pledged to use "all lawful means" to overturn the Brown decision. Only Senators Estes Kefauver (page 614) and Albert Gore of Tennessee, and Lyndon B. Johnson of Texas, refused to sign.

President Eisenhower said nothing in public, but privately he told an adviser, "Feelings are deep on this, especially where children are concerned. . . . All we can do is keep working toward a goal and keep it high. And the fellow who tries to tell me that you can do these things by force is just plan nuts."

Use of force. Eisenhower may not have wanted to use force to support integration, but in September 1957 he reluctantly did just that. The crisis took shape in late August when Central High School of Little Rock, Arkansas, prepared to admit black students. Arkansas Governor Orval Faubus ordered the state National Guard to stop the nine black students who had applied for admission. Over the denials of city and school officials, Faubus claimed that he had acted to avoid rioting around the school. When the Federal Court ordered him to cease his efforts to block integration, he withdrew the Guard.

Violence broke out a month later as gangs of whites roamed the area of the school, attacking blacks. Convinced that there was great public danger, Eisenhower acted. He ordered the Arkansas National Guard placed under federal control and sent a thousand paratroopers to assure the safety of the black students. In the years to come the federal government would many times have to use its power to enforce court desegregation orders.

A seat on the bus. Not only in the schools were blacks insisting on their rights. In Montgomery, Alabama, on December 1, 1955, black seamstress Rosa Parks sat down in the bus after a long day's work. Alabama law ruled that blacks must obey when a bus driver ordered them to give up their seats to whites. Mrs. Parks bravely decided to assert her right as a paying pas-senger. She refused to give her seat to a white man.

Mrs. Parks was arrested, found guilty, and fined ten dollars. Other Montgomery blacks also refused to put up with injustice and were arrested for the same "offense." They then agreed to boycott the bus company until people were allowed to sit on a first-come, first-served basis.

Since 75 per cent of the bus passengers were black, a long boycott would bankrupt the bus company. As the boycott expanded, a 26-year-old black clergyman, Martin Luther King, Jr., became increasingly active as its leader. He said, "This is only a conflict between justice and injustice."

King and 114 other black leaders were indicted by a white grand jury for interfering with trade. At his trial, King was fined a thousand dollars and court costs. But the boycott continued. King organized a car pool to provide transportation for blacks. This time he was arrested for operating a business without a license.

The Supreme Court settled the issue. It declared segregation on public transporta-

The first day of integrated schooling at Central High School, Little Rock, Arkansas.

633

tion to be unconstitutional. King went free 381 days after Mrs. Parks refused to give up her seat. Another barrier had fallen.

Black voters. In Congress, too, things were changing. In August 1957 a Civil Rights Act was passed, the first since Reconstruction. It established a six-member Civil Rights Commission and a Civil Rights Division in the Department of Justice. The Act also prohibited the use of force to prevent people from voting. For getting the new law through the Senate, much credit was due to Senator Lyndon Johnson of Texas, a state of the Old Confederacy.

In 1960 the Civil Rights Act was further strengthened. Federal judges could now actively help black citizens to register as voters.

New tactics. While school desegregation was stalled by legal maneuvering, blacks were working in other ways to gain social equality. The Montgomery bus boycott had produced a black leader in the Reverend Martin Luther King, Jr., and it had shown how to change unjust laws in an effective new way.

King and other religious people formed the Southern Christian Leadership Conference. Boycotts were undertaken against restaurants, theaters, stores, and other businesses. Nationwide chains were special targets for the civil rights movement. The chains usually followed "local custom" in their operation. This meant that they were segregated in the South but integrated in other parts of the country. When blacks were arrested for demanding service at a chainstore lunch counter, for example, it could affect the chain throughout the country. As word of the incident spread, northern blacks and whites who sympathized with their cause would refuse to patronize the chain's local outlets.

As the 1950s ended, lunch counter "sit-ins," often carried on by black students, were just getting under way. They were the spearhead of a movement that would bring much greater change in the next ten years.

Convicted and fined, but sure of victory, Martin Luther King, Jr., greeted by wife and followers.

TRY THIS!

Write an account of the changes in laws and customs governing race relations from the 1890s to the 1950s. Imagine you are an older person who remembers those early years. Look in the index of this book, under "blacks," for the information you need.

3. COMPLACENCY AND CONFORMITY

"Sometimes at night," one woman observed in 1948, "when a blind wasn't pulled all the way down we noticed mysterious blue light flickering in a living room across the street. Occasionally it was accompanied by sounds of laughter or gunshots." A few years later the "mysterious blue light" could be seen in homes all across the nation. Americans had found a new form of entertainment—television.

A toy for millions. Though invented in the 1920s, television's development was delayed by the depression and World War II. In the 1950s sales rose sharply. By 1957 Americans had plugged in forty million sets and could tune in to nearly 500 television stations.

Every afternoon the familiar words, "It's Howdy Doody time," announced the favorite program of millions of youngsters. Children everywhere plopped down before the family set and watched with delight. Some people thought that television would strengthen family ties by encouraging people to spend more time at home. Others were discouraged that television offered little that was educational or thought provoking. Only an occasional dramatic production rose above the seemingly endless cycle of comedies, mysteries, quiz shows, and westerns. This led Newton Minow, Chair-

---

Read here of how

A new means of communication appeared.
It changed politics and buying habits.
Women, like blacks, made little progress.
Soviet scientists startled the world.

---

man of the Federal Communications Commission, to call television a "vast wasteland."

The image-maker. It wasn't long before politicians discovered that television was a powerful tool for getting themselves known by the public. During the 1952 campaign Richard Nixon used it to save his political neck. Shortly after he was named the Republican candidate for Vice President (page 614), the press uncovered a sensational story: for several years, Nixon had been receiving money from a "secret fund" put together by some wealthy businessmen. The fund amounted to more than 18,000 dollars. There was nothing illegal or really secret about the fund. But the story, coming out as it did, threatened to hurt the Republican campaign. Some top party leaders demanded that Eisenhower drop Nixon from the ticket and replace him with someone untouched by scandal.

Nixon decided to appeal to the public. For half an hour he spoke on nationwide television. He denied any wrongdoing and described his modest financial circumstances. The funds, he said, had been used only for office and travel expenses.

Nixon admitted to accepting only one gift—a cocker spaniel puppy named Checkers, which his two daughters loved, and "regardless of what they say about it, we're going to keep it." Instantly known as the "Checkers Speech," Nixon's appearance was a smashing success. Republican headquarters was flooded with telegrams and letters supporting him. Nixon stayed on the ticket.

The "Checkers Speech" was the most effective early use of television in a national political campaign. From then on, no can-

Richard M. Nixon delivers his "Checkers Speech" and makes political history.

didate could ignore it. (Ironically, in the 1960 presidential campaign television helped defeat Nixon. He was bested in a series of televised debates by a better-looking, more accomplished performer, John F. Kennedy.)

"Private hoggishness." Even sooner than politicians, advertisers had discovered the possibilities of television. Program breaks were the perfect place to promote the latest household gadget or show off the sleek lines of a new car. Manufacturers spent millions to find the kind of commercials that brought the widest response. Their clever ads were hard to resist, espe-

cially for the young. In one survey 94 per cent of the mothers interviewed said their children asked them to buy products advertised on television.

In many cases television ads created an artificial demand for products. True happiness, viewers were told, could be theirs if they bought a new car, tried a different toothpaste, wore the latest fashions, acquired a new refrigerator, or ate the right cereal.

Television advertising increased the "buy, buy, buy" spirit of consumers. Many thoughtful men and women were worried about the extent to which television was shaping consumer buying habits. They were troubled by the growing desire for material goods. One writer concluded that the 1950s was "the age of the slob" when "the loudest sound in the land has been the oink and grunt of private hoggishness."

No better vocation? Social critics were also concerned that television was setting standards for the way people lived and thought. They felt it encouraged them to follow certain life-styles. The push to conform was particularly felt by women. Girls were encouraged to play with dolls so they could learn to be "little mothers." Women were told that their place was in the home, and that they would find happiness if they married "the right man" and raised a family. Only rarely did either movies or television feature a working woman with a successful career. Instead, cheery actresses played housewives and mothers, devoted to husband and family.

Women's magazines told their readers that raising a family was "the ultimate measure of success." To a group of college women Adlai Stevenson (page 615) said, "there is much you can do about our crisis in the humble role of housewife. I could

A single week's work and supplies for this American housewife. Why does she look happy?

wish you no better vocation than that." Stevenson added that housewives were important because they could "influence man and boy."

Security first. Despite the pressure to marry and stay at home, more women than ever before went to work in the 1950s. Marriage appeared to be no barrier. Between 1940 and 1960 the number of wives who were employed doubled. But most women could get work only as teachers, nurses, secretaries, or salesclerks. The few

women who did do the same work as men were usually paid less than their male co-workers.

Independent-spirited women fretted at being treated as second-class citizens. Some dedicated women, following the tradition of the suffragists (page 421), tried to promote the cause of women's rights. These *feminists* argued that society had to be made aware that women were as much individuals as men. But in the 1950s most women found it hard to resist conforming to society's picture of them.

Men, too, experienced pressure to conform to social standards. The ambition of most college men seemed to be landing a

The car dealer believes that these are the greatest developments of the 1950s. What happened to the Edsel?

safe, high-paying job with a big corporation. One writer looked over a graduating class and found them "curiously old before their time. Above everything else, security has become their goal."

An abrupt awakening. To a nation concerned with financial security and social conformity, the fall of 1957 brought a terrible shock. In October the Soviet Union sent the first artificial satellite—*Sputnik I*—into orbit around the earth. The Space Age had begun, and the world could never be the same again.

United States fear of the Soviets had been somewhat lulled during the period of affluence. Now it awoke. Soviet science seemed to be years ahead. Some Ameri-cans believed that the nation's concentration on consumer goods had given the USSR first place in the Cold War. Others noted that there seemed to be no sense of national purpose and wondered if the nation's schools were teaching the right subjects. To many it seemed clear that the United States needed new direction.

 TRY THIS!

1. Account for the effect of television on politics and advertising.   2. Tell how television failed to help women in the 1950s.   3. Write an editorial on the year 1957, commenting on the Soviet lead in the space race.

4.   SEEKING AN ACCOMMODATION

In the 1950s Americans grew accustomed to international crises. One might occur on some unheard of Asian island. Or an East European city like Berlin or Budapest might suddenly burst into the news. In the later 1950s American attention was often focused on the Middle East.

Playing both sides. Established in 1948, the state of Israel looked to the United States for material aid and moral support. When surrounding Arab states launched

---

Read here of how

Egypt wanted a canal and a dam.
The U.S. joined the USSR against the West.
The U.S. failed to get an arms agreement.
And found a problem on its own doorstep.

---

an attack on the new nation in 1948, President Truman solidly backed the Israelis. This angered the Arabs, who became more friendly with the Soviet Union.

Secretary of State John Foster Dulles worried about the Arab ties with communism. This was partly because 60 per cent of the world's oil reserves were in the Middle East. A special source of worry was the Egyptian leader, Gamal Abdel Nasser. To gain Nasser's good will, Dulles offered him funds for one of the Egyptian's pet projects—the Aswan Dam. It was to be an enormous hydroelectric project on the Nile River. Nasser accepted United States assistance but continued to take money and military aid from Communist countries. Dulles had little use for "nations which play both sides." For him, "neutralism" was immoral, and he withdrew the offer of American aid in mid-July 1956.

639

Nasser proved to be as headstrong as Dulles. On July 26, he seized the Suez Canal, which was owned by a British-French company. The Suez, connecting the Mediterranean and the Red Sea, was Europe's lifeline to Asia. Nasser planned to pay for the Aswan Dam out of the profits from the canal.

Alarmed by Egypt's growing strength, Israel sent troops into the Sinai Peninsula on October 29, 1956. Two days later, Britain and France joined the assault, bombing Egyptian cities and retaking portions of the Suez Canal.

Crackling language. The British, French, and Israelis had not informed the United States of their decision. President Eisenhower exploded when told of the invasion. A reporter on the scene recalled that "the White House crackled with barrack-room language the like of which had not been heard since the days of General Grant."

The President had good reason to be angry; the Anglo-French action put the United States in a difficult position. How could the United States maintain its opposition to attacks on independent nations, yet support its allies when they did that very thing? To make matters worse, the Soviets threatened to intervene unless the invaders withdrew. They said they would send Russian troops to Egypt and launch nuclear missiles against Britain and France. At the same moment, the UN was debating the fate of Hungary (page 621). World War III seemed close to breaking out.

In spite of his angry explosion, Eisenhower dealt cautiously with the crisis. The United States sided with the Soviet Union and demanded that all foreign forces pull out of Egypt. With the two superpowers

Gamal Abdel Nasser wanted to unite the Arabs of the Middle East against western imperialism.

against them, the invaders had little choice. Britain and France backed out of the canal zone and Israel withdrew from the Sinai.

A painful episode. The United States paid a price for its role in the Suez Crisis. America's two principal allies had been humiliated. Shaken leaders in London and Paris blamed Dulles. They reasoned that the Secretary's clumsy handling of Nasser had triggered the entire affair. Certainly, if Dulles had shown more patience with the Egyptians, the painful episode might have been avoided.

Following the Suez crisis, Egypt drew closer to the Soviet Union. Further Communist penetration of the Middle East became likely. To head it off, in early 1957 the President proclaimed what came to be called the "Eisenhower Doctrine." It offered United States military help to any Middle Eastern nation "requesting assistance against armed aggression from any country controlled by international communism." The doctrine was put to work in the summer of 1958. Washington feared that pro-Nasser elements in the Middle Eastern country of Lebanon were on the verge of a takeover. The President sent 14,000 Marines into the country to keep a right-wing government in power.

The Eisenhower Doctrine succeeded in preserving a pro-United States government in Lebanon, but it failed to deal with the real causes of unrest in the Middle East. These were poverty, nationalism, opposition to Israel, and the presence in Arab countries of Palestinian refugees. The latter had left their homes during the 1948 war that broke out between Israel and its Arab neighbors.

Spy in the sky. Throughout his years in the White House, Eisenhower hoped to achieve some sort of peaceful arrangement with the Soviet Union. In 1955, the President met with other leaders of the "Big Four"—Britain, France, and Russia—at Geneva (page 618). Nothing much came of Eisenhower's proposals for mutual disarmament, but the "spirit of Geneva" indicated that West and East could at least discuss their differences. When Dulles died in 1959, the President took a firmer hold on foreign-policymaking.

Eisenhower welcomed Soviet Premier Nikita Khrushchev to tour the United States. At Camp David, the presidential retreat in Maryland, the two leaders laid plans for a major summit conference to be held in Paris in May 1960. The United States looked forward to the meeting as a chance to reduce the tensions of the Cold War.

The Paris meeting blew up in Eisenhower's face. A few weeks before the conference opened, the United States was caught spying on the Soviet Union. On May 1, 1960, the Soviets shot down an American U-2 jet flying high over the USSR. At first Washington denied responsibility for the flight. The United States Central Intelligence Agency concocted a story that the U-2 was a weather plane which had gone off course. But when Eisenhower learned that the Russians had taken the U-2's pilot prisoner, he admitted the true nature of the flight.

U-2 pilot Francis Gary Powers in a Moscow courtroom. He was later exchanged for a Soviet spy.

Castro had been a high school athlete (baseball, basketball, track). He brought better education and medical care to the Cuban people but failed to restore the nation's prosperity.

The U-2 affair played into Khrushchev's hands. He and his advisers had decided that a meeting with the United States would not be in the interest of the Soviet Union. The U-2 incident gave the Russian leader an excuse to break up the Paris summit meeting.

A thorny problem. As the Eisenhower administration drew to a close, United States prestige throughout the world fell sharply. Eisenhower was forced to cancel a good-will visit to Japan because of anti-American riots. Even in the Caribbean—once called a United States lake—unsettling events commanded attention.

On January 1, 1959, Fidel Castro, a popular revolutionary, seized control in Cuba. At first most people in the United States welcomed Castro's rise to power. He was, after all, replacing a corrupt dictator, Fulgencio Batista. The bearded Cuban even appeared on American television programs. But Cuban-United States relations fell apart rapidly after Castro declared himself a follower of Marx and Lenin (in other words, a Communist) and started to woo the Soviet Union.

The Eisenhower Adminstration responded by cutting imports of Cuban sugar and stopped exports to Cuba. Large-scale aid from the Soviet Union became Cuba's chief source of necessary goods. Then, just before leaving office early in 1961, Eisenhower broke diplomatic relations with Castro's government. Eighteen days later, the thorny problem was handed over to a new President, John F. Kennedy.

TRY THIS!

On an outline map of the world, indicate all the places you can that became trouble spots for the United States between 1945 and 1960. Give dates and briefly explain the circumstances that led to each confrontation.

ROUNDUP

Who?
William Levitt
Oliver Brown
Rosa Parks
Martin Luther King, Jr.
Gamal Abdel Nasser
Fidel Castro

What?
Suburbia
baby boom
G.I. Bill
FHA
Brown v. Board of Education
Civil Rights Act of 1957
Southern Christian Leadership Conference
sit-ins
"vast wasteland"
Checkers Speech
Sputnik
Aswan Dam
Suez crisis
Eisenhower Doctrine
U-2 incident

Where?
Suez Canal
Aswan Dam
Sinai Peninsula
Lebanon

KNOW THIS

An Affluent, Mobile Society
1. Why was there an economic boom after World War II?
2. What groups of Americans did *not* share in the postwar prosperity?
3. Describe the population shifts of the late 1940s and 1950s.
4. How did the population shifts affect the older cities?
5. Why were so many Americans drawn to the South, the West, and the Southwest in the 1950s?

Civil Rights in the 1950s
1. What reasons did the Supreme Court give for its *Brown v. Board of Education* decision?
2. Why didn't President Eisenhower speak out on school segregation? What action did he take in Little Rock?
3. What were the reasons for the Montgomery bus boycott?
4. What new tactics were used in the bus boycott?
5. Why were chain stores so often targets of civil rights demonstrators?

Complacency and Conformity
1. What politician made the first effective use of television?
2. How did advertisers use television?
3. How did television encourage a particular way of life for American women? For American men?
4. What limitations were placed on working women during the 1950s?
5. How were Americans jolted from their contentment in 1957?

Seeking an Accommodation
1. What led up to Egypt's seizing of the Suez Canal?
2. How did Israel, Britain, and France react to the seizing of the canal?
3. Why did United States allies blame John Foster Dulles for the Suez crisis?
4. What was "the spirit of Geneva"? What ended it?
5. What foreign problem surfaced at the end of Eisenhower's Administration? What steps did the outgoing President take?

DIG HERE!

As the United States has grown, its cities have passed through a number of crises. The most recent followed the middle class's moving to the suburbs. Choose one city that you know well or want to know more about, and do an in-depth study. Deal with these topics:

A. What geographic features helped the city's growth—or hurt it?
B. What historical developments affected the city (for example, railroads or the rise of industry)?
C. Make a map of the central city and its suburbs. What is the population of the city? Of the entire metropolitan area? Has the population been growing recently, or shrinking?
D. Does the city have established ethnic neighborhoods (Chinese, Italian, etc.)? Can you show these on your map?
E. Do some industries dominate the city? Are they growing? Has new business come to the city lately?
F. What forms of transportation serve the metropolitan area?
G. What cultural advantages does the city offer? Are there theaters? A performing-arts center? An art gallery? Any colleges?
H. What has been done about slums, housing, race relations? Are there urban-renewal projects?

Besides books, magazines, and encyclopedia articles on your city, consult Habenstreit, *Making of Urban America,* Messner; Hoag, *American Cities,* Lippincott; Trettan, *Cities in Crisis,* Prentice; Wade, *Cities in American Life,* Houghton.

THINK ABOUT IT

1. Eisenhower did not approve of the *Brown* decision, but he enforced it to the best of his ability. Compare his action with that of Andrew Jackson on the Cherokee claims (pages 191–192). Do you feel that either President acted correctly? Why? Defend your answer.
2. In the Suez crisis, the United States sided with Egypt and the USSR against Britain, France, and Israel. What happens when a powerful nation acts against its friends on a matter of principle? Does it gain prestige, or lose it?

DO IT!

1. Have members of your class tell how far and how often their families have moved in the last ten years. If the class were a sample of the U.S. population, what would they be saying about the country?
2. Hold a debate or panel discussion on the value of television for news, education, and entertainment. Is it a "vast wasteland"?

THEN AND NOW

Is it right for nations to spy on each other by high-altitude planes or satellites? In an age of nuclear weapons and intercontinental missiles, is it safer for nations to know one another's plans and capabilities? Explain.

TEST YOUR HISTORY

1. Why did the United States become more concerned with world affairs in the 1930s?
2. What role did the United States play in the first years of World War II?
3. How did the nation enter the war?
4. What were some effects of World War II on the U.S. home front?
5. What military reverses did the United States suffer in 1942?
6. When and where did the tide turn for the Allies?
7. How was victory achieved in Europe? In the Pacific?
8. What troublesome decisions were made at the Yalta Conference?
9. What problems did the United States face just after the war?
10. How and why did Allied wartime cooperation end?
11. How did the United States carry out its policy of containment?
12. Why was Truman able to win election in 1948?
13. What caused the Red Scare that followed World War II?
14. What were some results of the United States occupation of Japan?
15. Why was Chiang Kai-shek unable to hold China?
16. What caused the war in Korea?
17. How was the Korean conflict settled?
18. What policies did the Eisenhower Administration follow at home? In foreign affairs?
19. What kinds of progress did blacks make in the 1950s?

VI
REVIEW

FURTHER READING

Brooks, J., *The Great Leap: The Past Twenty-five Years.* Harper, 1966.

Esposito, V. J., ed., *A Concise History of World War Two.* Praeger, 1964.

Ferrell, R. H., ed., *America in a Divided World.* Harper, 1974.

Goldman, E., *The Crucial Decade and After: America, 1945–1960.* Random, 1961.

Hodgson, G., *America in Our Time: From World War II to Nixon.* Doubleday, 1976.

Kirkendall, R. S., *Global Power: The United States Since 1941.* Allyn, 1972.

Leuchtenburg, W. E., *The Age of Change,* Vol. 12, *Life History of the United States.* Time, 1974.

Liddell Hart, B. H., *A History of the Second World War.* Putnam, 1971.

Phillips, C., *The Nineteen Forties.* Macmillan, 1974.

Rosenberg, E., *Our Times: America Since World War Two.* Prentice, 1976.

Taylor, A. J., *The Second World War: An Illustrated History.* Putnam, 1975.

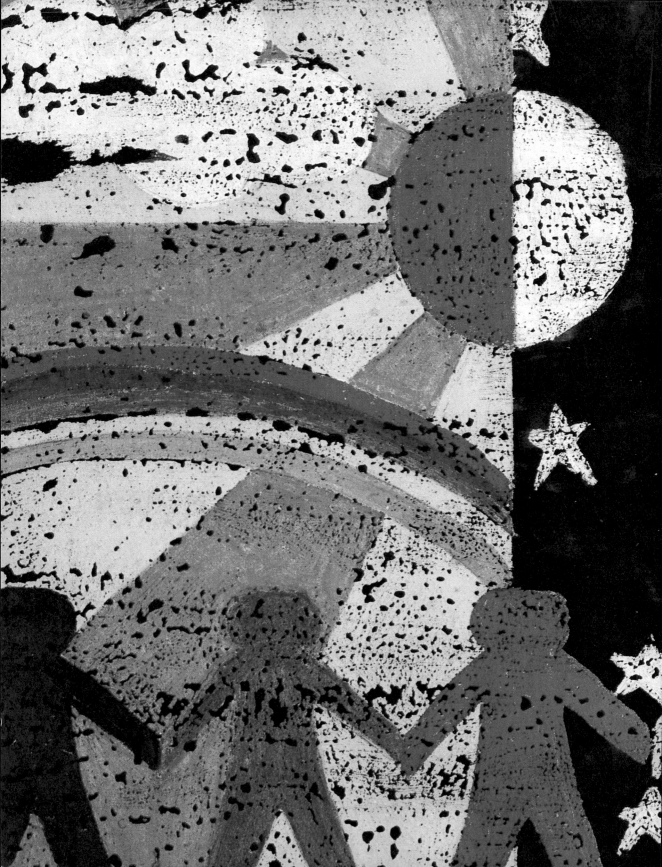

VII

A NEW DIRECTION

Our country—this great Republic—means nothing unless it means the triumph of a real democracy, the triumph of popular government, and, in the long run, of an economic system under which each man shall be guaranteed the opportunity to show the best that there is in him.

Theodore Roosevelt
"The New Nationalism"   647

The Nation Begins to Build a Great Society

28

In the midst of their affluence, Americans discovered the hidden poor, like this Appalachian coal miner. The Great Society programs were for them.

1. PROMISE OF THE NEW FRONTIER

Inauguration Day, 1961, dawned cold and clear in Washington, D.C. Drifts of snow had piled up the evening before. But thousands of workers cleared the avenues of Washington in time for the ceremonies. By the next day, the Democrats were ready to celebrate their recapture of the White House.

At twelve noon, John F. Kennedy, at 43 the youngest man ever elected to the Presidency, took the oath of office. In his inaugural address he pledged the nation to pay any price or bear any burden to assure the survival of liberty. Kennedy asked Americans to put their country before selfish interests: "Ask not what your country can do for you—ask what you can do for your country." Thus did the President set the tone of the new administration.

In the hours that followed, thousands passed in review before the White House as Kennedy and his wife, Jacqueline, looked on. It was a joyous beginning to a very brief term of office. The spirit and youthful energy of the President promised a new beginning for the country.

A close election. Kennedy had almost failed to make it. The 1960 election had been one of the closest. Just over 100,000 votes separated Kennedy from Richard Nixon. Almost 69 million ballots had been cast. The electoral count gave Kennedy 303 votes to Richard Nixon's 219.

The campaign had centered around a series of televised debates (page 634). Senator Kennedy was probably helped most by the debates. He had been less well known than Vice President Nixon. The debates showed up greater differences in personality and "style" than on major issues. Nixon kept warning the country that Kennedy was inexperienced, and Kennedy kept repeating that he wanted to "get the country moving again."

Kennedy's religion turned out not to be an issue. He clearly stated that his being a Catholic would in no way conflict with his loyalty to the Constitution.

"He did everything." After eight years of Eisenhower's conservatism, Washington in 1961 bubbled with plans for new social programs and promises of reform. A flood of college professors, many from Harvard, arrived to take positions in the new Administration. Historians, economists, political scientists, and social planners poured out ideas on how to move the country in new directions. Nothing like it had been seen since the first hundred days of the New Deal (pages 516–521).

At the center of this activity was a new President who seemed to be doing every-

Read here of how

Kennedy launched a New Frontier.
But it failed to meet its promise.
The black protest movement surged ahead.

TIME CHART

thing and going everywhere. Kennedy's energy and interests appeared unlimited. In his first two months in office he issued 32 official messages and legislative proposals, made 12 speeches, released 22 executive orders, sent 28 messages to foreign leaders, and held 7 press conferences. (Eisenhower had been content to issue five official messages in his first two months as President.) One journalist reported of Kennedy, "He did everything today except shinny up the Washington Monument."

Widespread problems. Only later would it become apparent that the Kennedy Administration accomplished less than all the activity suggested. Federal aid,   649

"The torch has been passed to a new generation of Americans," Kennedy said at his inaugural.

for example, was proposed to advance education and health. But Congress turned down programs to aid public schools and to provide medical insurance for the elderly. However, the minimum wage was raised and extended to cover more workers. Public funds were used to stimulate growth in depressed areas, where unemployment was high. And federal aid was advanced to colleges and universities.

None of these programs touched the deep-rooted problem of poverty. Between a fifth and a quarter of all the people in the United States had incomes too low to meet their basic needs. Millions of Americans had too little food, poor housing, and not enough medical care. Only in the mid-1960s would a determined effort be made to deal with those widespread problems.

Basic rights denied. The campaign to win equal rights for all citizens surged ahead during the Kennedy years. Kennedy gave full support to the Supreme Court decision outlawing school segregation (page 631). And the Justice Department, headed by his brother Robert F. Kennedy, enforced the Civil Rights Acts of 1957 and 1960 (page 634).

Through the first half of the 1900s, no part of the life of black Americans had been free from segregation. This was most obvious in the inferior schools built for black children. But it could also be seen on buses and trains where blacks had to sit in certain sections. Segregation cut deep in the armed forces, where blacks served in separate units. Theaters and other places of entertainment had segregated seating. Even some churches had separate pews for blacks or closed their doors to them altogether.

Despair over the lack of job opportunities found angry expression in the comment of blacks that "we're the last hired and the first fired." Throughout a large part of the country, blacks could not vote in elections. Nor could they run for office in many areas where they were a majority of the population. Too often, even the basic right to a fair trial was denied when lynch law took the place of justice (page 489).

Some aspects of segregation had been attacked in the 1940s and 1950s, but not until the 1960s did the whole federal government get solidly behind the movement to do away with inequality in American life.

Graduation to full citizenship. Nowhere was determination to resist change stronger than in Mississippi. In the fall of 1962, a black man, James Meredith, tried to enter the state-supported University of Mississippi. Officials of the university had no intention of allowing Meredith to register for admission, however. And the governor of Mississippi supported them.

Federal marshals accompanied Meredith when he went to the campus to regis-

ter. President Kennedy appealed for peaceful desegregation of the university. However, a mob gathered at the university and rioting broke out. Dozens of federal marshals were injured and two people were killed. Finally, Kennedy sent federal troops in to restore order. Meredith was at last allowed to register. Federal marshals protected him as he attended classes.

The closed system of segregation was also challenged in Alabama. In southern cities such as Birmingham, water fountains, waiting rooms, and rest rooms were marked *Colored* and *White.* A black person could not even be served at a soda fountain

The 1963 Civil Rights march on Washington (page 652) seen from the Lincoln Memorial.

(page 634). Police acted quickly whenever there was any protest. Martin Luther King, Jr. (page 633), had decided to center his attention on Birmingham. When blacks led by King planned a Good Friday protest march in 1963, the Birmingham public-safety commissioner forbade it. King marched anyway and went to jail.

"I have a dream." In the weeks that followed, hundreds of black high school students joined King. It was their "graduation into full citizenship," one explained. Demonstrations and arrests continued. An uneasy peace was shattered in the fall when four little black girls were killed in the bombing of their church. King's emphasis on peaceful protest against such violence won him respect and admiration throughout the nation.

Against a backdrop of violence that saw 14,000 demonstrators jailed during the summer of 1963, Martin Luther King, Jr., led a peaceful demonstration in the na-tion's capital. The "march on Washington" brought together some 200,000 people. They were showing their support for King's commitment to nonviolent protest against racism.

Singing "We Shall Overcome" and calling for "Freedom now," the crowd walked peacefully as millions watched on television. On the steps of the Lincoln Memorial, King appealed, "I have a dream that one day this nation will rise up, live out the true meaning of its creed: 'We hold these truths to be self-evident, that all men are created equal.' "

 TRY THIS!

1. Compare the beginnings of the Kennedy Administration with Franklin Roosevelt's "Hundred Days." **2.** Describe Martin Luther King's use of nonviolence. Was it effective? Why?

2.   THE KENNEDY FOREIGN POLICY

In his inaugural address, John F. Kennedy made clear that he meant to continue the United States role as the free world's chief defender. "Let the word go forth from this time and place, to friend and foe alike," he declared, "that the torch has been passed to a new generation of Americans . . . tempered by war, disciplined by a hard and bitter peace."

Ambitious programs. An early act of the new administration was the creation of the Peace Corps. This agency recruited thousands of Americans to work as teachers, health advisers, and technicians in countries around the world. Here was a practical gesture of friendship to develop-ing countries in Africa, Asia, and Latin America. In its call for service without financial reward, the Peace Corps appealed to the idealism of many Americans. Young people—and some not so young—used their talents, training, and experience to

Read here of how

The Cold War heated in the Kennedy years.
There were international crises.
But some easing of tension.
The New Frontier ended in assassination.

A Latin American view of the Kennedy-Khrushchev missile crisis. What was Castro's role?

help other people acquire modern technology and improve their lives.

To the nation's southern neighbors, Kennedy also offered a new program of economic assistance, the Alliance for Progress. It promised twenty billion dollars in aid over a period of ten years. Its goal was to help Latin American countries upgrade their housing, medical services, and education and to expand industrial and agricultural production. Another of its aims was to bring about in Latin America a fairer distribution of national income, price stability, and tax reform.

The Alliance was an ambitious program. At least part of its purpose was to change the conditions that had brought about Communist control in Cuba. However, as with other well-intentioned programs for Latin America, the Alliance never fully lived up to its promise.

A blow to United States prestige. In Cuba, less than a hundred miles from Florida, the Kennedy administration faced the unfriendly government of Fidel Castro (page 642).

After Castro seized power in 1959, he had begun calling for an end to United States political and economic influence in Cuba. Relations worsened when the Castro government took over the Cuban property of United States corporations.

The Eisenhower Administration responded by cutting off trade with Cuba and breaking diplomatic relations. It also secretly authorized a plan to overthrow Castro. The plan, masterminded by the Central Intelligence Agency (CIA), called for an invasion of Cuba by Cuban exiles. When Kennedy took office, he was told about the CIA plan. With some reluctance he agreed to the invasion but ordered that no United States forces take part.

In April 1961 a small group of Cuban exiles landed at the Bay of Pigs on Cuba's southern coast. The result was a disaster for the invaders. They had expected help from the Cuban people but got none. And the Cuban armed forces remained loyal to Castro. Most of the invaders were quickly captured.

The total collapse of the invasion strengthened Castro's hold on Cuba and seriously damaged United States prestige. Meanwhile, the Soviet Union was planning new tests of American determination.

"We need your freedom." In June 1961, the new President met in Vienna, Austria, with the Soviet dictator, Nikita

653

Khrushchev. The Soviet leader took an extremely hard line in their talks. Kennedy viewed this as meaning that Khrushchev intended to force the western powers out of Berlin (page 595).

The Bay of Pigs disaster had led Khrushchev to think of Kennedy as an inexperienced leader who would be frightened off by Soviet threats. Khrushchev's attitude stiffened the President's resolve. To show his intention of defending Berlin, Kennedy asked Congress to increase military expenditures. He also called up military reserves and ordered the drafting of many more men for service.

In August, the Berlin crisis took a dramatic turn. The Communist government of

East Berlin built a 25-mile wall topped with barbed wire to seal off its zone from West Berlin. Two years later President Kennedy visited West Berlin. He declared to the people of that city that the United States would "risk its cities to defend yours because we need your freedom to protect ours."

Confrontation in the Caribbean. Kennedy faced another Cold War crisis in October 1962. United States spy planes discovered that Soviet technicians were building missile bases in Cuba, only 90 miles from Florida. The missiles would threaten the whole southern United States. President Kennedy demanded that Khrushchev remove the missiles from Cuba. He also ordered the navy and air force to blockade "all offensive military equipment under shipment to Cuba."

Thousands of Eastern Europeans found ways to get under, over, and through the Berlin wall.

For a few tense days, the world waited to see if a third world war would explode. But in the end Khrushchev backed down. He agreed to remove the missiles in exchange for a promise that the United States would not attack Cuba. Kennedy accepted the proposal, and the Cuban missile bases were shut down.

Reducing Cold War tensions. The missile crisis had been a close call for world peace. United States and Soviet leaders agreed that steps should be taken to reduce the risk of nuclear war. One result of the agreement was the installation of a "hot line" between Moscow and Washington. This gave the American and Soviet governments a means of direct communication in case of an emergency that might lead to all-out war.

Kennedy achieved another thaw in the Cold War by signing a limited test-ban treaty in August 1963. The United States, the Soviet Union, and Great Britain thereby agreed to regulate the testing of nuclear weapons. The three nations pledged not to explode them in the atmosphere, under water, or in outer space. Underground testing was allowed to continue because it caused little fall-out.

A stunned nation. As 1963 drew to an end, Kennedy's attention was turning toward the 1964 presidential election. Concerned about a feud between liberal and conservative Democrats in Texas, the President flew there in November for a speaking tour. On Friday, Nov. 22, as Kennedy rode in an open car through downtown Dallas, shots rang out. Television and radio stations interrupted their programs to report that the President had been shot. Within minutes, a shaken country learned that its young President, John Kennedy, was dead.

Less than two hours later Lyndon B. Johnson took the oath of office as President. He did so aboard *Air Force One*, the presidential plane, minutes before it took off to carry the body of his slain predecessor from Dallas to Washington. Mrs. Johnson stood on one side of the new President; on the other side, her suit still spattered with blood, was the widow of President Kennedy. The new Chief Executive was sworn in by Judge Sarah Hughes, an old Texas friend.

At almost the same moment, the Dallas police arrested Lee Harvey Oswald for murdering the President and a Dallas policeman who had tried to question him. Two days later, as the nation mourned, television viewers watched the police preparing to transfer Oswald from one jail to another. Before the horrified eyes of millions, Jack Ruby, a Dallas nightclub operator, stepped out of the crowd of onlookers and shot the prisoner dead. A stunned nation could hardly believe what it saw.

The Warren Commission. A commission headed by Chief Justice Earl Warren was appointed to investigate the circumstances of the assassination. Ten months after the crime, the Warren Commission issued a report saying that Oswald was the only assassin, and that he acted on his own. In the years following, this conclusion was challenged. Those investigating on their own claimed that there was more than one assassin in Dallas, and that Oswald had received help. They refused to accept the Warren Commission's findings. More than sixty books were written, each offering a different account of the tragedy.

The story of the assassination took a strange turn in 1976. A committee of the United States Senate revealed that the CIA might have been involved in a plot to

Kennedy's funeral climaxed three days of public mourning and almost continuous TV coverage.

assassinate Fidel Castro before the Kennedy murder.

It also appeared that the FBI had not given the Warren Commission all the information it had about Kennedy's slayer, Lee Harvey Oswald. These revelations led to demands that Congress hold its own investigation of the 1963 assassination.

TRY THIS!

1. Describe John F. Kennedy's efforts to build friendships for the United States. **2.** Explain the miscalculation that resulted in the Bay of Pigs disaster. **3.** Show how the Cold War both intensified and thawed during the Kennedy administration.

3. PROGRAMS OF THE GREAT SOCIETY

President Lyndon Baines Johnson was a tall, restless Texan who, his wife said, "acted as if there is never going to be a tomorrow." Before becoming Vice President in 1961, Johnson had been the Democratic majority leader in the Senate. A shrewd man, he had the reputation of being a master politician who knew how to get things done and was not above twisting arms and being a little devious to get what he wanted (page 634).

Johnson had graduated from a small Texas college, and he suspected that eastern intellectuals looked down on him. For example, he said in an interview, "I don't believe that I'll ever get credit for anything I do in foreign affairs, no matter how successful it is, because I didn't go to Harvard." But Johnson had a quick intelligence, and he was determined to be a successful President. Above all, he wanted to win the Presidency in his own right.

"We have talked long enough." Johnson decided that his first goal would be to carry out the unfinished business of the Kennedy Administration. Only three days before his death, Kennedy had repeated his hope of doing something to solve the problem of poverty. He had also wanted to provide medical insurance for the elderly, greater aid for education, and more civil

rights legislation. Johnson saw in the national grief a chance to get quick congressional approval for these programs.

Five days after the assassination, Johnson acted. Speaking to a packed Congress, the President called for passage of the Kennedy programs. About a new civil rights bill, Johnson said, "We have talked long enough in this country about equal rights. . . . It is time now to write . . . it in the books of law."

A war on poverty. President Johnson committed his Administration to a "war on poverty" and pressed Congress for prompt action. A number of programs were launched as a result of passage of the Economic Opportunity Act. Local participation was emphasized as the key to meeting the poverty problem. Rather than having distant government officials determine what was best for the poor, people themselves would decide on programs for their own communities.

The Job Corps was established to provide employment and training for young people 16 to 21 years old. Job-training programs for adults were also created. And low-interest loans were made available to companies willing to hire the unemployed. Work-study programs were started for college students. Farmers and rural businesses received federal loans. The VISTA program sent people with special skills to work among the nation's poor.

Johnson's long congressional service was put to effective use in rounding up support for his legislation. Besides the poverty program, he got Congress to pass the Urban Mass Transit Act, the Housing Act, the Nurse Training Act, a food-stamp program, and the Wilderness Areas Act. A

Read here of how

A new President took office.
And won a vote of confidence on his own.
He tackled a variety of social problems.
And built up a tide of expectations.

657

OTHER GREAT SOCIETY LEGISLATION
(1965–1968)

WATER QUALITY ACT (1965). Required states to control water pollution.

CLEAN AIR ACT (1965). Ordered exhaust controls on all new cars.

HIGHWAY BEAUTIFICATION ACT (1965). Required states to control billboards and junkyards along federal highways.

HIGHER EDUCATION ACT (1965). Set up first federal scholarships for college students.

PUBLIC WORKS AND ECONOMIC DEVELOPMENT ACT (1965). Gave grants and loans to help depressed areas. Built airports, parks, and other public facilities.

NATIONAL FOUNDATION FOR THE ARTS AND HUMANITIES (1965). Established to give financial assistance to individuals and institutions in the creative arts.

CLEAN RIVERS RESTORATION ACT (1966). Set up a program to fight water pollution.

PUBLIC BROADCASTING ACT (1967). Established nonprofit corporation to aid educational TV and radio stations.

HOUSING AND URBAN DEVELOPMENT ACT (1968). Authorized funds to build 1.7 million housing units and to help low-income families rent or buy houses.

WILD AND SCENIC RIVERS ACT (1968). Protected sections of eight rivers from commercial development.

CIVIL RIGHTS ACT (1968). Outlawed discrimination in the sale or rental of private housing.

sweeping Civil Rights Act was also adopted. Johnson's astonishing performance set the stage for the presidential election of 1964.

A choice, not an echo. Lyndon Johnson had a secure claim to the Democratic nomination for President in 1964. The only question was who would be his running mate. Kennedy loyalists wanted it to be the former President's younger brother, Robert. But Johnson chose Senator Hubert H. Humphrey of Minnesota. The Republican Party swung to the right and chose a conservative, Senator Barry Goldwater of Arizona. Goldwater campaigned on the claim that he offered the country "a choice, not an echo."

When the voters went to the polls, they completely rejected Goldwater's conservatism. Johnson won 16 million more votes than his opponent and received an electoral vote of 486 to 52. And Congress was overwhelmingly Democratic. The stage was set for a period of reform legislation unmatched since the New Deal.

One for Harry. After the 1964 election, Johnson continued pushing Congress for enactment of his program. His "Great Society" included demands for expanded health care, increased funds for the War on Poverty, more help for education, extended civil rights legislation, a Medicare act, and Medicaid.

Johnson once said he wanted to be remembered as "the health and education President." Twenty years earlier, Harry S. Truman had pressed Congress to set up a national medical insurance program. But nothing had come of it. Among great industrial nations, only the United States lacked such protection for its citizens. Now President Johnson called for a program to provide hospital insurance for people over

65 who were covered by Social Security. For a small payment, these citizens could receive doctors' services as well as home health care. This was Medicare. Medicaid was to assist the needy and disabled who were not covered by Social Security.

Employing all his skills of persuasion, Johnson won Congress's approval for both programs. In July 1965 an aged and delighted Harry S. Truman watched as the President signed Medicare and Medicaid into law. "This one," Johnson declared, "was for Harry."

"Could anybody do better?" Aid to education was also high on Johnson's list of national needs. The Elementary and Secondary School Act gave funds to school districts on the basis of the number of needy

students. Always looking for dramatic effect, Johnson signed the Education Bill in the one-room Texas school where he had begun his education. Watching him sign was the elderly woman who had been his teacher.

The Medicare and education bills were just the tip of the legislative iceberg. As Congress yielded to Johnson's pressure for legislation, Senator Goldwater called it the "Xerox Congress." Some reporters complained that they lost count of the flood of reform measures (chart on page 658). In a single session of the 89th Congress, almost ninety major Administration bills were enacted into law.

In the White House, President Johnson was far from content. Restlessly he looked for still more ways to make American society better. And he grew uncomfortable as critics condemned his free-wheeling style. Frustrated, the President raged, "What do

VISTA (Volunteers in Service to America) carried the Peace Corps idea (page 652) to the poorer sections of the United States.

they want—what *really* do they want? I'm giving them boom times and more good legislation than anybody else did, and what do they do—attack and sneer! Could FDR do better? Could anybody do better? What do they want?" With the flood of Great Society programs, Johnson had triggered a soaring level of expectations. More and more, Americans expected to have problems solved today, not tomorrow.

TRY THIS!

1. Give some reasons for Johnson's success in getting legislation through Congress. How important were a) Johnson's personality, b) his experience and ability, c) the mood of the country, and d) the nature and seriousness of the problems dealt with? 2. Review the list of typical Great Society legislation on page 658. What kinds of problems did these measures tackle? Do the same problems face the country today? Explain.

President Johnson was genuinely convinced that he could wipe out poverty and human misery through dedication and hard work for others.

4. THE IMPACT OF REFORM

Nowhere was the rising level of expectations clearer than in the black community. After centuries of discrimination, blacks were being listened to. The protest movement and the resulting changes were called "a black revolution."

"An idea whose time has come." Two pieces of legislation were passed to meet the demand for equality. The civil rights law Johnson had called for was adopted in 1964. The Senate debate ended when a Republican leader declared the reform was "an idea whose time has come."

The Civil Rights Act of 1964 attacked injustice in several ways: (1) It said that hotels, restaurants, parks, and other public places could not be segregated. (2) It authorized the Attorney General to bring law suits against segregated schools. (3) It forbade employers to discriminate against anyone on the basis of race, color, religion, national origin, or sex. (4) It blocked the

Read here of how

A black revolution got under way.
And it was supported by new laws.
The Supreme Court expanded old rights.
In all, a more just society emerged.

The sign the policeman holds tells the story. The Civil Rights Act of 1964 answered its question.

use of literacy tests designed to keep blacks and others from voting. (Such tests had often been unfairly rigged.)

A year later, the Voting Rights Act of 1965 made *any* use of literacy tests illegal. With two blows, the federal government had swept away much of the ancient baggage of segregation.

People, not trees. A Supreme Court decision in 1964 gave greater weight to each citizen's vote. *Wesberry v. Sanders* had to do with the unequal number of people in congressional districts. The Court ruled that congressional districts within a state had to be as nearly equal as possible in population. "One person, one vote" was to

be a guiding principle. Another decision applied this principle to election districts of state legislatures. Chief Justice Earl Warren said of these decisions, "Legislators represent people, not trees or acres."

Three amendments to the Constitution have further widened voting rights. The Twenty-third Amendment (1961) gave the residents of Washington, D.C., the right to take part in presidential elections. The Twenty-fourth Amendment (1964) said the states could not require voters to pay a poll tax before exercising their rights at the ballot box.

When the Court ruled that Congress could lower the voting age to eighteen in federal but not state elections, Congress and the state legislatures settled the issue by passing the Twenty-sixth Amendment (1971) allowing eighteen-year-olds to vote.

A march for freedom. Martin Luther King, Jr. (page 633), played a major role in ensuring the passage of the 1964 and 1965 Voting Rights Acts. His was a loud voice pointing out that millions of southern black citizens had never been able to vote. And he kept a steady pressure on the nation to do something about this injustice.

Selma, Alabama, became a symbol of the problem. In 1965 Selma was a city of about 28,000 people. Out of 15,000 black adults, only 325 were registered to vote. Efforts to get additional blacks registered in

Selma had little success. Public demonstrations were broken up with clubs, whips, and tear gas. The crisis worsened with the murder of two people. One was James Forman, a local black civil rights worker; the other, James J. Reeb, a white Unitarian minister from Boston.

King and other black leaders decided on a march to Montgomery, the state capital. With federal protection, the Selma civil rights workers set out on the 54-mile walk. Along the way, their numbers swelled to 25,000 as whites and blacks from around the country joined them. This five-day "freedom march" was the high point of the nonviolence movement. A more explosive period was about to begin.

A skillful leader. The Supreme Court had given a cutting edge to much of the civil rights legislation. In the *Brown* decision of 1954, the Court had said it was illegal to segregate schools on the basis of race (page 631). But this was only the first of the drastic changes brought about by the Supreme Court over the next fifteen years.

During this period the Court became known as "the Warren Court," after its Chief Justice, Earl Warren. Before his appointment to the Court by President Eisenhower in 1953, Warren had been active in California politics. As the state's attorney general, he had played a major role in the internment of Japanese Americans during World War II (page 568). This was hardly the basis for supposing that he would take a strong interest in protecting citizen rights. But Warren proved skillful in leading the Supreme Court to decisions that significantly advanced civil liberties.

A controversial decision. In a series of cases from 1961 to 1972, the Supreme Court steadily expanded the legal protection of persons facing trial. *Gideon v. Wainright* (1963) guaranteed every person charged with a serious crime the right to a lawyer's advice. If such a person could not afford to hire counsel, the local court would have to appoint one. In 1972, a further decision expanded this protection to persons accused of any crime punishable by a jail sentence.

Earl Warren and reporters leaving the White House in October 1968.

The Warren Court's most controversial ruling was delivered in 1966. In *Miranda v. Arizona,* the Court stated that police must inform prisoners that they have the right to remain silent, and that anything they say can be used against them. Also, prisoners are entitled to have a lawyer present when answering police questions. In the decision *In re Gault* (1967), the Court said that juveniles, too, were entitled to the full protection of the law.

The Court's efforts to protect the rights of individuals accused of wrongdoing were not always popular. Shortly after the *Miranda* decision, a poll showed that 65 per cent of the public felt that criminals were being treated too gently. It was often argued that criminals were being protected and their victims ignored.

Overruling the Court. The Warren Court defended other rights of individuals. Some of these were also widely criticized. One decision barred prayers and Bible readings in public schools. The Court's purpose was to uphold the First Amendment. However, many parents insisted that they wanted prayers said in their children's schools. Anger also erupted at the overturn of obscenity laws which the Court said were too loosely drawn and often interfered with free speech. Nor were all citizens happy over the Court's support of busing as a legitimate means of integrating schools. Many also disagreed with the Court's protection of the rights of Communists and other radicals.

With the resignation of Chief Justice Warren and the appointment of Warren

664

Burger in 1969, some critics thought the Court would become less active. To an extent, it did. But in some areas the Burger Court continued to make controversial decisions. In 1972 it rejected the Justice Department's claim that it had the right to tap telephones without a warrant. Shortly after, in a confused five-to-four decision, the Court ruled that the death sentence, as it was being used, was unconstitutional.

Then in *Roe v. Wade* (1973) the Court held that state laws barring abortions violated the rights of women. Both the death-sentence and the abortion decisions caused wide criticism. A movement was started to overrule the Court by constitutional amendment allowing states to ban abortions. And states changed their laws to meet the Court's objections to capital punishment.

No time for sorting out. Sweeping changes were started during the Kennedy and Johnson years, and the Supreme Court pushed them along. The War on Poverty probably reduced by almost half the number of poor people in the United States. And many of the worst injustices in the lives of black Americans were removed.

By 1965, Congress had gone about as far as it could to end segregation through legislation. And the Supreme Court had given new meaning to the Constitution's protection of individual rights. The overall goal of both was the building of a more just society. But, as in any such effort, there was protest and unease. Whenever traditional ways of thinking and behaving are challenged, people are likely to be disturbed.

For all his lack of patience and criticism of his opponents, President Johnson had set the country on a new course, one that led toward a society in which more Americans would have a share.

 TRY THIS!

1. List the important legislation, constitutional amendments, and court decisions on voting rights in the 1960s. How was each of these important? **2.** Write arguments for and against *Miranda* and other controversial decisions of the Warren Court.

The artist, Marisol, made this carving of President Johnson, *LBJ*, almost seven feet tall. What is she saying about the President and his family?

665

Roundup

KNOW THIS

Promise of the New Frontier

1. To what can John F. Kennedy's victory in 1960 be credited?
2. How did Kennedy's performance measure up to his Administration's promises?
3. What programs of the "New Frontier" got through Congress?
4. Describe the situation of black Americans in the early 1960s.
5. What steps did the Kennedy Administration take to help blacks?

The Kennedy Foreign Policy

1. What two foreign-aid programs were started by the Kennedy Administration?
2. In what two ways did Khrushchev test the United States after the Bay of Pigs incident?
3. Why was Berlin so important to the western nations?
4. What reduced Cold War tension in the early 1960s?
5. Describe the circumstances of President Kennedy's assassination. Why were there so many doubts surrounding the tragedy?

Programs of the Great Society

1. What sort of personality did Lyndon Johnson have? What was his background?
2. What were the chief programs of the Johnson Administration?
3. How was Johnson able to get such a large amount of legislation through Congress?
4. Who were the candidates in the 1964 election? What were its issues and its outcome?
5. Why did the Great Society programs fail to satisfy so many people? Why did Johnson feel frustrated?

The Impact of Reform

1. What were the chief provisions of the Civil Rights Act of 1964?
2. How did Congress, the Constitution, and the Supreme Court expand voting rights in the 1960s?
3. What was Earl Warren's background? What did he do, as Chief Justice, that was surprising?
4. Why were the Warren Court decisions controversial?
5. What were some successes and failures of social legislation in the 1960s and 1970s?

DIG HERE!

The 1960s and 1970s saw the growth of the civil rights movement. Choose one of these groups and investigate their struggle: black Americans, Mexican Americans, American Indians, Oriental Americans, the elderly, women.

A. Is unequal treatment still a problem for the group? Can you find any recent charts showing income, education, employment, and housing for that group?
B. What organizations were formed by members of the group in the 1960s and 1970s? What techniques did the organizations use? Were they effective?
C. What leaders represented the group nationally in the 1960s and 1970s? Write a one-page biography of one of them.
D. What laws or government programs were planned to assist the group during the 1960s and 1970s? What were the strengths and weaknesses of these laws or programs?

Find some books and articles on the group you have chosen. Consult some of the following: Glasrud, *Promises: A Portrayal of Nonwhites in the United States*, Rand; the Ethnic Groups in the United States Series: *Mexican Americans, Jewish Americans, Japanese Americans, Black Americans*, Prentice; Levitan, Johnston, Taggart, *Minorities in the United States*, Public Affairs; Mencarelli and Severin, *Protest Three: Red, Black, Brown Experience in America*, Eerdmans; Ryan, *Womanhood in America*, Watts; Steinfeld, *Cracks in the Melting Pot*, Glencoe.

THINK ABOUT IT

1. When people have been long oppressed, token improvements in their condition make them impatient for justice. This is called the revolution of rising expectations. How can the term be applied to the civil rights movement?
2. Which of these, do you think, was most important in putting over the Great Society programs: public feeling about the Kennedy assassination, Johnson's skill as a politician, Democratic majorities in Congress—or something else entirely? Give reasons.

DO IT!

1. Make a bulletin-board display about the Great Society programs. Indicate which you think had the most lasting effects.
2. Report on what Henry David Thoreau and Mohandas Gandhi believed about nonviolence.

THEN AND NOW

Political leaders sometimes surprise us by acting in unexpected ways. Harry Truman was such a person (page 584); so was Earl Warren. Herbert Hoover (page 498) and Franklin Roosevelt (page 512) were too. How can you account for the seeming changes? Did greater responsibility bring it about? Or did the leader have qualities few had known about? Are there leaders now whose performance has been considerably better—or worse—than expected? Explain.

Stress and Cultural Change

29

Faith in the nation's future gave Americans hope for the 1960s. But as the decade ended, optimism died. There was unrest in the cities, bitterness and distrust among the young, dissatisfaction with the leaders of government and business. Few remembered when times had been so bad.

The United States as the only major power to come out of World War II undamaged. Not only were its industries intact but it also had the atom bomb. At this point American power was unequaled. The United States seemed to have escaped the revolutions and conflicts that plagued the rest of the world. But under the surface feelings of unrest were stirring. In the late 1960's, opposition to American involvement in a Southeast Asian war brought many of those feelings to the surface. Meanwhile, discontent among minorities mounted to challenge traditional values.

1. A PROBLEM IN SOUTHEAST ASIA

In 1947 India was split into the independent states of Pakistan and India. It was the beginning of a birth of freedom for almost all of the vast British Empire. The Dutch colonial empire disappeared as Indonesia (the Dutch East Indies—map on page 577) won its independence after three years of war. More peacefully, in 1946 the United States, fulfilling the pledges of the Tydings-McDuffie Act of 1936, recognized the independence of the Philippines.

Where European governments resisted colonial demands, bitter, drawn-out wars were fought. Without exception, these wars ended in the defeat of the colonial powers. Nowhere was this struggle to have a deeper effect on the United States than in Southeast Asia, the territory known as French Indochina.

A hot war in Southeast Asia. French Indochina was made up of the three small nations of Cambodia, Laos, and Vietnam (map on page 678). From the 1920s onward, underground revolutionaries were working to make the region independent of France. When the Japanese invaded Southeast Asia in 1941, an underground movement openly resisted Japanese occupation. Briefly, in 1945–1946, Ho Chi Minh, the veteran revolutionary leader in Vietnam, proclaimed the "Democratic Republic of Vietnam." But the French quickly moved in large forces to restore their control. That was the beginning of a war that did not end until 1975.

United States involvement in Southeast Asia came slowly. American officials were fearful that a victory by Ho Chi Minh would mean the spread of Communist

---

Read here of how

France fought to stay in Indochina.
Ike did not want a land war in Asia.
But the U.S. feared a Communist take-over of Vietnam.
So Kennedy and Johnson sent troops.

IME CHART

1955	The U.S. sends military advisers to Vietnam.
1964	The Tonkin Gulf Resolution is adopted.
1965	The Watts riots occur.
1967	Newark and Detroit erupt.
1968	The Tet offensive takes place.
1968	Martin Luther King, Jr., is assassinated.
1968	Robert Kennedy is assassinated.
1968	Richard Nixon is elected President.
1972	The Equal Rights Amendment passes Congress.

---

power into the area. At the outbreak of the Korean War, in 1950, President Truman ordered an increase in aid to the French and sent a military mission to help them in their effort to put down the revolution in Southeast Asia.

By the time Eisenhower took office, the French were losing the war. But the new President rejected any suggestion that the United States intervene. "No one could be more bitterly opposed," he said, "to ever getting the United States involved in a hot war in that region than I am."

Eisenhower was repeating the same military arguments used when MacArthur had wanted to expand the Korean War (page 613). Even when the French base at Dien Bien Phu (dee-EN bee-EN FOO) was attacked by Ho Chi Minh's forces, Eisenhower held off. Dien Bien Phu fell in May 1954, and the French lost the war.

An international conference was held the same year in Geneva. It was agreed that Laos and Cambodia would become independent states and that Vietnam would be divided at the 17th parallel. The Communist Viet Minh would control the North with Hanoi as their capital. The pro-French Vietnamese forces would have Saigon and the region south of 17° north latitude. It was also agreed that elections would be held in 1956 to determine the future of the divided country.

Above the limit. The United States did not sign the Geneva Agreements, but it did promise that it would not try to undo them. In the late summer of 1954 Eisenhower decided to give South Vietnam the means of defending itself against "subversion or aggression through military means."

In early 1955 the first United States military advisers arrived in Southeast Asia to begin training South Vietnamese forces. By 1956 there were more military advisers than the 342 allowed by the Geneva Agreements. And the promised elections were not held because, the United States said, Communist activity made a fair vote impossible. By 1959 a Saigon government allied with the United States was fighting guerrilla forces called the Viet Cong (who were allied to the Communist North) for control of South Vietnam.

A growing war. Ngo Dinh Diem (NO DIN ZEE-em), premier of South Vietnam, at first seemed able to maintain control. But Diem failed to carry out the land reforms he had promised, and the influence of his family grew steadily. Diem also failed to follow democratic procedures. By 1960 the Diem government was increasingly criticized at home and in the United States.

When John F. Kennedy became President, he was at first alarmed and then dismayed by the Diem government. In 1963 he suddenly withdrew United States support from Ngo Dinh Diem. Shortly afterward, Diem was overthrown and murdered.

The new military leadership in South Vietnam turned out to be as undemocratic as Diem. They were just as unwilling to bring about social and land reform or to do away with government corruption. To the dismay of United States military authorities, the Army of the Republic of Vietnam (ARVN) seemed unable to subdue the Viet Cong (National Liberation Front). The United States military missions of "special forces" and "advisers" grew to more than 20,000 by the time of Kennedy's assassination. In the 1964 presidential campaign, Barry Goldwater (page 658) left no doubt that he would increase American forces, while President Johnson seemed to be promising that he would not.

An expanding struggle. In the summer of 1964 President Johnson announced that U.S. naval forces had been fired on by North Vietnamese ships in the Gulf of Tonkin. Congress then adopted the "Tonkin Gulf Resolution." It authorized the President to "take all necessary steps, including the use of armed force," to keep the North Vietnamese in check. Only two senators, Wayne Morse of Oregon and Ernest Gruening of Alaska, voted against the resolution.

Johnson had already ordered air strikes against North Vietnamese military targets. Without anyone quite realizing it, the stage had been set for full-fledged war. Early in February eight Americans were killed in South Vietnam, and President Johnson ordered air attacks on the Ho Chi Minh Trail, the supply line between North Vietnam and the Viet Cong forces in the South.

Quickly now, the scale of air warfare grew until North Vietnam was enduring worse bombings than those directed against Germany and Japan in World War II. Far from reducing the scale of fighting, they expanded it until only a large United States commitment could tip the balance. American field commanders and military planners promised that more men and material would insure victory. By 1968 Johnson had sent an army of more than 536,000 to Southeast Asia.

Guerrilla warfare. Like most guerrillas, the Viet Cong depended on support from the civilian population. As a result, some of the war effort had to be directed against nonmilitary targets. Only in this way would the Viet Cong (the VC) be denied the food and shelter they needed. Thousands of men, women, and children of all ages were killed, wounded, or burned in a warfare that the television screen made horribly real. Americans saw on their evening news the full effect of napalm (fire) bombs and other weapons.

Furthermore, since the bulk of the victims were Asians, many felt that the war had racist overtones. However, once committed to fight, Johnson and his advisers pressed grimly on, even though Eisenhower's earlier fears of an endless and inconclusive land war in Asia were coming true. The United States seemed to be engaged in a "no-win" contest.

 TRY THIS!

1. Describe the steps by which Southeast Asia became a United States concern.
2. Try to guess how these Americans would have reacted to the United States' part in the Vietnam War: a) President Franklin Roosevelt, b) President Truman, c) General Marshall, d) Senator Joseph R. McCarthy, e) General MacArthur, f) President Eisenhower, g) Senator Goldwater.

A South Vietnamese family fleeing the bombardment of their village in 1965.

As Lyndon Johnson swept to election victory in 1964, it seemed that black Americans were being quickly drawn into the mainstream of American life. Civil rights agitation in 1964 shifted toward gaining the vote for southern blacks. Through the summer of that year thousands of blacks and whites, many of them college students, worked to get black voters registered in Mississippi and other parts of the South. When Johnson asked Congress to set federal voter-registration standards, he climaxed his speech by repeating the civil rights slogan, "We shall overcome." The 1964 and 1965 civil rights laws and the Poll Tax Amendment (pages 660–661) brought about the registration of more than half the eligible blacks in the southern states. The struggle for voting rights was practically won.

Black power. New issues related to jobs, housing, education, welfare, and medical care came to the forefront. Moreover, these issues were growing in the North. There, black protest involved considerable violence. In 1966, when Martin Luther King, Jr., launched a campaign for open housing in Chicago, he faced organized resistance that he said was worse than anything the civil rights movement had met in Alabama. A growing number of black leaders openly spoke of the need to mobilize "black power" to defend their rights.

Black militancy had existed before the 1960s. Throughout the long history of the black American, there were leaders who despaired of making changes through legal, peaceful means. Even in the days of slavery they had called for armed resistance to oppression (page 246). In the 1960s the most publicized militant black group was the Nation of Islam, better known as the Black Muslims. They had begun in the 1930s as a small, secret religious sect under Elijah Muhammad. Their numbers began to grow rapidly in the late 1950s, and by 1962 they numbered around 100,000 black men and women. Elijah Muhammad died in

WE WANT BLACK POWER

Read here of how

The civil rights movement took a new turn.
Black ghettos exploded in violence.
Two black leaders were assassinated.
And the ghettos stayed poor.

Malcolm X confers with Muslim leaders while traveling the Middle East.

1975. When his son, Wallace Muhammad, succeeded him, the organization's name was changed to "The World Community of Islam in the West." At this time, it began to admit whites to membership.

A worldwide struggle. Much of the Muslims' influence in the early 1960s came from the work of Malcolm X. (Black Muslims dropped their family names as coming from slave days.) Malcolm was Elijah Muhammad's Chief Minister. He pushed black nationalism and denounced white society. Like Marcus Garvey (page 490), he told blacks to be proud of their history and culture and to find meaning in their own culture rather than as part of white society. Malcolm rejected integration. He also rejected nonviolence, insisting that blacks defend themselves from white attack.

In 1963 Malcolm broke with Elijah Muhammad, and traveled to the Middle East and Africa. Upon his return to the United States, he had somewhat softened his antiwhite feelings. He accepted the teachings of the Koran, the Muslim holy book, on brotherhood. He also understood that the struggle of American blacks was part of a worldwide effort by nonwhite peoples to win liberty and equality.

In 1965 Malculm X was assassinated. The killers were very likely acting for the enemies of the slain leader. After his death, *The Autobiography of Malcolm X* was published. This immensely popular book gave many whites, for the first time, some understanding of the experiences of black people.

"Black is beautiful." In 1966 the slogan

Black Pride

The styles and colors of Africa served to remind American blacks of their proud past.

"black power" gave a new direction to black efforts. Some whites thought it meant that blacks should attack them. Stokely Carmichael, who first used the phrase, insisted that it meant blacks should organize themselves into an effective force. They should look to other blacks rather than to whites for leadership. In their own communities, blacks should run the businesses, own their own homes, and control the schools and other agencies that served them. Above all, black power recognized that integration was second. First came the need to improve economic conditions among the mass of blacks. To reinforce the point, increased emphasis was put on black pride, expressed in another Carmichael slogan, "black is beautiful."

Better conditions? As the talk of black power grew, newspapers and magazines increasingly spoke of the "black revolution." These words took on a threatening sound when large-scale violence erupted in northern cities. The first outbreak occurred in the Watts section of Los Angeles, in August 1965. It was set off by a seemingly minor incident over the arrest of a black motorist.

Only after five days was the Watts riot put down by the National Guard. As many as 10,000 blacks looted and burned stores, wrecked cars, and attacked police and firemen. When the upheaval was over, 34 persons (most if them black) were dead, more than 4,000 had been arrested, and some fifty million dollars' worth of property lay in ruins.

Behind the grim statistics was a shocking story. A full 30 per cent of all adult males in Watts were unemployed. The income of its residents had declined by more than 8 per cent between 1959 and 1965. The residents without cars found commuting to their jobs (there were few jobs in Watts) both expensive and time-consuming. Even such a basic service as hospital care was not to be found in the community. Yet conditions in most black slums were even worse than in Watts.

Two societies. The Watts riot was a forerunner of more than seventy disturbances that shook American cities through the next two years. The climax came in Newark and Detroit. Newark, New Jersey, was more than 52 per cent black. Its black unemployment rate was four times the national average. Much of the city was made up of ancient tenements. In its vast housing projects crime, drugs, and poverty were an everyday part of life. The city government run by the white minority was corrupt. The mayor would shortly be imprisoned for accepting bribes.

In July 1967 the explosion occurred. The police had beaten up a black taxicab driver. For the next five days, both the police and the National Guard used live ammunition to restore order. When the violence subsided, 26 blacks were dead and a large area of Newark was a burned-out ruin.

Ten days after Newark, Detroit was shattered by six days of violence. The nation's cities seemed to have become battlegrounds. When the Detroit riot was over, 43 people were dead, hundreds injured, and well over 7,000 under arrest. Some 5,000 people were homeless, 1,300 buildings were in ruins, and a quarter of a billion dollars' worth of damage had been done.

The question of why it had all happened was partially answered in the report of the Kerner Commission. President Johnson had established the Commission in 1967. Its report showed that in the midst of affluent America there still existed pockets

of crushing poverty and of unrelieved hopelessness. In the black ghettos nothing ever seemed to get better. "What white Americans have never fully understood—but what the Negro can never forget—is that white society is deeply implicated in the ghetto," the Report noted. "White institutions created it, white institutions maintain it, and white society condones it." The Report concluded, "Our nation is moving toward two societies, one black and one white—separate and unequal."

"To do God's will." On April 4, 1968, Martin Luther King, Jr., was killed by a sniper's bullet. He was shot while standing on the balcony of a Memphis motel. The assassin was later identified as James Earl Ray, a white man.

King had lived with threats of violence for so long that he had come to accept them. The day before his death, he had given an address in which he said, "I just want to do God's will. And he's allowed me to go up to the mountain, and I've looked over and I've seen the Promised Land. I may not get there with you. But I want you to know tonight that we as a people will get to the Promised Land." On King's tomb in Atlanta was inscribed, "Free at last, free at last, thank God Almighty I'm free at last."

The violent death of a man who had given so much for nonviolence led to massive riots in Washington, D.C., Chicago, and a hundred other towns and cities. It was 1967 all over again.

The overcrowded ghettos. Almost a quarter of all Americans lived in the deepest poverty. Mexican Americans, Puerto Ricans, Orientals, Appalachian whites, American Indians, and the aged made up a disproportionate number of the poor, but black Americans had special problems.

From the earliest years of the nation, immigrant groups had lived in their own

676 Not since the 1870s (page 371) had American cities seen disturbances like those of 1967 and 1968.

sections of cities—the "ghettos." But by the second or third generation the descendants of these immigrants had usually started buying homes in better neighborhoods. This, however, was not happening for black people. Their ghettos were generally old, worn-down areas with bad housing, high rents, and poor schools. Efforts by blacks to move elsewhere met with white opposition, and often with violence.

An unresolved question. Economic conditions were particularly bad in the ghettos. A large number of blacks in places like the Near North Side of St. Louis had migrated from the worn-out farms of the South. Earlier immigrants were absorbed into the unskilled working force that manned the factories, but black people had to face a decreasing demand for unskilled labor. The result was an unemployment rate for blacks almost always twice that of whites. Among teenaged blacks unemployment rates ran well over 50 per cent. After World War II black income levels averaged about half that of whites.

The result was a ghetto that could not be dissolved. Many whites saw the entrance of blacks into previously all-white jobs as a threat to their security. As whites moved out of central cities into the suburbs, they took with them a substantial part of the tax money needed to maintain city services. And many of the city's industries also moved out into the suburbs, reducing the job opportunities of ghetto dwellers.

Whites, and also some blacks, found proposals to integrate schools through busing unacceptable. Yet in a black ghetto the neighborhood school was racially segregated. How to bring into existence a truly integrated society which was also color-blind remained the great unresolved question facing the American nation.

 TRY THIS!

Briefly summarize the views of five black leaders discussed in this and earlier chapters: Booker T. Washington (page 343), W.E.B. DuBois (page 344), Marcus Garvey (page 490), Martin Luther King, Jr. (page 633), Malcolm X (page 673), and Stokely Carmichael (page 675). What similarities and differences do you find?

3.   A TIME OF NATIONAL QUESTIONING

The violent upheavals in the cities and the deepening war in Vietnam caused many

Read here of how

The Viet Cong surprised their enemies.
Student protests erupted.
Johnson decided not to run.
Nixon promised better government.

Americans to question the goals of their society. The questioning resembled the soul-searching stirred up by the antislavery movement before the Civil War.

Hawks and doves. In the colleges and universities the examination of society's goals was especially deep and intense. The widening conflict in Vietnam brought antiwar "teach-ins." The issues raised by the war were discussed at length by students and their professors. As the draft calls increased to 40,000 a month in 1968, thou-

677

The main enemy supply route was in neutral territory. Just one U.S. problem in the Vietnam War.

sands of young men refused to serve. Some fled to Canada or other countries. In the same year of 1968, the number of Americans fighting in Vietnam approached 600,000, and a militant peace movement took shape. The toll of American dead passed ten thousand and antiwar feeling grew. The previous year alone over 6,500 Americans died in the rice paddies, mountains, and jungles of Vietnam.

Also in 1968 five senators led by the majority leader, Mike Mansfield of Montana, went to Vietnam at the request of President Johnson. They returned to report that the United States was caught in an "open-ended war"—that is, one for which the outcome could not be foreseen. In the United States, Martin Luther King, Jr., concluded that the war had become the major obstacle to the advancement of black people. As the scope of the war grew, massive antiwar protests took place in the streets of cities across the nation. The United States was splitting between the "hawks" who favored the war and the "doves" who opposed it.

"I thought we were winning." Military leaders in Vietnam and Administration spokesmen in Washington kept announcing that the war was approaching its end. General William C. Westmoreland, the United States commander in Vietnam, assured a joint session of Congress, "We have reached an important point when the end begins to come in view." But secret CIA reports emphasized that, despite heavy bombings of North Vietnamese supply routes and bases, the flow of supplies and reinforcements to the Viet Cong grew steadily. And worse was to come.

On January 30, 1968, the New Year, called Tet, was celebrated throughout South Vietnam. During the previous weeks, special Viet Cong units had been moving into South Vietnamese cities. As the rest of the country slept off its celebrations, some 60,000 Viet Cong struck in Saigon, the ancient capital city of Hué (HWAY), and dozens of other places. Military bases, government buildings, radio and power stations, American and other embassies, railroad and highway facilities, airports, and police stations were targets.

The arrival of thousands of new troops from the United States enabled the Americans and the South Vietnamese army to regain control. But the two months of fierce fighting that followed the Tet offensive saw

American combat deaths reach 23,000. One senator, speaking for many, asked, "What happened? I thought we were supposed to be winning this war."

The privileged young. For Americans, college had always been a place to get a degree and have some fun before settling down to the business of earning a living. Unlike foreign university students, those in the United States rarely took part in intensive political activity. Most spent their extra time planning the big football or basketball weekends. But in the early 1960s a change took place. More and more colleges became centers of political action.

In 1964, on the Berkeley campus of the University of California, an upheaval erupted in the Free Speech Movement. Students struck out at traditional discipline and demanded that they be given more control in university policy. It was the beginning of a protest movement that reached a peak in 1968. By then the main issues were the war and civil rights. Campus radicals organized in groups like Students for a Democratic Society (SDS) and moved to bring political action to the colleges and universities.

An amazed nation watched as more than one hundred campuses became the scene of demonstrations. For a week in late April, students occupied five buildings at Columbia University and were removed only when New York City police were called in. Across the country at San Francisco State College, a bloody student strike lasted from late 1968 to early 1969.

Within the student groups, some moved to more radical positions. The Weather-men, for example, called for acts of terrorism to bring the distant war home to America. The violence that had exploded in the ghettos now struck the colleges of the privileged young.

"The huge world will come round." When Lyndon Johnson became President,

Colleges and universities had to call in local police to deal with student protests and riots, as happened at Columbia University.

he had proclaimed his desire to bring Americans together. By 1968 the nation was more dangerously split than it had been since Civil War days. In the Senate, J. William Fulbright of Arkansas, Chairman of the Senate Foreign Relations Committee, came out against the war. He accused the Administration of planning to enlarge the fighting. And Senator Eugene McCarthy of Minnesota decided to enter the Democratic primaries against President Johnson.

McCarthy's decision was surprising. Ordinarily, a President in office has complete control of his party. Even in 1912, the immensely popular Theodore Roosevelt was not able to unseat the unpopular William Howard Taft (page 417). In 1968 there was the added point that Americans have never switched Presidents in wartime. They accepted the principle that one should never "change horses in the middle of the stream."¹ McCarthy decided to act when no one else seemed willing to take on Johnson. He appeared to believe what Ralph Waldo Emerson had said, "If a single man plant himself on his convictions and there abide, the huge world will come round to him."

Again, political violence. In New Hampshire's first-in-the-nation presidential primary, it was clear that Eugene McCarthy had struck a responsive chord. Not only did he get 42 per cent of the Democratic votes but won 5,511 Republican ballots as well. This put him only a few hundred votes behind Johnson. It was a humiliation for the President.

The New Hampshire primary had three important results. Robert F. Kennedy, brother of the late President Kennedy and at that time a senator from New York, also decided to enter the race. He had behind him the thousands of loyal Kennedy followers. On March 31 Johnson announced that he would withdraw in order to avoid involving the Presidency in "the partisan divisions that are developing in this political year." And less than a month later Vice President Hubert Humphrey threw his hat into the ring.

In the primaries that followed, Robert Kennedy generally ran ahead, but everyone knew that California would be his real test. On June 4, 1968, Kennedy won a narrow victory, but as he was leaving the hotel after his victory speech, a Jordanian immigrant named Sirhan B. Sirhan shot him. Two days later he died of his wounds. Again the nation reeled under the impact of political violence. Robert Kennedy was buried in Arlington Cemetery, only a few feet from his assassinated brother, President John F. Kennedy.

A complicated election. When the Democrats assembled in Chicago late in August, the party seemed split beyond repair. Various radicals, as well as thousands of students who had worked for McCarthy, poured into the city. Mayor Richard Daley of Chicago, the last of the big-city bosses, was determined to have law and order at any cost. Americans watched as television screens showed police using tear gas and clubs to break up marches. Some innocent bystanders were caught up in the violence and also beaten.

On the floor of the convention hall, the party organization steamrollered the nomination of Hubert H. Humphrey. Senator Edmund Muskie of Maine was chosen to run for Vice President. The Republicans, meeting in Miami earlier in the month, had chosen Richard M. Nixon and Governor Spiro Agnew of Maryland as their presidential and vice presidential candi-

dates. Governor George C. Wallace of Alabama and General Curtis LeMay were the candidates of the conservative American Independent Party.

In the campaign, most Democrats decided they had nowhere to go but into Humphrey's camp, and so he steadily improved his standing. Nixon's supporters insisted that he had a plan to end the war in Vietnam but could not reveal what it was until after the election. Nixon also focused on the South and on widespread discontent with student riots and black protests. His running mate, Spiro Agnew, appealed to conservatives with the intention of cutting

Youth and others opposing the war joined forces in Eugene McCarthy's presidential campaign.

into Wallace's support. Wallace kept denouncing "left-wing theoreticians, briefcase-totin' bureaucrats, ivory-tower guideline writers, bearded anarchists, smartaleck editorial writers, and pointy-headed professors."

When the voters went to the polls on November 5, 1968, Richard Nixon won by a narrow plurality. Like Lincoln, Wilson, and Kennedy, he failed to get a clear majority of the vote. His electoral count was 301 to Humphrey's 191 and Wallace's 46.

Almost 10 million ballots had been cast for Wallace.

When Richard M. Nixon took the oath of office on January 20, 1969, he called upon Americans to stop shouting at one another and pledged that government would become more responsive to the needs of ordinary citizens. It seemed that a new leaf was being turned.

 TRY THIS!

1. Show how Americans were badly shaken by the Tet offensive in Vietnam. **2.** Explain why there were student riots on so many college campuses. **3.** Tell why President Johnson was unable to control his own party and win renomination in 1968.

4.   THE GROWTH OF A COUNTERCULTURE

As the country reeled from riots, student protests, and general violence, a major change in cultural values was taking shape. Because of the increasingly massive technological changes they had experienced, many Americans began to look longingly backward to an earlier, simpler time. City life was too complex; a few rejected it for a return to the land and in some cases to communal living (page 201). These Americans put aside competition and adopted a life-style based on cooperation.

With the interest in what was seen as a more natural way of living came a wish to eat only natural foods grown with organic rather than chemical fertilizers. The old interest in conservation took a new form— concern for the environment. Millions supported efforts to clean up the air and water and to end the use of pesticides such as DDT. Americans felt uneasy as they read that automobiles daily threw 10,000 tons of carbon monoxide plus 2,000 tons of hydrocarbons into the air over Los Angeles. Similar conditions in the atmosphere caused an estimated eleven billion dollars' worth of property damage throughout the country each year. Evidence pointed to such physical consequences as lung and heart diseases and cancer. It was not only trees and plants that suffered from poisoned air but also human beings.

Generation gap. Traditional music reflected the concern with earlier values. The new folk songs of such performers as Joan Baez, Pete Seeger, and Bob Dylan openly criticized established authority. Dylan's "The Times They Are a-Changing" emphasized the growing split between the values of the young and those of their parents.

Increasingly, newspapers and magazines commented on the existence of a "generation gap." Long hair was introduced by a British musical group, the Beatles, early in the 1960s. It quickly became the badge of the rock star. And it was the young male's declaration of independence from the crewcut of his father. Dress codes that had called for suits, neckties,

Read here of how

Some Americans turned away from technology and competition.
A generation gap developed.
More women became aware of being exploited.
And they demanded full equality.

682

DON'T TRUST ANYONE OVER **30**

SUPPORT OUR BOYS IN VIETNAM

FLOWER POWER

I AM A HUMAN BEING: DO NOT FOLD, SPINDLE OR MUTILATE

Counterculture

Children mystified their parents with endless talk of John, Paul, George, and Ringo (below). Young people took up life-styles the older generation could not accept. The commune at left occupied a former pig farm. But the two cultures still communicated through slogans (above).

skirts, and nylons gave way to jeans, sandals, and "doing your own thing."

Much more alarming was the move into drug experiments. Where school parties had once ended in beer bashes, the new generation experimented with marijuana. In some instances with tragic results, it also tried more dangerous drugs. And as traditional values were questioned, interest grew in Eastern religions, popular psychology, and meditation.

A worthwhile effort. Underlying all the questioning of the counterculture, as it was soon being called, there was a tendency to substitute impulse for logic and careful planning. The counterculture undermined long-established standards. At its best, it allowed for the emergence of a more open, balanced, and frank perspective on life. At its worst, it could make heroes out of murderers and misfits.

Basically, the counterculture was part of an effort to find a new set of values on which Americans could agree. A close look suggests that the counterculture was going back to the American belief in the worth of the individual. In a world grown impersonal, regaining control of the institutions that shaped people's everyday lives was a worthwhile effort.

A new feminism. Along with other challenges to traditional values in the 1960s, the campaign for women's rights was renewed. Twice before during periods of reform American women had demanded equal rights as human beings. In the time of Andrew Jackson (page 204) and again in the Progressive Era (page 384), feminist leaders had claimed for women a fair share of the opportunities offered by American society.

The groundwork for the new women's movement was laid earlier in this century.

Women have always done "men's work" in wartime. Now they have a legal right to such jobs.

After the 1920s growing numbers of women had attended college. During the Second World War many women for the first time took jobs outside their homes. When victory came, 300,000 women war workers were fired, but at least they had shown that they could do so-called "men's work." Even more important, the practice of family planning was adopted by a large part of the population.

By the early 1960s many women were questioning the roles into which society seemed to place them. In a book called *The Feminine Mystique* Betty Friedan identified the problem in a way that caught the attention of many women. She argued that women were forced by society's expectations to limit their goals in life to getting married and raising a family. Friedan's book made many girls and women wonder why they should accept this limitation. Men, after all, were expected by society to try to develop their talents, interests, and abilities to the fullest.

The women's movement that started in the 1960s recognized the achievements of the feminists of the early 1900s. Many of its demands were much like those of the Seneca Falls Declaration of 1848 (page 207). But the new movement drew far greater numbers of women. Moreover, its supporters used a greater variety of methods in working for their goals. They demonstrated, and they set up effective organizations. These included the National Organization for Women (NOW), the Women's Equity Action League, and the National Woman's Political Caucus. To fight discrimination in jobs, some women sued employers for rights guaranteed in the Civil Rights Act of 1964 (page 660). Growing numbers of women ran for political office and sought entry to law and medical schools.

Women also renewed the drive to add an Equal Rights Amendment to the Constitution. Such an amendment had first been proposed in the early 1920s. In 1972 Congress approved ERA, as the amendment was called, and sent it on to the states. If adopted, it would provide that "equality of rights under the law shall not be denied or abridged by the United States or by any state on account of sex" (Appendix).

By the mid-1970s the women's movement had made a clear impact on American society. Books explaining the movement poured from the presses, and many of the aims and concerns of the movement were voiced in a magazine called *Ms.* While some books also attacked the movement, opinion polls revealed a growing sympathy for the women's cause on the part of many men. Textbook publishers and authors discovered that women had been part of American life from the beginning and began recording that fact in their books. Male politicians and business managers were promising to recognize women's ability to serve as administrators and executives. And more women were actually finding it possible to rise to higher levels in government, business, and the professions.

Another effect of the movement was showing up in American marriages. Among some young couples it was no longer assumed that the husband would be the breadwinner and that the wife's job would be temporary or would take second place. While the future of the women's movement is not at all clear, it seems certain that women's life patterns, work opportunities, and political influence will be vastly different in the years ahead from what they were at mid-century.

 TRY THIS!

1. Collect some evidences of the counterculture of the 1960s from (a) the words of popular songs, (b) the subject matter of films, (c) high-school and college courses.
2. Describe some permanent changes in American life brought about by the counterculture.

ROUNDUP

Who?

Ho Chi Minh
Ngo Dinh Diem
Malcolm X
Stokely Carmichael
William C.
    Westmoreland
J. William Fulbright
Eugene McCarthy
Robert Kennedy
Hubert Humphrey
George Wallace
the Beatles
Betty Friedan

What?

Viet Cong
Tonkin Gulf Resolution
black power
Kerner Commission
Tet offensive
Students for a
    Democratic Society
New Hampshire
    primary
generation gap
counterculture
NOW
ERA

Where?

Dien Bien Phu
17th parallel
Hanoi
Saigon
Gulf of Tonkin
Ho Chi Minh Trail
Hué

KNOW THIS

A Problem in Southeast Asia

1. How did the United States become the supreme world power just after World War II?
2. Trace the beginnings of the Vietnamese independence movement.
3. What decisions were made at the 1954 Geneva conference? What part did the United States play?
4. Why did the United States increase its activity in Southeast Asia during the 1950s and early 1960s?
5. How was the Vietnam War enlarged after 1964?

Black Demands at Home

1. How did the civil rights movement change in the 1960s?
2. In what ways were the final views of Malcolm X unlike those of the Black Muslims?
3. What conditions were behind the riots in Watts and other United States cities?
4. How was the experience of early immigrants and poorer urban whites unlike that of American blacks?
5. What position did the Kerner Commission Report take on ghettos? On American society?

A Time of National Questioning

1. Why was the Tet offensive an unexpected development?
2. What led to the student riots of 1968?
3. Why did President Johnson withdraw from the 1968 campaign?
4. Who were the three leading presidential candidates, and what were the issues, in that election?
5. What was the outcome of the 1968 election?

The Growth of a Counterculture

1. In the 1960s, why did some Americans become disillusioned with technology?
2. How did the counterculture first make itself felt?
3. In what ways did the counterculture affect ideas and attitudes?
4. What prepared the way for the women's movement of the 1960s and 1970s?
5. What demands were women making in the 1970s?

DIG HERE!

Research *one* of these aspects of the environmental crisis: (a) land use (residential, agricultural, commercial, industrial, wilderness), (b) water pollution, (c) air pollution, (d) noise pollution, (e) the population explosion, or (f) energy and fuel resources. Use the following questions as a guide to your research:

A. Throughout most of their history, what policy have Americans followed with regard to this part of their environment? Has that policy contributed to present problems?
B. What problems does the nation face in this area today?
C. Are there current programs or projects intended to deal with these problems? How are the programs organized? Are they private or public (government-sponsored)? How are they being paid for? Have they been effective? Why, or why not?
D. What other solutions for the problem have been suggested? Which do you favor? Why?
E. What sacrifices will be needed to overcome the problem you are investigating? Are most people willing to make these sacrifices? Explain.

Use the books on page 710 to find answers. Those by Graham and Herbert will be especially useful. So will the report of the Energy Policy Project.

THINK ABOUT IT

1. The United States is still a powerful nation (perhaps the most powerful in the world). But it is no longer supreme, as in the later 1940s. What caused the change? Could that change have been prevented?
2. Why did women's groups in some states oppose the Equal Rights Amendment? Can any one group have both equality of rights *and* special protection? Why, or why not?

DO IT!

1. Using the *Readers' Guide to Periodical Literature,* find some articles on one of these topics of the late 1960s: the war, the draft, drugs, rock music, new lifestyles. Report to the class on your topic.
2. Find out whether your state ratified (accepted) or rejected the Equal Rights Amendment. Report on any campaign for or against this amendment in your community.

THEN AND NOW

The problem of poverty among blacks and other American minorities was not solved by the Great Society program. Why not? If a similar program were undertaken today, what past mistakes could be avoided?

687

The Republic Enters Its Third Century

30

America's hope has always been in its youth. At the beginning of the nation's third century, this Indian girl could stand for all those—women, nonwhites, and others—who had been prevented from taking a full part in the life of the nation. The 1970s promised something better for all.

1. THE PRESIDENCY OF RICHARD NIXON

When Republican President Richard M. Nixon took office in 1969, both houses of Congress were firmly in the hands of the Democratic Party. This had not happened to any President since Zachary Taylor (1849–1850). Nixon said he wanted a Cabinet that would represent a cross section of the country's population. As it turned out, however, his Cabinet members were all well-to-do, white, male Republicans, and all successful businessmen. They appeared to reflect, as did Nixon himself, what one newsmagazine called "cool competence."

Not in the Cabinet, yet about to make a deep impression on foreign policy, was German-born Henry Kissinger. He was the icily brilliant Presidential Assistant for National Security. Within the Executive Office the staff was efficiently directed by H. R. Haldeman and John R. Ehrlichman.

Remote and unreachable. Nixon's journey to the White House had been long and persistent. Narrowly defeated for the Presidency in 1960 (page 649), he had returned to California, run for the governorship, and suffered a stinging defeat. In his concession speech he lashed out resentfully at reporters, vowing that he was finished with politics.

Nixon next joined a New York City law firm, but he also campaigned vigorously for Goldwater in 1964 and for Republican congressional candidates in 1966. His demonstration of party loyalty got him the presidential nomination in 1968.

Nixon seemed to be a cold man, uncomfortable in the normal give-and-take of politics, though he was a seasoned campaigner, a former Congressman, and a former Vice President. At the same time, he appeared to be in complete control of his Administration. Underneath the efficiency was a love of secrecy and the will to hold on to power. Through much of his Presidency, Richard Nixon remained remote and unreachable.

"Man on the moon." Six months after Nixon took office, the United States celebrated the success of a project begun eight years earlier. On the order of President Kennedy, the country's space program had set out to "put a man on the moon" before 1970. On July 20, 1969, astronauts Neil Armstrong and Edwin "Buzz" Aldrin, Jr., stepped out of the spacecraft *Eagle* and began their "moonwalk." Television cameras beamed the astounding technological achievement to earth and the whole country stayed glued to their sets to watch the event.

Read here of how

A new Presidency began with high hopes.
Nixon tried to win conservative support.
But the country was at war in Vietnam.
And antiwar protests led to tragedy.

TIME CHART

1969	The My Lai incident is revealed.
1969	The first moon landing is made.
1969	Nixon announces the Vietnamization policy.
1970	The Kent State tragedy occurs.
1972	Nixon visits Communist China.
1972	Nixon visits Moscow.
1972	The Watergate break-in takes place. Nixon is re-elected.
1973	The Watergate investigation begins.
1974	President Nixon resigns. Gerald Ford becomes President.
1976	The nation celebrates its Bicentennial.
1976	Jimmy Carter is elected President.

A proud President Nixon awaited Armstrong and Aldrin on the carrier *Hornet,* when the astronauts returned to earth four days later. Over 24 billion dollars had, as of that date, gone into the country's space program.

A conservative trend. In 1948 the Republicans held only 2 per cent of southern congressional seats. But by 1972 they had almost a third. During the 1950s and 1960s the Republicans had cut into Democratic strength in the South. At one time or another in those twenty years, Republicans had held the governorships of Florida, Arkansas, Tennessee, Virginia, North Carolina, and South Carolina.

By 1968, the Republicans had hopes of again becoming the majority party. Nixon began appealing to conservative feeling in

689

the South and elsewhere. One part of his plan was to change the Supreme Court.

Chief Justice Warren (page 663) had retired from the Court in 1968. President Johnson had wanted to replace him with Justice Abe Fortas. However, Justice Fortas was forced to withdraw from consideration and to resign from the Court. It had come to light that while he was a justice, he had accepted money from a man convicted of illegal stock-market activities.

Nixon, on taking office, appointed Warren Burger as Chief Justice. However, the Senate refused to approve two men whom Nixon proposed as replacements for Justice Fortas. The first was federal Appeals Judge Clement Haynsworth of South Carolina. He was rejected on grounds that he had taken part in cases where he had a financial interest. A second federal judge, G. Harrold Carswell of Florida, was then rejected on grounds that he had defended segregation and insulted civil rights lawyers in court.

Angrily, Nixon denounced the Senate's refusal to confirm his nominees, declaring, "I cannot successfully nominate to the Supreme Court any federal . . . judge from the South who believes as I do in the strict [interpretation] of the Constitution." Finally, in May of 1970, the Senate approved Nixon's third choice, Appeals Judge Harry A. Blackmun of Minnesota.

New action in Vietnam. Meanwhile, the long-drawn-out war in Vietnam continued its bloody course. Barely a month after Nixon entered the White House, United States troops suffered heavy casualties as Communist forces launched new attacks. Nixon reacted by ordering heavy bombings in Cambodia to cut off the flow of supplies to the North Vietnamese and their Viet Cong allies (map on page 678).

The Image of Nixon isn't entirely clear!

To cartoonist Robert Osborn, and many other people, Richard Nixon was a very complicated man.

But the President was preparing for a new course of action. On November 3, 1969, he announced on television that he planned ". . . the complete withdrawal of all United States ground combat forces and their replacement by South Vietnamese forces." This was Nixon's "Vietnamization" policy. He also announced that the United States would assume responsibility for training and equipping South Vietnamese forces to prepare them for their combat role. "Vietnamization" looked like a return to the beginning of the war, when the United States had first sent its soldiers to train Vietnamese forces.

Deepening divisions. Six months earlier, the American people had been stunned to learn that their troops had killed over 500 unarmed South Vietnamese civilians in a tiny village called My Lai (ME LYE). The killings had taken place on March 16, 1968, a full year before the information became public. An investigation was started. Two years later, Lieutenant William L. Calley, Jr., a platoon commander at My Lai, was tried and found guilty of murdering 22 Vietnamese.

At first President Nixon had denounced the My Lai affair as a "massacre." But Calley's conviction and life sentence roused protests throughout the country. Many of them came from supporters of the war effort, but some were from people who objected to the fact that Calley's sentence was so severe. Higher officers who had covered up the My Lai affair were acquitted or got only reductions in rank and reprimands.

In the face of the protests, Nixon announced that he would review Calley's sentence. When this raised additional objections, the President changed his mind. Clearly, the Vietnam War was deepening the divisions among the American people.

A spreading conflict. The antiwar movement was stepping up its protests. In mid-October 1969, across the country, millions demonstrated for an end to the fighting. A month later, a quarter of a million protesters jammed Washington, D.C., in a "March Against Death." It marked a beginning of even greater violence.

On April 30, 1970, Nixon announced that a combined American-South Vietnamese force had crossed into Cambodia (map on page 678). Its purpose was to deny the Communists safe bases from which to attack South Vietnam. This was necessary, the President explained, to insure the successful withdrawal of the United States forces.

Although Washington claimed success, the clearest outcome of the invasion was an increase in enemy strength. Communists took control of half of Cambodia, until then a neutral country. Americans feared that the war in Southeast Asia was going to spread further rather than die out. And nowhere was this feeling more evident than in the colleges of the United States.

Invitation to tragedy. On 415 college and university campuses, tens of thousands of students went on strike. Once again, in the spring of 1970, Columbia, Berkeley, and Harvard were engulfed in protests against the war. But this time the disturbances spread as well to quiet places like Kent State University in Ohio. There, National Guard troops were called out. Ohio's governor bluntly warned, "We're going to use every weapon of law enforcement to drive [the protesters] off the campus." Vice President Spiro Agnew added to the uproar when he described the students as "a bunch of hoodlums."

The worst of the trouble had already seemed over at Kent State, when National Guardsmen ordered a group of students to break up. In the clash that followed, the soldiers chased some stone-throwing youths. Under circumstances that are still in doubt, the troops fired at some students, many of whom had just left their classes and were standing by, watching out of curiosity. Thirteen students were shot; four of them—two girls, two boys—were killed. In a subsequent grand jury hearing, the National Guardsmen were released from all charges. Nixon observed, "When dissent turns to violence, it invites tragedy."

On the weekend of May 9, 1970, about a hundred thousand students poured into Washington, D.C., to protest the war. Thousands of federal troops were called out to put down any violence or any attempt to disrupt the work of the federal government. Both Nixon and Vice President Agnew called the protesters "bums."

On May 14 two students were killed at Jackson State College in Mississippi by

691

As the war continued, not all protests against it were violent.

state police. On Wall Street a student protest was met with violence as thousands of "hard hat" workers in the building trades broke up the demonstration.

Inside protests. The political dissent also reached into the Administration. Walter J. Hickel, Secretary of the Interior, objected to the course that Nixon had been following with the young people. Hickel also protested Vice President Agnew's freewheeling verbal attacks on them. Nixon responded by firing Hickel and six other officials of the Department of the Interior.

Meanwhile, the office of Attorney General John Mitchell was planning a truly dangerous course of action. The Adminis-

tration would place FBI and CIA spies inside the protest movement. Only the objections of FBI Director J. Edgar Hoover put a stop to this plan.

 TRY THIS!

1. Trace the main events of Richard Nixon's career from its beginning in the Truman years (page 601). How did he come to prominence? What offices did he hold? What reverses did he have? What circumstances brought him to the Presidency in 1969?
2. Show why the antiwar protests became more intense in the 1970s.

2.   A NEW COURSE IN FOREIGN AFFAIRS

Congress in 1969 and 1970 was gravely concerned about the course of the war in Vietnam. On the last day of 1970 it voted to repeal the Tonkin Gulf Resolution (page 670). President Nixon regarded the action of Congress as unimportant and having no effect on United States military involvement.

The number of United States troops in Vietnam was steadily cut back, until in 1971 it was a third less than in 1968. However, as the ARVN (Army of the Republic of South Vietnam) took larger responsibility for carrying on the war, United States air involvement grew. Flights of giant B52's raked north-south supply routes. In April of 1972 they again bombed Hanoi and the port of Haiphong in North Vietnam.

An end of fighting. Since November 1968 the United States and the South Vietnamese had been holding peace talks with the North Vietnamese and Viet Cong in Paris. From the beginning the talks had been bogged down, and no one any longer expected much from them. However, early in 1972 Nixon revealed that his National Security Adviser, Henry Kissinger, had also been meeting secretly with the North Vietnamese. The President said that he was stepping up the pressure because the North Vietnamese were stalling.

Read here of how

The U.S. got out of Vietnam.
Nixon eased Cold War tensions in Moscow.
And he made diplomatic history in China.
Then the U.S. helped to make peace in the
   Middle East.

Early in May 1972 Nixon ordered the mining of Haiphong harbor and other North Vietnamese ports to prevent delivery of war equipment. He also ordered heavy bombing of all military targets in the North. The bombing would be kept up, the President declared, until the North Vietnamese agreed to a cease-fire and the release of all American prisoners.

Nevertheless, troop withdrawals still went on. On August 13, 1972, the last American combat forces left South Vietnam. Two months later Nixon ordered a halt to the air attacks. But in December the bombing of the Hanoi and Haiphong areas was resumed. Kissinger had concluded that a settlement could not be reached at the peace table, and the talks had been broken off.

China and the Soviet Union finally persuaded Hanoi to go back to the peace table. On December 30, the bombing ended. A month later, on January 27, 1973, a cease-fire agreement was signed.

By March nearly 600 American prisoners of war were released; the fate of hundreds more remained unknown. Direct American involvement in the war had ended. For the United States, the human cost was 46,079 killed and 303,640 wounded.

Eliminating the danger of war. In the general field of foreign policy the Nixon Administration blazed a new trail. The President was determined to end the Cold War. Although the Secretary of State until 1973 was William P. Rogers, the key figure in shaping U.S. foreign policy was Henry Kissinger.

As a boy, Kissinger had fled with his family to the United States to escape Nazi persecution. At Harvard he won wide recognition as a foreign-policy expert. He also served as Nixon's assistant for national security.

Nixon's and Kissinger's stand on the Vietnam War had appeared to be this: The free world would be safe only if friend and foe alike believed in the strength of the United States. Nixon and Kissinger also sought *détente* (day-TAHNT), a relaxing of strain in the relations between countries. In particular, they wanted to eliminate the chance of war with the Soviet Union.

On November 24, 1969, Nixon and the Soviet Russian President Nikolai V. Podgorny signed the Nuclear Nonproliferation Treaty. The superpowers and sixty other nations agreed to limit nuclear weapons. Only France and China refused. Two years later, the United States, the USSR, Britain, and France signed an agreement reducing the tensions over the Berlin situation (page 654). In 1972 the Seabeds Arms Treaty limiting the use of nuclear weapons beneath the ocean was ratified.

"We have laid out a road map." In the delicate negotiations over the control of nuclear weapons, Kissinger played a central role. He arranged the meetings between Nixon and the Soviet leader Leonid Brezhnev. In late May of 1972, Nixon spent nine days in Moscow. It was a triumphal occasion. In a hall of the Kremlin, the first U.S. President to visit Moscow and his Soviet hosts signed seven agreements. They covered cooperation in science and technology, health research, arms control, environmental protection, space exploration, commercial relations, and the avoidance of naval and air incidents. Both countries also agreed to push ahead with the Strategic Arms Limitation Talks (SALT).

President and Mrs. Nixon are entertained by Chou En-lai in Peking.

694

Nixon returned home with the definite evidence that the Cold War was over. Henry Kissinger summed up the results when he said, "We have laid out a road map." Following that "map," Brezhnev visited Washington in mid-June of 1973. Again the two countries stated their plans for reducing armaments. A later conference, in June 1974, pushed efforts to expand trade and commerce.

Balance of power. Through the 1950s, no one had taken a harder line against the recognition of Communist China than Nixon. It therefore came as a complete surprise when he announced in July 1971 that he had accepted an invitation to visit the People's Republic. Arrangements had been made in a secret conference between Kissinger and the Chinese Prime Minister, Chou En-lai (JOE en-LYE).

What the visit would mean became clear in October 1971. The UN General Assembly admitted the Peking government to the United Nations and expelled the Taiwan government of Chiang Kai-shek (page 608). The Nixon Administration went through the motions of criticizing the UN action but privately accepted it.

On February 21, 1972, the *Spirit of '76*, with President Nixon aboard, landed at Peking. The United States had taken a giant step toward recognizing the Communist government of China. Shortly after their arrival, Nixon and Kissinger were invited by Chou En-lai to visit the almost legendary Mao Tse-tung (pages 607–608). Only then were the Chinese people told that Nixon was visiting their country. The streets filled with curious crowds.

In the negotiations that took place, the United States made a major gesture. It acknowledged that Taiwan belonged to China. Neither the United States nor China

Kissinger shuttles between Israel and Egypt.

agreed to full diplomatic relations, but both agreed to set up liaison offices for conducting diplomatic business.

For Kissinger, the agreement was a major achievement. He believed in the "balance of power." The United States had now established friendly relations with both China and the Soviet Union. From here on, Peking and Moscow would have to guess which side the United States would take if the strained feelings between China and the USSR led to war. In September 1973 Nixon made Kissinger Secretary of State.

Shuttle diplomacy. The long dispute between Israel and the Arab states (pages 639–640) broke into full warfare on Octo-

695

ber 6, 1973. Attacking without warning on the solemn Jewish holy Day of Atonement, Yom Kippur (YOM ki-POOR), Egypt and Syria took Israel by surprise. Heavily armed by the Soviet Union, the attacking forces threatened Israel's existence.

A massive United States aid program allowed the Israelis to gain the upper hand. For a short time this brought the Soviet Union and the United States to the verge of war. The crisis passed when the Soviets agreed to a United Nations peacekeeping force from the smaller member states of the UN. By the time a cease-fire went into effect on October 25, 1973, Israeli forces had occupied large areas of Egypt and Syria.

To bring about the Middle East cease-fire Kissinger resorted to "shuttle diplomacy." That is, he made a steady round of visits to the capitals of the three countries, Cairo, Damascus, and Jerusalem. As a result of his efforts, Israel yielded to Egypt some territory in the Sinai peninsula. Israel also allowed the reopening of the Suez Canal. In the late spring of 1974, Kissinger persuaded Israel and Syria to accept a truce on their border. Kissinger's policy had edged the Middle East toward a settlement of its long-standing disputes.

 TRY THIS!

1. Explain how the Nixon-Kissinger foreign policy was intended to keep the United States strong and at peace. Tell how the policy was applied in Vietnam, Moscow, and Peking. **2.** From a map, show why the Middle East became a friction point for the United States and the USSR.

3.   DEVELOPMENTS AT HOME

By the late 1960s, Americans were realizing that the air they breathed and the waters surrounding them were so polluted that life itself was threatened. The people of the United States were paying a heavy price for their vast industrial achievements (page 624). Every day in Manhattan, people on the streets were breathing twice the safe amount of carbon monoxide. The problem was even clearer when an oil well erupted off Santa Barbara, California, and covered miles of white beach with a gummy crude-oil surface, destroying fish and sea birds.

Something finally happened in 1970. Under the National Enviromental Policy Act, all government bodies had to say in detail how any bills they presented would affect the enviroment. The Act placed these matters under a three-member Council of Environmental Quality. Much attention was given to the environment on April 22, 1970, which was celebrated across the country as Earth Day.

Sweet air and clean water. Under pressure for more action, Congress set up the Environmental Protection Agency. And Congress put tight environmental controls

---

Read here of how

Air and water pollution became a problem.
The government moved to solve it.
The President wanted to "win big" in 1972.
And he triggered a national scandal.

---

on more than 755 million acres of federally owned lands. In answer to the Santa Barbara oil spill, Congress passed the Water Quality Improvement Act of 1970.

The 1970 Act established harsh penalties for those polluting waterways. Further, it made them responsible for damages up to 14 million dollars. The Federal Water Pollution Control Act Amendment of 1972 set water standards to be achieved by 1985, and it authorized the spending of 25 billion dollars in federal funds to clean up water pollution.

The Clean Air Act of 1970 set rigid standards to remove most pollutants from automobile exhausts. In addition, over a billion dollars was set aside for cleaning up the air. If all these programs were carried out as Congress required, Americans might once again live in a country whose air would be as sweet to smell as when the first settlers arrived. And their water might again be as clean and drinkable as when the Indians roamed the banks of American streams.

Citizen action. Rachel Carson's *Silent Spring* (1962) had shown how chemical pesticides might cause cancer and other deadly diseases. In late 1972 Congress passed the Federal Environmental Pesticide Control Act. Shortly after its passage, a ban was placed on the use of DDT.

During the same years, Ralph Nader, a brilliant young lawyer, became interested in consumer protection. His first book, *Unsafe at Any Speed* (1965), pointed out the built-in dangers of American cars. Nader's research forced car manufacturers to recall large numbers of defective models. His investigation of the meat industry led to the Wholesome Meat Act of 1967, which provided for federal inspection of meats, and control over its purity.

Can this be a glimpse of the future?

Nader's activities attracted hundreds of young volunteer workers, nicknamed "Nader's Raiders." As Ralph Nader himself explained it, "The biggest job in this country is citizen action. Politics follows that."

Startling revelations. Along with their solid achievements, the members of the Nixon Administration showed another, darker side. The President and his advisers

697

Will "Watergate" become part of the language? Sculptor Miles Carpenter seems to think so.

were unusually concerned about secrecy. They had privately raged when leaks from within the Administration gave the press information on the handling of the Vietnam War and other foreign-policy matters. The White House was furious when in June 1971 *The New York Times* published the Pentagon Papers.

The Pentagon Papers were an extensive top-secret study of the American involvement in Vietnam. The study had been put together in 1967 by 35 experts from the government and from universities, at the request of then Secretary of Defense Robert McNamara. The papers contained such startling revelations as the fact that President Lyndon Johnson had ordered the Tonkin Gulf Resolution (page 670) drawn up months before the supposed incident took place.

"I stole nothing." Surprisingly, President Nixon did not know of the study until the *Times* began to print it. On the advice

of Attorney General John Mitchell, he directed the Justice Department to halt the publication by court order. *The Times* temporarily stopped printing the documents, but the *Washington Post* and the *Boston Globe* then began to do so. Shortly, by 6 to 3 vote, the Supreme Court upheld the papers' right to print the documents.

Daniel Ellsberg, one of those who had worked on the Pentagon Papers for the government, was the person who had turned them over to the newspapers. Ellsberg, however, insisted "I stole nothing, and I did not commit espionage. I violated no laws, and I have not intended to harm my country."

Nixon was now determined to put an end to such disclosures. A secret crew, dubbed the Plumbers, was set up by his domestic adviser to stop the "leaks."

A night to remember. Frank Wills was a watchman at the Watergate apartment/business complex in Washington, D.C. On the evening of June 17, 1972, Mr. Wills found some tape on a door in the complex and called the police. As a result, five men were caught burglarizing the headquarters of the Democratic National Committee. One of them was James McCord, security chief of the Committee to Re-elect the President (CREEP). The others were refugees from Castro's Cuba.

One of those caught in the Watergate was carrying with him the name and phone number of E. Howard Hunt, who had an office in the White House. As was later revealed, Nixon aides immediately began trying to cover up the fact that the burglary had White House connections.

On October 10 the *Washington Post* charged that the Watergate break-in was just the tip of "a massive campaign of political spying and sabotage . . . directed by officials of the White House and the Committee to Re-elect the President." In January 1973 the Watergate burglars went on trial before a stern federal judge, John J. Sirica.

The White House's attempted coverup began to fall apart when James McCord sent a letter to Judge Sirica. It stated that others had been involved in the break-in, that *perjury* (lying under oath) had taken place in the courtroom, and that the defendants were under political pressure to keep quiet and plead guilty. At this point, Congress began to take an interest. On February 7, 1973, the Senate set up a special seven-member investigating committee chaired by Sam J. Ervin of North Carolina. Ervin became a popular figure when the Watergate hearings were televised.

Four more years. The Watergate break-in was part of the presidential election of 1972. In the long primary campaign that year, Democratic Senators Hubert Humphrey of Minnesota and Edmund Muskie of Maine lost out to Senator George McGovern of South Dakota. He picked as his running mate R. Sargent Shriver, brother-in-law of the late President Kennedy.

Governor George Wallace of Alabama (page 681) ran impressively in the primaries, but he was shot and seriously wounded during a rally in Maryland. Unable to continue campaigning, Wallace withdrew. The Republicans renominated Nixon and Agnew, hoping for "Four more years!"

George McGovern campaigned by calling for an end to the Vietnam War and for major economic reforms. The Republican candidates' campaign was funded on a scale never seen before. It may have reached over sixty million dollars. Nixon, who had squeaked by with a bare plurality in 1968, raced on to an overwhelming victory. He had a majority of eighteen million votes; his electoral count was 520 to McGovern's 17.

Only Massachusetts and the District of Columbia had cast their lot with McGovern. In the months that followed, as the Watergate scandal grew, Massachusetts motorists bought bumper stickers saying, "Don't blame me! I'm from Massachusetts!"

Not fit to serve. It was an extraordinary triumph for the President. But within months the victory had come to nothing. Throughout 1973 the Nixon Administration reeled from repeated blows. One came from Vice President Agnew.

Spiro Agnew had been serving as governor of Maryland when Richard Nixon chose him for a running mate in 1968. In the late summer of 1973, the *Wall Street Journal* charged that during his governorship, Agnew had accepted payments from contractors doing business with the state. Furthermore, there was evidence that the payments had continued even while Agnew was Vice President. As a result of a grand-jury investigation, Agnew was charged with income-tax evasion. On October 10, 1973, the Vice President resigned his office and was allowed to plead "no contest" on a tax charge.

The Twenty-fifth Amendment (Appendix) provides for filling the office of Vice President between elections. This makes sure that there will always be someone to take over if the President dies, resigns, or is unable to serve.

The President names a new Vice President, who must then be confirmed by a majority vote of the House and Senate. This part of the Twenty-fifth Amendment has been used twice, once in 1973 when

699

Richard Nixon appointed Gerald Ford, and again in 1974 when Ford appointed Nelson Rockefeller.

The Twenty-fifth Amendment also sets up procedures to follow when the President is not fit to serve. This may mean relieving the President of the responsibilities of the office for a while, or actually forcing the President to resign.

 TRY THIS!

1. Explain why people did not become concerned about the environment until the 1960s. 2. Show how Richard Nixon's past political experiences made him especially eager to "win big" in 1972. 3. Describe the series of events by which the Watergate affair became a national issue.

4. WATERGATE AND A LOST PRESIDENCY

The findings about Watergate set the stage for the biggest political scandal in the nation's history. The Ervin Committee hearings (page 699) went on through the spring and early summer of 1973. They soon showed that former Attorney General Mitchell, White House aides H. R. Haldeman and John Erlichman, former Secretary of Commerce Maurice H. Stans, acting FBI Director L. Patrick Gray, and Attorney General Richard Kleindienst, as well as dozens of lesser Administration figures, had all been involved in breaking the law. The most devastating testimony came from John Dean, the presidential counsel, who implicated the President.

The President's men. As the Watergate story became known, it became apparent that the conspiracy went far beyond Watergate. Members of the White House

Read here of how

Watergate revealed widespread corruption.
Nixon was forced to resign.
An unelected President took office.

staff admitted that they had lied to juries, and that the White House had ordered phone taps, the opening of mail, and burglaries. Many of the illegal acts had been to get information against journalists, politicians, professors, and others not friendly to the Administration.

The President's men had tried to forge documents "proving" that John F. Kennedy had ordered the murder of South Vietnam's President Ngo Dinh Diem (page 670). Hugh Sloan, the treasurer of CREEP, told of vast sums the 1972 Nixon campaign had collected dishonestly from corporations and private individuals. Much of the money had found its way into the White House to pay for illegal activities, and the FBI and CIA had helped with the coverup. In July, Alexander Butterfield, a former presidential assistant, testified that all conversations in the presidential offices were tape-recorded. This meant that proof of John Dean's charges against Nixon existed.

"A smoking gun." In the later part of the Watergate investigation, Archibald Cox of the Harvard Law School was appointed special prosecutor to press the case. Both he and the Ervin Committee went to court to obtain some of the White House tapes; Nixon opposed them. On October 20, 1973, the President fired Attorney General Elliot L. Richardson and his deputy William D. Ruckelshaus. Both had refused to dismiss Cox as special prosecutor. Finally, Solicitor General Robert H. Bork assumed the post of acting Attorney General and got rid of Cox. The wholesale firings became known as the Saturday Night Massacre.

Public outrage forced Nixon to agree to turn over tapes to Judge Sirica. On one tape, an eighteen-minute part appeared to have been intentionally erased. At this point, the House Judiciary Committee under Peter Rodino of New Jersey moved to bring impeachment proceedings against Nixon.

On July 27, 1974, the committee voted 27–11 to impeach the President. The charges were that he had deliberately obstructed the Watergate investigation, tried to protect those responsible for the break-in, and had hidden other unlawful acts. Nixon was further charged with violating the constitutional rights of American citizens, obstructing justice, and breaking the legal restrictions Congress had placed on executive agencies.

On August 5, Nixon reluctantly complied with a July 24, 1974 Supreme Court order to release three more recordings to federal prosecutors. These revealed beyond doubt that the President had been involved in the coverup from the beginning. Nixon's doom was sealed. Even the President's Republican supporters said that this piece of evidence was like a "smoking gun" in the hands of a suspected criminal. Three days later, as millions watched and listened, Richard Nixon, faced with certain conviction by the Senate, resigned.

An appointed President. The next morning, surrounded by his family, a shaken Nixon left the White House for the last time. At 11:35 A.M. on August 9, 1974, as his plane flew over Kansas, the Nixon Presidency ended. Thirty minutes later, Vice President Gerald R. Ford was inaugurated, the first President to be appointed to that high office.

For a quarter century, Gerald Ford had represented a Michigan congressional district. For nine years he had been Republican leader in the House of Representatives. A thoroughly decent man, he was totally at home in small-town America.

The new President was warm and responsive in his dealings with individuals,

701

President Ford and Mrs. Betty Ford greeting friends and well-wishers.

but he seemed less sympathetic to the problems of people in a group. Those who knew Ford best emphasized his matter-of-fact openness. In the aftermath of Nixon's fall, Gerald Ford seemed unusually solid and reliable.

No deal. Nixon's resignation did not end the Watergate affair. Upon his return to his home in San Clemente, California, Nixon faced the possibility of a trial—even of a prison term. But on September 8, 1974, President Ford gave Nixon a pardon for all federal crimes that he had committed.

Millions of Americans were outraged. It seemed to them that a double standard of justice was being applied, one that allowed the powerful to escape the conse-

quences of criminal acts. Even more disturbing to many Americans was the failure of Nixon to admit his guilt. He simply acknowledged that he had made mistakes.

An angry Congress took control of the former President's tapes and papers and stated that none could be destroyed without its consent. In an unprecedented action, President Ford appeared before a congressional committee to insist, "There was no deal." He explained that he had granted the pardon because a trial might only deepen the divisions within the country. The time had come, he pleaded, "to put Watergate behind us."

Watergate tornado. Watergate did not go away. Numerous officials of the Nixon Administration stood trial—and went to

DIG HERE!

Through thirty chapters you have learned how Americans have worked, played, suffered, and rejoiced. Their history has lasted for over two centuries. For this final exercise, make predictions about the twenty-first century. What will the United States be like in 2000 A.D.? Answer the questions as they apply to a) government, b) the economy (jobs, business, labor unions), c) family life, d) education, e) minority-group relations, f) the environment, g) urban areas, h) leisure time.

A. Name the three most important changes you expect to take place by 2000 A.D.
B. Which of our present problems will disappear or seem much less serious by the year 2000? How will they have been resolved?
C. What new problems will Americans face in the twenty-first century?

The books listed on page 710 will offer ideas, especially those by Ehrlich, Freeman, Perloff, and Toffler.

THINK ABOUT IT

1. Those accused during the Watergate and related investigations claimed that the need for "national security" justified their deeds. Was this a reasonable excuse? Explain.
2. Have Presidents been playing a stronger role than Congress has, in dealing with economic depressions and wars since the 1920s? Should Congress play a bigger role in decision-making? Would that be possible during such serious crises as wars and depressions? Why, or why not?

DO IT!

1. Set up a panel discussion on possible U.S. responses to some future Arab oil boycott. Have panel members deal with alternate energy-sources.
2. Create a bulletin-board display about leisure activities of the 1970s.

THEN AND NOW

President Nixon had the largest White House staff in history. They shielded him from the public, from members of Congress, even from his own Cabinet. What was dangerous about that situation? What steps could be taken to keep any other President from doing the same thing?

TEST YOUR HISTORY

1. Why did the Presidency of John Kennedy seem like a new beginning?
2. What successes and what failures did Kennedy have?
3. What new social programs did Lyndon Johnson begin?
4. Why was the Great Society a disappointment to many?
5. How did the U.S. become involved in Vietnam?
6. What were some effects of the black power movement?
7. What conditions in the black ghettos led to the riots of the 1960s?
8. How was Lyndon Johnson driven from office?
9. What conditions was the counterculture reacting against?
10. What demands did the women's movement make in the 1970s?
11. What organizations did women form and what successes did they have?
12. How did Nixon hope to rebuild the Republican Party?
13. What caused new student protests in 1970?
14. How was U.S. involvement in Vietnam finally ended?
15. What new direction did Nixon take with the USSR?
16. How did President Nixon change U.S.-China policy?
17. What new environmental policy was begun in the 1970s?
18. What was Watergate about?
19. In what sense was Gerald Ford an "unelected" President?
20. How was Carter's candidacy and election unusual?

VII
REVIEW

FURTHER READING

Ehrlich, P., *The End of Affluence.* Ballantine, 1974.

Energy Policy Project, *Exploring Energy Choices.* Ford, 1974.

Fernandez, B. J., *Opposition: Images of American Dissent in the Sixties.* DaCapo, 1968.

Freeman, W. H., *Cities.* Scientific American, 1973.

Graham, F., *Since Silent Spring.* Houghton, 1970.

Herbert, F., ed., *New World or No World.* Ace, 1970.

Michener, J. A., *The Quality of Life.* Lippincott, 1970.

Murphy, E. F., *Governing Nature.* Quadrangle, 1970.

Nicholson, M., *The Environmental Revolution.* McGraw, 1970.

O'Neill, W. L., *Coming Apart.* Quadrangle, 1973.

Perloff, H., *The Future of the U. S. Government.* Braziller, 1971.

Toffler, A., *Future Shock.* Bantam, 1971.

Toffler, A., *Learning for Tomorrow.* Random, 1974.

 APPENDIX

THE DECLARATION OF INDEPENDENCE

In Congress, July 4, 1776
The Unanimous Declaration of the Thirteen United States of America

WHEN in the course of human events it becomes necessary for one people to dissolve the political bands which have connected them with another, and to assume among the powers of the earth the separate and equal station to which the laws of nature and of nature's God entitle them, a decent respect to the opinions of mankind requires that they should declare the causes which impel them to the separation.[1]

We hold these truths to be self-evident, that all men[2] are created equal, that they are endowed by their Creator with certain unalienable rights, that among these are life, liberty, and the pursuit of happiness. That to secure these rights, governments are instituted among men, deriving their just powers from the consent of the governed; that whenever any form of government becomes destructive of these ends, it is the right of the people to alter or to abolish it, and to institute new government, laying its foundation on such principles and organizing its powers in such form, as to them shall seem most likely to effect their safety and happiness. Prudence, indeed, will dictate that governments long established should not be changed for light and transient causes; and accordingly all experience hath shown, that mankind are more disposed to suffer, while evils are sufferable, than to right themselves by abolishing the forms to which they are accustomed. But when a long train of abuses and usurpations, pursuing invariably the same object, evinces a design to reduce them under absolute despotism, it is their right, it is their duty, to throw off such government, and to provide new guards for their future security. Such has been the patient sufferance of these colonies; and such is now the necessity which constrains them to alter their former systems of government. The history of the present King of Great Britain is a history of repeated injuries and usurpations, all having in direct object the establishment of an absolute tyranny over these states. To prove this, let facts be submitted to a candid world.

He has refused his assent to laws, the most wholesome and necessary for the public good.

He has forbidden his governors to pass laws of immediate and pressing importance, unless suspended in their operation

---

[1] *The Declaration has been modernized in spelling, capitalization, and punctuation.*

[2] *"Men" is used here to mean "humanity" or all human beings.*

till his assent should be obtained; and when so suspended, he has utterly neglected to attend to them.

He has refused to pass other laws for the accommodation of large districts of people, unless those people would relinquish the right of representation in the legislature, a right inestimable to them and formidable to tyrants only.

He has called together legislative bodies at places unusual, uncomfortable, and distant from the depository of their public records, for the sole purpose of fatiguing them into compliance with his measures.

He has dissolved representative houses repeatedly, for opposing with manly firmness his invasions on the rights of the people.

He has refused for a long time, after such dissolutions, to cause others to be elected; whereby the legislative powers, incapable of annihilation, have returned to the people at large for their exercise; the state remaining in the meantime exposed to all the dangers of invasion from without and convulsions within.

He has endeavored to prevent the population of these states; for that purpose obstructing the laws for naturalization of foreigners, refusing to pass others to encourage their migrations hither, and raising the conditions of new appropriations of lands.

He has obstructed the administration of justice, by refusing his assent to laws for establishing judiciary powers.

He has made judges dependent on his will alone, for the tenure of their offices, and the amount and payment of their salaries.

He has erected a multitude of new offices and sent hither swarms of officers to harass our people, and eat out their substance.

He has kept among us, in times of peace, standing armies without the consent of our legislatures.

He has affected to render the military independent of and superior to the civil power.

He has combined with others to subject us to a jurisdiction foreign to our constitution, and unacknowledged by our laws; giving his assent to their acts of pretended legislation:

For quartering large bodies of armed troops among us;

For protecting them, by a mock trial, from punishment for any murders which they should commit on the inhabitants of these states;

For cutting off our trade with all parts of the world;

For imposing taxes on us without our consent;

For depriving us, in many cases, of the benefits of trial by jury;

For transporting us beyond seas to be tried for pretended offenses;

For abolishing the free system of English laws in a neighboring province, establishing therein an arbitrary government, and enlarging its boundaries so as to render it at once an example and fit instrument for introducing the same absolute rule into these colonies;

For taking away our charters, abolishing our most valuable laws, and altering fundamentally the forms of our governments;

For suspending our own legislatures, and declaring themselves invested with power to legislate for us in all cases whatsoever.

He has abdicated government here, by declaring us out of his protection and waging war against us.

He has plundered our seas, ravaged our coasts, burnt our towns, and destroyed the lives of our people.

He is at this time transporting large armies of foreign mercenaries to complete the works of death, desolation, and tyranny, already begun with circumstances of cruelty and perfidy scarcely paralleled in the most barbarous ages, and totally unworthy the head of a civilized nation.

He has constrained our fellow citizens taken captive on the high seas to bear arms against their country, to become the executioners of their friends and brethren, or to fall themselves by their hands.

He has excited domestic insurrections amongst us, and has endeavored to bring on the inhabitants of our frontiers, the merciless Indian savages, whose known rule of warfare is an undistinguished destruction of all ages, sexes, and conditions.[3]

In every stage of these oppressions we have petitioned for redress in the most humble terms. Our repeated petitions have been answered only by repeated injury. A prince whose character is thus marked by every act which may define a tyrant is unfit to be the ruler of a free people.

Nor have we been wanting in attentions to our British brethren. We have warned them from time to time of attempts by their legislature to extend an unwarrantable jurisdiction over us. We have reminded them of the circumstances of our emigration and settlement here. We have appealed to their native justice and mag-

[3] *Here Jefferson was reflecting the common prejudices of his day.*

nanimity, and we have conjured them by the ties of our common kindred to disavow these usurpations, which would inevitably interrupt our connections and correspondence. They too have been deaf to the voice of justice and of consanguinity. We must, therefore, acquiesce in the necessity, which denounces our separation, and hold them, as we hold the rest of mankind, enemies in war, in peace friends.

We, therefore, the representatives of the United States of America, in General Congress assembled, appealing to the Supreme Judge of the world for the rectitude of our intentions, do, in the name, and by authority of the good people of these colonies, solemnly publish and declare, that these united colonies are, and of right ought to be, free and independent states; that they are absolved from all allegiance to the British Crown, and that all political connection between them and the State of Great Britain is and ought to be totally dissolved; and that as free and independent states, they have full power to levy war, conclude peace, contract alliances, establish commerce, and to do all other acts and things which independent states may of right do. And for the support of this declaration, with a firm reliance on the protection of divine Providence, we mutually pledge to each other our lives, our fortunes, and our sacred honor.

THE
CONSTITUTION
OF THE UNITED STATES
OF AMERICA

The Constitution, modernized in spelling, capitalization, and punctuation, is printed below in the wider column to the left. For greater convenience, various headings and subheadings have been added in italic type (like this: *LEGISLATIVE DEPARTMENT, The Congress,* and *a. Election and term of members*). Those portions of the Constitution that are no longer in effect are also printed in italic type (like this: *which shall be determined*). The superior numbers which are found throughout the text ([2]) refer to the explanatory notes in the narrower column to the right.

Preamble

WE THE PEOPLE of the United States,[1] in order to form a more perfect union, establish justice, insure domestic tranquillity, provide for the common defense, promote the general welfare, and secure the blessings of liberty to ourselves and our posterity, do ordain and establish this Constitution for the United States of America.[2]

1. The Constitution says that the sovereign power belongs to the people.
2. The Preamble states the overall purposes of the Constitution.

Article One. LEGISLATIVE DEPARTMENT

Section 1. The Congress

All legislative powers herein granted shall be vested in a Congress of the United States, which shall consist of a Senate and House of Representatives.[1]

Section 2. The House of Representatives

a. Election and term of members. The House of Representatives shall be composed of members chosen every second year by the people of the several states,[2] and the electors[3] in each state shall have the qualifications requisite for electors of the most numerous branch of the state legislature.[4]

b. Qualification of members. No person shall be a representative who shall not have attained to the age of twenty-five years, and been seven years a citizen of the United States, and who shall not, when elected, be an inhabitant of that state in which he shall be chosen.

c. Apportionment of representatives and of direct taxes. Representatives and direct taxes[5] shall be apportioned among the several states which may be included within this Union, according to their re-spective numbers,[6] *which shall be determined by the whole number of free persons, including those bound to service for a term of years,[7] and excluding Indians not taxed,[8] three fifths of all other persons.[9]* The actual enumera-tion shall be made within three years after the first meeting of the Congress of the United States, and within every subsequent term of ten years, in such manner as they shall by law direct.[10] The number of representatives shall not exceed one for every thirty thousand, but each state shall have at least one representative; *and until such enumeration shall be made, the State of New Hampshire shall be entitled to choose three; Massachusetts, eight; Rhode Island and Providence Plantations, one; Connecticut, five; New York, six; New Jersey, four; Pennsyl-vania, eight; Delaware, one; Maryland, six; Virginia, ten; North Carolina, five; South Carolina, five; and Georgia, three.*

d. Filling vacancies. When vacancies happen in the representation from any state, the executive authority thereof shall issue writs of election to fill such vacancies.[11]

e. Officers; impeachment. The House of Representatives shall choose their Speaker and other officers; and shall have the sole power of impeachment.[12]

1. The Senate repre-sents the states equally; in the House, member-ship is divided among the states according to population.
2. There is a new House every two years.
3. The voters.
4. This is the only vot-ing qualification in the original Constitution.
5. A direct tax is usually paid by the person on whom it is imposed; an indirect tax is usually shifted to the consumer.
6. Amendment 16 now permits Congress to levy an income tax (a direct tax) without apportion-ment.
7. Indentured servants.
8. Indians are now citi-zens.
9. "Other persons" here meant slaves.
10. A national census is taken every ten years. A law now provides that Congress shall re-appor-tion membership of the House among the states after each census.
11. A special election is held in the state to fill a vacancy in the House.
12. Only the House has power to impeach a civil official of the United States. The Senate tries cases of impeachment.

717

Section 3. The Senate

a. Number and election of members. The Senate of the United States shall be composed of two senators from each state, chosen *by the legislature thereof,*[13] for six years; and each senator shall have one vote.

b. Classification. Immediately after they shall be assembled in consequence of the first election, they shall be divided as equally as may be into three classes. *The seats of the senators of the first class shall be vacated at the expiration of the second year, of the second class at the expiration of the fourth year, and of the third class at the expiration of the sixth year,* so that one third may be chosen every second year;[14] *and if vacancies happen by resignation, or otherwise, during the recess of the legislature of any state, the executive thereof may make temporary appointments until the next meeting of the legislature, which shall then fill such vacancies.*[15]

c. Qualifications of members. No person shall be a senator who shall not have attained to the age of thirty years, and been nine years a citizen of the United States,[16] and who shall not, when elected, be an inhabitant of that state for which he shall be chosen.

d. President of Senate. The Vice President of the United States shall be President of the Senate, but shall have no vote, unless they be equally divided.[17]

e. Other officers. The Senate shall choose their own officers, and also a President pro tempore,[18] in the absence of the Vice President, or when he shall exercise the office of President of the United States.

f. Trial by impeachment. The Senate shall have the sole power to try all impeachments. When sitting for that purpose, they shall be on oath or affirmation. When the President of the United States is tried, the Chief Justice shall preside; and no person shall be convicted without the concurrence of two thirds of the members present.[19]

g. Judgment in case of conviction. Judgment in cases of impeachment shall not exceed further than to removal from office, and disqualification to hold and enjoy any office of honor, trust, or profit under the United States; but the party convicted shall nevertheless be liable and subject to indictment, trial, judgment, and punishment, according to law.[20]

Section 4. Election and Meetings of Congressmen

a. Method of holding elections. The times, places, and manner of holding elections for senators and representatives shall be prescribed in each state by the legislature thereof; but the Congress

13. Amendment 17 changes this provision.

14. The terms of only one third of the Senate's members run out in any election year.

15. Amendment 17 provides for special elections to fill Senate vacancies, as in the case of the House. The state legislature, however, may give the governor power to make a temporary appointment until the next regular election.

16. Qualifications for a senator were made higher so that the Senate might include older and more experienced persons.

17. This is the only duty assigned in the Constitution to the Vice President.

18. Called "President pro tem." ("Pro tempore" means "for the time being.")

19. Impeachment is one occasion which requires a two-thirds vote of those present.

20. If the Senate finds an officer guilty, it may only remove that person from office and disqualify him or her from holding another United States government position. However, the person may also be tried in the courts for the same offense.

may at any time by law make or alter such regulations, except as to the places of choosing senators.[21]

b. *Meeting of Congress.* The Congress shall assemble at least once in every year, *and such meeting shall be on the first Monday in December, unless they shall by law appoint a different day.*[22]

Section 5. Rules of Procedure

a. *Organization.* Each house shall be the judge of the elections, returns, and qualifications of its own members,[23] and a majority of each shall constitute a quorum to do business; but a smaller number may adjourn from day to day, and may be authorized to compel the attendance of absent members, in such manner, and under such penalties as each house may provide.

b. *Rules of proceedings.* Each house may determine the rules of its proceedings,[24] punish its members for disorderly behavior, and with the concurrence of two thirds, expel a member.[25]

c. *Journal.* Each house shall keep a journal of its proceedings, and from time to time publish the same, excepting such parts as may in their judgment require secrecy;[26] and the yeas and nays of the members of either house on any question shall, at the desire of one fifth of those present, be entered on the journal.

d. *Adjournment.* Neither house, during the session of Congress, shall without the consent of the other adjourn for more than three days, nor to any other place than that in which the two houses shall be sitting.

Section 6. Compensation, Privileges, and Restrictions

a. *Pay and privileges of members.* The senators and representatives shall receive a compensation for their services, to be ascertained by law, and paid out of the Treasury of the United States.[27] They shall in all cases, except treason, felony, and breach of the peace, be privileged from arrest during their attendance at the session of their respective houses and in going to and returning from the same; and for any speech or debate in either house, they shall not be questioned in any other place.[28]

b. *Holding other offices prohibited.* No senator or representative shall, during the time for which he was elected, be appointed to any civil office under the authority of the United States which shall have been created, or the emoluments[29] whereof shall have been increased during such time; and no person holding any office under

21. Congressional elections are held on the Tuesday after the first Monday in November of the even-numbered years. Congress now also provides for a secret ballot in these elections.

22. See also Amendment 20.

23. Either house may decide on the election or qualifications of a member, but it may not consider qualifications other than those found in Article One, Section 2, paragraph b, and Section 3, paragraph c.

24. These cover the duties of officers and committees and the order and means of conducting business.

25. Voters may then reelect the expelled member.

26. The Congressional Record is issued daily during sessions of Congress.

27. This provision served to strengthen the federal government, since it made members of Congress federal officials.

28. In effect, a member of Congress cannot be sued for any statement made in Congress or in a congressional committee.

29. Salary or other payment.

the United States shall be a member of either house during his continuance in office.

Section 7. Mode of Passing Laws

a. Revenue bills. All bills for raising revenue shall originate in the House of Representatives;[30] but the Senate may propose or concur with amendments as on other bills.

b. How bills become laws. Every bill which shall have passed the House of Representatives and the Senate shall, before it become a law, be presented to the President of the United States;[31] if he approve he shall sign it, but if not he shall return it, with his objections, to that house in which it shall have originated, who shall enter the objections at large on their journal and proceed to reconsider it. If after such reconsideration two thirds of that house shall agree to pass the bill, it shall be sent, together with the objections, to the other house, by which it shall likewise be reconsidered, and if approved by two thirds of that house, it shall become a law. But in all such cases the votes of both houses shall be determined by yeas and nays, and the names of the persons voting for and against the bill shall be entered on the journal of each house respectively. If any bill shall not be returned by the President within ten days (Sundays excepted) after it shall have been presented to him, the same shall be a law, in like manner as if he had signed it, unless the Congress by their adjournment prevent its return, in which case it shall not be a law.[32]

c. Approval or disapproval by the President. Every order, resolution, or vote to which the concurrence of the Senate and House of Representatives may be necessary[33] (except on a question of adjournment) shall be presented to the President of the United States; and before the same shall take effect, shall be approved by him, or being disapproved by him, shall be repassed by two thirds of the Senate and House of Representatives, according to the rules and limitations prescribed in the case of a bill.

Section 8. Powers Granted to Congress[34]

The Congress shall have power

a. To lay and collect taxes, duties, imposts, and excises,[35] to pay the debts and provide for the common defense and general welfare of the United States; but all duties, imposts, and excises shall be uniform throughout the United States;

30. Tariff or income-tax measures are examples. By custom, bills appropriating money also originate in the House. Actually the Senate also exerts considerable influence over revenue bills.

31. Before a bill is sent to the President, it must be passed in identical form by both houses. Differences are usually worked out in a conference committee having members from both houses.

32. This clause provides a way that a bill may become law without the President's signature and also for a "pocket" veto.

33. "Necessary" here means necessary only if a measure is to have the force of law. Procedural votes (for instance, on Congress's own rules) are not included.

34. Section 8 is one of the most important in the Constitution. A few other powers are granted to Congress, but the most important are listed here.

35. Congress under the Articles of Confederation had lacked the power to levy taxes. This power was of great importance in the growth of the national government.

b. To borrow money on the credit of the United States;[36]

c. To regulate commerce with foreign nations, and among the several states, and with the Indian tribes;[37]

d. To establish a uniform rule of naturalization, and uniform laws on the subject of bankruptcies throughout the United States;[38]

e. To coin money, regulate the value thereof and of foreign coin, and fix the standard of weights and measures;

f. To provide for the punishment of counterfeiting the securities and current coin of the United States;

g. To establish post offices and post roads;

h. To promote the progress of science and useful arts by securing for limited times to authors and inventors the exclusive right to their respective writings and discoveries;[39]

i. To constitute tribunals inferior to the Supreme Court;

j. To define and punish piracies and felonies committed on the high seas and offenses against the laws of nations;

k. To declare war,[40] grant letters of marque and reprisal,[41] and make rules concerning captures on land and water;

l. To raise and support armies, but no appropriation of money to that use shall be for a longer term than two years;[42]

m. To provide and maintain a navy;

n. To make rules for the government and regulation of land and naval forces;

o. To provide for calling forth the militia to execute the laws of the Union, suppress insurrections, and repel invasions;

p. To provide for organizing, arming, and disciplining the militia, and for governing such part of them as may be employed in the service of the United States, reserving to the states respectively the appointment of the officers and the authority of training the militia, according to the discipline prescribed by Congress;[43]

q. To exercise exclusive legislation in all cases whatsoever over such district (not exceeding ten miles square) as may, by cession of particular states and the acceptance of Congress, become the seat of the government of the United States,[44] and to exercise like authority over all places purchased by the consent of the legislature of the state in which the same shall be for the erection of forts, magazines, arsenals, dock-yards, and other needful buildings; and

36. Borrowing is generally done by selling government bonds or certificates of indebtedness.

37. This important power was not exercised by Congress under the Confederation.

38. Bankruptcy legislation was largely left to the states until 1898.

39. This clause is the basis of patent and copyright laws.

40. Congress alone has the power to declare war. But a situation may develop in which Congress feels that it has little choice.

41. This power to commission privateers (page 97) to prey upon enemy commerce has not been used since the War of 1812.

42. By this means Congress may retain control of the military.

43. This provision makes it possible for the federal government to regulate the National Guard.

44. The District of Columbia is governed under this clause.

r. To make all laws which shall be necessary and proper for carrying into execution the foregoing powers, and all other powers vested by this Constitution in the government of the United States, or in any department or officer thereof.[45]

Section 9. Powers Denied to the Federal Government

a. The migration or importation of such persons as any of the states now existing shall think proper to admit[46] *shall not be prohibited by the Congress prior to the year one thousand eight hundred and eight, but a tax or duty may be imposed on such importation, not exceeding ten dollars for each person.*

b. The privilege of the writ of habeas corpus shall not be suspended, unless when in cases of rebellion or invasion the public safety may require it.[47]

c. No bill of attainder[48] or ex post facto law[49] shall be passed.

d. No capitation or other direct tax shall be laid, unless in proportion to the census or enumeration herein before directed to be taken.[50]

e. No tax or duty shall be laid on articles exported from any state.[51]

f. No preference shall be given by any regulation of commerce or revenue to the ports of one state over those of another;[52] nor shall vessels bound to or from one state be obliged to enter, clear, or pay duties in another.

g. No money shall be drawn from the treasury, but in consequence of appropriations made by law; and a regular statement and account of the receipts and expenditures of all public money shall be published from time to time.

h. No title of nobility shall be granted by the United States; and no person holding any office of profit or trust under them shall, without the consent of Congress, accept of any present, emolument, office, or title, of any kind whatever, from any king, prince, or foreign state.

Section 10. Powers Denied to the States[53]

a. No state shall enter into any treaty, alliance, or confederation; grant letters of marque and reprisal; coin money; emit bills of credit; make any thing but gold and silver coin a tender in payment of debts; pass any bill of attainder, ex post facto law, or law

45. This implied-powers clause is the basis for much legislation not specifically authorized elsewhere. Under it the taxing power and the commerce clause have been stretched.

46. In other words, slaves.

47. This writ prevents unreasonable imprisonment. A person arrested can demand to be charged with a specific crime or released. The Constitution does not say who may suspend the writ. Lincoln did so during the Civil War, but the Supreme Court later held that the action must be authorized by Congress.

48. A legislative measure that condemns a person without a trial in court.

49. Legislation that would make an act a criminal offense after it was committed.

50. This provision necessitated the enactment of Amendment 16 to permit the levying of an income tax.

51. To assure the South that exports would not be taxed.

52. The purpose here was to insure equal treatment for all ports.

53. For the powers reserved to the states, see Amendment 10.

impairing the obligation of contracts; or grant any title of nobility.[54]

b. No state shall, without the consent of the Congress, lay any imposts or duties on imports or exports, except what may be absolutely necessary for executing its inspection laws; and the net produce of all duties and imposts laid by any state on imports or exports shall be for the use of the treasury of the United States; and all such laws shall be subject to the revision and control of the Congress.

c. No state shall, without the consent of Congress, lay any duty of tonnage; keep troops[55] or ships of war in time of peace; enter into any agreement or compact with another state or with a foreign power; or engage in war, unless actually invaded or in such imminent danger as will not admit of delay.

54. Some of these powers are also denied to the national government; others may be exercised by the national government but not by the states.

55. This does not prevent a state from having a militia (Amendment 2).

Article Two. EXECUTIVE DEPARTMENT

Section 1. President and Vice President

a. Term of office. The executive power shall be vested in a President of the United States of America. He shall hold his office during the term of four years,[1] and, together with the Vice President, chosen for the same term, be elected as follows:

b. Electors. Each state shall appoint, in such manner as the legislature thereof may direct, a number of electors, equal to the whole number of senators and representatives to which the state may be entitled in the Congress; but no senator or representative, or person holding an office of trust or profit under the United States, shall be appointed an elector.[2]

Former method of electing President and Vice President.[3] The electors shall meet in their respective states and vote by ballot for two persons, of whom one at least shall not be an inhabitant of the same state with themselves. And they shall make a list of all the persons voted for and of the number of votes for each; which list they shall sign and certify, and transmit sealed to the seat of government of the United States, directed to the President of the Senate. The President of the Senate shall, in the presence of the Senate and House of Representatives, open all the certificates, and the votes shall then be counted. The person having the greatest number of votes shall be the President, if such number be a majority of the whole number of electors appointed; and if there be more than one who have such majority, and have an equal number of votes, then the House of Representatives shall immediately choose by ballot one of them for President; and if no person have a majority, then from the five highest on the list the said house shall in like manner choose the President. But in

1. The four-year term without limitation as to re-election was a compromise.

2. Instead of placing the election of the Chief Executive directly in the hands of the voters, the Constitution provided for the selection of electors. The electors, in turn, would choose a President. Today electors usually are prominent party members whose votes are pledged to a given candidate.

3. This section has been changed by Amendment 12, adopted in 1804.

choosing the President the votes shall be taken by states, the representation from each state having one vote; a quorum for this purpose shall consist of a member or members from two thirds of the states, and a majority of all the states shall be necessary to a choice. In every case, after the choice of the President, the person having the greatest number of votes of the electors shall be the Vice President. But if there should remain two or more who have equal votes, the Senate shall choose from them by ballot the Vice President.

c. Time of elections. The Congress may determine the time of choosing the electors, and the day on which they shall give their votes; which day shall be the same throughout the United States.[4]

d. Qualifications of the President. No person except a natural-born citizen, *or a citizen of the United States, at the time of the adoption of this Constitution,* shall be eligible to the office of President;[5] neither shall any person be eligible to that office who shall not have attained the age of thirty-five years, and been fourteen years a resident within the United States.

e. Vacancy. In case of the removal of the President from office or of his death, resignation, or inability to discharge the powers and duties of the said office,[6] the same shall devolve on the Vice President;[7] and the Congress may by law provide for the case of removal, death, resignation, or inability, both of the President and Vice President, declaring what officer shall then act as President; and such officer shall act accordingly, until the disability be removed or a President shall be elected.[8]

f. The President's salary. The President shall, at stated times, receive for his services a compensation, which shall neither be increased nor diminished during the period for which he shall have been elected, and he shall not receive within that period any other emolument from the United States, or any of them.[9]

g. Oath of office. Before he enter on the execution of his office, he shall take the following oath or affirmation: "I do solemnly swear (or affirm) that I will faithfully execute the office of President of the United States, and will to the best of my ability, preserve, protect, and defend the Constitution of the United States."

Section 2. Powers of the President

a. Military powers; reprieves and pardons. The President shall be Commander-in-Chief of the Army and Navy of the United States, and of the militia of the several states, when called into the actual service of the United States.[10] He may require the opinion, in writing, of the principal officer in each of the executive departments, upon any subject relating to the duties of their respective

4. The popular vote for electors takes place every four years on the Tuesday after the first Monday of November. In mid-December the electors meet in their state capitals and cast their electoral votes.

5. A natural-born citizen is one who is a citizen at birth. This may include a child born to American parents living outside the United States.

6. One purpose of the Twenty-fifth Amendment is to clarify the way in which presidential disability may be determined.

7. Tyler, the first Vice President to succeed to the Presidency because of the death of the incumbent, took the title as well as the powers and duties of the Presidency and thus set a precedent.

8. The Twenty-fifth Amendment practically assures that there will always be a Vice President to succeed.

9. Congress has now fixed this salary at 200,000 dollars per year plus an expense account.

10. The President may use his military powers to see that the laws are carried out.

offices,[11] and he shall have power to grant reprieves and pardons for offenses against the United States, except in cases of impeachment.

b. Treaties; appointments. He shall have power, by and with the advice and consent of the Senate, to make treaties, provided two thirds of the senators present concur;[12] and he shall nominate and, by and with the advice and consent of the Senate, shall appoint ambassadors, other public ministers and consuls, judges of the Supreme Court, and all other officers of the United States, whose appointments are not herein otherwise provided for, and which shall be established by law;[13] but the Congress may by law vest the appointment of such inferior officers as they think proper in the President alone, in the courts of law, or in the heads of departments.[14]

c. Filling vacancies. The President shall have power to fill up all vacancies that may happen during the recess of the Senate, by granting commissions which shall expire at the end of their next session.

Section 3. Duties of the President

He shall from time to time give to the Congress information of the state of the Union[15] and recommend to their consideration such measures as he shall judge necessary and expedient; he may, on extraordinary occasions, convene both houses, or either of them,[16] and in case of disagreement between them with respect to the time of adjournment he may adjourn them to such time as he shall think proper; he shall receive ambassadors and other public ministers;[17] he shall take care that the laws be faithfully executed,[18] and shall commission all the officers of the United States.

Section 4. Impeachment

The President, Vice President and all civil officers of the United States shall be removed from office on impeachment for, and conviction of, treason, bribery, or other high crimes and misdemeanors.

Article Three. JUDICIAL DEPARTMENT

Section 1. The Federal Courts

The judicial power of the United States shall be vested in one Supreme Court and in such inferior courts as the Congress may

11. No provision is made in the Constitution for the Cabinet or for Cabinet meetings. But the existence of executive departments is implied here.

12. The President or his representatives draw up the treaty which is then submitted to the Senate for ratification.

13. Ratification of appointments requires simple majority.

14. Congress has given the Civil Service Commission responsibility for determining the fitness of most job applicants and for ranking them on civil service lists from which appointments are made.

15. Washington, John Adams, Wilson, Franklin Roosevelt, and all recent Presidents have delivered important messages to Congress in person. Others only sent written messages.

16. Special sessions are here provided for.

17. This clause gives the President the power to recognize a foreign government.

18. Actually, the laws are carried out by the various departments and by special commissions and agencies, but it is the President's responsibility to see that this is done.

from time to time ordain and establish.[1] The judges, both of the Supreme and inferior courts, shall hold their offices during good behavior[2] and shall, at stated times, receive for their services a compensation which shall not be diminished during their continuance in office.

Section 2. *Jurisdiction of the Federal Courts*

a. Federal courts. The judicial power shall extend to all cases, in law and equity, arising under this Constitution, the laws of the United States, and treaties made, or which shall be made, under their authority; to all cases affecting ambassadors, other public ministers, and consuls; to all cases of admiralty and maritime jurisdiction; to controversies to which the United States shall be a party; to controversies between two or more states; *between a state and citizens of another state;* between citizens of different states; between citizens of the same state claiming lands under grants of different states, and between a state, or the citizens thereof, and foreign states, citizens, or subjects.[3]

b. Supreme Court. In all cases affecting ambassadors, other public ministers, and consuls, and those in which a state shall be a party, the Supreme Court shall have original jurisdiction.[4] In all the other cases before mentioned, the Supreme Court shall have appellate jurisdiction, both as to law and fact, with such exceptions and under such regulations as the Congress shall make.

c. Rules respecting trials. The trial of all crimes, except in cases of impeachment, shall be by jury;[5] and such trial shall be held in the state where the said crimes shall have been committed; but when not committed within any state, the trial shall be at such place or places as the Congress may by law have directed.

Section 3. *Treason*

a. Definition of treason. Treason against the United States shall consist only in levying war against them or in adhering to their enemies, giving them aid and comfort.[6] No person shall be convicted of treason unless on the testimony of two witnesses to the same overt act, or on confession in open court.[7]

b. Punishment of treason. The Congress shall have power to declare the punishment of treason, but no attainder of treason shall work corruption of blood, or forfeiture except during the life of the person attainted.[8]

1. The organization of the Supreme Court and the establishment of lower courts was left to Congress.

2. Federal judges are appointed for life and may be removed only by impeachment.

3. In general, there are two reasons why cases come before the federal courts: (1) because of the nature of the case, for example, a case arising under the Constitution, federal laws, treaties, or affecting ships on the high seas or in United States waters; (2) because of the nature of the parties involved: the United States, a state, an ambassador, etc.

4. Only the special cases listed here start in the Supreme Court. Much of the Supreme Court's work has to do with cases appealed from lower federal courts or from state courts.

5. Here a jury trial is provided only for criminal cases. Amendments 5 and 6 supplement this and 7 extends it.

6. Note that the Constitution defines treason.

7. It is difficult to convict anyone of treason.

8. The punishment of treason cannot be extended to a traitor's relations.

726

Article Four. THE STATES AND THE FEDERAL GOVERNMENT

Section 1. State Records

Full faith and credit shall be given in each state to the public acts, records, and judicial proceedings of every other state.[1] And the Congress may by general laws prescribe the manner in which such acts, records, and proceedings shall be proved, and the effect thereof.

Section 2. Privileges and Immunities of Citizens

a. Privileges. The citizens of each state shall be entitled to all privileges and immunities of citizens in the several states.[2]

b. Extradition. A person charged in any state with treason, felony, or other crime who shall flee from justice and be found in another state shall, on demand of the executive authority of the state from which he fled, be delivered up, to be removed to the state having jurisdiction of the crime.[3]

c. Fugitive slaves. No person held to service or labor in one state, under the laws thereof, escaping into another shall, in consequence of any law or regulation therein, be discharged from such service or labor, but shall be delivered upon claim of the party to whom such service or labor may be due.[4]

Section 3. New States and Territories

a. Admission of new states. New states may be admitted by the Congress into this Union; but no new state shall be formed or erected within the jurisdiction of any other state; nor any state be formed by the junction of two or more states, or parts of states, without the consent of the legislatures of the states concerned, as well as of the Congress.[5]

b. Power of Congress over territory and property. The Congress shall have power to dispose of and make all needful rules and regulations respecting the territory or other property belonging to the United States; and nothing in this Constitution shall be so construed as to prejudice any claims of the United States, or of any particular state.

1. For example, a will legally drawn up in New Jersey would be approved in Connecticut courts even though it did not meet the requirements of Connecticut law.

2. A citizen of Oregon going into California would be entitled to all the privileges of a citizen of California. See Amendment 14.

3. Usually the governor surrenders such a person. The governor may, however, exercise his or her judgment. There is no way to force the surrender of the accused.

4. This statement referred to the return of fugitive slaves. Amendment 13 meant it was no longer in effect.

5. The power of admitting new states is here given Congress. No state may be deprived of any of its territory without its consent.

Section 4. Guarantees to the States

The United States shall guarantee to every state in this Union a republican form of government,[6] and shall protect each of them against invasion; and on application of the legislature, or of the executive (when the legislature cannot be convened), against domestic violence.[7]

Article Five. METHOD OF AMENDMENT

The Congress, whenever two thirds of both houses shall deem it necessary, shall propose amendments to this Constitution, or, on the application of the legislatures of two thirds of the several states, shall call a convention for proposing amendments, which, in either case, shall be valid to all intents and purposes, as part of this Constitution, when ratified by the legislatures of three fourths of the several states or by conventions in three fourths thereof,[1] as the one or the other mode of ratification may be proposed by the Congress; provided that *no amendments which may be made prior to the year one thousand eight hundred and eight shall in any manner affect the first and fourth clauses in the ninth section of the first article; and that* no state, without its consent, shall be deprived of its equal suffrage in the Senate.[2]

Article Six. GENERAL PROVISIONS

a. Public debt. All debts contracted and engagements entered into, before the adoption of this Constitution, shall be as valid against the United States under this Constitution as under the Confederation.

b. Supremacy of the Constitution. This Constitution, and the laws of the United States which shall be made in pursuance thereof; and all treaties made, or which shall be made, under the authority of the United States, shall be the supreme law of the land;[1] and the judges in every state shall be bound thereby, anything in the Constitution or laws of any state to the contrary notwithstanding.

c. Oath of office; no religious test. The senators and representatives before mentioned, and the members of the several state legislatures, and all executive and judicial officers, both of the United States and of the several states, shall be bound by oath or affirmation to support this Constitution; but no religious test shall ever be required as a qualification to any office or public trust under the United States.[2]

6. Congress may exercise this power by refusing to admit senators and representatives from a state.

7. The federal government intervenes upon request. If national interests are threatened, the President may intervene even over the protests of the state.

1. Amendments may be added in four ways:

(1) An amendment may be proposed by two thirds of both houses of Congress and ratified by the legislatures of three fourths of the states or (2) ratified by special conventions in three fourths of the states.

(3) An amendment may be proposed by a special convention called upon application of two thirds of the state legislatures and ratified by three fourths of the state legislatures or (4) ratified by special conventions in three fourths of the states.

2. Note this further protection for the states with smaller populations.

1. The supreme law consists of: (a) the Constitution, (b) laws passed by Congress in harmony with the Constitution, and (c) treaties.

2. Any religious qualification is ruled out.

Article Seven. RATIFICATION OF THE CONSTITUTION

The ratification of the conventions of nine states shall be sufficient for the establishment of this Constitution between the states so ratifying the same.[1]

1. Delegates had been instructed to revise the Articles of Confederation, and unanimous consent of the states was required for such amendments.

Amendments to the Constitution

Amendment 1 (1791).[1] Freedom of Religion, Speech, and the Press; Right of Assembly

Congress shall make no law respecting an establishment of religion, or prohibiting the free exercise thereof; or abridging the freedom of speech, or of the press; or the right of the people peaceably to assemble, and to petition the government for a redress of grievances.[2]

1. In general the Bill of Rights protects the individual against the exercise of undue power by the federal government.
2. All individuals are free to worship as they see fit. They may speak, write, or print anything they wish, except that they may not slander or libel others nor advocate overthrow of the government by violence. Citizens may meet together for any lawful purpose provided they do not interfere with the rights of others. Finally, the people are free to petition the government to correct grievances.

Amendment 2 (1791). Right to Keep and Bear Arms

A well-regulated militia being necessary to the security of a free state, the right of the people to keep and bear arms shall not be infringed.[3]

3. In the late 1700s the militia was the country's chief defense.

Amendment 3 (1791). Quartering of Troops

No soldier shall, in time of peace, be quartered in any house without the consent of the owner, nor in time of war, but in a manner to be prescribed by law.[4]

4. Forbids the assignment of troops to private homes, except in wartime.

Amendment 4 (1791). Limiting the Right of Search

The right of the people to be secure in their persons, houses, papers, and effects against unreasonable searches and seizures shall not be violated, and no warrants shall issue but upon probable cause, supported by oath or affirmation and particularly describing the place to be searched and the persons or things to be seized.[5]

5. The government may not search a home or arrest a person without good cause.

Amendment 5 (1791). *Rights of the Accused and of Property*

No person shall be held to answer for a capital or otherwise infamous crime, unless on a presentment or indictment of a grand jury, except in cases arising in the land or naval forces, or in the militia, when in actual service in time of war or public danger; nor shall any person be subject for the same offense to be twice put in jeopardy of life or limb; nor shall be compelled in any criminal case to be a witness against himself, nor be deprived of life, liberty, or property, without due process of law; nor shall private property be taken for public use without just compensation.[6]

Amendment 6 (1791). *Further Rights of Accused Persons*

In all criminal prosecutions, the accused shall enjoy the right to a speedy and public trial by an impartial jury of the state and district wherein the crime shall have been committed, which districts shall have been previously ascertained by law, and to be informed of the nature and cause of the accusation; to be confronted with the witnesses against him; to have compulsory process for obtaining witnesses in his favor; and to have the assistance of counsel for his defense.[7]

Amendment 7 (1791). *Rules of the Common Law*

In suits at common law, where the value in controversy shall exceed twenty dollars, the right of trial by jury shall be preserved, and no fact tried by a jury shall be otherwise re-examined in any court of the United States than according to the rules of common law.[8]

Amendment 8 (1791). *Excessive Bail, and Punishment, Prohibited*

Excessive bail shall not be required, nor excessive fines imposed, nor cruel and unusual punishments inflicted.[9]

Amendment 9 (1791). *Rights Retained by the People*

The enumeration in the Constitution of certain rights shall not be construed to deny or disparage others retained by the people.[10]

6. (a) Except for the armed forces in wartime, people may not be tried for crime unless they have been indicted by a grand jury. (b) They may not be tried a second time for the same offense. (c) No one is required to testify against himself or herself. (d) "Life, liberty, or property" may not be taken from anyone except by regular legal proceedings. (e) Private property may not be taken by the government without fair payment.

7. Those accused of a crime (a) are entitled to a prompt public trial before an impartial jury, (b) must be clearly told what the charge against them is. (c) Witnesses against them must give testimony in their presence, (d) the government must help them secure witnesses in their favor, and (e) they must be provided a lawyer.

8. Except in minor cases, civil suits may be tried before a jury.

9. A person accused of a crime may, in most cases, be released from jail by posting a bond that he or she will not run away.

10. This listing of certain rights does not imply that people do not have rights not so listed.

Amendment 10 *(1791). Powers Reserved to the States and to the People*

The powers not delegated to the United States by the Constitution, nor prohibited by it to the states, are reserved to the states respectively, or to the people.

Amendment 11 *(1798). Limiting the Powers of Federal Courts*

The judicial power of the United States shall not be construed to extend to any suit in law or equity commenced or prosecuted against one of the United States by citizens of another state or by citizens or subjects of any foreign state.[11]

Amendment 12 *(1804). Election of President and Vice President*

The electors shall meet in their respective states and vote by ballot for President and Vice President, one of whom, at least, shall not be an inhabitant of the same state with themselves; they shall name in their ballots the person voted for as President, and in distinct ballots the person voted for as Vice President, and they shall make distinct lists of all persons voted for as President, and of all persons voted for as Vice President, and of the number of votes for each, which lists they shall sign and certify, and transmit sealed to the seat of the government of the United States, directed to the President of the Senate; the President of the Senate shall, in the presence of the Senate and House of Representatives, open all the certificates and the votes shall then be counted; the person having the greatest number of votes for President shall be the President, if such number be a majority of the whole number of electors appointed; and if no person have such majority, then from the persons having the highest numbers not exceeding three on the list of those voted for as President, the House of Representatives shall choose immediately, by ballot, the President. But in choosing the President, the votes shall be taken by states, the representation from each state having one vote; a quorum for this purpose shall consist of a member or members from two thirds of the states, and a majority of all the states shall be necessary to a choice.[12] And if the House of Representatives shall not choose a President whenever the right of choice shall devolve upon them, *before the fourth day of March next following,* then the Vice President shall act as President, as in the case of the death or other constitutional disability of the President. The person having the greatest number of votes

11. This amendment prevents a state from being sued by a citizen of another state or of a foreign country.

12. Amendment 12 establishes the present procedure in the Electoral College. Today the national conventions of the major parties nominate candidates for the Presidency and Vice Presidency. At the presidential elections in November voters cast their ballots for electors who are usually pledged to vote for the candidates nominated by the conventions.

In December the President and the Vice President are voted for separately by the electors in the state capitals. The lists of candidates with the votes for each are sent to the President of the Senate, who opens them in the presence of both houses.

If no candidate for President receives a majority, the election goes to the House, where the members vote by states for the three highest candidates. Each state casts one vote. A quorum consists of at least one member from two thirds of the states, and a majority of all the states is necessary for a choice.

as Vice President shall be the Vice President, if such number be a majority of the whole number of electors appointed, and if no person have a majority, then from the two highest numbers on the list, the Senate shall choose the Vice President; a quorum for the purpose shall consist of two thirds of the whole number of senators, and a majority of the whole number shall be necessary to a choice.[13] But no person constitutionally ineligible to the office of President shall be eligible to that of Vice President of the United States.

Amendment 13 (1865).[14] *Slavery Abolished*

Section 1. Abolition of Slavery. Neither slavery nor involuntary servitude, except as a punishment for crime whereof the party shall have been duly convicted, shall exist within the United States or any place subject to their jurisdiction.

Section 2. Enforcement. Congress shall have the power to enforce this article by appropriate legislation.

Amendment 14 (1868). *Civil Rights Guaranteed*

Section 1. Definition of Citizenship. All persons born or naturalized in the United States, and subject to the jurisdiction thereof, are citizens of the United States and of the state wherein they reside.[15] No state shall make or enforce any law which shall abridge the privileges or immunities of citizens of the United States; nor shall any state deprive any person of life, liberty, or property, without due process of law; nor deny to any person within its jurisdiction the equal protection of the laws.[16]

Section 2. Apportionment of Representatives. Representatives shall be apportioned among the several states according to their respective numbers, counting the whole number of persons in each state, excluding Indians not taxed. But when the right to vote at any election for the choice of electors for President and Vice President of the United States, representatives in Congress, the executive and judicial officers of a state, or the members of the legislature thereof, is denied to any of the male inhabitants of such state, being twenty-one years of age and citizens of the United States, or in any way abridged, except for participation in rebellion, or other crime, the basis of representation therein shall be reduced in the proportion which the number of such male citizens shall bear to

13. If no candidate for Vice President receives a majority, the Senate chooses a Vice President from the two highest candidates. Again, a quorum consists of two thirds, and a majority of the whole number of senators is necessary for a choice.

14. Amendments 13, 14, and 15 resulted from the Civil War. In general, Amendment 13 freed the slaves, Amendment 14 was intended to guarantee civil rights to the freedmen, and Amendment 15 gave them the right to vote.

15. This is the only definition of citizenship in the Constitution.

16. Section 1 protects citizens against unjust actions on the part of state governments.

Many Supreme Court decisions related to segregation have been based in part on Amendment 14. Intended primarily as a protection for the freedmen, it also became a protection to corporations. The Supreme Court held a corporation to be a person within the meaning of this amendment, and it declared unconstitutional many state laws which denied to a corporation the equal protection of the laws.

the whole number of male citizens twenty-one years of age in such state.[17]

Section 3. Disability Resulting from Insurrection. No person shall be a senator or representative in Congress, or elector of President and Vice President, or hold any office, civil or military, under the United States, or under any state, who, having previously taken an oath as a member of Congress, or as an officer of the United States, or as a member of any state legislature, or as an executive or judicial officer of any state, to support the Constitution of the United States, shall have engaged in insurrection or rebellion against the same, or given aid or comfort to the enemies thereof. But Congress may by vote of two thirds of each house remove such disability.[18]

Section 4. United States Debt Valid; Confederate Debt Void. The validity of the public debt of the United States, authorized by law, including debts incurred for payment of pensions and bounties for services in suppressing insurrection or rebellion, shall not be questioned. But neither the United States nor any state shall assume or pay any debt or obligation incurred in aid of insurrection or rebellion against the United States, or any claim for the loss or emancipation of any slave; but all such debts, obligations, and claims shall be held illegal and void.[19]

Section 5. Enforcement. The Congress shall have power to enforce by appropriate legislation the provisions of this article.

Amendment 15 (1870). *Right of Suffrage*

Section 1. The Suffrage. The right of citizens of the United States to vote shall not be denied or abridged by the United States or by any state on account of race, color, or previous condition of servitude.[20]

Section 2. Enforcement. The Congress shall have power to enforce this article by appropriate legislation.

Amendment 16 (1913). *Income Tax*

The Congress shall have power to lay and collect taxes on incomes, from whatever source derived, without apportionment among the several states and without regard to any census or enumeration.[21]

17. This section was intended to solve the political problem created by the freeing of the slaves. Each freedman would now count as one in apportioning representatives. Since this would increase the representation of the southern (Democratic) states, the Republicans wanted to make sure that blacks, who were generally favorable to the Republican Party, were protected in the right to vote. This provision of Amendment 14 was never put into effect.

18. This provision deprived the southern states of many leaders during Reconstruction.

19. Section 4 silenced any doubt about the validity of the national debt but outlawed the Confederate debt. Confederate bonds were worthless. The former owners of slaves would receive no payment for them.

20. Amendment 15 limits the power of the states by denying them the right to exclude citizens from voting because of race, color, or previous condition of servitude.

21. Amendment 16 grants to Congress power to levy a tax on incomes without reference to population.

Amendment 17 (1913). *Direct Election of Senators*

a. Election by the people. The Senate of the United States shall be composed of two senators from each state, elected by the people thereof, for six years; and each senator shall have one vote. The electors in each state shall have the qualifications requisite for electors of the most numerous branch of the state legislatures.[22]

b. Vacancies. When vacancies happen in the representation of any state in the Senate, the executive authority of such state shall issue writs of election to fill such vacancies: provided that the legislature of any state may empower the executive thereof to make temporary appointments until the people fill the vacancies by election as the legislature may direct.

c. Not retroactive. This amendment shall not be so construed as to affect the election or term of any senator chosen before it becomes valid as part of the Constitution.

Amendment 18 (1919). *National Prohibition*[23]

Section 1. Prohibition of Intoxicating Liquors. After one year from the ratification of this article the manufacture, sale, or transportation of intoxicating liquors within, the importation thereof into, or the exportation thereof from the United States and all territory subject to the jurisdiction thereof for beverage purposes is hereby prohibited.

Section 2. Enforcement. The Congress and the several states shall have concurrent power to enforce this article by appropriate legislation.

Section 3. Limited Time for Ratification. This article shall be inoperative unless it shall have been ratified as an amendment to the Constitution by the legislatures of the several states, as provided in the Constitution, within seven years from the date of the submission hereof to the states by the Congress.

Amendment 19 (1920). *Extending the Vote to Women*

Section 1. Woman Suffrage. The right of citizens of the United States to vote shall not be denied or abridged by the United States or by any state on account of sex.[24]

Section 2. Enforcement. The Congress shall have power to enforce this article by appropriate legislation.

22. Amendment 17 provides for direct election of United States senators. The qualifications needed to vote for senators are the same as for the lower branch of the state legislature.

23. Wartime Prohibition restrictions caused the country to "go dry" sooner than was specified in the amendment. Although Section 2 provided for enforcement by states and federal government, the national act was so strong that little power was left to the states. In Section 3 the idea of limiting the time for ratification by the state legislatures was first introduced. Amendment 21 repealed Amendment 18.

24. Amendment 19 further limited the power of the states to determine who may vote.

Amendment 20 (1933). The "Lame Duck" Amendment

Section 1. Terms of President, Vice President, and Congress. The terms of the President and Vice President shall end at noon on the 20th day of January, and the terms of senators and representatives at noon on the 3rd day of January, of the years in which such terms would have ended if this article had not been ratified; and the terms of their successors shall then begin.[25]

Section 2. Sessions of Congress. The Congress shall assemble at least once in every year, and such meeting shall begin at noon on the 3rd day of January, unless they shall by law appoint a different day.[26]

Section 3. Death of the President-elect. If, at the time fixed for the beginning of the term of the President, the President-elect shall have died, the Vice President-elect shall become President. If a President shall not have been chosen before the time fixed for the beginning of his term, or if the President-elect shall have failed to qualify, then the Vice President-elect shall act as President until a President shall have qualified; and the Congress may by law provide for the case wherein neither a President-elect nor a Vice President-elect shall have qualified, declaring who shall then act as President, or the manner in which one who is to act shall be selected, and such person shall act accordingly until a President or a Vice President shall have qualified.[27]

Section 4. Choice of President by the House. The Congress may by law provide for the case of the death of any of the persons from whom the House of Representatives may choose a President whenever the right of choice shall have devolved upon them, and for the case of the death of any of the persons from whom the Senate may choose a Vice President whenever the right of choice shall have devolved upon them.[28]

Section 5. Effective Date. Sections 1 and 2 shall take effect on the fifteenth day of October following the ratification of this article.

Section 6. Limited Time for Ratification. This article shall be inoperative unless it shall have been ratified as an amendment to the Constitution by the legislatures of three fourths of the several states within seven years from the date of its submission.[29]

Amendment 21 (1933). Repeal of Prohibition

Section 1. Repeal of Amendment 18. The eighteenth article of amendment to the Constitution of the United States is hereby repealed.[30]

25. Before 1933 many members of the "short session" of Congress meeting in December of even-numbered years had been defeated in the November elections. They were called the "Lame Ducks." Amendment 20 caused the terms of senators and representatives to end on January 3 instead of on March 4.

26. The regular session of the newly elected Congress begins two months instead of thirteen months after the election.

27. Section 3 makes provision for filling the office of President in case of death or failure to qualify before the time fixed for the beginning of that term.

28. In case the election is thrown into Congress and any of the candidates die, Congress may decide what to do.

29. As in the case of Amendment 18, a time limit was placed upon ratification.

30. During the 1930s, arguments in favor of Amendment 18 were no longer as strong as they had been. It was desirable to put people to work, to find uses for grain, and to gain sources of tax revenue.

735

Section 2. States Protected. The transportation or importation into any state, territory, or possession of the United States for delivery or use therein of intoxicating liquors, in violation of the laws thereof, is hereby prohibited.[31]

Section 3. Limited Time for Ratification. This article shall be inoperative unless it shall have been ratified as an amendment to the Constitution by conventions in the several states, as provided in the Constitution, within seven years from the date of the submission hereof to the states by the Congress.[32]

Amendment 22 *(1951). Presidential Term*

Section 1. Definition of Limitation. No person shall be elected to the office of the President more than twice, and no person who has held the office of President, or acted as President, for more than two years of a term to which some other person was elected President shall be elected to the office of the President more than once. But this article shall not apply to any person holding the office of President when this article was proposed by the Congress, and shall not prevent any person who may be holding the office of President, or acting as President, during the term within which this article becomes operative from holding the office of President, or acting as President during the remainder of such term.[33]

Section 2. Limited Time for Ratification. This article shall be inoperative unless it shall have been ratified as an amendment to the Constitution by the legislatures of three fourths of the several states within seven years from the date of its submission to the states by the Congress.

Amendment 23 *(1961). Presidential Voting in the District of Columbia*

Section 1. Appointment of Electors. The District constituting the seat of government of the United States shall appoint, in such manner as the Congress may direct: A number of electors of President and Vice President equal to the whole number of senators and representatives in Congress to which the District would be entitled if it were a state, but in no event more than the least populous state; they shall be in addition to those appointed by the states, but they shall be considered, for the purposes of the election of President and Vice President, to be electors appointed by a state; and they

31. Section 2 was designed to protect states that had laws prohibiting the use of liquor.

32. Section 3 was unique in that Congress made provision for the submission of this amendment to conventions in the states. Ratification proceeded with unusual speed, and Amendment 21 was proclaimed a part of the Constitution before the end of 1933. The procedure followed gave the people an opportunity to express their views on the question of Prohibition in voting for delegates to the state conventions.

33. The authors of the Constitution placed no limit on the number of terms a President might serve. Presidents Washington and Jefferson, however, decided against a third term. This practice became an unwritten custom observed by succeeding Presidents until 1940, when Franklin D. Roosevelt was elected for a third term. This amendment did not apply to President Truman, who was in office when it was adopted.

shall meet in the District and perform such duties as provided by the twelfth article of amendment.[34]

Section 2. Enforcement. The Congress shall have power to enforce this article by appropriate legislation.

Amendment 24 *(1964). Poll Tax Prohibited*

Section 1. Prohibition in National Elections. The right of citizens of the United States to vote in any primary or other election for President or Vice President, for electors for President or Vice President, or for senator or representative in Congress, shall not be denied or abridged by the United States or any state by reason of failure to pay any poll tax or other tax.[35]

Section 2. Enforcement. The Congress shall have power to enforce this article by appropriate legislation.

Amendment 25 *(1967). Presidential Disability*

Section 1. Succession of the Vice President. In case of the removal of the President from office or of his death or resignation, the Vice President shall become President.[36]

Section 2. Replacing the Vice President. Whenever there is a vacancy in the office of the Vice President, the President shall nominate a Vice President who shall take office upon confirmation by a majority vote of both Houses of Congress.[37]

Section 3. The Vice President as Acting President. Whenever the President transmits to the President pro tempore of the Senate and the Speaker of the House of Representatives his written declaration that he is unable to discharge the powers and duties of his office, and until he transmits to them a written declaration to the contrary, such powers and duties shall be discharged by the Vice President as Acting President.[38]

Section 4. Determining Presidential Disability. Whenever the Vice President and a majority of either the principal officers of the executive departments or of such other body as Congress may by law provide, transmit to the President pro tempore of the Senate and the Speaker of the House of Representatives their written declaration that the President is unable to discharge the powers and duties of his office, the Vice President shall immediately assume the powers and duties of the office as Acting President.[39]

34. Amendment 23 permits residents of Washington, D.C., to vote in presidential elections. Before this amendment was adopted, they had not voted for President, because the Constitution provided that only states should choose presidential electors.

35. No citizen may be prevented from voting in a national election because of not having paid a poll tax or other tax.

36. Vice Presidents have always assumed the full powers of office when the President died.

37. In the unlikely event that the President and Vice President died or were incapacitated at the same time, the Speaker of the House would be next in line, followed by the President pro tem of the Senate and the members of the President's Cabinet in order as their offices were created.

38. The President can acknowledge incapacity and temporarily assign all functions to the Vice President.

39. If the President is incapacitated but unable or unwilling so to inform Congress, the Vice President and a majority of the Cabinet can take this action.

Thereafter, when the President transmits to the President pro tempore of the Senate and the Speaker of the House of Representatives his written declaration that no inability exists, he shall resume the powers and duties of his office unless the Vice President and a majority of either the principal officers of the executive department or of such other body as Congress may by law provide, transmit within four days to the President pro tempore of the Senate and the Speaker of the House of Representatives their written declaration that the President is unable to discharge the powers and duties of his office.[40] Thereupon, Congress shall decide the issue, assembling within forty-eight hours for that purpose, if not in session. If the Congress, within twenty-one days after receipt of the latter written declaration, or, if Congress is not in session, within twenty-one days after Congress is required to assemble, determines by two-thirds vote of both Houses that the President is unable to discharge the powers and duties of his office, the Vice President shall continue to discharge the same as Acting President; otherwise, the President shall resume the powers and duties of his office.

40. Note that the Vice President and a majority of the Cabinet can override the President's decision to resume duties. Congress, however, must agree with this judgment.

Amendment 26 *(1971). Lowering the Voting Age*

Section 1. Eighteen-year-olds may vote. The right of citizens of the United States who are eighteen years of age or older to vote shall not be denied or abridged by the United States or by any state on account of age.[41]

Section 2. Enforcement. The Congress shall have power to enforce this article by appropriate legislation.

41. This amendment was adopted because the Supreme Court had ruled that the Voting Rights Act of 1970 permitted eighteen-year-olds to vote only in the elections of federal officials.

Proposed Amendment 27. *Equal Rights for Women*

Section 1. No abridgment of rights. Equality of rights under the law shall not be denied or abridged by the United States or by any state on account of sex.[42]

Section 2. Enforcement. The Congress shall have the power to enforce, by appropriate legislation, the provisions of this article.

Section 3. Effective date. This amendment shall take effect two years after the date of ratification.

42. This amendment was approved by Congress in March 1972 and put before the states for ratification.

NO.	PRESIDENT	TERM	PARTY	ELECTED FROM	DEEDS AND HAPPENINGS
1.	George Washington (1732–1799)	1789–1797	None	Virginia	Set countless precedents (form of address, the Cabinet). Demanded respect for office.
2.	John Adams (1735–1826)	1797–1801	Federalist	Massachusetts	Made peace with France, putting nation above party. First occupant of White House.
3.	Thomas Jefferson (1743–1826)	1801–1809	Democratic–Republican	Virginia	Expanded executive power by Barbary "war," Louisiana Purchase. Set two-term tradition.
4.	James Madison (1751–1836)	1809–1817	Democratic–Republican	Virginia	Accepted some views of his foe Hamilton (tariff, Bank). Driven from capital by British.
5.	James Monroe (1758–1831)	1817–1825	Democratic–Republican	Virginia	Monroe Doctrine set course of Latin American relations. Redid White House in French style.
6.	John Quincy Adams (1767–1848)	1825–1829	National–Republican	Massachusetts	Able, experienced, well-prepared, but a poor politician. Only son of a President to serve.
7.	Andrew Jackson (1767–1845)	1829–1837	Democratic	Tennessee	First westerner, first "outsider." A strong, personal administration. Acted with firmness.
8.	Martin Van Buren (1782–1862)	1837–1841	Democratic	New York	A clever politician. Not re-elected because of a depression. Later a strong free-soiler.
9.	William H. Harrison (1773–1841)	1841	Whig	Ohio	Served only one month. Oldest ever elected (67). First to die in office.
10.	John Tyler (1790–1862)	1841–1845	Whig	Virginia	First Vice President to succeed to office. Won "squatter" rights to public lands.
11.	James K. Polk (1795–1849)	1845–1849	Democratic	Tennessee	Settled Oregon dispute, reduced tariff, acquired California and Southwest from Mexico.
12.	Zachary Taylor (1784–1850)	1849–1850	Whig	Louisiana	Hero of Mexican War. Last slaveowner to serve, but opposed Compromise of 1850.
13.	Millard Fillmore (1800–1874)	1850–1853	Whig	New York	Accepted Compromise of 1850. Fugitive Slave Law. Denied nomination in 1852.
14.	Franklin Pierce (1804–1869)	1853–1857	Democratic	New Hampshire	Gadsden Purchase. Accepted Kansas-Nebraska Bill. Neglected "Bleeding Kansas."
15.	James Buchanan (1791–1868)	1857–1861	Democratic	Pennsylvania	Under southern influence. Could not stop secession. Only unmarried President.
16.	Abraham Lincoln (1809–1865)	1861–1865	Republican	Illinois	One of the great Presidents. Saved the Union and ended slavery. First to be assassinated.
17.	Andrew Johnson (1808–1875)	1865–1869	Republican	Tennessee	Unable to deal with Congress or solve Reconstruction problems. Impeached.
18.	Ulysses S. Grant (1822–1885)	1869–1877	Republican	Illinois	A failure as President. His Administration was corrupt, but did begin civil service reform.
19.	Rutherford B. Hayes (1822–1893)	1877–1881	Republican	Ohio	Ended Reconstruction. An upright man, but may have benefited from a "stolen" election.
20.	James A. Garfield (1831–1881)	1881	Republican	Ohio	Last President born in a log cabin. Assassinated by disappointed office-seeker.
21.	Chester A. Arthur (1830–1886)	1881–1885	Republican	New York	Continued civil service reform. Vetoed Chinese Exclusion.
22.	Grover Cleveland (1837–1908)	1885–1889	Democratic	New York	Tried to reduce tariff and help the South. Defeated by electoral, not popular, vote.
23.	Benjamin Harrison (1833–1901)	1889–1893	Republican	Indiana	Grandson of ninth President. Favored high tariffs and generous pensions.
24.	Grover Cleveland (1837–1908)	1893–1897	Democratic	New York	Only President to serve a split term. Favored gold standard. Blamed for depression.

NO.	PRESIDENT	TERM	PARTY	ELECTED FROM	DEEDS AND HAPPENINGS
25.	William McKinley (1843–1901)	1897–1901	Republican	Ohio	Favored big business, high tariffs, and imperialism. Assassinated.
26.	Theodore Roosevelt (1858–1919)	1901–1909	Republican	New York	Understood and tried to deal with problems of industrial era. Youngest to serve (42).
27.	William H. Taft (1857–1930)	1909–1913	Republican	Ohio	A disappointment to progressives, but pursued antitrust action. First presidential golfer.
28.	Woodrow Wilson (1856–1924)	1913–1921	Democratic	New Jersey	Successful domestic program. Led nation to victory in World War, but failed at peace.
29.	Warren G. Harding (1865–1923)	1921–1923	Republican	Ohio	A corrupt Administration, like Grant's. Some excellent Cabinet appointments.
30.	Calvin Coolidge (1872–1933)	1923–1929	Republican	Massachusetts	An inactive President, but highly popular. Left office just before 1929 crash.
31.	Herbert Hoover (1874–1964)	1929–1933	Republican	California	Able and experienced but did not understand politics. Failed to deal with depression.
32.	Franklin D. Roosevelt (1882–1945)	1933–1945	Democratic	New York	Depression and World War II President. Set new government/business relations.
33.	Harry S. Truman (1884–1972)	1945–1953	Democratic	Missouri	Served during postwar readjustments, Cold War. Made decision to use atom bomb.
34.	Dwight D. Eisenhower (1890–1969)	1953–1961	Republican	New York	Tried to ease Cold War and reduce spending at home. Oldest to serve (70 at term's end).
35.	John F. Kennedy (1917–1963)	1961–1963	Democratic	Massachusetts	Youngest ever elected (43). Wanted a more active Presidency. Assassinated.
36.	Lyndon B. Johnson (1908–1973)	1963–1969	Democratic	Texas	Ambitious program of social legislation bogged down by Vietnam War.
37.	Richard M. Nixon (1913–)	1969–1974	Republican	New York	Opened relations with China, eased tensions with USSR. Watergate scandal. Resigned.
38.	Gerald R. Ford (1913–)	1974–1977	Republican	Michigan	First "non-elected" President (under Twenty-fifth Amendment).
39.	Jimmy Carter (1924–)	1977–	Democratic	Georgia	First since Taylor from Deep South. First since Wilson with no Washington experience.

1488	Portuguese round the tip of Africa.
1492	Columbus makes his first voyage.
1513	Ponce de León discovers Florida.
1519	Cortés finds Mexico City.
1565	St. Augustine, Florida, founded.
1585	First English colony started.
1588	Spanish Armada defeated.
1603	Champlain explores the northeast.
1607	Jamestown founded.
1608	French found Quebec.
1619	House of Burgesses meets.
1619	First blacks arrive at Jamestown.
1620	Plymouth founded.
1624	Dutch establish New Amsterdam.
1630	Puritans settle Boston.
1664	English take New Netherland.
1692	Witchcraft trials held in Massachusetts.
1704	Boston *News-letter* appears.
1735	John Peter Zenger tried for libel.
1759	Wolfe captures Quebec.
1763	Britain controls North America.
1765	Stamp Act Congress meets.
1773	Boston Tea Party held.
1775	Fighting breaks out between colonists and British.
1775	Washington commands Continental Army.
1775	Quakers start first American antislavery society.
1776	Independence declared.
1777	Battle of Saratoga won.
1777	Congress proposes Articles of Confederation.
1778	French Alliance signed.
1781	Virginia leads in giving up western lands.
1781	Cornwallis surrenders at Yorktown.
1783	Treaty of Paris signed.
1785	Land ordinance adopted for Northwest.
1786	Annapolis Convention meets.
1786	Shays' Rebellion takes place in Massachusetts.
1787	Constitutional Convention meets.
1788	Constitution ratified.
1789	Washington inaugurated. New government begins.
1790	Public debt reorganized.
1791	Bill of Rights ratified.
1793	Eli Whitney invents cotton gin.
1794	Western Pennsylvania farmers rebel.
1795	Jay's, Pinckney's, and the Greenville Treaties ratified.
1796	John Adams elected second President.
1798	Alien and Sedition Acts passed; Kentucky and Virginia Resolutions adopted.
1800	Undeclared war with France ended.

1801	Jefferson elected third President.
1803	*Marbury v. Madison* decided.
1803	Louisiana purchased from France.
1804	Lewis and Clark expedition begins.
1805	Britain begins seizing U.S. ships.
1807	Aaron Burr tried for treason.
1807	*Leopard* attacks *Chesapeake.*
1807	Embargo stops trade with Europe.
1808	Madison elected fourth President.
1811	Tecumseh defeated at Tippecanoe.
1812	Second war with England begins.
1813	Francis Lowell organizes the Boston Manufacturing Company.
1814	Capital attacked and burned.
1815	Treaty of Ghent ends war.
1816	Second U.S. Bank chartered.
1816	American Colonization Society founded.
1816	James Monroe elected fifth President.
1818	Jackson invades East Florida.
1819	Adams-Onís Treaty is signed.
1820	Missouri Compromise agreed upon.
1822	Americans begin settling Texas.
1823	Monroe Doctrine announced.
1824	John Quincy Adams elected sixth President.
1825	Erie Canal completed.
1828	Tariff of Abominations passed.
1828	Andrew Jackson elected seventh President.
1831	William Lloyd Garrison begins publishing *Liberator.*
1831	Nat Turner leads slave uprising.
1832	Nullification threatens Union.
1832	Jackson vetoes Second Bank charter.
1835	Newspaper first uses term "manifest destiny."
1836	Congress adopts "gag rule."
1836	Cherokee moved to Oklahoma.
1836	Jackson issues Specie Circular.
1836	Martin Van Buren elected eighth President.
1836	Texas wins independence from Mexico.
1837	Business panic breaks out.
1840	William Henry Harrison elected ninth President.
1841	John Tyler becomes tenth President.
1842	Webster-Ashburton Treaty negotiated.
1842	*Commonwealth v. Hunt* gives labor right to organize.
1844	James Polk elected eleventh President.
1845	United States annexes Texas.
1846	Oregon dispute settled.
1846	Elias Howe invents sewing machine.
1846	War with Mexico begun.
1848	Seneca Falls Convention meets.
1848	Zachary Taylor elected twelfth President.

1848	Treaty of Guadalupe-Hidalgo ends war with Mexico.	1877	Rutherford B. Hayes elected nineteenth President.

1848   Treaty of Guadalupe-Hidalgo ends war with Mexico.

1850   Millard Fillmore becomes thirteenth President.

1850   Congress passes Compromise of 1850.

1851   William Kelly develops blast furnace.

1852   Franklin Pierce elected fourteenth President.

1853   Congress authorizes mapping of transcontinental railroad routes.

1854   Stephen A. Douglas introduces Kansas-Nebraska Bill. Republican Party is born.

1856   James Buchanan elected fifteenth President.

1856   Civil War breaks out in Kansas.

1857   Chief Justice Roger Taney announces Dred Scott decision.

1857   Hinton R. Helper publishes *The Impending Crisis of the South.*

1858   Lincoln and Douglas debate in Illinois.

1859   John Brown raids arsenal at Harper's Ferry.

1860   Abraham Lincoln elected sixteenth President.

1860   South Carolina secedes from Union.

1861   Six states follow South Carolina. Confederate States of America formed.

1861   Fort Sumter fired upon. First Battle of Bull Run is fought.

1862   McClellan tries to take Richmond. *Monitor* meets *Merrimac (Virginia).*

1862   Homestead Act passed.

1863   Emancipation Proclamation goes into effect.

1863   South loses at Gettysburg and Vicksburg.

1864   Sherman marches to sea.

1865   Lee surrenders to Grant. Lincoln assassinated.

1865   Andrew Johnson becomes seventeenth President.

1867   Congress passes First Reconstruction Act.

1867   Alaska purchased.

1868   President Johnson impeached.

1868   The Fourteenth Amendment ratified.

1869   Ulysses S. Grant becomes eighteenth President.

1869   American Woman Suffrage and the National Woman Suffrage Associations founded.

1869   First transcontinental railroad finished.

1871   Treaty of Washington signed.

1873   Treasury stops buying silver.

1876   Sioux and Cheyenne defeat Seventh U.S. Cavalry.

1876   Disputed Tilden-Hayes election held.

1877   *Munn v. Illinois* upholds Granger laws.

1877   Last federal troops withdrawn from South.

1877   Rutherford B. Hayes elected nineteenth President.

1878   California ceases to be officially bilingual.

1878   Bland-Allison Silver Purchase Act passed.

1880   James A. Garfield elected twentieth President.

1881   Chester A. Arthur becomes twenty-first President.

1882   Standard Oil Trust is organized.

1882   Congress bars "undesirables" from immigration.

1884   Grover Cleveland elected twenty-second President.

1886   *Wabash v. Illinois* reverses *Munn.*

1886   Haymarket riot alarms nation.

1886   AFL established.

1887   Dawes Allotment Act passed.

1887   Interstate Commerce Commission formed.

1887   Electric streetcars appear in Richmond, Virginia.

1888   Benjamin Harrison elected twenty-third President.

1889   Jane Addams founds Hull House.

1890   Sherman Antitrust Act passed.

1890   Sherman Silver Purchase Act passed.

1892   Populists adopt Omaha Platform.

1892   Grover Cleveland elected twenty-fourth President.

1893   Sherman Silver Purchase Act repealed.

1894   President Cleveland intervenes in Pullman strike.

1895   Booker T. Washington proposes the "Atlanta Compromise."

1895   *U.S. v. E. C. Knight* undermines Sherman Act.

1896   Supreme Court establishes "separate but equal doctrine."

1896   McKinley wins "free silver" election. Becomes twenty-fifth President.

1898   Spanish-American War fought.

1898   Hawaii annexed.

1898   U.S. acquires Puerto Rico, Guam, and the Philippines.

1899   Open Door Policy announced.

1901   U.S. Steel becomes first billion-dollar corporation.

1901   McKinley is assassinated; Theodore Roosevelt becomes twenty-sixth President.

1902   Phillippine Insurrection ended.

1902   Chinese exclusion made permanent.

1902   Northern Securities Case filed.

1902   Newlands Act passed.

1902	Anthracite coal strike settled.
1903	Panama Canal Treaties signed.
1904	Roosevelt Corollary stated.
1905	Treaty of Portsmouth negotiated.
1906	NAACP founded.
1906	Algeciras Conference held.
1906	"Gentlemen's Agreement" reached.
1906	Hepburn Act passed.
1906	Pure Food and Drug Act and Meat Inspection Acts passed.
1907	Work begun on Panama Canal.
1908	Taft elected twenty-seventh President.
1912	Wilson elected twenty-eighth President.
1913	Income Tax and Senate Election Amendments ratified.
1913	Federal Reserve Act passed.
1914	Clayton Antitrust Act passed.
1914	World War I begins.
1915	*Lusitania* sunk.
1915	Ku Klux Klan reorganized.
1916	Germany makes *Sussex* pledge.
1916	Pancho Villa raids New Mexico.
1916	Wilson re-elected.
1917	Literacy test for immigrants adopted.
1917	Germany resumes unrestricted submarine warfare.
1917	Zimmermann telegram revealed.
1917	United States declares war.
1918	AEF goes into battle.
1918	Armistice signed.
1919	Paris Conference meets.
1919	Prohibition Amendment ratified.
1919	Race riots break out in northern cities.
1920	Marcus Garvey's Universal Negro Improvement Society meets in New York.
1920	Senate rejects Versailles Treaty for last time.
1920	Women's Suffrage Amendment ratified.
1920	Warren Harding elected twenty-ninth President.
1921	Washington Armament Conference meets.
1923	Harding dies. Calvin Coolidge becomes thirtieth President.
1924	Teapot Dome Scandal erupts.
1924	National Origins Act adopted.
1927	Stock market boom begins.
1928	Kellogg-Briand Pact signed.
1928	United States announces end of Roosevelt Corollary.
1928	Herbert Hoover elected thirty-first President.
1929	Stock market crashes.

1931	Hoover declares war-debt moratorium.
1931	Japan invades Manchuria.
1932	Stimson Doctrine proclaimed.
1932	Norris-LaGuardia Act signed.
1932	Bonus Marchers reach Washington.
1932	Franklin D. Roosevelt elected thirty-second President.
1933	New Deal begins.
1933	Bank Holiday declared.
1933	NRA, AAA, and other emergency New Deal legislation passed.
1933	United States adopts Good Neighbor Policy toward other American nations.
1935	WPA, Wagner Act, and Social Security Act passed.
1935	NRA declared unconstitutional.
1935	Italy conquers Ethiopia. First Neutrality Act passed.
1936	AAA declared unconstitutional.
1936	Germany and Italy give aid to Franco.
1937	Japan launches full-scale war on China. "Cash and carry" policy adopted.
1937	Roosevelt fails to change Supreme Court.
1938	Fair Labor Standards Act passed.
1938	Hitler invades Austria and Czechoslovakia.
1939	Germany and Soviet Union invade Poland; World War II begins.
1940	France surrenders to Germany. United States begins to mobilize. Roosevelt wins third term.
1941	Lend-Lease Act passed.
1941	Germany invades USSR.
1941	Japan attacks Pearl Harbor.
1942	Allies stop Axis forces in Pacific, Africa, and USSR.
1943	Italy falls.
1944	Allies invade Normandy.
1944	Roosevelt wins fourth term.
1944	Philippines retaken.
1945	Yalta Conference held.
1945	FDR dies. Harry Truman becomes thirty-third President.
1945	United Nations established.
1945	Potsdam Conference divides Germany.
1945	World War II ends.
1946	Employment Act passed.
1947	Congress passes Taft-Hartley Act.
1947	United States undertakes policy of containment.
1947	Truman Doctrine announced.

1947	Marshall Plan launched.
1948	Soviets blockade Berlin. Airlift undertaken.
1948	Truman wins second term.
1949	Communist forces take over China.
1949	Soviets explode atom bomb.
1949	NATO Treaty signed.
1950	North Korea invades South Korea. United States sends troops.
1952	Dwight D. Eisenhower elected thirty-fourth President.
1953	Korean conflict ended.
1954	Army-McCarthy hearings held.
1954	Supreme Court hands down *Brown* decision.
1955	"Big Four" conference held at Geneva.
1955	Montgomery bus boycott launched.
1955	U.S. sends military advisers to Vietnam.
1956	Highway Act passed.
1956	Crisis occurs over Suez Canal.
1956	Hungarians revolt against Soviet rule.
1957	Eisenhower Doctrine announced.
1957	Little Rock Central High School integrated by federal order.
1957	Soviets send up first Sputnik.
1958	U.S. Marines land in Lebanon.
1959	Castro takes over in Cuba.
1959	Nikita Khrushchev visits United States.
1960	The USSR shoots down U.S. spy plane.
1960	John F. Kennedy is elected thirty-fifth President.
1961	CIA-planned invasion of Cuba fails.

1961	Berlin Wall built.
1962	University of Mississippi desegregated.
1962	Cuban missile crisis threatens war.
1963	Martin Luther King, Jr., leads marches on Birmingham and Washington.
1963	Kennedy assassinated. Lyndon Johnson becomes thirty-sixth President.
1964	Johnson launches war on poverty.
1964	Tonkin Gulf Resolution adopted.
1965	Watts riots occur.
1967	Newark and Detroit erupt.
1968	Tet offensive takes place.
1968	Martin Luther King, Jr., assassinated.
1968	Robert Kennedy assassinated.
1968	Richard Nixon elected thirty-seventh President.
1969	My Lai incident revealed.
1969	First moon landing made.
1969	Nixon announces Vietnamization policy.
1970	Kent State tragedy occurs.
1972	Nixon visits Communist China.
1972	Nixon visits Moscow.
1972	Equal Rights Amendment passes Congress.
1972	Watergate break-in takes place. Nixon re-elected.
1973	Watergate investigation begins.
1974	President Nixon resigns. Gerald Ford becomes thirty-eighth President.
1976	Nation celebrates its Bicentennial.
1976	Jimmy Carter elected thirty-ninth President.

DEPENDENCIES

Dependency	Date of Acquisition	Population (1970 Census)	Area in Square Miles	Capital or Principal City
Puerto Rico	1899	2,712,033	3,435	San Juan
Guam	1899	84,996	212	Agana
American Samoa	1900	27,159	76	Pago Pago
Panama Canal Zone	1904	44,198	553	Balboa
Virgin Islands	1917	62,468	133	Charlotte Amalie
		2,930,854	4,409	

No.	State Name	Date of Admission	Population (1970 Census)	No. of Representatives (1977)	Area in Square Miles	Capital
1	Delaware	1787	548,104	1	2,057	Dover
2	Pennsylvania	1787	11,793,909	25	45,333	Harrisburg
3	New Jersey	1787	7,168,164	15	7,836	Trenton
4	Georgia	1788	4,589,575	10	58,876	Atlanta
5	Connecticut	1788	3,032,217	6	5,009	Hartford
6	Massachusetts	1788	5,689,170	12	8,257	Boston
7	Maryland	1788	3,922,399	8	10,577	Annapolis
8	South Carolina	1788	2,590,516	6	31,055	Columbia
9	New Hampshire	1788	737,681	2	9,304	Concord
10	Virginia	1788	4,648,494	10	40,817	Richmond
11	New York	1788	18,190,740	39	49,576	Albany
12	North Carolina	1789	5,082,059	11	52,586	Raleigh
13	Rhode Island	1790	949,723	2	1,214	Providence
14	Vermont	1791	444,732	1	9,609	Montpelier
15	Kentucky	1792	3,219,311	7	40,395	Frankfort
16	Tennessee	1796	3,924,164	8	42,244	Nashville
17	Ohio	1803	10,652,017	23	41,222	Columbus
18	Louisiana	1812	3,643,180	8	48,523	Baton Rouge
19	Indiana	1816	5,193,669	11	36,291	Indianapolis
20	Mississippi	1817	2,216,912	5	47,716	Jackson
21	Illinois	1818	11,113,976	24	56,400	Springfield
22	Alabama	1819	3,444,165	7	51,609	Montgomery
23	Maine	1820	993,663	2	33,215	Augusta
24	Missouri	1821	4,677,399	10	69,686	Jefferson City
25	Arkansas	1836	1,923,295	4	53,104	Little Rock
26	Michigan	1837	8,875,083	19	58,216	Lansing
27	Florida	1845	6,789,443	15	58,560	Tallahassee
28	Texas	1845	11,196,730	24	267,338	Austin
29	Iowa	1846	2,825,041	6	56,290	Des Moines
30	Wisconsin	1848	4,417,933	9	56,154	Madison
31	California	1850	19,953,134	43	158,693	Sacramento
32	Minnesota	1858	3,805,069	8	84,068	St. Paul
33	Oregon	1859	2,091,385	4	96,981	Salem
34	Kansas	1861	2,249,071	5	82,264	Topeka
35	West Virginia	1863	1,744,237	4	24,181	Charleston
36	Nevada	1864	488,738	1	110,540	Carson City
37	Nebraska	1867	1,483,791	3	77,227	Lincoln
38	Colorado	1876	2,207,259	5	104,247	Denver
39	North Dakota	1889	617,761	1	70,665	Bismarck
40	South Dakota	1889	666,257	2	77,047	Pierre
41	Montana	1889	694,409	2	147,138	Helena
42	Washington	1889	3,409,169	7	68,192	Olympia
43	Idaho	1890	713,008	2	83,557	Boise
44	Wyoming	1890	332,416	1	97,914	Cheyenne
45	Utah	1896	1,059,273	2	84,916	Salt Lake City
46	Oklahoma	1907	2,559,253	6	69,919	Oklahoma City
47	New Mexico	1912	1,016,000	2	121,666	Santa Fe
48	Arizona	1912	1,772,482	4	113,909	Phoenix
49	Alaska	1959	302,173	1	586,412	Juneau
50	Hawaii	1959	769,913	2	6,450	Honolulu
	District of Columbia		756,510	1 (non-voting)	67	
			203,184,772	435	3,615,122	

745

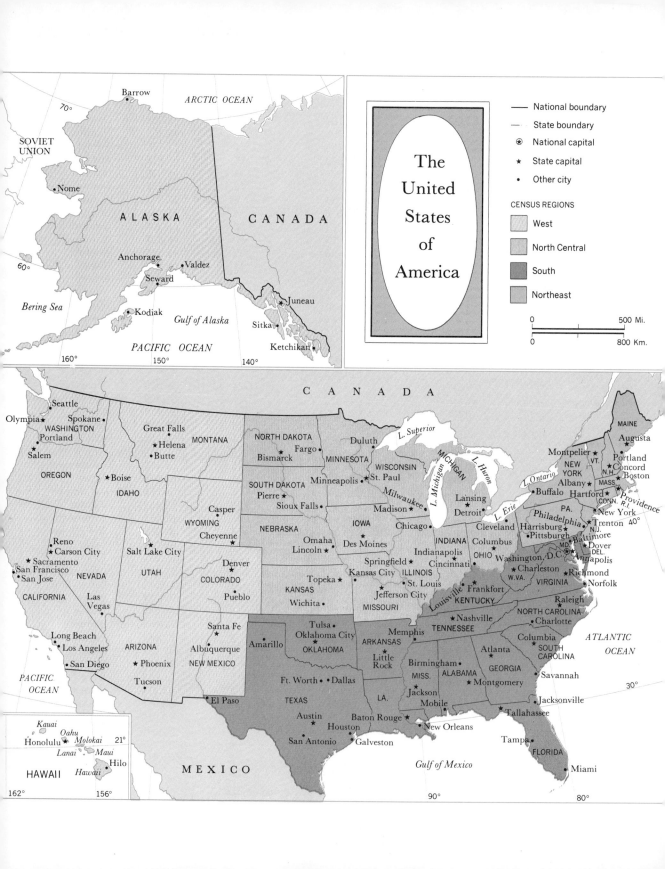

The United States of America

ARCTIC OCEAN

SOVIET UNION

70°

Barrow

Nome

ALASKA

CANADA

60°

Anchorage
Valdez
Seward

Bering Sea

Kodiak

Gulf of Alaska

Juneau

Sitka

PACIFIC OCEAN

Ketchikan

160°   150°   140°

National boundary
State boundary
National capital
State capital
Other city

CENSUS REGIONS
West
North Central
South
Northeast

0   500 Mi.
0   800 Km.

CANADA

Seattle
Olympia ★
WASHINGTON
Portland
Salem
OREGON

Spokane

Great Falls

MONTANA
★ Helena
Butte

★ Boise
IDAHO

NORTH DAKOTA
Fargo
Bismarck
MINNESOTA

Duluth

L. Superior

SOUTH DAKOTA
Pierre ★
Sioux Falls

WISCONSIN
Minneapolis ★ St. Paul
Milwaukee

L. Michigan

MICHIGAN

L. Huron

MAINE
Augusta

Montpelier ★
NEW
YORK
VT.
Portland
Concord
N.H.
Boston

Lansing
Detroit

L. Ontario
Albany
Buffalo
Hartford
MASS.
Providence
R.I.
CONN.

Reno
Carson City ★
Sacramento ★
San Francisco
San Jose
NEVADA

Salt Lake City ★
UTAH

Casper
WYOMING
Cheyenne ★

NEBRASKA
Omaha
Lincoln ★

IOWA
Des Moines

Madison ★

Chicago

INDIANA
Indianapolis ★

Columbus
OHIO

Cleveland
L. Erie
Pittsburgh

PA.
Harrisburg ★
Philadelphia

New York

Trenton
N.J.
40°

CALIFORNIA

Las
Vegas

Denver ★
COLORADO
Pueblo

Topeka ★
KANSAS
Wichita

Kansas City
ILLINOIS
Springfield ★
St. Louis
Jefferson City ★
MISSOURI

Cincinnati

Louisville
Frankfort ★
KENTUCKY

Washington, D.C.
Annapolis
MD.
Dover
DEL.

Charleston
W.VA.
VIRGINIA
Richmond
Norfolk

Long Beach
Los Angeles
San Diego

ARIZONA
★ Phoenix
Tucson

Santa Fe ★
Albuquerque
NEW MEXICO

Amarillo

Tulsa
Oklahoma City ★
OKLAHOMA

Memphis
ARKANSAS
Little
Rock

Nashville
TENNESSEE

NORTH CAROLINA
Raleigh ★
Charlotte

Columbia ★
SOUTH
CAROLINA

Raleigh

ATLANTIC
OCEAN

PACIFIC
OCEAN

El Paso

TEXAS

Ft. Worth Dallas

Austin ★
San Antonio

Houston
Galveston

LA.
Jackson ★
MISS.
Baton Rouge ★

Birmingham
ALABAMA
★ Montgomery
Mobile

Atlanta ★
GEORGIA

Savannah

Jacksonville

New Orleans

Tallahassee ★

Tampa

30°

Kauai
Oahu
Honolulu ★ Molokai
Lanai Maui
Hilo
HAWAII Hawaii

21°

MEXICO

Gulf of Mexico

FLORIDA
Miami

162°   156°

90°   80°

cover photograph—Elliot Erwitt, Magnum; painting—Joseph H. Hindley, VIEW OF POESTENKILL, NEW YORK, c. 1855 (detail), The Metropolitan Museum of Art, Gift of Edgar William and Bernice Chrysler Garbisch, 1963; sculpture—(front) Collection of Michael and Julie Hall, photograph The Brooklyn Museum, (back) Collection of Mrs. Jacob Kaplan

Maps by Dick Sanderson

Contents and Appendix art from pages 51, 196, 317, 400, 516, 556, 688, 87, 291, 256, 615, 598

1 FLAG GATE, Museum of American Folk Art, NYC

2–3 de Woiserie, NEW ORLEANS, 1803, Chicago Historical Society (detail)

14–15 Albert Bierstadt, WIND RIVER COUNTRY, 1860, Photo the Kennedy Galleries, courtesy of Mr. and Mrs. Britt Brown (detail)

16–17 John White, the Trustees of The British Museum (detail)

18 the Trustees of The British Museum

21 (top and bottom right) Museum of the American Indian; (bottom left) courtesy the Frank H. McClung Museum, University of Tennessee

22 Museum of the American Indian, Heye Foundation

28 the Trustees of The British Museum

28–29 the Trustees of The British Museum

30 Museum of the American Indian, Heye Foundation

31 courtesy Museum of Cultural History, Los Angeles, Photo by Susan Einstein

33 Rare Book Division, New York Public Library, Astor, Lenox and Tilden Foundations

35 John White, 'SECOTAN,' 1587, the Trustees of The British Museum (detail)

37 (top) The Metropolitan Museum of Art; (bottom) the Trustees of The British Museum

38 Meynell, slave deck, mid-19th century, National Maritime Museum, London

42 I. Obel Planatarum ser Stripirmin, 1576

46 Department of Antiquities, Ashmolean Museum, Oxford

49 Peabody Museum, Salem, Photo Mark Sexton

51 Philadelphia Museum of Art, Given by John T. Morris

53 New York Public Library

56 Embroidery, anonymous American, Museum of Fine Arts, Boston, M. and M. Karolik Collection

59 THE PLANTATION c. 1825, The Metropolitan Museum of Art, Gift of Edgar William and Bernice Chrysler Garbisch, 1963 (detail)

60 (top) Prints Division, New York Public Library, I. N. Phelps Stokes Collection

61 (top) Sinclair Hamilton Collection, Princeton University

60–61 (bottom) The New York State

Historical Association, Cooperstown (detail)

63 Ann Parker and Avon Neal

64 Johnson, OLDTIME SCHOOLS AND SCHOOL BOOKS, 1904

65 The National Gallery of Art

68 Private Collection

72 Bohdan Hrynewych

73 ANCO

80 W. D. Cooper, HISTORY OF NORTH AMERICA (London, 1789) (detail)

81 (portrait only) courtesy the Massachusetts Historical Society (detail)

83 unknown American artist, Attack on Bunker's Hill, with the Burning of Charlestown, The National Gallery of Art, Washington, Gift of Edgar William and Bernice Chrysler Garbisch (detail)

86 Metropolitan Museum of Art

87 All from Anne S. K. Brown Military Collection, Brown University Library, Providence, R.I.

88 The Rhode Island Historical Society

89 J. O. J. Frost, Glover's Marblehead Regiment, private collection

92 Concord Antiquarian Society (detail from a lace handkerchief)

93 Anne S. K. Brown Military Collection, Brown University Library, Providence, R.I.

96 The New-York Historical Society

98 (top) Peabody Museum, Salem (detail); (bottom) courtesy The Henry Francis du Pont Winterthur Museum

99 The London *Times*

102 ANCO

105 Free Library of Philadelphia

109 The Historical Society of Pennsylvania (detail)

112 The Metropolitan Museum of Art, Rogers Fund, 1945

118–119 L. M. Cooke, SALUTE TO GENERAL WASHINGTON IN NEW YORK HARBOR, The National Gallery of Art, Washington, Gift of Edgar William and Bernice Chrysler Garbisch (detail)

120 American Antiquarian Society

122 Amos Doolittle after Peter Lacour, 1790, Prints Division, New York Public Library, Astor, Lenox and Tilden Foundations, I. N. Phelps Stokes Collection

123 New York State Historical Association, Cooperstown

125 The New-York Historical Society

127 American Antiquarian Society

128 (both) American Antiquarian Society

131 J. Peale, WASHINGTON REVIEWING THE WESTERN ARMY AT FT. CUMBERLAND, MARYLAND, 1794, The Metropolitan Museum of Art, Gift of Edgar William and Bernice Chrysler Garbisch (detail)

136 University of Hartford Collection

138 Courtesy Vermont Historical Society

142 Jefferson Flag, 1800, Smithsonian Institution

145 Library of Congress (detail)

147 (left) Horned toad, collected by Lewis and Clark, drawn by C. W. Peale, American Philosophical Society; (right) pheasant of the Rockies from the journals of Lewis and Clark Expedition, Missouri Historical Society

148 (top) Rare Book Division, The New York Public Library, Astor, Lenox and Tilden Foundations; (bottom) The National Gallery of Art

149 THE QUILTING PARTY, c. 1854, artist unknown, Abby Aldrich Rockefeller Folk Art Collection, Williamsburg, Virginia

153 Rare Book Division, The New York Public Library, Astor, Lenox, and Tilden Foundations

155 U.S. Constitution, Peabody Museum, Salem

159 Yale University Art Gallery, Mabel Brady Garvan Collection

160 Library of Congress

164 BUNKERHILL, 1838, Huge, Courtesy of the Mariner's Museum, Newport News, Virginia (detail)

169 Massachusetts mail stage line, based on 1815 poster, Museum of Fine Arts, Boston, M. and M. Karolik Collection

170 The New-York Historical Society (detail)

171 Mary Keys, LOCKPORT ON ERIE CANAL, NY, 1832, Munson-Williams-Proctor Institute, Utica, New York

173 Prints Division, I. N. Phelps Stokes Collection, New York Public Library, Astor, Lenox and Tilden Foundations

174 ANCO

178 University of Hartford Collection

183 "We Go For the Union," anonymous artist, The National Gallery of Art, Gift of Edgar William and Bernice Chrysler Garbisch (detail)

186 George Caleb Bingham, CANVASSING FOR A VOTE, 1852, Collection of William Rockhill Nelson Gallery of Art, Atkins Museum of Fine Arts, Kansas City, Missouri (detail)

188 J. H. Whitcomb, OUR PRESIDENT—OLD HICKORY, Museum of Fine Arts, Boston, M. and M. Karolik Collection

193 Mark F. Boyd Collection, Otto G. Richter Library, University of Miami

195 (top) Kansas State Historical Society; (bottom) The Chase Manhattan Bank, Numismatic Collection

196 The Mattatuck Museum, Waterbury, Connecticut

198 E. W. Clay, METHODIST CAMP MEETING, 1836, The New-York Historical Society (detail)

200 (top) Gift of Miss Lucy T. Aldrick, Museum of Art, Rhode Island School of Design; (bottom) QUAKER MEETING, c. 1790, Museum of Fine Arts, Boston, Bequest of Maxim Karolik (detail)

203 (top) anonymous American, THE WATERCOLOR CLASS, the Art Institute of Chicago, The Emily Crane

748

426-427 Library of Congress
428 Courtesy of Michael and Julie Hall
433 Chicago Historical Society, MAINE, 1898
434 Chicago Historical Society, BATTLE OF SAN JUAN, 1899
436 (top) National Archives; (bottom) U.S. Naval Photograph
439 J. Lie, THE CONQUERERS: CULEBRA CUT, PANAMA CANAL, 1913, Metropolitan Museum of Art, George A. Hern Fund
444 N. R. Farbman, Time-Life Picture Agency/Courtesy of National Palace of Belles Artes and Literature, Mexico City
446 Brown Brothers
450 Smithsonian Institution
454 Culver Pictures, Inc.
455 Norman Wilkinson, from L'Illustration (May 15, 1915)
458 Courtesy of Eleutherian Mills Historical Library
459 National Archives
461 UPI
462 John T. McCoy, Jr., DOG FIGHT, 1918
463 Smithsonian Institution
467 Imperial War Museum
471 UPI
474 William E. Donze, M.D., photo copyright Henry Austin Clark, Jr.
478 Tom Lovell, SMOKE FILLED ROOM
479 Culver Pictures, Inc.
481 Culver Pictures, Inc.
482-483 Brown Brothers
485 Missouri Historical Society
486 Ben Shahn, BOOTLEGGING, Museum of the City of New York
487 John Steuart Curry, BAPTISM IN KANSAS (1928) Oil on canvas, 40" × 50", collection of the Whitney Museum of American Art
489 Jacob Lawrence, THE MIGRATION OF THE NEGRO (1 Panel), The Phillips Collection, Washington
490 Brown Brothers
491 Norton Gallery and School of Art, West Palm Beach, Florida
494 Library of Congress
496 DIES IRAE, Rosenberg, The Estate of Carl Zigrosser, Courtesy of the Philadelphia Museum of Art
497 UPI
499 UPI
500 Isaac Soyer, EMPLOYMENT AGENCY, 1937, Collection of the Whitney Museum of Art
503 UPI
504 UPI
507 UPI
508 (top) The Bettmann Archive; (bottom) Culver Pictures, Inc.
509 (left) Culver Pictures, Inc.; (right) Collection of Ben M. Hall
510 Dallas Museum of Fine Arts, Dallas Art Assoc. Purchase
513 UPI
516 The Bettmann Archive

520 Department of the Interior
522 The Butler Institute of American Art American Heritage Picture Collection
525 photo The Boston Athenaeum
527 copyright 1935 (renewed) 1963 by the Conde Nast Publications, Inc.
529 UPI
532 Brown Brothers
534 Department of the Interior, Washington
538-539 U.S. Department of Defense
540 Franklin D. Roosevelt Library, Hyde Park
542 UPI
543 UPI
545 UPI
546 Wide World
550 UPI
551 UPI
552 UPI (all)
555 UPI
556 Stanley King Collection
557 Franklin D. Roosevelt Library, Hyde Park
560 U.S. Army
562 Franklin D. Roosevelt Library, Hyde Park
563 Franklin D. Roosevelt Library, Hyde Park
565 Franklin D. Roosevelt Library, Hyde Park
566 UPI
568 National Archives
571 Franklin D. Roosevelt Library, Hyde Park
575 U.S. Defense Department, Washington
578 UPI/ACME
580 Franklin D. Roosevelt Library, Hyde Park
581 Franklin D. Roosevelt Library, Hyde Park
584 UPI
586 Ben Shahn, 1948, Harry S. Truman Library
587 Robert Osborn, INFLATION, 1950'S
588 UPI
590 Miguel Covarrubias, 1942, copyright 1942 Conde Nast Publications from the Franklin D. Roosevelt Library, Hyde Park (detail)
592 UPI
593 Harry S. Truman Library
595 Imperial War Museum
596 UPI
597 Eve Arnold, Magnum
598 University of Hartford Collection
599 UPI
600 UPI
601 UPI
602 UPI
606 Robert Osborn
608 Eastfoto
610 Rene Burri, Magnum
612 Acme Photo
614 UPI
615 University of Hartford Collection
616 State Historical Society of Missouri

619 UPI
620 UPI
621 Stern, Black Star
624 Popular Culture Library, Bowling Green State University
626 Bern Keating, Black Star
627 ANCO
628 Bruce Davidson, Magnum
629 (top) Wayne Miller, Magnum; (bottom) Joe Munroe, Photo Researchers
632 Ben Shahn, SUPREME COURT, Des Moines Art Center, James D. Edmundson Fund, 1964
633 Wide World Photos
634 Wide World Photos
636 UPI
637 Nina Leen, Time-Life Picture Agency © Time, Inc.
638 Carl Iwasaki, Time-Life Picture Agency © Time, Inc.
640 Rene Burri, Magnum
641 UPI
642 Lee Lockwood, Black Star
646-647 Beth Miller, U.S. Committee for UNICEF
648 Bill Strode, Black Star
650 Paul Schutzer, Time-Life
651 Robert Kelley, Time-Life
653 Jimmy Scott, Courtesy of Topaze
654 Stern, Black Star
656 UPI
659 Bill Strode, Black Star
660 Lyndon Baines Johnson Library
661 Bruce Davidson, Magnum
662-663 James H. Karales
664 UPI
665 MARISOL, LBJ. (1967) Painted Wood Construction, Collection, The Museum of Modern Art, New York, Gift of Mr. and Mrs. Lester Avnet
668 John Cayea, THE AMERICAN EAGLE, 1974
671 UPI
672 Wide World Photos
673 UPI
674 (all) Charles Moore, Black Star
676 Dennis Brack, Black Star
679 Claus Meyer, Black Star
681 Owen Franken, Stock, Boston
683 (top left) Bonnie M. Freer, Photo Trends; (bottom) © King Features-Subafilms, Ltd., 1968
684 Art Seitz, Black Star
688 Bob Towers, Black Star
690 Robert Osborn
692 Owen Franken, Stock Boston
694 Magnum
695 Black Star
697 Elliot Erwitt, Magnum
698 Collection, Herbert W. Hemphill, Jr.
701 Robert Pryor
702 Dennis Brack, Black Star
705 Shelley Katz, Black Star
706 Steven Scher, Black Star
716 John Bellamy, BELLAMY EAGLE, Peabody Museum, Salem, photo Mark Sexton

INDEX

751

757

759

N

761

765

430; Foraker, 438
Tarleton, Banastre, 91
Taxation, British, of colonies, 71, 77, 78; to pay war debts, 126; and protective tariff, 127; whiskey, 131. *See also* Income tax
Taylor, Zachary, 265, 266, *267,* 269, 271, 272, 273, 274
Tea, tax on, 79
"Teach-ins," 677
Teamsters Union, 525
Teapot Dome scandal, 475, 479
Technology, 480, 486; in World War II, 570, 576; and environmental protection, 707
Tecumseh, 22, 143, 156, 157, 165
Teheran Conference, 579
Telegraph, 262, 267
Television, 635–636, 658, 689; Army-McCarthy hearings on, 603; political events on, 613, 635–636, 649, 704; Watergate hearings on, 699
Teller, Edward, 576
Teller Amendment, 437
Temperance movement, 202–204, 387; women in, 208
Tenant farming, 232, 390, 519
Tenements, 221, 225, 354, 378
Tennessee, 131, 132, 299, 321, 332, 391
Tennessee Coal and Iron Co., 410
Tennessee Valley Authority (TVA), 518, *519,* 533
Tenochtitlán, *28,* 29, 30, 31
Tenure of Office Act, 334
Territorial expansion, 143, 146–147, 167, 197, 230, 256–257, 261, 262–263, 264, *270,* 351, 428–431
Tet offensive, 678
Texas, U.S. claim to, *166,* 167; cattle in, 237; as independent nation, 257, 259, 260, 261; annexation of, 257, 262–263; Americans in, 257–259; and Mexican War, 265–266; secession of, 293; new industry in, 630
Textile manufacturing, 97, 99, 216, 221, 222
Thomas, George H., 304, 311
Thomas, Norman, 561; quoted, 384
Thoreau, Henry David, 197, 199, 267, 288
Thurmond, J. Strom, 598

Ticonderoga, Battle of, 82, 90
Tidewater region, 57
Tilden, Samuel, 331, 341, 383
Timbuktu, 36–37
Tippecanoe, Battle of, 143, 156
Tobacco, 44–46, 54, 57, 69, 70
Tobacco Road (Caldwell), 511
Tokyo, bombing of, 570
Toleration, Act of, 54
Tonkin Gulf Resolution, 670, 693, 698
Tories, 87–88, 97
To Secure These Rights, 598
Town meeting system, 49
Townsend, Francis, Townsend movement, 528
Townshend, Charles, 78, 79
Townships, 101–102
Trade, European exploration for, 23, 24, 25, 32; Far East, 24, 97, 98, 267; slave, 25, 36–39, 57, 69, 264; as reason for settlement, 54; colonial, 55, 56, 68–70, 72, *73,* 77; triangular, 69, *70;* and "enumerated articles," 69–70, 77; in West Indies, 133, 134; embargo on, 80, 143, 153, 154, 215, 544–545, 546; free-trade policy, 264; restraint of, 369, 373; and naval power, 429; in World War I, 451–452; with Latin America, 542
"Trail of tears," 193
Transcendentalism, 199
Transportation, and growth of the West, 164, 168–173; public, desegregation of, 633–634
Treasury Department, 111, 121, 122, 124, 129
Trench warfare, 461–462
Trent, British boarding of, 310
Trenton, Battle of, 89
Tripoli, war with, 152–153
Trist, Nicholas P., 269, 270
Truman, Harry S., 569, 577, 584–588, 589, 591, *592,* 594, 595, 597–598, 602, 608, 614–615, 639, 658, 659, 669; in World War II, 561, 575; and 1948 election, 585, 598–600; and Korean War, 610, 611–613
Truman Doctrine, 585, 592–594
Trustbusting, 409–412, 415
Trusts, 369, 410, 420–421
Tubman, Harriet, 246
Tunisia, invasion of, 571–572

Turner, Nat, 237, 246, 247
Turnpikes, 170
Tuskegee Institute, 343, *344*
Twain, Mark, 354
Tweed, William Marcy, Tweed Ring, 382–384
Tydings, Millard, 603
Tydings-McDuffie Act, 669
Tyler, John, 196, 257, 260, 261, 262, *598*
Typewriter, 367, 388

U

U-2 incident, 625, 641–642
U-boats, 453, 454, 456, 457. *See also* Submarines
Underground Railroad, 246
Underwood Tariff, 419
Unemployment, 195, *494, 500,* 501, 506, 512, 533, 543, 617, 650, 703; aid in, 518, 522–524
Union, Act of (British), 72
Union Pacific Railroad, 356, 358
Union Party, 530
Unions, 222, 223, 371–373, 521, 526, 600; right to form, 215, 221, 458, 524, 525, 533; opposition to, 372, 525, 587; and strikes, 413, 525, 532, 587; protection of, 421; in World War I, 458; setbacks for, 484, 497; and Wagner Act, 524–525. *See also* Labor
Unitarianism, 199
United Auto Workers, 532, 587
United Mine Workers, 413
United Nations, 580, 581, 585, 589–590, 695; and Korean War, 610, 611, 618, 696
"United Order," 199
United States (warship), 137
U.S. v. E. C. Knight Co., 369
United States Steel Corp., 410
Universal Negro Improvement Association, 475, 490
Unsafe at Any Speed (Nader), 697
Urbanization, 223–225. *See also* Cities
Urban Mass Transit Act, 657
U.S.A. (Dos Passos), 511
Utah, 199, 270, 388, 408, 421

V

Valley Forge, 90

CDEFGHIJ-KR-79

HETERICK MEMORIAL LIBRARY
973 S5462t c.2   onuj
Shenton, James Patri / These United States

3 5111 00024 7290